AMERICA'S FOREIGN POLICY:

Drift or Decision

AMERICA'S FOREIGN POLICY:

Drift or Decision

By
Martin E. Goldstein

SR Scholarly Resources Inc.
104 Greenhill Avenue · Wilmington, Delaware 19805

Scholarly Resources Inc.
104 Greenhill Avenue
Wilmington, Delaware 19805

Library of Congress Cataloging in Publication Data
Goldstein, Martin E.
  America's foreign policy.

  Includes bibliographies and index.
  1. United States—Foreign relations—1945–.
2. United States—Foreign relations administration.
I. Title.
JX1417.G63   1984   327.73   84-20221
ISBN 0-8420-2209-0

The Truman Doctrine thus represented the first link in a "chain of steel" that the West placed around Soviet communism in order to contain it. Numerous other links were soon forged. In a successful effort to overcome the Soviet blockade of Berlin, the West mounted an airlift of supplies to the capital of the former Reich. As a means of boosting the economies and confidence of Western Europe, a likely target of Soviet penetration, the United States transferred about $12 billion in goods and services under the Marshall Plan. In 1949 the United States joined its first peacetime alliance, the North Atlantic Treaty Organization (NATO). Later expanded to include 16 members, NATO was designed to blunt a Soviet military drive into Western Europe. When Communist Ho Chi Minh led Vietnamese nationalists against the reimposition of French control in Indochina, America contributed to France's war effort.[4] When American aid and advice failed to sustain Jiang Jieshi against his Communist foes in China, the United States signed a security treaty with the Chinese Nationalists in Taiwan in 1954 (since abrogated by Washington) and recognized Jiang's regime as the rightful government of all of China. This military treaty was accompanied by other security pacts designed to encircle the Communist bloc with American military power. The United States entered into the Southeast Asia Collective Defense Treaty (SEATO) in 1954 (with Australia, France, New Zealand, Pakistan, Thailand, the Philippines, and the United Kingdom); the ANZUS Pact in 1951 (with Australia and New Zealand); the Inter-American Treaty of Reciprocal Assistance (Rio Pact) in 1947 (with nearly all the states of Latin America including Cuba, which was expelled in 1962); and bilateral security treaties with the Philippines (1951), South Korea (1953), and Japan (1960). Although it did not join, America supported the Central Treaty Organization (CENTO) formed in 1955 by Iran, Iraq, Pakistan, Turkey, and Great Britain. Through executive agreements, the United States also made defense arrangements with such countries as Iran, Spain, Israel, Liberia, and Thailand. Thus, as the decade of the 1950s drew to a close, America found itself allied with over forty other states against Communist expansion. Washington supplemented these alliances with military and economic aid. American intervention in Korea, the Bay of Pigs landing in 1961, the Cuban missile confrontation in 1962, and the sustained US effort in Vietnam were all part of the containment policy.

The orthodox interpretation of the Cold War, as we have seen, attributes United States-Soviet tension to Soviet aggressiveness. But affairs of diplomacy, no less than affairs of the heart, rarely admit to a single interpretation. (Clearly, the Soviet Union does not accept the orthodox view presented here.) Revisionist historians place primary blame for the Cold War upon the United States and its Western allies. While currently accepted by a minority of historians,[5] this interpretation merits our examination.

To begin with, the revisionists place much more emphasis upon the economic component of the national interest than do the conventional historians of the period. While the orthodox interpreters portray America as seeking to preserve its security and values against alien threats, revisionists assert that the United States has acted aggressively to secure overseas markets and raw materials and to impose American values upon other lands.

The revisionists perceive a pattern of Western belligerence toward Soviet communism since the 1917 revolution that brought Lenin and his Bolshevik followers to power. Immediately after the revolution, the West gave assistance to the Russian Whites who were conducting rear-guard action against the "Reds" in hope of toppling the Communist regime. When this effort failed, the United States took until 1933 to recognize the Communist government and welcome it into the international community of nations. During the 1930s, England, France, and the United States repeatedly rebuffed Soviet overtures to create a collective security pact against the Nazi menace. Then, at Munich in 1938, without consulting Moscow, the West gave Germany the go-ahead to seize Czechoslovakia. In Soviet eyes, Hitler was being encouraged to move eastward. Stalin responded by signing the Non-Aggression Pact with Germany in August 1939.

Even when the Soviet Union and the West became allies, as the result of Hitler's attack on Russia in June 1941, the West continued its pattern of hostility, according to revisionists. Because of the tremendous losses suffered by the Red Army and the civilian population, Stalin repeatedly called for the opening of a second front in Europe; but it was not until 1944 that the Allies landed at Normandy. Were not the Western Allies hoping that Germany would expunge communism from Russia, so that they could then go in and pick up the pieces? In arranging the terms for Italy's surrender, England and the United States shut the Soviets out of the negotiations and set in place a conservative, pro-Western government. Indeed, wherever their military forces were in control at the end of the war, the West installed pro-Western governments and went to great efforts to neutralize local Communists, who had played extremely significant roles in the Resistance. The Yalta agreement to hold democratic elections in liberated territory, the revisionists suggest, was a thinly disguised effort to place in Eastern

Europe regimes that were bound to be hostile to the Soviet Union. When in 1945 Russia asked the United States for a $6 billion credit for postwar reconstruction, the State Department incredulously replied (months later) that they had lost the request; however, Washington granted a similar loan to England almost immediately. After the war Washington insisted that Russia, but not France or Great Britain, repay its Lend-Lease loans. The primary purpose for dropping the atom bomb on Japan was not to bring about its defeat, which revisionists claim could have been achieved with incendiary air attacks, but to demonstrate the terrible consequences of a new weapon that would be deployed against Moscow if the need arose.

In the revisionist view, the Russians were especially angered by Western behavior toward postwar Berlin. Decimated twice in the same century by German aggression, the Soviet Union was determined to keep Germany weak. The West, on the other hand, predicated West European economic recovery on a revitalized and prosperous German state. In violation of previous agreements, the United States, Great Britain, and France decided to fuse their three occupation zones, create a new West German currency, and authorize West German leaders to form a separate state. In Russian eyes, the West was priming Germany for another drive toward Moscow.

Revisionists further argue that actions taken allegedly for defensive purposes by the West, particularly the United States, were actually attempts to unseat communism and extend America's economic sway around the world. Thus, the revisionists interpret America's security commitments as aggressive actions designed to intimidate the Soviet Union and contribute to the downfall of communism. They assert that the military and economic aid given by the United States to approximately one hundred other states was not motivated by altruism or defense but was—and is—an effort to make these regimes dependent on American largesse. Such countries could then not refuse to grant economic favors to American corporations, such as easy access to markets and raw materials at advantageous prices. The containment policy, say the revisionists, is really a veil to conceal the expansionist thrusts of the United States.[6]

Which interpretation is correct, the orthodox or the revisionist? Both sides are able to muster evidence in support of their arguments. Yet, much of the relevant information, particularly the perceptions and intentions of Soviet leaders as well as some Americans, remains secret, perhaps never to be revealed. From today's vantage point, it remains impossible to confirm or deny either with finality. It may be, however, that future historians will perceive a similarity between the Cold War and the kind of episode that occurred count-less times in the Old West. Suppose that two gunfighters, Ivan and Sam, come to town. Each has heard of the other's orneriness, and each knows that the other would like to establish his supremacy by gunning down the other. While neither is really sure that the other wishes to risk his life by drawing, both must assume that a shootout remains possible. In order to intimidate the other and possibly drive him out of town, each man capitalizes on whatever chance he gets to enhance his reputation as a sharpshooter and quick draw. To enhance his security, each gunslinger forms a gang of other cowboys around himself. Before long, Ivan and Sam find themselves in an extremely touchy situation, not unlike that between the United States and the Soviet Union today. Each one prefers to stay alive. Ideally, each would like to do so and at the same time establish his superiority over the other, but not in a shootout, because that would be too risky. Also, each has taken a number of measures, basically though not totally for defensive purposes, such as arming himself and forming a gang. In Sam's eyes, these measures only confirm his suspicion that Ivan is out to bushwhack him; Ivan feels the same way. Consider their predicament. If Sam tries to shoot Ivan, Sam risks being shot, and vice versa. But suppose Sam seeks to terminate the feud by appearing unarmed before Ivan, who would be carrying his six-shooter. Would Ivan reciprocate Sam's peaceful move, or would he take advantage of a once-in-a-lifetime opportunity and empty his six-gun into Sam?

The imaginary confrontation described here suggests a third source of the Cold War, namely, mutual misunderstanding and misperception. In this view, neither side started the Cold War, but rather it developed through a series of actions and reactions.

How can Sam and Ivan break out of their dilemma? The answer would seem to be that each must test the other's intentions by probing actions not likely to have life-and-death consequences. In foreign policy, such actions include cultural exchange, trade, tech-nological exchange, limited arms control, travel, tourism, and the like. The responses to these gestures provide a measure of each country's willingness to coexist on a cooperative basis. As we shall see, both the Soviet Union and the United States have engaged in such activities.

A Period of Détente

The diplomatic sparring that characterized United States-Soviet relations in the late 1940s and 1950s reached a turning point in 1962 with the effort of the Soviets to emplace missiles in Cuba. President Kennedy reacted to this maneuver by imposing a naval blockade around Cuba. Secretary of State Dean Rusk epitomized this tensest confrontation in US-Soviet relations: "We and the Russians were eyeball to eyeball, and Russia blinked." Had Soviet ships run the blockade, nuclear war probably would have resulted. Realizing this, Soviet Premier Nikita Khrushchev respected the blockade and negotiated the withdrawal of Soviet missiles already in Cuba in return for the United States removing its missiles from Turkey.

The missile crisis underlined the need to limit US-Soviet rivalry so as to avoid future marches to the brink of war. This fear that unbridled competition might lead to nuclear war led to a series of agreements between the United States and the Soviet Union, beginning in 1963 with the installation of a Hot Line between the White House and the Kremlin. The Hot Line accord was followed by a series of other agreements including the Limited Test Ban Treaty to prohibit atmospheric and underwater nuclear testing (1963); the pact to open consulates in each other's country (1964); a Moscow-New York air link (1966); the Outer Space Treaty to disallow the use of space for military purposes (1967); the Astronauts Rescue Treaty (1968); the Nonproliferation Treaty to control the spread of nuclear weapons (1968); the agreement to share information on scientific and technical subjects (1972); a massive grain deal (1972); SALT I (1972), signed during President Richard Nixon's visit to Moscow; and the Vladivostok Accord to continue the process of limiting strategic weapons (1973). In 1975 the United States and the Soviet Union attended the thirty-five-nation Conference on Security and Cooperation in Europe, which confirmed European boundaries (including the division of Germany) and committed all parties to respect human rights. In 1976 the two nations signed a pact limiting the size of nuclear detonations permitted under the Limited Test Ban Treaty. Numerous trade agreements were concluded. In 1979, President Carter initialed Salt II and sent the treaty to the Senate for ratification.

If East-West relations in the détente era in Europe have yielded disappointment, détente outside of Europe has yielded a severe disillusionment for those who expected a moderation of Soviet behavior.
President Reagan, Eureka College commencement address, 1982

This period of mutual accord became known as détente, a French word meaning the relaxation of tensions. But despite détente, US-Soviet competition continued. Moscow lent assistance to one of the three factions fighting in Angola, and this aid, as well as Cuban troops, proved decisive in that struggle. In 1973, the Soviets encouraged the Arabs to attack Israel, and they supported a coup by pro-Soviet leaders in Southern Yemen. Throughout the period of American involvement in Vietnam, Moscow supplied assistance to its Communist ally, while at the same time urging Hanoi to negotiate. Toward the end of the 1970s, tensidn between Washington and Moscow increased. President Carter angrily denounced the presence of a Soviet combat brigade in Cuba. In 1979 the Soviet army crossed into Afghanistan to put down an uprising against the Soviet-dominated government in Kabul. The following year the United States boycotted the Moscow Olympics.

The Controversy over Human Rights

The most contentious issue in US-Soviet relations during the Carter presidency concerned human rights. With a tendency to view political matters in terms of good and evil, President Carter pledged to make respect for human rights a key objective of American foreign policy. In pursuit of this goal, Carter established in the State Department a new Bureau of Human Rights and Humanitarian Affairs.

Carter's human-rights policy had a firm grounding in diplomacy as well as morality. In 1975, the heads of state from Canada, the United States, and all the countries of Europe, thirty-five leaders in all, gathered at the Helsinki Conference on Security and Cooperation in Europe. This meeting was called to settle a wide range of European disputes, including boundary questions dating back to the Second World War, with particular reference to German borders. The conference's Final Act, which recognized the permanence of existing boundaries, as the Soviets desired, also called upon the signatories to respect human rights.

The Soviet Union never claimed to accept human rights in the Western sense of the term. According to the ideology of Marxism-Leninism, the Communist party knows what is best for the populace, and whatever the party ordains advances the human rights of everyone in the society.

Carter and his aides fired especially loud verbal salvos against the Kremlin's treatment of dissidents, such as Alexander Solzhenitsyn, and Andrei Sakharov, and restrictions placed on Jews who wanted to leave Russia. The Soviet Union reacted to Carter's criticism with mounting fury. The Kremlin accused Carter of unwarranted interference in Russia's internal affairs, conduct prohibited by the Helsinki accords. Such verbal assaults, said the Russians, were just as uncalled for as if the Soviets were to criticize America for having so few black or Hispanic corporate officers. In a speech to the Supreme Soviet in October 1977, Premier Brezhnev went on the offensive.

> What real rights and freedoms are guaranteed to the masses in present-day imperialist society? The "right" of tens of millions to unemployment? Or the "right" of sick people to do without medical aid, which costs a vast sum of money? Or else the "right" of ethnic minorities to humiliating discrimination in employment and education, in politics and everyday life? Or is it the "right" to live in perpetual fear of the omnipresent underworld of organized crime and to see how the press, movies, television and radio go out of their way to educate the younger generation in a spirit of selfishness, cruelty and violence?[7]

The acrimony over human rights all but dispelled the atmosphere of détente by the time of Ronald Reagan's election in 1980.[8]

Trade, Technology, and Emigration

Another contentious facet of US-Soviet relations has been trade and technological exchange. These issues have become closely linked with Soviet emigration practices and Moscow's treatment of Poland.

Prior to 1972, trade between the Soviet Union and the United States was negligible. At the same time, Soviet emigration policy, especially toward Jews, was extremely restrictive. In 1970, for example, the Soviets granted exit visas to only 1,000 Jews. As détente gathered speed in the early 1970s, relations between the superpowers took a turn for the better. The Vietnam War was drawing to a conclusion and a major agreement had been signed to resolve the perennial problem of Berlin. The improving state of US-Soviet relations culminated in May 1972, when Nixon journeyed to Moscow to sign SALT I and other agreements providing for increased US-Soviet cooperation. One of these agreements provided for the formation of a trade commission to settle such outstanding economic issues as Russia's World War II Lend-Lease debt and to plan for large-scale economic interchanges. In July 1972, the United States signed a three-year agreement to sell the Soviets at least $750 million of American wheat, corn, and other grains, the largest grain transaction between two countries in history. Three months later, the recently established joint trade commission concluded a three-year trade pact, which included settlement of Russia's World War II debt and a United States promise to request most-favored-nation (MFN) status for Soviet imports. MFN means that a state will levy against incoming goods a tariff no higher than the lowest tariff charged against similar goods coming from any other country. Without MFN treatment from the United States, Soviet products would be priced out of the American market, and this would have stymied the Nixon administration's efforts to boost détente through trade.

In accordance with this trade agreement, Nixon submitted to Congress in 1973 a piece of legislation known as the Trade Reform Act. This act covered a broad range of issues, including authority to reduce trading barriers against industrialized countries and plans to enable developing lands to increase their exports to the United States. The most controversial aspect of the proposed legislation, however, involved authority to extend credits and MFN status to the Soviet Union. At this juncture the question of Soviet emigration policy entered the picture.

Unhappy with Soviet restrictions on emigration, Senator Henry M. Jackson (D.-Wash.) and Representative Charles A. Vanik (D.-Ohio) attached an amendment to the Trade Reform Act requiring the Soviet Union in effect to provide assurances that it would allow increased emigration. This modification, known as the Jackson-Vanik Amendment, infuriated the Soviets. To understand this reaction, we must gain some familiarity with the Soviet outlook on freedom of movement.

Westerners are accustomed to regarding freedom of travel as an inalienable right, which government may abridge only under the most unusual of circumstances. The Soviet Union, like most Communist countries, takes an entirely different view. In Soviet eyes, citizens raised and educated by the state owe a duty to the state and should not be permitted to leave except under abnormal conditions. The more schooling the citizen has had, the larger the debt the citizen owes to the state. This qualification has a special effect upon Jews, who tend to be the most educated minority in the Soviet Union. The Soviets also feel that emigration policy is an internal matter and therefore not properly the subject of legislation by the American Congress. In consequence of this outlook, the Soviet Union denounced the Jackson-Vanik Amendment and refused to provide public assurances of easier emigration rules.

Kissinger, then in the Ford administration, sided with the Soviets, although not because he approved of their restrictions on freedom of travel. In testimony before the Senate Finance Committee in March 1974, Kissinger explained his position.

> The most painful aspect of this debate . . . centers around the question of respect for human rights in the Soviet Union.
>
> This is not a dispute between the morally sensitive and the morally obtuse. It is, rather, a problem of choosing between alternatives.
>
> I do not oppose the objective of those who wish to use trade policy to affect the evolution of Soviet society; it does seem to me, however, that they have chosen the wrong vehicle and the wrong context. We cannot accept the principle that our entire foreign policy—or even an essential component of that policy such as a normalization of our trade relations—should be made dependent on the transformation of the Soviet domestic structure. . . .
>
> Détente is not rooted in agreement of values; it becomes above all necessary because each side recognizes that the other is a potential adversary in a nuclear war. To us, détente is a process of managing relations with a potentially hostile country in order to preserve peace while maintaining our vital interests. In a nuclear age, this is in itself an objective not without moral validity.
>
> Since détente is rooted in a recognition of differences—and based on the prevention of disaster—there are sharp limits to what we can insist upon as part of this relationship. We have a right to demand responsible international behavior from the U.S.S.R.
>
> But with respect to basic changes in the Soviet system, the issue is not whether we condone what the U.S.S.R. does internally; it is whether and to what extent we can risk other objectives—and especially the building of a structure for peace—for these domestic changes. I believe that we cannot, and that to do so would obscure, and in the long run defeat, what must remain our overriding objective—the prevention of nuclear war.[9]

In arguing for defeat of the Jackson-Vanik Amendment, Kissinger further contended that the Soviets were allowing many more Jews to leave than previously. As we have seen, the Soviets granted only 1,000 exit visas to Jews in 1970; this figure grew to 13,022 in 1971; 13,681 in 1972; and 34,733 in 1973.[10] Kissinger maintained that quiet diplomacy was producing results, but that the insistence on a Soviet public pledge would only bring about a reduction in emigration.[11]

Congress, however, remained unconvinced, and in 1974 it passed the Jackson-Vanik Amendment. In reaction, the Soviets angrily declared that they would no longer be bound by the 1972 trade agreement. Thereafter, as Table 2–1 indicates, American imports from Russia languished instead of rising markedly as Nixon, Kissinger, and Ford had hoped. Aside from grain, which they continued to purchase from the United States, the Soviets turned to Western Europe and Japan for the products they sought.

During my first press conference as President ... I pointed out that as good Marxists-Leninists the Soviet leaders have openly and publicly declared that the only morality they recognize is that which will further their cause, which is world revolution. ...

Let us pray for the salvation of all those who live in totalitarian darkness, pray they will discover the joy of knowing God.

But until they do, let us be aware that while they preach the supremacy of the state, declare its omnipotence over individual man, and predict its eventual domination of all peoples of the earth—they are the focus of evil in the modern world.

President Ronald Reagan, speech to the National Association of Evangelicals, Orlando, March 8, 1983

Despite the dent that the Jackson-Vanik Amendment put in détente, the Soviet Union began shortly thereafter to allow more Jews to leave. The principal reason for this seems to have been a desire to improve the likelihood of negotiating a second SALT agreement with the United States. In 1975, the Soviets, still angered over the collapse of the trade pact, permitted only 13,222 Jews to leave. In 1976, this figure rose to 14,261, and the following year saw another small increase to 16,737. In 1978, as the SALT talks moved toward a conclusion, the Kremlin granted 28,864 exit visas to Jews, and, in 1979, the year Carter sent the SALT agreement

TABLE 2–1: US-SOVIET TRADE, 1971–79 ($ millions)

	1971	1972	1973	1974	1975	1976	1977	1978	1979
Exports to Russia	160.5	483.6	1,187.1	611.9	1,836.0	2,305.9	1,623.5	2,249.0	3,400.0
Imports from Russia	56.8	95.4	214.6	349.5	256.0	220.6	234.3	953.8	700.0

Source: *Congressional Quarterly*, January 12, 1980. Copyright © 1980 by Congressional Quarterly Inc. Reprinted by permission of Congressional Quarterly Inc.

to the Senate, the figure rose to a record 51,000.[12] During the same period, US-Soviet trade also accelerated, largely due to Russia's need for imported grain. In addition, many of the cooperative ventures arranged during Nixon's 1972 visit to Moscow were being implemented, from joint research in cancer prevention to the sharing of information on weather patterns. In 1977, the United States and the Soviet Union renewed for another five years their 1972 pact on cooperation in science and technology, by which time the two countries were working together on forty-seven scientific projects.

Détente, as we have observed, does not take the place of competition; it only sets limits to it. Under President Carter, US-Soviet relations experienced one of those downturns that is entirely consistent with the "limited adversary relationship"[13] that has existed between the two powers. Carter angered the Soviets by criticizing their human-rights record, and he further aroused their ire in 1977 by proposing very deep arms cuts that would leave the Soviets at a strategic disadvantage. The decline in relations accelerated at the close of 1979, when Soviet troops invaded Afghanistan to halt the threatened drift of that nation out of the Soviet orbit.[14] Although some writers, such as George Kennan, labeled the Soviet move as essentially a *defensive* measure (protection of a fellow Socialist regime), the Carter administration read it as a sign of a new adventurousness in Soviet foreign policy. President Carter insisted the Soviet invasion called for a strong American response, not only because the invasion marked the first use since World War II of Soviet troops outside the Socialist bloc but also because Washington feared the Soviets might have designs on the nearby Persian Gulf.

In reaction to the Soviet aggression, President Carter asked the Senate to postpone consideration of the SALT II treaty. He also announced a trade embargo against the Soviet Union applicable to agricultural products (except for grain yet to be shipped under previous agreements) and any items incorporating "high technology." In the summer of 1980 Washington boycotted the Moscow Olympics and pressured other governments to do the same.

In the early years of the Reagan administration, US-Soviet relations grew even more distant. President Reagan intensified curbs on the transfer of high-technology equipment, seeking (unsuccessfully) to pressure European firms to deny the Soviets machinery to be used in the construction of a natural gas pipeline from Russia to Western Europe. Many of the joint endeavors of the détente years were not renewed. President Reagan held the USSR responsible for most of the ferment in the Third World, especially Central America. The Soviets complained that Washington was seeking to exclude it from Middle East diplomacy. Both powers entered head-long into an arms race, while negotiations on strategic weapons (START) and intermediate-range nuclear missiles in Europe were suspended in 1984. Détente had given way to enmity in US-Soviet relations.

Toward the end of 1982, Soviet leader Leonid Brezhnev died and was succeeded by Yuri V. Andropov and then Konstantin U. Chernenko. In a state such as the Soviet Union, where policies are not rooted in public consent, a change in leaders can portend sharp policy swings. Whether that would be the case of the Soviet Union under Chernenko was not discernible by the middle of 1984.

Clearly, Chernenko needs a major success of some sort in order to solidify his succession. This is necessary because the Politburo, the highest decision-making body in the Soviet Union, is not uniformly behind Chernenko. While both the military and the KGB appear to support him, these organizations are traditional rivals, and the military is not yet certain Chernenko will cater to their interests. A stunning victory, whether at home or abroad, would do much to cement his position as Andropov's successor. In the foreign policy realm, two approaches suggest themselves. Should the United States and the Soviet Union sign a major arms-control agreement, Chernenko could hold himself out as a man of peace who can negotiate with the Americans without giving in to them. If such an accord with the United States proves unobtainable, Chernenko might turn to a more imperialist tack. Perhaps he would seek a major victory in Central America, by helping leftists come to power in El Salvador or a neighboring country. Alternatively, he might seek to boost Soviet fortunes in Africa or the Middle East. Clearly, Chernenko could not afford to allow any nation presently in the Soviet fold, and Poland in particular, to strike out on its own, for then he would be open to accusations of failure to defend the Socialist coalition.

Chernenko's need for a visible success affords some leverage to President Reagan. He might seek to drive an even harder bargain at arms-control negotiations in the hope that Chernenko will come around. Too heavy a hand in these talks, however, could backfire. Chernenko cannot let himself be seen as giving away advantages unilaterally. Should President Reagan require this, the Soviet leader might conclude that the victory he needs can better be achieved through foreign intervention. The outcome of such considerations is likely to become known as the 1980s unfold.

We are now in a position to gain some insights into the operation of the analytic model of foreign policy depicted in Fig. 1–1. For illustrative purposes, let us consider the 1974–1975 breakdown of the US-Soviet trade agreement. (The following account is greatly simplified for purposes of explaining the model.) The desire on the part of both powers to put their relations on a friendlier footing, an aspect of the State System, provided momentum toward a trade agreement, signed in 1972. This pact had numerous effects (feedback) on actors in the policy-making process. The trade agreement proved offensive to those who espoused the values of freedom of movement and religion. Through the feedback process, the pact triggered the actions of certain Pressure Groups, elements of Public Opinion and the Media to influence the government (Political System) in various ways. The Values referred to above also affected Public Opinion, Pressure Groups, and the Media, as well as government officials (Political System). These combined effects produced a Foreign Policy action, namely, a demand that the Soviets pledge to increase Jewish emigration. As we have seen, this insistence resulted in Soviet renunciation of the trade agreement; such behavior falls under the model's component State System. The Soviet rebuttal then produced its own effects (feedback) on elements of the model. For many Americans, it confirmed the merits of sticking by their Values of religious freedom and freedom of movement. It also affirmed the Tradition of standing up to dictatorial regimes. The Russian reaction had numerous effects on the Political System. The Agriculture Department, having lost the prospect of massive grain sales, had to seek other means of servicing the farm community. The president and his special assistant for national security (Kissinger) considered the abrogation of the trade agreement a setback for détente and therefore searched for other ways of cementing US-Soviet friendship. Pressure Groups whose members stood to lose money from loss of sales to the Soviet Union vented their anger upon the government (Political System), while those whose members preferred to have nothing to do with the Soviet Union showered praise upon Washington. Respective elements of Public Opinion and the Media did likewise. All these forms of behavior in turn yielded other Foreign Policy actions, which then impacted upon the State System.

The preceding discussion has mentioned only a few of the consequences and effects of each action, in order to illustrate the analytical model. It is worth stressing that the main purpose of the model is to provide categories so as to enable one to analyze foreign policy in a systematic manner. As an intellectual exercise, one could take other foreign policy episodes and try to work them through the model.

THE UNITED STATES AND CHINA

The United States and the Communist Revolution

China has long held the fascination of Americans. Home of one-fourth of the human race, China used to be viewed as a land of brightly colored silks, exotic spices and teas, and intricately woven rugs. For over a century, American textile merchants dreamed of the profits that would accrue if only each person in China would add one inch of cloth to his or her shirttail. (The modern version has each citizen of China drinking one Pepsi or taking one aspirin per day.) The missionary impulse has also shaped American attitudes toward China; Senator Wherry perhaps expressed the apotheosis of America's evangelical spirit in declaring, "With God's help, we will lift Shanghai up and up, ever up, until it is just like Kansas City." Despite America's long-time enchantment with China, American relations with the Asian colossus have shown a mixed record.

To begin an exploration of American relations with China, it is useful to observe that the most critical development in recent Chinese history was the humiliation of China at the hands of the West, beginning with the British defeat of China in the Opium War of 1839–42. During the remainder of the nineteenth century, European states carved out spheres of influence in China, thereby eviscerating the country's sovereignty. Using methods borrowed from the West, Japan further diminished Chinese self-pride by defeating her in the war of 1894–95. When the fanatical members of the Boxer sect sought in 1900 to oust foreign influence, several Western countries (including the United States) forcefully put down the movement and imposed a peace treaty including a large indemnity.

To comprehend the enormous impact of these successive humiliations upon the Chinese, one must have some familiarity with China's traditional view of itself in relation to the rest of the world.[15] For nearly five thousand years, the Chinese found themselves surrounded by Asiatic tribes that they perceived as decidedly inferior in almost all respects. Having no experience with people who were their equals, the Chinese evolved a world view that placed them at the center of the universe. Everyone else lived on the fringes and was clearly of a lower order—"barbarians" the Chinese called them. Chinese world maps typically placed China squarely in the middle, surrounded by seas dotted with tiny islands that represented the rest of the world; all the islands combined would not occupy an area as large as one province of China. Thus, the Greeks at the time of Aristotle and England during the Elizabethan age were, in the Chinese view, all one with the primitive tribesmen who crossed the barren deserts of Central Asia. The ceremony of the kowtow epitomizes China's perception of its relations with the rest of the world. Every ambassador to the Imperial Court was expected to perform this elaborately orchestrated series of bows before the Chinese royalty there assembled. When in 1793 Lord Macartney, leader of a trade mission from Great Britain, refused to perform the kowtow, the Chinese emperor denied him an audience and sent the following message to King George:

> You, O King, are so inclined toward our civilization that you have sent a special envoy across the seas to bring to our Court your memorial of congratulations on the occasion of my birthday and to present your native products as an expression of your thoughtfulness. On perusing your memorial, so simply worded and sincerely conceived, I am impressed by your respectfulness and friendliness and greatly pleased.
>
> The Celestial Court has pacified and possessed the territory within the four seas. . . . As a matter of fact, the virtue and prestige of the Celestial Dynasty having spread far and wide, the kings of myriad nations come by land and sea with all sorts of precious things. Consequently there is nothing we lack, as your principal envoy and others have themselves observed. We have never set much store on strange or ingenious objects, nor do we need any more of your country's manufactures.

The country that was about to embark upon the industrial revolution and defeat the armies of Napoleon must have regarded such an epistle with more than one raised eyebrow!

Had the Chinese regarded themselves as one among many more-or-less equal societies, their humiliations at the hands of the West would not have been so traumatic. As it was, however, the Chinese found themselves humbled by the very lesser beings they so scorned. The Chinese made several unsuccessful attempts to eject foreign influence, including the Boxer Rebellion and boycotts of alien products. None of the attempts to reverse China's humiliations was successful. A rather small group of Chinese intellectuals had a very different idea of how to achieve the renewal of Chinese self-esteem. In July 1921, these intellectuals formed the Chinese Communist party. Among those present was the son of a small farmer; the young man's name was Mao Zedong (Mao Tse-tung). For a time the Communists cooperated with the ruling Nationalist party of Jiang Jieshi (Chiang Kai-shek) against the hated foreigner. In 1927, however, Jiang feared that the Communists, whose followers had radically increased in numbers, represented a challenge to his own authority, and he turned against them. After Jiang massacred numerous Communists in Shanghai—an event retold by André Malraux in the novel *Man's Fate*—Mao led the remnant of his adherents on the epic Long March of five thousand miles to the protective caves and hills of Yenan. Although this ordeal was much more arduous than the struggles of George Washington's troops at Valley Forge, the two exercises in adversity served a similar purpose: a call to extreme sacrifice that fortified the resolve to struggle against all odds. Practically all of China's present-day leaders were present on the Long March.

In 1937, the Japanese launched full-scale war against China. In face of this attack, the Nationalists and the Communists set aside their enmity to combine forces against the invader. Throughout the war against Japan, however, each Chinese party maneuvered to place itself in the more favorable position for resumption of the civil conflict that was certain to follow. Sure enough, no sooner were the Japanese defeated in 1945 than the Communists and the Nationalists resumed hostilities against each other. By this time the Communist forces were greatly strengthened, owing in large part to the poor leadership that Jiang had demonstrated during the struggle. Despite large quantities of aid supplied by the Americans, Jiang's forces were no match for the Communists, and, in 1949, Mao's troops sent Jiang and his dwindling forces scurrying in flight to the island of Taiwan, one hundred miles off the Chinese coast. The Communists now had an opportunity of their own to exact revenge against the despised foreigner and to make up for China's mortification during the last century.

The Korean War and the Hardening of American Policy

At the time of the Chinese Communist victory, American foreign policy was in a troubled state. We have seen how the wartime alliance with the Soviet Union disintegrated. Now China had joined the Soviets, creating a massive, powerful Communist machine that threatened to engulf all of Eurasia. Already, Vietnamese Communists led by Ho Chi Minh were waging a struggle against the reimposition of French control in Indochina. The future stability of Japan was far from certain. In Europe the "Iron Curtain" had descended.

American policy regarding China was put on hold. Would the Communists consolidate their victory by capturing Taiwan? Would Jiang find the means to reverse his military defeat? Would the Communist regime collapse from within? While American officials in Washington were pondering such questions, American diplomats in China were bearing the brunt of Chinese Communist resentment against the United States. Indeed, the new rulers of China so harrassed and mistreated American representatives that Washington recalled its diplomatic staff in January 1950. At the same time, Chinese propaganda had embarked upon a vitriolic "Hate America" campaign.

The reasons for Chinese Communist animosity toward the United States, which led to a break in diplomatic relations in January 1950, are not difficult to unearth.[16] Although America had been less rapacious than most other Western countries during the dismemberment of China in the previous century, the United States had not been entirely blameless. The Open Door Notes of 1899 and 1900 represented an American effort to gain an entry to the China trade before the Europeans had completely parcelled out China among themselves. In Chinese eyes, America resembled a bank robber who arrived late at the scene and still wanted a share of the spoils. By the time the Communists had defeated their Nationalist foes, the United States was unquestionably the leading Western power. In their almost fanatical hatred of the West, the Chinese were bound to choose America as their foremost enemy of the moment. Then too, the Communists had not forgotten American aid to Jiang during the closing years of the civil war. Finally, American hostility toward anything Communist was well known, and the new authorities in China deemed it only proper to return such sentiment in kind.

The Korean War finally determined America's response to the Communist revolution in China and also solidified American policy toward China up to the time of President Nixon's journey to Peking in 1972. The Chinese decision in October 1950 to send 300 thousand troops to Korea marked a turning point in Sino-American relations. In American eyes, such intervention offered proof of Chinese expansionism, which the containment policy was devised to prevent. Washington made no allowance for Peking's perception that its involvement in Korea was necessary for *defensive* purposes—that is, to deter United Nations (mostly American) forces from crossing into China, as General Douglas MacArthur was urging.[17]

> **We do not recognize the authorities in Peiping for what they pretend to be. The Peiping regime may be a colonial Russian government—a slavonic Manchukuo on a larger scale. It is not the government of China. It does not pass the first test. It is not Chinese. It is not entitled to speak for China in the community of nations.**
> Dean Rusk, after the Chinese Communist revolution

With Beijing's military intervention, Chinese and American troops were fighting each other on the wintry slopes of Korea. Denouncing Chinese Communist "aggression," Washington determined to oppose the Communist regime in Beijing and extended diplomatic recognition to Taiwan as the government of all China, as Jiang claimed. This commitment was solidified when the United States signed a security treaty with Taiwan in 1954 and thereafter provided it with economic and military assistance amounting to over $6 billion. For many years Washington prevented the mainlanders from taking the Chinese seat occupied in the United Nations by the Nationalists on Taiwan. The United States imposed a trade embargo upon China and pressured its allies to follow suit. Now the containment doctrine was being applied to China as well as the Soviet Union. The configuration of world politics was bipolar, with the United States and Western Europe at one extremity and the Sino-Soviet bloc at the other.

For the next twenty years, Sino-American relations remained frozen in the mold of hostility shaped by events surrounding the Korean War. Internally, China proceeded to create a Communist society by eliminating landlords and rich peasants, collectivizing farms, nationalizing industry and doing away with all opposition to the authority of the Communist party. On the international front, having finally succeeded in eliminating foreign prerogatives, China set about restoring its ancient status as a great power.

The Sino-Soviet Split

When the Communists came to power in China, and thereby joined their resources with those of the Soviet Union, the position of the Western world seemed more precarious than ever. Few Western diplomats dreamed of prying apart these twins of Communist power. Perhaps if the West had made such an attempt, Russian and Chinese anger at such meddling would have acted as cement to keep them together. As it turned out, the Sino-Soviet split developed not as a result of Western diplomatic machinations but due to causes organic to the relations between the two powers themselves. The chasm that opened in the early 1960s continues to hold out enormous opportunities and challenges for American diplomacy.

In 1950, one of the West's greatest fears came to pass, for in that year the Soviet Union signed a thirty-year treaty of friendship with the People's Republic of China. The grand Communist alliance was born. According to this pact, each side committed itself to refrain from using force in the settlement of mutual disputes. More troubling, from the standpoint of American diplomacy, were provisions for trade and for Soviet assistance to the new member of the Communist camp. To American policymakers, the Communist menace looked more threatening than ever.

Underlying the Sino-Soviet accord, however, were fundamental though little-perceived differences between the two countries. The Chinese in particular nursed grievances that extended back to the previous century. Among the European powers that wielded a scalpel in the dismemberment of China in the late nineteenth century was Imperial Russia. China has never forgiven the Russians. A 1954 map published in China showed nineteen territorial claims covering approximately 500 thousand square miles that China leveled against the Soviet Union. As Fig. 2–1 reveals, two of the largest of these areas are located in northwestern and northeastern China. These lands were ceded to Russia when China was weak and had no choice but to sign various unequal treaties forced upon her by European powers. In addition to seizing territory, Russia established a sphere of influence in Manchuria and practically administered the region as a Russian province. In 1924 the Soviet Union converted Outer Mongolia, originally part of China's empire, into a Soviet protectorate. (The Republic of Mongolia is today a Soviet satellite.) As communism in China arose partly in response to foreign intrusions, it should come as no surprise that Mao and his fellow leaders demanded the return of these lands.

If a real-estate dispute makes up the core of the Sino-Soviet rift, there are other divisive factors that comprise the outer shell. The Chinese are resentful that Stalin provided such meager assistance during their long struggle for power. During the closing months of World War II, the Soviet army liberated the Chinese province of Manchuria from the Japanese and then proceeded to dismantle and send back to the Soviet Union a large part of the Chinese heavy industry located there. In 1945 Stalin signed a treaty of friendship

FIGURE 2-1: SOVIET-CHINESE TERRITORIAL DISPUTES

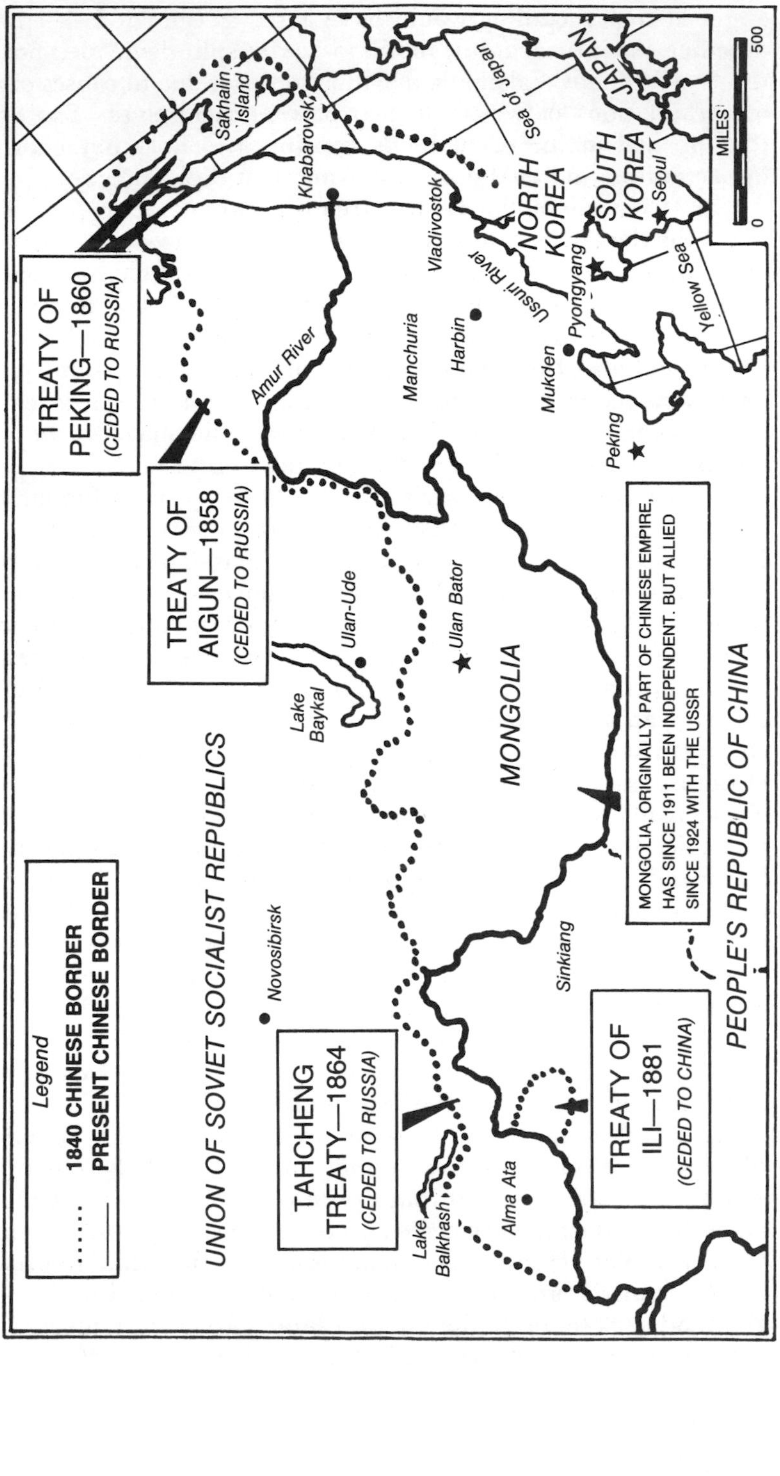

Legend

•••••• **1840 CHINESE BORDER**
——— **PRESENT CHINESE BORDER**

TREATY OF
PEKING—1860
(CEDED TO RUSSIA)

TREATY OF
AIGUN—1858
(CEDED TO RUSSIA)

TAHCHENG
TREATY—1864
(CEDED TO RUSSIA)

TREATY OF
ILI—1881
(CEDED TO CHINA)

MONGOLIA, ORIGINALLY PART OF CHINESE EMPIRE,
HAS SINCE 1911 BEEN INDEPENDENT. BUT ALLIED
SINCE 1924 WITH THE USSR

UNION OF SOVIET SOCIALIST REPUBLICS

PEOPLE'S REPUBLIC OF CHINA

Novosibirsk

Lake
Balkhash

Alma Ata

Sinkiang

Lake
Baykal

Ulan-Ude

Ulan Bator

MONGOLIA

Amur River

Khabarovsk

Vladivostok

Manchuria

Harbin

Mukden

Ussuri River

Peking

Pyongyang

Seoul

NORTH
KOREA

SOUTH
KOREA

JAPAN

Sea of Japan

Yellow Sea

Sakhalin
Island

MILES

0   500

and alliance with Jiang, just at the time when the Communists were preparing to renew their civil war against him. During the last phase of this struggle, 1945–49, Stalin advised Mao to seek a compromise settlement with Jiang, for Stalin (rightly) feared the consequences of a rival giant in the Communist camp.

The resentments over past treatment were compounded by several doctrinal disputes about the "true" meaning of Communist ideology. Much more was at stake in these doctrinal differences than the academic question of which party correctly interpreted Marxism-Leninism. By the early 1960s the Soviet Union and China were vying for leadership of world communism. The allegiance of millions of people to one side or the other depended to some extent upon which one proffered the more acceptable interpretation of Communist ideology. Thus, the doctrinal debate was a form of power politics conducted with verbal cannonades.

Still heady after their own successful revolution, the Chinese insisted that violent wars of national liberation represented the only way for Communists to come to power. The Russians demurred, insisting that in some cases Communists could attain power by parliamentary means. This view led the Soviets to maintain harmonious relations with the "bourgeois" governments of many states. China accused the Soviets of sacrificing their Communist brothers on the altar of Soviet national interests. The Soviets asserted that the Chinese were displaying recklessness, especially in the nuclear age.

A second doctrinal dispute concerned relations with the West. The Soviet Union maintained that peaceful coexistence was possible and that communism would triumph by outperforming Western economies and political systems and thereby attracting the uncommitted nations to the fold. Besides, Moscow said, the alternative to peaceful coexistence was nuclear war. China took the opposite view, insisting that only a violent confrontation could unseat the Western powers.

A third major ideological conflict concerned the pace of transition to a Communist society. The Chinese insisted that once Communists attained control of the government, they should bring about a rapid transition to a total Communist society, including establishment of communes and nationalization of industry. The Soviets counseled a more gradual approach.

By 1960 the Sino-Soviet rift was a prominent feature of the international political landscape. In that year the Soviet Union recalled the thousands of scientists and technicians it had sent to

China to assist in such fields as agriculture, communications, industrialization, education, transportation and scientific research. The Russians also terminated economic aid. When China attacked India in 1962 in a border dispute, the Soviet Union sided not with its Socialist ally but with the world's largest democracy. In the spring of 1969 fighting between Soviet and Chinese soldiers along the Ussuri River resulted in the deaths of hundreds on each side. The Soviets even began to hint at a preemptive nuclear strike against China. Ironically, as a result of the Sino-Soviet feud, the Soviet Union has become the only Communist state practically surrounded by hostile Communist nations.

The Chinese—"nine hundred million axe handles."
Soviet poet Yevgeny Yevtushenko

As the decade of the 1980s opened, China and the Soviet Union each appeared to be engaged in a contest to contain the influence of the other. The 1950 Treaty of Friendship and Cooperation between them was left to expire in 1980 with no attempts at renewal, signaling a lack of interest in repairing relations. In the Communist struggle for primacy, the enormous imbalance of resources—except for people*—in favor of the Soviet Union would seem to favor that contestant, at least in the near term. Indeed, by the 1980s the Soviets had largely succeeded in encircling China. Along the 4,500 mile border that separates the two countries, the Soviet Union had forty-five divisions or approximately 450 thousand soldiers. These forces were equipped with Russia's most advanced tanks, helicopters and surface-to-air missiles. The advanced SS–20 medium-range missile could be found at some points. These ground forces were supported by some five hundred bombers and fourteen hundred fighter planes, the latter quite capable of dealing with China's aged force of bombers.[18] To China's east, the Soviets strengthened their Pacific fleet, which is far stronger than China's fledgling navy. The Soviet fleet is now bolstered by naval and air facilities developed at Cam Ranh Bay and Danang in Vietnam, a Soviet ally on China's southern flank. By signing a treaty of friendship and cooperation with Vietnam, the Soviets appear intent on preventing China from

---

*A Soviet diplomat offers this scenario of a war with China. "The first day we capture 100 thousand Chinese prisoners. The second day a million. The third day 10 million. The fourth day 100 million. The fifth day we surrender."

filling the void left by the ebb of American influence in Southeast Asia. To China's southwest, Russia's friendship treaty with India and the puppet regime installed in Afghanistan in 1979 further circumscribe Chinese influence.

The question of warfare between Russia and China has occupied the attention of strategists since the outbreak of the Sino-Soviet dispute. Most analyses of this issue begin with the observation that in all respects other than manpower the Soviet Union has far greater quantities and much more modern equipment than China. Even in cases where the Chinese have plentiful supplies, they tend to be old and obsolete. For example, the Chinese have a large air force, but their MIG-19s are no match for the Soviet Union's MIG-25s, MIG-23/27s, and SU-19s. The Chinese manufacture many tanks, but their T-54s and T-59s could not hold the field against Russia's T-64s and T-72s. While the Chinese are not lacking in artillery, they have very weak fire control and communications capabilities. Chinese infantry remains vulnerable to Soviet air power and mechanized divisions. The Soviets are far ahead of the Chinese in chemical warfare. It would take several years and an astronomical outlay of funds for the Chinese to gain the capability of defending themselves against a Soviet conventional attack. According to a 1979 study by the US Department of Defense, the cost of such a program would range between $41–$63 billion.[19] The study not only doubted China's willingness to divert such funds from economic-development projects but also questioned China's capacity to utilize high-technology weapons needed for defense, given the fairly low level of technical sophistication prevalent in the People's Liberation Army. Although China has intermediate-range nuclear missiles that could reach some Soviet cities and has tested a missile of intercontinental range, China would suffer grievous losses in a city-for-city exchange. Therefore, it is likely to attack Russia only in desperation. Ironically, the massive buildup of Soviet forces along the border might well stimulate the Chinese into constructing the type of military force that the Russians fear.

The Soviet Union, on the other hand, would appear to have a number of military options against China. One option that does not seem feasible would be an attempt to occupy China and turn it into a satellite along East European lines. Like the Japanese invaders in World War II, the Soviets would no doubt find themselves drowned in a Chinese ocean. Less extreme measures cannot be ruled out, however. As Lucian W. Pye observes, the Soviets could strike at places along the border where population is sparse or where most of the residents are not ethnic Chinese (and therefore not too likely to resist).[20] Sinkiang province, for example, is one-third as large as the United States but has only 20 million inhabitants, half of whom are Turkic minorities unhappy with Beijing's rule. Alternatively, the Soviets could follow the tactic used by China against India in 1962; that is, they could occupy a salient of territory along the border but not penetrate so deep as to allow themselves to be surrounded by Chinese forces. Any of the above steps would humiliate China and dampen its pretensions to great-power status. Their long-term advantage is much less obvious, however.

The Sino-American Détente

The widening chasm between the two Communist giants provided an opening for American foreign policy, if only the United States could place relations with China on a friendlier footing. During the 1960s, just when Sino-Soviet relations were turning uglier, the Cultural Revolution in China and the Vietnam War blocked any efforts to make American ties with Beijing more amicable. Toward the end of that decade, however, both of these impediments began to recede, making an improvement in Sino-American relations possible.

The Pragmatists Replace the Maoists

Ironically, it was Mao's ideological zeal that helped pave the way for better relations between Beijing and Washington. As Mao surveyed the situation in China in the early 1960s, approximately fifteen years after the Communists had come to power, he was disturbed by the course the revolution was taking. The more he looked, the more he found resemblances to the ossified bureaucratic society of the Soviet Union. Scorning Russia's "goulash communism" for its stagnation and complacency, Mao launched the Great Cultural Revolution in order to revive China's revolutionary spirit.

The Cultural Revolution, begun in 1966, can be seen as a revolution within a revolution. Mao encouraged China's youth to challenge the authority of calcified senior officials who seemed more interested in enjoying their privileges than in serving the people. To rekindle the revolution's egalitarian ideal, Mao closed the country's schools and urged the young people to organize into Red Guard units and remove recalcitrant government officials. To overcome society's tendency to divide into privileged and under-privileged classes, Mao forced people with expert knowledge (and healthy incomes) into the farmlands to reacquaint them with peasant labor. It was not unusual for a research physicist to pick cotton alongside a factory manager or the designer of machine tools. These toilers were replaced back home by peasants and soldiers who came from the ranks of the people. As a result, China's economy was slowly grinding to a halt.

Fulfilling Oscar Wilde's witticism that nothing succeeds like excess, the Cultural Revolution had profound if short-lived effects upon China. It is not clear whether those persons dismissed from their posts and sent into the fields experienced a renewal of their commitment to an egalitarian society or merely made the best of a bad situation. What is clear, however, is that during the height of the Cultural Revolution the orderly administration of the country practically disintegrated; factories manned by unskilled workers turned out inadequate supplies of shoddily made goods; an entire generation of students was denied basic educational skills; and the country's level of technical and scientific expertise plummeted as swiftly as the fabled fishing ducks of the Yangtze River.

Those who opposed the Cultural Revolution believed that China had less need of revolutionary fervor than of orderly administration and technological progress. We shall call these people the pragmatists, a label that describes their outlook on the requirements of a modernizing Chinese state. Today, leading pragmatists include Deng Xiaoping, the most powerful figure in China, Prime Minister Zhao Ziyang, and party chairman Hu Yaobang. The pragmatists prized efficiency over ideological purity. They insisted education should include basic skills as well as Marxism-Leninism. They believed in rewarding expertise and achievement, not just revolutionary fervor. In the foreign policy realm, the pragmatists set aside two practices of their predecessors, namely, the promotion of revolution in such far-flung regions as central Africa and ideological denunciations of the United States and other Western states; they insisted that China could profit from dealing with other countries, a rejection of the notion of strict self-reliance practiced during the Cultural Revolution.

The Nixon Summit

After a prolonged internal struggle, the pragmatists emerged triumphant by 1970. This transformation, together with America's withdrawal from Vietnam, provided the needed opening for American diplomacy. The compelling factor that drew America and China together was shared opposition to the extension of Soviet influence.

Both China and the United States now identified the Soviet Union as their principal adversary. In one of the most surprising turnabouts in diplomacy since World War II, President Nixon stunned the world by announcing that he would visit Beijing in February 1972. Before an astonished television audience, President Nixon strode along the Great Wall, visited the court of Chinese emperors, and held conversations with Chairman Mao.[21] In the space of a few days, the two leaders reversed over two decades of hostility between their countries.

The 1972 summit did not itself place Sino-American relations on a normal footing. The two governments had yet to exchange ambassadors and conclude the series of agreements necessary to permit the fluid exchange of people and goods. But the trip did symbolize the intention of both countries to take these steps. The most concrete byproduct of the meeting was the joint communiqué issued at its conclusion. Known as the Shanghai Communiqué, the document dealt with the single most troublesome issue dividing the two nations—Taiwan.

At the time of the Korean War, the United States decided to recognize the Taipei regime as the rightful government of all China, enacted a trade embargo against the mainland, and concluded a treaty of mutual defense with Jiang Jieshi. The Communist government regarded these actions as hostile and unwarranted interference in China's internal affairs, as it regarded Taiwan as a part of China and not a separate country. In the Shanghai Communiqué the United States said:

> The United States acknowledges that all Chinese on either side of the Taiwan Strait maintain there is but one China and that Taiwan is part of China. The United States Government does not challenge that position.

Thus, the United States agreed not to challenge Beijing's interpretation. However, Washington was in no haste to abandon its ally Taiwan, particularly after the disastrous war in Vietnam, for that would make America appear to be an entirely unreliable partner. American credibility represented the keystone in the arch of collective defense. Since so many countries had linked their security to the United States, doubts concerning America's willingness to come to their defense would dislodge that keystone. The entire structure of collective defense would crumble.

Chairman Mao appreciated Nixon's position. In a very significant concession—perhaps a measure of how dearly China wanted

America as a counterbalance to the Soviet Union—the Chinese agreed to place the Taiwan issue on the back burner. "We can do without them for the time being, and let it come after one hundred years," Mao told Nixon.[22] The Shanghai Communiqué made no mention of America's mutual defense treaty with Taiwan or the presence of nearly ten thousand American military personnel—mostly in connection with the war in Vietnam—on the island.

Before Air Force One lifted off from the Chinese mainland, the United States and China had reached one of the historic agreements of the postwar world. The two leaders had in effect renounced the use of force between them, agreed on the necessity to contain Soviet influence, undertook to promote trade and people-to-people exchanges, and agreed to set aside the issue of Taiwan for a while.

Uneasy Collaboration

The Nixon visit seemed to dissolve the obstacles in the path of harmonious Sino-American relations so easily that many observers expected full diplomatic recognition and normal relations to follow immediately. By the time this occurred, however, neither President Nixon nor Chairman Mao, who died in 1976, was any longer in office.

The Chinese insisted that the United States meet three conditions before full diplomatic relations could be established. These were that the United States:

(1) break diplomatic relations with Taiwan,
(2) remove all American military forces from Taiwan,
(3) terminate the mutual defense treaty with Taiwan.

Fearful of appearing to be an unreliable ally in the wake of the Vietnam debacle, the United States did not find these conditions easy to accept, particularly as China refused to make a public commitment not to invade Taiwan by force. Eventually, however, President Carter did accept these conditions, and on January 1, 1979, the United States extended formal diplomatic recognition to the government in Beijing. In announcing the decision, Secretary of State Vance said that it was made with the assumption that China would not use force against Taiwan. "We stated very clearly what our expectations were, and they have not contradicted that," Vance said on "Meet the Press."[23]

American conservatives, including Ronald Reagan, pounced on Carter's actions as the treacherous abandonment of a loyal and deserving ally. Once in office, however, Reagan has continued his predecessor's policy. Meanwhile, trade between the United States and Taiwan continues to flourish, overshadowing trade between America and the mainland (see Fig. 2–2). In 1982, US trade with the mainland totaled $5.2 billion. (By way of contrast, Sino-Soviet trade amounted to only $316 million in that year.)[24] The United States has become China's third largest trading partner after Japan and Hong Kong. Although the United States has granted China most-favored-nation status, American imports from China have remained at a modest level, consisting mainly of textiles, petroleum products, bristles and feathers, antiques and handicrafts, and non-ferrous metals. China's principal import from the United States has been grain (over eight million tons in 1981). The Chinese are also interested in American technology, and they have complained that the United States has been too restrictive in sharing advanced technology with China. Expanding Sino-American trade must overcome obstacles posed by American producers of textiles and footwear. These groups persuaded the United States to impose quotas against Chinese imports in 1983. To protest these moves, China for a time ceased buying American grain. Such commercial sparring

FIGURE 2–2: AMERICAN TRADE WITH CHINA AND TAIWAN

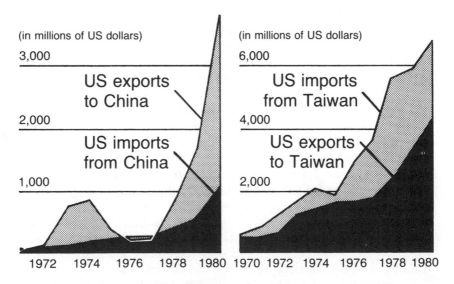

Source: *The New York Times*, June 14, 1981. Based on Department of Commerce Data. Copyright © 1981 by the New York Times Company. Reprinted by permission.

resulted in a 15 percent decline in Sino-American trade from 1982 to 1983, when such trade totaled $4.4 billion. By 1984, however, there were signs of better commercial accord. A textile agreement was signed, some twenty Chinese-American business ventures were under way, and several American companies were engaged in the search for oil off China's coast.

A continuing source of tension in Sino-American relations is American military assistance to Taiwan. Under the Taiwan Relations Act, approved by Congress after Washington established diplomatic relations with Beijing in 1979, the United States maintains unofficial relations with Taiwan and is committed to supplying "such defense articles and services in such quantity as may be necessary to enable Taiwan to maintain a sufficient self-defense capability." China denounced American arms sales to Taiwan as an infringement of China's sovereignty over the island. In August 1982, the United States and China signed a joint communiqué in hope of overcoming this problem. In the document, Washington agreed not to exceed the level of arms sales to Taiwan in any given year since normalization and to reduce them gradually, although no timetable was included. (In 1979, the United States shipped about $800 million worth of arms, the highest amount to date.) The Chinese, for their part, said the peaceful reunification of Taiwan with the "motherland" was "a fundamental policy." For years Washington has sought a Chinese pledge not to use force to integrate Taiwan with the mainland; the Chinese have refused to do so, arguing that relations with Taiwan are an internal matter. In practical terms, the 1982 formula states that China intends to reunify the country peacefully, and that in consequence Washington will gradually reduce arms sales to Taiwan. While the 1982 communiqué defused immediate tensions, the Chinese have since voiced complaints that reductions of American arms sales to Taiwan are not proceeding fast enough. This issue is likely to cloud Sino-American relations for some time to come.

The joint pursuit of containing the Soviet Union gives rise to the question of whether the United States should provide military assistance to China.[25] Valid arguments can be found on both sides of this issue. Bolstering Chinese military capabilities would continue to tie down and perhaps even increase the number of Soviet forces along the border with China, currently estimated at fifty divisions. American military assistance to China, by aggravating Sino-Soviet tensions, would in all likelihood prolong the state of animosity between the Communist rivals, a condition from which the United States derives benefits. Such aid would also make more concrete China's stake in strong ties with the United States.

American military aid would furthermore boost the political standing of the pragmatists in Beijing, who need to demonstrate some advantages from their policy of accommodation with the United States. At home, American military sales would reduce per-unit costs to America's armed forces, keep assembly lines in operation, and reduce the balance of payments deficit.

Opponents of American military aid to China cite the worsening in US-Soviet relations likely to result. They have also expressed the fear that such a measure would constitute the first step down the slippery slope of a perceived commitment to China's integrity. If China should be threatened later on, the United States would be faced with a choice between honoring this commitment or being pilloried as an undependable ally. Critics with a particular interest in arms control fear that American military aid to China might stimulate an Asian arms race against China, Russia, and Japan, all of whom have historic reasons to distrust one another. Strong advocates of human rights do not believe that the United States should provide military assistance to a country, such as China, that systematically violates those rights. Other critics fear that supplying arms might embolden Beijing to pursue a policy of imperialism. Still others observe that a rifle or a missile that is one day pointed toward Moscow may on another day be aimed at Washington, particularly if the two Communist giants should compose their differences.

Obviously, the question of military aid to Beijing admits of no easy answer. However, by providing Beijing with military assistance that is basically defensive, it might be possible to accentuate the advantages of such aid while meeting many of its objections. Defensive equipment might include radar, surface-to-air missiles (an anti-aircraft weapon), communications gear, sonar systems and helicopters.

The Reagan administration has displayed a willingness to sell such equipment to China, but Beijing's leaders have not shown much enthusiasm for such purchases. The Chinese seem more intent on rebuilding their economy and enhancing their technical prowess than engaging in a major military buildup.

UNITED STATES-SOVIET-CHINESE RELATIONS

The rise of China as a world power has stimulated talk of a US-Soviet-Chinese triangle in world politics. This triangle (as depicted in Fig. 2–3) is not equilateral; the three powers are located at

FIGURE 2–3: MODEL OF US-SOVIET-CHINESE RELATIONS

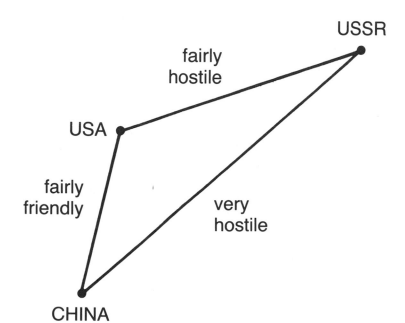

The distances between the points approximate the degree of friendliness or hostility between the countries shown.

various distances from each other, reflecting different degrees of hostility and friendliness. At the beginning of the 1980s one could diagram the three-power triangle as shown above.

The French analyst Michel Tatu suggests that this triangular relationship contains a built-in dynamic. Since no state can be equally hostile to two other states, each of the three states chooses a principal adversary. For the United States and China, the principal adversary is the Soviet Union. The latter's prime opponent is China. According to Tatu, the following principles apply to the triangular relationship:

(1) The existence of adversary number one leads to collusion with the other power.

(2) Each state seeks to minimize collusion between the other two.
(3) It is in the interest of each to bluff or blackmail its principal adversary by threatening collusion with the remaining power.
(4) The surest way for any power to provoke the other into collusion is to display undue aggressiveness.[26]

One can find numerous applications of these principles. The recent improvement in Sino-American relations may be traced in large measure to common opposition to the Soviet Union (principle 1). By consolidating better relations with China, Washington clearly hopes to minimize collusion between the two major Communist powers (principle 2). The Chinese similarly seek to perpetuate suspicions between Moscow and Washington (using what little leverage they have). The third principle finds expression in the phrase "China card," which describes Washington's efforts to apply pressure on Moscow by threatening to sell military-related items to China. Henry Kissinger has warned Washington against overplaying its hand, however.

> Any attempt to manipulate Peking might drive China into detaching itself from us, perhaps to reexamine its options with the Soviet Union, to gain control of its own destiny. Equally, any move by us to play the Chinese card might tempt the Soviets to end their nightmare of hostile powers on two fronts by striking out in one direction before it was too late, probably against China.[27]

At the moment, the Soviets offer the best illustration of the fourth principle; their invasion of Afghanistan resulted in President Reagan's offer to sell military goods and some high-technology equipment to China. Soviet support for the Vietnamese invasion of Kampuchea and machinations in the Horn of Africa have also nudged the United States and China closer together.

The above illustrations suggest that as the suitor courted by Beijing and Moscow, Washington retains the largest degree of leverage in the great-power triangle. While this may be true for the present, this temporary advantage should not obscure the complexity of the three-sided relationship or the need for deft diplomacy. Several of these complexities are discussed below.

It is clear, to begin with, that the nature of the dispute between Russia and China goes deeper than the differences between Washington and either power. Washington's concerns have to do with geopolitics. Kissinger writes, for example, that neither he nor President Nixon could accept a Soviet assault against China. If Russia humiliated China and reduced it to impotence, the Soviets could hurl the entire weight of their military force against Europe. Furthermore, American inaction in the face of Soviet aggression against China would incline Japan and Western Europe to bow to Soviet blackmail, as these countries became convinced of American impotence or indifference to the fate of its allies.[28] Similarly, Washington would oppose the forceful extension of Chinese power against Japan or Southeast Asia.

In contrast to the Sino-Soviet rift, the rivalry between the United States and Russia (and the recently ended hostility between the United States and China) did not spring from historical enmity. In the US-Soviet instance, such competition arose almost by accident; the Soviet Union sought to expand after World War II and the United States happened to be the only power in position to stop her. In the case of Russia versus China, however, antagonism springs less from what each does than what each stands for. Each of these rivals represents a threat to the other's domination of the worldwide Communist movement. Russia's imperialistic behavior toward China in the previous century and Stalin's indifferent assistance to Mao have left deep resentments in China. Failing gigantic blunders by American diplomacy, the enmity between the Soviet Union and China is likely to outlast the rivalry between the United States and either of the other two powers.

For the time being, the United States appears to be in the most favored position of the three powers. China finds itself at the other extreme, surrounded as it is by the Soviet Union and its allies and greatly disadvantaged by the Soviets in terms of military power. But Soviet diplomacy has not been noticeably successful in the US-Soviet-Chinese triangle. In all likelihood, Moscow assumed that détente with Washington would place a brake on the improvement of Sino-American relations. The Soviets also hoped that Chinese leaders who replaced Mao might take a more cooperative stance toward the Soviet Union. Neither of these expectations has materialized, however. Instead, the Soviet Union finds itself on poor terms with both China and the United States. The nightmare of a two-front war continues to recur in Moscow. Indeed, the United States, China and Japan appear to be drawing together in an implicit coalition against the Soviet Union.

In terms of the stability of each bilateral relationship, the general equivalence of military power between the United States and the Soviet Union holds out prospects of a stable if prickly relationship. Least stable of the three relationships is that between the Soviet Union and China. Here we find two states with an enormous disparity of military power coupled with intense enmity. In 1982–83, the Chinese moved a little closer to the Soviets, out of pique with American arms sales to Taiwan as well as trade and technology restrictions. The implications of such moves remain unclear at present. For many years to come, the Soviets will be tempted to launch a preemptive strike (perhaps nuclear) against China. America's sale of high-technology items and military equipment to China could well hasten such attacks, on the ground that delay would only permit the Chinese to become stronger. For the moment, military clashes between China and the United States seem out of the question. Should the United States show itself to be a weak opponent of the Soviet Union, however, the Chinese may decide they have no choice but to repair relations with the Soviets. To avoid this situation, America must strive to maintain its resolve against the Soviet Union sufficiently to keep China as an ally. At the same time, Washington must not allow US-Soviet relations to deteriorate to the point at which either side contemplates nuclear war. Such a balancing act is destined to pose an extraordinary challenge for American diplomacy.

FOR DISCUSSION

Which view of the origins of the Cold War seems more valid, the orthodox or revisionist interpretation?

Does Soviet foreign policy appear to be guided by the tenets of Marxism-Leninism or by the dictates of Soviet national interests?

Is détente a prudent goal for American foreign policy? If not, what objectives should the United States pursue with regard to the Soviet Union?

Should the United States sell military equipment to China?

Describe the consequences for American foreign policy of a rapprochement between Moscow and Beijing.

READING SUGGESTIONS

Butterfield, Fox. *China: Alive in the Bitter Sea*. New York: Times Books, 1982.
Horowitz, David. *The Free World Colossus*. New York: Hill and Wang, 1965.
Jacobsen, C. G. *Sino-Soviet Relations Since Mao: The Chairman's Legacy*. New York: Praeger, 1981.

Kennan, George F. *Russia and the West under Lenin and Stalin*. New York: Mentor Books, 1962.

Pillsbury, Michael. "U.S.-Chinese Military Ties?" *Foreign Policy*, Fall 1975.

Pipes, Richard. *U.S.-Soviet Relations in the Era of Détente*. Boulder, Colo: Westview Press, 1981.

Solomon, Richard H., ed. *The China Factor: Sino-American Relations and the Global Scene*. Englewood Cliffs, NJ: Prentice-Hall (for the American Assembly and the Council on Foreign Relations), 1981.

Stoessinger, John G. *Nations in Darkness: China, Russia and America*, 2nd ed. New York: Random House, 1975.

NOTES

1. It is possible to argue that some of the practices associated with the Watergate episode were made palatable to high government officials by the persistent violation of basic American principles by the US government. The same can be said regarding certain illegal activities undertaken by American intelligence agencies within the United States, including wiretapping and mail tampering.

2. George F. Kennan, *Russia and the West under Lenin and Stalin* (New York: Mentor Books, 1962).

3. Later, Kennan altered his views on containment. He said he never meant the United States should use only military force to oppose Soviet expansion but should rely primarily upon political and economic support for threatened regimes. He also wrote that the United States should not seek to contain communism everywhere but only in those regions deemed vital to American interests (a concept we might call "selective containment"). The evolution of Kennan's views may be found in George F. Kennan, *The Nuclear Delusion* (New York: Pantheon Books, 1982).

4. However, Washington did not accede to France's request in 1954 for American air power. For an account of this refusal, see Chalmers M. Roberts, "The Day We Didn't Go to War," *Reporter*, XI (September 14, 1954): 31–35.

5. Revisionist explanations of the Cold War may be found in the following studies: Gar Alperovitz, *Atomic Diplomacy: Hiroshima and Potsdam* (New York: Random House, 1965); D. F. Fleming, *The Cold War and Its Origins, 1917–1960*, 2 vols. (New York: Doubleday, 1961); David Horowitz, *The Free World Colossus* (New York: Hill and Wang, 1965); Gabriel Kolko, *The Roots of American Foreign Policy* (Boston: Beacon, 1969); Harry Magdoff, *The Age of Imperialism: The Economics of U.S. Foreign Policy* (New York: Monthly Review Press, 1969).

6. Many revisionists link the containment policy to the "military-industrial complex." In this view, the same people control both. Thus, they gain economically at home through the promotion of a foreign policy that benefits them abroad.

7. *New York Times*, October 5, 1977.

8. In a report filed at the end of 1979 evaluating implementation of the Helsinki accords, the State Department concluded:

> After four years of experience, it can be said that neither the optimists nor the pessimists have been proven correct. The Helsinki conference did not lead immediately to extensive changes in the repressive practices of some nations, nor to universal implementation of the principles embodied in the Final Act. It did not transform the world, but it did make a beginning. We have seen genuine efforts by many countries to fulfill their obligations to human rights, security, and cooperation; and we have seen the Final Act grow to become a standard of civilized conduct which even those who sometimes flout its provisions cannot ignore.

US, Department of State, *Implementation of Helsinki Accord, June 1–November 30, 1979,* 7th semiannual report (Washington: Government Printing Office, 1979), p. 2.

9. US, Department of State, *Testimony by Secretary of State Kissinger before the Senate Committee on Finance,* March 7, 1974 (Washington: Government Printing Office, 1974).

10. *New York Times,* April 4, 1979.

11. In actuality, Kissinger's predictions proved questionable. After a falling off in 1974, Jewish emigration from Russia rose steadily, as the figures in the text demonstrate, despite Carter's public criticism of Russia's human-rights record. Of course, we are unable to estimate how many Jews would have been permitted to leave had the United States followed Kissinger's advice.

12. Emigration figures from *New York Times,* April 4, 1979, and October 1, 1980. While most Jews leaving Russia designate Israel as their destination, over half make their way to the United States. As of 1980, experts estimated a total of between 2 and 2.6 million Jews still in Russia out of a total Russian population of 240 million. In 1980, after the collapse of détente, Russia permitted only 21,000 Jews to emigrate.

13. The phrase is that of Marshal Shulman, a leading State Department adviser on Soviet affairs during the Carter years.

14. Specialists estimated that approximately 100 thousand Soviet troops were in Afghanistan as late as 1983.

15. For a graphic portrayal of China's traditional outlook, see John G. Stoessinger, *Nations in Darkness: China, Russia and America,* 2nd ed. (New York: Random House, 1975), Chapter 2.

16. For a revealing account of Chinese resentment toward the United States, see John K. Fairbank, "Why Peking Casts Us as the Villain," *New York Times Magazine,* May 22, 1966. Fairbank's book, *The United States and China,* 4th ed. (Cambridge: Harvard University Press, 1978) is the standard work on Sino-American relations.

17. The Chinese had repeatedly warned that they would intervene if UN forces approached too near their border.

18. These estimates are based on reports emanating from NATO headquarters in Brussels as reported in *New York Times,* May 21, 1980.

19. Ibid., January 4, 1980.
20. Lucian W. Pye, "Dilemma for America in China's Modernization," *International Security*, IV (Summer 1979): 3–19.
21. Kissinger graphically describes his secret journey and the Nixon summit in *White House Years* (Boston: Little, Brown, 1979), Chapters 18, 19, and 24.
22. Ibid., p. 1062.
23. *New York Times*, December 18, 1978.
24. *New York Times*, March 7, 1983.
25. For two provocative discussions of this question, see Michael Pillsbury, "U.S.-Chinese Military Ties?" *Foreign Policy* (Fall 1975): 50–64, and A. Doak Barnett, "Military Security Relations between China and the United States," *Foreign Affairs*, LV (April 1977): 584–97.
26. Michel Tatu, *The Great Power Triangle: Washington-Moscow-Peking* (Paris: The Atlantic Institute for International Affairs, 1970).
27. Kissinger, p. 763.
28. Ibid.

Chapter 3
The United States, Allies, and the Third World

In the previous chapter, we examined two important members of the state system. Here, we study America's principal allies—Western Europe and Japan—as well as developing countries. The actions of all these members of the state system have an impact upon the United States through the feedback mechanism illustrated in Fig. 1–1. As that diagram also suggests, foreign-policy actions taken by the United States affect these other states. We shall discover many instances of these interactions in the pages that follow.

THE UNITED STATES AND WESTERN EUROPE

Ever since World War II, a close relationship with the nations of Western Europe has formed the pedestal of American foreign policy. Indeed, as far back as World War I, it has been a cardinal principle of American foreign policy to prevent any single power from controlling the people and resources of Western Europe. Were there no other reason for American participation in these global conflicts, Washington would have intervened to prevent Germany from conquering the continent. Any country that rules all of Europe's resources would represent an intolerable threat to the United States.

FIGURE 3–1: US TRADE, 1980
    ($ billions and percentages)

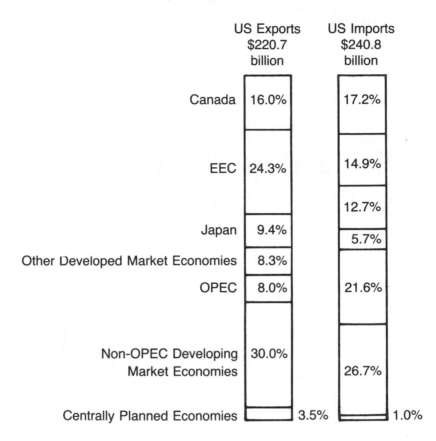

Source: *U.S. Foreign Policy and the Third World: Agenda 1982* by Roger D. Hansen and Contributors for the Overseas Development Council. Copyright © 1982 by the Overseas Development Council. Reprinted by permission of Praeger Publishers and the Overseas Development Council.

Importance of Western Europe to the United States

Why is Western Europe of such importance that America has twice in this century sent her sons to die in its defense? There are several answers to this question. Most of the small number of democratic countries in the world are situated in Western Europe. Here too are most of the economically advanced states. Thus, in the political and economic realms, the United States and Europe share many of the same concerns. Many Americans take a natural interest in Western Europe as the land from which their forebears sailed for the United States decades or centuries ago. Western Europe also buys a substantial portion of American exports; it attracts a significant amount of American private investment; and it supplies many essential imports to American consumers (see Fig. 3–1). In a strategic sense, the nearly 300 million people of Western Europe possess a combination of technological prowess, economic resources, managerial capability, and philosophical outlook to constitute a formidable concentration of military power. Two European states (Great Britain and France) possess nuclear weapons, and several others have the capacity to do so. Were Western Europe's military and economic power to fall into hands hostile to the United States, the resulting tilt in the world's balance of power would seriously jeopardize American security.

To substantiate America's interest in preserving the integrity of Western Europe, the United States presently stations approximately 300 thousand troops on the continent, 250 thousand of them in West Germany. In case of hostilities involving Western Europe and the Soviet Union, these American forces would almost certainly become engaged. Indeed, Washington hopes that the likelihood of such entanglement will deter the Soviets from striking westward. The annual cost of America's military commitment to Europe approaches $15 billion (approximately 50 percent greater than Japan's entire military budget).

Evolution of American Relations with Western Europe

Immediately after World War II, the continent of Europe lay in smoking ruins. Food and jobs were scarce. General strikes by discontented mobs threatened to break out and destroy what little was left of political authority. Many Americans feared that, having just saved the continent from Hitler, they were about to see it fall prey to Soviet communism. This threat stemmed from two sources. Internally, economic conditions were such that many Europeans were prepared to adopt any system that promised them relief. In countries such as France and Italy, where Communist voting strength was one-third the total, lawful takeover of the government by Communists was a real possibility. Externally, the Soviet army stood poised on the frontiers of Western Europe, with no effective military power to block its advance should it choose to move.

To blunt the threat of communism, the United States decided to make major economic and military commitments to Western Europe (an example of the State System's effect on a country's Political System). As a means of blocking the internal threat of communism, America launched a massive economic aid program known as the Marshall Plan. Under this program, the United States gave approximately $12 billion to the nations of Western Europe to help them place their economies back on their feet and restore the confidence of the people in democracy and free enterprise. Announced in 1947, the Marshall Plan proved so successful that the United States was able to terminate it in 1951; the internal Communist threat had been largely overcome. (The United States also offered recovery aid to Eastern Europe and the Soviet Union, but this assistance was rejected for fear that it would lead to interference in the internal affairs of these countries.)

Meanwhile, however, the Red Army had ensured the triumph of Communist regimes in Eastern Europe, which fell under Moscow's thumb. This army now stood on the verge of Western Europe, and many feared that Stalin would give the command to attack. To deter such an assault, the United States took the lead in forging a military alliance of West European and North American countries. This pact, known as the North Atlantic Treaty Organization (NATO), was formed in 1949 and represented America's first peacetime alliance. NATO's original members were Belgium, Canada, Denmark, France, Great Britain, Iceland, Italy, Luxembourg, the Netherlands, Norway, Portugal and the United States. In later years, Greece, Turkey, West Germany and Spain joined. To sharpen NATO's teeth, the United States supplied military aid to the new coalition.

Considering Europe's history of near-constant warfare, a military pact embracing such nations was an historic event in itself. The United States, however, strove in the years that followed for an even more epoch-making development, the unification of Western Europe. Such a coalescence would not only put an end to Europe's fratricidal wars but would also create a united front against Soviet communism. Beginning with the Marshall Plan, the United States lent its support to various collaborative efforts by the states of Western Europe.

A major initiative was formation of the European Coal and Steel Community in 1951, which later expanded its functions and evolved into the European Common Market (1958). The Common Market, known officially as the European Economic Community, now includes ten nations. These nations charge a common tariff against outsiders' goods and engage in several joint economic endeavors. The United States lent its support to and joined the Organization for European Cooperation and Development (OECD). Today, the OECD supports a permanent multinational staff and provides a forum where the industrial democracies including Japan can concert their policies—or attempt to do so—on a wide range of economic concerns that include monetary policy, trade barriers, energy, and policy toward the developing world. Scores of other intra-European organizations have also come into existence, so that today there is practically no sphere of life toward which at least one European organization does not direct its activities.

Ironically, the very successes of American policy toward Europe have given rise to certain difficulties for the United States. American policymakers assumed that a rejuvenated Europe would pursue common policies with the United States regarding Western security, economic matters, and relations with the non-European world. As matters turned out, however, American and European interests have diverged on several occasions. For example, France, Portugal and Belgium resented America's half-hearted support of their efforts to retain control over their colonial empires. Europe extended lukewarm support or maintained an embarrassed silence regarding American actions in Vietnam. European tariff and investment policies have sought to protect their markets from what Europeans perceive as excessive American penetration. When Great Britain, France and Israel invaded Egypt in 1956, after Nasser nationalized the Suez Canal, the United States, in a bid to court Arab sympathies, sided with Egypt, forcing the invasion to an early end. The episode had a lasting impact in that it planted doubts in Europe about American reliability. France decided to build its own nuclear force as insurance against a repetition of what it viewed as American perfidy and withdrew from NATO's integrated military organization in order to maximize France's autonomy in military matters.

It is probably unavoidable that allied nations experience some strains in their relations. By virtue of differing geographical location, internal needs, overall capabilities and historical traditions, they are bound to have interests that vary to some extent. As the next section will reveal, such conflicts certainly exist in the Atlantic Alliance. As we review these differences, however, we should not lose sight of the many common bonds that unite the United States and Canada with the nations of Western Europe. Statesmen in all these capitals reveal by their actions a realization that their economic well-being and national security depend upon one another's acting in concert.

Current Issues in US-West European Relations

Policy toward the Soviet Union

It is one of the paradoxes of recent history that the countries of Western Europe, the most likely targets of Soviet aggression, have displayed less concern than the United States about a Soviet thrust westward. Many West Europeans, especially West Germans, have developed a vested interest in détente and are extremely reluctant to dismantle the structure of cooperative East-West relations that has been erected over the years. To a much greater extent than Americans, West Europeans count on trade with the Soviet Union and Eastern Europe to help them cope with inflation, recession, and unemployment (see Table 3–1). Western Europe has agreed with the Soviets to construct a pipeline that will bring large additional quantities of natural gas from Russia to Western Europe. In reply to President Reagan's objections that the pipeline will render Western Europe overly dependent upon the country that is the continent's principal threat to peace and will produce revenue for additional military spending, the Europeans insist they need alternatives to volatile Middle East oil supplies. Because of détente, 200 thousand Germans were allowed to leave Russia and Eastern Europe in the 1970s. In the same period, 50 thousand East Germans were

TABLE 3–1: EAST-WEST TRADE (In millions of dollars)

	US Exports to E. Eur. & USSR	US Imports from E. Eur. & USSR	Total Trade
1970	352	216	568
1975	2,780	626	3,406
1978	3,670	1,410	5,080
1980	3,850	1,376	5,226
	W. Eur. Exports to E. Eur. & USSR	W. Eur. Imports from E. Eur. & USSR	Total Trade
1970	5,838	6,227	12,065
1975	21,698	18,204	39,902
1978	26,195	26,219	52,414
1980	35,823	44,121	79,944

Source: Compiled from data in United Nations, *Monthly Bulletin of Statistics*, May 1982, pp. xxx–xxxii.

permitted to join their families in the West. Détente has opened the land approaches from West Germany to Berlin; families that had been separated for years are now able to visit and telephone each other.

Whether in the realm of economics or defense—as we shall see in the next section—the countries of Western Europe are less willing than the United States to make sacrifices to oppose Soviet expansionism. This reluctance springs from a reduced perception of the Soviet threat compared to the American view.

I believe in the unity of the West as the foundation for any successful relationship with the East. Without Western unity, we will squander our energies in bickering while the Soviets continue as they please.
President Ronald Reagan, Eureka College commencement address, 1982

Sharing the Defense Burden
Ever since the creation of NATO, the United States has accused its European allies of failing to contribute a fair share of the common defense. Europe's reluctance to boost defense spending reflects in part a lesser perception of the Soviet threat, as mentioned before. In recent years, the United States has been devoting approximately 5 percent of its gross domestic product to defense, compared to 3.5 percent for most European members of NATO. In the early 1980s, the US accounted for nearly two-thirds of NATO's annual military expenditures, although the United States produces only one-half the gross domestic product of the alliance. The Europeans counter that they supply the bulk of troops stationed on the continent.

The issue of burden-sharing took on new urgency in the late 1970s, as US-Soviet relations began to deteriorate and new data revealed that the Soviets were militarily outbuilding the West by large amounts. In 1977 the NATO countries agreed to increase their military spending by 3 percent annually after inflation. While the United States and some of its European allies have fulfilled this pledge, the declining economies of some allied states have caused them to fall short of this goal.

As the Soviets began in the late 1970s to flex their military muscles in Africa and Southwest Asia, the United States urged Europe to widen its military commitments. Indeed, it is only because the United States counters Soviet threats worldwide that the Europeans can afford to spend so little on defense, Washington asserts. If the United States were to mothball its intercontinental missiles and bombers, Europe would be left hostage to Soviet power. In particular, the Pentagon has encouraged Europe to contribute to a credible deterrent in the Persian Gulf, since Europe would be the first to suffer should the Soviets gain control of this strategic waterway. French deployments in northern Africa and the Persian Gulf are not enough, American officials insist.

Credibility of America's Commitment to Europe

If Soviet troops seized a sixty-mile strip of territory in West Germany and then threatened to destroy New York and Washington if the United States counterattacked, would America honor its commitment to European defense? Would the United States be willing to trade Boston for Bonn or Los Angeles for Lisbon?

In NATO's early years this issue did not arise. Soviet weapons could not reach American cities, so Europeans had little reason to doubt that America would honor its security commitment. In 1957, however, the Soviet Union launched the Sputnik rocket, demonstrating that Soviet missiles could hit the territory of the United States. By the mid-1960s, the Kremlin possessed a substantial arsenal of such missiles, tipped with nuclear warheads. America's stake in a European war dramatically changed, as now US participation could result in missile attacks on its own cities. The Europeans grew understandably nervous that the United States might prefer to settle with the Soviet Union at Europe's expense rather than risk such destruction. Europe's fears were heightened by the Kennedy administration's adoption of the doctrine of "flexible response." Under this military doctrine, the West would meet a Soviet assault at the same level of conflict as employed by the aggressors, rather than destroying Soviet cities with nuclear missiles. In other words, if the Soviets launched a tank assault against western Europe, NATO would retaliate in kind rather than attack the Soviet heartland—as called for by the previous military doctrine of "massive retaliation." This alteration led many Europeans to suspect that the United States was looking for a way to avoid Soviet attacks on American cities. If flexible response did not work, would America take the ultimate step of attacking Soviet territory in order to save Western Europe?

Despite strong verbal commitments to European defense by every recent American president, lingering doubts about America's willingness to defend Europe persist. In France, such doubts have led to the strengthening of an independent nuclear force. To confirm its commitment, the United States has continued to station fighting men and women in Europe. Their function is largely symbolic; that is, they function as a "plate-glass window" to ensure that any Soviet attack on Europe would necessarily involve the United States. Nonetheless, some Europeans point out that at the signing ceremony for the NATO treaty in 1949, the US Marine Band played the then current hit, "It Ain't Necessarily So."

The Matter of Consultation

Europe's doubts about the depth of America's commitment were fed by the unfortunate American habit in NATO's early years to dictate to its allies rather than consult with them. In what is perhaps an overstatement, former Senator Eugene J. McCarthy wrote, "American allies are treated as if they were enemies—or, at best, as highly unreliable allies to be consulted as little as possible, to be left uninformed, and to be forced, whenever possible, to accept US policies and support US programs."[1]

Consultation refers to a method of decision making whereby partners discuss an issue and reach a decision through the interplay of ideas and opinions. In the years immediately following NATO's formation, however, the United States was so much stronger than even the combined power of its allies that Washington developed the practice of making decisions affecting the alliance without consulting Europe. The decision to respond to Soviet aggression in Europe by attacking Russia's heartland (the doctrine of massive retaliation, adopted during the Eisenhower years), as well as the shift to flexible response, was taken unilaterally by the United States. Europe, made proud by its long tradition of sovereign splendor, strongly resented such treatment at the hands of a relative upstart in world politics. By the late 1960s Europe's protests began to penetrate Washington's veil of arrogance and numerous consultative organs were established. Through such bodies, NATO has forged common policies on such issues as SALT, troop reductions in Europe, and the development of a new intermediate-range nuclear missile to counter Russia's deployment of the SS-20 missile and Backfire bomber. To deal in a consultative manner with Russia's military buildup in Europe and measures for modernizing NATO's response, the alliance has established a High-Level Group. It has also created a Special Group on Arms Control to develop proposals in this area. NATO's foreign and defense ministers meet once a year, and annual economic summits among leading Western powers inevitably touch on security concerns.

Despite advances made in the area of consultations, Washington still offends its allies periodically by unilateral actions. For example, shortly after coming into office, President Carter pressured NATO countries to accept on their territory a new American weapon called the neutron bomb. This weapon seemed ideal for warfare in Europe's urbanized setting, as it produced casualties by the spread of deadly radiation rather than heat and blast. Branded by its opponents as a weapon that preserves buildings while killing people, the neutron bomb was designed to halt a Warsaw Pact tank assault against Western Europe without at the same time obliterating the territory it was supposed to protect. Some Europeans objected that a certain amount of damage through heat and blast was bound to occur, and they feared its deployment would lower the nuclear threshold. After strongly urging Western European governments to persuade their citizens to accept the weapon, President Carter then unilaterally decided against deployment, embarrassing several of these governments. President Reagan subsequently elected, without extensive consultation, to develop and deploy the weapon.

American Globalism Versus European Regionalism

In contrast to the situation that prevailed just fifty years ago, America is now a global power while Europe's concerns are largely regional. As a global power, the United States is concerned with events that occur everywhere; a revolution in Central America or an oil discovery in the South China Sea affects American interests. Europe, having shed its colonies, is far less affected by developments outside the European continent. To express this dichotomy, Arnold Wolfers has dubbed the United States a "hub" power. As Figure 3–2 illustrates, American interests are affected by events anywhere on the "rim." Europe, as a "rim" power, is scarcely touched by occurrences that take place elsewhere on the rim. Of course, the distinction can be overdrawn; the distribution and price of petroleum and other scarce resources most certainly bear on Europe's well-being. Nevertheless, the difference in perspective between a hub power and a rim power helps explain some of the clashes between the United States and its NATO partners. Europeans had difficulty in discerning how the outcome of the Vietnam War could affect themselves (or the United States for that matter). American interventions in Cuba, the Dominican Republic, and Chile generally drew no more than a yawn from Europe. After Iranian revolutionaries seized American hostages in 1979, Europe expressed its sympathies but refused to freeze Iranian assets as Washington

FIGURE 3-2: UNITED STATES AS A "HUB" POWER

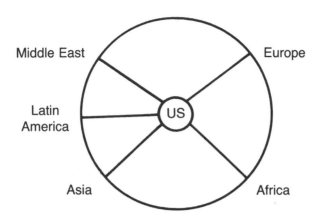

requested. Following the Soviet invasion of Afghanistan, several European states did not join the United States in boycotting the Moscow Olympics and halting grain and high-technology sales to the Soviet Union. In the 1973 Middle East war, Europe (Portugal excepted) denied its bases to American planes carrying supplies to Israel, for fear of antagonizing Arab oil producers.

These episodes make clear that NATO is least united on threats that emanate from outside Europe. However, should the strategic stand-off in Europe continue to hold, it would appear that the greatest hazards to Western Europe are likely to stem from outside. This realization has led some commentators to call for a reevaluation of NATO so as to give the alliance a role in defending the West's interests worldwide. For the present, the United States is bearing that burden almost alone.

Economic Disputes
A group of nations with advanced industrial economies almost inevitably experience a certain degree of economic conflict. As in the case of the security issues discussed above, however, it is important to bear in mind that underlying the topsoil of occasional disagreement rests a bedrock of like-mindedness. To a steadily increasing extent, the industrial countries of the North Atlantic area realize that the prosperity of all is joined together. It is also important to recall that while we can separate economic and security concerns for analytical purposes, in reality the two are intermixed. If the

members of NATO face mounting unemployment, inflation and phlegmatic economic growth, they will be reluctant to boost military spending. Furthermore, economic adversity could induce nationalistic economic policies, generating resentments that impede cooperation in the security sphere. Similarly, of course, sharp disagreements over security issues could interfere with economic cooperation.

During Europe's economic recovery following World War II, the United States accommodated itself to high European tariffs, judged necessary to protect reviving industry. Washington also accepted the preferential tariffs Europe extended to its colonies and former colonies, as well as monetary inconvertibility. Once Europe recovered its economic health, Washington assumed, these special privileges would disappear, and a grateful Europe would open its doors to American goods. When the European Common Market was formed, the United States accepted the organization's discriminatory tariffs against outsiders, including America, for the sake of boosting the EEC's prospects for success.

Washington's toleration of these practices unquestionably helped Europe to prosper, and that prosperity contributed to the stability of democracy and the thwarting of communism. By the 1960s, however, the United States felt it was time for Europe to admit more American goods and investment. In the face of European reluctance to take such measures, American companies found a way of avoiding the EEC's tariffs by setting up manufacturing plants within those countries. This practice became so common that some Europeans expressed the fear that America was "taking over" European industry. Just as some Americans today chafe at Arab investment in the United States, many Europeans and Canadians have expressed reservations about Americans making important decisions about the size, location, establishment and termination of manufacturing plants and other forms of investment abroad. After the passage of the Trade Expansion Act by Congress in 1962, several European (and American) tariffs were reduced as a result of negotiations that lasted from 1964–67 (known as the Kennedy Round). In April 1979, the major trading nations approved a new trade package at Geneva after five and a half years of negotiations. These arrangements lower existing tariffs by one-third over an eight-year period and also curb other obstacles to trade.

A. W. DePorte explains that US-European economic difficulties can be divided into three types: monetary, Third World policy (especially energy), and the combined challenge of inflation and unemployment.[2]

Monetary Problems

Starting in the 1950s, the United States began running balance of payments deficits; that is, the amount of funds flowing out of the United States exceeded those coming in. These deficits fueled international trade, as nations holding US dollars could use them to purchase goods from other nations, when the exporter would prefer not to accept payment in the importer's currency. However, there were limits to the US deficit that could not be topped without calling into question the worth of the dollar. To restrain the deficit, Washington resorted to various means, including the encouragement of exports, limitations on the expenditures of tourists, "buy American" provisions in foreign aid bills, and arrangements with West Germany to help offset the costs of stationing American troops there. To assist Washington's efforts, the central banks of the major trading nations cooperated to minimize the impact of monetary difficulties. However, these steps failed to stem America's spiraling deficit, which totaled $9.8 billion by 1970. Worried by the huge amounts of dollar holdings abroad, the Nixon administration took drastic and unilateral action. In 1971 the United States suspended the convertibility of dollars into gold and imposed a 10 percent surcharge on dutiable imports. Termed the "Nixon shocks" by Japan, these measures produced a major crisis in American relations with both that country and Europe. After months of feverish negotiations, conducted in a rather heavy-handed manner by Secretary of the Treasury John Connally, Washington agreed to cancel the surcharge and reshuffle exchange rates. This reshuffling had the effect of devaluing the dollar (making it cheaper for foreigners to buy American goods). As even these steps failed to place a brake on America's mounting deficit, the trading nations agreed to suspend fixed exchange rates and let currencies float against each other according to supply and demand. This scheme has worked tolerably well. But it was just when the industrialized democracies had managed to work out their monetary difficulties that a new set of problems threatened to dwarf these issues. These new dilemmas emanated from the developing world, and they centered around energy.

Third World Policy—Energy

A detailed examination of the energy crisis is reserved for Chapter 13. Here we shall look at some preliminary problems of Western unity in the face of the energy "crunch." In 1973, the OECD countries enjoyed a balance of payments surplus of $11 billion, even after factoring in the American deficit. In that year, however, war in the Middle East led Arab oil producers to suspend shipments to some Western countries (particularly the United States), and then to start ratcheting up the price of oil. By 1974 the OECD surplus had become a deficit in the amount of $22 billion.[3] This deficit rose to approximately $80 billion by 1980.

Many observers feared that price hikes by the Organization of Petroleum Exporting Countries (OPEC) would demolish the structure of economic cooperation erected by the OECD countries. Would not each country rush separately to OPEC with special "deals" involving investment preferences, military assistance, measures against Israel, and technological aid? However, no such scramble occurred. Instead, the major oil importers decided to consult and evolve joint policies. Australia, Austria, Great Britain, Belgium, Canada, Denmark, West Germany, Greece, Ireland, Italy, Japan, Luxembourg, the Netherlands, New Zealand, Norway, Spain, Sweden, Switzerland, Turkey and the United States formed the International Energy Agency and agreed to a scheme for sharing oil if world supplies plummeted more than 7 percent. In 1979 the United States agreed in Tokyo with Canada, France, Great Britain, Italy, Japan and West Germany to reduce their future oil imports, each country setting its own target; the United States agreed to limit its imports to 8.5 million barrels per day through 1985. The conferees further agreed to consider international ventures in the development of synthetic fuels.

Despite these and other cooperative efforts by the West and Japan, the rising price of energy and the always-present threat of future oil embargoes have caused some friction within the ranks of the industrialized world. EEC recognition of the right of Palestinians to self-determination and territory seized by Israel in successive Middle East wars clearly reflect a desire to gain the good graces of Arab oil exporters. Similarly, the refusal by several European countries to freeze Iranian assets, as the United States requested following the seizure of American hostages in 1979, manifested a reluctance to offend the Moslem world, to which most OPEC states belong.

Inflation and Unemployment
Chronic inflation began in the United States, Western Europe and Japan in 1973 along with the climb in OPEC oil prices. Normally, an inflated economy is treated by applying deflationary measures

(such as higher interest rates) that slow down the pace of economic activity and therefore produce some unemployment. When the Western economies took such steps, however, they found themselves saddled not just with mounting unemployment—always a touchy political problem—but with continuing inflation as well. This combination of inflation, slow economic growth and high unemployment has gained the label of "stagflation." Persistent stagflation has accentuated the gap between the relatively healthy economies of the United States, West Germany, and Japan and the economies of most other OECD nations. An effective remedy for stagflation has yet to be found.

Despite temptations to follow beggar-thy-neighbor economic policies to overcome stagflation, the OECD nations have managed to retain their commitment to cooperation. Some of these countries have devised a new forum, the economic summit, to deal with the entire range of economic problems discussed here. The first of these gatherings of heads of state took place in Rambouillet, France, in 1975. These summits, now held annually, have included the heads of state of Canada, France, Great Britain, Italy, Japan, West Germany, the United States, and occasionally other Western nations. While the achievements of these meetings have been rather slim, the sessions do preserve the spirit of cooperative endeavor in meeting problems common to all the industrialized democracies. If they remain baffled by their economic problems, at least they remain baffled together.

In this section we have examined the importance of Western Europe to the United States and traced the evolution of US-European relations since World War II. To build West European strength and confidence, the United States lent military and economic assistance to the continent, and Washington became a leading member of such organizations as NATO and the OECD. However, the very success of America's endeavors provided Western Europe with the leeway to assert its own interests, which have not always coincided with those of the United States. We have examined some of the differences between the United States and Western Europe, including burden-sharing, the credibility of America's commitment to defend Europe, the issue of consultation, American globalism versus European regionalism, and various economic disputes. Still, despite these factors, the United States and Western Europe find themselves in harmony most of the time. Like all alliances, the Atlantic Alliance undergoes strains, but the essence of the partnership has not yet been threatened.

THE UNITED STATES AND JAPAN

Japan has been called an economic giant, a military pygmy, and a political curiosity. Such a description may well conceal the fact that, for the next decade at least, the most consequential Asian power from the standpoint of American foreign policy is bound to be not China but Japan. The Land of the Rising Sun, now boasting the world's highest gross national product (after the United States), exerts sufficient economic power to overshadow China's military or political influence. Like the nations of Western Europe, Japan has been an American ally since World War II. This fact has led some analysts, such as President Carter's national security assistant, Zbigniew Brzezinski, to propose that the United States join with Western Europe and Japan to form a tripartite coalition of like-minded nations. This coalition of democratic industrial nations would cooperate to raise their standard of living, ensure their security, and devise common policies toward the developing world. Let us examine more closely the nature of Japan and its importance to the United States.

An island chain extending approximately two thousand miles along China's eastern flank, Japan occupies about the same area as the state of California. Upon these islands dwell approximately 110 million people, about one-half the population of the United States. The world's sixth most populous state generated in 1980 a per capita gross national product (GNP) of $9,890, compared with $290 for China.[4] As Asia's most prosperous state, Japan leads the world in producing ships, radios and commercial vehicles, and ranks second in motor vehicles, computers, cotton yarn, aluminum, copper, crude steel, cement, fishing, rayon and acetate. With a military force numbering only one-quarter million men, Japan's considerable influence in world affairs stems from its economic might. Yet, Japan's economic power is constrained by factors of geography. Japan is poor in natural resources and arable land. The country lives by foreign trade. It imports approximately half of its food supply, all of its oil (mostly from the Middle East), and huge quantities of raw materials that it exports as finished products. To cut off Japan from the world environment would be to remove the life-support system from a voyager in outer space. Japan must export or die.

Japan's importance to America's national interest springs from her economic muscle and her military potential. After Canada, Japan is America's largest trading partner, while America ranks as Japan's top trading power. US-Japanese trade exceeded $60 billion in 1982, with Tokyo enjoying a $20 billion surplus. Japan buys about 9.5 percent of American exports and supplies approximately 13 percent of America's imports (see Fig. 3–1). America takes nearly one-third of Japan's exports and supplies over one-fourth of her imports. These figures reveal Japan's very large role in America's economic well-being, and vice versa. While Japan's military forces presently have no mission beyond territorial self-defense, the first half of this century exposed the extent of the nation's military potential. It remains very important to the security component of America's national interest that Japan not array this incipient military power against the United States. A Russo-Japanese alliance or a Sino-Japanese alliance, directed against Washington, would gravely upset the balance of power against America. In summary, as a trading partner and a latent military power, Japan is of enormous importance to the United States.

The Occupation and the Security Treaty

Japan's development as an economic titan is all the more remarkable considering the enormous destruction the country suffered in World War II. At the war's conclusion, the United States feared a renewal of Japanese aggression to avenge the island-nation's defeat. To preclude this threat—more in America's imagination than in Japan's mind—the United States occupation forces instituted three programs: demilitarization, democratization, and economic growth.

Demilitarization was expressed in Article 9 of the Japanese constitution, written by General Douglas MacArthur, commander of the occupation forces, and accepted by the Japanese people. Unique among constitutions, Article 9 rejects military force as an instrument of national policy. The article states:

> Aspiring sincerely to an international peace based on justice and order, the Japanese people forever renounce war as a sovereign right of the nation and the threat or use of force as means of settling international disputes.
>
> In order to accomplish the aim of the preceding paragraph, land, sea, and air forces, as well as other war potential, will never be maintained. The right of belligerency of the state will not be recognized.

This remarkable provision does not preclude the existence of any military forces whatever. Today, Japan has a Self-Defense Force of 240 thousand men. However, Article 9 is generally assumed to prohibit the development of offensive forces with the capability of operating beyond the home islands.

Democratization was as successful as demilitarization. The new constitution created a constitutional monarchy based on the British system of government. The legislature, called the Diet, plays the dominant role in the government. The majority party in the Diet selects the prime minister, and he and his cabinet are responsible to the Diet. The constitution further provides for an independent judiciary and guarantees civil rights. Since its creation in 1955, the Liberal-Democratic party (conservative in outlook despite its name) has governed the country. It is opposed by a composite of leftist parties, including the Socialists, the Komeitos, the Democratic Socialists, and the Communists, a small, faction-ridden party lacking funds.

At the outset of the occupation, Washington decided to dissolve the huge financial-industrial combines, called *zaibatsus*, that had provided the base for Japan's military power and make Japan a land of small shopkeepers and farmers. However, it soon became evident that the United States needed a strong ally in Asia, and the *zaibatsus* were let stand. A program of land distribution in rural areas improved the farmer's lot and created a class of conservative growers.

Japan's status as a formal ally of the United States was created by a mutual security treaty signed in 1951, revised in 1960, and renewed in 1970 for an indefinite period. The treaty as it now reads provides for an American guarantee of Japanese security, in return for which the United States gains the right to maintain bases and other facilities in Japan. Interestingly, the treaty does not obligate Japan to respond if American forces or territory are assaulted. US bases and facilities may be used not only for the defense of Japan but to maintain peace and security (as defined by Washington) throughout Asia. America has used these facilities, strategically located on the rim of the Asian mainland, to support its military efforts in Korea and Vietnam. As of 1980, nearly 50 thousand American men and women were stationed at 112 locations throughout Japan. In a "prior-consultation" note appended to the treaty, the United States agreed not to use Japanese bases for combat operations outside Japan or to introduce nuclear weapons into Japan without the consent of the Japanese government.

While most Japanese accept the necessity of preserving this treaty, there can be no doubt that the treaty wounds Japanese pride by placing the country's defense in outside hands. For years the opposition, centered in the Socialist party, argued that the treaty serves the interests of the United States more than Japan. The Socialists asserted that the treaty endangers Japanese security by threatening to drag Japan into a war fought in the name of American foreign policy. Citing the absence of any threat to Japan, they insisted the treaty was not only unnecessary but that it prevented Japan from conducting an independent foreign policy. Those who accepted the treaty as a necessary evil observed that America's security umbrella shelters Japan from any threat that might develop. Furthermore, they said, the security arrangement allows Japan to concentrate its energies and resources on economic development instead of military defense. (Japan spends just under 1 percent of GNP on national defense, compared to 5 percent for the United States.) Proponents add that, to the extent that American and Japanese foreign policy objectives in Asia coincide, American bases in Japan serve the goals of Japanese foreign policy.

For the United States, the benefits of the security treaty are manifest. As mentioned, America has used its bases in Japan, sometimes called an "unsinkable carrier," to support military campaigns in Korea and Vietnam. America's commitment to Japan ties that country to the American alliance system and impedes the growth of a Sino-Japanese or Russo-Japanese alignment against the United States. Japan's reliance upon America's security guarantee also offers the United States a certain amount of leverage in the trade disputes between the two countries.

Following several years of cordial relations, American relations with Japan plummeted in 1971 to their lowest level since World War II. This deterioration was due to what Japan referred to as the three Nixon "shocks." The first of these shocks concerned China. For years Japan had refrained from consolidating friendly ties with China at Washington's insistence. Washington's abrupt reversal of its own policy toward China, without any prior consultation with Japan, aroused fears that America might take other actions in the future without considering Japan's interests. Such anxieties were heightened by the reduction of American forces in Asia and continued talk of no more American wars on that continent.

The China shock was quickly followed by two others—the suspension of the dollar's convertibility and a 10 percent surcharge on imports (which has since been lifted)—both aimed in large part at Japan's trade surplus with the United States. These episodes raise the issue of US-Japanese economic relations.

US-Japanese Economic Strains

As we have seen, Japan is America's second largest customer, while the United States buys more from Japan than does any other country. The substantial amount of trade between these countries means that economic decisions taken in one capital are bound to have a considerable impact in the other. The underlying difficulty in US-Japanese economic relations centers around Japan's growing trade surplus with the United States. This surplus currently approaches $20 billion annually. The United States would like Japan voluntarily to restrict exports to America and make it easier for American firms to sell goods in Japan. In America's eyes, the Japanese engage in some questionable trade practices. The Japanese government, for example, subsidizes research undertaken by some high-technology firms, thus lowering production costs and thereby reducing the price of the finished product. Many Americans also feel that Japanese tariffs are unjustifiably high, now that the country no longer need protect its industry as in the rebuilding period following World War II. Furthermore, Americans assert that the Japanese have fashioned a shield of complicated administrative regulations that blocks the entry of American goods into Japan. The frustration resulting from these factors is heightened by the conviction in many quarters that Japan has prospered in large part because it has received from America a free ride on defense, and because America was so helpful in bringing about Japan's postwar recovery.

The Japanese, on the other hand, contend that the above arguments are no more than a set of excuses for the declining productivity in the United States as compared with Japan. The Japanese insist that their trade surplus stems from the fact that Japan makes goods more cheaply and better than their American counterparts. Let Detroit produce a less expensive, better-made car, Japan says, and Americans will cease buying Toyotas and Hondas and Datsuns. The Japanese further contend that they have little choice but to export. Nature has endowed Japan with few natural resources. The country must import 88 percent of its energy, over 60 percent of its grain, and 100 percent of its iron ore, bauxite and copper.[5] Japan uses its export revenues to pay for these imports. While Americans accept Japan's need to export, they cite Japan's worldwide trade surplus (close to $15 billion in 1981) as evidence that Japan's economic vitality allows for limitations on its exports to the United States and the opening of Japan to more American goods.

Sales of Japanese automobiles and trucks in the United States have generated considerable ill-will against Japan. In 1979, 17 percent of all cars sold in the United States were made in Japan. In 1982 this figure rose to 22 percent, despite a 1981 agreement by Japan to limit the export of cars to 1.68 million vehicles annually. The flood of imports from Japan and Europe threw the American automobile industry into one of its worst slumps as the 1980s began. Detroit laid off workers in record numbers. The auto industry appealed to Washington for relief. The Carter administration, however, refused to place quotas on imports, arguing that such action would make consumers pay higher prices for cars and result in increased oil consumption by America's less fuel-efficient automobiles. The United Auto Workers union wants Japan to assemble its cars in the United States, so as to provide jobs for American workers. The union also advocates quotas or higher tariffs on foreign cars. These are sensitive issues in Japan. Automobiles account for 20 percent of Japan's exports, and one out of ten industrial workers is engaged in car-related production. The Japanese do not wish to throw their own people out of work. Furthermore, Japan hesitates to build plants in America for fear that they will become idle once Detroit retools to produce the kinds of cars Americans want. Nonetheless, Honda has announced plans to build an assembly plant in Columbus, Ohio, and General Motors and Toyota are planning to jointly produce automobiles in Fremont, California. At the same time, the United States is asking Japan to lower or remove its 10.4 percent tax on foreign-made automobile chassis and its 5.3 percent tax on foreign automobile parts; this would make it easier to sell American cars in Japan.

Much the same situation arises in connection with color television sets, but in this area the two countries have evolved an agreement that may prove a model applicable to other items in dispute. By 1977, Japan had captured 35 percent of the American market for color televisions. American industry and its workers asked President Carter for relief. That year the Carter administration approved an agreement with Japan to limit Japanese exports of color TVs over the next three years to 1.56 million "complete" color television receivers and 0.19 million "incomplete" sets annually. This agreement has reduced Japan's share of the American market by a considerable extent. There are also serious trade disagreements regarding Japanese import quotas on agricultural goods and sales of Japanese textiles and steel in the United States.

There can be little doubt that sentiment for erecting trade barriers against Japan has been growing in America. This attitude was perhaps best expressed in 1977 by the late George Meany, president of the AFL-CIO: "Foreign trade is the guerrilla warfare of economics—and right now the United States economy is being ambushed. . . . Free trade is a joke and a myth. . . . The answer is fair trade, do unto others as they do unto us—barrier for barrier— closed door for closed door."[6] The anger of the American worker found support in a 1977 AFL-CIO report estimating job losses due to imports (not just from Japan) at 300 thousand in textiles and apparels, 150 thousand in electronics and electrical machinery, 100 thousand in steel and other primary metals, and 70 thousand in shoes.[7] If Japan refuses to take steps to restrict exports to America and open its country to American goods, there is a strong prospect that Congress will enact quotas and tariffs against Japan. Such actions will probably lead Japan to further question America's willingness to come to its defense, and could induce Japan to consolidate military ties with China and try to improve its relations with the Soviet Union. Either of the above actions would destabilize the international politics of Asia and complicate American foreign policy. Thus, for political as well as economic reasons, it is in America's interest to resolve the trade dispute with Japan—though no easy solution appears in sight.

Japan's Role in Asia

Military Forces

Its mission greatly circumscribed by Article 9 of the constitution, Japan's Self-Defense Force numbers 240 thousand men. The Japanese habitually limit their defense expenditures to just under 1 percent of GNP; in 1983 they spent approximately $12 billion on defense, eighth highest in the world. Yet Japan's military forces are only half the size of South Korea's and don't begin to match China's 4.3 million soldiers. In addition to their defense outlays, the Japanese spend close to $1 billion annually to defray maintenance costs of American bases on Japanese soil.

Beginning in the mid-1970s, Japanese attitudes toward military policy started to change. Up to that time, most Japanese tolerated the Self-Defense Force with some reluctance, preferring to leave national defense to the hands of the United States. As confidence in America began to ebb, however, more and more Japanese began to appreciate the need for indigenous military power. Today, most Japanese support the Self-Defense Force, including 73 percent of the Socialists, traditionally opposed to the military.[8] The current debate in Japan no longer centers on whether to maintain a military force but on how much larger it should be. There seems to be little sentiment in Japan for conscription, the deployment of military forces outside the home islands,[9] repeal of Article 9, or even increasing the proportion of GNP allocated to defense. Most serious proposals concern means of upgrading existing forces, such as by equipping them with more advanced weapons. Meanwhile, Japanese forces have begun to participate in naval exercises with the United States, Canada, Australia, and New Zealand. Virtually no Japanese advocate the acquisition of nuclear weapons, although Japan remains fully capable of developing such armaments. Japanese memories of World War II remain too vivid to consider this option. Besides, military strategists realize that Japan's urban density renders the country an ideal target for a nuclear attack, which a Japanese nuclear capability could invite. Only if the international situation gravely deteriorated and Japan were convinced that America would not come to her defense would Tokyo contemplate obtaining nuclear weapons.

The frustrating thing is the Japanese don't always believe us when we say we're committed to defending them. We say the security treaty is the anchor of our Far East policy. They say, "An anchor? That's something you can pick up and run with!"

US embassy official quoted by Henry Scott-Stokes,
"It's All Right to Talk Defense Again in Japan,"
New York Times Magazine, February 11, 1979

Despite the waning of Japan's distaste for a military force, the Japanese have given no sign of agreeing to the demands of the Reagan administration for bolstering Japan's military role in Asia. The United States would like Tokyo to upgrade its navy so as to be able to take over defense of 1,000 miles of sea lanes around Japan. This measure would enable the United States to release more ships in the Pacific fleet for duty in the area of the Persian Gulf. In order to undertake this responsibility, Japan would have to build up its navy well beyond present levels. So far, Japan has refused to appropriate the funds to do so.

Japanese-Soviet Relations

Japanese relations with the Soviet Union have been marinated in hostility for an extended period dating back to the Russo-Japanese War of 1904–05 and including Russia's intervention against Japanese forces in the closing days of World War II. At war's end, the Soviets seized southern Sakhalin and the entire Kurile Islands chain, including four islands just off Japan's northern waters. These four islands, over which Russia has no historic claim, comprise the core of Japanese-Russian animosity today and have prevented the signing of a formal peace treaty ending the state of war between the countries. In late 1979, the Soviets further angered Japan by constructing military facilities and moving 10 thousand soldiers to these islands.

This territorial dispute extends to a conflict over fishing. Both the Soviet Union and Japan are major fishing nations. The waters surrounding the contested islands are particularly abundant with fish. The Soviets have detained thousands of Japanese fishermen who insist on harvesting the waters around the islands.

Recently, the United States and China have suggested that Japan join them in an anti-Soviet coalition. Tokyo's recent uncertainty concerning America's commitment inclines Japan against making an irrevocable break with Moscow, however. Many Japanese would like the opportunity to invest in the extraction of resources from Siberia, which the Soviets encourage. Large-scale joint exploitation of Siberia, as well as sharp increases in Japanese-Soviet trade, have been held up by the territorial dispute. (Nonetheless, Japan ranks second only to West Germany among Russia's non-Communist trading partners.) Should US-Japanese relations sour, Tokyo would have no choice but to reach an accommodation with the Soviet Union, unless Japan engaged in a major arms buildup. Several observers fear that the economic conflict between Tokyo and Washington could lead to such an impasse, which would represent a severe setback for American foreign policy.

Japanese-Chinese Relations
As opposed to the Soviet Union, the Japanese feel a marked cultural and racial affinity toward China. Additionally, Japan's surplus of capital and China's abundance of labor suggests a marriage of economic convenience.

Following in the wake of Nixon's visit to Peking, Japan and China established diplomatic relations in 1972. Relations between Tokyo and Peking proceeded smoothly if unspectacularly until 1978. In that year, China and Japan signed a Treaty of Peace and Friendship, followed by an $80–$100 billion trade agreement to extend over thirteen years. Japan will buy oil and coal, while China is to receive industrial plants and technology. At China's insistence, the former agreement included a phrase opposing the efforts of any power to establish "hegemony" in Asia, a Chinese code word for Soviet expansionism. The Japanese, however, insisted that the treaty also contain a provision that the pact would not affect relations between the signatories and third parties; this was an effort to soften the anti-Soviet tenor of the document and reflects Tokyo's desire to maintain correct if not cordial relations with Moscow.

Following these agreements, trade between Japan and China began to expand. In 1979, it stood at $6.5 billion, approximately twice the figure for 1977 and one-seventh the amount of Japanese trade with the United States. While Japan accounts for 20 percent of China's exports and over one-third of China's imports, China absorbs only 2.5 percent of Japan's exports and supplies a slightly lower proportion of Japan's imports.[10] In December 1979, Japanese Prime Minister Ohira visited Peking and signed a government-to-government loan program. The leaders of both countries pledged to increase exchanges in economics, cultural affairs, science and technology. More than any other country, Japan is playing a critical role in China's modernization.

The Soviets take a dim view of the Peking-Tokyo axis. They can be expected to level threats should either China or Japan significantly boost its military power. Both Asian nations will in that case look to the United States for protection, generating the prospect of continued tension between Moscow and Washington. Indeed, it may turn out that the close ties between Tokyo and Peking, to the extent they are directed against the Soviet Union, will greatly complicate efforts by Washington and Moscow to place their relations on a better footing. Should America at some point decide to reduce its support of China or Japan in the hope of solidifying friendlier ties with the Soviet Union, Washington faces the prospect that either or both of these Asian states will perceive no possibility other than accommodation with Moscow. It appears that for the immediate future the United States must choose between supporting China and Japan or reaching for friendlier relations with the Soviet Union. Only with an extraordinary degree of luck will Washington be able to have it both ways.

Japan, Western Europe, and the United States

During the previous decade, a group of scholars and prominent officials joined to form an organization called the Trilateral Commission. Headed by Zbigniew Brzezinski, later to become President Carter's national security adviser, the commission also included then Governor Jimmy Carter. The commission's purpose was to explore ways of consolidating ties among the three nuclei of industrial democracy: the United States and Canada, Western Europe, and Japan. These three centers share many interests and hold similar views about the shape of the world they hope to see evolve. They share a belief in the preeminent value of self-government through representative institutions and in basic civil liberties and civil rights. They share an interest in stable and growing economies and in the continuing and orderly growth of trade, access to markets, raw materials (particularly Middle Eastern oil), investment opportunities, and sound monetary arrangements that will facilitate such economic interchange. Under the Trilateral concept, accepted by President Reagan and his leading assistants, the United States, Japan, and the NATO nations would cooperate in the international sphere, particularly in the areas of security, trade, and policy toward the developing world. Sometimes it was suggested that formal security arrangements among the United States, NATO, and Japan be established. It was further hoped that economic progress of these developed states would stimulate economic growth in the less developed countries, as a prosperous industrialized world would buy more goods from the developing countries.

We have already explored two sides of this triangle, the one connecting the United States with Western Europe and the one that joins the United States and Japan. Turning to the Western European-Japanese side, we find that the line connecting these two parties is dotted rather than heavy and solid. In other words, relations between these two centers of the industrialized world remain sporadic and limited in magnitude. For example, Japan accounts for only 1 percent of the EEC's exports and supplies slightly over 2 percent of the EEC's imports.[11] In the security sphere as well, the extent of interaction is slight. The parties display a tendency to view the Asian and European theaters as things apart, with minimal effort to plan for one region by reference to exigencies in the other. Michael Pillsbury suggests, as a step in the opposite direction, exchanges of visits between NATO and Japanese defense officials. He goes on to propose that such consultations might include discussion of circumstances under which Japan would attempt to bottle up the Soviet Far Eastern Fleet in the Sea of Japan in case of general war.[12] The Atlantic Council of the United States, a public policy interest group, endorses Pillsbury's suggestion and further proposes that Japan and NATO join the United States in creating a deterrent force to protect the Persian Gulf from Soviet incursion. As the Japanese constitution outlaws the use of force as a tool of national policy, the council urges Tokyo to devote a major new effort to support research and development of alternative sources of energy.[13]

Standing in the way of such cooperation in the security sphere are economic conflicts between Japan and Western Europe that mirror the commercial disputes between Japan and the United States. Since 1968 Japan has enjoyed a trade surplus with the countries of the Common Market, which approached $10 billion in 1982.[14] Like the United States, Europe has complained that Japan makes it inordinately difficult for foreigners to sell their goods, particularly agricultural items, in Japan. Europe also laments that Japanese manufactured imports are throwing Europeans out of work; consequently they have asked Japan voluntarily to restrict exports to Europe. The Japanese response has been essentially identical to what they have told the United States.

While the vision of the Trilateral Commission has yet to be fully realized, the United States, Japan and Western Europe have begun to concert their actions in a number of ways. All are members of the OECD. Their leaders meet regularly to talk about such matters as energy, monetary and fiscal policy, trade, food and preservation of the environment. Most of the trade engaged in by these states flows from one to the other. While three-sided coordination in security matters has been minimal, economic collaboration has laid the foundation for a cohesive community among the world's leading industrial democracies.

THE UNITED STATES AND THE THIRD WORLD

The abrupt emergence from colonialism of over one hundred states in the two decades following World War II ranks as one of the greatest transformations of the state system in history. Today, most of the world's people live in these developing states, often referred to collectively as the Third World. This term came about as a convenient way of distinguishing among the states of the Western alliance (First World), those of the Soviet bloc (Second World) and all the rest (Third World). The Third World is composed of approximately one hundred twenty states. It embraces an astonishing variety of political and economic systems, from affluent Saudi Arabia to poverty-stricken Bangladesh, from democratic India to authoritarian Ethiopia.

In recent years, Third World countries have become increasingly important to the United States in economic terms. Of the

twenty largest American trading partners, eleven are developing
countries (see Table 3–2); these eleven countries account for more
than 25 percent of American trade. In the last decade, developing
countries have increased in significance, both as suppliers of US
imports and purchasers of American exports, compared to the
industrial market economies (Fig. 3–3). Developing countries supply 90 percent of America's petroleum imports. The Third World
also supplies the United States with much of its imports of key
metals and raw materials (Fig. 3–4). By the end of 1980, US direct
investment in developing countries totaled $52.3 billion, up from
$14.8 billion in 1967.[15] Several Third World states are important
to America because they occupy strategic locations. The states in
the vicinity of the Persian Gulf offer examples.

TABLE 3–2: TWENTY LARGEST US TRADING PARTNERS, 1980
($ billions and percentages)

*The twenty largest US trading partners, in terms of total merchandise transactions, include eleven developing
countries, which together account for more than 25 percent of all such transactions and 33 percent of all
US imports. Mexico is the third largest trading partner of the United States.*

	Total Transactions	Exports	Imports
Canada	$ 76.9	$ 35.4	$ 41.5
Japan	51.5	20.8	30.7
Mexico	27.6	15.1	12.5
West Germany	22.7	11.0	11.7
United Kingdom	22.5	12.7	9.8
Saudi Arabia	18.3	5.8	12.5
France	12.7	7.5	5.2
Nigeria	12.1	1.2	10.9
Taiwan	11.1	4.3	6.8
Netherlands	10.6	8.7	1.9
Venezuela	9.9	4.6	5.3
Italy	9.8	5.5	4.3
Korea, Rep.	8.8	4.7	4.1
Belgium-Luxembourg	8.6	6.7	1.9
Brazil	8.0	4.3	3.7
Libya	7.6	0.5	7.1
Hong Kong	7.4	2.7	4.7
Algeria	7.1	0.5	6.6
Indonesia	6.7	1.5	5.2
Australia	6.6	4.1	2.5
Total, 20 Countries	$346.5	$157.6	$188.9
Total US Trade	$461.5	$220.7	$240.8
11 Developing Countries as % of Total US Trade	**27.0%**	**20.5%**	**33.0%**

Source: *U.S. Foreign Policy and the Third World: Agenda 1982* by Roger D. Hansen and Contributors
for the Overseas Development Council. Copyright © 1982 by the Overseas Development Council. Reprinted
by permission of Praeger Publishers and the Overseas Development Council.

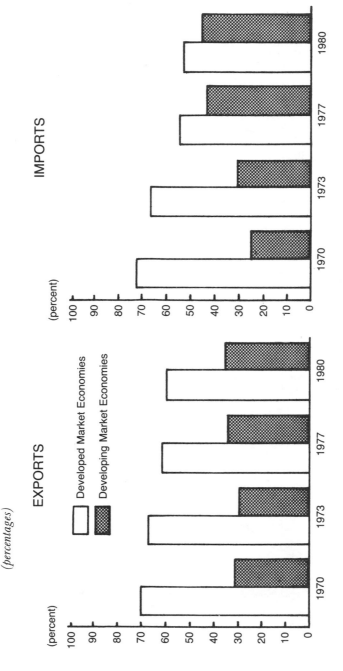

FIGURE 3-3: US EXPORTS TO AND IMPORTS FROM DEVELOPED AND DEVELOPING COUNTRIES AS SHARE OF TOTAL US EXPORTS AND IMPORTS

(percentages)

Source: U.S. Foreign Policy and the Third World: Agenda 1982 by Roger D. Hansen and Contributors for the Overseas Development Council. Copyright © 1982 by the Overseas Development Council. Reprinted by permission of Praeger Publishers and the Overseas Development Council.

FIGURE 3–4: US IMPORTS OF SELECTED METALS AND MINERALS
(percentages of total imports)

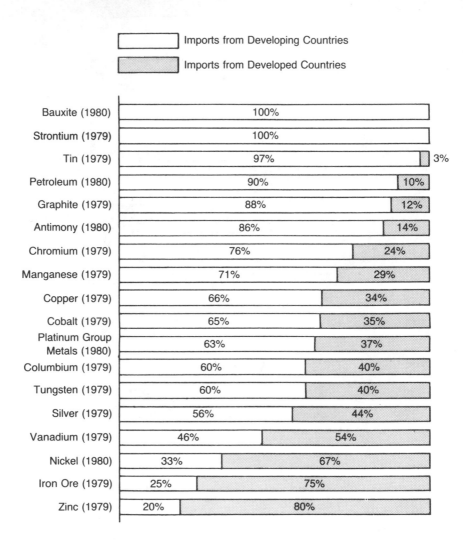

Source: *U.S. Foreign Policy and the Third World: Agenda 1982* by Roger D. Hansen and Contributors for the Overseas Development Council. Copyright © 1982 by the Overseas Development Council. Reprinted by permission of Praeger Publishers and the Overseas Development Council.

The significance of the Third World to the United States makes all the more vexing the fact that many of these states regard America as an obstacle to their cherished dreams of modernization. Of course, not all developing states take this attitude, but the fact remains that the United States is not overburdened with friends in the developing world. To understand why this is the case, we must analyze Third World nationalism.

Nationalism in the Third World

"The people of Africa, Asia and Latin America, because of ages of colonialism, have been robbed of their gold, their diamonds, their cotton, their silk, their ivory, their spices, their drugs, their rubber, their oil, their animal wealth, and many times even robbed of their fabulous museums, including their dead kings and queens."[16] This complaint, voiced by a Third World representative in the General Assembly, highlights one of the main themes of Third World nationalism, namely, an anti-Western bias. As the leading Western power, the United States bears the brunt of this perception, which Third World states claim to be accurate in light of history.

Nationalism is a state of mind. In essence, it expresses an awareness of belonging to a nation and a desire to perpetuate that relationship. In the Western world, nationalism is normally based on such concepts as common language, shared experiences, and cultural unity. Many Third World countries, however, are composed of groups of people whose differences overshadow their shared characteristics. The 100 million people of Nigeria, for example, speak 250 different tongues and are divided into 250 different tribal groups.

Lacking the cultural and linguistic unity of Western states, citizens of many Third World countries have in common only the struggle against colonialism. Leaders use this formative experience as a foundation for building nationalism. One of the most effective ways of establishing national identity and cohesion is to mobilize the populace against an alleged alien foe, in this case the West. Once again, the United States, as the West's foremost power, offers a ready target. The doctrines of Marxism-Leninism have also inclined numerous Third World leaders against the West, especially as these tenets place responsibility for Third World backwardness not upon the deficiencies of developing countries themselves but rather on their former colonial masters.

If anti-Westernism represents a negative pillar of Third World nationalism, then economic modernization constitutes a positive stanchion. The effort to modernize and industrialize can engage the joint energies of a nation, much in the way that space shots have fostered national pride in the United States. However, as modernization has progressed, conflict with the West has arisen once again. States entering the modern age have called for a New International Economic Order, which would involve, among other things, lower Western tariffs, freer export of Western technology, stable prices for raw materials, tolerance for cartels (such as OPEC), greatly increased economic aid and other economic benefits. Western resistance, particularly at a time of stagflation, has reinforced the antagonism between the developed and the underdeveloped world that stemmed from colonialism. How have these factors affected American foreign policy?

America's Response to Third World Nationalism

The rise of Third World nationalism has created dilemmas for American foreign policy just as it has established opportunities for American diplomacy. To better appreciate America's response to Third World nationalism, we shall examine a few instances.

In their hearts, most Americans were clearly on the side of Third World nationalists striving for national independence. Americans could easily identify with young nations that wished to cast off the yoke of distant power. The United States barely participated in the Western scramble for colonies in the late nineteenth century, contenting itself with the Philippines, Samoa, Guam, Hawaii, and little else. As World War II drew to a close, Americans generally hailed the end of the colonial era, which they regarded as contrary to the cherished American principle of self-determination.

Were it not for the Cold War, the United States would no doubt have opposed colonialism in action as well as thought. However, America's growing rivalry with the Soviet Union injected another consideration into America's attitude toward the Third World. In order to carry out the policy of containment, the United States needed Western Europe as an ally. Furthermore, the strategy of containment included opposition to pro-Communist regimes in the new states of the Third World. These factors led to numerous American interventions that clashed with the anticolonial principle of noninterference in the internal affairs of other countries. The situation in Indochina illustrated America's dilemma.

During World War II, the Japanese ousted the French from their colony of Indochina (comprising the present states of Vietnam, Laos, and Cambodia). Immediately after the war, Paris asked the United States for ships to transport French soldiers back to Indochina to reassert French control. The United States, traditionally opposed to colonialism, refused.

Meanwhile, in Europe the Cold War had taken shape. Washington favored a rearmed West Germany. France, wary of past German aggression, opposed such a move so long as so much of France's resources were tied up in Indochina. Paris agreed to accept German rearmament only if America would help with the struggle in Southeast Asia. Regarding Europe as far more important than Southeast Asia to the national interest, both for political and economic reasons, the United States acceded to France's conditions and began to aid Paris. In December 1952, the outgoing Truman administration approved $60 million for support of France's war in Indochina. By 1954 the United States was financing 75 percent of France's expenditures in Southeast Asia.

In the spring of that year, the French decided to leave Indochina after the battle of Dienbienphu. By this time, the United States was fully committed to the effort to halt Communist expansion worldwide. Presuming that Ho, with the backing of the Soviet Union and/or China, would seek to assert control over all of Southeast Asia, the United States gradually escalated its involvement in Vietnam during the following years.

Elsewhere, the United States followed a similar pattern. While expressing verbal support for the self-determination of colonial peoples, America assisted its Western friends in their colonial wars. Thus, Washington provided military aid to Portugal, which was fighting to retain control of Angola and Mozambique. Washington also supported the French effort to hold on to Algeria. For many Third World nationalists, America's willingness to support its Western friends in their colonial struggles bedimmed Washington's verbal support for the principle of self-determination.

An even more critical factor giving rise to Third World bitterness toward the United States has been Washington's willingness to intervene in developing countries to suppress what America has perceived as Communist threats. These interventions have been part of the containment policy. A few examples will illuminate the point.

The United States has always regarded the Caribbean region as crucial to American security, one reason being the importance of the Panama Canal. As far back as the nineteenth century, Washington acted to counter threats to American interests in Latin America. Today Latin America is the location of over half of US direct investment in the Third World. The perceived menace of communism has led the United States to continue its activist policy in the region. When in 1951 American leaders identified a threat to this region by the government of leftist Jacobo Arbenz Guzman in Guatemala, the CIA helped unseat the new regime.

Several years later, the United States found itself confronted with a Communist regime on its very doorstep in Cuba. Having aided Fidel Castro in overthrowing the harsh dictatorship of Fulgencio Batista, the United States was sorely shaken when Castro later proclaimed that he was a Communist. Determined to expunge communism from the hemisphere, the United States secretly trained a brigade of Cubans and landed them in Cuba at the Bay of Pigs (1961). The sorry defeat of these forces is well known.

Castro's survival wreaked panic in the corridors of government buildings throughout Washington. Conditions in Latin America— widespread poverty and rule by a privileged few—made the region ripe for Communist revolution. In addition, Castro publicly proclaimed that he would sow revolution throughout the continent. The fear of Castroism led the United States to intervene in the Dominican Republic in 1965 to prevent Juan Bosch, a leftist with Communist support, from gaining power.

American fears of Communist penetration of Latin America can be seen in the United States policy toward Chile. Chile is as far away from the United States as the Middle East. Yet, Washington intervened in that country for the purpose of opposing another left-leaning government in the Western Hemisphere. In 1970 Chile held a popular election for president. One of the three candidates was Salvador Allende. Allende clearly had intentions of making radical changes in Chile. He was also decidedly anti-American, often blaming the United States for Chile's travails. Denouncing "imperialist exploitation" and "American monopolies," Allende proclaimed his intention to seize land from large holders and distribute it to the peasants, and nationalize the country's banks and major industries, including American copper mines. The other two candidates, one a centrist and the other conservative, were much more to Washington's liking than Allende. When the votes were tallied, Allende received 36.2 percent of the ballots, more than the other candidates but well under half the votes cast. The Chilean electoral system provides that, in cases where no presidential candidate receives a majority of the electoral vote, the legislature will select the chief executive. At this juncture, President Nixon ordered the CIA to intervene to prevent the accession of Allende.[17] At first, Nixon directed the CIA to offer bribes to Chilean legislators to induce them to vote for one of the other candidates. When this scheme proved unworkable, Nixon told the CIA to foment a coup before the legislature met to pick the president. The planning for this operation—dubbed Track II—was held so closely that neither the American secretary of state nor the American ambassador in Chile was informed. The CIA did make contact with the commander-in-chief of the Chilean army, General Schneider, but he refused to undertake a coup. The CIA then contacted other military officers, but finally concluded they lacked the capacity to overturn the government. Plans for the coup were abandoned, and Allende was elected president. Fulfilling Washington's fears, the new head of state appointed a number of Communists to his cabinet. Within a year of his election, he reestablished diplomatic relations with Cuba, invited Castro for a state visit that lasted nearly a month, and concluded with a joint communiqué that affirmed the "common struggle" and "common outlook of both governments and peoples in analyzing the world situation."[18]

After Allende's electoral victory, the American ambassador in Santiago, Edward Corry, reported, "Chile voted calmly to have a Marxist-Leninist State. It will have the most profound effect on Latin America and beyond; we have suffered a grievous defeat."[19] Kissinger's own estimation of the consequences of Allende's election is expressed below:

> Allende's election was a challenge to our national interest. We did not find it easy to reconcile ourselves to a second Communist state in the Western Hemisphere. We were persuaded that it would soon be inciting anti-American policies, attacking hemisphere solidarity, making common cause with Cuba, and sooner or later establishing close relations with the Soviet Union.[20]

It seems likely that if left to himself Allende would have fallen. Practically all elements of society had turned against him, due to an annual inflation rate of 300 percent and severe shortages of basic household items. Nonetheless, Washington intervened by restricting loans and credit to Chile and secretly funneling money to striking truckers to sustain them while out of work. The economy came to a complete standstill, and this situation led the nation's military to mount a coup against Allende. During the course of the confusion, the ousted president committed suicide.

In the case of Chile, one can make a strong case that American intervention was not only unnecessary but counterproductive, in that it revived accusations of big-stick diplomacy and created a new anti-American martyr in Latin America. The regime that replaced Allende, one with which the United States is rightly identified, is one of the most brutal military dictatorships in the Western Hemisphere. The United States itself, under President Carter, condemned the Chilean government for systematic repression of human rights.

President Reagan has singled out Central America as the region where America must make a stand against Marxist inroads. In 1983 he sent American Marines to unseat the Communist-supported regime in Grenada. In El Salvador, he has extended military and economic aid to the government, which is fighting a guerrilla war against forces the White House claims are armed and trained by Cuba and Nicaragua. At the same time, Washington is providing covert assistance to irregulars in Nicaragua, who are struggling to unseat the Marxist government that replaced the dictatorship of the Somoza family. Large-scale military maneuvers in Honduras underline Washington's keen interest in preventing Communist governments from coming to power in Central America.

The national security of all the Americas is at stake in Central America. If we cannot defend ourselves there, we cannot expect to prevail elsewhere. Our credibility would collapse, our alliances would crumble and the safety of our homeland would be put in jeopardy.
President Reagan, address before joint session of Congress, April 27, 1983

In another effort to combat communism in the Third World, the CIA in 1953 toppled Premier Mohammed Mossadegh of Iran, a left-leaning leader who threatened to nationalize Western oil companies. In his place the United States installed the shah, who remained at the helm until overthrown by Moslem followers of Ayatollah Khomeini in 1979.

When Great Britain, France and Israel invaded Egypt in 1956, after Nasser had nationalized the Suez Canal, the Soviet Union sided squarely with its new Middle Eastern ally. This gesture cemented Nasser more firmly than ever in the Soviet camp and helped him outlast the onslaught. Buoyed by his survival, Nasser redoubled his efforts to place supporters in other Arab capitals. In 1957, when pro-Nasser officers sought to unseat King Hussein of Jordan, a friend of America, Eisenhower ordered the 6th Fleet to the eastern Mediterranean and gave Jordan $20 million in military aid. The following year pro-Nasser forces threatened President Camille Chamoun of Lebanon. To sustain this pro-Western leader, Eisenhower cited the Eisenhower Doctrine and dispatched Marines to the beleaguered country. The American troop landing was more symbolic than strategic, as it met no response other than the startled gazes of bathers at the seashore. Chamoun would have survived without the Marines, but the American action underlined Washington's support of pro-Western forces in the Middle East.

In the Far East, the attempt to contain communism was played out on a much larger scale. The victory of the Communists in China in 1949 triggered the application of containment in Asia. In the years following the triumph of Mao Zedong's forces, the United States signed bilateral security treaties with Japan, Taiwan and the Philippines. In 1950 Truman sent American forces to Korea. We have already discussed America's support of France in the Indochina war. After the conclusion of this struggle, Secretary of State John Foster Dulles traveled to Manila to put his signature on the treaty establishing the Southeast Asia Treaty Organization (SEATO). The SEATO pact never displayed the unity of an alliance, but it did provide a conduit for the transfer of enormous quantities of American military and economic aid to its members (Pakistan, Philippines, Thailand, Australia, New Zealand, Great Britain, France and the United States). The United States also signed a separate security pact with Australia and New Zealand (the ANZUS treaty). Subsequently, South Vietnam, Laos and Cambodia were brought under SEATO's defense umbrella. If one peers at a map, it is easy to perceive the American strategy of drawing a cordon of steel, reinforced by American military might, around the eastern periphery of what was then called the Sino-Soviet bloc. This cordon stretched from South Korea (with which Washington signed a bilateral security treaty in 1953) southward through Japan, the Philippines and Taiwan to those states of Southeast Asia willing to associate themselves with the United States, and then westward to Pakistan and the southern tier. (It might be noted that while American policymakers viewed these pacts as links in containment, many Third World leaders saw them as evidence of American imperialism.)

Of course, the most momentous instance of American intervention in Asia occurred in Vietnam. The fundamental motive behind America's intervention in that country, as well as Cambodia and Laos, was to contain Communist expansion. In the case of Southeast Asia, Chinese communism was the threat against which the United States took arms. Just as American policymakers had earlier assumed that the Chinese were taking orders from Moscow, most took it for granted that Ho Chi Minh was receiving direction from Beijing. It was further assumed that if Asian communism went unopposed in Indochina, it would be only a matter of time until the expansionist-minded Asian Communists reached toward the shores of California. Thus, Asian communism had to be stopped in Indochina in order to avoid a much wider war later on.

Subsequent developments in Southeast Asia have cast considerable doubt on much of this reasoning. Falling back into their age-old pattern of hostility, the Vietnamese and the Chinese have become rivals. The Vietnamese, while intent on controlling Laos and Cambodia, give little evidence of seeking to extend their hegemony across a wider area. The depth of Sino-Soviet antagonism gives further indication of how erroneous were American assumptions about a monolithic Communist force sweeping across the Pacific Ocean toward America's shores. In assessing American actions, it must be borne in mind that these points were far from evident at the time that Washington decided to play a role in the affairs of Asia. American policy was undoubtedly misguided, but the country's intentions were not dishonorable.

In the eyes of many Third World nationalists, however, Washington's interventionist inclinations display evidence of a smug and uncaring attitude toward the Third World. The United States has seemed to regard developing countries as pawns in the great-power game, countries not to be taken seriously for their own sakes. While American leaders spoke loudly about self-determination, CIA agents were busy overthrowing Third World governments. Few Third World leaders share Washington's urgency about stopping communism; indeed, many regard the United States as posing as large a threat as the Soviet Union or China. To some, containment was no more than a cloak to hide Washington's desire to dominate the economies of Third World states. In many ways, America has seemed to be little different from the colonial powers of old.

President Carter showed an awareness of these attitudes, and during his tenure in office he evinced a reluctance to intervene in the Third World. Thus, instead of rushing to the support of General Anastasio Somoza Garcia of Nicaragua when his government was attacked by leftists, Carter persuaded Somoza to step down. This action infuriated American conservatives, who warned that Somoza's opponents, the Sandinista National Liberation Front, were Communists wearing the disguise of nationalism. Carter's decision to return control of the Panama Canal to the Panamanians gave further evidence of his sensitivity to Third World nationalism. President Reagan has reversed many of Carter's policies, including tolerance for the Sandinistas, and has dispatched military assistance teams to several pro-American regimes in Central America.

The continent of Africa, large enough to contain the United States, Western Europe, and India, scarcely engaged American interest until well after World War II. However, American policy toward South Africa, lying at the southernmost tip of the continent, reveals another dimension of America's response to Third World nationalism.

The earliest inhabitants of South Africa arrived in the seventeenth century, and they happened to be white. A group of Dutch settlers landed in the empty territory just thirty-two years after the Pilgrims put into shore at Plymouth Rock. In later years, blacks trickled down to the territory, and at present they outnumber the whites over four to one. The Dutch, known as Afrikaaners (after their dialect), often cite the fact that, unlike other white people in Africa, they preceded the blacks and have no family or land in Europe to which they can return. They insist that they are as African as the blacks who followed them to South Africa.

During the nineteenth century, the Dutch settlers were joined by British, who eventually gained control of the area and attached it to the British Empire. In 1910 the Union of South Africa, an independent state, was formed. This became the Republic of South Africa in 1960, one year before it bolted the British Commonwealth. By 1980 the population breakdown was as follows: 18,648,000 blacks (called Bantus), 4,320,000 whites (mostly Afrikaaners and some English), 2,385,000 coloreds (people of mixed racial stock), and 746,000 Asiatics (mostly Indians).

South Africa has been a particular object of controversy due to the practice of apartheid. Apartheid means separateness. As originally formulated, the doctrine of apartheid held that every race has a unique destiny and a distinct cultural contribution to make to the world. Accordingly, each race should remain separate and develop along its own individual lines. Highly questionable from a biological standpoint, apartheid is the official doctrine of the government of South Africa. In its "pure" form, the doctrine implies that all races should have equal opportunities to work out their own destinies—a variant of the "separate but equal" doctrine rejected by the US Supreme Court in 1954. As applied by the ruling Nationalist party of South Africa, however, apartheid has been a device for maintaining the privileges of the white minority at the expense of the black majority.

South Africa's prosperity—it has by far the highest GNP per capita in Africa—has been based for years on the exploitation of cheap black labor. While the blacks work for subsistence wages, the whites lead a life of relative privilege. The availability of such cheap labor has also attracted a large amount of foreign investment (including American) that has returned handsome profits. It is this system that apartheid is designed to perpetuate.

Apartheid is based on a series of laws enacted since the Nationalist party came into power in 1948. In order to provide for the separation of races, the Group Areas Act (1950) applied racial zoning to urban areas. A few years later the legislature passed a law providing for the creation of homelands for black tribes. These large areas, called Bantustans, set apart from the cities, will eventually house all the tribes, with a separate area for each. There is nothing resembling equality between these areas and the sections where white people dwell. The Bantustans are all located in remote, desolate areas far from the vast mineral wealth that underlies much of the country, making the Bantustans essentially labor reserves for white-owned industry. In 1962 the government passed the General Law Amendment Act, popularly known as the "Sabotage Act." This law says that anyone who commits certain acts, from trespass to murder, to "further or encourage . . . any social or economic change" in the country may be sentenced, without jury trial, to penalties ranging from forced isolation to death. The Terrorism Act (1967) authorizes arrest without warrant, solitary confinement, and indefinite detention. Additional legislation stipulates what occupations blacks may pursue and where they may live. Blacks and whites are not permitted to intermarry, and sexual relations between whites and coloreds or blacks are against the law. Blacks are not represented in the government nor permitted to hold government jobs or serve as officers in the military. Pass laws require nonwhites to carry with them at all times a pass which authorizes them to live or work in designated areas. Anyone caught without a pass is subject to punishment. Men who work in the mines and industry live in camps nearby for twelve to eighteen months at a time before returning to their Bantustans; however, they are not permitted to bring their families with them. Educational facilities are completely segregated. The system of apartheid is buttressed by a police force armed with the most modern weapons. While some whites (mostly those from Britain) oppose apartheid, they are outnumbered by those who have vowed to protect it with their lives.

PRETORIA, South Africa (AP)—Ambulance apartheid may have killed an African man who lay dying in a Pretoria street after he was struck by an automobile.

The Rev. Father P. B. Stein, a Roman Catholic priest, says he called an ambulance after he saw the man in the street but that an ambulance for whites only arrived at the scene.

He said that instead of taking the seriously injured man to a hospital the two white attendants radioed for an ambulance for blacks and stood around waiting for it.

"They did nothing for the man, who was lying in the street in the rain," said Father Stein. "They did not even throw a blanket over him."

The priest said an ambulance with black attendants finally arrived and took the injured man to hospital but he died within minutes.

News dispatch from South Africa, May 1975.
Reprinted by permission of AP Newsfeatures.

For many years the blacks in South Africa docilely accepted this discrimination. However, the movement for liberation and human dignity that was sweeping Africa finally made its way down to the southern reaches of the continent. In 1960 a crowd of blacks gathered around the Sharpville police station to protest a regulation that blacks carry passes. The police reacted with a volley of shots, killing sixty-seven of the unarmed demonstrators, many of whom were shot in the back while fleeing. Pictures of the Sharpville massacre were featured in newspapers around the world. Other disturbances occurred from time to time. In 1976, black students in Soweto, the black workers' suburb of Johannesburg, protested against having to use the Afrikaans language in their segregated schools. When police broke up the demonstration, riots erupted throughout the country and many government buildings were burned. In these disturbances the government arrested hundreds of black leaders and over six hundred blacks were killed.

These developments did not go unnoticed by the rest of the world, particularly the states of black Africa. In 1963 the United Nations passed an arms embargo against the country, with American support. A more inclusive embargo was imposed in 1977. Every year the South African question is debated in the United Nations, and in recent years some members have sponsored resolutions to oust South Africa from the organization. The fact remains, however, that the other states of Africa have little leverage over their southernmost neighbor. That is why they have turned to the United States to apply corrective action.

Were South Africa one of those sleepy backwater outposts so richly described in the novels of Joseph Conrad, the United States would not be faced with the dilemma it confronts today with regard to that country. In point of fact, however, South Africa is the most thriving country in all Africa. Approximately three-fourths of the non-Communist world's gold comes from South Africa. The country is the non-Communist world's largest producer of platinum and antimony. It also possesses the world's largest known deposits of uranium, manganese, chrome, vermiculite and fluorspar. In addition, South Africa is a major producer of diamonds, copper, and asbestos.

Aside from these mineral deposits, South Africa is important to the United States and other Western countries for its strategic location. A large proportion of the Western world's imported oil travels in tankers from the Persian Gulf around the Cape of Good Hope to the United States or Western Europe. Control of the Cape is a strategic asset, one that the United States would certainly hate to see pass into hostile hands (which some feel may well happen if the blacks gain control of the country and invite Soviet or Cuban assistance, a not unfamiliar pattern in Africa). The US Navy has been badgering for port facilities on or near the Cape in order to prevent unfriendly forces from gaining control of these vital sea lanes. NASA currently maintains a satellite-tracking station in South Africa, and the US Air Force has a similar facility. While the United States does not need a port facility in South Africa in order to keep the shipping lanes open, no other country in southern Africa seems likely to grant port facilities to a Western power. Therefore, military planners deem it essential that South Africa remain in nonhostile hands.

While not essential to America's well-being, the US government also cannot ignore the private investment of American firms in South Africa. Such investment amounts to approximately $1.5 billion, nearly one-third the total of all American private investment in Africa. The American portion of foreign investment in South Africa represents about 15 percent of all foreign investment in that country. If American investment were withdrawn, as many opponents of South Africa demand, the effect would be felt but would hardly bring down the South African government. Indeed, it is debatable who would be most affected by such a move, the white population or the blacks, who would be unable to secure alternative employment.

For the various factors mentioned above, the United States has a higher stake in the future of South Africa than in any other country on that continent. The importance of South Africa to the United States conflicts with the antipathy that most Americans feel toward apartheid. American policy has reflected the dilemma posed by these two forces.

In considering alternative American policies toward South Africa, it must be remembered that American leverage in that country is limited. Without outside assistance, internal security forces are capable of handling internal dissent. South Africa's military forces are sufficiently strong to overcome even a massed attack by neighboring states. The nation has the technology to build nuclear weapons, and there is some speculation that it already has a small stockpile. As we have observed, the extent of American investment in South Africa is not wide enough to give Washington much control over the government. In sum, any steps the United States might take short of outright military intervention, which practically no one advocates, are not likely to induce great changes among people who identify their very existence with white supremacy.

The United States has abided by the arms embargo enacted by the United Nations. The principal effect of this embargo, however, has been to render South Africa self-sufficient in armaments. Aside from the arms embargo and occasional denunciations of apartheid in speeches by public officials, American policy toward South Africa can reasonably be described as business as usual. The United States has evinced no urgency to alter the country's racial policies. This relaxed attitude can best be explained by South Africa's economic contribution to the West, the country's strategic location, and, less significantly, American investment.

Third World states have consistently denounced the United States for not taking sterner measures against South Africa. Many of these states would have America discourage or prohibit future investment in South Africa, impose a total trade embargo, close American consulates, recall its ambassador, or completely sever diplomatic relations. The more radical states would have Washington actively aid the small pockets of black guerrillas who intermittently attack military patrols and police outposts. For the reasons we have discussed, the United States is unlikely to take such measures. Thus, South Africa will probably remain a sore point in American relations with the Third World for some time to come.

To the northwest of South Africa lies Namibia (formerly South-West Africa), a land of 900 thousand inhabitants, 90 percent of whom are black. Namibia is one of the world's few remaining colonies. Following World War I, the League of Nations mandated it to South Africa. The purpose of the mandate system was to prepare the mandated territories for eventual self-government. Namibia is the only mandated territory that has not obtained national independence. In the case of Namibia, the United States has lined up firmly with the other states in Africa to demand that South Africa yield its colony. South Africa, for its part, is reluctant to do so. The South African government takes comfort from the existence of another white-ruled nation nearby, and South Africa has little interest in being completely bordered by black-ruled states (who could provide sanctuary and military training to black guerrillas). Discussions with South Africa over granting independence to Namibia have been moving at a desultory pace for years.

As of 1983, movement toward a settlement was held up by South African insistence that Cuban troops leave Angola before Namibia receives independence. The Angolan government claimed that the Cubans, numbering 25 thousand in 1983, were invited in to protect Angola against South African military incursions aimed at combatting black guerrillas fighting for Namibian independence. Angola has said it will send the Cubans home only after Namibia gains independence, at which time, presumably, South Africa will not be able to threaten Angola from positions inside neighboring Namibia. Washington has supported the South African position, and negotiations are continuing over this impasse. While the United States has relied on diplomacy to urge South Africa to give up Namibia, the Soviets have earned the gratitude of black Africa by providing assistance to the South-West Africa People's Organization (SWAPO), a black guerrilla organization fighting for Namibia's independence. South Africa has branded SWAPO a Communist organization.

In Namibia as elsewhere in Africa, the United States appears to black Africa to be doing little to bring about black majority rule. Concrete Soviet assistance to resistance fighters has gained for Moscow far more credit in Third World eyes than US rhetoric.

Foreign Aid

In reviewing America's response to nationalism in the Third World, we have thus far focused on political and military intervention. This response took an additional form, namely, foreign aid.

The term foreign aid is highly misleading. "International self-help" would be a much more accurate term. This description is more apt because the United States, like any aid-giver, dispenses assistance to other countries primarily to help itself. To be sure, such aid can and often does benefit the recipient. However, its fundamental purpose is to aid the donor. The self-interested element of foreign assistance was clearly spelled out by Secretary of State Muskie in a 1980 address to the Foreign Policy Association in New York City:

> Let me emphasize that these [foreign aid] programs involve far more than our humanitarian instincts. They bear strongly on our national interests. For the fact is that we have a deep and growing stake in developing countries. We cannot get along without them as trading partners and markets; as sources of essential materials; as necessary partners in efforts to address pollution and population, the proliferation of nuclear weapons and countless other issues touching all of our lives. . . . Our own economic health is bound up with theirs. . . .
>
> These programs are important for another reason. With them, we have an opportunity to influence events in crucial areas of the world. Without them, our power to shape events is drastically diminished. . . .
>
> Declining American aid, and declining American influence, would also help the Soviets exploit internal instability in Nicaragua, in El Salvador, and in many other places where the Soviets are prepared to exploit tensions to expand their power and to limit Western influence.
>
> Finally, the decline of American aid and influence would hamper our efforts to settle dangerous disputes and build peaceful, democratic solutions.[21]

Seen in this light, foreign aid is hardly the "giveaway" that its opponents brand it. Like diplomacy, military power and propaganda, foreign aid is a tool of influence. Of course, one should not deny the humanitarian component of foreign assistance. Americans do like to help others, and this is certainly one reason underlying America's aid program. However, it is not the strongest reason, as shown by the fact that American aid goes not to the neediest but to those lands where the United States wishes to exert influence (see Table 3–3).

Foreign aid may be divided into two categories, military and economic, and each of these can be further classified as a loan or a grant. Table 3–4 summarizes these forms of aid for the United States between the years 1946 and 1980. These figures reveal a moderate decline in military aid as a proportion of total foreign

TABLE 3-3: MAJOR RECIPIENTS OF US ECONOMIC ASSISTANCE, FY 1980 COMMITMENTS ($ millions)

15 Major Recipients	Agency for International Development			P.L. 480	Other[2]	Total Economic Assistance[3]
	Economic Support Fund[1]	Development	Total			
Egypt	865.0	—	865.0	301.4	—	1,166.4
Israel	785.0	—	785.0	1.0	—	786.0
India	—	103.2	103.2	118.3	—	221.5
Turkey	198.0	—	198.0	0.1	—	198.1
Indonesia	—	82.7	82.7	113.7	—	196.4
Bangladesh	—	80.3	80.3	77.0	—	157.3
Sudan	40.0	30.1	70.1	26.3	—	96.4
Philippines	20.0	39.7	59.7	18.8	4.8	83.3
Portugal	40.0	—	40.0	38.0	—	78.0
Jordan	69.0	—	69.0	3.7	—	72.7
Somalia	5.0	12.3	17.3	50.0	—	67.3
Sri Lanka	—	31.4	31.4	28.9	—	60.3
Pakistan	—	—	—	58.1	0.5	58.6
El Salvador	9.1	43.2	52.3	5.5	0.6	58.4
Dominican Republic	—	34.6	34.6	19.7	1.5	55.8
Total, 15 Recipients	2,065.7	422.9	2,488.6	860.5	7.4	3,356.5
Total, All Recipients	2,183.0	1,879.0	4,062.0	1,436.0	2,075.0	7,573.0

[1] Assistance to countries of special interest to the United States under specific programs, such as Indochina Postwar Reconstruction, Middle East Special Requirements Fund, and Assistance to Portugal and Portuguese Colonies in Africa. Formerly Security Support Assistance.

[2] Consists of Peace Corps, capital subscriptions and contributions to international lending organizations such as the Inter-American Development Bank, and grants to programs such as the International Narcotics Control Program.

[3] US "economic assistance" is equivalent to the aid reported to DAC as "official development assistance" (ODA). However, "economic assistance" figures represent gross commitments in fiscal years, while ODA figures are net disbursements or net flows in calendar years.

NOTES: In FY 1980, 80 countries received P.L. 480 assistance, 71 received assistance from AID, and the Peace Corps was active in 46 countries.

Source: U.S. Foreign Policy and the Third World: Agenda 1982 by Roger D. Hansen and Contributors for the Overseas Development Council. Copyright © 1982 by the Overseas Development Council. Reprinted by permission of Praeger Publishers and the Overseas Development Council.

TABLE 3–4: FOREIGN ECONOMIC AND MILITARY AID PROGRAMS,
1946–80 ($ millions)

Economic aid shown here represents total US economic aid—not just aid under Foreign Assistance Act. Major components in recent years include AID, Food for Peace, Peace Corps, and paid-in subscriptions to international financial institutions, such as IBRD, and IDB. Cumulative totals for 1946–1980 are true totals net of deobligation; annual figures, however, are gross unadjusted program figures. Military aid includes Military Assistance Program (MAP) grants, foreign military credit sales, service-funded programs, and excess defense articles.

PERIOD OR YEAR	Total economic and military aid	ECONOMIC AID			MILITARY AID		
		Total	Loans	Grants	Total	Loans	Grants
1946–1980, total	**229,106**	**141,635**	**47,365**	**94,270**	**87,471**	**17,355**	**70,116**
1946–1952	41,661	31,116	8,518	22,598	10,545	—	10,545
1953–1961	43,358	24,053	5,850	18,203	19,305	161	19,144
1962–1969	50,254	33,392	15,421	17,972	16,862	1,620	15,242
1970–1980	97,678	56,746	19,652	37,095	40,934	15,630	25,303
1970	6,568	3,676	1,389	2,288	2,892	70	2,822
1971	7,838	3,442	1,299	2,143	4,396	743	3,653
1972	9,021	3,940	1,639	2,301	5,080	550	4,530
1973	9,472	4,117	1,391	2,726	5,356	550	4,805
1974	8,510	3,906	1,150	2,756	4,604	1,396	3,208
1975	6,916	4,908	1,679	3,229	2,009	750	1,259
1976	6,412	3,878	1,759	2,119	2,535	1,442	1,093
1976, TQ[1]	2,603	1,931	840	1,091	672	494	178
1977	7,784	5,594	2,083	3,511	2,190	1,411	779
1978	9,014	6,661	2,530	4,131	2,353	1,601	752
1979	13,845	7,120	1,900	5,220	6,725	5,173	1,552
1980	9,695	7,573	1,993	5,580	2,122	1,450	672

— Represents zero.

[1]Transition quarter, July–Sept.

Source: US Bureau of the Census, *Statistical Abstract of the United States: 1981* (Washington: GPO, 1981), p. 841.

assistance. In 1980, for example, America extended $2,122 million in military aid but over three times that amount ($7,573 million) in economic aid. Through the mid-1970s, most military assistance was extended through the Military Assistance Program, scheduled to be phased out in fiscal year 1981. Under this program, Washington offered military equipment, defense services (such as operation of military communications) and training to other countries on a grant basis (no repayment required). Today the United States continues to provide these forms of assistance, but in almost all cases foreign governments pay for them. From the inception of military aid after World War II up to the present, Washington has used this instrument of diplomacy to pursue the policy of containing

Soviet expansion. Until the 1960s, most American military assistance went to allied nations in Western Europe. Once European recovery took hold, the United States began to direct military assistance to Third World nations menaced by communism. Table 3–5 reveals the recipients of American military aid from 1962 to 1980. Recipients of the largest amounts include Taiwan, Kampuchea (formerly Cambodia), South Korea, Laos, Thailand, Vietnam, Greece, Turkey, Egypt and Israel. The latter two have received substantial infusions of military aid since the Camp David meeting of 1978 as an inducement to reach a settlement of the differences between them. The vast bulk of American military ties with other countries presently consists of government-to-government arms transfers. These are discussed in some detail in Chapter 11. The remainder of this chapter focuses primarily on economic assistance.

For most of the post-World War II era, the underlying motive for US aid to the Third World has been to combat Communist penetration. In communism, many Third World leaders find a weapon for wounding the Western colonialist. The rapid if uneven industrialization of Communist Russia offers an attractive model for the development of poorer lands. Washington has believed that aid would offset the nutrients that have made some Third World soil so fertile to communism, namely, hunger, poverty, disease, and similar causes of human misery. At the same time, Washington has hoped Third World countries would utilize aid to achieve one of their most cherished goals, modernization. Aid could also lay the groundwork for political stability, a necessary prerequisite for economic development. Finally, Washington has trusted that its aid would bind recipients to America with hoops of gratitude.

The aid program known as the Alliance for Progress provides an illustration of American thinking. After the failure of the Bay of Pigs invasion, the United States had a great fear that Castro would seek to spread revolution throughout Latin America. If any region seemed ripe for communism, it was Latin America. In many countries the masses lived in squalor while a few families wallowed in luxury. Channels of public protest were choked off by brutal dictatorships. Similarities to pre-Bolshevik Russia were painfully obvious to American policymakers.

Having failed to eradicate Castro by force, President Kennedy decided to neutralize Castro's appeal through foreign aid. His instrument was the Alliance for Progress, announced with great fanfare in 1961. The alliance envisioned a ten-year expenditure of $10 billion to promote modernization and democracy in Latin

TABLE 3–5: US MILITARY AID BY SELECTED COUNTRIES, 1962–80
($ millions)

For years ending **Sept. 30**, except as indicated. Military aid data include Military Assistance Program (MAP) grants, foreign military credit sales, International Military Education and Training, and excess defense articles.

REGION AND COUNTRY	1962–1980[1] Total	Percent grants	1978, total	1979, total	1980, total
Total	**57,795.0**	**70.0**	**2,353.0**	**6,725.0**	**2,122.0**
Near East and So. Asia[2]	**22,394.6**	**44.2**	**1,480.8**	**6,007.5**	**1,484.2**
Egypt	1,501.4	.9	.2	1,500.4	.8
Greece	2,122.9	53.0	175.0	172.3	147.6
India	146.4	81.0	.3	.5	.3
Iran	844.7	40.3	—	—	—
Israel	12,911.6	40.7	1,000.0	4,000.0	1,000.0
Jordan	979.2	54.6	127.4	109.6	79.3
Lebanon	117.4	93.2	.6	43.1	22.4
Pakistan	208.1	95.1	.6	.5	—
Saudi Arabia	223.7	.4	—	—	—
Turkey	3,299.8	70.0	175.4	180.3	208.3
East Asia[2]	**28,921.7**	**91.6**	**452.1**	**345.0**	**283.9**
China, Taiwan	1,893.9	70.9	24.1	(z)	(z)
Indonesia	397.1	60.5	58.1	34.8	33.1
Japan	240.9	85.6	—	—	—
Kampuchea	1,196.8	100.0	—	—	—
Korea	5,851.8	79.3	276.8	238.4	130.5
Laos	1,481.9	100.0	—	—	—
Malaysia	149.8	.4	17.1	8.0	7.3
Philippines	599.2	75.6	37.3	31.7	75.5
Thailand	1,246.3	86.3	38.6	32.1	37.4
Vietnam	15,797.9	100.0	—	—	—
Europe[2]	**1,856.0**	**69.7**	**165.0**	**192.7**	**157.9**
Denmark	71.1	100.0	—	—	—
France	62.8	.8	—	—	—
Italy	268.5	99.9	—	—	—
Norway	199.0	100.0	—	—	—
Portugal	162.3	100.0	—	—	—
Spain	985.6	51.1	137.0	164.4	125.9
Latin America[2]	**1,741.8**	**46.2**	**79.2**	**30.9**	**21.1**
Argentina	261.5	33.0	—	—	—
Bolivia	79.9	71.2	.8	6.7	.3
Brazil	413.9	34.3	—	—	—
Chile	146.0	57.1	—	—	—
Colombia	188.1	44.0	52.2	13.0	.3
Dominican Rep.	38.5	83.9	.7	1.0	3.5
Ecuador	77.7	50.1	10.7	.4	3.3
Guatemala	40.2	73.1	—	—	—

TABLE 3-5 (continued)	1962–1980[1]		1978,	1979,	1980,
	Total	Percent	total	total	total
REGION AND COUNTRY		grants			
Honduras	31.3	48.9	3.2	2.3	3.9
Nicaragua	30.6	73.9	.4	(z)	—
Paraguay	30.0	98.7	.6	—	—
Peru	166.2	48.6	8.9	5.5	3.3
Uruguay	57.6	68.0	—	—	—
Venezuela	121.5	22.6	.1	—	—
Africa[2] **.................**	**1,083.7**	**33.2**	**125.4**	**96.7**	**118.9**
Ethiopia	224.3	84.0	—	—	—
Kenya	109.4	.3	27.4	10.4	20.5
Morocco	308.4	15.9	44.2	46.1	25.9
Sudan	33.3	.5	.2	5.3	25.4
Tunisia	167.0	28.3	26.1	21.1	15.6
Zaire	156.9	25.4	19.5	9.8	6.9
Oceania and					
other	**94.9**	**.3**	**—**	**—**	**—**
Interregional	**1,702.2**	**98.8**	**50.9**	**52.3**	**56.4**

— Represents zero.   Z Less than $50,000.
[1]From 1962 to 1976, years ended June 30. Includes transition quarter, July 1, 1976 to Sept. 30, 1976.
[2]Includes amounts not shown separately. Regional totals include aid to entire regions or subregions.

Source: US Bureau of the Census, *Statistical Abstract of the United States: 1981* (Washington: GPO, 1981), p. 841.

America. The major flaw in the concept, and the one that contributed to its undoing, was the requirement that the small class of Latin American oligarchs spread their wealth through land distribution and higher wages and permit democracy to take hold. While the oligarchs welcomed transfusions of American aid, they strongly opposed the social, economic and political changes that the alliance demanded. Having developed selfish exploitation to a fine art, they saw nothing in the alliance for themselves if they had to yield their privileged status.

It is not even certain that American aid officials had a clear image of the kinds of changes the alliance would ultimately produce. The general assumption was that the alterations caused by the alliance would occur in an orderly manner, and that the United States could calibrate the rate of change with ease. However, there is strong reason to believe that the development process is not so tidy. Once the impoverished perceive the glint of gold, they want not just a few grains but all their pockets can hold. Similarly, the rich generally do not give up their privileges without a fight. Once the snowball of social change begins to roll downhill, there is no

saying who or what might cling to it. Experience reveals that local
Communists try strenuously to make a bid for power during times
of social change.

**Those who make peaceful revolution impossible will
make violent revolution inevitable.**

President John F. Kennedy

In all likelihood, had the aid program continued, Washington
would have had to choose between radical and disorderly change,
on the one hand, and maintenance of the status quo, on the other.
With few exceptions, the United States has in such situations come
down on the side of the conservatives. Thus, it is not clear that the
United States was or is ready for the kind of changes that would
follow in the wake of a comprehensive development program. In
any event, the alliance failed to achieve its goals and gradually
withered away during the Johnson administration. (President
Reagan has sought to revive the concept on a smaller scale with
an aid program to the countries of the Caribbean.)

Foreign aid has never attracted a wide constituency in the United
States. While America remains the world's largest donor of foreign
assistance, comparison with other industrial countries reveals that
the United States ranks far from highest in terms of willingness to
help others. Figure 3–5 indicates that the United States falls well
below the average of aid as a percentage of GNP given by members
of the Development Assistance Committee (the foreign aid arm of
the OECD). In 1980, for example, the United States ranked thir-
teenth among the seventeen DAC countries in aid as a percentage
of GNP. While the United States devoted .27 percent of GNP to
aid, the DAC average was .37 percent. Figure 3–6 compares American aid (ODA, or official development assistance) with spending
for other purposes. As that graph reveals, Americans spent six times
as much money on alcoholic beverages as on foreign aid in 1980.
Adjusted for inflation, American aid was actually less in 1980 than
it was in 1961.

American policy toward the Third World reflects the national
interest of the United States in its three components: security,
economic prosperity, and the American way of life. The United
States seeks to maintain friendly ties with Third World nations that
sit astride strategic waterways and land formations, such as the
Persian Gulf and the Panama Canal. Washington tries to gain

FIGURE 3–5: US OFFICIAL DEVELOPMENT ASSISTANCE IN COMPARISON WITH ALL OTHER DAC COUNTRIES, 1965–80
(as percentage of GNP)

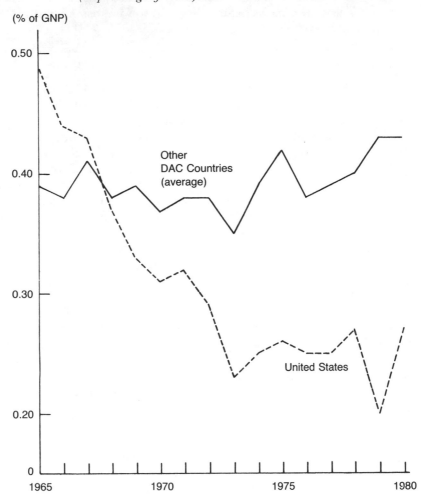

NOTES: Finland and New Zealand not included until 1970. Portugal not included after 1972. US ODA amounted to 2.79 percent of GNP at the beginning of the Marshall Plan in 1949. The abnormally low figure for US ODA for 1979 is largely due to the timing of enactment of legislation concerning US contributions to multilateral organizations and programs.

Source: *U.S. Foreign Policy and the Third World: Agenda 1982* by Roger D. Hansen and Contributors for the Overseas Development Council. Copyright © 1982 by the Overseas Development Council. Reprinted by permission of Praeger Publishers and the Overseas Development Council.

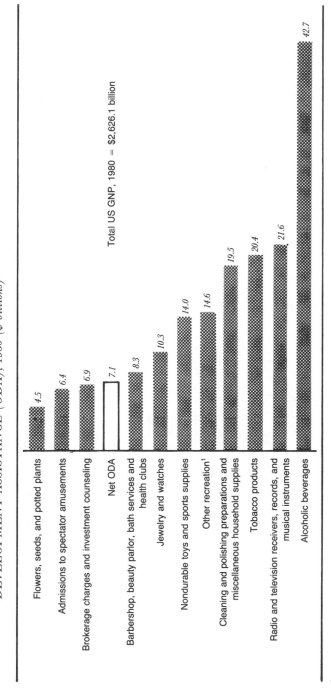

FIGURE 3–6: SELECTED US PERSONAL CONSUMPTION EXPENDITURES AND NET OFFICIAL DEVELOPMENT ASSISTANCE (ODA), 1980 ($ billions)

Total US GNP, 1980 = $2,626.1 billion

Flowers, seeds, and potted plants	4.5
Admissions to spectator amusements	6.4
Brokerage charges and investment counseling	6.9
Net ODA	7.1
Barbershop, beauty parlor, bath services and health clubs	8.3
Jewelry and watches	10.3
Nondurable toys and sports supplies	14.0
Other recreation[1]	14.6
Cleaning and polishing preparations and miscellaneous household supplies	19.5
Tobacco products	20.4
Radio and television receivers, records, and musical instruments	21.6
Alcoholic beverages	42.7

[1]Expenditures on pets and pet care, cable television, lotteries, camping, photo studios, and film processing.

Source: *U.S. Foreign Policy and the Third World: Agenda 1982* by Roger D. Hansen and Contributors for the Overseas Development Council. Copyright © 1982 by the Overseas Development Council. Reprinted by permission of Praeger Publishers and the Overseas Development Council.

access to states that produce key resources essential to national defense and a strong economy. The government also wishes to create and maintain profitable investment opportunities for American firms and develop markets for American goods. The United States tries to bolster Third World regimes that share America's belief in private enterprise and democracy. Naturally, America's national interest on occasion conflicts with the interests of some Third World states or other developed states that are pursuing their own national interests in the Third World. Such clashes generally lead to either diplomatic adjustment or war.

FOR DISCUSSION

Compare the importance of Western Europe and Japan to the United States.

Explain the "credibility" problem that the United States has with regard to its allies.

What bearing do economic disputes between allies have on cooperation in the security sphere?

How would international politics, particularly in Asia, be affected if Japan were to acquire nuclear weapons? What actions by the United States might lead Japan to develop or refrain from developing such weapons?

Would greatly increased cooperation among Japan, Western Europe, and the United States, as urged by the Trilateral Commission, justify the accusation that the rich countries are engaged in a conspiracy to deprive developing countries of their share of the earth's bounties?

Develop a rationale for either increasing or decreasing American economic aid.

What dangers face the United States if it sides with the forces of radical change in the Third World? If it sides with the status quo?

READING SUGGESTIONS

Barnds, William J. ed. *Japan and the United States: Challenges and Opportunities.* New York: New York University Press, 1979.

Grosser, Alfred. *The Western Alliance: European-American Relations since 1945.* New York: Continuum, 1980.

Hansen, Roger D. and Contributors for the Overseas Development Council. *U.S. Foreign Policy and the Third World: Agenda 1982*. New York: Praeger, 1982.

Pillsbury, Michael. "A Japanese Card?" *Foreign Policy* (Winter 1978–79): 3–31.

Rothstein, Robert L. *The Third World and U.S. Foreign Policy*. Boulder, CO: Westview Press, 1981.

Scalapino, Robert A. "Asia at the End of the 1970s," *Foreign Affairs*, vol. 58, no. 3, 1980, pp. 693–737.

NOTES

1. Eugene J. McCarthy, "Look, No Allies," *Foreign Policy*, no. 30 (Spring 1980): 12.
2. A. W. DePorte, *Europe Between the Superpowers* (New Haven: Yale University Press, 1979).
3. These figures come from DePorte, p. 208.
4. Roger D. Hansen and Contributors for the Overseas Development Council, *U.S. Foreign Policy and the Third World* (New York: Praeger, 1982), p. 156.
5. Saburo Okita, "Japan, China and the United States: Economic Relations and Prospects," *Foreign Affairs*, vol. 57 (Summer 1979): 1090–1110.
6. *Congressional Quarterly Weekly Reports*, January 21, 1978, p. 104.
7. Ibid.
8. Michael Pillsbury, "A Japanese Card?" *Foreign Policy*, no. 33 (Winter 1978–79), p. 4.
9. According to Pillsbury, any one of the five following factors could push Japan in the direction of large-scale rearmament:
    (1) breakdown in US-Japanese security arrangements;
    (2) serious conflict between the US and the USSR;
    (3) Sino-Soviet rapprochement;
    (4) deterioration in Sino-American relations;
    (5) major changes in the Korean military balance.
    Pillsbury, "A Japanese Card?"
10. Okita, p. 1106. These percentages refer to 1977.
11. Hakoshima Shin'ichi, "Mutual Ignorance and Misunderstanding—Causes of Japan-EC Economic Disputes," *Japan Quarterly*, XXVI (October-December 1979), p. 483.
12. Pillsbury, "A Japanese Card?"
13. The Atlantic Council of the US, *The Common Security Interests of Japan, the United States and NATO* (Washington, 1980).
14. *New York Times*, January 20, 1983.
15. Hansen *et al.*, p. 144.
16. Quoted in Frederick H. Hartmann, *The Relations of Nations* (3rd ed.; New York: Macmillan, 1967), p. 550.

17. The following account is based upon Cord Meyer, *Facing Reality: From World Federalism to the CIA* (Washington: University Press of America, no date), pp. 181–190.

18. Henry A. Kissinger, *White House Years* (Boston: Little, Brown, 1979), p. 683.

19. Ibid., p. 653.

20. Ibid., p. 654.

21. Quoted in *New York Times*, July 8, 1980.

Chapter 4
The Influence of
Political Culture

The preceding two chapters described major actors in the state system, and the development of US policy toward them during the period since World War II. As Fig. 1–1 shows, members of the state system affect the making of American foreign policy through the feedback mechanism; that is, they influence the country's ever-changing values, beliefs, and traditions, its public opinion, pressure groups, and media, and its political system. These elements, in turn, act together to produce foreign policy. Chapters 4 through 10 deal with these various components of the policy-making process. The present chapter examines values, beliefs, and traditions. Chapter 5 covers public opinion and pressure groups, and Chapter 6 takes up the media. Chapters 7 through 10 focus on important members of the political system including the president, the National Security Council, the State Department, the Defense Department, the intelligence community, and Congress. The remaining three chapters address specific problems in American foreign relations.

ELEMENTS OF POLITICAL CULTURE

When the members of a new presidential administration begin to occupy their government offices in downtown Washington, they often swell with enthusiasm for making fundamental changes in policy, both domestic and foreign. Each new chief executive wants to chart paths no one has yet trod, to forge a special place in history for the new administration. President Carter, for example, vowed to reduce arms sales and make the observance of human rights by other countries the keystones of his foreign policy. Domestically, he promised a reform of the welfare system, a reduction of government personnel, and a comprehensive energy program. Yet, as his term came to a close, many observers felt that little had changed. President Reagan was somewhat more successful, particularly in reducing the size and scope of government and in fashioning a military buildup; yet, fundamental alterations in American political practice were hard to discern.

Previous administrations have had the same experience, whose pervasiveness suggests that something beyond the control of individual policymakers serves to anchor policy to well-tried channels. This is not to imply that change never occurs. The New Deal of the 1930s and the foreign policy of containment represent real transformations of American practices. But it does seem to require a violent storm of outside forces to unearth the anchor that fastens American policies to their regular berths. In the absence of such upheavals, American policy, both foreign and domestic, displays a remarkable degree of continuity.

What is this anchor to which we have referred? Some would suggest it is "political culture." Political culture may be thought of as those values, beliefs, and traditions that affect the political behavior of a state in recognizable patterns over a period of time.

Values refer to that which a person or group considers to be good. Such assumptions cannot be proven or disproven; they spring from inner convictions about the way things ought to be. Some of the values held dear by most Americans include individual freedom, national self-determination, and freedom of religion. The citizens of states recently liberated from colonial domination might embrace the values of freedom from foreign control, rapid economic development, and national unity. People crystallize their own values as a result of personal experiences in their early years, political socialization by various groups, and indoctrination by parents and schools. Values do not prescribe specific actions to take in response to a particular problem, but they do bend the individual toward certain kinds of solutions and away from others. They establish certain attitudes or leanings that people call into play when a problem arises. For example, an American policymaker who holds firmly to the value of self-determination might insist on extremely persuasive reasons before approving American intervention in a foreign election in order to assist a particular candidate.

Beliefs refer to assumptions about the nature of reality. Some beliefs common in the United States are that foreign aid leads to stability and democracy, and private ownership of the means of production ensures maximum productivity. In Communist countries, contrasting beliefs are that government ownership of the means of production ensures the greatest fairness in distributing wealth, and political power automatically flows to those who control the means of production.

As in the case of values, an individual may embrace beliefs that lead to conflicting actions. For example, a person who thinks that a state should help its allies (value judgment) might approve a program of military aid to help an ally put down a colonial uprising. A simultaneously held belief that colonialism breeds instability might lead to second thoughts about such assistance.

Policymakers are influenced by beliefs as well as values. Woodrow Wilson, for example, believed that secret diplomacy, the balance of power and autocracy led to war. Accordingly, when he arrived in Paris at the conclusion of World War I to participate in the forging of a new world, he sought to abolish these practices from the international state system.

Traditions refer to patterns of behavior exhibited by a nation over a lengthy interval of time. Traditions are often derived from the values and beliefs that prevail in a state. For much of American history, the tradition of isolationism defined the country's orientation toward Europe. The Soviet Union is noted for its traditions of hostility to foreigners and the constant search for outlets to the sea. China has a long tradition of insularity—a tradition in process of erosion—while Japan has a tradition of borrowing from other cultures.

While there is general agreement that political culture affects foreign policy, little consensus exists regarding the precise nature or extent of political culture's impact. It is sometimes tempting to explain the entirety of a state's foreign policy by reference to political culture, as though the people who select these policies do not matter. Yet, various studies lead to the conclusion that the identity of those people often does make a difference, and that a different group of persons would produce a different foreign policy.[1] The model presented in Fig. 1–1 illustrates the manner in which political culture makes its influence felt. According to this model, the nation's values, beliefs, and traditions affect the policy-making process in two ways. In the first place, these components of political culture have an impact upon public opinion, pressure groups, and the media, all of which in turn influence policy formulation by placing demands upon the political system. But the individuals who are engaged in making policy—the president, the Cabinet, the Executive Office, indeed all members of the political system—are also influenced by political culture. After all, these people have presumably spent most of their lives immersed in America's political culture. Put another way, political culture provides a setting for the formation of foreign policy, and all Americans who participate in foreign policy are touched by that setting, though to varying degrees.

The remainder of this chapter will examine some of the values, beliefs, and traditions of the United States that affect American foreign policy. Of necessity, the discussion will be selective. Entire books have been written on America's national character.[2] We shall restrict ourselves to those facets of political culture that influence foreign policy.

ISOLATIONISM

In the aftermath of Vietnam, America's first military defeat since the War of 1812, many Americans urged their government to avoid further involvements overseas. "No more Vietnams!" was the cry of the day. For a time, America heeded this call, refraining from large-scale intervention in military conflicts in Angola, the Horn of Africa, Rhodesia (now Zimbabwe), and Iran.[3] Such abstention harks back to one of the best-established traditions in American foreign policy, isolationism.

Isolationism represents a form of behavior characterized by a rejection of world politics. An isolationist state refrains from joining military alliances. It may trade with other states, but such commerce represents only a small proportion of its economic activity. The attitude of isolationist states toward foreign involvements resembles the way most of us feel about visiting the dentist: we would prefer the experience to be as brief and infrequent as possible.

Isolationism made a great deal of sense for a geographically isolated, young, and vulnerable America trying to establish itself. The settlers who first came to these shores had already made a deliberate decision to detach themselves from the European continent, a decision reinforced by the difficulty of communicating with the Old World. Rather than looking to foreigners for guidance, they regarded themselves as conductors of a great experiment in social and political organization. These early Americans believed that their political and economic system represented an ideal toward which the Old World could only stumble.

Domestically, there were real dangers to political stability if the new republic sided with one European state at the expense of another. At the time, all American citizens were "hyphenated Americans" and, while they displayed no desire to return to their mother countries, they did care about how their former homelands fared in the wars of Europe. Were America to take sides in these wars, the citizenry would become hopelessly divided. Besides, Americans had other tasks to occupy themselves. There were vast spaces to settle, cities to build, roads to construct, and canals to build. The great abundance of the land beckoned for industries to develop. When Americans found themselves embroiled in foreign conflicts—as in the War of 1812, the Mexican War, the war with Spain, and both world wars—they displayed great eagerness to liquidate their involvement as quickly as possible and return to domestic undertakings.[4]

Externally, too, Americans had good reason to shun the political and military imbroglios of Europe. The fledgling republic did not need to worry greatly about the outcome of foreign wars, insulated as she was by the Atlantic and Pacific oceans—termed America's "greatest liquid asset" by historian Thomas A. Bailey. America was also shielded from the consequences of Europe's wars by the British navy. Locked in perpetual dispute with the land powers of Europe, the British had no desire to see her rivals establish footholds in the Western Hemisphere. Since the British navy commanded the seas, London was in a position to enforce her wishes. Happily for the United States, these preferences coincided with America's goals and interests.

George Washington, in his Farewell Address of 1796, provided one of the earliest statements of American isolationism:

> Europe has a set of primary interests, which to us have none, or a very remote relation. Hence she must be engaged in frequent controversies, the cause of which are essentially foreign to our concerns. Hence, therefore, it must be unwise in us to implicate ourselves, by artificial ties, in the ordinary vicissitudes of her politics, or the ordinary combinations and collisions of her friendships and enmities.
>
> Our detached and distant situation invites and enables us to pursue a different course. . . .
>
> Why forego the advantages of so peculiar a situation? Why quit our own to stand upon foreign ground? Why, by interweaving our destiny with that of any part of Europe, entangle our peace and

prosperity in the toils of European ambition, rivalship, interest, humor, or caprice?

'Tis our true policy to steer clear of permanent alliances with any portion of the foreign world. . . .

Taking care always to keep ourselves, by suitable establishments, in a respectable defensive posture, we may safely trust to temporary alliances for extraordinary emergencies. . . .

While Washington stressed the imprudence of American involvement with the Old World, John Quincy Adams emphasized the moral degradation that such involvement might produce:

Where ever the standard of freedom and independence has been or shall be unfurled, there will be America's heart, her benedictions, and her prayers. But she goes not abroad in search of monsters to destroy. She is the well-wisher to the freedom and independence of all. She is the champion and vindicator of her own. She will recommend the general cause by the countenance of her voice, and by the benignant sympathy of her example. . . . Otherwise she might become the dictatress of the world. She would no longer be the ruler of her own spirit.

During most of the eighteenth and nineteenth centuries, the United States adhered to the doctrine of isolationism. Americans concentrated on the great domestic challenges alluded to previously. In the early nineteenth century, however, Americans began to get nervous about the possibility of European involvement in Latin America. During the Napoleonic Wars, which concluded in 1815, Spain's New World colonies declared their independence. The conservative monarchs of Europe, which had formed a "Holy Alliance," threatened to bring these new states back under Spanish rule. Most Americans sympathized with the fledgling republics in Latin America. The citizens of the United States equated their earlier struggle against England with the efforts of Latin America to retain its freedom. As a democracy, America felt an affinity for the republican governments south of the Rio Grande. Americans also contemplated a vigorous trade with Latin America and did not relish competition from Europe. Furthermore, a European presence in Latin America seemed to threaten the security of the United States.

Like the Americans, the British sympathized on a philosophical basis with the republican regimes of Latin America. In her rivalry with the autocratic states of Europe, Britain was hardly anxious to see these states fortify themselves through the acquisition of colonies. In addition, the British, like the Americans, looked forward to trading with Latin America and frowned upon competition from the rest of Europe.

In order to discourage Europe from intervening in Latin America, President James Monroe issued his now-famous Monroe Doctrine in 1823. The Monroe Doctrine was clearly an expression of American isolationism. "Separated as we are from Europe by a great Atlantic Ocean," Monroe declared, "we have no concern in the wars of the European governments nor in the causes which produce them. The balance of power between them, into whatever scale it may turn its various vibrations, cannot affect us." Monroe went on to warn the European governments not to intervene in the Western Hemisphere. At the time, the British extended similar admonishments, and it was these latter ones that the rest of Europe heeded. Americans could congratulate themselves on the enunciation of great principles, but Britain deserved credit for providing the muscle that would back up President Monroe's message.

Heeding the isolationist impulse, the United States hoped to remain out of World War I, the great global struggle that marked the beginning of the end of Europe's domination of world politics. When the war erupted in 1914, the United States remained on the sidelines, and it was only in 1917, the year before the guns fell silent, that the United States did participate. In a subsequent section of this chapter, we shall explore the reasons for America's intervention. For the moment, however, we may note that it was only with the greatest reluctance that the United States abandoned isolationism and became involved. Let us remember that Woodrow Wilson won election to his second term in 1916 with the slogan, "He kept us out of war." At the conclusion of that conflict, the United States returned to its isolationist tradition by refusing to join the League of Nations. America's abstention from the league was not the principal cause of its failure, but it did contribute to the organization's demise. It took the United States several more years to learn that global power struggles do not cease when the gunsmoke clears, but only enter a new, less violent phase.

In the interval between the world wars, isolationism reigned supreme in the United States. Congress passed the Hawley-Smoot tariff, the highest in the nation's history, thereby signifying America's lack of interest in solving the world's economic ills through cooperation. Great Britain displeased America in 1931 by abandoning the gold standard, and most of America's World War I allies (except Finland) repudiated their debts to the United States. These actions only confirmed the long-standing American perception of Europe as devious and dishonorable and better left to its own devices. It was in an effort to leave Europe in precisely such a position that Congress passed various pieces of neutrality legislation in the later 1930s, as war clouds were gathering over the Continent. It occurred to few Americans that the best way of preventing war was to indicate firmly in advance to potential aggressors that the array of forces against them was so formidable that they could not possibly succeed. Most Americans, believing that a European war was imminent, preferred policies that would spare America the casualties suffered in World War I. The neutrality laws prohibited traffic in arms and loans to warring states, and they required the president to keep Americans off the merchant vessels of belligerents. These acts were designed, in part, to prevent a recurrence of the grievances that dragged America into World War I, but they also served notice to Hitler—falsely, it turned out—that he could count on US abstention from a European war.

World War II drew the United States out of its isolationist cocoon. At the conclusion of that struggle, the country planned to return to isolationism, as indicated by the precipitous demobilization of America's armed forces. Now that the war was over, the United States, in characteristic fashion, saw no purpose in retaining this instrument of diplomacy that could help police the peace.

The reluctant reentry of the United States on the world scene and the adoption of containment make it tempting to conclude that the isolationist impulse in American foreign policy is moribund. However, designs that have been etched into the bedrock of a nation's political culture for nearly two centuries are not so easily erased. The isolationist tradition continues to shape American foreign policy. Consider the words of President Kennedy, no isolationist in deed:

> We must face the fact that the United States is neither omnipotent nor omniscient . . . that we cannot impose our will upon the other 94 percent of mankind—that we cannot right every wrong or reverse each adversity—and that therefore there cannot be an American solution to every world problem.

President Nixon who, like Kennedy, did not hesitate to utilize the various tools of diplomacy in order to advance America's interest, also displayed a leaning toward isolationism. Clearly reacting to American frustration with the seemingly endless war in Vietnam,

Nixon issued a statement at Guam in 1969 designed to prevent future massive American interventions abroad. In this statement, he pledged that, while the United States would uphold all its security commitments, any actual fighting would be done by citizens of lands under assault, either from within or from without. The United States would provide material support if the case warranted it, but American soldiers would not fight for the survival of other countries, as they had done in Vietnam. Since the end of American involvement in Vietnam, the United States has not sent large expeditionary forces to fight overseas. During the 1960s and 1970s, Americans exhibited a great impatience to turn inward. Great masses of Americans concentrated their political efforts on issues dealing with consumerism, pollution, racial and sexual equality, and the like. While the climate of the post-World War II world has not been conducive to American isolationism, that well-established tradition in American foreign policy does not seem to have expired.

George F. Kennan, reflecting on the consequences of American isolationism, has been led to

> sometimes wonder whether in this respect a democracy is not uncomfortably similar to one of those prehistoric monsters with a body as long as this room and a brain the size of a pin; he lies there in his comfortable primeval mud and pays little attention to his environment; he is slow to wrath—in fact, you practically have to whack his tail off to make him aware that his interests are being disturbed; but, once he grasps this, he lays about him with such blind determination that he not only destroys his adversary but largely wrecks his native habitat. You wonder whether it would not have been wiser for him to have taken a little more interest in what was going on at an earlier date and to have seen whether he could not have prevented some of these situations from arising instead of proceeding from an undiscriminating indifference to a holy wrath equally undiscriminating.[5]

Isolationism has contributed to a bias in the American education system that renders the nation less prepared than it might otherwise be to cope successfully with the outside world. So long as America remained essentially isolationist, the country's schools saw little need to prepare their graduates to interact with other nations. The study of foreign languages and cultures received little emphasis. When, after World War II, Americans had to deal regularly with other countries—in the Middle East, southern Asia, and Indochina, for example—they had little knowledge and background upon which to draw. American education continues to reflect the isolationist outlook in foreign policy. Few Americans bother to learn other languages. Public school systems generally require students to study American history, but the history of other lands is optional. Even college courses in world history concentrate almost exclusively upon events in Western Europe and North America, relegating to footnotes regions where the majority of the world's population lives.

Finally, the relative indifference of most Americans to foreign policy, one of the by-products of isolationism, has amplified the opportunities for those who are so interested to influence the government. Many interested groups seek to persuade the government that their particular interests are identical to the national interest, as we shall see in Chapter 5. While such groups do not control American foreign policy, the lack of interest of most citizens in the subject does give pressure groups more influence over policy making than would otherwise be the case.

LEGALISM-MORALISM

A second component of political culture is what Kennan has called legalism-moralism.[6] This represents a conviction that power conflicts among states can be superseded by the acceptance of legal rules and restraints, and it also expresses a faith that once such rules are written down, states will abide by them. Legalism-moralism further presumes that states will subordinate their selfish interests to the cause of a peaceful and orderly world, if only such a pathway is pointed out to the men and women who determine foreign policy. Proponents of this outlook place great stock in international law, world public opinion, collective sanctions, arbitration and mediation. Kennan described the concept in these words:

> The tendency to achieve our foreign policy objectives by inducing other governments to sign up to professions of high moral and legal principle appears to have a great and enduring vitality in our diplomatic practice. It is linked, certainly, with the strong American belief in the power of public opinion to overrule governments. It is also linked, no doubt, with the pronounced American tendency to transplant legal concepts from the domestic to the international field: to believe that international society could—and should—operate on the basis of general contractual obligations, and hence to lay stress on verbal undertakings rather than on the concrete manifestations of political interests.[7]

Perhaps the best way of perceiving how legalism-moralism has influenced American foreign policy is to examine various facets of the concept. We begin with America's sense of mission.

Sense of Mission

From the time of the early settlers down to the very present, Americans have believed themselves charged with a special mission. Often, this feeling has involved a belief in the unique virtue of American society. James Russell Lowell's "A Fable for Critics," published in 1848, illustrates this feeling of separateness from and superiority to the Old World:

> Forget Europe wholly,—your veins throb with blood,
> To which the dull current in hers is but mud; . . .
> O my friends, thank your god if you have one, that he
> Twixt the Old World and you sets a gulf of a sea; . . .
> To your own New-World instincts contrive to be true, . . .

Of course, Lowell neglected to mention the British navy which, by insulating the United States from Europe, made it possible for Americans to detach themselves from the political struggles of the Old World.

America's vision of itself as a chosen people springs from the practically unique success of the new nation in solving problems that plagued other nations. While older societies continued to wallow in poverty, the United States attained the highest standard of living in the world. While other societies were torn asunder by ethnic conflicts, the US forged a melting pot. Elsewhere, revolution seemed the normal method of changing governments; in America, orderly elections sufficed. To be sure, American society is far from perfect. Women and certain minorities, such as Native Americans, Hispanics, and blacks, have not shared equally in the American dream. But when Americans look about themselves and compare their society to others, many do not find it difficult to reach the conclusion that America indeed is superior.

A sense of mission continues to energize American foreign policy. President Kennedy referred to it in these words:

> We dare not forget today that we are the heirs of that first revolution.
> Let the word go forth from this time and place, to friend and foe alike,
> that the torch has been passed to a new generation of Americans—

born in this century, tempered by war, disciplined by a hard and
bitter peace, proud of our ancient heritage—and unwilling to witness
or permit the slow undoing of those human rights to which this nation
has always been committed, and to which we are committed today
at home and around the world. With a good conscience our only
reward, with history the final judge of our deeds, let us go forth to
lead the land we love, asking His Blessing and His help, but knowing
that here on earth God's work must truly be our own.

What are the consequences of America's self-image as a chosen
people? Convinced of their own superiority, Americans have sometimes felt obliged to export the American way abroad. Such an
impulse springs from admirable motives. After all, if the American
system brings so many blessings to citizens of the United States,
should they not seek to confer these blessings on other people? This
outlook has led some Americans to insist that other countries adopt
a free-enterprise economic system and a political system based on
American democracy. To non-Americans, such pressure often
smacks of extreme arrogance and self-righteousness. All too frequently, the beneficent attempt to implant the American way of
life is directed toward lands that may be singularly infertile to the
American seed. In many ways, America is not a typical country,
and so its own experience cannot be readily transplanted. America
has enjoyed unprecedented material abundance and political stability. Lands plagued by deep poverty and chronic political chaos—
conditions that prevail in most countries—find it difficult to adopt
the American way of life. To provide just one illustration, it is an
adage of economics that one cannot have investment, the basis for
economic growth, without savings. But the peasant who tills a small
plot that must feed seven children has nothing left over to save,
and an impoverished society is unable to accumulate savings.
Therefore, an American-style, private-enterprise economy that relies
on individual saving and investment is not likely to experience
substantial growth. Frustrated by the failure of their institutions
to take root elsewhere, Americans sometimes blame other societies
for laziness or stupidity, not realizing the more fundamental reasons
that prevent a successful transplant.

Moralism

Another facet of legalism-moralism is moralism itself. Moralism
refers to the standard a nation uses to evaluate foreign policy options.
Some nations weigh foreign policy alternatives on the basis of selfish

national interest. At the other extreme lies moralism. Moralism represents the selection of foreign policy based on moral grounds. If an action is judged moral, that is the policy states should adopt. Nations should reject immoral policies. The United States has had a long history of not only basing its own actions on morality but expecting other nations to do the same. Sometimes the meaning of moralism has been extended to include self-righteousness. Thus, on occasion Washington has reserved for itself the privilege of judging what is best for other countries, whether they agree or not. The Bay of Pigs invasion illustrates this concept, to the extent that the landing represented an effort to improve the lot of Cubans by eliminating communism. We shall return to this notion later in this section.

A recent example of moralism can be found in connection with the 1962 Cuban missile crisis. In the deliberations over how to respond to the Soviet emplacement of missiles in Cuba, many options were considered, including a surprise air strike against the existing missile sites. President Kennedy's brother Robert explained why this tactic was rejected:

> Whatever validity the military and political arguments were for an attack in preference to a blockade, America's traditions and history would not permit such a course of action. Whatever military reasons [former Secretary of State Dean Acheson] and others could marshal, they were nevertheless, in the last analysis, advocating a surprise attack by a very large nation against a very small one. This, I said, could not be undertaken by the U.S. if we were to maintain our moral position at home and around the globe. Our struggle against Communism throughout the world was far more than physical survival— it had as its essence our heritage and our ideals, and these we must not destroy.[8]

Eventually the president chose to place a blockade around the island, a tactic which worked brilliantly.

American foreign policy presents numerous instances of moralism. By examining some of these cases, we can gain a fuller understanding of the concept.

Thomas Jefferson is often credited with initiating the strain of moralism in American foreign policy. At the time of his presidency, the Barbary Pirates—Arab clans that controlled sections of territory along the Mediterranean coast of Africa—preyed on shipping that coursed that body of water. The Europeans, who were the principal victims, were willing to pay protection money; this was far cheaper than providing naval escorts. When confronted with the problem,

President Jefferson rejected this policy, which had been followed by his predecessors. Instead, he dispatched the navy to teach the pirates a lesson; America would not pay protection money to anyone. (Hence the reference in the Marine Corps song to "the shores of Tripoli.") After the Americans left, the Barbary Pirates returned to their gainful employment in the Mediterranean, but at least the United States had stood for principle.

The Spanish-American War of 1898 affords another example of moralism. Under Spanish rule, conditions in Cuba were truly abominable for the Cubans. The widespread suffering of the people prompted formation of guerrilla units which engaged Spanish troops in sporadic combat. To bring an end to this rebellion, Spain sent Captain General Valeriano Weyler (nicknamed "Butcher" Weyler in America) to Cuba. His strategy was to round up those Cubans loyal to Spain and place them in resettlement camps; Cubans who refused to go were considered outlaws and were shot. (This policy bears marked similarities to the "strategic hamlet" program carried out by American forces in Vietnam during the 1960s.) As the camps housed "friendly Cubans," they were supposed to provide adequate shelter, sanitation, food, and other necessities of life. However, few of these requirements were ever supplied, and disease and starvation became rampant. At the same time, the Spaniards levied burdensome taxes upon the suffering Cubans. All these conditions were worsened by the worldwide depression of 1893, which drastically reduced world demand for Cuba's main export, sugar.

Many Americans were moved by the plight of the Cubans, only ninety miles from America's shores. The "yellow press" sensationalized a situation already grim enough, leading many Americans to feel that the United States, in the name of humanity, should assist their neighbors. As the situation in Cuba deteriorated, riots broke out in Havana in December 1897. To safeguard American lives and property, President McKinley sent the battleship *Maine* to Havana's harbor. In February 1898, an explosion of undetermined origin destroyed the ship, sending 260 American sailors to their watery graves. Prodded by the yellow press, Americans concluded that Spain had been responsible for the explosion and urged that the United States take military action. With a certain reluctance, McKinley yielded to the swelling chorus that called for intervention in Cuba. In March, the United States sent Spain an ultimatum: agree to an armistice with the Cubans and abandon the policy of concentration camps, or war would be declared. Spain actually agreed to these conditions, and fighting could have been averted. However, war fever was so high in the United States that

Spain's reply was rejected as coming too late. In April Washington declared war.

Why did America launch this war? It was certainly not for reasons of national security, since neither Cuba nor Spain represented any threat to the United States. It is true that certain American investors in Cuba wanted the United States to take action to safeguard their holdings, but although these people had a voice in American foreign policy, they hardly controlled it. The major excuse for the war can be found in moralism. Americans were morally outraged at the behavior of Spain and wanted to aid the Cubans.

Considering the origins of the war, the actual fighting and its consequences took curious turns. Although the purpose of the war was to free the Cubans, the first engagement occurred in the Philippines, where Commodore George Dewey destroyed Spain's Pacific fleet and seized the islands. It was two months later that the United States destroyed Spain's main fleet near Santiago, Cuba. Shortly thereafter Teddy Roosevelt's Rough Riders—their horses actually left behind in Florida—raced up San Juan Hill with the smell of victory in their nostrils. Spain sued for peace, and Cuba gained her independence. In return for a payment of $20 million, Spain ceded the Philippines to the United States. The United States, in keeping with its moralistic outlook, did not regard this acquisition as imperialist expansion—equivalent to the seizures of territory by Great Britain, France, Belgium and other Europeans at the time—but rather as an "unselfish" move toward preparing less civilized people for independence. Spain also ceded to America the islands of Guam and Puerto Rico. Hawaii, an independent state, joined the United States voluntarily during the war. Most diplomatic historians date the origins of America's rise to world power from the Spanish-American War.

No single individual illustrates the principle of moralism better than Theodore Roosevelt. Roosevelt spoke often of a "peace of righteousness," which was to be based on a virile America that vigorously employed its power in the name of virtuous causes. The United States, he thought, should use its power to create a better world. (A close connection between moralism and America's sense of mission emerges quite markedly in Roosevelt's outlook.) The fiery orator divided the states of the world into two categories: civilized enlightened ones and uncivilized barbaric ones. The former nations had a responsibility to uplift and civilize the latter, even at the expense of war. In 1905 he wrote, "Just war is in the long run far better for a nation's soul than the most prosperous peace obtained by acquiescence in wrong or injustice." This outlook led Roosevelt to send the Great White Fleet around the world and to send the Marines into Latin America on numerous occasions to help set their affairs in order. These latter forays exemplify the self-righteous facet of moralism discussed earlier.

America's entry into World War I affords a classic instance of moralistic behavior. Woodrow Wilson perceived this epic conflict as a question of principle. The Allies were fighting for liberty, self-determination, democracy, freedom of the seas, and the rights of neutrals. Germany and her "cohorts" represented barbarism, authoritarianism and militarism, trampling the rights of small inno-cent nations and murdering helpless civilians. Consider Wilson's war message to Congress on April 2, 1917:

> We are now about to accept gauge of battle with this natural foe to liberty and shall, if necessary, spend the whole force of the nation to check and nullify its pretensions and its power. We are glad, now that we see the facts with no veil of false pretense about them, to fight thus for the ultimate peace of the world and for the liberation of its peoples, the German peoples included: for the rights of nations great and small and the privilege of men everywhere to choose their way of life and of obedience. The world must be made safe for democracy. Its peace must be planted upon the tested foundations of political liberty. We have no selfish ends to serve. We desire no conquest, no dominion. We seek no indemnities for ourselves, no material com-pensation for the sacrifices we shall freely make. We are but one of the champions of the rights of mankind. We shall be satisfied when those rights have been made as secure as the faith and the freedom of nations can make them.

Notice the absence in these words of any reference to America's national security. No mention is made of the perils America would face if Germany succeeded in overrunning Europe. There is no hint that the master of Europe could then turn against the United States, and that therefore the United States must join the struggle before this happened. Indeed, one year before America entered the war Wilson declared, "With the objects and causes of the war we are not concerned. The obscure foundations from which its stupendous flood has burst forth we are not interested to search for or explore." Wilson brought the American people into the war to defend certain moral principles. Is it any wonder, then, that after the conflict the American people perceived no need to participate in the postwar peace arrangements? The Allied victory represented the triumph of the moral principles in which the war was fought. For America, the struggle was over. If America's principles had been vindicated, what need was there to participate in the League of Nations? Germany's defeat meant that the United States had achieved its war aims, and therefore could go back to its domestic concerns. Few Americans appreciated the need to maintain a balance of power on the continent of Europe in order to preserve America's security.

We live in a world in which total war would mean catastrophe. We also live in a world that's torn by a great moral struggle—between democracy and its enemies, between the spirit of freedom and those who fear freedom.

In the last 15 years or more, the Soviet Union has engaged in a relentless military buildup, overtaking and surpassing the United States in major categories of military power, acquiring what can only be considered an offensive military capability. All the moral values which this country cherishes—freedom, democracy, the right of peoples and nations to determine their own destiny, to speak and write and to live and worship as they choose— all these basic rights are fundamentally challenged by a powerful adversary which does not wish these values to survive.

President Reagan, speech to Los Angeles World Affairs Council, March 31, 1983

Moralism has remained a strong component of American foreign policy up to the present day. The effort to prevent Communist expansion after World War II was portrayed as a campaign on the part of the "free world" to combat the forces of totalitarianism and atheism. America justified the long and bitter struggle in Vietnam in terms of preserving the freedom of the South Vietnamese people and guaranteeing them control over their own destiny. President Carter's initial enthusiasm for promoting human rights abroad offers another illustration of the strong pull of moralism over American foreign policy.

Moralism has had a number of consequences, both positive and negative, for US foreign policy. On the positive side, moralism has led the United States to work steadily for goals that it perceives will contribute to a better world (although other countries do not always share these perceptions.) In support of the peaceful settlement of disputes, the United States has from time to time supported the arbitration of boundary and territorial conflicts; Theodore Roosevelt mediated the settlement of the Russo-Japanese War in 1905, and various American presidents have sought to mediate a resolution of the Arab-Israeli conflict. In an effort to help less fortunate peoples, the United States has given billions of dollars to other countries and international organizations. Apart from conquering the continent from Native Americans and seizing one-third of Mexico, the United States has taken practically no territory as the spoils of military victory, despite her position on the winning side in two world wars.

From the domestic standpoint, moralism has on more than one occasion served to unite and energize the American population behind foreign policy. Lacking the moral fervor generated at the time, it is questionable whether America would have kept its factories humming around the clock in order to supply her World War II allies with materials to prosecute the war. As we shall see in Chapter 5, the average American takes little interest in foreign policy most of the time. While a measured presentation of the virtues of a particular foreign policy may not excite the average citizen, he or she can be mightily aroused by a moral appeal. Furthermore, by masking the subtleties of foreign policy, moralism can serve to unite the American people on a course of action. Thus, moralism can generate mass support for the foreign policy of the United States.

Sober analysis suggests, however, that despite America's often noble intentions, the negative results of moralism have outweighed the positive ones. Because they are convinced that their cause is just, Americans often approach foreign policy as a crusade. Just as crusaders are not prone to compromise with their opponents, so moralistic nations hesitate to compromise with theirs. This attitude builds rigidity into foreign policy. It becomes difficult to abandon an ill-advised policy once it is associated with an overarching principle. Crusading nations fight wars until they achieve total victory; compromise peace settlements are seen as the surrender of high principle. In their negotiations with other states, crusading nations similarly prefer total victory to compromise. Moralism has led Americans to regard foreign policy as a struggle between two extremes or mutually exclusive alternatives to global issues. Americans are not comfortable with partial solutions, such as the neither-war-nor-peace relationship with the Soviet Union. How often have Americans expressed an impatience to settle the Cold War once and for all, perhaps suppressing the inescapable conclusion that nuclear war would remain the price of such a final outcome? Yet, as Cecil Crabb notes, Americans are content with partial solutions to domestic problems, such as urban decay, poverty, crime, and alcoholism.[9] The world of international politics rarely admits to total victory, whether in warfare or in negotiations. In the nuclear age, total victory may simply not be worth the destruction entailed. Thus, the United States is reluctantly learning to live with limited wars, that is, wars fought with limited means for limited ends. Americans were not comfortable with the compromise truce that marked the cessation of hostilities in Korea, nor did they enthusiastically embrace the limitations placed on the fighting in Vietnam.

In our intractable world, crusades are likely to fail or succeed only in part. America did not meet with total success in World War I, World War II, the Cold War, Korea, or Vietnam. At the end of each of these episodes, many Americans, frustrated and disgruntled, favored a return to isolationism. That is the great danger of moral crusades. When they fail, as they often do, the crusaders are tempted to dismiss the object of their efforts as no longer worthy. As the decade of the 1980s began, many Americans, smarting from Vietnam, were prepared to withdraw from world politics. A marked hesitancy against US participation in foreign conflicts lingers to this day. Whether this yearning for isolationism is wise, given American interdependence with many portions of the globe, is a question worth pondering.

The presumption of moral rectitude that accompanies many American foreign-policy efforts brings with it another consequence. Once a person decides that his or her cause is just, it is an easy leap to conclude that whatever means are used to forward that cause must also be just. Moral crusaders from the Spanish Inquisitors to Robespierre have reasoned thus, leading to unmentionable atrocities committed in the name of morality. This attitude finds expression in the words of the American soldier holding a cigarette lighter to a Vietnamese thatched hut while proclaiming, "We have to destroy this village in order to save it." Inspired by moral self-righteousness, Americans in recent years have engaged in numerous practices whose moral virtue is open to question, including:

support for military and civilian dictators (Iran, South Korea, Philippines);
intervention in the internal affairs of other countries (Dominican Republic, Guatemala, Iran, Indonesia, Grenada);
training of foreign police in techniques of torture and assassination (Uruguay, Iran);
efforts to assassinate foreign leaders (Castro, Lumumba).

Discounting of Force

When the moon is in the second house,
And when Jupiter aligns with Mars,
Then peace will rule the planets
And love will steer the stars.
This is the dawning of the Age of Aquarius. . . .

The lines above come from the musical production "Hair," perhaps the most popular American musical extravaganza of the 1960s and 1970s. The Age of Aquarius refers to an era when people behave with decency and consideration toward one another, and when nations renounce violence and behave in the spirit of cooperation. Although the song hails the faint beginnings of the Aquarian Age, the United States, in its attitude toward military force, has frequently acted as though that era had dawned many decades ago. More specifically, the United States has often behaved as though military force were not important in foreign policy, as though foreign policy objectives could be achieved without backing up diplomacy with military force. This is what we mean by the discounting of force. Through much of its history, the United States has behaved as though the mere exhortation of legal and moral principles would induce other nations to act in conformity with them, as though a morally superior America could shame other states into acting virtuously (as defined, of course, by the United States). While since World War II the United States appears to have learned much about the relationship between force and diplomacy, it displayed striking naiveté about this connection until that time.

It is perhaps understandable, given America's experiences, that the new nation should underestimate the significance of force in the political process. With the one great exception of the Civil War, the United States has been able to settle its internal conflicts with minimal resort to force. While countless other states have been routinely torn by internal violence, America has succeeded in integrating a multiplicity of ethnic groups into the "melting pot" with a remarkable degree of domestic tranquility. This was made possible, in large part, because of the great abundance of wealth in the United States. It seemed that whenever a new wave of immigrants demanded higher incomes and greater access to opportunity, there were always sufficient quantities of these to pass around without penalizing those who had already entered the economic mainstream. It is no small wonder that Americans developed faith in the processes of negotiation, mediation and judicial settlement.

Since these mechanisms had worked so well on the domestic scene, was there any reason to doubt their effectiveness internationally? Americans have always displayed an eagerness to negotiate over foreign policy impasses. This sometimes places the United States at a disadvantage against an adversary who has little intention of compromising but can capitalize on America's abiding faith in discussion as a means of resolving conflict.

In foreign affairs, Americans also have had reason to discount the role of military force. After the short-lived British landing on American shores in the War of 1812—resulting in the burning of Washington—the United States did not need to fear attack from abroad for approximately one hundred fifty years. This was because the two oceans, patrolled by the British navy (which did not wish to see its European rivals establish footholds in the New World), shielded America from the power politics of Europe. Because the American people for so long enjoyed external security without a large military force, they easily reached the conclusion that military power was not required to protect the country. Having been involved in so few foreign conflicts during the period leading up to World War II, many Americans came to believe that international clashes occur not because of fundamental conflicts of interest but rather on account of misunderstandings, wily and power-hungry statesmen, the influence of munitions makers, or other factors, all of which could be rectified. Thus, Americans to this day wax enthusiastic about cultural exchange and personal diplomacy, believing that such activities can eliminate war. Americans still have difficulty in accepting the fact that between certain states there may be very real and fundamental conflicts of interest, and that the source of international hostility may lie not with a failure of one country to understand another but with the very accurate perception by one country that another state covets its land and resources.

The discounting of force reveals itself in several episodes in American foreign policy. After proclaiming his famous "doctrine," President Monroe took no steps to support it with a strong navy; instead, Washington entrusted enforcement to the British fleet. After circulating the Open Door notes of 1899 and 1900, the United States showed no inclination to police respect for Chinese integrity with military force. In urging the American people to join him in declaring war upon Germany, President Wilson made little mention of the peril to American security were the war to be won by Germany. Accordingly, the American people refused to join the League of Nations or take any part in maintaining a balance of power in Europe. Instead, in passing the Neutrality Acts in the 1930s, the

United States went out of its way to detach itself from Europe. A greater appreciation for the role of force in international affairs would have led the United States to take precisely the opposite course. Indeed, as late as 1940, after Hitler's tanks had already stormed across Poland, Congress passed a law to institute a military draft by only a single vote!

When World War II drew to a close, the United States concluded that it could no longer afford to behave as it did after World War I, when it renounced the League and abandoned Europe. The US took the lead in establishing the United Nations and helping the war-torn participants to recover. Yet, it continued to discount the role of force. Understandably enough, American families wanted their sons in uniform to return home from Europe and the Pacific. The war over, America sped its troops back home and practically disbanded the armed forces. Again, the United States showed little understanding of the importance of military force in supporting diplomacy. The Soviet Union, now in control of Eastern Europe, was not so naive.

We can summarize much of the above by observing that up to the end of World War II, the United States exhibited little comprehension of the famous dictum of the nineteenth-century Prussian General Carl Maria von Clausewitz that war is the continuation of politics by other means. This statement refers to the fact that states remain locked in perpetual conflict; sometimes this conflict is prosecuted by diplomacy, sometimes through economic tactics, sometimes by propaganda, and sometimes by war. (These various tools of statecraft are not mutually exclusive.) Peace and war, in this view, are not opposites but rather represent points along a spectrum of intensity of conflict. The United States, in contrast, has tended to view peace and war as poles apart. During peacetime, the isolationist impulse has prevented the nation from taking a great interest in foreign affairs. Only when it is morally outraged by the behavior of another nation does it turn to foreign policy, and then with a vengeance. America fights a moral crusade to stamp out evil. Once this purpose is accomplished, the United States returns to its internal pursuits. Regarding foreign policy as a temporary nuisance, the United States displays little interest in fashioning postwar settlements that will prevent future wars, and in deploying sufficient power to ensure their success. Thus, after World War II the United States was prepared to withdraw its forces from Europe and let events there take their course.

It does appear that now the United States has learned to appreciate the significance of military power in world affairs. In time of peace, America currently maintains substantial military forces in being. While Americans might debate whether to build a particular weapons system or to deploy the armed forces in a specific instance, most Americans seem to have accepted, if reluctantly, the need to support American diplomacy with military power.

PRAGMATISM

Two small-town mayors were discussing their methods at a national conference on local government. One explained that he constantly read books about model cities and studied academic theories about administrative procedures. The second mayor said she came to the office every day with her head uncluttered by distant visions and took each problem as it arose. She likened her job to that of a forest ranger, putting out small (and occasionally large) fires wherever they arose in city government. The second of these executives illustrates another component of American political culture: pragmatism. According to Webster's *Seventh New Collegiate Dictionary*, pragmatism means "a practical approach to problems and affairs." The pragmatic or practical approach can be contrasted with a theoretical or ideological approach.

The early settlers in America had little choice but to develop a pragmatic approach to the problems they confronted. Their choice was limited to pragmatism or starvation. There were countless tasks to perform merely in order to survive, including growing food, building shelters, establishing a system of governance, building roads and harbors, constructing markets, and creating all the other factors essential to living. Since the frontier continued to march westward, Americans had to repeat these efforts each time new land was cleared. There was little time or reward for philosophizing. In order to establish a flourishing society, America needed to develop the qualities of hard work and ingenuity, talents for which America today is justly renowned.

Kenneth Keniston has aptly observed that "ours is a how-to-do-it society, and not a what-to-do society."[10] Based on the legacy of the past, Americans take an engineering or crisis-management approach to problems. It is characteristic of the pragmatist to peer over the next hill but not to gaze at the horizon. In other words, the pragmatists concern themselves less with long-range visions than with meeting each problem as it arises. Americans are prepared to let the long run take care of itself. Impatient with theoretical analysis, they like to see results, and they like them quickly.

They are much more comfortable with the visible and concrete than the abstract and intangible. For example, the American people were mesmerized by the sight of the first moon walk, but they showed little interest in the fundamental knowledge about the universe that has been obtained as a result of the space program.

Pragmatism has had a decided impact on American foreign policy. It is responsible for the often-voiced accusation that the United States does not even have a foreign policy. Such a statement does not mean that the United States fails to take any foreign actions; rather, it means that the nation often appears to lack a long-run foreign-policy program, a set of goals it hopes to achieve over the next twenty, fifty or hundred years. By contrast, the Soviet Union does have such a blueprint, although it is arguable whether Soviet policymakers adhere to it. The Soviet long-range program follows the dictates of Marxism-Leninism, which call for the eventual triumph of communism throughout the world. Accordingly, Moscow's foreign policy, at least in part, takes direction from this objective. The United States holds out no comparable vision of a future world it is trying to create. American foreign policy often appears reactive, particularly to the initiatives of Communist regimes. These criticisms all spring from America's pragmatic approach to problems and from the country's bias against planning. Rather than follow a foreign policy blueprint, the United States handles each problem as it arises, relying on its qualities of ingenuity, improvisation, and experimentation. This approach in part accounts for the disproportionate share of lawyers and businessmen who are appointed to top foreign policy-making positions. In order to succeed in law or business, an individual must learn the techniques of problem solving. Such people are accustomed to coping with unforeseen problems as these arise. However, since they frequently have not developed a distant vision of the future, it is often difficult to discern any pattern other than self-preservation in American foreign policy.

The early history of the State Department's Policy Planning Staff illustrates the American preference for improvisation over long-range planning. This unit was created in the late 1940s to prepare long-range plans for American foreign policy. Some of State's most capable officers were assigned to it. However, the Policy Planning Staff rarely succeeded in influencing foreign policy. Since the organization embraced such talented individuals, these people were often called away to work on specific problems that arose unexpectedly, leaving them little time for planning. Indeed, such individuals found that they were most highly valued not when engaged in planning but when employed in "putting out fires," as crisis management is sometimes called. The remainder of the State Department often paid little heed to the planning documents produced by the Policy Planning Staff. Thus, when a crisis arose, department officers did not first consult the Policy Planning Staff's "thought papers" but instead dealt with the issues as best they could.

The manner in which the United States fought in Vietnam provides another illustration of America's bias against planning for the future. No American officer, in the early days of that conflict, ever planned for an expeditionary force of half a million men. Rather, America's longest war escalated incrementally as each new military problem surfaced. One day, Americans were stunned to learn that they were involved in a major military effort.

America's pragmatic heritage, while it facilitated the building of a great nation, has also prejudiced Americans in favor of rapid results. However, in navigating the obscure and hazardous shoals of foreign policy, a speedy passage often ends on the rocks of disaster. Nonetheless, the American people typically demand fast action, and a president who cannot produce stands little chance of getting reelected. Presidents obtain little public support when they justify an action that will bear fruit perhaps ten or twenty years in the future. Furthermore, in foreign policy debates that take place in the upper reaches of the bureaucracy, advocates of a policy that will yield dividends only years ahead find themselves at a disadvantage. The foreign assistance program illustrates these problems. Much of American foreign aid goes to countries that lack an infrastructure such as that existing in Europe at the end of World War II. American postwar aid to Europe satisfied the American craving for speedy results, because the Europeans could absorb American assistance into their economic framework so as to reconstruct their economies. But many Third World recipients of American aid have no such infrastructure to rebuild; they must start from scratch. The first step might be a literacy program, accompanied by the construction of markets and roads. In order to produce the savings that yield investment in capital goods—goods that produce other goods—these countries must raise their standard of living above the subsistence level. Feudal economic and political systems must be replaced with new structures that provide opportunities for industrious people to rise in society. Perhaps most difficult of all, it is necessary to inculcate the values of hard work and (incongruously for pragmatists who demand quick results) postponement of gratification in societies that have always lived from hand to mouth. Seen in such a light, economic development is a task for the long-distance runner, not the sprinter. While it may not take Third World countries as long to industrialize as it took Western Europe, such an economic transformation is not going to occur in the space of a decade. Many Americans, accustomed to seeing quick results, have grown frustrated with economic aid.

Americans are also impatient with the new doctrines of limited war made necessary by the destructive force of strategic missiles. Many Americans reverberate with sympathy to the words of General Douglas MacArthur, "In war there is no substitute for victory." Yet, in recent decades, Americans have learned to live, albeit uneasily, with such substitutes. America had the capacity to push the North Koreans far north of the 38th Parallel, had it been willing to engage the Soviet Union and China in full-scale combat. Similarly, there is no doubt that the United States could have obliterated North Vietnam, but only at the risk of a nuclear confrontation with the Soviet Union and China. It has been difficult for many Americans to adjust to fighting "with one hand behind their backs"— usually the hand that grasps a nuclear weapon. Americans would much prefer the total and unconditional surrenders that ended both world wars to compromise settlements that marked the conclusions of the fighting in Korea and Vietnam. Yet, the advent of nuclear weapons seems to leave the United States—and other countries facing nuclear foes or foes with nuclear allies—with little choice other than limited war.

Following World War II, the pragmatic strain in American foreign policy became much more pronounced than ever before. In an effort to halt Communist expansion, the United States concluded security agreements with over forty other countries, distributed billions of dollars in military and economic aid, and intervened in the political affairs of states as far apart as Laos and Guatemala, Iran and Italy.

LIBERALISM

Lexicographers might one day cite liberalism as the most overworked word of the twentieth century. The number of meanings ascribed to this term is almost countless. Yet the word cannot mean all things to all people and at the same time communicate anything. For our purposes, liberalism will refer to a set of values clustered around the sanctity of the individual. The most prominent champions of this idea include Jean Jacques Rousseau, John Locke, John Stuart Mill and Jeremy Bentham. These thinkers gave rise to the school of thought known as classical liberalism. Proponents of this philosophy believe that an individual has the right to manage his or her own life in any way he or she desires, so long as no harm is caused to any other individual. If it were possible to live tolerably without government, that would be ideal. However, some degree of government appears indispensable, if only to organize self-defense, put out fires, and subdue criminals. Any form of government naturally restricts individual freedom. The liberal accepts this limitation but insists that government should base itself on consent of the governed.

Internationally, liberalism has found its clearest expression in the idea of self-determination, explained here by Thomas Jefferson in a letter to Thomas Pinckney:

> We certainly cannot deny to other nations that principle whereon our government is founded, that every nation has a right to govern itself internally under whatever form it pleases, and to change these forms at its own will; and externally to transact business with other nations throughout whatever organ it chooses. . . .

Self-determination means that each nationality has a right to govern itself. In contrast, under an empire one nationality rules all the others and nearly without exception discriminates against them. Many liberals believe that the lack of self-determination is one of the principal causes of war. Indeed, as one surveys the world today, many of the states experiencing violent conflict seem beset by the desires of minorities to gain more control over their own destinies.

Liberalism has inclined the United States to support other regimes that cherish liberal values. Thus, it has linked its own future to the states of Western Europe, Australia, New Zealand, Canada, and Israel. Generally, the United States is quick to support experiments in democratic government as they arise in other lands. However, contradictory values here frequently led to US support for undemocratic governments, and to US intervention designed to thwart the establishment of a democratic government (as in the Philippines at the turn of the century) or to overturn the results of a democratic election (as in the case of the Allende government in Chile).

PRIVATE ENTERPRISE AND OPTIMISM

In the same year that an upstart nation in the New World issued its Declaration of Independence, an English economist and philosopher named Adam Smith published a book entitled *The Wealth of Nations.* Both publications proved extremely influential. The former justified the severing of political ties between a nation and its foreign oppressor. The latter provided the rationale for the economic system we know today as capitalism.

In his monumental book, Smith argued that national output and economic well-being are maximized if each individual acts in his or her own selfish interest. If each producer of goods seeks to maximize profit, the dynamic of competition will spur each to produce the best product for the lowest possible price. The "unseen hand" of the marketplace regulates the economy according to the laws of supply and demand. Producers that cannot compete are forced to produce something else, for which their talents are better suited. Consumers vote for the goods they wish fabricated by purchasing these commodities and leaving the others to perish on the shelf. The mechanism of the marketplace thus transforms individual selfishness into the general economic good.

What is government's role in this process, according to Smith? The British theorist believed that by interfering with the operation of the marketplace, government would only hinder the optimal production and exchange of goods and services. Government should restrict itself to creating the proper climate for the operation of the private enterprise system. It should maintain law and order, manage the currency, determine weights and measures, oversee patents, copyrights and trademarks, but it should not play a direct role in the production and exchange of goods. *Laissez-faire* (to leave alone) is the term used to describe such government abstention.

Smith recognized that the system he charted would not work to everyone's advantage. An individual who could not produce at a sufficiently low cost to sell his wares would suffer during the interval while he learned another trade. Some people are generally inept, and these unfortunate souls would have to live in poorhouses, maintained by charity and/or government. But if government took a hand in the economy and tried to ensure a more equal distribution of goods and services, the result would be subsidized inefficiency, and that would only reduce the total amount of goods and services produced. Besides, said Smith and his followers, it is in the natural order of things that some people are more talented than others, and these people are entitled to greater rewards. The writings of Charles Darwin a century later seemed to confirm this notion, for Darwin theorized that in nature the strong survive and the weak perish. Surely, God must have meant it so.

The economic system of private enterprise or capitalism that Adam Smith described is basically the one adopted by the United

States at the time of its founding. In those days, of course, business was conducted by individual farmers and small shopkeepers. Today's corporate giants were unknown. In the nineteenth century large corporations began to develop, particularly in railroading and oil. These firms, with their enormous financial assets, could and did undercut their smaller competitors, ruthlessly driving them out of business. The unfettered play of the marketplace, it turned out, could foster monopolies, which could then produce at any cost because there was no competition to fear. Furthermore, large masses of workers were suffering at the hands of unscrupulous entrepreneurs. More and more people called for the government to do something, and so government regulation was introduced to keep the private enterprise system well-tuned. Antitrust legislation was enacted to break the power of such companies as Standard Oil. Labor unions arose. As the twentieth century unfolded, a vast panoply of government regulatory agencies, including the Federal Trade Commission and the Interstate Commerce Commission, came into being. Today, the government takes a large hand in regulating the economy, using such instruments as the Federal Reserve System and the federal budget. The latter helps set national priorities and allocate resources between the public and private sectors. Despite the pervasive role of government in regulating the economy, one suspects that most Americans regard government interference as a necessary evil, albeit one not likely to disappear. (Certainly, Ronald Reagan's 1980 electoral pledge to reduce the scope of government struck a responsive chord among voters.)

A lingering nostalgia for the nearly pure private-enterprise system of days gone by colors American foreign policy. The United States exhibits a decided preference in favor of regimes where government interference in the economy is minimal. Few states today approximate the *laissez-faire* model touted by Adam Smith, but there are marked differences in degree of government involvement. The deeply ingrained American notion of private enterprise has also inhibited the US government from controlling the operations of American corporations abroad, even when they adversely affect the interests of the United States. This tendency mystifies many other countries, where business firms cannot write an order without government approval. Such countries find it difficult to accept the idea that the American government may not interfere in the operations of American companies without due process of law. (Of course, many corporate practices are subject to government regulation.) In a poor country with a population of five or six million, the decision by an American corporation to open or close a mine or a plantation can have drastic effects on the host nation's economy and political stability, just as the decision where to locate a railroad junction in the nineteenth century American Midwest could create a boom town or a ghost town. Yet, such decisions may well be made in the boardrooms of the American corporation with little or no direction from Washington, not to mention the host country.

America is known as the most materialistic society on earth. Materialism means an affection for things, and no people love things so much as Americans. For most Americans, bigger is better and more is better. "The business of America is business," Calvin Coolidge is reported to have said, and it is certainly true that the primary preoccupation of Americans is to produce and accumulate things. Not only do Americans like things, but they tend to judge the worth of an individual not in terms of his or her integrity or compassion or the like, but in terms of the things a person owns. "What kind of car does he drive?" is a question often asked by someone who wants a rapid reading on the general standing in society of another person. America's intoxication with things often reveals itself in a fascination for gadgets. No people are more receptive to new products than Americans, whether it be miniature calculators or electronic garage-door openers, microwave ovens or digital watches. Americans can't wait to get their hands on the latest video game or home computer. Such attitudes, of course, reflect a receptivity to experimentation and inventiveness, which in turn manifests itself in the substantial efforts Americans devote to research and development. The continual quest to discover new and better solutions to problems accounts in no small part for America's phenomenal economic growth.

American materialism, an outgrowth of private enterprise, has affected American foreign policy, especially toward nations of the Third World. Since individual Americans grow discontented when deprived of economic goods, Americans have a tendency to identify such deprivation abroad with revolution. It has long been a tenet of American foreign aid that poverty breeds instability, which in turn affords opportunities for Communists to seize power. Foreign aid is therefore seen as a means of overcoming the discontent that leads to such upheavals. Only recently have some thinkers begun to suggest that aid itself might be a cause of revolution, in that it can lead to the erosion of fundamental values and social structures (such as the extended family), without supplying new integrating mechanisms in their place. American aid programs are not likely to succeed in societies where the people place little importance on material goods, and where basic discontent springs from other causes. In such countries as Pakistan, Iran (after the shah) and Lebanon, political instability remains chronic, yet the causes appear to have little to do with the availability of material goods.

Lastly, Americans exude optimism. No matter how gloomy his projection of the future may be, the typical American ends his forecast on a note of good cheer. The quality of optimism is readily understandable in a people who have known little but success throughout their history. The United States has succeeded in gaining independence, conquering a continent, creating a mighty industrial base, winning nearly every major war it fought, and fostering one of the highest living standards in the world. At the same time, the US has maintained a remarkable degree of civil tranquility— the Civil War being a major exception—and political liberty. From the earliest days of the Republic, America was a land of opportunity. So long as a person was industrious and displayed a modicum of ingenuity, he or she stood a good chance of success. America offered fertile land and commercial prospects. Individuals were not limited in their climb up society's ladder by the nobility of their blood. Of course, people have had to work hard in order to prosper. But the point is that it has been far easier to flourish in America than in almost any other society in the world. It is true that blacks and other minorities as well as women have been denied equal opportunities. While no claim is being made here that the United States is or ever was a perfect society, it has provided more opportunity for getting ahead than almost any other land.

Due to the nation's remarkable record in overcoming obstacles, most Americans welcome challenges and remain convinced that they can be met. This attitude has led Americans to undertake a great many ambitious tasks both at home and abroad. Whereas other nations, their expectations tempered by a checkered history, might hesitate to play a vigorous part in world politics, the United States since World War II has adopted an extremely active role in direct contradiction of its isolationist tendencies. Americans are convinced they can affect events, and so they try.

Optimism leads not only to an activist foreign policy but sometimes tempts Americans to tackle problems beyond their powers. For instance, Americans fully expected that foreign aid would give an enormous boost to poorer lands, enabling them to take off into the wild blue yonder of self-sufficiency within a relatively short period of time. The United States further expected that those receiving foreign aid would attain political stability within a democratic framework and later display gratitude to their benefactor. With the exception of a very few recipients such as Israel, this succession of events has not materialized. Unrealistic expectations fueled by optimism present the hazard that Americans will grow disillusioned and withdraw from undertakings that require sustained amounts of time and energy. Today, for example, American enthusiasm for foreign aid approaches its nadir.

In the wake of Watergate, Vietnam, inflation, energy shortages, and the nuclear threat, is American optimism waning? Even if the future looks dimmer to Americans now than it did to previous generations, it seems safe to say that the underlying optimism in America's political culture will survive for years to come.

CONCLUSIONS

This chapter has tried to show how American political culture— its political values, beliefs, and traditions—affect the foreign policy of the United States. The main cultural tendencies surveyed were isolationism, legalism-moralism, pragmatism, liberalism, private enterprise, and optimism. Although not an exhaustive list, these elements have an important influence on American foreign policy. The nature and extent of that influence is a question that deserves further consideration.

It should be clear that political culture is an extremely amorphous concept; like a hearty soup that contains many flavors, it includes various ingredients whose contribution to the final product is difficult to measure. Some of the components of political culture are mutually contradictory, at least in some circumstances. Consider, for example, the contrast between pragmatism and legalism-moralism. It seems contradictory for a state to embrace in its heritage one force that leads to cynical interventions in affairs of other countries and another force that gives rise to self-righteous moralism. It seems similarly contradictory for a state to at one time retreat behind a wall of isolationism and at another time to carry a sense of mission to other lands with all the fervor of a crusader. Might not some of President Carter's turnabouts in foreign policy be attributable to the conflicting pulls of different elements of American political culture? The strong stand in favor of human rights adopted at the outset of his administration evidences the presence of legalism-moralism. The softening of this theme by 1980 suggests that pragmatism was at war with legalism-moralism.

Carter's shift in policy toward the Soviet Union from accommodation to confrontation, following the invasion of Afghanistan, was
perhaps partly the product of tension between these same two
elements of political culture.

In a recent study, John Stoessinger divides American policymakers into two categories, crusaders and pragmatists.[11] Crusaders,
such as Woodrow Wilson, manifest a missionary zeal to improve
the world. They make decisions on the basis of preconceived notions
as opposed to the facts of a case. If the facts contradict these
preconceived ideas, crusaders set aside the facts. Burning with an
almost religious intensity, crusaders reject courses of action that
differ from their preferences. Pragmatists, by contrast, base their
actions on the facts of a given situation, not preconceived ideas
about what needs to be done. Given to sober reflection, they consider various alternatives before selecting a foreign policy action.
If their policy choice proves unwise, they are prepared to reverse
field. Harry Truman and Henry Kissinger were pragmatists.
According to Stoessinger, most of the major American foreign policy
decisions of this century have been made by very few individuals,
sometimes as few as a single person. America has swung like a
pendulum between the two poles of "Sunday evangelism and week-
day realism."

Alternation between two such opposite extremes is consistent
with the view that states are extremely complex social organizations
containing contradictory forces. This poses a difficulty for assessing
the exact relationship between political culture and foreign policy.
It is extremely precarious to predict a state's foreign policy only
by reference to its political culture, as there is no way of telling
which element in the political culture will predominate at a particular juncture. It is much easier to explain a foreign policy action
in terms of political culture after the event occurs. As an analytical
tool, therefore, political culture has its limitations.

One way in which political culture can help us understand
foreign policy is to hypothesize that political culture sets limits to
the foreign policy actions a state is likely to take. We have already
seen that the Kennedy administration rejected an air strike against
Soviet missiles in Cuba in 1962 because of moral objections against
conducting a Pearl Harbor in reverse. Another illustration of this
limit-setting process arose toward the end of World War II. As
Allied leaders were contemplating the nature of the postwar world,
Stalin laid on the table a plan for preventing a resurgence of German
militarism. The Soviet head of state suggested that the victors

simply murder the 50,000 officers in the German armed forces. Roosevelt, joined by Churchill, vetoed this proposal without hesitation. Did the political culture of America and Great Britain influence Roosevelt and Churchill to reject Stalin's plan? While proof is lacking, it seems safe to suggest that political culture had much to do with their decision.

The model in Chapter 1 indicates that political culture in itself does not make foreign policy. People make foreign policy. This observation introduces another complication into the relationship between political culture and foreign policy. Political culture must be filtered through the individuals who influence foreign policy decisions and those who make such decisions. A detailed examination of who these people are is reserved for a future chapter. However, we must pause to inquire whether all the persons involved are similarly influenced by political culture. To make the issue clearer, consider two extreme cases. J. Vaughan Patterson is a fictional investment banker born of wealthy parents in Bryn Mawr, Pennsylvania, and educated at Choate School, Yale University and Columbia Law School. He is presently an assistant secretary in the State Department. Alvin Lewis was born in the Bronx, dropped out of school after the tenth grade, and dries automobiles at a carwash. Both of these imaginary characters influence American foreign policy, the former as a policymaker and the latter as a voter and perhaps a member of one or more interest groups. Both were raised in the US and spent their lives immersed in America's political culture. Yet, can we say that these men would express the same foreign policy preferences in the event of a crisis? The investment banker has known a life of success and self-pride. He is an educated and cultured individual. He feels comfortable at gourmet restaurants, art museums, and corporate board meetings. Lewis's life experiences are just the opposite. Can we hypothesize with any confidence that both men, as products of American political culture, would think alike on matters of foreign policy? The answer is not at all obvious. However, if it seems that the two individuals would be likely to think differently on some matters, then we must inquire whether there does not exist in America something approaching a foreign policy elite whose outlook and policy choices depart from the world view of the average American. Alternatively, it may turn out that the policy-making establishment represents a cross section of the American people. Each possibility suggests a different kind of relationship between political culture and foreign policy.

FOR DISCUSSION

Which elements of American political culture most strongly affect foreign policy today? Provide examples to support your conclusions.

Did Vietnam squelch the missionary impulse in American foreign policy?

Compared to other factors that affect foreign policy, how strong an influence is political culture?

What new elements of political culture do you see emerging as America enters the twenty-first century? How will these new elements shape foreign policy?

Select another country and explain how its political culture influences its foreign policy. Compare and contrast this country with the United States.

Choose a current major problem in American foreign policy and predict how America's political culture is likely to shape Washington's response.

What elements in America's political culture would seem to account for the Reagan administration's strong interest in combatting leftist forces in Central America?

READING SUGGESTIONS

Almond, Gabriel, and Verba, Sidney. *The Civic Culture: Political Attitudes and Democracy in Five Nations*. Princeton: Princeton University Press, 1963.

Brogan, D. W. *Politics in America*. Garden City, New York: Doubleday, 1960.

Commager, Henry Steele. *The American Mind: An Interpretation of American Thought and Character Since the 1880s*. New Haven: Yale University Press, 1950.

De Tocqueville, Alexis. *Democracy in America*. Various editions.

Kennan, George F. *American Diplomacy, 1900–1950*. New York: Mentor, 1951.

Lipset, Seymour Martin. *The First New Nation*. New York: Basic Books, 1963.

Mills, C. Wright. *The Power Elite*. New York: Oxford University Press, 1956.

Potter, David M. *People of Plenty: Economic Abundance and the American Character*. New York: Collier-Macmillan, 1971.

Stoessinger, John G. *Crusaders and Pragmatists: Movers of Modern American Foreign Policy*. New York: Norton, 1979.

Toffler, Alvin. *Future Shock*. New York: Random House, 1970.

NOTES

1. See, for example, John G. Stoessinger, *Crusaders and Pragmatists: Movers of Modern American Foreign Policy* (New York: W. W. Norton and Company, 1979).
2. One of the finest such volumes is the classic study by Alexis de Tocqueville, *Democracy in America.* Although written over a century ago, this Frenchman's observations have a startlingly current ring. D. W. Brogan, *Politics in America* (Garden City, N.Y.: Doubleday, Anchor, 1960) offers a cogent and more up-to-date analysis of American society. While not written strictly about America's political culture, Alvin Toffler's *Future Shock* (New York: Random House, 1970) contains a penetrating description of modern America. *The Greening of America*, by Charles A. Reich (New York: Random House, 1970), presents a controversial view of the American character from the standpoint of the "counter-culture" that emerged in the 1960s.
3. While avoiding the temptation to intervene militarily in these conflicts, the United States did employ economic and political measures to influence events. Thus, isolationism in these instances was not total, a reflection of America's position in the contemporary world. A rationale for a contemporary policy of isolationism may be found in Robert W. Tucker, *A New Isolationism: Threat or Promise* (New York: Universe Books, 1972).
4. The urge to concentrate on internal concerns remains strong in the United States. Max Lerner has written in *America as a Civilization* that both isolationists and interventionists share this ultimate goal. The latter press the government to use its economic and military power abroad in order to shape a world that will permit America once again to concern itself with domestic tasks.
5. George F. Kennan, *American Diplomacy, 1900–1950* (New York: Mentor Books, 1951), p. 59.
6. Ibid., pp. 82–89.
7. Ibid., p. 44.
8. Robert F. Kennedy, *Thirteen Days* (New York: W.W. Norton and Company, 1971), pp. 16–17.
9. Cecil V. Crabb, Jr., *American Foreign Policy in the Nuclear Age*, 3rd ed. (New York: Harper and Row, 1972), p. 31.
10. Quoted in Howard Bliss and M. Glen Johnson, *Beyond the Water's Edge: America's Foreign Policies* (Philadelphia: J.B. Lippincott, 1975), p. 110.
11. John G. Stoessinger, *Crusaders and Pragmatists* (New York: Norton, 1979).

Chapter 5
Public Opinion and
Pressure Groups

Like values, beliefs and traditions, public opinion and pressure groups represent inputs into the political system (see Fig. 1–1). Like the political system itself, public opinion and pressure groups are affected by the nation's values, beliefs and traditions. Furthermore, public opinion and pressure groups are influenced by the impact of American foreign policy upon the international state system; such influence makes itself felt through the feedback mechanism. Thus, American military action in Vietnam eventually turned public opinion against further foreign interventions, at least for some time. A host of pressure groups became active in urging reduced military spending and the curtailment of American military (and other) activity abroad. These forces exerting pressure upon the political system produced a president, Jimmy Carter, who pledged to do these very things.

WHOSE OPINION?—FOUR MODELS

Many of us have been brought up to believe that the American political system rests on public opinion. The entire purpose of representative government, it is often said, is to translate the preferences of the citizenry into government policy. In this conception, government acts much like a bookie who places bets on instructions

145

from clients. A close examination of the role of public opinion reveals, however, that the relationship between opinion and policy is much more complex than the simple proposition suggested above. In order to help us explore this relationship, it will be helpful to depict American society as shown in Fig. 5–1.

The pyramid depicted in Fig. 5–1 divides American society into four different segments. We shall refer to each segment in describing four separate propositions about the influence of the public upon foreign policy. The entire pyramid represents the whole of American society, and we shall refer to it in discussing the proposition that each adult citizen has an equal effect upon policy. We call this the one-person, one-vote—or democratic—theory. The broad band near the top of the pyramid represents a select portion of the public. We shall make reference to this group in examining the theory of pluralism. This approach states that only a limited portion of the public, those people organized in pressure groups, have a meaningful say over government policy. The entire shaded section at the summit represents an even smaller number of citizens, those we shall mention in analyzing the power elite theory. This theory maintains that only those citizens who comprise a power elite make a

FIGURE 5-1: AMERICAN PUBLIC OPINION

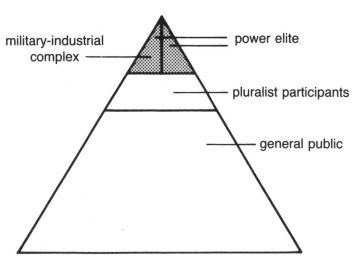

consequential input to policy. Finally, the left-hand portion of this shaded segment stands for a still smaller number of persons, those included in the military-industrial complex. Our fourth proposition states that only these individuals have a determining impact upon foreign policy. Let us explore these possibilities.

One-Person, One-Vote

One-person, one-vote remains a cherished American ideal because it states that all voters have an equal voice in determining policy. Indeed, the notion of one-person, one-vote underlies the entire concept of democratic government. For this very reason, it is disturbing to proponents of democracy to learn that this concept has almost no validity in actual practice. We may like to think that the vast majority of the citizenry thoroughly investigates a problem, gathers all relevant data, weighs all the pros and cons of all possible outcomes, and then makes a choice that it conveys unambiguously to the government. However, between this ideal and reality lie various qualities of public opinion: apathy, ignorance, inconsistency, permissiveness, and personality. We shall examine these in turn.

Apathy.

An American institution of higher learning issues an annual award to the student club that most perfectly carries out the intents expressed in its charter. Every year the Apathy Club garners the award; it has never met. Observers have found that a large majority of the American public displays hardly more interest in foreign policy. For example, a 1974 study asked respondents to name the two or three problems they would most like government to act upon. Table 5-1 reveals the low priority that most members of the public accorded foreign policy. While these figures might differ during intervals of extreme international tension, the evidence suggests that the priorities expressed in Table 5-1 are valid most of the time.

Many members of the public simply lack an opinion on numerous issues of foreign policy. How many Americans lose sleep over such issues as the need for a naval base on Diego Garcia in the Indian Ocean, the advisability of supplying military aid to Morocco in its fight against Polisario soldiers, or the tariff the United States should level against imports of light industrial goods coming from

TABLE 5-1: PERCENTAGE OF POPULATION MENTIONING
         PROBLEM BY CATEGORY

(December 1974)	
Economy	80
Energy crisis, oil shortage (primarily domestic)	11
Foreign policy	13
Government corruption	15

Source: adapted from John E. Reilly, ed., *American Public Opinion and U.S. Foreign Policy,
1975* (Chicago, Chicago Council on Foreign Relations, 1975), p. 10. Reprinted by permission
of the Chicago Council on Foreign Relations.

Central America? Citizen apathy calls into doubt the validity of
the democratic model. Apathetic persons rarely or never participate
in the affairs of state. Indeed, few of them even vote. How can
such individuals have the same impact upon government as those
people who discuss issues, contribute money to political campaigns
and pressure groups, and regularly appear at the polls? Indeed,
one wonders how the government is capable of finding guidance
in a citizenry that lacks an opinion. Returning to an earlier
analogy, government often finds itself in the position of a bookie
who receives a call telling him to place a bet on a horse of his own
choice.

Ignorance.
Public apathy concerning foreign policy is matched by public ignorance. Numerous studies of public opinion support this conclusion.
In 1978, only half the American population knew that the United
States imported any oil, at a time when nearly half the nation's oil
consumption came from abroad.[1] In 1964, 25 percent of the American people were unaware that there was a Communist government
in mainland China; an additional 29 percent did not know that an
alternative Chinese government existed on Taiwan. In that same
year, only 58 percent of the American people thought that the
United States was a member of NATO, while 38 percent believed
that the Soviet Union was a member (despite the fact that the
alliance was formed to blunt a Soviet attack). In 1966, as in 1950,
only two-thirds of the American people were able to name the
secretary of state.

      After a careful review of these and other data, Free and
Cantril[2] classified American public awareness of foreign policy as
follows:

Well informed	26%
Moderately well informed	35%
Uninformed	39%

The low level of public knowledge regarding foreign policy cannot be attributed to the absence of information. Such material abounds, particularly in the media. The United States ranks among the leading countries in the world in terms of literacy and enrollment in higher education. On everyday issues of foreign policy, most Americans are simply not interested.

The low level of public knowledge about foreign policy, coupled with a general lack of interest, raises the question of how well the nation would prosper should the government allow itself to be guided by public opinion. We shall return to this consideration at a later point in the chapter.

Inconsistency.

It is not uncommon for the American public to favor two mutually exclusive courses of action, or to prefer a certain objective but reject the path required to attain it. Americans may support defense spending but resent the taxes required to pay for it. They may champion the cause of human rights in the Soviet Union while desiring better relations with Moscow, not realizing that the Soviets take great offense at external interference in their domestic affairs.

Gabriel A. Almond, reflecting upon the inconsistency of American opinion, has suggested that the word "mood" is preferable to "opinion" as a description of the views of most Americans. Mood can be contrasted with an intellectual thought process based on facts and objective analysis. Where public policy affects personal interests, Americans are prone to develop opinions based on facts and reason. This thought process most often occurs with regard to those matters that touch everyday personal lives, such as zoning, public school issues, taxes or Social Security policy. On the more remote issues of foreign policy, however, most citizens do not trouble to inform themselves. Consequently, their viewpoints are likely to be based on emotional considerations. These emotional factors, not tethered to firm facts, are subject to constant change, just as the emotional states of people undergo ceaseless turmoil. American interest in foreign policy increases with a crisis, but even in crises the typical reaction is one of mood. Often a crisis generates a vague apprehension or anger, which soon evaporates when the crisis passes.[3]

The inconsistency of American public attitudes toward foreign policy gives the president considerable leeway. The president can nearly always find some support among the public for any action taken. Often, presidential action is the catalyst needed to crystallize public opinion. For example, there was little public opinion for President Kennedy to follow in deciding whether to commit military advisers to Vietnam. It was only after Johnson had sent half a million troops there that public sentiment began to form.

Permissiveness.

One might expect that a combination of public apathy, ignorance and inconsistency would afford the government considerable leeway in foreign policy. Studies show that this indeed is the case.

A foreign policy crisis nearly always boosts presidential popularity. Such an event elicits a rally-'round-the-flag reaction, as the public sees the nation pitted against an alien foe. In June 1950, just before the North Koreans stormed across the 38th Parallel, 37 percent of those polled approved the way Truman was doing his job while 45 percent did not. One month later, after the invasion, the corresponding figures were 46 percent and 37 percent. In April 1958, Eisenhower's popularity rating was 49 percent as the country suffered a recession and saw the Soviets launch the first satellite (Sputnik). In the summer of that year, Eisenhower sent a Marine landing force to Lebanon; his popularity rose to 58 percent.[4] Table 5–2, based on Harris polls, reveals the significant increase in support for sending American troops into Cambodia that materialized *after* President Nixon sent troops there in May 1970. It is interesting to note that the best educated citizens evinced the greatest increase in support for the measure.

The figures reported below suggest that the public rallies around the president in time of military action, summit conferences, and other types of highly visible and consequential international events. Indeed, there is evidence to support the contention that the public responds positively, at least in the short run, to whatever the president does when the national interest is seen in jeopardy. The populace appears to prefer a chief executive who takes firm, decisive action. There is even evidence to sustain the conclusion that in time of crisis the public will support a president who bungles the job. The Bay of Pigs invasion of Cuba in the spring of 1961 is generally regarded as a foreign policy disaster for the United States. Yet, just after the landing party was decimated on the beaches, Kennedy's popular standing attained its summit, 83 percent approval.[5]

TABLE 5–2: PUBLIC SUPPORT FOR VARIOUS FORMS OF INTERVENTION IN CAMBODIA, BEFORE AND AFTER ACTUAL INTERVENTION

	APRIL 1970 (BEFORE)			
	Send troops	Send advisers or conduct bombings	Stay out	Not sure
Race				
White	7%	25	58	10
Black	6%	10	64	20
Education				
Eighth grade or less	4%	13	62	21
High school	8%	22	59	11
College	8%	28	56	8

	MAY 1970 (AFTER)				
	Send troops	Send advisers	Conduct bombings	Stay out	Not sure
Race					
White	42%	14	8	29	7
Black	9%	21	3	56	11
Education					
Eighth grade or less	30%	5	7	44	14
High school	36%	19	8	31	7
College	50%	13	7	26	4

Source: Barry B. Hughes, *The Domestic Context of Foreign Policy* (San Francisco: W. H. Freeman and Co., 1978), p. 109. By permission of Louis Harris and Associates, Inc.

At the same time, we must add that public approval does not last forever. Once the atmosphere of crisis dissipates, the public evaluation of presidential performance nearly always reverts to precrisis levels. The populace tends to support the president in times of crisis because he symbolizes the nation. He alone provides a pole around which the people can rally. To reject the president is to reject one's country.

The permissiveness normally displayed by most members of the public greatly expands the boundaries within which the president may operate. The chief executive can virtually count on public support in time of national danger. At such a moment, when the public has the greatest stake in the outcome, public opinion becomes least significant. Indeed, it is at such junctures that the chief executive seems most able to create and mold the attitudes of the public. Rather than forcing its views upon the occupant of the White House, the public seems anxious for guidance from the nation's leader. At the same time, we must add that public approval does not last

forever. Once the atmosphere of crisis dissipates, the public evaluation of presidential performance nearly always reverts to precrisis
levels. Popular support in times of crisis stems from the fact that
the president symbolizes the nation rather than from public agreement with the president's policies.

Opinion and Personality.
Some studies suggest that opinion may have less to do with facts
than with personality. Smith, Bruner and White, for example, classify opinion according to the following types: object appraisal, social
adjustment, and externalization.[6] These categories are differen-
tiated by the function that an opinion performs for the opinion
holder. Object-appraisal opinions are formed for the purpose of
understanding something. In reaching an object-appraisal opinion,
an individual carefully studies a situation, weighs available information, and forms a conclusion based on the evidence. Social-
adjustment opinions are formed in order to win friends. Thus, a
new member of an assembly-line team might adopt the views of
fellow workers so as to be liked by them. Externalization opinions
serve unconscious emotional needs. A man may hate his father, but
he realizes it is not acceptable in most societies to dismember one's
own sire. Such a person might seek other outlets for his antipathy,
such as foreign nations or minorities like blacks and Jews. A man
who doubts his masculinity might compensate by calling for large
military expenditures and military intervention at the slightest
provocation.

The purpose that an opinion serves has a bearing on the ease
with which an opinion can be altered. Object-appraisal opinions
are most easily changed, since they are based on facts that can be
verified or proven false. If a person eats a certain food and gets a
sick stomach every time, that person soon learns to shun that food.
Foreign policy views rarely confront such irrefutable evidence, however. So long as these views serve their social or emotional purposes,
a person may have little reason to change them. Rational argument
will not cause a person to alter social-adjustment or externalization
opinions, because such opinions have only the most tenuous connection with facts. In addition, the ease of changing one's opinion
is related to the intensity with which one espouses that opinion. In
general, people hold social-adjustment and externalization opinions
more dearly than object-appraisal opinions, because the first two
serve very basic social and emotional needs. Consequently, these
opinions are difficult to alter.

The connection between opinion and personality has disturbing implications for a democratic polity. Is it really a good idea for government to be guided by people whose opinions on foreign policy are determined by social adjustment or externalization? Correspondingly, what guarantee is there that key leaders in government, including the president, do not form some of their opinions on the basis of unconscious social or emotional needs?[7]

A Working Model.

It should be quite obvious by now that the actuality of public opinion in the United States bears little resemblance to the role or nature of public opinion as conceived in an ideal model of democracy. The public, especially as regards foreign policy issues, is apathetic, ill-informed, inconsistent and permissive. Public opinion may be based on an objective appraisal of the facts, but it may just as frequently be grounded in unconscious emotional needs. Many citizens fail to participate in the political process, and among those that do there is substantial difference in the degree of their involvement. All citizens do not affect government equally. Accordingly, many observers have discarded the simple notion that the general public affects policy on the basis of one-person, one-vote. Instead, numerous champions of popular democracy have accepted a scheme for classifying public opinion suggested by Gabriel A. Almond in his classic study, *The American People and Foreign Policy.*

Almond divides the general public into three segments: the mass public, the attentive public and the policy and opinion elite. The mass public numbers from 75 to 90 percent of the adult population of the country. Members of this group know and care little about foreign policy. Their views are not based on the analysis of facts but rather on gut feelings; hence these views or moods are subject to great fluctuation. The mass public is generally content to follow the president's leadership on matters of foreign policy. In effect, it remains outside the opinion-policy relationship. In time of war or other spectacular crises, the mass public rouses itself from its slumber but, like a confused hulking beast, it is usually content to be led. The mass public's greatest impact on foreign policy occurs when it helps select the leaders of the country (by voting). In picking leaders that share its values, the mass public does help set a tone for foreign policy. But on a day-to-day basis, the mass public plays no role in the determination of foreign policy.

A much smaller number of persons, perhaps 10 percent of the country's adult population, Almond places into the attentive public.

Members of the attentive public are informed and interested in foreign policy. They are likely to read the *New York Times*, the *Washington Post*, or some other quality metropolitan newspaper. Many belong to organizations such as the Foreign Policy Association, which engages in educational activities, the League of Women Voters, or the Council on Foreign Relations. They read books and periodicals, attend seminars and lectures, and send letters to their congressional representatives and to the White House. The views they hold have some basis in fact and thus are not so volatile as the moods of the mass public.

The attentive public serves as an audience for the discussion of foreign policy alternatives proposed by the policy and opinion elite. Decision makers make serious efforts to win the support of the attentive public, for the attentive public acts as a crucial link between the opinion makers and the mass public. Members of the attentive public discuss issues with their co-workers, clients, students, parishioners, and others, thereby transmitting ideas and information to (and from) the mass public and affecting the public mood on various issues. The attentive public also influences decision makers, for they find it difficult to act without the consent of sizable segments of this group. In consequence, the attentive public comes closer than the mass public to fulfilling the role of an active inquiring citizenry in the democratic political system.

Almond terms the third category of the public the policy and opinion elite. These are the people who formulate the policy options that the attentive public discusses. This group is very small, constituting perhaps only one or two percent of the adult population. James N. Rosenau estimates that there may be no more than 50 thousand persons in this category.[8] Typical members include a syndicated columnist, a professor who writes a treatise on military policy, a staff member of the House Armed Services Committee, an editorial writer for *Newsweek*, a retired admiral or a US senator. The ideas generated by the policy and opinion elite are debated by policymakers (not considered part of public opinion as used here) as well as the attentive public. The policy and opinion elite give the attentive public clues about which issues are important; if the elite ignores an issue, the attentive public is likely to follow suit. On the other hand, active debate of an issue by the elite places it high on the agenda of topics debated by the attentive public. Members of the policy and opinion elite can have significant influence over government policy. Before joining the government, Henry A. Kissinger's writings on military policy affected America's military doctrines. Former cabinet members Dean Acheson and Robert M.

Lovett served on the president's private policy-making group at the time of the Cuban missile crisis. In domestic matters, Ralph Nader is held largely responsible for the consumer movement, and Michael Harrington's book *The Other America* was said to inspire the war on poverty waged by Presidents Kennedy and Johnson. As a columnist, Walter Lippmann had enormous influence over both foreign and domestic policy.

Public Opinion as a Constraint.

It is tempting to conclude from the passive role of the vast majority of the public that public opinion plays a negligible part in the foreign policy process. In the short run, the president has virtual freedom to take practically any desired measures, including war. Public support for the president has been uniformly high in the early stages of a war. Should such an effort be brought to a successful conclusion within, say, a period of a year, the public will no doubt applaud the performance. But the patience of the mass public is not without limits. Should the president pursue a faltering policy for a sustained interval, the public will bestir itself and demand a termination of the venture. This insistence became quite clear to the chief executive once battalions of American bodies came home in coffins from Vietnam.

The eminent diplomatic historian Dexter Perkins has ably expressed the role of the public as a constraint on policy in the following words.

> In a democratic state, the details of policy, indeed even the major decisions, are and ought to be based on special knowledge. But these decisions have to be taken in a climate of opinion which is created by public sentiment, and which defines the limits of action. No president of the United States, for example, could launch a preventive war. The national ethos forbids it. No president could launch upon an ambitious career of foreign conquest; the deep-seated assumptions of the average American forbid it. The *tone* of our foreign policy is not set in the White House or in the State Department, but in the great body of the citizenry.[9]

Former Secretary of State Dean Rusk once remarked, "One thing is very clear in our society, and that is that a president cannot pursue any policy—any important policy over any period of time—without the understanding and support of the American people."[10]

Public opinion, to repeat, will eventually compel a president to alter a policy for which it does not care. It is possible to think of the relationship between government and the mass public in terms of a game of pool. The president, cue stick in hand, circles around the felt-topped table searching for clever angles and wise strategies. He decides which balls to dispatch into the waiting pockets. The gleaming wooden walls surrounding the surface of the table represent the public. The walls play a limit-setting role. Sometimes they box in the players, and on occasion they provide opportunities to make winning shots. In either case their role is mostly passive. It is the government, symbolized by the president, who determines strategies and calls the plays within the rather broad confines of the public's limitations.

It is now appropriate to question the desirability of the one-person, one-vote model. Recall some of the features of public opinion. It leans toward ignorance and apathy and inconsistency. Many opinions rest less on cognitive processes than on emotional ones, serving social-adjustment and externalization needs rather than the need to understand an issue objectively. The question arises: should the government construct its policies on such a foundation? Or would the country better prosper by allowing only rational and knowledgeable persons to influence the course of policy? If governmental decisions can be likened to the choices made by experts, we can rephrase our question as follows: If you were responsible for choosing a site to build a tunnel under a river, would you be guided by the inhabitants of the river bank or would you consult a civil engineer?

These are troubling issues for believers in the desirability of the democratic model. Clearly, the American creed places the destiny of the nation in the hands of the people, shortcomings and all. But does practice follow this creed? This question can be explored by examining some other models of the opinion-policy relationship.

The Pluralist Model—Interest Groups

Numerous observers of the American scene have suggested that the connection between public opinion and government policy is best described by the model of pluralism. The pluralist model states that the public affects the course of policy through the activity of interest groups. An interest group—sometimes called a pressure group—consists of a number of people with shared interests who organize to influence government to respond to those interests. Interest groups usually concern themselves with a very narrow range of issues. Interest groups are generally selfish; that is, they usually pressure government to act in a manner that would benefit their own members, not the entire country. Examples of interest groups include the American Farm Bureau Federation, the United Auto Workers, the American Medical Association and the American Legion. According to the pluralist model, every citizen is represented by one or more such groups. Each group has representatives—called lobbyists—in Washington who try to influence government policy. The precise number of interest groups is not known, but they surely number in the thousands. The State Department once estimated that over half the sixty-five hundred national interest groups (the total is only a guess) display an interest in foreign policy.[11] According to the pluralist model, the struggle for influence over policy resembles a multisided tug of war in which each interest group attempts to pull the government in its own direction while resisting the tugs of others. From this contest policy emerges.

In its ideal form, pluralism is not at all inconsistent with democracy. The model presumes that all Americans are members of interest groups, and that the pressures exerted by these groups upon government enable the public to affect policy. If voting allows the citizen to influence policy only on occasion, pressure groups allow the citizen to exert an impact every day. Americans are famous for being a nation of joiners. People rush out to become members of the PTA, the Rotary or other civic groups, labor unions and other occupational associations, church or synagogue groups, recreational organizations such as the Miniature Figure Collectors of America, ethnic societies and racial groups. Many citizens belong to more than one group, such as an imaginary Jewish (B'nai B'rith) doctor (American Medical Association) who collects guns (National Rifle Association) and whose daughter attends school (PTA). It has been suggested that one reason for the inconsistency of American public opinion lies in the fact that many citizens are pulled in different directions simultaneously by the different interest groups to which they belong.

While the pluralist model may appear to be in harmony with democratic government, we must pause to inquire whether all Americans are in fact represented by interest groups. Upon closer inspection, it would appear that the more affluent members of society stand a better chance than poor persons of having their preferences represented by pressure groups. In this view, pluralism becomes a form of elitism in which only the upper layers of society have an opportunity to influence government. Furthermore, not all groups possess identical resources. Most interest groups depend upon their members for financial support, and it stands to reason that the wealthier the membership, the larger the dues that can be assessed. The size of the membership also affects available resources. Groups that represent consumers and the poor are typically run out of cluttered offices in shabby buildings, while business and larger groups often occupy the tall glass structures that crenelate the Washington skyline.

Aside from their possibly undemocratic character, interest groups have come under fire for many reasons. As we have seen, interest groups are selfish; few of them strive to promote the "national" interest. What assurance is there that the taffy pull of pressure groups will produce a confection healthful for the entire country? If interest groups work for the narrow (often economic) benefit of their members, then who speaks for the more noble ends of democratic government, such as equal opportunity, freedom from governmental abuse, and the right to life, liberty and the pursuit of happiness?

At the same time, it cannot be denied that interest groups perform some valuable functions. They supplement the representation of public wishes otherwise confined to the voting process. By sounding an alarm when government policy threatens the interests of their members (and probably other citizens as well), pressure groups act as watchdogs. They may also generate new ideas which then become government policy.

It has often been noted that pressure groups are more active, not to mention more effective, on domestic rather than foreign-policy issues. However, since their impact on foreign policy cannot be ignored, it is well to examine the major kinds of interest groups that participate in foreign policy.

Business Groups.
These organizations often have clear interests in economic aspects of foreign policy. Formerly, business appeared most anxious to protect its domestic market from foreign competition; the textile, steel, shoe and automobile industries still pursue this objective. Today, most business groups seek to penetrate, preserve and expand foreign markets.

As we shall discover with regard to other types of interest groups, there is no single business point of view on all issues. While it is safe to say that most business pressure groups direct their efforts toward trade barriers (tariffs, import quotas, and the like), some groups prefer higher barriers and some prefer lower ones. Even within certain industries differences exist. Wool growers want a high tariff on imported raw wool; clothing and fabric makers would reduce these tariffs. Such clashes make it difficult sometimes for broad-based business interest groups, such as the National Association of Manufacturers or the US Chamber of Commerce, to take firm positions on trade barriers. On balance, American business since World War II has supported free trade. However, the following pressure groups took protectionist stances on the 1970 trade bill: American Textile Manufacturers' Association, National Cotton Council, American Footwear Manufacturers' Association, and the National Machine Tool Builders' Association. Oil and coal industries also take protectionist positions. In the arena of pluralism, business groups must struggle not only among themselves but also against other forms of pressure groups, in the hope of affecting American policy.

Labor Groups.
Like most business groups, labor takes an internationalist outlook. Foreign markets mean jobs for workers who produce goods for export. Foreign markets mean jobs for workers who produce goods for export. At the same time labor has taken protectionist stands to shelter domestic employment. Before World War II labor groups were instrumental in maintaining the Chinese Exclusion Law, designed to keep out workers who might be willing to work for very low wages. Today labor is vehemently opposed to illegal immigration, particularly from Mexico and Latin America. In addition, the AFL-CIO, labor's prime voice, supports legislation and executive action to halt the employment of people who gain illegal entry to the United States. Since 1972 labor has lobbied for passage of the Burke-Hartke Foreign Trade and Investment Act, or variants thereof, which would establish quotas on all imports on a category-by-category basis and make it less profitable for large multinational corporations to invest overseas (instead of creating jobs in America) by eliminating foreign tax credits. Labor also attacks the Export-Import Bank, which it says involves American taxpayers in subsidizing the export of American technology, production and jobs. The Overseas Private Investment Corporation, which insures overseas investments of American corporations, also is condemned by labor organizations.

Like business, labor groups sometimes take opposing positions. The AFL-CIO was formed in 1955 as an umbrella organization to represent approximately 17 million workers (out of a national work force of 70 million) in two hundred separate unions. On the question of free trade, unions in export industries (farm machinery) favor fewer restrictions while workers in industries facing stiff foreign competition (automobiles, steel) want more. In this respect, labor and management in the same industry often support each other.

Agricultural Groups.

Like business and labor, the agricultural sector of the nation has long been active in foreign policy. In common with the other two groups, agricultural interests occasionally find themselves arrayed against each other, thereby reducing their impact upon American foreign policy. Agriculture has had a minimal influence over those facets of foreign policy unrelated to farming.

The National Farmers Union is the smallest of the three principal agricultural pressure groups in the United States. Claiming a membership of one-quarter million farm families, the union concerns itself with the well-being of small farmers as opposed to agribusiness. Since its founding in 1902, the union has taken an internationalist stance in foreign policy, expressing support for international organizations, world law and foreign aid. It has criticized wheat deals with the Soviet Union on the ground that they benefit the large grain traders and not the small wheat producers.

At the other end of the spectrum sits the American Farm Bureau Federation, the largest, most conservative and most influential of the agricultural interest groups. The federation often finds itself aligned with big business and against labor. For example, it has supported the legalized importation of Mexican farm laborers. Mirroring the interests of large farmers, the federation supports increased agricultural exports. It has protested against European Common Market policies that discriminate against American agriculture.

The oldest farmers' organization is the National Grange, founded in 1867. Most of its members come from New England and the mid-Atlantic states. The grange occupies a political position that stands between the other two agricultural organizations. Like them, it favors the lifting of trade barriers.

These agricultural organizations, like business and labor pressure groups, favor foreign policy actions that enhance the economic interest of their members. They all support the expansion of agricultural exports. On other issues, the agriculture lobby has little impact on foreign policy. The declining influence of agricultural interest groups no doubt reflects the steady diminution of America's farm population, now 10 percent of the total population. Further-more, differences of opinion on nonagricultural matters among the different interest groups weaken their impact on American foreign policy.

Other Groups.

Other sectors of society have also formed pressure groups to influ-ence American foreign policy by doing battle in the pluralist arena. Women's organizations, such as the League of Women Voters (LWV) and the Women's International League for Peace and Free-dom (WILPF), have taken foreign policy positions, usually in sup-port of conciliatory stances. The LWV favors liberalized trade, including reductions of tariffs and import quotas, as well as foreign aid for economic development and preferential trade policies toward less-developed countries. The LWV also remains a strong supporter of the United Nations. The WILPF is a far more idealistic orga-nization, leaning in the direction of world government and unilat-eral disarmament.

Several religious organizations have sought to affect foreign policy. The National Council of Churches of Christ in America represents Protestants. A more recent Protestant group, the Amer-ican Council of Christian Churches, takes more conservative and militantly anti-Communist positions. The American Council crit-icized the National Council for favoring diplomatic recognition of mainland China. Neither group performs a great deal of lobbying in Washington.

Jewish organizations, on the other hand, are extremely active, generally in support of the state of Israel. Ever since the founding of the Jewish state in 1948, these organizations have had a signif-icant impact upon American foreign policy. In his memoirs, Eisen-hower's special assistant, Sherman Adams, attested to the influence of the Jewish lobby.

> Any attempt to give aid to the Arabs always met with opposition behind the scenes in Washington, where the members of Congress were acutely aware of the strong popular sentiment in this country for Israel. Had the members of Congress either underestimated or overlooked the strength of such feeling they would have been quickly reminded of it by the alert representatives of the many well-organized pro-Israel lobbies that were always effective and influential in the Capitol. Consideration for the great body of private opinion in the United States favoring Israel was a large factor in every government decision on the Middle East issues, especially in the [Suez] crisis.[12]

Jewish groups are well organized and well financed, giving them far more influence than one would expect considering the total number of Jews in the United States (5.8 million, or less than 3 percent of the population in 1979). Since Jews have gravitated toward large cities, they have been able to influence voting in states where large metropolitan areas are located, such as New York and California. Often overlooked in assessing the influence of the Jewish lobby is the fact that the overwhelming majority of the American people support Israel, although the size of that majority may have shrunk in the last few years.

Ethnic minorities also attempt to sway American foreign policy. Vocal Irish and German minorities were partly responsible for the delayed entry of the United States into World Wars I and II. More recently, citizens of East European origin have attempted, without notable success, to persuade the United States to take strong measures to ease Soviet hegemony over Eastern Europe. These groups have also urged more generous immigration quotas from Eastern Europe. Their small numbers keep such groups from having much influence over foreign policy.

Let us now inquire into the overall impact of pressure groups upon American foreign policy. Recall that interest groups generally take stands on issues that affect the pocketbooks of their members. We would expect, therefore, that in the realm of foreign policy, pressure groups have the largest impact on economic matters. That conclusion seems warranted by the facts, with the important exception of ethnic lobbies. Let us also remember that each organized sector of the economy (business, labor, agriculture) speaks in a cacophony of tongues, thereby sending competing messages to government. In short, pressure groups often neutralize each other, leaving the government relatively free of their influence to select those policies it deems best serve the national interest.

Lack of information further affects the degree of influence pressure groups exert over foreign policy. Traditionally, information has been a source of power for interest groups, particularly on domestic matters. Many domestic policy lobbyists are experts in their own right or employ experts on their staffs. Government officials generally welcome the assistance such experts can provide (although lawmakers remain aware that such "expertise" may be biased).

As regards foreign policy, the situation with regard to information is likely to be far different. What lobbyist can equal the information resources of the Department of State, or Defense, or the CIA? Much of the relevant information may be classified, depriving the lobbyist of access to it. On foreign policy matters that lack a direct, visible effect upon the pocketbooks of interest-group members, lobbyists may be at a loss to know the attitudes of their membership. Furthermore, interest groups are much less able to deliver the votes of their members on issues that do not affect their livelihood; this too weakens the persuasive power of lobbyists on foreign policy matters.

What conclusions can we offer regarding the strength of interest groups in the determination of foreign policy? It would seem that such organizations have only marginal influence as regards those issues that attract broad public interest and have major consequences for the well-being of the entire nation. Thus, on matters such as SALT, military cooperation with allies and relations with China, pressure group impact is small. On more specialized issues, particularly of an economic nature, interest groups may have much greater clout. The general apathy of the public concerning such items as textile quotas, seabed mining and steel dumping affords interest groups much latitude to influence government policy. (Recall, however, that not all pressure groups will advocate the same policy outcome.) On these kinds of issues, therefore, interest groups are likely to become heavily involved and may have an important impact on the determination of policy.

A Power Elite?

The two models of public influence upon foreign policy thus far considered assume that the general public has some input to the policy process. But may it not be the case that a privileged elite makes foreign policy solely to serve its own narrow interests?

The most persuasive argument that a power elite runs America may be found in the now classic study by C. Wright Mills entitled *The Power Elite*, published in 1956. Mills argues that power resides in the military, corporate and governmental domains, and that the individuals at the summits of these sectors control America. Furthermore, Mills added, the people who dwell at such rarified heights make up an informal interlocking directorate. These individuals know each other, see each other socially and at business, and experience a conscious awareness that they constitute a ruling class, albeit untitled. What sets these persons apart from the rest of society is their "superior character and energy." Members of the power elite share similar origins and education; their careers and life styles are also similar. The power elite comes from the upper third of the nation's income and occupational pyramids. Their fathers came from professional and business strata. They are native-born Americans of native-born parents, and mostly come from the East. They are mainly Protestant, especially Episcopalian or Presbyterian, and almost entirely white and male. Most members of the elite graduated from eminent universities, a high proportion holding diplomas from the Ivy League. Their children attend private schools or they go to public schools in the well-manicured suburbs where their homes are located. In many respects, the life experiences of this elite differ from those of the typical American. Members of the elite rarely face job layoffs, lost unemployment checks, denial of credit, rejected school applications, unhealthy diets, unaffordable medical expenses, and the like. While subject to the disappointments that affect all ordinary mortals, the elite enjoys material advantages that make these burdens easier to bear. Because these people have so many attributes in common, they are comfortable in moving from boardroom to government office and back again. What is more common than to learn of a retired general who becomes a director of a large corporation, a corporate president invited to join the Cabinet, a corporate lawyer asked to head a regulatory commission, or a member of the White House Office who returns to lead an investment banking firm on Wall Street? The members of the power elite pass through a trio of revolving doors that lead from big business to big government to the Pentagon. Whichever of the three institutions they lead, members of the power elite make the decisions that have national (and sometimes international) consequences. The power-elite thesis does not state that a small handful of people make all the important decisions in the nation, but rather that many different individuals from the top stratum of society make these decisions. The thesis does not postulate a conspiracy of power. Indeed, it hardly matters which persons actually initial policy papers expressing final decisions, since members of the power elite share a common outlook and set of objectives for the country. They are all substitutable one for the other. Like unclaimed suitcases on an airport conveyor belt, certain names like Clark Clifford, Cyrus Vance, Paul Nitze, Paul Warnke and Henry Kissinger keep coming 'round.

If somewhat less than 10 thousand individuals make the crucial decisions for America, then what role does the mass public and interest groups play? There is no denying that interest groups display considerable activity. However, in the minds of power-elite theorists, the result of pressure-group conflict is a stalemate that only affords the elite more leeway to make decisions that will shape the future. The general public is even less significant. These people are the "sheep in sheep's clothing," to use Vance Packard's words, willing to be led in almost any direction by the power elite. There may be deserts or swamps where the public refuses to tread, but they exist at such distances from the normal locus of policy that they hardly constitute significant limits on the course preferred by the power elite. This hypothesis is consistent with the permissive nature of public opinion we have already noted. The pliability of public opinion in the power-elite theory brings to mind an observation about the world of advertising, namely, that people buy products not because they need them, but because they are told they need them. For centuries, the world managed without deodorant, but today many individuals would no sooner think of leaving the house without using this product than they would consider going to work stark naked. Similarly, the power elite tells the public how it must think and act, and unless these suggestions are absolutely preposterous, the public will buy the "product." Democracy is thus turned on its head.

If a power elite does indeed make the most important decisions affecting American foreign policy—and domestic policy as well—then we must ask whether the elite reflects only their own narrow interests or the interests of all of American society. Is there, in other words, a sense of *noblesse oblige* among the elite that compels them to behave in a manner benefiting the vast bulk of Americans who will never join the Million Mile Club or see their names listed in the Social Register? Barry Hughes suggests that members of the elite display a greater willingness to involve the country in international relationships than does the general public.[13] Thomas Dye and L. Harmon Ziegler have found that the elite is more committed to democratic processes than the general public, except in times of crisis.[14] One is struck by the infrequency with which the mass public turns against government policies. Such acceptance may be traceable to a remarkable degree of docility among the American public or to a similarity in outlook between the masses and the elite. The elite would appear to resemble a giant redwood that towers above the rest of the trees but whose roots are one with the matted floor of the forest. After all, members of the elite do brush against members of the general public. They attend baseball games, buy on credit, watch countless hours of television, suffer the inconvenience of faulty automobile repairs, undergo marital stress, go to shopping malls—in short, immerse themselves in American culture. It is far from unthinkable that the elite should share, at least to some extent, the outlook upon life common to most Americans.

A Military-Industrial Complex?

A variant of the power-elite approach says that a narrow portion of the elite, called the military-industrial complex, runs America. The so-called military-industrial complex is composed of those individuals and organizations that advocate high defense spending, often for selfish economic purposes. Does such a complex exist, and does it guide the fortunes of the United States?

Ironically, it was a former general, Dwight D. Eisenhower, who first alerted the country to the hazards of the military-industrial complex. In his oft-quoted farewell address he said,

> In the councils of government we must guard against the acquisition of unwarranted influence, whether sought or unsought, by the military-industrial complex. The potential for the disastrous rise of misplaced power exists and will persist.

Who are the members of the military-industrial complex? Obviously, the top brass of the armed services are included. In addition, leading executives of major defense contractors, such as General Dynamics, Lockheed, and United Technologies, would qualify. Certain members of Congress are often mentioned, particularly members of the committees from both houses on armed services and appropriations. In some variants of the military-industrial complex theory, labor unions are mentioned, since approximately 3.5 million workers are employed in defense industry. Universities and research organizations, such as the Rand Corporation and the Hudson Institute, are said to belong, as many of their multimillion dollar contracts stem from military-related research. It has been estimated that nearly half the research performed in America relates in some way to defense. Veterans organizations—the American Legion (2.7 million members), AMVETS (1.5 million members) and Veterans of Foreign Wars (¼ million members)—are often included. Certain "military support organizations" are also said to be members. The Navy League, for example, produces the journal *Sea Power*, which has a circulation of 55 thousand and conducts regional "sea power" seminars, which invariably stress the need for more and bigger warships. The Air

Force Association and the Association for the US Army join with the Navy League in supporting high levels of military preparedness. A number of organizations such as the American Ordnance Association, the National Security Industrial Association, and the Aerospace Industries Association bind together defense industry and the military services in favor of large military forces and the development of new weapons systems.

What integrates these units into a "complex" is an interlocking arrangement in which each reinforces the other in support of high defense spending and a high level of military preparedness—too high in both cases, claim critics. The interlocking directorate is alleged to operate in the following manner. The military chiefs ask Congress for unnecessarily high defense appropriations, in order to enhance the status of their organizations and their own self-esteem. In return for the location of military installations within their districts, representatives and senators on the Armed Services and Appropriations committees approve the military's request. Research organizations and universities provide the rationale for these expenditures, thereby persuading the general public that they are necessary for national defense. Defense workers and their families elect candidates who favor high defense spending, so that the former can retain employment. Defense contractors use a portion of their profits to contribute to the election campaigns of candidates known to be friendly toward defense spending. Veterans organizations, whose membership exceeds 5 million, urge their members and their families to vote for defense-minded candidates. Military support organizations also throw their support behind government officials who favor lofty levels of defense spending. The remainder of the country, which is not organized against unnecessarily high defense spending, is helpless to prevent the military-industrial complex from having its way, so the theory goes. (The combined effects of all these efforts led Senator Eugene McCarthy to quip, "We don't declare war anymore; we declare national defense.")

The "links" in this interlocking directorate consist of personal contacts as well as common interests. A study by Senator William Proxmire found 2,072 retired military officers at work in 100 major defense firms in 1968. Many of these individuals maintained contacts with active-duty officers, so that the defense contractors gained an "in" with the military. These informal ties are said to assist defense industry in gaining military contracts. The Pentagon employs over three hundred "legislative-liaison" specialists whose job it is to convince members of Congress to vote for military requests.

Furthermore, corporate executives are in a position to do large favors for legislators in return for votes in support of military spending. They also wine and dine military procurement officers in the hope of getting orders.

Critics of the military-industrial complex do not question the need for national defense. But they do insist that the *excessive* military spending advocated by the military-industrial complex is detrimental to the rest of the country. Money used to build unneeded weapons is siphoned away from schools, hospitals, housing and other social needs. The mere existence of weapons stockpiles encourages their use, contributing to what some have called the militarization of American foreign policy. Other countries, particularly the Soviet Union, respond to American military expenditures, resulting in a dangerous and costly arms spiral that leaves the country no more secure despite astronomical arms outlays.

How valid is the theory of a military-industrial complex? As we have seen, there is no shortage of evidence to support the contention that a military-industrial complex exists. Consider also the following information, taken from Senator Proxmire's study. In 1968 the United States was committed to spend $38.8 billion in prime military contracts. Two-thirds of this sum went to 100 firms (many of whom, it must be said, subcontracted considerable work). Ninety percent of military contracts, the senator found, are typically arranged through negotiation, not through competitive bidding. Cost overruns are frequent.[15]

But is the military-industrial complex really as cohesive and all-powerful as its critics claim? Consider the following words of Aaron Wildavsky, a long-time observer of the military:

> The outstanding feature of the military's participation in making defense policy is their amazing weakness. Whether policy decisions involve the size of the armed forces, the choice of weapons systems, the total defense budget, or its division into components, the military have not prevailed.[16]

Were a military-industrial complex in charge of foreign policy, one would not have expected restrictions on the use of force in Vietnam or ratification of SALT I (including subsequent cancellation of the ABM system). In 1971, Lockheed Aircraft, the nation's largest defense contractor, appealed to the federal government for a large loan to prevent it from going bankrupt. The Senate approved the loan, but only by a single vote. Scholars who have investigated the military-industrial complex have found no systematic relationship between congressional votes on military spending and either the amount of military spending in their districts or states or the number of defense-related jobs in their constituencies.[17] Thus, it would appear that neither defense contractors nor the military exert substantial leverage over the people in Congress who determine levels of defense spending. Fig. 5–2 reveals, furthermore, that defense spending as a percentage of federal budget outlays has declined steadily since 1960.

What conclusions can we draw about the military-industrial complex? It would seem that there are certain elements in society whose interests are served by high defense spending. It is also reasonable to conclude that such elements try to persuade the government to keep defense spending at a high level. No doubt the

FIGURE 5–2: DEFENSE SPENDING AS A PERCENTAGE OF FEDERAL EXPENDITURES

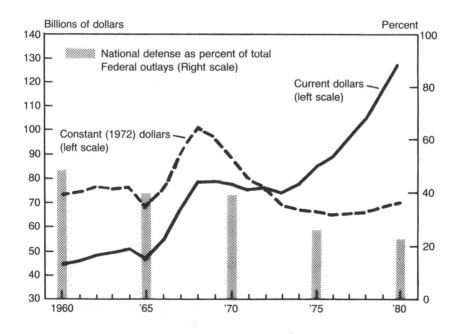

Source: U.S. Department of Commerce, Bureau of the Census, *Statistical Abstract of the United States: 1980*, p. 367.

hiring of retired military men by defense firms helps these companies obtain certain contracts, negotiate favorable terms, and justify cost overruns. The lavish corporate entertainment of military procurement officers in all likelihood lubricates these points of contact. However, the proposition that a military-industrial complex *controls* foreign policy remains debatable. In the struggle to shape American policy, the military-industrial complex must compete against other forces. Sometimes the complex emerges on top, but frequently it loses out in this competition. Before one can offer a final conclusion on the existence or role of a military-industrial complex, one must await the findings of further empirical research.

Whose Opinion?—Conclusion

Having just examined four different models of the public's impact upon foreign policy, let us recapitulate some of our findings.

We began our inquiry by examining the one-person, one-vote model so cherished by the classical theorists of democratic government. With infrequent exception, we discovered, the general public is content to let government make foreign policy decisions for the nation. Most members of the general public are uninterested in foreign affairs except when their personal lives are touched, usually by war. Public apathy is matched by lack of knowledge, inconsistency and permissiveness. We explored the poorly understood connection between opinion and personality, and we made reference to Gabriel Almond's division of the public into the mass public, the attentive public and the elite. The mass public, as we have seen, affects foreign policy by selecting the national leaders that will choose the policies and make the responses that will guide the nation through the shoals and eddies of international relations. Beyond that, the mass public's role is minimal. In extremely rare cases, perhaps once every two or three decades, the public may refuse to follow the government's lead, as eventually occurred in the case of Vietnam. Thus, political leaders are aware that the public can set limits to policy initiatives.

The pluralist model presents a quite different picture of the public's impact upon foreign policy. In the pluralist image, the public is organized into interest groups. Each citizen belongs to one or more such groups. It is through the struggle among these various interest groups that the public makes its preferences felt in the political system. Upon closer inspection, however, we found that as often as not one set of interest groups offsets another, providing the government with little guidance concerning the public prefer-ence. Furthermore, the overwhelming majority of interest groups concern themselves with domestic policy, where the outcome has a greater bearing on the narrow—often economic—interests of their members. Therefore, we concluded that pressure groups often do not play a very large role in the formulation of foreign policy. We also observed that interest groups are much more likely to represent the better educated, more well-off members of society than the underprivileged, calling into question the democratic nature of pluralism.

We then considered the possibilities that a power elite or a military-industrial complex controls foreign policy. As in our dis-cussion of the other two models, we found evidence to support each of these theories, but we also encountered data that calls these models into question.

It would be satisfying if we could verify one of these four models to the exclusion of the others. We must admit, however, that the findings of social science research do not yet permit us to take such action. Each theory continues to draw its advocates as well as its detractors, and there seems to be sufficient data to arm these intel-lectual warriors with a full complement of weaponry. One day, perhaps, further investigation will reveal which of these models most closely approximates reality.

THE OPINION-CONVERSION PROCESS

No matter what the nature of public opinion may be, it must somehow be communicated to policymakers in order for democracy to work. The flow of opinion from the citizenry to policymakers is known as the opinion-conversion process. This process encompasses two levels of activity. At the upper level, decision makers—elected officials and bureaucrats—determine American foreign policy. At the lower level the general public discusses and debates various policy alternatives. It is conceivable, of course, that there is no communication between the two spheres. Decision makers may pay little attention to the wishes of the public. On some issues public opinion may not have coalesced by the time government must decide. Policymakers may tailor policy to what they believe public desires to be, but their estimates may be in error. It is also possible that government officials may consciously ignore public opinion but coincidentally happen to select options that the public favors.

Should any of these possibilities characterize the opinion-conversion process, it would be difficult to make a case for the existence of democratic government in the United States. If we assume, however, that some degree of communication between the two levels takes place, then to that extent the opinion-conversion process can be said to operate. In a democratic political system, opinion-conversion operates primarily through voting and the activities of pressure groups, political parties, and the bureaucracy. (We shall ignore demonstrations and other less typical forms of opinion-conversion.)

Voting

Models of democratic government pay great homage to voting. Indeed, the secret ballot, so rare in today's world, is often heralded as the very hallmark of democratic government. Voting is the principal means whereby the vast electorate supposedly communicates its policy preferences to government officials, who then translate these wishes into policy. Should the public be displeased with the decisions of its elected officials, it can "throw the rascals out" at the next election.

In order for electoral control of government to work in the realm of foreign policy, voters must possess basic information about major foreign policy issues; they must care enough about such issues to affect their vote, and they must be able to distinguish between the positions of parties and candidates on these foreign policy issues.

We have already found good reason to question the first two of these conditions. It turns out that voters are frequently unable to perceive significant differences between candidates and parties on foreign policy issues.

In the presidential elections of 1964, 1968 and 1972, when Vietnam was presumably in the forefront of voters' minds, nearly half the respondents in national surveys said that they failed to see either party as taking a "stronger stand" on Vietnam.[18] Consider the 1964 election in which Lyndon B. Johnson defeated Barry Goldwater. During the campaign, Johnson pledged restraint on Vietnam, while Goldwater advocated a policy of victory. The voters appeared to have a clear choice, at least on this important issue. Johnson won by a landslide. However, consider the results from the standpoint of opinion-conversion. Sixty-three percent of those favoring withdrawal voted for Johnson, but so did 52 percent of those favoring "a stronger stand even if it means invading North Vietnam," as did 82 percent of those who preferred to "keep our soldiers in

Vietnam, but try to end the fighting."[19] How was President Johnson to read his mandate? A majority of both hawks and doves supported him. By 1968 the overwhelming majority of the public opposed the war. Yet in that year's presidential election, Vietnam hardly figured because most members of the public correctly perceived no significant difference between the stands of Hubert H. Humphrey and Richard M. Nixon on that issue. This is not to say that the electorate never discerns differences between candidates and parties, but only that such is often the case. When it is so, it is difficult to argue that the opinion-conversion process is working as intended.

Another requirement of democratic politics is that elected representatives be aware of constituent preferences. Lacking such knowledge, representatives could reflect voter wishes only by chance. Warren E. Miller and Donald E. Stokes conducted a study in the 1960s to determine how familiar were congressmen with the foreign-policy views of their constituents. The two political scientists interviewed 116 members of Congress about voter preferences and also examined their voting records. They then compared these findings with constituency opinion on foreign policy. The results proved disturbing from the standpoint of democratic government. The correlation between voter opinion and congressional voting was 0.2, very low. This study suggests that congressional voting on foreign policy bears little relation to what voters want. Furthermore, the investigators found a low correlation (0.32) between the attitudes of voters and the attitudes of their representatives on foreign policy issues. Finally, the researchers learned that members of Congress entertained inaccurate perceptions of the views of their constituents on foreign policy.[20]

Findings such as those above leave one uneasy concerning democratic control of American foreign policy. Moreover, it must be remembered that usually less than half the voting age public casts a ballot in congressional elections, and only slightly more than a majority votes in presidential elections. Even if representatives attempted to express voter preferences, their behavior would be based on only about half of the potential electorate.

From these studies, it can be argued that on specific foreign policy questions that arise day to day, the opinion-conversion process as expressed through voting does not work. On a much broader level, however, a different conclusion seems justified. In voting, citizens do not attempt to tell policymakers how to behave on a daily basis. Rather, voters select representatives whose general views approximate their own. These officials are then largely free to act as they wish until the next election. At that time, the electorate can turn them out of office. This process brings to mind the driver who steers by peering in the rear view mirror. Voters, in other words, tell their representatives either that they liked or disliked past actions, but there is little guidance concerning what elected officials should do in the future. Of course, elections are incapable of indicating public wishes concerning unforeseen crises. Did President Kennedy obtain any voter mandate on the Cuban missile crisis, or did President Carter get a voter preference on how to handle the seizure of hostages in Iran?

Other Forms of Opinion-Conversion

Opinion-conversion may also occur through interest groups, political parties and the bureaucracy. Interest groups can affect policy by means of several techniques, including:

    providing technical information in support of their position to government officials;
    organizing telegram and letter-writing campaigns;
    sending representatives to testify at legislative and executive hearings;
    conducting face-to-face meetings with government officials;
    contributing to electoral campaigns;
    conducting public persuasion campaigns in the hope that the general public will then apply pressure on elected officials.

Since interest groups are more active in domestic than foreign policy, it follows that their opinion-conversion efforts are more likely to bear fruit in domestic than foreign policy matters. Furthermore, many of the activities mentioned above are less applicable to the executive branch, which dominates in foreign policy, than to the legislative branch.

Political parties provide another channel for opinions to reach government officials. In reality, however, many obstacles impede the smooth flow of opinion by means of this route. In the first place, a growing proportion of citizens are registering as independent voters, depriving them of influence over political party platforms. Secondly, people who do join parties do so for a variety of purposes, the party's foreign policy plank often being one of the weaker reasons. Due to the low level of party discipline in the American political system, wide divisions frequently exist within each party over any policy issue; some Republicans are more liberal than certain Democrats, while some southern members of the Democratic party are stauncher conservatives than certain Republicans. From the vantage point of philosophical consistency, it makes no sense for Ronald Reagan and Congressman John Anderson to share the same party label (Republican); by the same token, Democratic Senators Edward Kennedy and John Stennis stand at opposite ends of the political spectrum. (The above consideration has led some observers to suggest a new party alignment of liberals against conservatives to replace what they believe to be a meaningless dichotomy between Republicans and Democrats.) The low level of interest on foreign policy matters displayed by most citizens raises questions about whether most people even know the foreign policy positions of their political parties. On foreign policy matters, political parties, like interest groups, are generally a weak instrument for converting public opinion into public policy.

Finally, we turn to the bureaucracy. Do federal departments and agencies make any effort to ascertain public wishes?

Bernard C. Cohen studied the attitudes of State Department officials toward public opinion.[21] Cohen found that most officers in State agreed with an office director who said, "To hell with public opinion. . . . We should lead, not follow." According to Cohen, State is far more interested in selling the department and its views to the public than in discovering what the public wants and adjusting policy thereto. The State Department has no office assigned the responsibility of systematically analyzing public opinion. The department's handling of mail from members of the public confirms a barely concealed contempt for public opinion. Some officers dismissed these letters as a measure of opinion, on the ground that people write only when discontented. Said one official, "The policy officers must make decisions on the basis of what is the best thing for the United States. If the public doesn't understand the issue, the only solution is to educate the public." "It is a fair conclusion . . . that this machinery for opinion gathering and analysis does not work very well," Cohen concluded.[22]

Does Opinion-Conversion Work?

A fundamental assumption underlying democracy states that government policy is based upon public opinion. The opinion-conversion process refers to the means by which the people make their views known to government officials. We have examined four facets of opinion-conversion: voting, interest groups, political parties, and the bureaucracy. In none of these cases could we find strong evidence of an effective mechanism for the transmittal of public desires to government officials, as regards foreign policy matters. The conclusion is therefore inescapable that the opinion-conversion process does not work very effectively in the realm of foreign policy. We now turn to an even more unsettling prospect from the standpoint of democratic foreign policy, namely, the question of government manipulation of public opinion.

GOVERNMENT MANIPULATION OF PUBLIC OPINION

"No president is obliged to abide by the dictates of public opinion. . . . He has a responsibility to lead public opinion as well as respect it—to shape it, to inform it, to woo it, and win it. It can be his sword as well as his compass." These words, penned by Kennedy's special assistant, Theodore Sorensen, suggest a conception of the opinion-policy relationship that differs from one normally associated with democratic government. Secretary of State John Foster Dulles echoed a similar thought: "A Secretary of State who waited for public opinion of the right kind to develop before taking action is derelict in his duty."[23]

These statements, both by individuals that occupied high government posts, imply that government not only has the right to lead public opinion, but has the duty to do so. When couched in such terms as "lead" or "guide," this form of government initiative does not sound so devious. However, the line between "guidance" and "manipulation" can grow very hazy indeed. For example, when President Truman sent soldiers to Korea in 1950 and then attempted to persuade the American people that such action was necessary to the national welfare, was he guiding or manipulating public opinion?

It is incontrovertible that government officials try to influence public opinion on many matters. There is also ample evidence that the public often swings behind decisions after they are taken. On the face of it, then, it would appear that a good case can be made for the presence of government manipulation. However, can we attribute public acquiescence to "manipulation" or to something far less sinister, namely, the appreciation by the public of what is good for them? Where does manipulation end and leadership begin? Perhaps the distinction lies in the use of duplicity or the deliberate distortion of material facts.

In this day and age, no government could function if it always consulted the public before acting. Every day the government makes hundreds of decisions. Even operating at such a pace, government is frequently accused of lethargy. On the numerous issues concerning which the public lacks an opinion, public attitudes would provide little guidance to government officials anyway. Can one truly criticize government officials for acting first and explaining later? These officials, and most particularly the president, seek to influence public opinion in many ways, including press releases, speeches, press conferences, radio and television broadcasts. The Bureau of Public Affairs at the State Department also conducts briefings in Washington and holds regional seminars, and it mails out materials presenting State's point of view. Can such activities be labeled education or manipulation? Perhaps we can conclude that if officials offer the complete truth as they believe it to be, they are sincerely trying to educate or guide the public. However, if they omit important details or tell outright lies, then they can be accused of manipulation. Sometimes even this test presents difficulties. No official can be expected to say all he or she knows about a problem, for the simple reason that it would take too long and no one would continue paying attention. Therefore, he or she must select those facts deemed most essential. People can err in making such choices. If such error, usually evident only in hindsight, was deliberately made to mislead the public, then that official was in all probability guilty of manipulation. Another difficulty often arises, particularly in the beginning stages of a crisis; the actual truth may lie concealed. For example, disputes among specialists make it far from clear whether leftists in El Salvador are receiving large quantities of arms from Cuba and Nicaragua, as the Reagan administration claims. Governments cannot wait to act until historians have combed archives to determine what really happened. It is possible for government officials to be genuinely wrong in their perception of a situation. When they pass along such erroneous perceptions to the general public to justify a decision, are they guilty of manipulation? It would appear not.

In a political system that believes in the necessity of accountability to the public, a certain amount of government manipulation of opinion is probably inevitable. Government officials are constantly justifying their actions to the public. It would be truly amazing if not a little deceit crept into these presentations.

Whether or not manipulation occurs, it is clear that public gullibility has its limitations. We have already seen that the public insisted upon the termination of American participation in the

Vietnamese and Korean conflicts, and eventually the government complied. Were the public infinitely malleable, Nixon would not have been compelled to resign in disgrace. In fact, were it so easy to fool the public, every president that wished to should succeed in being elected to a second term.

Regardless of where the truth lies, there seems to be a strong suspicion among the public that government manipulation of opinion is not uncommon. One of the strongest checks against such deceit is a vigorous free press, and it is to that topic that we turn in the next chapter.

FOR DISCUSSION

What suggestions would you offer to improve the effectiveness of the opinion-conversion process?

What evidence can you cite to substantiate the accusation that the United States government manipulates public opinion?

Discuss the proposition that the characteristics of public opinion render it an unsound guide to government policy in foreign affairs.

How effective is public opinion as a restraint on government in foreign policy?

Discuss the hypothesis that a power elite or military-industrial complex makes American foreign policy.

READING SUGGESTIONS

Almond, Gabriel A. *The American People and Foreign Policy.* New York: Frederick A. Praeger, 1962.

Cohen, Bernard. *The Public's Impact on Foreign Policy.* Boston: Little, Brown, 1973.

Free, Lloyd A., and Cantril, Hadley. *Political Beliefs of Americans: A Study of Public Opinion.* New York: Simon and Shuster, 1968.

Klingberg, Frank L. "The Historical Alternation of Moods in American Foreign Policy." *World Politics,* IV (January 1952): 239–73.

Levering, Ralph B. *The Public and American Foreign Policy, 1918–1978.* New York: Morrow, 1978.

Mueller, John E. *War, Presidents and Public Opinion.* New York: Wiley, 1973.

Rosenau, James N. *Public Opinion and Foreign Policy.* New York: Random House, 1961.

NOTES

1. Thomas L. Brewer, *American Foreign Policy* (Englewood Cliffs, N.J.: Prentice-Hall, 1980), p. 64.

2. Lloyd A. Free and Hadley Cantril, *The Political Beliefs of Americans: A Study of Public Opinion* (New York: Simon and Shuster, 1968), pp. 60–61.

3. Gabriel A. Almond, *The American People and Foreign Policy* (New York: Frederick A. Praeger, 1962), p. 53.

4. Kenneth N. Waltz, "Electoral Punishment and Foreign Policy Crisis," in James N. Rosenau, ed., *Domestic Sources of Foreign Policy* (New York: The Free Press, 1967), pp. 272–73.

5. Waltz, pp. 272–73.

6. M. Brewster Smith, Jerome S. Bruner and Robert W. White, *Opinions and Personality* (New York: John Wiley, 1956).

7. For example, Alexander and Juliette George contend that Woodrow Wilson's inability to please his stern father accounted for his burning need to achieve great things and sponsor such high-minded concepts as the League of Nations. See Alexander L. and Juliette L. George, *Woodrow Wilson and Colonel House: A Personality Study* (New York: Dover, 1964).

8. James N. Rosenau, *Public Opinion and Foreign Policy* (New York: Random House, 1961), p. 71.

9. Dexter Perkins, *The Evolution of American Foreign Policy*, 2nd ed. (New York: Oxford University Press, 1966), p. 152.

10. Interview on NBC-TV, July 2, 1971.

11. Barry B. Hughes, *The Domestic Context of American Foreign Policy* (San Francisco: W. H. Freeman and Company, 1978), p. 156.

12. Quoted in Hughes, p. 179.

13. Hughes, pp. 69–73.

14. Thomas R. Dye and L. Harmon Ziegler, *The Irony of Democracy* (Belmont, Calif.: Wadsworth, 1970), pp. 18–20.

15. Hughes, p. 175.

16. Quoted in John Spanier and Eric M. Uslaner, *How American Foreign Policy Is Made*, 2nd ed. (New York: Holt, Rinehart and Winston/Praeger, 1978), p. 84.

17. Charles Gray and Glenn Gregory, "Military Spending and Senate Voting," *Journal of Peace Research*, V (1968): 44–54; Bruce Russett, *What Price Vigilance?* (New Haven: Yale University Press, 1970); Stephen A. Cobb, "Defense Spending and Foreign Policy in the House of Representatives," *Journal of Conflict Resolution*, XIII (September 1969): 358–69; Stephen A. Cobb, "The United States Senate and the Impact of Defense Spending Considerations," in Steven Rosen, ed., *Testing the Theory of the Military-Industrial Complex* (Lexington, Mass.: D.C. Heath, 1973), pp. 197–224.

18. Brewer, pp. 74–80.

19. Charles W. Kegley, Jr., and Eugene R. Wittkopf, *American Foreign Policy: Pattern and Process* (New York: St. Martin's, 1979), p. 221.

20. Warren E. Miller and Donald E. Stokes, "Constituency Influence in Congress," in Angus Campbell, Philip E. Converse, Warren E. Miller and Donald E. Stokes, *Elections and the Political Order* (New York: John Wiley, 1966).
21. Most of the material that follows is based on Cohen's excellent study, *The Public's Impact on Foreign Policy* (Boston: Little, Brown and Company, 1973).
22. Ibid., p. 48.
23. Quoted in Cecil V. Crabb, Jr., *American Foreign Policy in the Nuclear Age*, 3rd ed. (New York: Harper and Row, 1972), p. 170.

Chapter 6
The Media and
Foreign Policy

"If there is ever to be an amelioration of the conditions of mankind, philosophers, theologians, legislators, politicians and moralists will find that the regulation of the press is the most difficult, dangerous and important problem they have to resolve. Mankind cannot now be governed without it, nor at present with it." Those words, penned by John Adams in 1815, introduce us to an essential feature of modern government, the media.

Reference to the analytic model presented in Fig. 1–1 reveals that the media, along with public opinion and pressure groups, influence the policy-making process that produces the nation's foreign policy. Indeed, it is through the media that members of the public and pressure groups learn about government policy. These individuals and groups may then use the media to channel their views to government officials. In actuality, the role of the media is far more complex. As we shall have occasion to see shortly, the media are sometimes part of the policy-making process itself. Also, the media carry much of the feedback or information flows shown in the model.

Taken in their entirety, the media in America represent a vast ocean of words and pictures, including both the written press and the electronic press (radio and television). The former consists mainly of newspapers and magazines. Certain newspapers comprise what is often referred to as the "prestige press." Outstanding among

181

these publications is the *New York Times.* Other newspapers normally included in the prestige press are the *Washington Post, the Wall Street Journal,* the *Christian Science Monitor,* the *Los Angeles Times,* the *Baltimore Sun* and the *Saint Louis Post-Dispatch.* This select group of newspapers derives its name from the fact that many prestigious people, particularly leaders of government and big business, consult these newspapers on a regular basis. Thus, these publications have an impact that is far greater than their circulation would indicate. The newspaper with the highest circulation in America is the *National Enquirer,* whose impact on the political process may be said to be nil. The press also includes numerous weekly news magazines, the best known of which are *Newsweek, Time* and *U.S. News and World Report.* Other magazines, such as the *Atlantic Monthly* and *Harper's* also feature articles on public affairs from time to time.

Today, most people receive the news of the world through the electronic media, particularly television. Since few local TV stations send their own correspondents overseas, most of the news from abroad comes from the approximately 300 reporters who work for the three major networks. For most Americans, television now serves as the principal window on the world.

An exhaustive treatment of the media's role in the political process is beyond the scope of this book.[1] Here, we shall concern ourselves with the media as they affect foreign policy. We begin in the next section with an extended examination of the media's function in a political system. Thereafter, we shall consider some of the criticisms often made about the media and suggestions for improvement. Finally, we shall probe the issue of secrecy and foreign policy.

ROLE OF THE MEDIA IN A POLITICAL SYSTEM

Authoritarian and Democratic Systems Compared

No political system exists today in which the media do not play a role. The media have become no less integral to a political system than traffic lights are to a transportation system. Recognition of the media's importance is implied by the common description of the media as "the fourth estate." To gain an overview of the media's relevance, it is useful to examine the media's function in an authoritarian as compared with a democratic political system.

Briefly stated, an authoritarian political system is one in which the existing political leaders determine which policies will be adopted, with a minimum of popular input. In more extreme authoritarian systems, popular input does not exist at all.

In an authoritarian system, the government controls the media. Lenin expressed the rationale for such control as follows:

> Why should freedom of speech and freedom of press be allowed? Why should a government which is doing what it believes to be right allow itself to be criticized? It would not allow opposition by lethal weapons. Ideas are much more fatal things than guns.

The role of the media in an authoritarian system may be likened to the function of an intercom on a naval vessel. Just as the captain needs some method of telling the crew what to do, so an authoritarian government requires a way of announcing government policy to the populace. Through careful molding of media coverage, the government can also generate support for itself. Media exposés of government inefficiency, corruption and wrong-doing do not appear in authoritarian systems, except perhaps at a time of purges. Normally, however, the only news about the government is good news. The bad news is saved for enemies of the regime, both internal and external. Thus, the government can use the media to shape an image of infallible and dedicated officials striving valiantly against implacable foes who seek at every moment to destroy the nation.

In a democratic system the media's role is much more complex. Here, the government does not control the voices of mass communication. In fact, the undisciplined cacophony produced by such voices is often heralded as one of the defining characteristics of democracy. While the flow of media communications in an authoritarian system can be expressed by a straight line,

in a democratic system an information loop may be found.

In democratic systems, furthermore, the media often serve as an independent source of information as opposed to a passive conduit. Let us look at some of the major functions of the media in a democratic political system.

Informing the Public

Nearly all theorists of democracy agree that such a form of government works well only if the public is informed. The media carry a major responsibility for enlightening the public. As a means of educating the public, the media both present information and interpret it.[2]

The scope of the mass media is impressive. Over 1,700 daily newspapers with a combined circulation of 70 million readers arrive on the doorsteps of American households daily. According to an International Press Institute study, Americans spend about 18½ minutes per day reading 5 columns of news, of which only one-eighth consists of international news.[3] As already observed, network TV programs are the main source of information about foreign affairs for most Americans. Nearly 95 percent of American households own at least one television set, more than own bathtubs or telephones. It is estimated that approximately one-third of the country's adult population watches network news. The weekly news magazines reach about 5 percent of the adult population, while the prestige newspapers are read by 1 percent of American adults.[4]

How much does the media's prodigious outpouring of words affect the thinking of the American people? There are no precise answers to this question. One may hypothesize that if the media do not tell people what to think, they might very well tell people what to think about. In other words, the media appear to perform an agenda-setting function. If the media in a particular city devote large amounts of space to local crime, before long the people will begin to discuss the local crime situation; readers will write letters to the editor on the topic; neighborhood organizations will schedule meetings on crime in the streets. By calling the public's attention to a situation, the media can force the government to act or at least to explain why it is not acting. Such an instance arose in 1979, when the media reported that 2,500 Soviet combat troops were stationed in Cuba. In actuality, the troops had been there for several years and hardly represented a threat to American interests. Since the American people were ignorant of their presence, the government could afford to remain silent. When the media announced their presence, however, a public outcry followed. President Carter, campaigning for reelection, and smarting from accusations of softness and indecisiveness, insisted publicly that the Soviet Union remove its troops. The Russians refused, and Mr. Carter was forced to back down.

The agenda-setting capacity of the media was investigated in a study of media coverage of the 1968 presidential election in Chapel Hill, North Carolina. The researchers compared the media's definition of key issues with the public's definition of key issues. Citing a correlation of .967, the investigators concluded that the media have a determining impact on what the public deems to be the major issues of the day.[5] This finding helps us appreciate the American public's general indifference toward long-range issues, an area that the media often forsake in favor of more immediate problems.

Aside from helping the public identify the issues of the day, it is very difficult to characterize the media's effect on public attitudes. Contrary to the accusations of beleaguered government officials, there is no such thing as a media conspiracy. Media leaders hold no gathering at which they formulate a "media line." Different elements of the media speak in varying tongues, ranging from the conservative columns of the *National Review* and *U.S. News and World Report*, through the more balanced pages of *Time* and *Newsweek*, to the liberal paragraphs of *The New Republic*. The editorial pages of most newspapers carry columns by writers occupying different points along the political spectrum. The enormous variety of media sources dilutes the impact of any single one of them. Furthermore, the media must compete with other influences such as local and national opinion leaders, family members, peers and educators. If the media do display any persistent bias, it is perhaps an anti-government bias. While such an attitude would be unthinkable in an authoritarian system, it is quite proper in a democracy. One of the media's functions is to act as a check on government. Should the media find little to criticize, they are in all probability doing a less than diligent job. In this regard, it is worth noting that public officials on both the right and the left have complained of media bias. That is as it should be, for it indicates that the media are not allied with either political persuasion, but rather exhibit a healthy skepticism toward all brands of political power.

Expressing Public Opinion

A second function of the media is to express public opinion, particularly to government officials. Whether scientifically correct or not, many government officials equate public opinion and the press.

It is not just the content of news stories that supposedly mirrors public concerns. This service is also performed through the placement of stories (front page headline or back page filler), size of headlines, content of editorials and columns, and the reactions of opinion leaders and the general public (through letters to the editor) to the stories of the day. Some government officials regard the behavior of reporters as a barometer of public opinion. What questions do reporters pose? What issues do they fail to get excited about? On what topics do they continually press for more information? Whether these contacts take place in the office, at a social function or at a formal press conference, government officials often regard reporters as representing the informed public. Said one important official at State, "We all read the press pretty carefully. . . . So we know pretty well what the country is thinking."[6] By articulating the views of the unorganized members of the attentive public, the media supplement voting and interest groups as a channel of public influence over government.

Watchdog

Perhaps the most heralded duty of the press, unthinkable in an authoritarian society, is to act as a watchdog over government. Thomas Jefferson recognized this function as follows:

> No experiment can be more interesting than that we are now trying, and which we trust will end in establishing the fact, that man may be governed by reason and truth. Our first objective should therefore be, to leave open to him all avenues of truth. The most effectual hitherto found, is the freedom of the press. It is therefore the first shut up by those who fear the investigation of their actions.

More recently, journalists Joseph and Stewart Alsop echoed the same thought: "In a democratic society especially, unwatched politicians are always untrustworthy politicians."[7] One of the defining features of American democracy is the opportunity to "throw the rascals out" at the next election. Until that time arrives, however, the "rascals" can create a good deal of damage. A free press is one of the few day-to-day checks on the actions of government.

The media can fulfill the watchdog function by guarding against corruption, special interests, and lax (or worse) performance. Toward the close of the last decade, the media revealed that the government of South Korea, fearful of losing American support, had paid out large sums of money to a few congressmen in the hope that they would mobilize the US government behind the Seoul regime. The South Koreans used a lubricious rice trader who had set himself up in Washington society to make these surreptitious payments. In all probability, the revelation of this bribery, branded "Koreagate" by the media, caused more harm than good to Seoul's interests. It also served notice to members of Congress that accepting bribes carries risks.

As we saw in Chapter 5, pressure groups occasionally seek to influence foreign policy, particularly international trade issues. Through fear of exposure, the media discourage government officials from taking undue guidance from special interests. For example, when agribusiness interest groups were lobbying for gigantic grain sales to the Soviet Union, the media played a significant role in exposing drawbacks of that proposal, such as higher food prices in American supermarkets.

Laxness or downright incompetence is not unknown in government. In a business firm, such deficiencies are often revealed in the annual profit and loss statement. Government produces no such annual report, however. The media act as one of the few institutions in society that monitors government ineptness. Certainly, the abuses associated with Watergate would not have come to light in the absence of probing by the media.

The media might well be the only nongovernmental institution in American society with the power to confront the president and other officials directly. If the president says something foolish at a press conference it will appear foolish; presidential assistants can only attempt to rescue their chief after the fact. The same can be said for officials who face reporters on such programs as "Issues and Answers," "Meet the Press" and "Face the Nation." Reporters are in a position to tell government officials what they think of them in a way that subordinates are not. Many officials rarely receive such evaluations from their own staff, because negative criticism (even if sought) rarely paves the road to a promotion.

While the press conference leaves a government official standing before his or her inquisitors without the protective shield of assistants, some presidents have proven adept at turning the confrontation to their own uses. President Johnson, for example, often called press conferences during weekends, when few reporters were on the beat. Frequently he did not announce them in advance. Presidents can call on "friendly" reporters, and they can provide long-winded answers to trivial questions in order to take up time that might be devoted to embarrassing inquiries. President Carter sometimes treated his press conferences not so much as occasions for accountability as opportunities to announce new policies and offer persuasive reasons in their support.

Sometimes the media, through their watchdog role, can induce changes in policy. In Vietnam in 1963, three reporters—David Halberstam (the *New York Times*), Neil Sheehan (United Press International) and Malcolm Browne (Associated Press)—were consistently sending dispatches at variance with official government reports on the war's progress. Their accounts of the deteriorating position of the Diem regime in South Vietnam and the Byzantine intrigues in Saigon are credited with altering American support for Diem. Eventually, all three reporters won Pulitzer Prizes for their Vietnam coverage.

On occasion, the media's watchdog role can have curious effects. When President Kennedy assumed office, he expressed considerable doubt about the CIA's proposal to invade Cuba at the Bay of Pigs. By that time, the CIA had already assembled and trained an invasion force, awaiting in Nicaragua the call to action. One of the arguments that persuaded the dubious commander-in-chief to proceed with the invasion was consternation about stories the soldiers would tell if the US canceled the invasion.

The investigative activities of the media can also have unintended consequences for the manner in which government conducts its business. Fearful of a probing press, officials might prefer verbal agreements to written memoranda, possibly leading to later uncertainty about what was decided and leaving no written record for historians. Secretary of State Dean Rusk expressed such anxiety. "My habit was that I did not go around writing a lot of memoranda. I've been in government long enough to know it is not a good idea to spread papers all over the landscape."[8] Intimidated by a probing press, officials might be tempted to write self-justifying memos rather than creative policy analyses. In order to deflect media inquiries, officials might classify more documents than warranted by the dictates of security. To limit leaks, officials might keep information from those who could make helpful policy suggestions. One such instance occurred in July 1971, when Henry Kissinger journeyed to Peking to prepare for President Nixon's subsequent trip. To keep this spectacular mission secret, only half a dozen policymakers were informed. On July 10, the *Washington Post* ran a lead story describing the Pentagon's recommendation to transfer American nuclear weapons from Okinawa to Taiwan. To the Chinese, this would have been an extremely unfriendly act, and it must have bewildered them that elements of the US government contemplated such an action at the very moment when the president was preparing a visit to Peking.

Informing Policymakers About the World

Upon first glance, it might seem strange that a policymaker, having access to the world's most extensive intelligence and reporting network, would rely upon the media to learn about the outside world. Nevertheless, almost every policy official in government relies to some extent upon the media, especially the prestige press, to find out what's going on around the world. Supposedly, a *New York Times* reporter once asked Undersecretary of State Sumner Welles, "Do you know anything we don't know today?"

Welles replied, "Of course not, where do you think we get our information?"

While it remains true that officials at State, Defense, and other foreign policy agencies are plugged into a worldwide information network, all but the very highest officials receive information concerning only their narrow area of responsibility. Thus, the State Department desk officer for Thailand will receive all the telegrams that arrive from the embassy in Bangkok, but only a small proportion of the telegrams that come in from other Asian stations, not to mention the rest of the world. The handiest way for such an official to gain a worldwide view is to read the prestige press. Accordingly, it is not surprising to learn that a great many officials turn to the *Washington Post* or the *New York Times* first thing in the morning. Having absorbed the global view, an official gains a context in which to place his or her own area of responsibility. "You can't work in the State Department without the *New York Times*," an official there told one investigator. "You can get along without the overnight telegrams sooner."[9]

While he was American ambassador to India in the 1960s, John Kenneth Galbraith met with American reporters in New Delhi for one hour each Wednesday, and more frequently if things were active. Galbraith wrote that the information exchange at these meetings flowed in two directions. The ambassador learned from the reporters what Indian officials were revealing in their press conferences, background briefings, and press leaks. He also became privy to rumors circulating among members of the Indian parliament and press. Occasionally, Galbraith reported, journalists would call him to announce a story in the making. Naturally, the ambassador gave the reporters news concerning American policy and actions in India.[10]

Policymakers also value the media as a check against embassy reporting. A report in the media concerning a foreign government sometimes triggers a diplomatic probe. A policy official at State might read about an impending realignment of power in another country and then summon the ambassador from that country for confirmation.

Stories in the press about the outside world carry special importance for those members of Congress charged with checking on the executive's handling of foreign policy. Congressmen do not have access to the extensive reporting facilities of the CIA, the State Department or the Defense Department. Often they must rely upon the press for issues that need to be explored, policies about to be adopted (or already adopted), foreign policy actions taken, and events in other countries. Without the independent source of information that the press provides, Congress would be severely handicapped in carrying out its duties to investigate the executive branch of the government.

Communications Link Within the Government

The government of the United States is a huge sprawling complex made up of hundreds of different organizations. Presumably, all of these departments, agencies, commissions, and other groups are laboring toward the same purpose, namely, advancing the interests of the United States. Clearly, there is no mammoth coliseum where all three million workers in the federal government can gather to concert their efforts. In theory, the president commands these legions of bureaucrats, providing coherence to their efforts. However, the president lacks sufficient time and endurance to concern himself with the multitude of decisions the government makes every day. Coordination remains one of the gargantuan and largely unfulfilled tasks of government.

To some extent the media, particularly the prestige press, help solve the problem of coordination. They do so by binding together people in separate offices and buildings with the cement of common information. As we have observed, many government officials open the *New York Times* or the *Washington Post* upon arriving at the office. Thousands of influential people therefore start out the day with a common vision of problems to be confronted and solutions to be considered. In their biography of one of America's most influential journalists, Walter Lippmann, James Reston and Marquis Childs wrote, "When . . . Walter Lippmann returned not so long ago from Russia and later from Germany, his reports were part of the common conversation of the Capital. Every embassy . . . discussed them and reported them to their governments. Members of the Senate Foreign Relations Committee read them and questioned the Secretary of State on his points."[11]

The legwork engaged in by reporters also weaves a communications web within the government. A reporter may get the reaction of a senator on the Armed Services Committee to a military appropriations bill. The journalist may then go to an officer in the Pentagon for a reaction to the senator's views. In the process, the military learns about the perceptions of a key senator. Important speeches delivered in the House or Senate are sometimes summarized in the press, informing other legislators as well as people in the executive branch of the speaker's views. If the speaker has expressed doubt about a pet program, such a report may trigger an executive branch effort to target the speaker for further persuasion. Through their daily activities, reporters are constantly informing officials in one governmental office about actions being taken and the views held by people in other offices.

Bureaucratic Politics

As we shall see in Chapter 8, policy making resembles not so much a military chain of command as a poker game. In other words, various players seek to capitalize upon their (unequal) assets in order to prevail. Each player (department, agency, office, and so forth) strives to persuade the highest decision makers in government to adopt its preferred policy. For example, the Arms Control and Disarmament Agency might regard arms control as the best means of guarding American security; the Pentagon might favor a policy of arms racing in order to achieve that objective. Each of these agencies will try to convince the president to adopt its preference.

The media participate in these bureaucratic wars. To be more specific, the media can become involved in policy promotion, institutional promotion, and personal promotion. The first refers to an agency's attempts to advance its own policy preference; the second, to an agency's efforts to forward its own prestige; the third, to an individual's efforts to boost his or her own status. Some examples follow.

It was John Kenneth Galbraith, the American ambassador to India referred to earlier, who wrote, "I found it easier to bring my views to bear on the President of the United States by way of the *Washington Post* and its New Delhi correspondent than by way of the State Department."[12] Bernard C. Cohen, a foremost authority on the press and foreign policy, tells of a freshman congressman who wished to circulate his foreign policy ideas at the State Department, the White House, and among his congressional colleagues. Lacking direct access to influential officials because of his rookie status, the legislator succeeded in breaching the walls of power by writing a letter to the editor of the *New York Times*.[13]

Sometimes government officials use the press to generate support for or opposition to a proposed policy. In 1968 someone leaked a report that the Joint Chiefs of Staff were recommending an additional 206 thousand American troops be sent to Vietnam. The public outcry was so great that President Johnson decided against sending any more American forces there; from that point the American disengagement from Vietnam began. As an indication of the media's importance in bureaucratic politics President Johnson is reported to have told the editor of an influential newspaper that an editorial which supported his Vietnam policy was "worth two divisions to me."

With ritualistic regularity, the Pentagon engages in policy promotion and institutional promotion every year at budget-setting time. In the weeks preceding consideration of the federal budget, the military disseminates through the press analyses of America's military standing. Invariably, America's position is reported as declining. The Navy cannot guarantee free passage of the sea lanes without more ships. Unless the Air Force gets bigger and faster planes, it might as well surrender the skies without a dogfight. The Army pleads for more soldiers, tanks and artillery. To justify these requests, the military always seems able at this time of the year to unearth an intelligence study demonstrating an alarming Soviet military build-up. It is the military's hope that such publicity will heighten its chances of obtaining a fat slice of the federal budget.

The presidential press conference combines policy promotion with personal promotion. Although press conferences are frequently hailed as a means of making the president accountable to the people (and there is an element of truth to this), some chief executives have been able to use press conferences to their own advantage. Presidential press conferences are staged events. The president chooses a dignified setting, usually a podium flanked by the American flag. Behind that is spread a curtain tinted to enhance the president's complexion. Dressed in a dark suit and conservative necktie, the president enters the chamber and all the reporters rise, a throwback to an aristocratic tradition that Americans have shunned in other types of relationships. Invariably, media coverage is extensive. Knowing this, the president may begin with a policy announcement (policy promotion), and then call upon reporters to pose questions, aware of who is likely to ask "friendly" questions and who might proffer "hostile" ones. It is up to the president to allow follow-up questions. Even though no one can reasonably expect a president to know the answers to all questions, it is almost unheard of for the chief executive to answer a question with the words, "I don't know; I'll have to look that up." Such an answer would—at least in the minds of past presidents—create a poor image (personal promotion); presidents are supposed to be all-knowing. Finally, the president decides when the conference will end.

John Herbers, a former presidential press secretary, believes that press conferences serve the purpose of the president rather than the people.[14] As he observes, reporters display a great deal of self-restraint at these events. In an effort to maintain objectivity, they normally report what the president says; some newspapers carry verbatim reports of the conference. Rarely do reporters point out errors of fact or interpretation made by the chief executive. Nor do they typically challenge the president's solutions to policy questions.

A well-recognized type of policy promotion is the "trial balloon." President Kennedy used this technique to help him decide whether to appoint his brother Robert to be attorney general. The new occupant of the White House feared adverse reaction from the appointment of a family member to so important a post. Therefore, he floated a rumor that he was contemplating the appointment, carefully concealing the fact that he was the source. The press duly printed the story, citing an undisclosed authority. The president awaited the public reaction. If there were an angry protest, he could always deny that he had ever considered his brother. As it turned out, however, the public did not raise a fuss, and Robert Kennedy soon found himself ensconced at the Justice Department. The trial balloon allows an official to obtain public reaction to a potential policy before that policy is set in concrete. Since the identity of the individual who releases the balloon is usually concealed, he or she can disavow any responsibility for the policy. Without the media the trial balloon would have difficulty in getting off the ground.

Media as Policymaker

The media are sometimes responsible for suggesting foreign policy alternatives. This function is usually assumed by the press, especially the prestige newspapers. Television, by its very nature, seems less suited to provide policy advice. Television lacks the newspaper's central device for setting forth a point of view, namely, the editorial page. While network correspondents could present editorials, clearly identified as such, the networks are reluctant to do so for fear of antagonizing their station affiliates and sponsors. Television newspeople themselves are hesitant to present editorials for fear of losing their credibility; they also see their role less as policymakers than as transmitters of information.[15] Another complication, emanating from government itself, inhibits television from editorializing. The Federal Communications Commission has instituted a Fairness Doctrine, which calls upon television stations to provide air time for opponents of any points of view expressed by the station. Many station managers are averse to become involved in such time-sharing due to the high cost of television programming. The Fairness Doctrine seems also to have affected television documentaries. The standard formula for such programs calls for the presentation of various interpretations of the subject matter; viewers are then allowed to select the interpretation they prefer. The narrators rarely take sides. In the area of news and public affairs, TV prefers the role of photographer to that of painter.

The press offers an entirely different picture. The editorial page is an integral part of every newspaper. Many newspapers feature "op-ed" pages, where readers and commentators are invited to express their points of view. Among the prestige press, certain editorial writers and columnists often write expressly for government officials. In other words, they deliberately seek to influence what often amounts to only a handful of key officials (sometimes including the president) who are about to make a policy decision.

The press also occasionally directs its message toward foreign officials. As a critical juncture in the 1962 Cuban missile crisis, Premier Khrushchev offered to trade Soviet missiles in Cuba for American missiles in Turkey. Could it have been more than coincidence that on the previous day columnist Walter Lippmann, known to have close relations with American officials, had suggested such a trade in his newspaper column?

The most illustrious case in recent times of the media as policymaker concerned Fidel Castro and a *New York Times* writer. Former American Ambassador to Cuba Andrew Gardner tells it best in his testimony before a Senate Internal Security subcommittee:

> Three front-page articles in the *New York Times* in early 1957, written my (sic) the editorialist Herbert Matthews, served to inflate Castro to world stature and world recognition. Until that time, Castro had been just another bandit in the Oriente Mountains of Cuba, with a handful of followers who had terrorized the campesinos, that is the peasants, throughout the countryside. . . .
>
> After the Matthews article, which followed an exclusive interview by the *Times* editorial writer in Castro's mountain hide-out and which likened him to Abraham Lincoln, he was able to get followers and funds in Cuban [sic] and in the United States. From that time on, money and soldiers of fortune abounded. Much of the American press began to picture Castro as a political Robin Hood.[16]

Matthews's reports had a profound effect not only upon officials in the American government, but also on members of other governments and upon public opinion in many lands.

Channel of Communication to Other Governments

Sometimes the media participate in policy making simply by acting as a channel of communication to other governments. The media may serve as conduit for all kinds of information, including declaratory statements of policy (such as the State of the Union address), statements of American intentions, hints of a willingness to discuss a particular problem, and the reaffirmation of commitments to other states. Every time the president speaks, it is for the United States. Therefore, whenever the media carry a presidential address they are conveying American policy to other governments.

On occasion, the media play a more deliberate role in the interchange between governments. At the height of the Cuban missile crisis, a senior Soviet official in Washington asked ABC correspondent John Scali to convey a message to high level friends at the State Department. This communication contained the conditions under which the Soviets would remove their missiles from Cuba. Scali delivered the message, whereupon Secretary of State Dean Rusk instructed him to inform the Russians that the United States wished to discuss the proposal further. This interchange helped smooth the path for a resolution of the confrontation.

It should be clear from the foregoing that the media play a central role in the political process. They inform the public, express public opinion, act as a watchdog, inform policymakers about the outside world, serve as a communications link within the government, participate in bureaucratic politics, propose policy alternatives, and act as a channel of communication to other governments.

Institutionally, the media have proven to be hardy, lending validity to the words of Oscar Wilde: "In America, the President reigns for four years, but Journalism governs forever."

CRITIQUE OF THE MEDIA

A good part of the time, it can be said that the media do a meritorious job. As in any institution, however, there are flaws in the media. This section will focus on these deficiencies, ending with some suggestions about improving media performance.

Paucity of International News

One of the most frequently heard criticisms of American media points to the dearth of international news. Two recent studies seem to support this accusation. One study of 60 daily newspapers from nine countries during the week of May 24, 1970, revealed the following ranking (by place of publication) of foreign news as a proportion of all nonadvertising space:[17]

Area	Rank Order
Eastern Europe	1
Western Europe	2
Nonaligned	3
Soviet Union	4
United States	5

A 1973 study conducted by UNESCO of 100 countries found that the percentage of international programming on American television was the lowest (between 1 percent and 2 percent) of any of the countries observed.[18]

Most newspapers assign only a small proportion of news space to foreign news. An International Press Institute study of 93 American newspapers between October 1952, and January 1953 (the time of the Korean War), found the average proportion of foreign news to all news to be slightly over 8 percent.[19] Furthermore, the average space devoted to foreign dateline news by these newspapers (including headlines) was only 4.4 columns per day. A more recent study suggests that the amount of space allocated to foreign news has shrunk. This study holds that the average newspaper devotes no more than one-half of one column of newsprint per day to international events.[20]

As one might expect, the prestige newspapers offer far more coverage of international news. In addition, the number of American foreign correspondents appears to be declining. In 1975 there were 676 American full-time foreign correspondents, down from 929 in 1969. In 1975, 51 percent of these reporters were stationed in Europe and 23 percent were assigned to Asia, leaving the remaining 26 percent to cover the entire rest of the globe.[21] This geographic apportionment of correspondents is bound to influence the perceptions of the world held by readers of the press. Africa and Latin America receive little coverage, inclining many readers to regard them as of little importance in world affairs.

Since most Americans derive knowledge of international affairs from the media, it is distressing to learn how little time the average person spends in reading about foreign affairs. One study, conducted by the prestigious American Institute of Public Opinion, found that the American adult reads an average of 12 column-inches of foreign news each day (or about one-half column). The same study revealed that the average reader spends about two and one-third minutes on this material.[22] Thus, if the amount of foreign news that sees publication is small, the amount that is actually read is even smaller.

Commercialism

Executives in the media defend scanty coverage of foreign affairs by observing that the media in America are competitive. They must give their customers what they want or go out of business. If a newspaper places more emphasis on foreign news than its readers desire, the newspaper will not become a lone beacon of knowledge; instead, its light will be extinguished. Similarly, television news producers maintain that if their viewers want less foreign news than the station purveys, they will bestir themselves and turn the dial. In truth, there is no easy way to refute these arguments. The American media are mostly commercial ventures. Such commercialism accounts for many outstanding features of media performance. It is also the source of many of the media's problems.

Let us recognize, to begin with, that it costs an inordinate amount of money to operate a newspaper, a radio station, or a television station. It costs much more to operate an entire network. Radio and television stations cover these costs, and try to make a

profit, by selling time to advertisers. Newspapers rely on both advertising (two-thirds of revenues) and sales to gain revenues. In either
case, the key to profits lies with the size of the audience; an empty
theater does not fill the till.

In the television industry particularly, costs are staggering. Listed
below are estimated combined costs from the three major networks
for coverage of selected events in the 1970s:

Pope Paul's visit to US (1 day)	$10 million
A space flight	$ 1 million
A moon shot	$2½ million
Coverage of Middle East conflict (for year 1967)	$ 9 million
A national convention	$10 million
Vietnam coverage (entire year)	$ 5 million
1974 election night coverage	$8½ million

Nixon's trip to China—at least $3 million per network dur-
ing time Nixon was in China

The three networks spent a total of $30 million covering the 1968
presidential election campaign.[23] In 1982, each network spent
between $2 million and $4 million to cover the 11-week war in the
Falkland Islands. The weekly salaries for a standard three-person
news team—reporter, camera operator and sound technician—
stands in the area of $1,500. Each camera crew generates a large
amount of film, about 20 times as much as is shown on the screen.
Such film must be transported, processed and edited. In the early
1970s, NBC accountants used the rule of thumb measure of $14
for each foot of film used on a program, or $504 per minute. The
network further estimated that in 1968 each film crew accounted
for $500 thousand in expenditures.[24] As a consequence of these high
costs, news executives prefer to utilize as few crews as possible.
Furthermore, producers (the equivalent of editors in print journalism) are not happy when crews are standing around; they want
as many stories as possible from each crew. The television correspondent, unlike the newspaper reporter, is not permitted to spend
time gathering background information at bars, social events and
the like, in preparation for filing an in-depth story. Camera crews
are almost constantly on the go, or else they are dismissed.

To recoup these enormous costs and show a profit besides,
television relies upon advertisers. The price a station or network
can charge its advertisers depends on the size of the viewing audience. Even a slight increase in the size of the audience at prime

time viewing hours can mean a sizable increase in advertising revenues. In 1969, CBS Evening News sold its five minutes of commercial time at $28 thousand per minute. At that rate, the program grossed $36 million for the year, leaving a $13 million profit after deducting costs.[25]

In television news, the concept of "audience flow" is widely accepted. This concept states that if viewers are watching the local news on a particular channel, they will stay tuned to that station for the network news. In other words, the conviction prevails that most viewers don't care much which network news they watch. If this be the case, industry executives insist it makes little economic sense to increase the number of network news crews or to significantly alter existing formats. While such steps might improve program quality, they would not increase audience size. The notion of audience flow seriously reduces industry incentives to improve the quality of network news.[26]

The corporate structure of television networks also affects news programming. From its origins, television has been first and foremost an entertainment medium. Most of the industry's top executives have come up through show business, sales, research or advertising, but not the news. Their corporate outlook often inclines them to slight public affairs programming for the more lucrative shows that fall under the heading of entertainment. Such an attitude was largely responsible for the resignation in 1966 of Fred W. Friendly as president of CBS News. Friendly left because network executives overruled his decision to air Senate hearings on Vietnam and chose instead (in Friendly's words) "a fifth rerun of 'Lucy,' then followed by an eighth rerun of 'The Real McCoys.' " It is well known that few advertisers care to sponsor documentaries, which typically attract a very small audience. Networks cannot charge a very high advertising rate for such shows. Therefore, they must search for clients who sponsor such programs out of a desire to identify themselves with responsible corporate citizenship.

News Definition

The competitive nature of the media, reinforced by the necessity of showing a profit, affects the content of the news. This influence is most readily seen in the television industry where, it will be recalled, most Americans gain their knowledge about foreign policy.

"A volcano is news only when it erupts," commented an observer of the media. This remark highlights the all-important concept of news definition. A story is worth reporting, many executives believe, if it involves conflict, if it is dramatic, and (for television) if it is visual. These are the very qualities that characterize athletic competition, the perfect subject for media coverage. Perhaps the ideal news story, from this point of view, is a grisly murder. Reports of fires, train wrecks, floods and hurricanes rarely wind up on the cutting room floor.

How might the presentation of news as conflict affect consumers' outlook upon international affairs? With occasional exception, the only international stories that make the news are those that show governments and people in opposition. The media consumer barely receives a suggestion of the undeniable fact that most countries get along quite amicably most of the time. It would hardly be surprising if news consumers gained a distorted view of a world in ceaseless turmoil, with their own nation in constant jeopardy. If that be the case—and there is no empirical evidence to prove it—then might not those same consumers be inclined to adopt a suspicious and belligerent attitude toward other countries?

These trends are particularly in evidence in the case of television news. Here the emphasis is not only on conflict, but also on the visual. For many television news producers, the best stories are those that require no commentary; the picture tells the story. A CBS publication, *Television News Reporting*, makes this point:

> Television news properly emphasizes the frankly pictorial aspects of the news, thus respecting the nature of its own resources. By doing so, it can perform a unique service in making the viewer an eye-witness to much of the news as it happens. The largest and the smallest events are recorded by the camera in a fashion which makes seeing understanding.[27]

It is relevant to ask, however, whether seeing does make for understanding. The television camera usually records the moment of impact, but it rarely captures the background of an event. Pictures of bombings in Belfast tell the viewer nothing about the causes of the religious dispute in Northern Ireland. Film clips of the president warmly greeting a foreign head of state on the White House lawn tell the viewer nothing about the points of difference and agreement between their two nations.

It is worthwhile inquiring what television news consciously strives to avoid. Perhaps the worse bugaboo is the "talking head," a lengthy shot of a person talking. Such footage is the direct opposite of "action news." Indeed, television news—and newspaper reporting to a somewhat lesser extent—shies away from the cerebral. To lighten the fare, television broadcasters pepper their dialogue with "happy talk." However, most international developments are exceedingly complex. If viewers or readers are to gain an *understanding* of an event, they need an explanation. Yet, news executives are convinced that if they supply such analysis, most consumers will discard their product in favor of a less taxing competitor. Television news reports rarely exceed 350 words, far too few to explain any event more involved than a children's trip to the monkey house. Stories dealing with complicated ideas, long-term trends, and economics receive little media coverage, unless they can be translated into human interest stories, such as a picture of a distraught mother with her starving child dangling in her arms. The media obsession with events and personalities means that they rarely introduce their consumers to such fundamental issues as rising nationalism, the corrosive effects of ethnic diversity upon national unity, the impact of medical advances on population growth, the rise of the middle class in certain Third World nations, and the consequences of nuclear power for the proliferation of nuclear weapons. One wonders whether the media, structured as they are today, would have bothered to report the publication of *Origin of Species, The Communist Manifesto,* or the works of Sigmund Freud or Albert Einstein.

Television news is widely recognized today as no more than a headline service. This would not be so serious if the public then engaged in further investigation of world events. However, as we have seen, most members of the public obtain all the information they are going to get from television.

The near absence of explanatory segments on the news can give the public a distorted view of world affairs. In coverage of Latin American affairs, for example, the military coup has become almost a media cliché. Rarely do the media present the unspectacular developments that lead up to the takeover. It would be hardly surprising to learn that many Americans perceive Latin America as a land of wild-eyed revolutionaries, since few other types of stories about that region appear in the media. Even the attentive media watcher would gain barely a hint of the substantial economic development taking place in certain Latin American countries.

Many of the above news practices emerge with unusual clarity in the coverage of terrorism. Few incidents have more news appeal than a terrorist attack. The incident itself expresses conflict, and it offers splendid opportunities for dramatic film coverage. (One is reminded of pictures of the hooded terrorists who murdered Israeli athletes at the 1972 Munich Olympic Games.) The media exhibit such enthusiasm for covering terrorist actions as to render terrorists the "super entertainers of our time," in the words of Walter Laqueur, chairman of the International Research Council of the Center for Strategic and International Studies. Terrorists have learned how to exploit the media. "Don't shoot, we're not on prime time!" is not an unrealistic caricature of terrorist planning. For many terrorists, success itself is defined in terms of media coverage. And they have been extraordinarily successful. The Symbionese Liberation Army, with which Patricia Hearst became involved, never numbered over two dozen followers, yet it captured media attention for a full two years. However, for all the unstinting coverage of terrorism, how much explanation and analysis of the phenomenon has there been? All too often, the media will provide an exhaustive account of a hijacking or a bombing, complete with pictures and interviews with survivors; yet, the media will say almost nothing about the fundamental causes of the conflict that gave rise to the terrorist act in the first place.

Discontinuous Coverage

Another facet of the modern media is discontinuous coverage. Reporters hurriedly scamper in search of "today's" news. If it happened yesterday, it is already history. Discontinuous coverage is traceable in large part to the media's reporting methods. Outside of a few foreign cities where correspondents are regularly stationed, coverage usually proceeds as follows. When a crisis erupts, a TV network or newspaper rushes a correspondent and supporting staff to the scene. So long as the crisis remains "hot," extensive reporting continues. Once the crisis subsides, however, the correspondents are rushed to the newest trouble spot and the story disappears.

It is extremely difficult for the consumer of such news to gain a coherent picture of world events. Crises seem to arise in random fashion from one place to the next, like a loon breaking water at various spots on a lake. No pattern emerges. The media rarely supply the connective tissue that would explain the relationship between one crisis and another. It is no wonder that so many people give up any hope of comprehending international politics.

Reporting After the Fact

According to the media's definition, news is something that has already occurred. Even the few analytical segments that appear in the media usually pertain to past events. It is highly unusual for the media to act as an early warning device, alerting the public and government to major events over the horizon. This practice of reporting after the fact raises a dilemma for democratic government. A major function of the media is to supply information to the public so that it can intelligently influence government decisions. However, so long as the media continue to report what *did* happen as opposed to what *might* happen under various circumstances, the media are not preparing the citizenry to participate in policy making as well as it might. The public needs information about future possibilities as well as past certainties. The public also needs information at the early stage of policy formulation, if it is to influence government decisions. But here again, the media usually report a decision only after it has been taken. In brief, media consumers find themselves driving forward by looking through the rear-view mirror.

Wire Service Copy

Because of the vast expense, no more than a score or so of newspapers employ foreign correspondents. To obtain foreign news, most newspapers rely upon wire services, particularly the Associated Press and the United Press International. In a 1973 survey of the managing editors of 140 large newspapers, 70 percent of the respondents said that the Associated Press was their most important source of foreign policy news.[28] Radio stations similarly rely upon the wire services for foreign news.

In order to satisfy such a wide variety of subscribers, the wire services present the news in the form of an inverted pyramid. According to this formula, the writer places the most recent and dramatic event in the first paragraph and then works back to antecedent causes. A newspaper or radio station can then cut the story at any place and not sacrifice its timeliness. For a story on a large grain deal with the Soviet Union, for instance, a midwestern newspaper might want to carry the full wire service report. A coastal state newspaper might content itself with the first paragraph only.

Objectivity is another requirement of serving so many different kinds of customers. Wire service writers try to slant the news as little as possible, for fear of antagonizing some subscribers. To write such stories, reporters search for hard, indisputable, observable events: assassinations, coups, elections, wars and the like lend themselves to such reporting.

While such coverage may satisfy the economic needs of the wire services, one wonders how well it meets the requirements of an informed citizenry. As James Reston, one of the most respected of Washington reporters, suggests, the inverted pyramid may be fine for a story about a fire or a train wreck. However, he goes on to say, it is impossible to reduce the nuances of a Senate debate on China policy to one or two paragraphs.[29] The inverted pyramid, in short, encourages oversimplified reporting. The quest for perfect objectivity also deprives the reader or listener of important information. The public needs interpretive analysis if it is to comprehend the significance of an event. Interpretation, however, violates the code of objectivity, so the wire services provide very little of it. Even if a wire service report contains an analysis of an event, this point of the pyramid, which comes at the end of the story, is frequently not published.

Suggestions for Improvement

As the foregoing should make clear, the media are not without their maladies. As so often occurs in both medicine and politics, however, diagnosis is far easier than treatment. Before prescribing any remedies, it would be well to observe that, infirm as the American media may be, they show far more signs of vitality than their counterparts in most other countries.

One of the major problems plaguing media performance concerns the definition of news. We have seen that an event becomes news when laden with conflict and drama; television producers also favor pictorial stories. Thus, when the British and the Argentines clashed in 1982 over the Falkland Islands, scores of reporters descended upon the scene to cover the brief war. Before the hostilities, however, there were practically no journalists reporting on the simmering conflict between the two nations over possession of the islands.

The media would better serve their consumers if they would expand their definition of news to include the slowly gathering forces that lead to the "newsworthy" events of the day. This broader definition of news should also embrace the consequences of events. Too many journalists today conduct themselves according to James Reston's description: "Most of the time we rush from crisis to crisis like firemen, and then leave when the blaze goes out."[30] Reston suggests that the definition of news should also include ideas. The media, he says, are too event-centered; scientific discoveries and philosophical ideas deserve coverage too.

Many professional news people would agree in theory that the definition of news should be expanded. However, they would add, if a newspaper, radio or television station provides material that its customers reject, it will go out of business. Reston has wrestled with these considerations, which cannot be ignored so long as the media remain competitive, commercial ventures. Reston suggests that the media set aside a particular segment of their presentations for news analysis, background, forecasting, and other elements of a broadened concept of news. Precedents already exist in the press, as evidenced by special sections on business, sports and fashions. Following these examples, the media should make no special effort to jazz up their news analysis presentations to appeal to the general public, any more than editors attempt to enhance the appeal of stock market quotations by including photographs or funny stories. The media should recognize that there is a certain group in the population—the attentive public—that will consume such offerings out of genuine interest, not because they are enticed by slick marketing. Such a special section might include news analysis by selected experts, passages from noteworthy speeches, excerpts from outstanding periodicals and books, as well as philosophical musings on the issues of the decade (as opposed to the day).

THE ISSUE OF SECRECY

The time was April 1961. *New York Times* reporter Tad Szulc had one of the scoops of the decade, a story describing secret CIA training of a brigade of Cuban exiles in Nicaragua for the purpose of invading Castro's island.

When President Kennedy learned that the *Times* was about to feature the story on page one, just days before the invasion was to occur, he anxiously telephoned the publisher and asked him to kill the story. In the pages that follow, we shall consider the publisher's dilemma.

The Need for Openness

"A popular Government, without popular information, or the means of acquiring it, is but a Prologue to a Farce or a Tragedy; or, perhaps, both." So said James Madison in 1822 about the need to make information available in a democracy. His comments seem particularly apt with regard to the Bay of Pigs invasion, which managed to combine the defining characteristics of both tragedy and farce.

The clearest and most compelling rationale for openness states that it is impossible to conduct democratic government, unless the public has the information to guide and evaluate the actions of policymakers. Had the American people had the opportunity to debate the Bay of Pigs landing before its occurrence, they might well have averted a major foreign policy defeat for the United States.

The ideals of democracy are more fully realized if the people have a say in the early stages of policy formulation, rather than merely having the chance to express approval or disapproval after the fact. Veteran journalist Douglass Cater phrased this idea as follows:

> The reporter believes in the purifying powers of publicity. He is the sworn enemy of secrecy. He holds firm in the faith that "public opinion" must have an opportunity to express itself while policy is still malleable and has not been molded into unchangeable dogma.[31]

The liberal philosophers of the nineteenth century, and John Stuart Mill in particular, articulated another reason for free and open discussion. The more thoughts displayed in the market place of ideas, the better chance that the people will seize upon the idea that best realizes the true national interest. By tearing down some stalls in this market place, government may deprive its citizens of the best produce.

The cleansing light of public knowledge also keeps government on its toes. While there may be plausible reasons for withholding some information, many people feel that the government classifies far more documents than needed to protect national security. Some of these documents may have been classified in order to conceal government errors. In the early 1970s, a retired Pentagon security officer estimated that Pentagon files alone contained 20 million classified documents, and that only one percent to five percent of these truly needed to be kept secret to preserve national security.[32]

As historian and former White House adviser Arthur Schlesinger has written,

> If secrecy in some cases remains a necessity, it also can easily become the means by which Government dissembles its purposes, buries its mistakes, safeguards its reputation, manipulates its citizens, maximizes its power and corrupts itself.[33]

If governments were always wiser than citizens, then the case for openness might be rather weak. History has shown, however, that governments have only too often led their people like lemmings over unforeseen precipices down into treacherous waters below. The theory of democracy is based upon the premise that in the majority of cases the people are the best judges of their own welfare.

Returning to the Bay of Pigs incident, it is interesting to contemplate one of President Kennedy's remarks in the wake of the disaster. The *Times* did handle Szulc's story in a manner acceptable to Kennedy. The newspaper printed the story, but it omitted mention of CIA involvement and the imminence of the operation. The *Times* also buried the story on the inside pages. "If you had printed more about the operation," Kennedy later told *Times* managing editor Turner Catledge, "you would have saved us from a colossal mistake."

Should the *Times* have acted otherwise? Did not Szulc's full story qualify under the newspaper's slogan, "All the news that's fit to print"? Suppose the *Times* had printed the full story as planned on page one, under a banner headline. In all likelihood, the United States would have canceled the invasion. In that case, would the newspaper have received credit for averting a foreign policy debacle, or would it have incurred public wrath for spoiling a chance to rid the hemisphere of a Communist dictator?

Ivan and Carol Doig suggest a rule of thumb for coping with the issue of secrecy: if opposing governments are aware of the information in question, the case for hiding it from the American people is not persuasive.[34] The Bay of Pigs invasion clearly did not catch Castro by surprise. Within three days his soldiers rounded up those members of the invasion force not cut down on the beach. The existence of the secret training base in Nicaragua was fairly well known throughout Central America long before the invasion. Since Castro knew the outlines of the invasion plan—if not the precise date, location and troop strength involved—the only people that were caught by surprise were the American public. The partial suppression of the news by the *New York Times* deprived the American people from debating the merits of the invasion beforehand; it did not preserve the secrecy of an operation already known to Castro.

While the *New York Times* has incurred censure for withholding Tad Szulc's full story, consider the probable reaction to the newspaper's performance had the invasion been a rousing success. Would not the *Times* have been hailed for its distinguished judgment and patriotism? Such a question leads us to contemplate the case for suppressing information.

The Need for Secrecy

The Battle of Midway was the turning point in the Pacific War against Japan. The United States won that naval encounter largely because Washington had broken Japan's military code, unbeknownst to Tokyo. American commanders were understandably jubilant about access to Japanese military secrets; they fully intended to exploit their new knowledge following the victory at Midway. However, a Chicago newspaper got wind of America's extraordinary cryptographic achievement and published the news. The Japanese promptly changed their code, and America lost her ear on Japanese military planning.

In January 1980, a half dozen Americans hiding in the Canadian embassy in Teheran donned disguises and left Iran, along with the Canadian diplomatic staff. The Iranian regime of Ayatollah Khomeini was sorely miffed, for it was holding 54 Americans hostage in their own embassy in another part of town. Several news organizations had known for several weeks that the Canadians were sheltering the Americans, but they declined to publish the news. Indeed, Secretary of State Cyrus Vance had requested the *New York Times* not to publish the information, and the newspaper complied.

In which of these cases, if either, did the press live up to its highest ideals? The question leads us to consider the conditions under which the media are justified in withholding the news.

Arthur Schlesinger has suggested six justifications for denying information to the public:

  the content of diplomatic negotiations;
  the nature of intelligence operations;
  military plans, movements and weaponry;

information that might compromise a foreign government or American friends or agents abroad;

personal data given to the government on the presumption that it will remain secret, such as tax returns and medical records;

official plans and decisions which, if prematurely disclosed, would lead to speculation in lands or commodities, preemptive buying, private enrichment and higher costs to government.[35]

The first of these conditions is often cited, especially by diplomats, as a requirement for successful negotiation. The famous French diplomat Jules Cambon said, "The day secrecy is abolished, negotiation of any kind will become impossible." Anyone who has bargained for wares at an open market can understand the need for secrecy. You wish to buy a wicker basket for no more than $5. The wizened and frail-looking man behind the counter tells you he bought it for $10 but will sell it to you, as a special favor (based on a presumed friendship the basis of which is not in evidence) at cost. You tell him you have only $2 to spend. If he knew your top price were $5, he would never sell it to you for the $3.50 that he reluctantly accepted. In diplomacy the process is similar, although the stakes are usually higher. No country could hope to achieve anything beyond its minimal objectives if the press revealed them to the opposition. However, how can the people debate the merits of their government's negotiating objectives before it is too late, without knowing what it is the government seeks to obtain? It would seem that in this case the requirements of democratic foreign policy and successful negotiation are not easy to reconcile.

In conclusion, it can be said that the conflict over secrecy between government and the media arises from the different roles these two institutions play in society. It is the government's job to conduct foreign policy. To do so effectively, government officials sometimes would prefer to distort or even withhold information. The media have no responsibility for foreign policy. They see their role as obtaining and presenting information. The media need not worry about the effect of their actions upon foreign policy; only the government is saddled with that responsibility. If the media habitually sought government sanction before presenting information, the nation would lie in peril of a self-serving body of officials. Should the media automatically release all the information they acquire, foreign policy could suffer great harm.

The struggle between secrecy and openness is not a battle between right and wrong. Both the free circulation of information

and judicious restraint are essential to the functioning of democracy. Wherever democratic government is found, the conflict between
secrecy and openness will persist.

FOR DISCUSSION

How might the American political process differ if the government controlled the media? Would such control be likely to
strengthen or weaken foreign policy?

Describe the role of the media in bureaucratic policy making.

Would government-funded, noncommercial media make a
sounder contribution to foreign policy formulation than media operated for profit?

Would you favor a law making it a crime to print or broadcast
classified information, such as exists in Great Britain?

How might the manner in which the media cover international
events color the public's perception of conflict and cooperation in
the international state system?

READING SUGGESTIONS

Batscha, Robert M. *Foreign Affairs News and the Broadcast Journalist*. New York:
    Praeger, 1975.
Chittick, William O. *State Department, Press, and Pressure Groups: A Role Analysis*.
    New York: Wiley-Interscience, 1970.
Cohen, Bernard C. *The Press and Foreign Policy*. Princeton: Princeton University
    Press, 1965.
Davison, W. Phillips. "Diplomatic Reporting: Rules of the Game." *Journal of
    Communication*, XXV (Autumn 1975): 138–46.
McCombs, Maxwell E., and Shaw, Donald L. "The Agenda-Setting Function of
    Mass Media." *Public Opinion Quarterly*, XXXVI (Summer 1972): 176–87.
Nimmo, Dan. *Political Communication and Public Opinion in America*. Santa Monica,
    Calif.: Goodyear, 1978.
Reston, James. *The Artillery of the Press*. New York: Harper and Row, 1966.

NOTES

1. Two excellent studies are Bernard C. Cohen, *The Press and Foreign Policy* (Princeton: Princeton University Press, 1965) and Dan Nimmo, *Political Communication and Public Opinion in America* (Santa Monica, Calif.: Goodyear, 1978).
2. American media also influence the perceptions of people in other countries. The *New York Times* news service is sent to 136 of the world's major newspapers, many of them based outside the United States. Approximately 60 foreign newspapers subscribe to the *Washington Post—Los Angeles Times* joint news service. *Time*'s foreign circulation approaches 1.3 million, while *Reader's Digest* is received by some 100 million persons abroad. The United Press International has subscribers in 113 foreign countries. American television programs are immensely popular overseas; these consist mostly of entertainment, not public affairs shows. (Above information from W. Read, "Multinational Media," *Foreign Policy*, Spring 1975: 155–67.) The pervasiveness of American media has led to cries of "cultural imperialism." Thus, what a Berliner knows about Japan may well come through the American media. Furthermore, what many Third World inhabitants know about their own countries might derive from American coverage.
3. Douglass Cater, *The Fourth Branch of Government* (Boston: Houghton Mifflin, 1959), p. 171.
4. Figures cited in Thomas L. Brewer, *American Foreign Policy* (Englewood Cliffs, N.J.: Prentice-Hall, 1980), p. 72.
5. Maxwell E. McCombs and Donald L. Shaw, "The Agenda-Setting Function of Mass Media," *Public Opinion Quarterly*, XXXVI (Summer 1972): 176–87.
6. Reported in Cohen, p. 107.
7. Ibid., p. 35.
8. Leon V. Sigal, *Reporters and Officials* (Lexington, Mass.: D.C. Heath and Company, 1973), p. 185.
9. Cohen, p. 138.
10. John Kenneth Galbraith, "Why Diplomats Clam Up," in Louis M. Lyons, ed., *Reporting the News* (Cambridge: Harvard University Press, 1965), pp. 375–78.
11. Cited in Cohen, p. 245, note 21.
12. Quoted in Sigal, p. 135.
13. Cohen, p. 135.
14. John Herbers, *No Thank You, Mr. President* (New York: W. W. Norton, 1976).
15. Robert M. Batscha, *Foreign Affairs News and the Broadcast Journalist* (New York: Praeger, 1975), pp. 43–44.
16. Quoted in Cohen, pp. 44–45.
17. George Gerbner and George Marvanyi, "The Many Worlds of the World's Press," *Journal of Communication*, XXVII (Winter 1977): 52–66. For individual newspapers, the investigators found the *New York Times* devoted 16 percent of its news space to foreign news. The corresponding figures for the London *Times* and *Pravda* were 22 percent and 38 percent.

18. *Opening or Closing Our Window on the World?* Interim Report of the Council on International and Public Affairs Project on Language, Area, and International Studies and the Mass Media in the United States, New York City, February 19, 1979, p. 2.
19. Cohen, p. 115.
20. *Opening or Closing Our Window on the World?* p. 2.
21. John A. Lent, "Foreign News in American Media," *Journal of Communication,* XXVII (Winter 1977): 49.
22. Cohen, p. 251.
23. All the above figures come from Batscha, pp. 82–83.
24. Edward Jay Epstein, *News From Nowhere* (New York: Random House, 1973), Chapter 3.
25. Ibid.
26. The number of crews each network employs is not so large. For domestic coverage, each network relies on approximately ten regular crews plus three staff camera operators who can assemble crews on short notice. Each network also has camera crews in about ten foreign cities. Furthermore, the networks tend to station crews in the same cities. These allocations account for the fact that most domestic news stories originate from the same half-dozen cities, especially New York, Chicago, Washington and Los Angeles. Since it costs much more to send a crew to a remote location, most such news is simply announced with a graphic in the background. In 1982, ABC and CBS had 22 correspondents in 13 cities abroad, while NBC had 17 reporters in 13 foreign locations. The *New York Times,* in contrast, had over 30 full-time correspondents in 24 foreign cities, and *Time* magazine had 35 reporters in 22 overseas locations. (The *New York Times,* August 8, 1982, section II). Networks provide direct coverage to news that occurs where camera crews are normally located, and dispatch crews elsewhere for stories of unusual interest. Because of the high costs of satellite transmission, all but the most momentous of foreign film footage is shipped back by airplane. Producers ask foreign bureaus to produce "timeless" stories that can be shown any day.
27. Quoted in Batscha, p. 67.
28. Timothy Schiltz, Lee Sigelman, Robert Neal, "Perspective of Managing Editors on Coverage of Foreign Policy News," *Journalism Quarterly,* vol. 50 (Winter 1973): 717–21.
29. James Reston, *The Artillery of the Press* (New York: Harper and Row, 1966), pp. 14–16. This is an informed and still relevant study of the press and foreign policy.
30. Ibid., p. 83.
31. Cater, p. 19.
32. Reported in Arthur Schlesinger, Jr., "The Secrecy Dilemma," *New York Times Magazine,* February 6, 1972.
33. Ibid.
34. Ivan and Carol Doig, *News: A Consumer's Guide* (Englewood Cliffs, N.J.: Prentice-Hall, 1972), pp. 59–60.
35. Schlesinger, "The Secrecy Dilemma."

Chapter 7
The Constitution and
the Presidency

While the international state system, political culture, public opinion, pressure groups and the media comprise the environment in which foreign policy is conceived, it is the political system that formulates foreign policy (see Fig. 1–1). The political system is composed of the various elected and appointed officials, as well as career civil servants, who labor in the executive, legislative and judicial branches of government. The product of their efforts becomes the policy of the United States government.

This chapter and the three that follow will examine components of the political system that have a determining voice in the formulation and implementation of American foreign policy. The discussion will be selective, giving more emphasis to those individuals and groups that play decisive roles. It begins with the document that sets forth the very structure of the American political system.

THE CONSTITUTION

Located somewhere in the interior of the country is a railroad crossing where a north-south main line intersects an east-west main line at 90 degree angles. The crossing is controlled by block signals that halt one train if another train is proceeding through the crossing on the other track. Occasionally, however, the signal system fails and the trains collide. The signalling malfunction is not the result of a technical difficulty but rather the conscious design of a young boy who yearns occasionally for a wreck of his toy trains.

The model train layout here described may appear to have little to do with the American Constitution. In actuality, however, that document also lays the basis for collision, in this case among the three branches of the federal government, the executive, the legislative, and the judicial. Let us see how this came about.

It will be remembered that the United States Constitution was forged on the hearth of rebellion against tyranny. Patrick Henry hammered this fact into the consciousness of the world with his immortal words, "Give me liberty or give me death!" The colonists who came to the New World were fleeing from the prerogatives of monarchs who, with the notable exception of the British crown, ruled by "divine right." It is easily understandable, therefore, that the colonists wished to ensure that there would be no repetition of executive tyranny in the New World.

The lawyers, planters and businessmen who gathered in Philadelphia in 1787 to write a constitution for the United States were determined to place limits on executive power. "All power in human hands is liable to be abused," said James Madison, one of these delegates. The men who created the "miracle in Philadelphia" kept this maxim in mind.[1]

At the same time, the delegates realized that they needed an executive with the power to govern effectively. It would hardly do to create a head of state who was at the same time decapitated (in a figurative sense). The country needed a strong, vigorous chief executive to forge a sense of national unity and set a course for the country.

In short, the men who gathered in the intense heat of that Philadelphia summer were faced with a conflict. On the one hand, they sought to provide for an executive branch that was capable of governing the country. On the other hand, they wanted to make sure that this executive would not amass so much power as to threaten the very liberties the colonists had come to America to establish. This clash of objectives is sometimes known as the "Madisonian Dilemma." The founders coped with it in a particularly successful manner.

The delegates divided the structure of government into three parts, the executive, legislative and judicial branches. According to the principle of checks and balances, no single branch of government could force through its preferences without the cooperation of the other two. In the landmark decision *Marbury v. Madison* (1803), the Supreme Court declared itself authorized to void laws it held in violation of the Constitution.

Authority to raise funds was housed in Congress, affording that body a powerful rein on executive action. Should a president incur the displeasure of a sufficient proportion of the country, the Constitution provides for impeachment (the imminent threat of which led Richard Nixon to resign office in 1974). It is in connection with these instances of opposed power, or what presidential scholar Richard Neustadt calls "separate institutions sharing power," that the image of colliding trains gains relevance.

By all accounts, the charter drafted in 1787 was a resounding success. The American Constitution is the oldest written constitution still in effect. (The British Constitution, which antedates the American, does not exist in the form of a single written document.) But how adequate is the American Constitution for a world power? At a time when the oceans and the airspace sealed America off from foreign wars, the delegates to the Constitutional Convention were hardly concerned with designing a government that could play a leading role in world affairs. May not the very devices that inhibit tyranny at home prevent the government from acting with that decisiveness and dispatch necessary to protect the national interest? Might not a government too enfeebled by constitutional niceties find itself at a distinct disadvantage in dealing with authoritarian regimes not similarly incapacitated? Is it possible that the Constitution is out of date in a world that challenges America's interests at every turn? Does the president need more latitude to act with speed and secrecy than the Constitution allows? Yet, were the Constitution altered so as to confer upon the president the same scope for action possessed by Soviet leaders, would not the very democratic values that foreign policy is supposed to protect be in jeopardy?

These questions do not admit of easy answers. They do reveal, however, another dilemma of American democracy. The very devices in the Constitution that protect democracy at home may jeopardize it abroad. Before considering how the Constitution might need to be altered, however, let us examine some of its major provisions regarding foreign policy.

CONSTITUTIONAL PROVISIONS AND FOREIGN POLICY

Article 2—significantly not Article 1—sets forth the powers of the president and the executive branch. We shall concern ourselves here only with those powers that have to do with foreign policy; most of these can be found in Section 2.

The Constitution authorizes the president to:

serve as commander-in-chief of the army and navy;
make treaties with foreign powers with the advice and consent of the Senate, provided that two-thirds of the senators present concur;
appoint ambassadors and other representatives, with the advice and consent of the Senate;
receive foreign ambassadors.

Given the extensive involvement of the president and the remainder of the executive branch in foreign policy today, this list of powers is extraordinarily brief.

In foreign policy, as in all aspects of government, many powers have evolved in response to necessity. The presidential prerogative of receiving foreign ambassadors has been broadened to give the chief executive the authority to establish or break diplomatic relations with other governments. The president's right to conduct negotiations with other governments also extends from this grant of power.

Article 1 of the Constitution enumerates the powers of Congress. As regards foreign policy, the legislature's principal powers are as follows:

provide for the common defense and general welfare;
regulate commerce with foreign nations;
establish a uniform rule of naturalization;
declare war;
raise and support military forces;
make all laws which shall be necessary and proper for executing the above powers (as well as other powers not listed here).

A comparison of the powers delegated to the president and Congress reveals a startling degree of overlap and conflict. In their efforts to restrain executive power, the framers of the Constitution resolved to prevent the chief executive from making foreign policy according to whim, as did many of the kings in Europe. These whims, of course, often resulted in capricious wars that produced enormous government expenditures and loss of lives, the burdens of which were borne by the people who had no say over the decision to go to war. If we list some of the powers of the executive and legislative branches, we can readily see where the writers of the

Constitution applied the principle of checks and balances to foreign policy.

Powers of President	Powers of Congress
make treaties	provide advice and consent on treaties (two-thirds of senators present)
commander-in-chief	raise and support military forces; declare war
appoint ambassadors and other officials	provide advice and consent on appointments (Senate)

It is quite evident from the above that the Constitution builds conflict into three vital areas of foreign policy: treaty-making, war-making, and appointments. Executive-legislative conflict is also generated by constitutional provisions in two other areas, finances and legislation.

No government can conduct foreign policy without money. The Constitution stipulates that while the president may request funds for the operation of government, only Congress can appropriate them. The founders regarded the legislature's authority to provide funds as one of the principal checks on presidential power. Each year the president goes to Congress with hat in hand for money for a host of foreign policy needs, from paper shredders at CIA to the American contribution to the World Bank to the procurement of jet fuel for fighter-bombers. To run foreign policy, governments also need personnel, and this too costs money. The Constitution empowers Congress to raise money to pay the salaries and other expenses of the executive bureaucracy.

Many of the government's foreign policy programs cannot take effect unless Congress passes implementing legislation, and this affords the legislature another check on executive power. Trade agreements, cultural exchange pacts, immigration quotas, the development of elaborate new weapons systems, the lifting or imposition of quotas on imports—all these illustrate the kinds of subjects regarding which Congress must pass laws if the president's foreign policy is to leap from conception to implementation.

The Constitution, in sum, does not prescribe a neat division of labor between the executive and legislature for the conduct of foreign policy. Instead, it brings to mind our earlier image of two trains approaching each other at a crossover. There is in the Constitution what E. S. Corwin has labeled "an invitation to struggle" between the president and Congress for control of foreign policy.

Presidential Usurpation of Power

Someone with no knowledge of foreign policy apart from the Constitution might well conclude that Congress has the dominant role in American foreign relations. However, quite the opposite is the case. Over the years, and especially since World War II, a succession of presidents has accumulated a great deal of foreign policy authority at the expense of Congress. President Truman stated baldly, "I make foreign policy." Those words would no doubt cause great dismay among the founders who sought to balance presidential power. As shown in Chapter 10, it has been only since the 1970s that Congress has begun to react to this imbalance.

War Making.
The Constitution gives Congress the authority to declare war. Since World War II, however, various presidents have committed the armed forces to action without a war declaration, sometimes in precisely the manner that the founders wished to prevent. Under the commander-in-chief authority, presidents have sent American forces into combat in Korea (1950–53), Cuba (1961 and 1962), Lebanon (1958), Dominican Republic (1965), Vietnam, and Grenada (1984).[2] The 1962 Cuban missile crisis brought the world as close as it has come to nuclear war, yet Congress was shut out of the planning of this operation. Congress's power to declare war has in recent years acted as a negligible restraint upon the war-making capacity of the president.

Treaty Making.
From 1789 to the present, the Senate has rejected in entirety approximately one percent of the treaties submitted to it. The Senate has not completely rejected a treaty since 1940. The most notable rejection—indeed, the only notable rejection—was the Versailles Treaty marking the end of World War I. These figures might lead one to conclude that the Senate's treaty-making power has fallen into disuse. Before reaching such a judgment, however, we should note that most treaties are of a technical or commercial nature and do not involve issues vital to national security. Furthermore, it is difficult to gauge the extent to which presidents have negotiated treaties based on their estimates about what the Senate would accept. In the SALT II Treaty, for instance, President Carter was aware that the Senate would not approve an agreement giving the Soviets a numerical advantage in strategic weapons, as provided for in

SALT I, and he insisted on parity. Finally, the Senate has on several occasions altered portions of treaties without rejecting the entire document. Despite these caveats, it is difficult to dispute the conclusion that the Senate's authority to approve treaties has not significantly hindered the executive branch from concluding the agreements it has sought.

Appointments.

It is generally agreed that the president is entitled to choose higher-level administrators. One cannot expect opponents of the president's policies to execute those policies vigorously. Accordingly, the Senate, which has the constitutional power to approve appointments, has turned down only a negligible number of foreign policy appointments. On extremely rare occasions, the Senate indicates that it would be unlikely to approve a particular ambassadorial appointment, and the president withdraws the nomination. This happens so infrequently, however, that we can safely conclude that the Senate's power to approve appointments has not limited presidential latitude in the conduct of foreign policy.

Appropriations and Legislation.

Even in the other two areas of congressional authority, appropriations and legislation, the legislature has generally granted the president's requests. Perhaps the outstanding exception has been foreign aid, where Congress has often cut the president's request. The most sizable foreign policy appropriation, that for defense, often passes through Congress with only a few minor scars. In 1982, however, Congress refused to honor President Reagan's request for funds to deploy the MX missile, and in 1984 Congress appeared to be gearing up for a battle over the defense budget. Whether these developments signify a new trend remains to be seen.

It would seem, then, that despite the relatively equal constitutional division of authority in foreign policy between the legislative and executive branches, the executive branch clearly dominates the process today.

Historical Explanation of Presidential Power

In the early years of the Republic, American foreign relations were sufficiently minimal as to allow the executive-legislative relationship to evolve as the founders had foreseen. As late as 1870, the State Department housed only a secretary and 52 assistants.

Today, conditions are vastly different. The State Department now numbers 25 thousand individuals. The country participates in diplomatic relations with over 125 nations and has security treaties with 42 other states. Over 4,500 treaties and other international agreements are currently in force between the United States and other governments. The country is a member of over 70 international organizations, of which the most prominent is the United Nations. In a typical year, the United States sends delegations to over 600 international conferences, ranging from such topics as regulation of tuna fishing to limitation of industrial waste. Furthermore, the country's foreign relations are no longer conducted by a single department; scores of departments, agencies and commissions participate in the nation's diplomacy. The enormous complexity of American foreign policy today makes it exceedingly difficult for the average legislator, concerned with domestic as well as foreign matters, to grasp the entire picture. The executive branch, by contrast, resembles a giant funnel of information, with all key facts and figures flowing down to the president, who therefore stands in a position to comprehend the overall view of America's foreign relations. The president can perceive, for example, the connection between Washington's support for South Korea and Israel's willingness to refrain from deploying nuclear weapons (because of Israel's trust in American commitments). The typical legislator, however, stands outside the funnel and gains only occasional glimpses of the totality of the country's foreign relations. Until very recently, therefore, Congress has been willing to allow the chief executive a free hand in conducting the nation's foreign policy.

Technology has reduced the time available for making foreign policy decisions. Consider the difference in the time required to transmit diplomatic communications today compared with the pre-electronic age. To cite an illustration, on June 27, 1786, the American minister in London wrote to the secretary of state, beginning, "Sir: I have just received the letter you did me the honor to write on the first day of May. . . ." (57 days earlier). The minister then referred to a letter he had written March 4 and to which he had received no reply, no doubt because "we hear that the vessel which carried out that despatch sprung a leak at sea, put into Lisbon and did not sail thence until late in April."[3] Today, of course, diplomatic messages can be transmitted instantaneously, and heads of state must sometimes act rapidly in order to avoid disaster. It takes approximately 30 minutes from the time a missile leaves a silo in the Soviet Union before it reaches its target in the United States. The time it would take for a missile fired from a submarine off the

New Jersey coast to hit Washington, D.C. is much less. Had President Truman awaited an extended debate by Congress before sending troops to South Korea in 1950, the soldiers would have disembarked only to find the country occupied by North Korea. As the Cuban missile crisis revealed, there may be very little time between moves in a foreign policy contest; it is much easier for the president to assemble the necessary information and select a course of action than it would be for the 535 members of Congress to do so.

The complexity of foreign policy and the diminished interval for reaching decisions have led to an imbalance between the executive and legislative branches in conducting foreign policy that would horrify the founders if they could return to view their handiwork. The president clearly dominates the foreign policy process today.

PRESIDENTIAL EVASION OF CONGRESS

Over the years, a number of practices have evolved that permit the president to skirt several of the constitutional checks originally given to Congress.

Treaties

Presidents have discovered a way to circumvent legislative participation in the treaty making process. A chief executive who feels that the required number of senators might not approve a treaty can conclude an executive agreement with representatives (usually the head of state) of other governments. In terms of committing the United States, executive agreements are for all practical purposes equivalent to treaties. A pledge given by the American president is no less solemn or binding than a treaty. Like the latter, executive agreements commit the nation not just for the duration of the incumbent's term in the White House but until the agreement is terminated by one or both parties. The Paris peace agreement that terminated the Vietnam War (on paper if not on the battlefield) and the five-year freeze on offensive arms negotiated in SALT I were both executive agreements. The Destroyers-for-Bases deal with Great Britain in 1940, which clearly placed the United States on the side of the Allies well before America formally entered World

War II, was an executive agreement, as were the agreements reached at Yalta at the conclusion of that titanic struggle.

As a symptom of the growing executive predominance in foreign affairs after World War II, executive agreements have become much more common than previously. In the 150 years prior to 1939, the United States entered into 799 treaties and 1,182 executive agreements. Between 1946 and 1972, the nation concluded 368 treaties and 5,590 executive agreements.[4] Two political scientists, Loch Johnson and James M. McCormick, conducted a study of treaties and executive agreements concluded by the United States between January 1, 1946, and December 31, 1976.[5] These investigators identified 7,201 pacts that the United States entered into with other countries during this interval. Of these, 6 percent were formal treaties requiring Senate confirmation; 87 percent were statutory agreements concluded by the president pursuant to legislation; and 7 percent were executive agreements entered into by presidential authority. The authors also broke down the 7,201 instances into military and non-military ones. Here, they found 1,235 or 17.1 percent relating to military matters. These were divided into two types, administrative (secondary details such as the establishment of a military headquarters provided for in an alliance) and substantive. The latter category covers such matters as the formation of alliances, signing of peace treaties, establishment of military bases, transfer of military equipment, and other actions that commit the U.S. to policy positions. Between January 1, 1946, and August 9, 1974 (the day Nixon left office), the US entered into 1,196 substantive military commitments. These commitments break down as follows:

    42 (3.5%) treaties;
 1,003 (83.9%) statutory agreements;
   151 (12.6%) executive agreements.

In studying the 151 executive agreements, the authors concluded that many were extremely important, such as:

    use of Azores airbases by US (1947);
    placement of US troops in Guatemala (1947);
    establishment of US bases in the Philippines (1947);
    broad US military prerogatives in Ethiopia (1953);
    security pledges to Turkey, Iran and Pakistan (1959);

military use of British island of Diego Garcia in the Indian
Ocean (1966);

military use of Bahrein in the Persian Gulf (1971);

establishment of a military mission in Iran (1974).

Johnson and McCormick demonstrate that every presidential
administration since World War II has entered into a larger number of substantive, military executive agreements than treaties; the
Nixon administration was particularly prone to this practice. Furthermore, the authors found that most of the substantive military
pacts entered into after World War II took the form of executive
agreements, not treaties. This finding substantiates a lament registered by the Senate Foreign Relations Committee in a 1969 report:
"We have come close to reversing the traditional distinction between
the treaty as an instrument of a major commitment and the executive agreement as the instrument of a minor one."[6] As we shall
have occasion to see in Chapter 10, Congress has taken action to
ensure that the executive agreement as a method of bypassing the
legislature's constitutional role in foreign policy will no longer be
abused.

Appointments

Regardless of which governmental institutions have a hand in the
conduct of foreign policy, that policy is bound to reflect the preferences and outlooks of the key officials involved. The founders
understood this proposition quite well, which is why they wished
the Senate to play a role in the approval of top appointments. In
dealing with this matter, the members of the Constitutional Convention reached a compromise. They allowed the president to pick
key officials, but they gave the Senate the right to approve them.
This arrangement extends to ambassadors, Foreign Service officers,
military officers, Cabinet secretaries and other departmental officials, but it excludes career civil servants and White House aides.
While this sharing of responsibility would seem to divide the
appointment power evenly between the two branches of government, in practice the legislature has almost never turned down a
key foreign policy appointment. With very few exceptions, the Senate grants the president his "team." To avoid the embarrassment

of a rejection, the chairman of the Senate Foreign Relations Committee may inform the president that a particular nominee is likely to be refused; the president then normally withdraws the nomination.

Should the Senate indicate that it will not approve a particular individual, the president can still bring that person into the government by appointing the individual as a personal assistant. These intimate associates, who have no responsibility for running a department or agency, do not need congressional sanction. It is worth noting, however, that as policy making has moved from the Cabinet into the White House, personal assistants may wield more power than Cabinet secretaries. Under President Nixon, for example, Robert Haldeman and John Erlichman exercised more influence than any department secretary with the possible exception of Secretary of State Kissinger. Under President Wilson, Colonel House exerted enormous influence, as did Harry Hopkins under President Roosevelt. In the Carter White House, Hamilton Jordan influenced the president on a wide range of issues.

The president can also avoid Senate scrutiny of an appointment by filling a post while the Senate is in recess. These are called interim appointments. If the president appoints an individual for a specific task of short duration, the appointee's functions may have terminated by the time the Senate reconvenes. In 1951, President Truman sensed that the Senate would not confirm the appointment of Philip Jessup as Ambassador to the United Nations, on account of his leftist leanings. Therefore, Truman made the appointment while the Senate was in recess.

War-Making

Perhaps the most controversial area of executive-legislative conflict concerns authority over the nation's armed forces. The Constitution, as we have seen, designates the president as commander-in-chief. Congress, however, is empowered to declare war. The legislature also determines the size of the armed forces, raises money for their maintenance, approves new weapons systems, and authorizes funds for the purchase of weapons and equipment.

A president who deems it vital for the United States to participate in a war, but doubts Congress will concur, may take certain actions to achieve the objective. Franklin D. Roosevelt, for example, believed that a fascist victory in World War II would leave the United States indefensible should the aggressors turn toward the

New World. When, in 1938, he gave a speech calling for the "quarantining" of the aggressors, he was shouted down as a war-monger. Believing that presidents should lead as much as follow public opinion, Roosevelt proceeded to take actions that he knew—and hoped—would involve the United States in the war before it was too late. When Japan asked the United States to recognize a Japanese sphere of influence in Southeast Asia, Roosevelt refused. He also cut off shipments of American oil and scrap iron to the Tokyo regime. It came as no surprise to Roosevelt when the Japanese attacked, although the precise time and location of the assault was unknown to him. Once the United States is attacked, Congress is hardly likely to withhold a declaration of war. Roosevelt achieved his aim of getting into the war and affecting the outcome.

The president's ability as commander-in-chief to deploy forces abroad can also involve the United States in war, even without a congressional declaration. It was through this method that the United States joined combat in Korea and Vietnam. Due to the speed with which events unfold in the modern age, a congressional declaration of war seems almost obsolete. At most, it implies congressional recognition that hostilities have erupted. It is hard to imagine a case in which American forces are engaged in combat and Congress, in order to discipline the president, would refuse to support American troops. In the wake of Vietnam, presidents might be more inclined to request a declaration of war before committing American forces to long-term combat. However, the legislature's authority to issue such a declaration has barely restrained presidents when they have sought to involve the United States in armed hostilities.

The issue of authority over the armed forces came to a head in the 1960s and 1970s, largely due to the outcome of the largest "presidential war" in the nation's history, the war in Vietnam. In the eyes of many, a succession of presidents, advised by all the appropriate experts, had committed a grievous error. It was time, a good number of people believed, to return the war-making power to the place where the framers of the Constitution intended it should lie, namely, with the legislature. This argument was joined by those who agreed that Vietnam had been a major mistake, but who believed that modern conditions had superseded the ideas of 1787. The fact of one mistaken presidential war does not mean that all such wars must be misguided, they argued. Only the president, they added, had the capacity to act with decisiveness and dispatch; and despite the error of Vietnam, the president's sources of information surpass those of Congress. Besides, Congress is not infallible in matters of war and peace. If left up to the legislature, the US would probably have remained out of World War II until the country stood alone against the Axis powers. The Senate's rejection of the Versailles Treaty ending World War I is regarded by most knowledgeable persons as a grievous error.

If we inquire into the intent of the founders, we find their purpose rather clear. They wanted to prevent the president from waging war whenever it suited a whim, as so many European monarchs had done. The ultimate sufferers in such wars were the common people. In a letter to James Madison written in 1789, Thomas Jefferson wrote, "We have already given in example one effectual check to the Dog of War by transferring the power of letting him loose from the Executive to the Legislative body, from those who are to spend to those who are to pay." The president's powers as commander-in-chief were described by Alexander Hamilton in Federalist No. 69:

> The president is to be commander in chief of the army and navy of the United States. In this respect his authority would be nominally the same with that of the king of Great Britain, but in substance much inferior to it. It would amount to nothing more than the supreme command and direction of the military and naval forces, as first General and admiral of the confederacy, while that of the British king extends to the *declaring* of war and to the *raising* and *regulating* of fleets and armies—all which, by the Constitution under consideration, would appertain to the legislature.

From the early days of the Republic through the end of the nineteenth century, control over the armed forces worked largely as the founders had intended. During the 1800s, Congress declared war three times: the War of 1812, the Mexican War (1846), and the Spanish-American War (1898). While presidents during this period sought a declaration of war before engaging in large-scale hostilities, they also found occasion to use the armed forces without declaring war. Thomas Jefferson himself, while president, dispatched the Navy to suppress the Barbary Pirates in the early 1800s. American warships patrolled the seas in suppression of the slave trade. Such actions, being of a far less magnitude than an attack upon a foreign government, did not seem to warrant a declaration of war. Never was it spelled out just how extensive the use of force must be in order to qualify as a war. Thus, these early uses of force without congressional authorization afforded a precedent for the much larger operations of the recent twentieth century, such as Korea, Cuba, Lebanon and Vietnam.

The expansion of executive power over the armed forces began in the early years of the current century and gathered a full head of steam following World War II. A number of American presidents sent troops to China, Colombia, Cuba, the Dominican Republic, Haiti, Mexico and Nicaragua—all without declarations of war. Between the world wars, the United States did not engage in military actions of much significance. As World War II gathered force, however, Franklin D. Roosevelt seized the occasion to augment executive authority over the armed forces. As we saw earlier, Roosevelt feared the consequences of America's abstention from the conflict that was wracking Asia and Europe. Realizing the mood of the people and Congress was decidedly against intervention, Roosevelt took steps to boost the Allied cause and link the United States to the Allied war effort. We have remarked the 1940 executive agreement whereby the United States gave Great Britain about 50 overage (but still usable) destroyers in return for base rights in the Western Hemisphere. In 1941, Roosevelt committed American forces to the defense of Greenland and Iceland. After a German submarine fired upon the American destroyer *Greer*, which had radioed the submarine's position to the British, Roosevelt ordered American naval craft to shoot on sight German and Italian vessels west of the 26th Meridian. It is not unfair to say that by the time the Axis powers declared war on the United States in the wake of Pearl Harbor, this country was already engaged in an undeclared naval war in the Atlantic, undertaken by the president alone.

After World War II, the president's war-making power expanded like a mushroom cloud. Bolstered by a national consensus on the need to contain Communist expansion, a succession of presidents ordered American troops into action without first seeking a declaration of war. These episodes included Korea (1950), Lebanon (1958), Bay of Pigs (1961), Cuban missile crisis (1962), Dominican Republic (1965) and Vietnam. Testifying in 1966 before a Senate Preparedness subcommittee, Secretary of State Dean Rusk expressed the acme of executive supremacy over control of the military: "No would-be aggressor should suppose that the absence of a defense treaty, congressional declaration, or United States military presence grants immunity to aggression." The secretary seemed to be putting the world on notice that the president has the authority to use military force at any time; treaties and the like are only embellishments on the unlimited charter of presidential prerogative. The worst fears of the founders seemed to have materialized.

It would be a distortion to lay the blame for the perversion of the Constitution in this area upon the executive branch alone.

Clearly, the legislature was an accessory. At any point along the way, one or both houses of Congress could have passed a resolution deploring presidential usurpation of control over the armed forces. Congress could also have cut off funds for any of these military operations. Instead, Congress tamely acquiesced in the new arrangement; until, that is, the first plainly disastrous presidential war, Vietnam. Under President Eisenhower, Congress went so far as to assure the president *in advance* that he could use force. That episode occurred in 1957. Soviet communism seemed to be sweeping the Middle East, symbolized by a massive Egyptian-Czechoslovakian arms deal (1955), Soviet financing of the Egyptian Aswan High Dam and the presence of Soviet advisers in Syria. To provide emphasis to America's containment policy in the Middle East, Congress passed a joint resolution that became known as the Eisenhower Doctrine. Declaring that "preservation of the independence and integrity of the nations of the Middle East" was vital to American national interests, the resolution granted the president authority "to use armed force to assist any such nation or group of such nations requesting assistance against armed aggression from any country controlled by international communism." The following year, Eisenhower ordered 14 thousand Marines to land in pro-Western Lebanon to discourage threatened subversion and help President Chamoun preserve internal order. Encountering no resistance beyond the startled gazes of several tourists, these landing forces did not engage in combat.

During the early years of the Vietnam conflict, Congress on several occasions expressed its support for the presidential war by voting money for military action. The year 1964 marked the nadir of congressional influence over the use of force. In that year Congress passed the Gulf of Tonkin Resolution, a document that borders on congressional abdication of responsibility over the use of military force. President Johnson submitted the text of the resolution to Congress following an attack upon the American destroyer *C. Turner Joy*, which was allegedly cruising in international waters off the coast of North Vietnam. The North Vietnamese attack, carried out by P.T. boats, was portrayed by the president as a wanton assault upon an innocent American vessel on the high seas. Unknown to congressmen at the time, the destroyer had in previous days bombarded North Vietnam with its deck guns and engaged in electronic eavesdropping on North Vietnamese communications. President Johnson used the resolution, the text of which is printed in part below, to launch the air war against North Vietnam. On more than one subsequent occasion, Johnson cited the resolution, which passed the House unanimously and met but two dissenting votes in the Senate, to demonstrate that Congress supported the escalation of the fighting in Vietnam.

GULF OF TONKIN RESOLUTION, 1964 (Excerpt)

Be it resolved by the Senate and House of Representatives of the United States of America in Congress assembled, That *the Congress approves and supports the determination of the President as Commander in Chief, to take all necessary measures* **to repel any armed attack against the forces of the United States and to prevent further aggression.**

The United States regards as vital to its national interest and to world peace the maintenance of international peace and security in Southeast Asia. Consonant with the Constitution and the Charter of the United Nations and in accordance with its obligations under the Southeast Asia Collective Defense Treaty, the *United States is, therefore, prepared, as the President determines, to take all necessary steps, including the use of armed force,* **to assist any member or protocol state of the Southeast Asia Collective Defense Treaty requesting assistance in defense of its freedom. (Italics added).**

Chairman of the Senate Foreign Relations Committee J. William Fulbright, who led the Senate campaign to approve the document, later asserted that he had never meant to authorize a war without limit as to intensity or duration. These ex post facto exculpations have a distinctly hollow ring, however. It is quite a simple matter to voice support for the president without granting an unlimited charter to take military action for as long an interval as the president deems appropriate. The language of the resolution was quite clear in what it authorized the president to do. During Senate debate on the resolution, John Sherman Cooper of Kentucky inquired, "Then, looking ahead, if the President decided that it was necessary to use such force as could lead into war, we will give that authority by this resolution?" Senator Fulbright replied, "That is the way I would interpret it."[7] Furthermore, it is difficult to avoid the speculation that few if any members of Congress would have voiced second thoughts about the resolution if the president's subsequent military ripostes had brought the Vietnam War to a speedy and successful conclusion.

As is well known, however, just the opposite occurred. As American casualties began to mount with no end to the conflict in sight, the conviction spread that the cause of the debacle was the abuse of executive authority over the armed forces. Had the decision to engage in combat been left up to Congress, many claimed, the United States would never have gotten so deeply involved in the fighting. This argument totally ignores, of course, repeated congressional assent in the American role, expressed by the passage of the numerous military appropriations bills.

In 1973, the new constitutional righteousness culminated in passage of the War Powers Act. This bill seeks to reach a compromise between the necessity for speedy military action, which can be ordered only by the president, and the desirability of congressional deliberation and input before the United States commits itself to major military action. The bill allows for three types of emergency situations in which the chief executive may commit American forces without a congressional declaration of war: to repel or forestall an attack upon the United States; to repel or forestall an attack upon American forces situated outside the country; and to rescue endangered American citizens in certain well-defined situations. Aside from those emergency conditions, the president needs "specific statutory authorization," meaning a joint resolution or the like, to use military force in the absence of a declaration of war. Even when the president uses force in emergency situations, congressional permission must be obtained to continue the action beyond 60 days (or 90 if the president determines the troops are in danger). At any time during this 60 or 90 day period, Congress can terminate the operation by concurrent resolution, which is not subject to veto.

In allowing the president to send the military into action without previous legislative sanction, the War Powers Act takes notice of the occasional need for immediate military response. In the case of Korea, for example, the North Korean invaders might have swallowed all of South Korea in less than a week had not President Truman sent American forces into action. The legislation also takes notice of the fact that there may be times when it suits the country's interests to engage in combat without a declaration of war. Aside from calling into effect various emergency regulations, a declaration of war signifies a totality of commitment that may be inappropriate for limited wars and may later hinder a compromise settlement short of unconditional surrender.

The War Powers Act has been hailed as a great victory for champions of congressional control over the use of military force.

But will the law truly enhance the legislature's voice? It is hard to think of a single instance of presidential military action since World War II that would have been aborted had the War Powers Act been in effect. In virtually every case of presidential deployment of the armed forces, Congress, backed by public opinion, has rallied around the White House and "patriotically" supported the action. On the other hand, the bill might well have prevented Roosevelt from taking vital steps in 1940 and 1941 to bolster England's fortunes against a rampaging Germany. A clever president can always make a convincing case for military action; it is only long after the 60 day period has ended that the president's decision may appear to have been in error. Congress as well as public opinion supported Presidents Kennedy and Johnson in the early years of the war in Vietnam. Any legislator who voices doubt in the early weeks of a military action is vulnerable to accusations of unpatriotic conduct and refusal to support American fighting men (and, now, women). In the early months of a military campaign, the executive branch generally has a near monopoly over battlefield information. The president could make a persuasive case that victory is around the corner, and therefore Congress should not cut short a particular military action. The president could apply further pressure on Congress, as did Johnson and Nixon in the case of Vietnam, by asserting that expressions of doubt about the war effort give aid and comfort to the enemy and in themselves prolong the war. Public opinion invariably supports the president in time of crisis and opposes any action that suggests retreat or surrender. It would appear, in short, that the War Powers Act will not prevent future presidents from sending American troops into action. (The bill did not hinder President Reagan from sending troops to Lebanon or Grenada.) The bill's greatest effect might well be to prod future presidents into intensifying their public relations efforts to convince the people and Congress that the combat in question is in America's national interest and should be continued. Should Congress acquiesce, as seems likely, the law might also weaken whatever remains of Congress's rein over the president's war making ability.

The Debate over Presidential Predominance

Aside from the War Powers Act's consequences, it is worthwhile inquiring whether predominant authority over deployment of the armed forces *should* rest with Congress or the president. In the age of airplanes and the missile, speedy action can spell the difference between victory and defeat. We have already cited Korea as a case where a prolonged decision would have enabled North Korean forces to capture the entire peninsula. A careful review of crises since World War II reveals, however, few other instances in which a two or three day delay would have been critical. In the Cuban missile crisis, President Kennedy and his advisers took ten days to decide on a response; certainly there would have been time for a congressional debate while the executive branch was pondering its own decision. Furthermore, the careful calculation born of delay can prevent hasty emotional decisions later regretted. Such hesitation might have prevented the unnecessary American troop landing in the Dominican Republic in 1965 for the alleged purpose of heading off a Communist takeover. A cooling-off period might have revealed the emptiness of the Communist threat and have thereby kept the United States from antagonizing all of Latin America through the display of the unpopular "big stick."

Proponents of presidential predominance often point to the chief executive's unique access to information. In time of crisis, they say, only the president has all the information gathered by the intelligence services and operating agencies, and is therefore in the best position to make a decision. This question is often joined with the issue of expertise. Most foreign policy experts in the government reside in the executive branch. Few members of Congress have the knowledge, time or interest to immerse themselves in foreign policy. The president, commanding the government's very best information and expertise, is in a far better position than Congress to make correct decisions, according to this view. Critics of this contention invite one to consult the record. For most of the years following World War II, the executive has dominated foreign policy. Have all this intelligence information and expertise produced a satisfactory record? This is not the place to answer such an open-ended question with finality. Suffice it to say that many foreign policy observers remain unsatisfied with the post-World War II record of American foreign policy. Vietnam was the major debacle of this era, but critics cite other failures as well. Why, they ask, did it take so long for the United States to recognize that the Soviet Union was outspending America for military purposes? What accounts for the weakness of the American response to leftist movements in southern Africa? How is it possible to explain the overthrow of the shah of Iran, given extensive American involvement in that country? What accounts for the inability of the United States to persuade the oil producers to hold down the price of petroleum? Is there nothing the United States can do to shore up the flagging NATO alliance? Critics who dwell on these and other blunders would release important information to Congress, and let the lawmakers try their hand at foreign policy. If it be objected that providing information to 535 legislators is equivalent to releasing it to the world, then such information could be restricted to members of the Foreign Relations or Armed Services committees. Legislators, being closer than the executive bureaucracy to the people, have a better idea of what the populace wants in foreign as well as domestic matters, the argument concludes.

Perhaps the strongest case for a vital legislative voice in foreign policy concerns a paramount purpose of that policy, namely, the preservation of democracy itself. Foreign policy is designed to accomplish more than the protection of those chunks of real estate that make up the country. Foreign policy is also intended to preserve the values that make up the "American way of life," one of those values being democratic government. The undue preponderance of executive authority represents a threat to democracy. As Louis Brandeis, dissenting in *Myers* v. *U.S.* (1926), wrote:

> The doctrine of the separation of powers was adopted by the convention of 1787, not to promote efficiency but to preclude the exercise of arbitrary power. The purpose was, not to avoid friction, but, by means of the inevitable friction incident to the distribution of the governmental powers among three departments, to save the people from autocracy.

As the following passage makes clear, depriving Congress of the foreign policy role assigned to it in the Constitution subverts the very purpose of foreign policy.

> Foreign policy is not an end in itself. We do not have a foreign policy because it is interesting or fun, or because it satisfies some basic human need; we conduct foreign policy for a purpose external to itself, the purpose of securing democratic values in our own country. These values are largely expressed in *processes*—in the *way* in which we pass laws, the *way* in which we administer justice, and the *way* in which government deals with individuals. The means of a democracy *are* its ends; when we set aside democratic procedures in making our foreign policy, we are undermining the purpose of that policy. It is always dangerous to sacrifice means to ostensible ends, but when an instrument such as foreign policy is treated as an end in itself, and when the processes by which it is made—whose preservation is the very objective of foreign policy—are then sacrificed to it, it is the end that is being sacrificed to the means. Such a foreign policy is not only

inefficient but positively destructive of the purposes it is meant to serve.[8]

The question of legislative versus executive participation in the foreign policy process is not likely to be resolved soon, if ever. People of integrity will continue to advance valid arguments in support of each point of view. During the late 1960s and 1970s, many Americans were troubled by the practically unchallenged executive dominance of foreign policy in preceding decades. As we shall see in Chapter 10, this reaction led to a reassertion of congressional participation in foreign policy. In the early 1980s, the executive-legislative balance returned to the more nearly equal position foreseen by the Founding Fathers, although the executive branch remained clearly supreme.

PRESIDENTIAL ADVISERS IN FOREIGN POLICY

It has often been stated that the presidency is too big a job for any single person. The American president is not just head of government but also of state. The first role involves submitting legislation to Congress, appointing members of regulatory commissions and courts, campaigning locally on behalf of loyal members of the president's political party, determining policy priorities as reflected in the federal budget and fighting for them in Congress, rallying the citizenry behind the president's pet political projects, running for reelection to a second term, directing the massive federal bureaucracy, and conducting an enormous amount of other business. As head of state, the president signs treaties, makes July 4th speeches, welcomes foreign dignitaries, makes official trips abroad, greets delegations of students at the White House, and performs countless other duties. Many governments divide these duties between a prime minister (head of government) and president or king/queen (head of state). The combination of these two roles in the American presidency gives that office extraordinary power. With that power goes more responsibility than any one person can manage.

For assistance in carrying out these responsibilities, the president relies on a group of persons referred to as "the administration." These are not career civil servants but rather people appointed by the president; when the president's term of office expires, members of the administration also expect to leave. The administration includes the secretaries of Cabinet departments as well as undersecretaries and assistant secretaries. The White House Staff, to be described shortly, is also part of the administration, as are the directors of such agencies as the Agency for International Development and the Arms Control and Disaramament Agency. In addition, the people chosen by the above for their own staffs are part of the administration. The basic function of the administration is to ensure that the executive branch implements the president's policy. The members of an administration also help the president make policy. An administration may be compared to a giant bureaucratic octopus, with the head representing the president and the tentacles representing the people appointed by the president to run the various departments and agencies. The tentacles are supposed to carry out motions emanating from the head, not from their own volition. As we shall see, however, some of the tentacles have minds of their own.

❦ With the unprecedented degree of government activity that arose in connection with Franklin D. Roosevelt's New Deal, a new layer of presidential assistants came into being. These new assistants are gathered in the Executive Office, a now sprawling collectivity of organizations whose personnel total approximately 1,500 people. (See Fig. 7–1). Many of these individuals work in the Executive Office Building just west of the White House.

An even more intimate group of presidential advisers is housed in the White House itself. Appropriately enough, these individuals are known as the White House Staff, and they too are part of the Executive Office. As the responsibilities of government have expanded since World War II, the White House Staff has grown accordingly. In 1980 it numbered approximately 350. Their job is to help the president make policy and see to it that those policies are implemented effectively. The composition and assignments of the White House Staff change as the agenda of government changes. For our purposes, the most important member of the White House Staff is the president's special assistant for national security, a post held in recent years by Henry Kissinger (under Nixon), Zbigniew Brzezinski (under Carter), and George Allen, William P. Clark and Robert C. MacFarlane (under Reagan).

The special assistant joins the president and secretary of state as having primary responsibility for foreign policy. But why does the government need three individuals for the same task? Who in fact does have final responsibility for American foreign policy? In seeking to answer these questions, we come face to face with one of the most perplexing issues in the conduct of foreign policy, namely, the problem of coordination.

FIGURE 7–1: EXECUTIVE OFFICE OF THE PRESIDENT

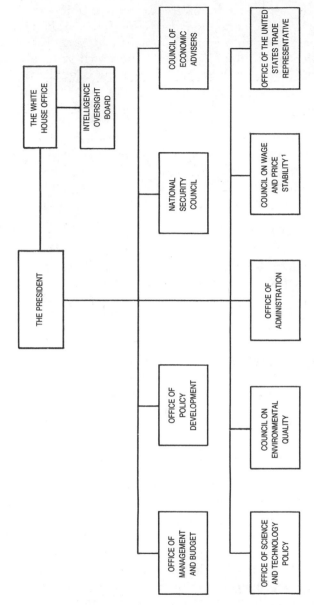

[1]The Council, with an appropriation authorization through the fiscal year ending September 30, 1981, became inactive as of June 5, 1981 due to a recession in funding. See Pub. Law 97–12 of June 5, 1981 (95 Stat. 74).

Source: Office of the Federal Register, *United States Government Manual*, 1981–1982, p. 821.

The Problem of Coordination

To comprehend the problem of coordination, imagine yourself present at a regatta featuring a race by eight-oared shells. One of the shells is exhibiting decidedly strange behavior. In the bow, the diminutive coxswain is barking orders through a small megaphone. One of the oarsmen, however, is back-paddling. Another is engaged in a splashing contest with yet a third. A fourth contemplates other matters while letting an oar trail in the water, and the fifth has jettisoned his oar altogether. The other three are dutifully rowing to the coxswain's beat. Obviously, any boat that displayed such antics would be lucky to stay afloat, let alone win a race.

While the analogy may be overdrawn, the US government behaves at times in a similar manner. At the helm sits the president, barking orders to the crew. But some of the crew members seek to torpedo the president's policy; others exhibit decided indifference; certain members are more interested in personal and organizational rivalries than the steady course of the vessel; and still others work diligently in support of their captain. Sometimes, the system works well enough and the craft makes a splendid showing. At other times, however, the ship of state founders on the shoals of cross-purposes. Let us explore this important problem more fully.

Crisis diplomacy aside, policy making is handled through standard bureaucratic procedures. Below, we take a typical policy issue and trace its likely development through the decision stage. While we are not here recounting an actual policy debate, we shall choose an issue that has arisen in recent years, namely, the question of whether to sell advanced fighter aircraft to Saudi Arabia.

This matter might become an issue for government consideration when a Pentagon weapons team, on an inspection and good will tour of the Middle East, receives a request for the aircraft from the Saudi high command. Upon returning to Washington, the leader of the team communicates the request to the secretary of defense, who then raises the issue either at a meeting of the National Security Council, at a luncheon with the secretary of state, or at an informal meeting with the president. The president or the special assistant for national security would then direct those departments and agencies with an interest in the matter and expertise on the subject to draft memoranda setting forth their views. Following the submission of these memoranda, a meeting of top officials from these organizations would be scheduled to recommend a policy. This recommendation would then go to the president for a final decision.

Which agencies and departments should the special assistant direct to submit memoranda? Certainly the State Department should be contacted. The CIA might be able to contribute important intelligence assessments. The Defense Department could surely shed light on whether the Saudis could fly and maintain the aircraft, as well as the extent to which the arms transfer would advance American security interests. But might not there be other departments and agencies with a rightful interest in the matter and helpful information to contribute? The Arms Control and Disarmament Agency, for example, might feel that the decision could have a telling effect on the chances for arms control in the Middle East, and so that agency would insist on being included in the policy debate. Since the potential sale would involve the sum of over a billion dollars, the Commerce Department would no doubt desire a say in the decision. Such a hefty sum would surely influence the nation's balance of payments, and so the Treasury Department would wish to submit a policy memorandum. Since Saudi Arabia has a determining voice in setting policies of the Organization of Petroleum Exporting Countries (OPEC), the Department of Energy would feel entitled to contribute its views. Finally, such a sale would have an effect on America's image abroad, and so the International Communications Agency, charged with creating a favorable impression of the United States overseas, would wish to submit a policy recommendation.

Like the design woven into an oriental rug, the decision-making situation gains in complexity as one moves in for a closer look. On most issues, the agencies and departments participating in the decision will not agree. Peering even closer, we find that within each of these units, considerable disagreement is likely to exist. Consider, for a moment, the views likely to prevail in different elements of the State Department as they are asked to contribute to State's draft on the sale of the airplanes. The Saudi desk is likely to approve the sale, as it would certainly enhance relations between the US and Saudi Arabia. But down the hall, the officers on the Israeli desk would argue most strenuously that such a transaction would antagonize America's only trustworthy and democratic ally in the Middle East, Israel. The Office of Politico-Military Affairs might favor the sale on the ground that it would fortify a pro-Western, anti-Soviet regime. The Bureau of Economic Affairs, still in State, might advocate the sale, as it would improve America's overall economic standing. Yet another unit in State, the Bureau of Congressional Relations, might oppose the transaction because the pro-Israeli faction in Congress would try to shoot it down, thereby complicating State's not too favorable relations with Congress across the board. Through a series of written drafts and discussions over the course of several weeks, the State Department will eventually evolve a single point of view on the proposed sale and submit its policy paper to the special assistant. Similar internal debates will occur in the other departments and agencies involved in the deliberations. Eventually, each will come forward with a memorandum setting forth its policy recommendations. These recommendations will not necessarily be restricted to a simple approval or disapproval of the sale. Each department may suggest that the sale be modified to include a larger or smaller number of airplanes, perhaps a mix of different types of aircraft, a variety of credit terms, or outright rejection of the sale.

The problem of coordination arises in orchestrating the policy debate. Over 40 departments and agencies are involved in American foreign policy; some of these groups are listed below:

Foreign Policy Departments and Agencies

Agency for International Development
Agriculture Department
American Battle Monuments Commission
Bureau of Narcotics and Dangerous Drugs
Central Intelligence Agency
Commerce Department
Customs Bureau
Defense Department
Energy Department
Environmental Science Services Administration
Export-Import Bank
Federal Aviation Administration
Federal Bureau of Investigation
Foreign Agriculture Service
General Services Administration
Health and Human Services Department
Housing and Urban Development Department
Immigration and Naturalization Service
Interior Department
Internal Revenue Service
Justice Department
Labor Department
Maritime Administration

National Aeronautics and Space Administration
National Science Foundation
Peace Corps
Public Health Service
Smithsonian Institution
State Department
Tennessee Valley Authority
Transportation Department
United States Information Agency (International Communi-
cations Agency)
United States Travel Service
Veterans Administration

While we often view the State Department as the primary foreign policy organization, less than 10 percent of all American personnel handling foreign policy are housed in State. The entire Foreign Service—the State Department's overseas cadre—numbers only 3,500, and many of these individuals can be found in Washington on their regular rotation home. Outnumbered and outfinanced—on both scales State is the smallest Cabinet-level department—the State Department is in no position to command other departments and agencies involved in foreign policy. Indeed, State is just another player among equals in the policy-making game; it lacks authority to issue orders to other Cabinet departments and their personnel telling them how to behave in matters of foreign policy. Nor is any other department or agency given the responsibility of orchestrating the policy-making process, a task which seems essential if the nation is to have a consistent and coherent foreign policy. Even the president, as titular head of the nation, participates in the policy debates less as a commanding general than an ardent suitor. It is in this sense that non-crisis policy making resembles the eight-oared shell mentioned earlier. While the president, in the end, is empowered to make the decision, top aides will desert the ship if they are constantly overruled. Consequently, the president often makes compromises just as the assistants do. Roger Hilsman, an assistant secretary of state in the Kennedy administration, describes the "politics of policymaking" in these words:

> In a major problem of foreign affairs, as we have said, the advo-
> cate of a particular policy—even if there is neither a rival advocate
> nor a rival policy—must build a consensus to support his policy in
> the different constituencies within the government and frequently
> outside as well. He needs the active co-operation and support of some,

the formal or informal approval of others, and at least the acquiescence of still others. He may prevail over the active opposition of one or another constituency, but rarely if it is from within the government and the enterprise is large. For even passive opposition can bring a large and complicated enterprise to failure, not by sabotage, but simply lack of enthusiasm. When there are rival advocates or rival policies, on the other hand, there is not only debate before the different constituencies, but competition for their support. Alliances are formed, and all the techniques of consensus-building appear—persuasions, accommodation, and bargaining.

Over some of this at certain times, the President may merely preside—if it is a matter of slight interest to him and has little impact on his position. But if *he* is an advocate or if the outcome affects *his* position and power, then the President, too, must engage in the politics of policymaking.[9]

It must be added that the constraints of time prevent the president from so intervening except on the most important of questions.

The problem of coordination reduces itself to three questions. (1) Who should identify the issues that need to be studied, so as to ensure that all important foreign policy questions are being considered? (2) Who should supervise the process whereby policy recommendations are developed? (3) Who should decide what policy to adopt once these recommendations have been submitted?

Should these responsibilities fall to the president, overburdened with duties as he is? Should the secretary of state take charge? Is the president's special assistant in the best position to handle these duties, acting as the alter-ego of the chief executive? Might not the vice president be suited for these tasks? Is an inter-agency body the best place to deliberate such matters? These queries suggest some of the solutions that have been posed to the problem of coordination. During the remainder of this chapter and throughout the next, we shall make frequent reference to this important problem, concluding with some suggestions for improving the policy process.

The Special Assistant for National Security

In recent years, an important presidential adviser on foreign policy has been the special assistant for national security. The special assistant's office is located in the White House, since it is part of the White House Staff.

Creating a special assistant for national security was one means of coping with the problem of coordination. Hand-picked by the president, the special assistant is in a position to stand above the operating departments (State, Defense, etc.) and coordinate their activities. While each department is responsible for a single facet of foreign policy (defense, propaganda, energy, etc.), the special assistant's jurisdiction embraces the entire foreign policy spectrum. Furthermore, as we shall see in the next chapter, each department and agency, in the course of policy debates, is inclined to provide data in support of its own policy preference. The special assistant, unencumbered by departmental prejudice, can evaluate such evidence objectively. Closeness to the chief occupant of the White House gives the special assistant the opportunity to direct the nation's foreign policy so as to mirror the preferences of the president.

The duties of the special assistant are not spelled out in any legislation. Each president decides what the special assistant should do. These responsibilities can be quite varied. The special assistant can render policy advice. In consultation with a staff of experts, the assistant can draft policy papers that are then circulated among the operating agencies for comment and possible modification. Some special assistants have taken responsibility for deciding which issues the policy-making community should study; this agenda-setting function often rises to the fore at the beginning of an administration. The special assistant can also engage in diplomatic negotiations, as did Henry Kissinger on a 1971 secret mission to Peking to arrange for Nixon's subsequent visit to that city, or assist in policy making when a crisis arises, as Zbigniew Brzezinski did in 1979 when Russia invaded Afghanistan. If the president so desires, the special assistant can be responsible for presenting a variety of options on a particular policy problem or for fashioning a consensus from the policy-making community and placing that consensus upon the president's desk.

The real organization of government at higher echelons is not what you find in textbooks or organizational charts. It is how confidence flows down from the President.
Secretary of State Dean Rusk

For purposes of illustration, we can identify two models of behavior for the special assistant. The "facilitator" model sees the special assistant as a neutral coordinator of the operating agencies. In such a role, the special assistant's own policy preferences are suppressed. The concern here is more with the creation and operation of a smoothly functioning policy-making process than with the proposals that this process generates. The special assistant's abilities as a mediator or broker are crucial in this role. The facilitator also sees to it that the operating departments and agencies are following the president's policies, even if the career experts believe these policies to be in error. The facilitator ensures that major foreign policy problems, to be distinguished from immediate crises, are being studied by the appropriate agencies, and takes account of intelligence projections to order contingency planning.

The other role model for the special assistant is the "advocate." In this conception of the office, the special assistant's main function is to make policy recommendations to the president, as one of the president's chief foreign policy advisers, competing with the secretary of state and the heads of other operating agencies in an effort to shape American foreign policy. Utilizing a separate staff of experts, the special assistant drafts policy papers and submits them to the president. Most recent special assistants have emphasized this advocate role, while combining with it certain duties of the facilitator.

Henry Kissinger combined both roles with great effect during the Nixon administration. Brzezinski also joined both roles under President Carter, although Brzezinski did not wield as much influence as Kissinger. Special assistants who are both facilitator and advocate gain an enormous degree of power. Not only do they have opportunities to influence the president, but they also control the access of rivals to the Oval Office. This is not to say that they will systematically intercept all competing ideas but that they may at times succumb to the natural urge to do so. By setting the foreign policy agenda, they can affect the outcome of inter-agency deliberations. Acting as a gatekeeper, the special assistant is in a position to limit contact between the president and the heads of operating agencies, and has a certain capacity to minimize the persuasiveness of rival ideas that are seeking their way toward the president.[10] It is perhaps easier to comprehend these models by examining the actual behavior of some past special assistants. In doing so, we must keep in mind the essential fact that the president has the largest influence over the role to be played by the special assistant. The president will convey a preference for a facilitator or an advocate or both; the special assistant will either conform or be asked to resign.

President Truman felt that the chief executive should play an active role in policy formulation, both foreign and domestic. He also had strong views on many topics, particularly foreign policy. Consequently, he viewed the special assistant as a facilitator rather than an advocate, and he solicited policy advice from his forceful secretary of state, Dean Acheson. Truman wished his aides to gather and place before him the views of his leading officials, so that he himself could make a decision based on the widest range of choices. It was the special assistant's job to collect these views and present them to the president.

President Eisenhower took a far more restrained view of the presidency than Truman. Eisenhower pictured himself as a sheriff, whose job it was to enforce existing laws and policies. Eisenhower's operating style was also radically different from that of his feisty predecessor. The mellow, relaxed, constantly smiling ex-general was far less inclined than Truman to participate directly in policy making, preferring to intervene at the last stage of policy formulation to make a final decision. Accustomed to the bureaucratic hierarchies found in the military, Eisenhower delegated a greal deal of authority to subordinates, who in turn directed the activities of various inter-agency study groups. While Truman would participate actively in day-to-day policy making, meeting and exchanging ideas frequently with Cabinet members and White House assistants, Eisenhower preferred to remain above the process and review policy recommendations after the bureaucracy had drafted them.

Eisenhower's first special assistant for national security was Robert Cutler. Like his successor, Cutler was more a facilitator than advocate. His primary duty was to supervise the elaborate organizational structure of the NSC and communicate the NSC's recommendations to the president. Had Cutler espoused stronger views on foreign policy, he would have run head on into conflict with Eisenhower's chief foreign policy adviser, Secretary of State John Foster Dulles. Indeed, Dulles's influence with Eisenhower was so great that the secretary's policy recommendations often superseded the recommendations that emerged from the channels that Cutler directed.

John F. Kennedy expressed his conception of the presidency as "a Chief Executive who is the vital center of action in our whole scheme of government." In this respect, he was much like Truman. Rejecting Eisenhower's caretaker approach, Kennedy involved himself personally in efforts to reshape both foreign and domestic policy. At first, Kennedy hoped that Secretary of State Dean Rusk would become his principal foreign policy adviser. However, Kennedy soon became disenchanted with Rusk and the State Department bureaucracy, and the president turned more and more to his

delayed, way-laid

special assistant for policy guidance. Under Kennedy, McGeorge Bundy and later Walt Rostow (who remained on during the Johnson presidency) became important policy advocates. Kennedy saw himself as a policy innovator, and took the initiative in identifying the issues on which the departments and agencies should work. Possessed of a clear conception of the new pathways he wished to chart, Kennedy was not content to allow his subordinates to choose which issues needed to be examined. Kennedy rarely called meetings of the White House Staff or the National Security Council, preferring instead ad hoc meetings with selected assistants when he deemed it necessary.[11] The persuasiveness of Bundy and Rostow with the president gave them considerable policy influence during the Kennedy administration. Both these special assistants followed the advocate rather than the facilitator role, as Kennedy had little use for the latter.

Under the tenure of Henry Kissinger, the special assistant attained its zenith of influence. Kissinger proved able to exploit the potentialities of both facilitator and advocate so as to practically make foreign policy, especially after Nixon became so preoccupied with Watergate that he devoted little attention to other matters. Brzezinski too combined the roles of facilitator and advocate. As Carter's term progressed, however, Brzezinski became an increasingly voluble advocate. Carter's special assistant had a major say in numerous policy areas, including normalization of relations with China, development of the MX missile, and the imposition of sanctions against the Soviet Union after its military intervention in Afghanistan.

The heightened importance of recent special assistants as policy advocates has brought into focus the rivalry between this office and that of secretary of state. So long as the special assistant remained a facilitator, this overlapping of responsibilities proved little cause for concern. However, Walt Rostow, Henry Kissinger and Zbigniew Brzezinski all overshadowed the secretaries of state serving with them. Such competition can have harmful results for foreign policy. When the special assistant and the secretary have different views, America's adversaries and allies, not to mention Congress and the public, get confused about who really speaks for the administration. Such a situation arose not infrequently under President Carter. Brzezinski held more hard-line views about relations with the Soviet Union than Secretary Vance, and there was often uncertainty about which position was accepted by the president. The rivalry between these two top aides can also interfere with the special assistant's duties as facilitator. If the president solicits foreign policy views from the special assistant, that person may be inclined to keep from the president the conflicting opinions of other top officials. If the special assistant does not allow various points of view to get through to the president, there may be no other channel for these opinions to follow. Thus, a special assistant who acts primarily as an advocate may isolate the president from debates in the foreign policy community, and this could interfere with the president's selection of the optimal foreign policy for the United States. Furthermore, if other top officials perceive the special assistant as a single-minded defender of a given point of view, they will seek to circumvent the assistant in order to reach the president. This is bound to disrupt the policy-making process and heighten divisiveness within an administration.

It might be said that the secretary of state could fulfill these tasks as well as the special assistant. However, the secretary is to some extent a prisoner of departmental prejudices. Of greater significance in accounting for the reduced role of the secretary, however, has been the disenchantment among recent presidents with the performance of the State Department and its head. This disappointment goes back to President Kennedy, who as we have seen lost faith in Dean Rusk's capacity to take a leading role in the formulation and execution of foreign policy. Regarding Nixon's view of the State Department, Kissinger had this to say:

> He had very little confidence in the State Department. Its personnel had no loyalty to him; the Foreign Service had disdained him as Vice President and ignored him the moment he was out of office. He was determined to run foreign policy from the White House.[12]

President Carter, particularly in the latter period of his term, often took his special assistant's hard-line advice over that of his secretary of state, and President Reagan fired Secretary Haig over policy and personality disputes.

Kissinger, who served as both special assistant and secretary of state, has reflected upon the proper roles for these two offices:

> I have become convinced that a President should make the Secretary of State his principal adviser and use the national security adviser primarily as a senior administrator and coordinator to make certain that each significant point of view is heard. If the security adviser becomes active in the development and articulation of policy he must inevitably diminish the Secretary of State and reduce his effectiveness. Foreign governments are confused and, equally dangerous, given opportunities to play one part of our government off against the other;

the State Department becomes demoralized and retreats into parochialism. If the President does not have confidence in his Secretary of State he should replace him, not supervise him with a personal aide.[13]

Despite this admonition, Kissinger, the special assistant, greatly overshadowed William P. Rogers, secretary of state during most of the Nixon administration.

Finally, it needs to be stressed again that it is the president who determines the relationship between the secretary of state and the special assistant. If the chief executive looks to the special assistant for policy advice, the latter will become an advocate rather than a facilitator. If the president displays more confidence in the secretary of state, as Truman did with Secretary Acheson, then the latter will predominate in foreign policy. The president may prefer to let the two aides fight it out between themselves for predominance. When this happens, however, the likelihood for a discordant administration rises dramatically. Again, Kissinger's words are instructive.

> In the final analysis the influence of a Presidential Assistant derives almost exclusively from the confidence of the President, not from administrative arrangements.... Propinquity counts for much; the opportunity to confer with the President several times a day is often of decisive importance, much more so than the chairmanship of committees or the right to present options. For reasons that must be left to students of psychology, every President since Kennedy seems to have trusted his White House aides more than his Cabinet. It may be because they are even more dependent on him; it may be that unencumbered by the pressures of managing a large bureaucracy the Presidential Assistants can cater more fully to Presidential whims; it may be as simple as the psychological reassurance conferred by proximity just down the hall.[14]

The ascending importance of the special assistant under Kissinger and Brzezinski has led some observers to insist that the position be more accountable. As we have said, the special assistant is appointed by the president without Senate confirmation. Unlike the secretary of state, who does require Senate confirmation, the special assistant need not (and usually does not) testify before congressional committees, under the doctrine of executive privilege. According to this doctrine, the president and the president's aides can discuss matters thoroughly only if persuaded that their exchanges will remain private. The special assistant, in short, is accountable to no one but the president. Given the special assistant's enormous influence, some people have called for Senate confirmation of the appointee, and some have even gone so far as to suggest that the office of the special assistant be elective. Neither of these ideas is likely to be implemented, however. Senate confirmation would dissolve the special personal relationship between the president and the special assistant, making the latter less dependent on the former's approval. Less closely linked to the president, the special assistant might be less zealous in carrying out the president's wishes. The president would in all probability hire someone else, beholden only to the White House, to take over many of the duties of the special assistant, thereby giving rise to the problem anew. If the special assistant were elected, there would be a question concerning who held final responsibility for American foreign policy, the president or the special assistant. This practice could lead to the existence of two chief executives: one for domestic policy and a new one, the elected special assistant, for foreign policy. In case of disagreement between these two individuals, which elected representative of the people should prevail? Electing the special assistant appears to be a remedy that is worse than the original ailment.

The Office of Management and Budget

As anyone who has managed a family checking account knows, decisions regarding expenditures are also decisions about program priorities. Put another way, budgetary decisions are also policy decisions. The Office of Management and Budget (OMB), part of the Executive Office, exists to help the president reconcile and choose among the various policy alternatives clamoring for funds. Thus, OMB also assists in the coordination of foreign policy.

OMB is headed by a director, who is appointed by the president with Senate confirmation (since 1974). The 650 professional staffers at OMB assist in the formulation of foreign policy in two ways. First, they help the president allocate funds between foreign and domestic programs. Secondly, they assist the chief executive in parceling out the money earmarked for foreign policy among different foreign policy objectives.

As the next fiscal year approaches, each department and agency submits to OMB a request for funds. Officials must justify their requests by explaining how the money will be used. The total of all these requests invariably exceeds available funds, and this condition of scarcity brings OMB into action. Working with the president, the director of OMB determines policy priorities and allocates funds to each executive department and agency. The president, while not determining exactly how many pennies to devote to each program, does indicate priorities to OMB's director. Often, the special assistant for national security is brought into these discussions, as are other presidential aides. The president's request for funds provides an indication of the order of priorities. In foreign policy, the budget request signals the relative importance the president attaches to foreign aid, military bases overseas, cultural exchange, new weapons systems, propaganda, refugee relief, energy exploration, and the like. Once OMB and the president assemble the federal budget, the document goes to Congress in January as a request for funds for the fiscal year beginning next October 1. Congress may then increase or diminish each line item, thereby forcing modification of the president's expectations and plans. Since few programs can be effected without money, the annual federal budget is one of the most important documents in the determination of both foreign and domestic policy.

OMB also assists in the efficient management of the executive branch. It provides technical assistance in the preparation of plans for organizational restructuring and helps with the orderly operation of departments as they presently exist. OMB also monitors the performance of executive agencies and evaluates the extent to which they are achieving their stated goals.

THE NATIONAL SECURITY COUNCIL

Shortly after the conclusion of World War II, two facts stared American policymakers squarely in the eyes. First, the end of the Second World War had not ushered in a period of peace and tranquility but had introduced an era of tension and conflict between the United States and the Soviet Union. Secondly, if the United States were to prevail in this conflict, the country needed a mechanism for making and implementing foreign policy across a wide global reach.

To meet this challenge, Congress in 1947 passed the National Security Act. This legislation created a new Department of Defense and provided that a civilian secretary head this Cabinet-level department. To ensure the coordination of foreign policy across the spectrum of political and military and economic fronts, the law established the National Security Council (NSC). As stated in the act, the role of the NSC is "to advise the President with respect to the integration of domestic, foreign, and military policies relating to the national security so as to enable the military services and other departments and agencies of the Government to cooperate more effectively in matters involving the national security." The act also created the Central Intelligence Agency and placed it under the National Security Council.

The NSC was the product of a perception that during the Second World War there had been insufficient consideration of the political consequences of military actions taken to win the war. It was perhaps understandable that Allied leaders, desirous of putting an end to the killing and destruction of property, sought to end the fighting as quickly as possible. In retrospect, however, some of the military decisions taken during the final years of the conflict seemed to have been shortsighted. For example, the decision to enlist Russian assistance in the struggle with Japan resulted in Soviet control of North Korea. Of even greater consequence was the decision to invade Europe at Normandy and drive eastward toward Berlin. Winston Churchill, with an eye to the post-war situation, urged the Allies to land instead in the Balkans and arc through Eastern Europe toward the German capital; this maneuver would leave Allied troops in control of Eastern Europe after the surrender of Germany. Churchill's plan was rejected because military leaders thought it would take longer and produce more Allied casualties than a Normandy landing. The latter plan left the Red Army in control of Eastern Europe, just as Churchill had feared. With the war over, many strategists became convinced that the British leader had been correct. More fundamentally, they were troubled by a seeming gap between military and political or diplomatic policy-making. The decision to land at Normandy was taken on purely military grounds; there had not been sufficient dialogue between the generals and the diplomats.[15] This chasm, it was feared, could in the future lead to the undertaking of political commitments, such as the defense of certain areas, without sufficient military resources. The achievement of better coordination between military policy and diplomatic policy was one of the primary purposes of creating the NSC. Thus, the NSC represents another way of contending with the problem of coordination.

A glance at the membership of the NSC reveals how this coordination between military and political planning is to occur. The National Security Act (as modified) specifies the following individuals as members of the NSC: president, vice president, secretary of state, and secretary of defense. By including the secretaries of state and defense, the NSC aspires to make sure that both military and diplomatic considerations are taken into account whenever the government reaches a foreign policy decision. The statute further names the director of the Central Intelligence Agency and the chairman of the Joint Chiefs of Staff as advisers to the NSC. These individuals are charged with contributing relevant policy advice to NSC deliberations. Furthermore, there is nothing in the statute to prevent the president from asking other officials to attend NSC meetings when their areas of responsibility are under consideration. Thus, as many as one or two dozen persons may attend meetings of the NSC.

In establishing the NSC, the authors of the National Security Act took care not to prescribe overly restrictive regulations for the operation of that body. The law says nothing about the frequency with which the NSC meets, nor does it compel the president or anyone else to follow NSC decisions. The NSC was designed as an advisory body to help the president make foreign policy. Presidents may rely on it extensively, as Eisenhower and Nixon did, or can practically ignore it, like Kennedy or Johnson. It is up to the president to decide whether to handle a problem through the NSC or to use other channels, such as private discussions with the special assistant, delegation to the State Department, or consultation with trusted friends. The president or, more typically, the special assistant, decides how frequently the NSC will meet, who shall attend, and what topics will be considered. The underlying point here is that the NSC is strictly an advisory body to be utilized as the president desires, either extensively (the Nixon-Eisenhower approach) or very little (the Kennedy-Johnson approach).

Both Nixon and Eisenhower viewed the NSC as the apex of an institutionalized system of policy formulation. Under each of these heads of state, the NSC served as the principal channel for foreign policy formulation. A look at the operation of the NSC under Nixon will make this approach clearer.

When President Nixon took office in 1969, he promptly announced that the NSC would be his principal forum for the formulation of foreign policy. Working closely with Kissinger, whom Nixon directed to oversee the NSC, the president designed a fairly elaborate bureaucratic structure for the handling of foreign policy. The main elements of this structure are depicted in Fig. 7–2.

Policy formulation in this system began with a proposal to study a particular foreign policy problem. The proposal might come from the State Department, the special assistant, the Treasury Department, the president, or elsewhere among the higher reaches of the

FIGURE 7–2: NATIONAL SECURITY COUNCIL UNDER .
PRESIDENT NIXON

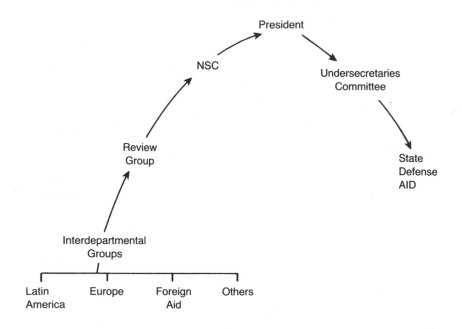

Auxiliary bodies: Defense Program Review Committee
Washington Special Actions Group
Verification Panel
Vietnam Special Studies Group

foreign policy bureaucracy. This proposal went to Kissinger; if he approved it, he would then send it to the appropriate Interdepartmental Group. These groups represented the lowest level within the NSC structure. Chaired by an assistant secretary of state, each group concerned itself with a geographic area or a topical area, such as foreign aid or energy policy. On each group sat a representative from Kissinger's office, the State Department (chairman), the CIA, the Defense Department, and other agencies invited by the chairman. After receiving an assignment from Kissinger, the chairman directed the group to study the issue and prepare a policy paper. Usually, the paper analyzed the assigned problem, summarized policy choices and analyzed the pros and cons of each course of action. The groups also prepared contingency papers on potential crises in their areas of responsibility.

Policy papers then proceeded to the Review Group, which acted as a clearing house for the full NSC. Chaired by Kissinger, the Review Group included representatives from the departments of State and Defense, CIA, the Joint Chiefs of Staff, and any other departments and agencies that had a significant interest in or expertise to contribute to the matter at hand. These representatives were generally at the next highest level above the assistant secretary. In going over papers submitted by the Interdepartmental Groups, the Review Group made sure they presented all realistic alternatives; that they set forth all relevant facts, including monetary costs of each policy alternative; and that the views of all the departments that worked on the document were fairly represented. Before the Review Group certified the paper as ready for NSC action, the group might write additional drafts of the document. The group then transmitted it to the NSC.[16]

*Under Presidents Nixon and Eisenhower, the NSC met on a regular basis, normally 30 or 40 times each year. During the Nixon administration, Kissinger scheduled the meetings, prepared the agendas, circulated material in advance, and often chaired the meetings. Sometimes Nixon would participate actively in the discussions, while at other times he mostly listened. Occasionally the NSC devoted several meetings over the course of many weeks to a single issue. Eventually, the council would agree upon a policy recommendation or set forth different recommendations complete with supporting material. Eisenhower, who rarely attended NSC meetings, insisted that the NSC produce a consensus that he could either accept or veto. Nixon, on the other hand, preferred a set of alternatives if the members could not reach agreement. In any case, at the conclusion of its deliberations, the NSC sent a document to the president with its recommendations. Nixon would then ponder the matter at a later time, usually in his accustomed manner of reflection in isolation, and come to a decision. He rarely made a decision at the NSC meeting itself.

Should the president approve an NSC recommendation, it is then necessary to see that the decision gets implemented. This was the task of the Undersecretaries Committee. The chairman of this body was the undersecretary of state, an assignment that gave State prime responsibility for policy execution. Leading officials from the same departments and agencies found on the other NSC units also served on the Undersecretaries Committee. The committee would assign tasks to the appropriate departments and agencies as called for in the president's decision, and it would review progress in executing decisions (reporting back to Kissinger).

The weeks or months it took for the entire NSC structure to complete a policy review meant that the organization was suited only to broad issues that did not require immediate resolution. Thus, the NSC might examine such issues as the role of tactical nuclear weapons in Europe, means of promoting democratic government in Latin America, the guarantee of oil supplies to the Western world and Japan, long-term strategy toward the government of South Africa, and the like. At times, however, unforeseen developments calling for rapid decisions arise in the conduct of foreign policy. To help the government cope with such situations, the NSC structure included the Washington Special Actions Group (WSAG). The WSAG drafted contingency plans for potential crises, setting forth the responsibilities of each department and agency in case the contingency materialized. WSAG also convened when a crisis occurred and attempted to resolve it.

The Defense Program Review Committee, another unit in the NSC structure, had the assignment under Nixon of reconciling foreign policy options with available resources. The committee evaluated the feasibility of foreign policy options in light of available funds. This procedure was designed to avoid the common practice of making foreign policy decisions only to discover that insufficient resources were available to implement them.

Every administration finds itself saddled with highly visible problems that require constant attention. To handle these issues, the NSC created topic-related sub-units. Each of these was responsible for a single problem area. Under Nixon, such groups were set up for Vietnam planning (Vietnam Special Studies Group), for SALT (Verification Panel) and for various other issues.

The Nixon-Eisenhower approach to the NSC has many virtues, but it is not without its flaws. Through the NSC's regular schedule of meetings and its multi-level structure, all the important foreign policy issues facing the United States are likely to receive consideration in due course. Involvement in NSC discussions also helps educate the top officials in government. We must remember that many, indeed most, of these individuals have come from the world of business and law and are likely to be unversed in foreign policy. Participation in NSC debates acquaints these officials with the nuances of the major policy issues of the day. Furthermore, the system as guided by Nixon (but not Eisenhower) is capable of bringing to the president various points of view and policy alternatives.

The deficiencies of the NSC system stem in large part from its bureaucratic nature. Bureaucracies rarely exhibit innovation. A famous passage by former Yale president A. Whitney Griswold is worth quoting in this context.

> Could Hamlet have been written by a committee, or the Mona Lisa painted by a club? Could the New Testament have been composed as a conference report?
> Creative ideas do not spring from groups. They spring from individuals. The divine spark leaps from the fingers of God to the fingers of man.

NSC deliberations have proven more valuable as educational tools and a means of keeping foreign policy up to date than as a vehicle for inducing creative change in that policy. All bureaucracies are conservative in that they tend to reinforce the status quo rather than lead to change. As discussed more fully in Chapter 8, several factors account for the conservative nature of bureaucracies. The difficulties involved in persuading many individuals with differing personal and organizational interests to agree on a new course of action often yield the conclusion to carry on as before, at least until a crisis forces a new decision. Proposing a new alternative is bound to offend fellow workers who profit personally and organizationally by existing arrangements. Individuals who work in bureaucratic organizations quickly learn that the best way to avoid making enemies is to "go with the flow" rather than dig new channels; such an outlook is hardly conducive to bold policy innovation. Accordingly, the elaborate NSC system engineered by Nixon and Kissinger would seem to be more suitable for a conservative president like Ronald Reagan than for one like Kennedy who aspired to make some fundamental alterations in American relations abroad.

Aside from conservatism, bureaucracies are also noted for duplication and delay, and the NSC system under the Nixon-Eisenhower approach is certainly not immune to such qualities. Before its final resolution, an issue might receive consideration at as many as a half dozen levels. What's more, the degree of specialized knowledge was likely to decrease at each higher level, since the higher one's responsibility, the more likely is one to be a generalist. The president is bound to be the broadest generalist of all.

The NSC system also presents the danger, somewhat realized under Eisenhower, that the president will become a prisoner of the NSC rather than its task-master. In a democracy, the people elect the president to carry out electoral pledges. If, however, the president comes to view options through NSC lenses, the election loses much of its meaning. This potential departure from democratic government is rendered more hazardous by the secrecy of NSC deliberations. Furthermore, members of the NSC staff—those specialists who help the various NSC bodies accomplish their work—do not testify before Congress and are not subject to congressional approval. To the extent that the NSC makes foreign policy, then, Congress loses the opportunity to question key officials closely. Thus, a highly secret bureaucratic structure is in a position to capture the president's mind. It must be said, however, that the tendency for this to occur under President Eisenhower alerted Nixon to the danger and he largely managed to avoid it. A less energetic or knowledgeable chief executive might not be so successful, however.

Many of these drawbacks to the highly institutionalized operation of the NSC became evident during the Eisenhower years. Determined to avoid such pitfalls, and personally averse to elaborate and cumbersome bureaucratic structures, President Kennedy adopted a much less formal approach to the NSC. Kennedy preferred to make foreign policy himself, with the assistance of advisers that he chose to help him on each particular problem. Much of the work performed by the NSC under Eisenhower was delegated to the State Department or one of the other executive units. When one of these agencies had prepared a staff study for presidential decision, Kennedy would meet with the head of that agency rather than call a meeting of the full NSC. Kennedy abolished Eisenhower's regular schedule of meetings, preferring to call a meeting when it seemed necessary. During the first six months of the Kennedy administration, the NSC met only 16 times. Favoring more personal conferences with fewer people in his office, Kennedy often met with members of the NSC but not in the context of NSC meetings. As a reflection of his distaste for elaborate bureaucratic mechanisms, Kennedy abolished the NSC's subsidiary organizations, roughly equivalent to the Interdepartmental Groups, Review Group and Undersecretaries Committee attached to the Nixon NSC. Kennedy relied at first on the State Department and later on the special assistant, rather than an interdepartmental organization, to oversee the implementation of foreign policy.

Like Kennedy, President Johnson allowed the NSC to fall into relative disuse. The Texan made many of his foreign policy decisions at the regular "Tuesday luncheon" meetings he held with the secretaries of state and defense, the national security adviser, and other selected officials. Also like Kennedy, Johnson preferred to reach decisions by working with selected advisers rather than relying upon a many-layered bureaucratic structure.

When Jimmy Carter came into office in 1977, he vowed to make several changes in American foreign policy, including a simplification of the Nixon-Kissinger NSC structure. Carter reduced the number of NSC committees to two. The Policy Review Committee, a Cabinet-level organization chaired by the Cabinet officer with prime responsibility for the issue at hand, met periodically to discuss foreign policy matters of a long-term nature.[17] Dr. Brzezinski headed the second NSC group, the Special Coordinating Committee, which dealt with shorter-term matters and appeared to exert more influence over foreign policy than the Policy Review Committee. Supplementing these formal bodies were the weekly luncheon meetings attended by the special assistant and the secretaries of defense and state. In his approach to the NSC, Carter leaned closer to the Kennedy-Johnson model than the Nixon-Kissinger model. In his first nine months in office, Carter held only seven formal NSC meetings. Nixon, by contrast, called 27 NSC meetings during his first six months. Like his Democratic predecessors, Carter reached many decisions outside the NSC framework. He further emulated Kennedy and Johnson by closeting himself with selected advisers to make important foreign policy decisions.

Like its alternative, the Kennedy-Johnson approach has its advantages as well as drawbacks. On the positive side, this way of conducting foreign policy poses fewer obstacles to boldness and decisiveness. When only three or four people need to clear a decision, there is much less likelihood that it will be diluted to suit the preferences of scores of decision makers with varied outlooks and bureaucratic interests. Thus, this *modus operandi* is perhaps better suited to a president who tries to be an innovator, as did Kennedy, rather than a president who wishes mainly to uphold the status quo. With fewer participants involved, decisions are likely to emerge in a shorter interval of time. This approach also affords an opportunity to infuse foreign policy with the president's own policy preferences. The president personally meets with assistants, urging them to study the important problems and suggesting satisfactory outcomes. The Eisenhower-Nixon model presumes that someone other than the president will energize the bureaucracy; as we have seen, this procedure carries the danger that foreign policy will bear only a slight resemblance to the president's personal vision of the country's interests.

The principal drawback to the Kennedy-Johnson approach is lack of systematic planning. Such a method of operation relies to a great extent on the wisdom and idiosyncrasies of the individual in charge. This person, usually the president, determines which foreign policy issues top officials will examine. Since no person or committee within the bureaucracy is charged with reviewing all areas of foreign policy, there is a danger of blind spots toward important foreign policy problems. Should the president deem a particular foreign policy issue insignificant, that issue will not receive study at the highest levels. For example, Johnson received criticism for ignoring American relations with Europe, because he was so absorbed with the matter of Vietnam. The Nixon-Eisenhower approach is much less dependent on the particular outlook of any single individual. The Kennedy-Johnson approach is also highly dependent on the energies and capabilities of a very few individuals. Only about a dozen top officials, assisted by their staffs, made the more important foreign policy decisions in the Kennedy-Johnson years. No one could expect this small number of persons to engage in as comprehensive a review of foreign policy as the scores of people involved in the NSC deliberations under Eisenhower and Nixon. A president who decides which persons will be involved in a foreign policy decision risks the exclusion of a variety of viewpoints and expertise. Presidents tend to appoint people who mirror their own outlook. By subjecting a foreign policy question to extensive review through the NSC system, the Nixon-Eisenhower approach affords persons with widely scattered viewpoints the opportunity to voice their opinions.

A further drawback to limiting policy making to a handful of top officials is the exclusion from policy planning of those subordinates who will be charged with the execution of policy decisions. By falling outside the decision-making process, these officials may fail to grasp certain nuances of policy and thus fail to implement policy as the small cadre of decision makers had intended. Under Johnson, this lack of full understanding was heightened by the habit of Rusk and McNamara to avoid discussing Tuesday luncheon debates with their subordinates.

In closing, it needs to be stressed again that the NSC is only one of several channels the president can rely on to help reach a foreign policy decision. Presidents come to office with their own individual operating styles; forcing them to behave according to a particular mold would only diminish their capacity to carry out their duties. Every president designs the NSC system according to personal preference. A method of operation that would work well under one president might prove a disaster under another. While we can offer some generalizations about different approaches to the NSC, it does not follow that a single approach should be adopted by every president.

CONCLUSION

In the present chapter, we have begun our exploration of governmental policy making by focusing upon the leading player, the president, and the president's immediate assistants. The Constitution sets forth the foreign policy powers of the chief executive and Congress. Rather than prescribing a neat division of labor, the Constitution deliberately brings the two branches into conflict over the conduct of foreign policy, particularly as regards treaties, warmaking, appointments, funding, regulation of the executive bureaucracy, and legislation with foreign policy implications (such as immigration). We have examined techniques used by various presidents to elude congressional control. We have also considered the individuals and offices that are at the chief executive's disposal to help formulate and execute foreign policy. Prominent among these are the special assistant for national security and the National Security Council. Both of these assist in managing the ever-present problem of coordinating the government's gargantuan policy-making machinery and making certain that important foreign policy problems are being attended to.

The president and the chief assistants comprise the decision-making core of the government. They make the most critical foreign policy decisions. However, they do not make all the foreign policy decisions that government is called upon to make daily. This task falls to the various executive departments and agencies that are situated just outside the inner core. These organizations are also responsible for implementing foreign policy decisions. The next chapter investigates these organizations in detail.

FOR DISCUSSION

How might the Constitution be modified so as to better equip the American political system to conduct a global policy of "perpetual crisis?"

Does the Constitution "tie the hands of the president" in making foreign policy?

Should the president and Congress be equal partners in formulating foreign policy, or should one branch predominate? What characteristics of each branch render it especially capable or incapable of making foreign policy?

How much power should the chief executive have to commit the nation's armed forces to combat?

Discuss the pros and cons of the War Powers Act of 1973.

Explain the problem of coordination. Why is it significant?

Discuss the virtues and drawbacks of placing the overall coordinating responsibility in the hands of 1) the president, 2) the special assistant for national security, 3) the secretary of state.

What are the advantages and disadvantages of using the National Security Council in the manner of Nixon-Eisenhower? Kennedy-Johnson?

READING SUGGESTIONS

Cronin, Thomas E., and Greenberg, S. D. *The Presidential Advisory System.* New York: Harper and Row, 1969.

George, Alexander L. *Presidential Decisionmaking in Foreign Policy.* Boulder, CO: Westview, 1980.

Janis, Irving L. *Victims of Groupthink.* Boston: Houghton Mifflin, 1972.

Johnson, Loch, and McCormick, James M. "Foreign Policy by Executive Fiat." *Foreign Policy* (Fall 1977): 117–38.

Kissinger, Henry. *White House Years.* Boston: Little, Brown and Company, 1979.

NOTES

1. The fear of arbitrary rule in this country did not disappear with the adjournment of the Constitutional Convention. In 1961, President Eisenhower in his farewell address warned about the hazards of a "military-industrial complex" that threatened to dominate America. President Nixon, by directing the FBI and the Internal Revenue Service to harass individuals with opposing political views, and by seeking to cover up the Watergate break-in of Democratic party headquarters, demonstrated some of the behavior that the Founding Fathers at Philadelphia feared would occur if they failed to restrain executive power.

2. Prior to World War II various presidents sent troops into action in the following episodes: Barbary Wars, Indian Wars, opposition to the Boxer Rebellion in China, and numerous instances in Latin America.

3. Cited in Cecil V. Crabb, Jr., *American Foreign Policy in the Nuclear Age* (New York: Harper and Row, 1960).

4. *New York Times*, May 1, 1972.

5. Loch Johnson and James M. McCormick, "Foreign Policy by Executive Fiat," *Foreign Policy* (Fall 1977): 117–38.
6. Ibid., p. 118.
7. United States, Senate, Committee on Foreign Relations, *National Commitments*, Report to Accompany Senate Resolution 187, 90th cong., 1st sess., November 20, 1967, p. 20.
8. Ibid., pp. 7–8.
9. Roger Hilsman, *To Move A Nation* (Garden City, N.Y.: Doubleday and Company, 1967), p. 561.
10. Memos from the foreign policy operating agencies went to President Carter through Special Assistant Brzezinski, who had the opportunity to place his own covering letter upon them. Brzezinski also saw the President every morning and normally met with him an average of four times a day. (Elizabeth Drew, "Brzezinski," *New Yorker*, May 1, 1978.)
11. Herbert Y. Schandler, writing about President Johnson during the Vietnam years, commented as follows on the dangers of personalized decision making as practiced by Johnson and Kennedy:

> It limits meaningful debate to a small and highly selected circle within the government. Indeed, as the importance of the issues becomes greater and has more political significance, the circle becomes even smaller. The president chooses the members of this circle and establishes the limits of their debate. Thus, the nature of the debate and the variety of the viewpoints expressed in this circle are of vital importance. But these individuals most certainly share the values and perspectives of the president and identify with his beliefs. They also must feel some personal loyalty and attachment to the man responsible for their very presence in that inner circle. This places an almost impossible burden upon the man within that circle who dissents from the apparent trend of the president's views. Such dissent at some point results in ostracism or even dismissal.

Herbert Y. Schandler, *The Unmaking of a President: Lyndon Johnson and Vietnam* (Princeton: Princeton University Press, 1977), pp. 329–30.
12. Henry A. Kissinger, *White House Years* (Boston: Little, Brown and Company, 1979), p. 11.
13. Ibid., p. 30.
14. Ibid., p. 47.
15. Such coordination was not totally lacking. The Committee of Three and the State-War-Navy Coordinating Committee provided a certain degree of coordination.
16. The extraordinary influence amassed by Henry Kissinger was due in part to his central position in the NSC structure. Kissinger assigned problems to the Interdepartmental Groups, and he also chaired the Review Group and the NSC. In addition, he supervised the activities of the NSC auxiliary bodies, such as the Verification Panel. Kissinger's influence was further bolstered by

the strong voice he exerted in those decisions taken by the president outside the NSC structure, such as preparations for Nixon's trips to Moscow and Peking, the decision to place American forces on worldwide alert during the 1973 Middle East war, and numerous decisions relating to Vietnam. Under President Ford, Kissinger's influence rose even higher, as the former Michigan congressman relied more heavily than his predecessor upon the foreign policy advice of others. Kissinger's position was likened to the master of a control tower in a freight yard, with 500 tracks leading in and one (Kissinger) leading out.

17. In a rare moment of pique, Senator Muskie expressed some dissatisfaction with Carter's foreign policy-making machinery. Specifically, he said that Policy Review Committee meetings rarely lasted beyond an hour, an interval he thought too brief to examine a complicated issue. At the weekly luncheon meetings he attended with Brzezinski and Defense Secretary Harold Brown, as many as 25 matters were served up in the space of one or two hours. Again, Muskie bemoaned the brevity of discussion held on each issue. See *New York Times*, August 10, 1980.

Chapter 8
The Executive
Bureaucracy

The first opinion to be formed of a prince and his intelligence
will depend on the men we see around him.

Machiavelli

Once upon a time there was a handsome young lion. He was
captured in the African jungle and brought to America, where he was
put on display in a zoo. This made the lion very unhappy because
he preferred the freedom of his wild native land and the companion-
ship of other jungle beasts. But after a time he became resigned to
his fate and made up his mind that if he had to live behind bars he
would be the best lion around.

In an adjoining cage there was another lion, an old and lazy one
with a negative responsibility and no signs of ambition or capability
of any kind. He lay all day in the sun, aroused no interest from visitors.
In sharp contrast, the young lion paced for hours back and forth in
his cage. He acted the true King of Beasts, rolling his maned head,
snarling, and baring his teeth. The crowds loved him. They paid no
attention to the indolent old lion asleep in the next cage.

The young lion appreciated the attention he was getting, but he
was annoyed by his failure to win adequate reward. Each afternoon
the zoo keeper came through the cages to feed the animals. The lazy
old lion, who made no effort to please the spectators, was given a big
bowl of red horsemeat. The young lion, now a star attraction, was
given a bowl of chopped-up oranges, bananas, and nuts. This made
him very unhappy.

"Perhaps," he mused, "I am not trying hard enough. I will improve the act." So he strutted longer and more spectacularly. To the snarls and gnashing of teeth he added frequent roars that shook the bars of his cage. The crowds got bigger. Thousands of citizens came to see his performance, and he was pictured on page one in the local newspaper.

But the diet did not change. Still the lazy lion got the red meat, and the young lion stayed on a vegetarian diet. Finally he could endure it no longer. He stopped the keeper with a challenge.

"I am getting sick and tired of this," he complained. "Each day you give that no-good lazy type next door a big bowl of meat, and you feed me oranges, bananas, and nuts. It is grossly unfair. I'm the star attraction, the lion that's doing all the work, and the one that gets the credits. Why am I not entitled to meat for dinner?"

The keeper did not hesitate with his reply.

"Young man," he said, "you don't know how lucky you are.

"Our Table of Organization in this zoo calls for one lion. You are being carried as a monkey."

Paul Dickson, *The Official Explanations*
(New York: Delacorte Press, 1980),
pp. 170–72.

THE BUREAUCRATIC SETTING

The anecdote above brings to mind just a sample of the criticisms we normally associate with bureaucracy. When asked how much bureaucracy is enough, most people would probably answer, "less." However, without bureaucracy the work of government would not get done. Meat would not get inspected; highways would not get built; and the nation would not field a military force. In this chapter we shall delve further into the American political process (see Fig. 1–1). We shall concentrate on those people who work for the president—not the immediate assistants, described in the previous chapter, but those charged with the everyday management of routine affairs that rarely come to public attention. Since most foreign policy actions do not concern crises, these fairly mundane decisions and actions of the executive bureaucracy shape American foreign policy to a very large extent.

The bureaucracy plays different roles in crisis and non-crisis situations. To highlight this difference, it is helpful to consider an analogy with a typical family confronted with two problems. In the first instance, the parents and two children are gathered around the breakfast table to discuss vacation plans for the coming summer.

Dad prefers the seashore, where he can do some deep-sea fishing. Mom suggests a mountain resort; she likes the cool air. The teenage daughter would just as soon stay at home, as she has recently become friendly with a young man down the block. The other youngster, a boy of seven, wants to go anywhere that requires an airplane trip; he has just decided to become a pilot. As the leisurely breakfast continues, each person sets forth arguments in favor of his or her preferred destination. Eventually, the family reaches a decision: they will spend one week at the seashore and one at the mountains; Sis can stay home for part of the time; the family will drive, not fly.

Now consider an entirely different situation. This time the family is watching television in an upstairs room just before going to bed. They hear a tapping noise downstairs and then the clatter of breaking glass. Someone has broken into the house. There is little time for protracted discussion. The parents exchange a few words, and the mother and children hurry into a bedroom, lock the door, and telephone the police. The father gathers his bathrobe around himself and gingerly steps into the hall. . . .

It is not necessary to finish the story in order to emphasize the differences between these two decisional settings. In a crude way, these situations are analogous to two types of decision situations in the federal government. The first example, vacation planning, is roughly similar to what we shall call the Bureaucratic Politics Model. The case of the intruder suggests the Unitary Actor Model. We shall consider the latter model first.[1]

The Unitary Actor Model

In their everyday discussion of foreign affairs, most people think and talk in terms of the unitary actor model of decision making. This model treats a state as a unitary actor; that is, it conceives of the state as having a single source of policy making. The following statements illustrate this approach. "The Soviet Union has built up its fleet in order to project its power." "Saudi Arabia is trying to hold down the price of oil." "If South Korea goes nuclear, North Korea is sure to follow." These statements portray government as analogous to a single individual making rational, calculated choices. As Graham T. Allison points out, deterrence and war-gaming are usually based on the unitary actor model: "the question of what the enemy will do is answered by considering the question of what a rational unitary genie would do."[2]

There are situations when policy making approaches the unitary actor model. Such situations, like the case of the intruder above, usually involve a crisis. Few people are involved in the decision. The situation leaves little time for lengthy debate or bureaucratic infighting. The outcome affects the whole country equally, and the Congress and general population rally around the president. Examples include Truman's response to the invasion of South Korea in 1950, Kennedy's decision to impose a blockade around Cuba in 1962, and President Carter's ill-fated effort to rescue American hostages from Teheran in 1980.

The Bureaucratic Politics Model

Far more common are decisions that approximate the bureaucratic politics model. This model roughly resembles our imaginary situation of vacation planning. Instead of a single or unitary actor, many persons and organizations seek to influence the decision. The final outcome may well represent a compromise among the desired outcomes of all participants. Most parties can live with the decision, although none may be thrilled with it. Different parties have varying degrees of influence in the debate; they don't bargain as equals. Let us explore this model in more systematic detail.

Given the thousands of decisions, foreign and domestic, that the federal government makes every year, it is obvious that only a small proportion goes to the president and the president's top assistants to decide. The rest are handled by the federal bureaucracy according to the bureaucratic politics model. A few examples include the defense budget, authorization of funds for the World Bank, laws setting immigration quotas, and legislation permitting the president to lower American tariffs in international negotiations.[3]

In essence, the bureaucratic politics model states that policy is the resultant of influences exerted by the various bureaucratic organizations involved in the decision. The policy decision represents a compromise among these organizations, not the decision a perfectly knowledgeable and rational mind would select (at least not usually). Bureaucratic politics is "the process by which people inside government bargain with one another on complex public policy questions."[4] Bureaucratic politics arises from at least four conditions:

(1) Issues cut across lines of organizational responsibility (for example, the balance of payments considerations of increasing the military assistance program);

(2) No single official has the power, wisdom or time to decide all important executive branch policy decisions himself or herself;

(3) Departments and agencies have different ideas about how to solve a particular problem;

(4) The various departments and agencies possess differing amounts of influence in the decision making process.

The latter two of these conditions call for some elaboration.

While all executive branch organizations seek to advance the national interest, they generally have different ideas about how best to achieve this goal. Take the question of national security. The Defense Department might insist the best means of promoting national security is to become stronger militarily than any other nation. But the Arms Control and Disarmament Agency might counter that security for one nation spells insecurity for another, and therefore the only way of truly enhancing national security is through arms control. The State Department might suggest that national security is best assured by having in power governments that share American preferences about the world order, and that therefore the US must be highly selective in choosing its friends. Stressing that no person is secure so long as he or she is dependent economically upon another, the Commerce Department might claim that the road to security lies through a favorable balance of trade. And Treasury might add that a strong currency is essential to national security. Of course, none of these positions is completely in error. Neither, however, does any single one guarantee the nation's security. The country must pursue all these avenues. The bureaucratic politics model becomes evident in settling this question: how much money should the government devote to each of these objectives? This question is answered every year when the government draws up its budget. Each department and agency argues as vociferously as it can for funds to implement its own programs, seen as the most significant way to achieve national security. Bureaucratic politics represents the process whereby the conflicting goals of governmental units are reconciled.

Roger Hilsman, an assistant secretary of state in the Kennedy administration, observed, "The relative power of these different groups of people included is as relevant to the final decision as the appeal of the goals they seek or the cogency and wisdom of their arguments."[5] Any student who has questioned a professor's grade is aware (usually painfully so) of this proposition. Some organizations are inherently more powerful in Washington debates than others. The Defense Department, with its large domestic constituency among defense contractors, their employees, and veterans, usually has far more clout than the State Department or the Agency for International Development, neither of which can look to a substantial body of supporters at home. An organization's effectiveness also depends to some extent upon the president. After the Bay of Pigs fiasco, President Kennedy downgraded the CIA and thereby weakened it in inter-agency debates. President Nixon had little faith in the State Department and often excluded it from the most sensitive policy issues, such as Nixon's journey to Peking and SALT deliberations. Former Foreign Service Officer Richard J. Barnet argues that the American tendency to resolve foreign policy dilemmas by force rather than negotiations results from the increased power of those agencies charged with the use of military power—particularly Defense and CIA. In his view, the military exigencies of World War II left these kinds of agencies in a strengthened position, while State and other organizations prone to negotiate rather than fight were disenfranchised.[6]

The lengthy debates and delicate compromises that characterize the bureaucratic politics model render this form of decision making more applicable to routine (which is not to say insignificant) matters than to crises. The mode of policy making also affects the kinds of decisions that emerge.

Decisions resulting from efforts to fashion a compromise among several departments and agencies, each with its own view of how to achieve the national interest, are not likely to steer the country down untried pathways. Bureaucratic policy making generally follows the middle of the road, as any other kind of acceptable consensus is difficult to produce. Abrupt departures from existing policy rarely emerge from the bureaucratic process. Indeed, bureaucratic policy making sometimes seems to function like an automatic pilot to prevent the country from straying off a given course. It would not be an exaggeration to state that a principal reason for the continuity of American foreign policy in recent decades lies with the large number of decisions reached through bureaucratic politics. At its best, bureaucratic politics can illuminate optimal policy choices through the clash of competing ideas. At the other extreme, the counter-balancing of forces can yield stalemate.

INFLUENCES ON THE POLICYMAKER

Whether a policymaker participates in a decision that follows the unitary actor model or the bureaucratic model, he or she is subject to certain pressures. These influences stem from the individual himself or herself (personality), the organization in which the individual works (organization), and the individual's position within that organization (role).

Personality

It would seem almost too obvious to state that a decision maker's personality affects the decisions he or she makes. Having said this much, however, we find ourselves at the entrance to a maze of queries about the nature of personality's influence upon decisions. Does everyone's personality affect decisions to the same degree? What competing factors, if any, override personality in the decision making process? Can we classify personality types so as to analyze systematically the impact of personality upon decisions? Does personality affect decision making equally for all types of decisions? Even if we could find answers to these and other questions, how might we gain access to the minds of particular decision makers and learn what transpired therein?

The questions above suggest that certain gaps in our knowledge of the psyche block a thorough investigation of personality's influence upon policy making. Nevertheless, several personality studies of governmental leaders have been made.[7] Alexander and Juliette George, for example, seek to explain Woodrow Wilson's behavior as president in terms of his upbringing at the hands of a stern and rigidly moralistic father.[8] The Georges attempt to demonstrate that much of Wilson's conduct, including his idealistic espousal of the League of Nations and his condemnation of the balance of power, stems from his inability to please his father in earlier years.

Richard J. Barnet suggests that practically all important figures in the national security bureaucracy share similar personality traits.[9] Barnet employs the term "bureaucratic machismo" to describe the personality of the typical policymaker. Toughness is the most highly prized virtue. Policymakers who recommend solving a foreign policy problem by use of force do not damage their reputations, even if overruled. However, those who recommend taking the issue to the United Nations, seeking negotiations, or doing nothing, quickly become known as "soft"; their reputations suffer even if they prove to be right! Barnet argues that departments and agencies that deal with questions of national security are not staffed by "tough" persons coincidentally. Such organizations select these people and promote them, while deliberately overlooking "softies."

In a more scientific study, Lloyd Etheredge found pronounced correlations between personality traits and foreign policy outlooks of government officials.[10] "What you decide depends ultimately on who you are," he concluded. According to Etheredge, highly dominant, ambitious, competitive and self-assertive decision makers tend to be mistrustful in both interpersonal relations and in their perceptions of the nation's adversaries. Such individuals are inclined to view the nation's opponents as aggressive and are prone to recommend hard-line policies. Less aspiring and domineering persons are more inclined to view the nation's adversaries as cooperative; these policymakers question the need for hard-line responses.

The Etheredge study raises disturbing questions about the basis of foreign policy. Do policymakers base their recommendations on objective facts, or do their conclusions merely reflect their own personalities? If, as Etheredge suggests, the latter is the case, then is there anything an adversary can do to convince competitive policymakers that it lacks aggressive designs? Similarly, will noncompetitive policymakers recommend amicable policies no matter how belligerently another nation may behave? Should Etheredge's findings be corroborated by other investigators, it might become necessary to revise our general understanding of how foreign policy is made.

Organization

A second influence upon a decision maker is the governmental organization to which he or she belongs. "Where you stand depends on where you sit," says an oft-quoted bureaucratic maxim. Each department and agency in the executive branch has a unique vision of the world and of the mission of American foreign policy. The Air Force sees the principal threat to America coming from Soviet strategic missiles and therefore advocates programs strengthening strategic deterrence. The Navy is more concerned with keeping open sea lanes and therefore wants additional ships. The Commerce Department tends to perceive America's well-being in terms of favorable trade. Organizations have a tendency to seek like-minded recruits, thus perpetuating distinctive organizational outlooks. Occasionally, when an organization does employ a person with views that differ from the dominant mind-set of the organization, that individual quickly learns the truth expressed in the maxim, "To get along, go along." Bureaucratic organizations have little tolerance for nonconformists. Promotions and the best assignments generally go to those who excel within the framework of the organization's general outlook. Nonconformists are usually shunted aside so that their influence on policy is minimized. Effectively neutralized, such individuals generally drop out or seek an organization more receptive to their views. Of course, such persecution may stifle creativity and soften the clash of ideas that helps bring to light the best policy.

Members of bureaucratic organizations also tend to favor foreign policy actions that result in advancement of their own organization's influence, prestige, budget and staff. Many bureaucrats genuinely believe that what is best for their organization is best for the country. For instance, intelligence officials may well believe that the nation's foreign policy can be no better than its knowledge about other countries. It follows that whatever enhances the capabilities of the intelligence services—be it added personnel, higher appropriations to pay for additional satellites, or better relations with congressional oversight committees—advances the objectives of American foreign policy. In short, bureaucrats tend to equate the national interest with the interests of their own organization. The battle to raise each organization's prestige becomes exceptionally fierce at budget time.

To boost their own prestige and influence in inter-agency debates, organizations often grasp for tasks performed by other organizations ("organizational imperialism"). Generally speaking, the more tasks an organization performs, the more influence the organization wields. This desire to expand the range of an organization's assignments accounts in part for the duplication for which government is so justly renowned.

The organizational influence upon decision makers helps us understand why policy debates so often end in compromise. The protagonists in these discussions approach a particular problem from the standpoint of what will best serve their own departments (and, by extension, the nation). Since each department has a different policy recommendation, conflict arises and the only acceptable solution takes the form of compromise.

The organizational factor also helps explain an uncommon though disturbing practice—the simultaneous pursuit of conflicting foreign policies by different government agencies. In Laos in 1960, for example, there was a civil war between pro-Western forces led by Gen. Phoumi Nosavan and neutralists led in the field by Kong Le and loyal to Premier Souvanna Phouma. During the fall of that year, the CIA funneled money and equipment to Phoumi, while State supplied the same to the neutralists. Two years previously, the CIA provided material support to rebels fighting the regime of Sukarno in Indonesia; at the same time State, unaware of this activity, assured a bewildered Sukarno that Washington was firmly on his side.

The government's slowness to alter foreign policy may be accounted for in part by the challenge that bold policy initiatives pose to an organization's standing in the bureaucratic pecking order. New functions and modes of operation threaten officials who benefit from existing routines and who therefore resist changes. Often the least disruptive course seems to be to let well enough alone.

The difficulties in mobilizing the bureaucracy behind a foreign policy decision result in another characteristic of bureaucratic politics—the tendency to put off decisions to the last possible moment (and occasionally even beyond). In the bureaucratic milieu, each decision entails hundreds of hours of work—preparing position papers, attending meetings, coordinating positions within one's own agency, and doing battle with other agencies. Bureaucrats normally have their in-baskets piled high enough without taking on the extra work involved in a new decision. Therefore, government often awaits a crisis to grapple with a problem.

Another consequence of bureaucratic politics is the occasional violation of existing policy by an individual or organization. The foreign affairs bureaucracy is so large and is engaged in so many activities at once that no one can monitor what everyone is doing. Top officials must rely on the willingness of subordinates to follow decisions already taken. But sometimes a maverick violates policy. Such an occurrence took place in 1972. President Nixon had ordered a halt in the bombing of North Vietnam in the hope of promoting negotiations. However, Air Force Lieutenant General John D. Lavelle, no friend of a negotiated compromise, ordered hundreds of bombing sorties against North Vietnam over a period of three months. It was reasonable on the part of Hanoi to assume that American policy had not changed at all, and that Nixon was lying to them and the American people in announcing a bombing halt. For his infraction, General Lavelle was retired with a demotion in rank. Such outright violations of existing policy do not occur too often.

A final impact of the organizational influence upon policy-makers has to do with the quality of their output. It has not infrequently been observed that the national security agencies are staffed by unusually competent people, but that the quality of their joint efforts is less than the total of the individual parts. This sad situation may prevail because the most powerful individuals in an organization generally have vested interests in the status quo. Accordingly, they reward staffers who reinforce the way things are.

People with creative ideas that challenge the status quo are viewed as threats by the powers that be. Department heads display little enthusiasm for reorganization plans that merge their units into a larger entity and rescind their titles. Too many persons in positions of power reward conservatism and timidity and penalize creativity, boldness and risk-taking. Talented individuals who engage in the latter forms of activity are eventually faced with two choices. Either they adapt to the tried and true ways of the organization or they leave. In short, the system has a tendency to neutralize its own capabilities.

Role

Like a policymaker's personality and the organization to which he or she belongs, that person's role in the organization also affects his or her decisions. Role refers to the particular office or position a person holds in a governmental organization. The presidency is a role, as is the agricultural attaché in Hungary or the CIA station chief in Montevideo. Role theory, as this type of analysis is sometimes called, assumes that a particular role carries with it certain expectations of behavior. No matter who occupies that role, the acts of that individual will be more or less identical to those of the incumbent's predecessor. Thus, regardless of an individual's outlook upon taking the post, any secretary of defense will press for larger military expenditures, while every secretary of commerce will seek to boost the country's exports. Role theory lies at the opposite extreme from personality theory, which holds that personality is the prime determinant of a policymaker's actions.

Jimmy Carter provides an example of how role affects performance. In the early days of his presidency, Carter took special pains to portray himself as a man of the people, "plain ol' Jimmy," the young man next door who grew up to become president. No doubt Carter wished to paint a contrast to his predecessor Nixon, who was noted for his aloofness and stiff formal manner. Carter's attempt to identify himself with "plain folks" was symbolized by his decision to forego the traditional inaugural limousine ride up Pennsylvania Avenue and instead walk. To the ceremony he wore a business suit, not the formal outfit selected by Ronald Reagan. Perhaps the most telling sign of Carter's attempts to shed the elitist manner of some of his predecessors was his decision to sell the presidential yacht *Sequoia*.

It did not take too long, however, for Carter to discover that, while the citizenry might feel affection for the "boy next door," it did not hold that figure in sufficient awe to permit vigorous presidential leadership. Foreign leaders felt uncomfortable with the "down home" ways at the White House and tended to denigrate the power of the United States. After a while, Carter and his close aides began to conform to their roles. Dark blue suits replaced the cardigan sweaters, and the president was seen boarding Air Force One unencumbered by a briefcase. At the end of his term, Carter's behavior conformed to the standard role of the chief executive of the United States.

While each role carries with it certain expectations and demands, role theory does allow for occasional individuals to transcend and redefine their roles. Franklin D. Roosevelt, for example, reshaped the role of president from caretaker to leader.

One of the corollaries of role theory is that to alter policy one should alter roles. Thus, when President Carter wished to stress human rights as an element of foreign policy, he established a new role or office in the State Department, assistant secretary of state for human rights, with specific responsibility for enforcing human rights. The Department of Energy—consisting, like all departments, of a cluster of roles—was established to ensure that energy concerns would be attended to.

We see then that there are three major influences on the decision maker: personality, organization and role. There is much more that we should like to know about these factors. Which one has the most or least impact upon a policymaker's behavior? Do the different factors have the same degree of influence for all types of decisions, from routine situations to national crises? How do these three factors interact with one another to yield a policy decision? Regrettably, we lack answers to such questions at present. We turn, therefore, to the relationship between bureaucrats and their boss, the president.

THE BUREAUCRACY VERSUS THE PRESIDENT

It is not very likely that the time will arise when it will be necessary to place a help-wanted advertisement to fill the presidency. Assuming such an occasion should arise, however, consider the following job notices:

Example I
Wanted: bold, innovative executive to draw up and implement American foreign policy. Must be able to choose among sharply different

policy alternatives; no wishy-washy compromiser need apply. Must be capable of issuing direct orders to federal bureaucrats and taking strong action to see that these orders are executed. Applicant should possess long-range vision of American foreign policy. Relevant previous experience: military commander or football coach. Good public relations skills an asset.

Example II

Wanted: individual with good human relations skills to resolve disputes among headstrong leaders of bureaucratic agencies. Must be able to detect points of compromise among competing bureaucratic positions. Must have ability to soothe ruffled feathers. Premium on pragmatic, short-run outlook. Tolerance for occasional defeat essential. Applicant should feel comfortable with existing American foreign policy. Relevant previous experience: labor arbitrator or corporate ombudsman. Good public relations skills an asset.

The first of these examples comes close to the common perception of the president as an energetic, forceful chief executive who makes bold decisions and oversees their execution. A more informed depiction of the president may be found in the second example. Except at rare intervals, usually involving the nation's very survival, the president behaves more like a broker than a cavalry leader. Consider the words of Richard Neustadt, former assistant to President Truman:

> Underneath our images of Presidents-in-boots, astride decisions, are the half-observed realities of Presidents-in-sneakers, stirrups in hand, trying to induce particular department heads, or Congressmen or Senators, to climb aboard.[11]

Graham Allison refers to presidential authority as an "extensive clerkship."[12]

These descriptions of presidential power owe a debt to the organizational influence on policymakers. We normally view department and agency heads and their assistants as instruments of presidential authority. But these individuals speak not just for the president; they speak also for the professionals who staff their organizations. Bureaucrats look to their chief for support. Technically, bureaucrats are career officials who do not enter and leave office with each new president. Since presidential appointees—not strictly bureaucrats—often head the organizations in which bureaucrats work, they are sometimes included in this discussion for convenience. Many of these career specialists know more about their subject than their chief or the president. If a department head fails to champion vigorously his or her staff's ideas in the inter-agency arena, the staff will rapidly lose interest in providing the expert advice it is supposed to supply. Offering such advice is not being "meddlesome"; on the contrary, the government needs such input in order to deal with the complex problems it faces. Just as one would not want the country to launch an invasion without consulting the military, so few would want the government to select a trade or energy policy without input from relevant specialists. The level of performance and morale in an agency will also decline if its head is invariably overruled or excluded from important policy decisions (a situation that occurred not infrequently with the Department of State in the Nixon administration). If the best minds in a particular department question the wisdom of a presidential policy, it is part of the secretary's role to bring these doubts to the attention of the president and urge a change of course. Several Cabinet secretaries also represent public constituencies that expect to be heard in the councils of government. The agriculture secretary speaks for farmers, just as the secretary of commerce speaks for the business community. When these constituents object to presidential policy, they demand that their spokespersons voice their complaints. These conflicting loyalties are what led Vice-President Charles G. Dawes to comment that "the members of the Cabinet are a President's natural enemies."

Some people are invited into an administration because they are prominent in their own right and bring a measure of public support to the government. For example, Andrew Young, Carter's ambassador to the United Nations, represented the black community and the liberal, civil rights movement. The president can overrule such personalities only at the peril of losing support among their backers. There can be little doubt that Carter lost support among blacks and liberals when he fired Andrew Young for holding conversations with official representatives of the Palestine Liberation Organization.

While a department or agency head cannot expressly refuse to carry out a presidential directive without losing his or her post, there are many ways to frustrate presidential policy. Jonathan Daniels, an aide to Franklin D. Roosevelt, explained how this works.

> Half of a President's suggestions, which theoretically carry the weight of order, can be safely forgotten by a Cabinet member. And if the President asks about a suggestion a second time, he can be told that it is being investigated. If he asks a third time, a wise Cabinet

officer will give him at least part of what he suggests. But only occasionally, except about the most important matters, do Presidents ever get around to asking three times.[13]

Even if a presidential decision is not ignored, there are numerous ways the bureaucracy can interfere with its implementation. Career specialists opposed to a presidential policy can withhold or slant information necessary to the execution of a policy. They can "uncover new information" to show why a chosen policy is not likely to work. Bureaucracies can delay implementation (claiming the need for additional time to study the situation) until the situation calling forth the policy has passed. Examples of bureaucratic frustration of presidential policy are numerous. President Truman, who had experienced the bureaucracy's capacity to frustrate presidential efforts, commented just before Eisenhower took over the Oval Office, "He'll sit here and he'll say, 'Do this! Do that!' And *nothing will happen*. Poor Ike—it won't be a bit like the Army." In 1961 President Kennedy instructed the State Department to negotiate the removal of American Jupiter missiles from Turkish soil. The president had concluded that the missiles, which stood exposed on their launching pads, were highly vulnerable and aggravated Soviet fears of encirclement without conferring significant benefits on the United States. Turkey, however, strongly wanted the missiles to remain as visible symbols of America's commitment, and State let the matter rest. The following year, when the United States placed a blockade around Cuba and insisted on the removal of Russian missiles, Moscow offered to trade its missiles in Cuba for the American Jupiters in Turkey. Kennedy was infuriated when he discovered that State had not carried out his instructions.

The bureaucracy's skill in scuttling presidential initiatives of which it disapproves led Richard Neustadt to observe that "presidential power is the power to persuade."[14] Despite the exalted office, the chief executive must fabricate a consensus behind policy preferences if they are to be translated into government action. This necessity carries with it the liability that the president, who is supposed to lead the government, may become its captive. Anyone who seeks to build a consensus must be prepared to compromise. A president who becomes little more than an arbiter of interagency disputes will be unable to impress his vision of the nation's destiny upon the government.

The president does have many resources available to persuade those whose consent is needed. The chief executive can offer to support a Cabinet officer's pet project in return for the latter's advocacy of a presidential initiative. Recalcitrant officials can be invited to the White House for breakfast to hear arguments for the president's point of view. The president can also apply indirect pressure on the bureaucracy by persuading the Congress and the public to support a given position, with the expectation that they will then pressure the bureaucracy to go along. Appreciating the need to coax others to jump on board the presidential bandwagon, Truman once said, "I spend most of my time urging people to do what they ought to do without being urged."

Having explored the influence of personality, organization and role upon policymakers, and having considered the relationship between the bureaucracy and the president, we now turn to the principal departments and agencies involved in formulating and implementing foreign policy.

STATE DEPARTMENT

Founded in 1789, the State Department was the first executive department in the United States government. As the first secretary of state, Thomas Jefferson was assisted by five clerks, a part-time translator of French, and two messengers. Today, the State Department employs a total of 27 thousand persons in Washington, 134 embassies abroad, approximately 120 consulates, and 10 special missions to international organizations (including the United Nations). The department has an annual budget of approximately $1.5 billion. Yet, in terms of both budget and personnel, State is the smallest of the executive departments. The Defense Department's budget is over 100 times as large as State's, and the personnel roster of the Postal Service is approximately 20 times as large.

Functions and Organization

In broad terms, the State Department has three principal functions. It advises the president on foreign policy; it helps implement foreign policy decisions; and it represents American citizens and their interests in dealing with other states.

At the top of the structure (see Fig. 8–1) sits the secretary, whose many duties include representation of the United States in foreign negotiations, provision of foreign policy advice to the president, persuasion of Congress to support the president's foreign

FIGURE 8-1: THE DEPARTMENT OF STATE

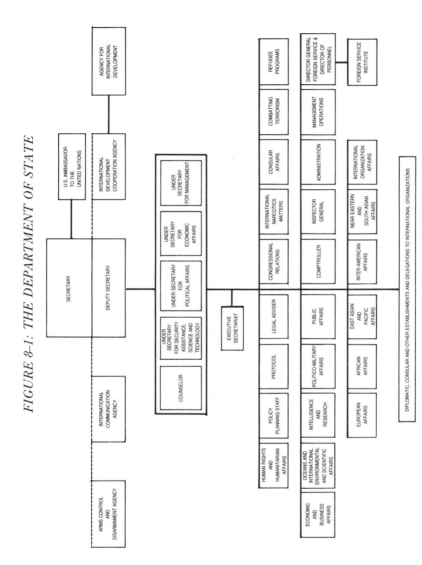

Source: *United States Government Manual, 1980–1981*, p. 429.

policy, and fabrication of public support through policy statements and press conferences.

Six executive-level individuals assist the secretary. The deputy secretary, the number-two person in the department, acts as the secretary's alter ego and carries out assignments as the secretary directs. For example, Warren D. Christopher, deputy secretary under Secretaries Vance and Muskie, was in charge of negotiating the release of American hostages held by Iran. During the secretary's absence from the country, the deputy secretary acts as secretary of state. The counselor gives advice on a wide range of issues, and other undersecretaries carry out duties as implied by their full titles.

Below this executive level are found the geographic and functional bureaus, each headed by an assistant secretary appointed by the president, as well as various other offices. It is at these levels that most of the department's daily work gets done. The executives at the top, together with the assistant secretaries in charge of the regional and functional bureaus, are responsible for making sure that the department reflects presidential preferences in foreign policy. These appointees are selected so that they will stamp the president's interpretation of foreign policy upon the department, just as assistant football coaches are expected to follow the game plan the head coach has devised.

As Figure 8–1 shows, there is a geographic bureau for each major region of the world. Each geographic bureau is broken down in a hierarchical manner, with a country desk officer—one for each country—at the bottom of the structure. The desk officer serves as the point of contact between the department and the American embassy in his or her country of responsibility. He or she also acts as the focal point in Washington for the activities of all American departments and agencies with programs in his or her country.

Functional bureaus exist because various tasks cut across regional boundaries and need to be coordinated. The duties of most of these bureaus are evident in their titles. The Bureau of Politico-Military Affairs is concerned with the relationship between military and political policy. It watches to see that the nation's military activities remain attuned to the country's political objectives. This bureau serves as a principal point of contact between the State Department and the Defense Department.

If one wishes to become an employee of the State Department today, one joins the Foreign Service. There are approximately 3,500 Foreign Service Officers (FSOs). Aside from the assistant secretaries and above, FSOs hold the most consequential positions at

State and in the field. These are the career professionals who view themselves as the foreign policy elite. FSOs normally spend two or three years at an overseas post and then return to Washington for a tour of similar duration. In line with the department's policy of producing highly skilled generalists who can serve anywhere, FSOs are rotated to various parts of the globe. Thus, a typical FSO might serve in Algeria, then in Uruguay, and then in France, with Washington assignments interspersed in between. Tours back home are meant to keep the FSO in touch with American interests and events, so that he or she can effectively implement American interests when transferred overseas. FSOs must constantly fight the temptation to develop an affection for the country where they are stationed, making them an advocate of that country's interests instead of their own country's objectives. Through years of service, an FSO can rise to become an ambassador—75 percent of American ambassadors have risen from the ranks of the Foreign Service. FSOs may also become deputy chiefs of mission (just below the ambassador) or high officials in the department (a certain number of assistant secretaries and higher officials are chosen from among the Foreign Service). Most FSOs, however, never reach these lofty heights.

Current Issues

Robert Lovett, a high State Department official in the Eisenhower years, reportedly compared the operation of the State Department to the love life of elephants. All the important business is done at a very high level; developments are accompanied by tremendous trumpeting; and, if any results are forthcoming, the period required is from 18 months to two years. There can be little doubt that the State Department has become a very busy organization. At the same time, there is general agreement that the department has lost considerable influence since the days when Truman looked to Secretary Dean Acheson for foreign policy advice, and Eisenhower gave Secretary Dulles wide scope to shape foreign policy. President Kennedy preferred to act as his own secretary of state, and Presidents Johnson and Nixon turned elsewhere for foreign policy guidance. Under Carter and Reagan, State has regained some of its prominence, but it has yet to recapture its stature of the Truman-Eisenhower period.

There is substantial agreement among foreign affairs specialists that the decline of State is largely due to the department's own shortcomings. According to I. M. Destler, State's central problem is a lack of responsiveness to the president. He divides this difficulty into six facets:

(1) State produces poor staffwork and analysis of issues;
(2) State is slow to respond to presidential requests;
(3) State displays resistance to new foreign policy approaches;
(4) State does not adequately implement foreign policy once it is decided;
(5) State fails to take the leadership in foreign policy, preferring to let others play this role;
(6) State seems unable to put its own house in order, clearly assigning responsibilities to officials and checking on their performance.[15]

Why does State get such low marks? An examination of working conditions within the department suggests some answers. Like most people, State Department personnel are interested in gaining promotion for superior achievement. The basic criterion for determining promotion is an "efficiency report" prepared annually by each individual's immediate superior. This procedure builds in a mechanism that discourages officers from aggressively challenging the views of higher level officials, with the result that policy papers may not be as closely scrutinized as they otherwise might be.

This tendency to accept what is handed down is reinforced by an attitude of caution that extends back to the 1950s, when Senator Joseph McCarthy sought to blame supervisors at State for the "loss" of China and other foreign policy failures. McCarthy claimed to have a list of 205 State Department officers who were known to the secretary as members of the Communist party. To clear the department of suspicion, Foreign Service Officers and State Department personnel were subjected to loyalty checks and other humiliating practices. Senior officials who had provided wrong advice were shunted off to uninfluential posts or dismissed outright. Many of State's most distinguished analysts left the department in disgrace. Although McCarthy never provided evidence to substantiate his charges—he was subsequently censored by the Senate—the effects of his assault are still felt today. To avoid blame for views that might later be questioned, some FSOs couch their reports in bland language laced with qualifiers. For example, instead of saying that a foreign leader is hostile to America, an FSO might report that the leader "displays a tendency, from time to time, to be critical of the United States."

The State Department appears enveloped in an outlook that pays homage to tradition and precedent. There is a strong tendency to abide by the status quo until it proves itself unsatisfactory beyond a doubt. By then, however, the situation may have worsened beyond repair.

Another condition of employment that detracts from State's performance is what Foreign Service Officer Robert Pringle calls a personnel logjam.[16] State has an oversupply of middle and senior-level officers. There are twice as many people in State's top four ranks as in the lower four. Many do not have enough to do to utilize their talents, so they are given make-work. Not only does this situation result in the under-utilization of talent, but it means that younger officers must wait longer to rise to policy-making positions. It is not uncommon for an FSO to wait 20 years or so to reach such a level. The lengthy interval during which the junior FSOs must await the retirement of senior officers saps the former of initiative and drive. By the time they occupy policy-making posts, they have already passed their peak productive years.

Still another factor that weakens State's contribution to foreign policy formulation and implementation concerns the department's perception of what properly constitutes diplomacy. Fashioned in the day when diplomacy consisted of elegant turns of phrase uttered by aristocrats in ruffled shirts, the Foreign Service continues to believe that the essence of diplomacy lies in the traditional tasks of representation, negotiation, and reporting. While no one would deny that these functions remain important, foreign policy today consists of a much wider range of activities. Many of these tasks require technical skills, such as those possessed by a commodities trade specialist, an agricultural aid officer, a scientist in the anti-satellite program, or a nutrition expert working in a Latin *barrio*. Yet, State continues to believe that these specialized activities remain peripheral to foreign policy. An internal State Department report concluded that the department

> has relied too long on the 'generalist' and has been slow to recruit and develop officers with the wide range of special aptitudes, skills and knowledge which the new diplomacy requires. Too many officers have been reluctant to master the intricacies of the new activities— agriculture, labor, commerce, finance, development economics, science, information and the like—which have become a standard part of our diplomatic operations abroad, and the Department has not done enough to encourage them to do so.[17]

The above attitude is reflected in State's recruitment of generalists and its scarcely concealed disdain for "technocrats." In consequence, State finds itself in a weak position to challenge the policy recommendations of agencies that specialize in less traditional aspects of foreign policy.

An additional condition of employment that hampers State's effectiveness concerns the limited opportunities available to FSOs within their own organization. Professionals in any organization naturally derive at least part of their incentive for outstanding performance by the hope of rising to the top. At the State Department, however, many top posts are filled from outside the Foreign Service (a situation which, incidentally, exacerbates the personnel logjam mentioned earlier). We have already spoken of the secretary and the secretary's chief assistants, few if any of whom are chosen from among career officials. While it used to be more common than today to choose ambassadors from the ranks of "fat cats" and presidential cronies, one-quarter of these positions continue to be filled from outside the Foreign Service. Furthermore, the posts that outsiders tend to fill are situated in the most desirable locations, such as Paris or London or Rome. Not only does this practice deprive the nation of outstanding talent in important positions, but it brings to power individuals with little commitment to improving the overall effectiveness of the department. Of course, some of these outsiders possess considerable expertise in foreign affairs.[18] They may also bring fresh blood into a conservative organization and help keep the department attuned to the president's policy. Nevertheless, the lack of opportunity at the summit of their profession has a dampening effect on the performance of the Foreign Service.[19]

The internal procedures within the department also detract from its output. Before the department dispatches instructions to an embassy, or an officer passes a policy recommendation to a higher level, the initiating officer must clear the document with certain other officers at a comparable level. Each time a document moves to a higher level it must first be cleared, a practice which if portrayed graphically would resemble a shrub which has been espaliered against a wall. Suppose, for example, that an officer wished to make a recommendation on selling fighter aircraft to Egypt. He or she would have to gain the approval, accomplished by a signature, of officers at a comparable level that concern themselves with the Middle East, with military assistance, and with Congress (because the legislature would eventually have to approve the sale). Each time the document moved to a higher level, similar clearances would be required. The rationale for this procedure is to ensure that all officers with relevant information participate in the decision. One undeniable consequence, however, is delay; officers whose approval is needed may be out of town or working on priority projects, rendering them unavailable for several days. The clearance procedure also tends to dilute policy statements, since there is a tendency to adopt general language to secure agreement.

The vertical equivalent of clearances is known as "layering." Like a salmon struggling to make its way upstream, a policy paper must be approved at several different levels or layers before it is adopted as a departmental recommendation. Passing each layer takes time and may also dilute the recommendation. Former Secretary Dean Rusk described the process as follows:

> ... When I read a telegram coming in in the morning, it poses a very specific question, and ... I know myself what the answer would be. But that telegram goes on its appointed course into the Bureau, and through the office and down to the desk. If it doesn't go down there, somebody feels that he is being deprived of his participation in a matter of his responsibility.
>
> Then it goes ... back up through the Department to me a week or 10 days later, and if it isn't the answer that I know had to be the answer, then I change it ... But usually it is the answer that everybody would know has to be the answer.[20]

The problems described in the previous pages obviously diminish the quality of the product that State puts out. A president who is convinced that better assistance can be obtained elsewhere than at State will turn to these other sources. When this occurs, however, the expertise accumulated by the career professionals at State goes to waste.

Alexander M. Haig, Jr., in his confirmation testimony before the Senate Committee on Foreign Relations, remarked,

> ... the most consistent articulation of policy is wasted if the professionals who must execute it are divorced from its formulation, and if their experience and skill are usurped in the name of confidentiality, haste or political sensitivity.
>
> The career personnel of the State Department and the Foreign Service are an unmatched, intellectual resource. ... If the United States is to act consistently and reliably in the world arena, it must use its career professionals. Their effective participation is imperative.[21]

The failure to call upon the State Department generates a vicious circle, in which a feeling of uselessness lowers morale, which in turn reduces the quality of State's product. The operation of this circle has led some recent presidents, especially Kennedy, Johnson and Nixon, to turn to their White House staffs and the Defense

Department for foreign policy guidance. The Defense Department seems more able than State to produce crisp analyses supporting a unified policy recommendation in a brief interval of time. It must be said, however, that many of the issues Defense treats lend themselves to quantifiable presentation, and this in itself gives a hard-hitting quality to its policy papers. For example, when the Pentagon argues in favor of placing more intermediate range missiles in Western Europe, it is able to cite statistics on Soviet and Western weapons to support its case. The State Department enjoys no such advantages in arguing the case for American support of such functions as the United Nations Year of the Child. Because the Defense Department's analyses often contain more data (numbers of tanks, planes, etc.) than State's, they often appear more precise. One must be on guard, however, against ignoring foreign policy complexities for the sake of a deceptive precision.

Another factor that has contributed to Defense's strong voice is the nearly ceaseless succession of alleged military threats to America since World War II. To meet these exigencies, the nation's leaders have first turned to the military, and the State Department has tended to take a back seat.

Personality, a factor that cannot be ignored in foreign policy analysis, has also contributed to the ascendancy of Defense over State. In recent years, most of the individuals who have occupied the secretary of defense's post have possessed more assertive personalities than their counterparts at State. Only Dulles, Kissinger and Haig have been strong advocates at State in the near past, while nearly every defense secretary has been an aggressive defender of that department's views. Hodding Carter III, Secretary of State Vance's press spokesman, had this to say about his boss:

> . . . I came to regard Cy Vance as one of the most decent, courageous and humane men American public life has seen. He knows the ins and outs of power in Washington . . . but he wouldn't fight dirty if his life depended on it. In many ways, his effectiveness in the Carter Administration's infighting was severely hampered precisely because he was instinctively so straight.[22]

What is disquieting to long-time observers of the State Department is that the inadequacies in conditions of employment and operating procedures that we have mentioned are far from new. Scores of studies of the State Department have been undertaken, and nearly all make mention of the same deficiencies. This lamentable situation gives one little reason to hope for improvement, unless a future president determines to perform surgery on State and stays in the operating room until the operation is complete.

Just as mention of the same inadequacies recur, so do recommendations for improvement. The most common proposal refers to the need to simplify and accelerate clearance procedures and paper flow. Critics also suggest that State make its policy papers tighter; that is, the papers should gather behind a specific point of view rather than qualify every option so that none stands out as the department's recommendation. (State's defenders insist that too much paring would obscure relevant complexities.)

A 1970 in-house study, conducted by 13 task forces, stressed the need for more creativity in State's output.[23] To reach this goal the study group recommended that the department:

emphasize creative aptitudes in recruiting employees;

alter performance evaluations to give more weight to creative work;

bring in outsiders, such as academics and private specialists, to serve on task forces to be formed when crises erupt;

heighten the exposure of regular personnel to outside wisdom through temporary personnel exchanges with other government agencies, business firms, professional and academic communities;

augment lateral entry, that is, recruitment of specialists into middle level positions instead of at the bottom rung.

The report stressed that the current promotion system, based on efficiency reports by one's superior, stifles creativity and inspires too much caution. Such a system encourages an employee to conform to his or her superior's views rather than forthrightly challenge them. To overcome this tendency, the study group recommended that after a probationary period of two to three years, during which the department closely monitors a new employee, an officer receive automatic promotions, unless his or her performance is found to be unusually good or poor. Further screening would be necessary before an officer is admitted to the top grades in the department. Such security would give officers the confidence to challenge accepted wisdom, the study group suggested.

Destler believes that if State is to have a stronger voice in policy making, it must become more responsive to the president.[24] In particular, the Department must be willing to challenge the expertise housed in other departments and agencies, write concise emphatic policy papers, respond quickly to presidential directives and requests, and take the broadest possible interpretation of its mandate to lead the nation in foreign policy formulation.

These and other analyses suggest that if State is to take its rightful place as the president's principal source of foreign policy advice, the department must make some far-reaching changes.

International Development Cooperation Agency

The International Development Cooperation Agency (IDCA) was established in 1979 to conduct policy planning, policy making, and policy coordination on international economic issues affecting developing countries. IDCA ensures that economic development objectives are considered for all executive branch decisions concerning trade, finance, monetary affairs, technology, and other economic matters. The agency was created to provide a focal point within the executive branch for American policies toward the developing world and for bilateral and multilateral aid programs conducted by the US government. The director of IDCA is the principal international development adviser to the president and the secretary of state. In turn, the director receives overall policy guidance from the secretary of state. IDCA's director shares responsibility with the secretary of the treasury for American participation in the World Bank and various regional developmental banks. The director also works with Agriculture Department officials in conducting the Food for Peace Program. Each year IDCA's director prepares a Development Policy Statement for the president, outlining recommendations concerning the nation's development priorities and allocation of funds. As the nation's principal economic development official, the director chairs the inter-agency Development Coordination Committee, which plans and coordinates the nation's economic development policy.

IDCA is composed of the following three elements: the Agency for International Development (AID), the Overseas Private Investment Corporation (OPIC), and the Institute for Scientific and Technological Cooperation. The first two of these organizations actually antedated IDCA.

Established in 1961 to administer the country's economic aid programs, AID currently conducts major efforts in population planning, food, education, health and energy. With a budget of $5.9 billion for fiscal 1981, AID operates in approximately 80 countries. Its main purpose is to foster long-term economic development. In some cases, however, AID draws from an Economic Support Fund to promote immediate political or economic stability in countries of special interest to the United States. Also, on rare occasion, AID has funneled clandestine funds to pro-American political groups overseas.[25] While providing policy input to IDCA and the State Department on economic development matters, AID's main charge is to carry out assistance programs by a number of means, including low interest loans, cash grants, technical training of nationals in recipient countries, and sending American technical experts abroad.

OPIC represents an alternative approach to the stimulation of foreign economic development. In contrast to the government-to-government programs carried out by AID, OPIC insures investments made by private firms that promote the economic development of less developed countries. By insuring such investment, OPIC eliminates risks that might otherwise discourage investors from placing funds in developing countries. Such risks include expropriation of property, inconvertibility of local currency holdings, and damage to property from war, revolution and insurrection. By encouraging such private investment, OPIC reduces the need for governmental aid. In addition, the investment opportunities created by OPIC generate jobs and export earnings for Americans.

The Arms Control and Disarmament Agency

Created in the same year as AID, the Arms Control and Disarmament Agency (ACDA) is a semiautonomous agency operating under the policy guidance of the Department of State.

The legislation creating ACDA specified that its director should be the "principal advisor to the secretary of state and the president on arms control and disarmament matters." The approximately 200 officials who work in ACDA assist the director in making recommendations on arms control to the president, the secretary of state, and the National Security Council. ACDA conducts studies and research on various aspects of arms control and contracts out research to private firms. ACDA's officers serve on inter-agency planning bodies concerned with arms control and they represent the United States in international arms control negotiations. The chief American negotiator in the Strategic Arms Limitation Talks (SALT)—renamed START by President Reagan—is often the director of ACDA. In the Reagan administration, however, this has not been the case. Even if ACDA's director heads the strategic discussions with the Soviets, the country's negotiating position may be developed elsewhere. Nixon and Kissinger issued instructions to ACDA chief and US SALT negotiator Gerard Smith. Some of the arms control initiatives that have involved ACDA in recent years include: START, mutual force reductions in Europe, a comprehensive nuclear test ban, agreement to limit anti-satellite satellites, a ban on chemical warfare, proliferation of nuclear weapons, conventional arms transfers, arms control in outer space and on the seabed, and the control of intermediate-range nuclear missiles in Europe.

DEPARTMENT OF DEFENSE

The Department of Defense (DOD) is the largest organization (aside from governments) in the non-Communist world. Its headquarters, the Pentagon, symbolizes DOD's mammoth size. This five-sided structure, the largest office building in the world, covers 34 acres and houses a work force of 27 thousand people. Pentagon tour guides are fond of pointing out that the edifice contains $17\frac{1}{2}$ miles of corridors, 100 thousand miles of telephone cables, 65 thousand light fixtures, 150 staircases and 19 escalators. During lunch hour, Pentagon workers may visit a department store, several banks, a drugstore, a laundry, a bakery, and a travel bureau, all without leaving the building. Overall, approximately three million persons (equal to the population of Connecticut) work for the Defense Department, one-third of them in uniform.

The Defense Department was created in response to the threat of aggression that many Americans perceived as emanating from the Soviet Union shortly after World War II. Having adopted the doctrine of containment, the United States needed to pull together the various instruments of national security scattered throughout the government. In particular, more coordination between the diplomats at State and the nation's military leaders was called for. Inter-service rivalry had to be mitigated in order to fortify the military arm of containment. The product of these perceptions was the National Security Act of 1947, which established the Central Intelligence Agency, the National Security Council, and the Department of Defense.

At the head of the DOD (see Fig. 8–2) sits the secretary of defense, a civilian appointed by the president with the advice and consent of the Senate. In addition to managing the department, the secretary is a primary adviser to the president and the NSC on military matters. Various amendments to the National Security Act have given the secretary increased authority over the armed forces. The 1958 Defense Reorganization Act significantly boosted the

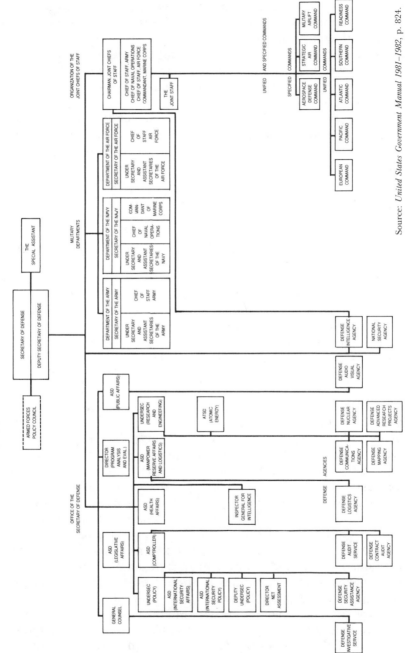

FIGURE 8-2: DEPARTMENT OF DEFENSE

Source: *United States Government Manual 1981–1982*, p. 824.

secretary's control over the military forces by virtue of the authority to assign the development and use of weapons systems to whichever military service the secretary chooses. This gave the secretary control over the enormous program of weapons research and the power to determine when new weapons would become operational and which service would employ them. The act also gave the secretary authority to transfer, abolish and consolidate military missions (such as continental defense or air support for naval craft) among the military services. Another source of the secretary's power over the armed forces lies in the control of military budgets. By allocating funds among the various armed services, the secretary largely determines the scope of their activities and missions.

No one could expect the secretary to perform these functions alone. Accordingly, a panoply of assistants, mostly civilians, has grown around the secretary. These approximately 2 thousand individuals are grouped in what is called the Office of the Secretary of Defense (OSD). As Figure 8–2 reveals, this "office" comprises a fairly sizable organization. A deputy secretary assists the secretary as the latter directs. The undersecretary for research and engineering is responsible for new weapons systems, including research, development, testing and procurement. Given the increasingly technical sophistication of weaponry, this post is one of the most important in the entire field of security policy. The undersecretary for policy is the secretary's principal assistant on political-military affairs, including arms control, intelligence collection and analysis, communication, command and control, the use of outer space, and the integration of departmental plans and policies with overall national security objectives, and is also the prime adviser on NATO matters. The deputy undersecretary for policy planning directs DOD's SALT Task Force, assists the secretary in long and mid-range policy planning for international security matters, and also formulates policy, for the secretary's approval, regarding strategic offensive and defensive forces, theater nuclear force capabilities, arms control, and nuclear targeting. The assistant secretary for program analysis and evaluation, in charge of force planning for the future, analyzes and evaluates the nation's military forces, weapons systems and equipment in light of projected threats and then makes recommendations to the secretary. The Defense Security Assistance Agency handles requests from other countries for military assistance and administers military aid programs, once they have been authorized at higher levels and approved by Congress.

One of the most important units within OSD is the Office of International Security Affairs (ISA), headed by a civilian assistant secretary (who also doubles as the principal deputy undersecretary for policy). Known as the "little State Department" in the Kennedy-Johnson years when it exerted considerable influence in formulating American foreign policy, ISA assists the secretary across the entire spectrum of political-military and economic affairs. Organized along functional and geographic lines that parallel the State Department, ISA and its 250 staffers (mostly civilian) participate in inter-agency bodies and advise the secretary of defense on a broad range of foreign policy concerns. Within the Defense Department, ISA offers a point of view that (sometimes) gives the secretary an alternative to the recommendations of the Joint Chiefs of Staff.

The Joint Chiefs (JCS) constitute a second major component of DOD. This organization consists of the heads of the four military services (the joint chiefs themselves) and a joint staff of 400 military officers. The president appoints the chiefs and selects one among them to be chairman.

The relationship between the secretary and the Joint Chiefs has never been an easy one, in part because their functions overlap to some extent. Both the secretary and the JCS have access to the president. Just as the secretary sits on the National Security Council, the chairman of the JCS attends its meetings in the capacity of military adviser. When the secretary and the JCS hold similar views, as often occurred when Melvin Laird and James Schlesinger were secretary (the Nixon and Ford administrations), the relationship between them is bound to be more cordial than when their views differ (as they often did under Secretary Robert McNamara in the Kennedy and Johnson years). A major area of contention is the military budget. The secretary has the final say over the allocation of funds, but is nevertheless supposed to consult the JCS, as they normally possess more military expertise than the secretary. Invariably, the secretary must pare the JCS budgetary requests, for the latter base their figures more on what they deem the nation needs rather than what the government can afford. Insofar as spending decisions shape military strategy, conflicts over budgets pierce to the heart of the nation's future military options. (One must remember that weapons systems typically take 7–10 years from conception to deployment.) In the lively tradition of inter-service rivalry, each service insists that its mission should take precedence, and that therefore it should receive a higher budgetary allocation than the others. The secretary must reconcile these demands with available resources and with military priorities as seen by the secretary and the president.

While the JCS has an input to many of the security policies that are the concern of the secretary, the main responsibilities of JCS concern military matters. In particular, JCS is responsible for preparing strategic military and logistics plans, reviewing personnel and logistics requirements in light of strategic plans, providing the secretary with statements of military requirements for use in preparing budgets, and advising the secretary regarding foreign military assistance and scientific research and development. As part of this effort, the JCS prepares war plans and engages in contingency military planning. In case of military conflict, the JCS directs the operations of military units in the field.

Civilian Control over the Military

Cognizant of the tendency in many countries for a military elite to seize control of the government, Americans have long believed in civilian control over the military. To ensure civilian supremacy over the military, the framers of the Constitution designated a civilian, the president, as commander-in-chief; they empowered Congress to raise and support the armed forces; and they authorized the Senate to provide advice and consent on military appointments. The National Security Act of 1947 specifies that the secretary of defense as well as the service secretaries be civilians.

But, it might be asked, has not the military slipped the civilian leash in recent years? Those who would answer this question in the affirmative cite the astronomical rise in military spending over past decades as well as American military involvement in such places as Cuba, Vietnam, the Dominican Republic, Iran, Korea, Lebanon, Cambodia and Grenada. A review of these decisions to deploy military force reveals, however, that these actions were not taken by the military over the heads of their civilian counterparts, but rather that the civilians themselves chose to use military force. Despite popular opinion, people in uniform do not always take a more "hawkish" stance than officials in pin-stripe suits. If the United States has shown an inclination to rely on military force, it is because a succession of presidents, legislators, secretaries of state and defense, and members of the public have felt military force to be an appropriate tool of foreign policy. Once the United States had elected to follow the containment doctrine, it was highly probable that the nation would turn to its armed forces. The military services have not obtained such high appropriations over the objections of the civilian sector. Indeed, on occasion Congress has appropriated more money for defense than the Pentagon requested. Let us recall that it was candidate Reagan, a civilian, who promised higher military spending in the 1980s.

The extreme opposite view, that the military silently awaits to be called, like a rifle resting in a rack, is similarly misguided. Because the stakes in the Cold War are so high, leading civilian officials constantly seek military assessments of global tension areas. Furthermore, the military feels duty-bound to make known its views on political-military affairs. The military has gained considerable expertise in evaluating the political implications of various military options. As noted earlier, there is evidence that the Pentagon produces more concise and persuasive policy papers on general foreign policy topics than the Department of State, and that this acumen has contributed to the undoubted increase in the Pentagon's influence in the policy-making arena. The growing importance of military assistance as a tool of foreign policy has also boosted the military's voice as a policymaker. Expertise among military officers is no longer limited to questions of technical military matters. Presidents, furthermore, seek the approval of the military, especially the Joint Chiefs, in taking military-related action. Thus, President Carter made a point of revealing the Joint Chiefs' support for the new Panama Canal treaty signed in 1977. Finally, the sheer size of the military, as well as its large domestic constituency, enhances the military's role in policymaking. The effect of DOD activities upon various sectors of the economy has inclined many Americans to support a large military effort for reasons that have little to do with external threat. Approximately 10 percent of American workers find themselves in military-related employment, whether they be makers of nuclear warheads, suppliers of tires to equip military jeeps, or manufacturers of telephone cable used in military installations. Some members of Congress vote for military projects primarily because they bring jobs to their districts. Other members, especially those serving on armed services and appropriations committees, sometimes vote for high military spending because to do otherwise would seem unpatriotic. (The State Department, by contrast, lacks such a broad-based American clientele. In the eyes of many Americans, the State Department speaks for the interests of foreigners at least as much as for Americans.)

US INFORMATION AGENCY

The US Information Agency (USIA) is the propaganda arm of the United States government. Known for some years as the International Communications Agency, USIA interprets the world through American eyes and ears to foreigners by use of various kinds of media, including radio, moving pictures, television, books, journals, and exhibits. With 204 posts in 27 countries (as of 1980), USIA also develops and administers programs for the international exchange of students, teachers, athletes, artists, and people in various professions. In performing their functions abroad, USIA officers work out of American embassies and other diplomatic missions. USIA operates several libraries and cultural centers in foreign countries. It broadcasts radio programs in English and 38 foreign languages. While it is an independent agency, USIA takes policy guidance from the State Department.

USIA also plays an advisory role in foreign policy formulation. The agency conducts studies of foreign opinion, which it relays to appropriate officers throughout the executive branch. USIA also advises the president, the secretary of state and the NSC regarding foreign opinion toward existing and proposed American foreign policy.

THE ECONOMIC AGENCIES

As the American economy has grown more complex, and as the destructiveness of modern weapons has rendered military force less usable for limited objectives, economic instruments of diplomacy have gained in importance. In Chapter 13, we shall explore some of America's foreign economic relations in detail. Here, we are interested in the role that economic agencies play in the formulation of foreign policy.

Logically speaking, one could make a persuasive case that the State Department, nominally responsible for the overall conduct of American foreign policy, should set the broad outlines of the country's foreign economic policy. In fact, however, State has had a rather weak voice in the determination of such policy. Instead, the economic departments have had a relatively free hand in shaping economic policy abroad. This latitude springs from three sources. In the first place, each of the economic departments enjoys a large, vocal and well organized domestic constituency. Business, farm and labor lobbies bring considerable pressure to bear upon and devote a good deal of support to the Departments of Commerce, Treasury, and Agriculture. This alliance is bolstered by the addition of certain congressional committees who view themselves as supporters of the departments they are charged with overseeing. Not only does State lack such domestic support, but it possesses less expertise in economic matters than those departments whose primary functions concern economic affairs. As we have seen, State continues to display a reluctance to master such technical aspects of foreign policy. The second factor weakening State's control over economic policy is the steady erosion of the traditional distinction between domestic and foreign matters. For example, the quantity of grain American farmers sell overseas affects farm incomes as well as the price of bread in American supermarkets. As has become painfully obvious to many Americans, the price that OPEC countries set for petroleum has a direct bearing on the price displayed on gasoline pumps. Bayless Manning has coined the term "intermestic" to describe the ever-growing list of items that have international as well as domestic implications.[26] Today, the nation's security may be undermined just as seriously by a shortage of key raw materials as by a military assault. Because economic matters have a clear domestic tie-in, the State Department must share responsibility for foreign economic policy with the domestically oriented agencies that have greater responsibility for and expertise in these areas. Thus, both State and Agriculture have responsibility for the Food for Peace Program. This sharing constitutes the third factor that weakens State's control over international economic policy.

Treasury Department

Since the days when Alexander Hamilton occupied the post, the secretary of the treasury has been the government's chief financial officer. Although the Treasury Department is much more concerned with such domestic matters as inflation, interest rates and employment than with international affairs, the department does have primary responsibility for international monetary affairs. The strength of the dollar in international currency markets is a primary international concern of the Treasury Department, as is international monetary reform. The department also concerns itself with the nation's balance of trade, balance of payments, trade agreements, and loans to developing countries.

The secretary enjoys a considerable say in foreign economic policy through formal roles in many international economic bodies. The secretary is the American representative to the International Monetary Fund, the International Bank for Reconstruction and Development (World Bank), the Asian Development Bank, the Inter-American Development Bank and the African Development Fund, and has a loud voice in decisions of the Export-Import Bank, an American institution that lends money to foreign governments so they can purchase American exports. The secretary is co-chairman of the US-Saudi Arabian Joint Commission on Economic Cooperation, co-chairman of the US-Israeli Joint Committee for Investment and Trade, a member of other Middle East joint commissions, co-chairman of the US-USSR Commercial Commission, co-chairman of the US-China Joint Economic Committee, chairman of the East-West Foreign Trade Board, and a member of joint trade and development commissions with Poland and Rumania. The secretary is also a member of various inter-agency bodies that formulate foreign economic policy.

The undersecretary for monetary affairs is responsible for such matters as international monetary affairs, trade and energy policy.

The primary unit within Treasury for international matters is the office of the assistant secretary for international affairs. This office advises and assists the secretary and the undersecretary for monetary affairs in formulating and executing policies regarding monetary, financial, commercial, energy and trade issues. The office is divided into units concerned with monetary matters, developing nations, trade and investment policy, and commodities and natural resources.

The Treasury Department houses the Bureau of Alcohol, Tobacco, and Firearms, the US Customs Service, and the US Secret Service. These units deal in part with such matters as the international drug traffic, illegal arms imports and exports, and protection of the president while abroad.

In recent years, Treasury has on occasion clashed with AID over the nation's development policy toward Third World countries. An ever increasing proportion of the nation's economic aid is being disbursed through international financial institutions, such as the World Bank, as opposed to bilateral assistance arrangements. Since the Treasury Department instructs American representatives to these institutions, Treasury has been gaining a larger say over the country's economic development policy at AID's expense.

Commerce Department

While the Commerce Department has a voice in many of the issues for which the Treasury Department has principal responsibility, Commerce is primarily charged with protecting and increasing America's foreign trade, especially exports. In pursuit of this task, Commerce conducts research on overseas trade and investment developments, advises the business community, and helps American business gain access to export markets. The department makes a large input into inter-agency policy on trade negotiations, international commodity and resource policy, and import and export policy. Department officials negotiate and administer various international trade agreements, such as those pertaining to textiles and television sets.

While Treasury has traditionally been more influential than Commerce in formulating foreign economic policy, the latter's role has been on the rise since the 1970s. America's first trade deficit in the twentieth century, which occurred in 1971, spurred the Commerce Department under Secretary Maurice Stans to make an all-out effort to boost American exports. Commerce's role was further strengthened by the Nixon administration's determination to make trade a girder in the structure of détente. The 1972 summit resulted in the establishment within Commerce of the Bureau of East-West Trade. This bureau has the function of helping American businesses develop trade with the Soviet Union and Eastern Europe; the bureau has also been effective in removing some American controls on exports of goods to Communist Eastern Europe. One measure of its success is the growth of US trade with the Eastern Bloc from one-half billion dollars in 1970 to five billion dollars in 1980 (see Table 3–1).

The department's Bureau of International Commerce works with the president's trade representative and other executive agencies in formulating policy for international trade negotiations. In 1980 the secretary of commerce established the International Trade Administration to promote world trade and strengthen the international trade and investment position of the United States. The US Travel Service, part of the Department of Commerce, stimulates foreign travel to the United States, thereby alleviating America's balance of payments deficit (thrown deep into the red as a result of higher prices paid for imported oil after 1973).

United States Trade Representative

The Office of the United States Trade Representative was established in 1963 as part of the president's executive office. Creation of this post manifested a recognition that international trade is an increasingly important factor in the nation's economic well-being. (By the end of 1980, exports accounted for nearly 20 percent of all goods produced by the United States, up from less than 12 percent in 1973.) The office is headed by the US Trade Representative, a Cabinet-level official with the rank of ambassador who is responsible directly to the president.

With input from other executive agencies, the Office of the United States Trade Representative is responsible for setting and administering overall trade policy. The US Trade Representative is the chief American negotiator at most multinational trade negotiations, including those conducted under the auspices of the General Agreement on Tariffs and Trade (GATT), the Organization for European Cooperation and Development (OECD), and the United Nations Conference on Trade and Development (UNCTAD). The trade representative may also conduct sensitive bilateral trade talks, such as those with Japan on that country's voluntary export restrictions to the United States. In addition, the trade representative chairs the Cabinet-level Trade Policy Committee, which determines the country's overall foreign trade policy, and serves as *ex officio* member on the board of directors of the Export-Import Bank and the Overseas Private Investment Corporation.

Agriculture Department

The US Department of Agriculture (USDA) works to develop and expand foreign markets for American agricultural products. Through a network of about 100 attachés located in approximately 70 different countries, the department reports on agricultural developments abroad and seeks new markets for American produce. USDA also manages the country's programs in agricultural assistance, cooperative research and scientific exchange. The department further seeks to reduce foreign barriers to American agricultural exports.

One of the USDA's major tasks in the international field is management of the Public Law 480 Program, more commonly known as Food for Peace. The Food for Peace Program aims at long-range improvement of the economies of developing countries. The United States provides low-interest, long-term credits to governments that purchase American farm commodities. These buyers then sell the goods and use the proceeds for self-help measures that generate economic development. Recent alterations of P.L. 480 allow the United States to write off repayments if the recipient country undertakes specified economic development projects with the revenues from the sales. In case of natural disasters, USDA sends food abroad without any expectation of repayment. Under the Commodity Credit Corporation Export Credit Sales Program, USDA offers financing at commercial or preferred rates to countries to enable them to buy American agricultural goods. This program seeks to expand American farm exports and is not part of the nation's economic assistance program. The department also recommends import quotas for certain agricultural commodities.

Members of the department's international wing, known as the Foreign Agricultural Service, help formulate policy for and conduct negotiations in bilateral and multilateral agricultural trade talks. These individuals participate in the regular meetings of such organizations as GATT, the Food and Agricultural Organization (FAO) of the United Nations, and the OECD. Like other attachés who are not State Department employees, these agricultural attachés report to their own department rather than through the ambassadors.

As do most of the economic agencies discussed here, USDA tends to support the immediate needs of its domestic constituency. The main clients of the Agricultural Department are farmers and those involved in agribusiness, large conglomerates like Ralston-Purina that engage in many aspects of commodity production, processing, and sales. Support for their constituencies sometimes involves the domestic departments in disputes with the Department of State, due to a difference in mission. The State Department, to some extent at least, concerns itself with the nation's longer-range goals, and it often objects when the economic agencies seek to promote their clients' immediate interests. As an illustration of such conflict, the State Department urged a boycott of American grain sales to the Soviet Union after Moscow invaded Afghanistan in 1979. The Agriculture Department was more concerned with obtaining profitable revenues for farmers and opposed the boycott (which was enacted in 1980). After vocal protests by the farm community, President Reagan lifted the embargo in 1981.

POLICY MAKING REVISITED: IMPROVING THE POLICY MACHINERY

Considering the complexity of foreign policy making in the executive branch, it is somewhat surprising that the government is able to formulate any foreign policy whatever. In this concluding section, we shall review some of the virtues and deficiencies of bureaucratic politics and then consider some suggestions for improving the policy machinery.

As currently structured, the system is not without advantages.[27] By the time the various departments and agencies have fashioned a bureaucratic compromise, there is broad agreement throughout the government about what course of action to take. This consensus minimizes the likelihood that any particular department or agency will seek to thwart chosen policy. The exercise of bureaucratic politics also ensures that many voices will be heard before the government reaches a decision. Such practice heightens the chances that the optimal policy will be revealed through the clash of competing alternatives. As we have seen, a great deal of planning and analysis goes into decision making; this too increases the probability that the best course of action will come to light. Finally, one of the often-cited drawbacks of the system, delay, is not without its advantages. How often have individuals and organizations taken hasty decisions in the heat of the moment, only to regret them at a later time? The time-consuming process of bureaucratic politics imposes a sobering interval upon governmental action and thereby reduces the system's capacity for rash emotional responses.

At the same time, we must realize that bureaucratic politics suffers from several deficiencies. One of these is the very delay just mentioned. While such intervals may impose a moment of reflection before government leaps to unconsidered action, they may also prevent government from capitalizing on opportunities of the moment. Events overseas will not wait for the American policy-making community to reach decisions. While the government is capable of responding swiftly in crises (thereby bypassing bureaucratic politics), developments short of crisis proportions can outpace the government's capacity to act. Thus, it took an unduly long time for the government to realize that the Sino-Soviet dispute represented a fundamental cleavage and not just a family feud or a trick to throw the West off guard. There are other drawbacks associated with bureaucratic politics. We have mentioned the tendency to compromise instead of making bold decisions. The difficulties in fashioning new policies sometimes result in adherence to existing policy until long after it no longer suffices. On some occasions the enormous efforts required to hammer out policy result in inaction. A process in which many departments and agencies examine the same issues in preparation for policy debates produces a large amount of duplication. Exposing divisions within the bureaucracy affords foreign powers the chance to drive a wedge into the policy-making machinery, playing off one or more departments against others. To illustrate, during the Carter administration the

Soviet Union attempted more than once to capitalize on differences between Secretary of State Vance, who went out of his way to look for points of agreement with Moscow, and Special Assistant Brzezinski, who took a much harder view of the Kremlin. Finally, when bureaucratic differences come out into the open, other nations may gain the impression that the United States is divided and lacks determination.

Many experts both within and outside government have examined the policy-making process in search of a better method. Many of these analyses have proceeded from the conclusion that the State Department, nominally the lead agency in foreign affairs, is incapable of playing this role effectively. This finding has little to do with the quality of individuals who work at State or the internal procedures of the department. Rather, there is strong agreement that State lacks the resources to oversee the entire "foreign affairs government." According to one estimate, State receives only about 7 percent of all the resources the government expends upon foreign policy.[28] The department's overseas personnel represent only 29 percent of the 21,500 officials who staff America's diplomatic missions.[29] Another impediment to the State Department's orchestration of foreign policy is State's lack of control over the career progress of individuals in other departments. Thus, a Treasury officer posted abroad who is faced with conflicting instructions from the Treasury Department and from the ambassador (representing State) is likely to follow the Treasury instructions, since superiors in that department will determine the individual's efficiency rating.

Because the State Department seems incapable of managing the entire foreign policy apparatus, several analysts have proposed the creation of a new "super agency" to oversee all the departments and agencies that participate in foreign policy, including State. Of the numerous variations on this theme, a representative example may be found in a suggestion by the Brookings Institution in 1960. This proposal called for a new Department of Foreign Affairs (the original name for the Department of State for a brief period in 1789) that would provide unified direction to foreign policy. The new department would be headed by a secretary for foreign affairs, a Cabinet-level officer appointed by the president. The new secretary would be responsible for the overall direction of foreign policy and would be the president's chief deputy in foreign affairs. The department of foreign affairs would be responsible for planning and directing foreign policy, not for implementation of policy. That task would fall to three operating organizations, the leaders of which would also sit in the Cabinet. The Department of State would be responsible for the day-to-day operation of foreign policy. A Department of Foreign Economic Operations would concern itself with America's foreign economic relations, including foreign aid. Finally, a Department for Information and Cultural Affairs would take the place of the US Information Agency.

Advocates of such a scheme discern a significant advantage in the unification of foreign policy direction in a single office. Since the president would appoint the secretary for foreign affairs, the chief executive would gain a strong hand over the direction of the nation's foreign policy. Yet, others detect in the idea more problems than advantages. The new department of foreign affairs would represent still another layer of organization in an already overly bureaucratic setting. This new layer would further remove those who make policy from the everyday realities of implementing policy. Conflicts between the secretary for foreign affairs and the secretaries of the operating agencies would surely arise; since all of these officials would possess Cabinet rank, the president would be compelled to resolve disputes. If the new secretary emerged supreme, it might become difficult to locate outstanding individuals to fill such roles as secretary of state. A secretary for foreign affairs who performed the role with great effectiveness might pose problems for the president. If the new secretary actually directed the nation's foreign policy, then which office would function as the nation's chief executive in foreign affairs? Would a president welcome a rival authority? If not, would the president on occasion seek to undercut the potential challenger just to maintain control? Other critics fear that an effective secretary for foreign affairs would insulate the president from the clash of foreign policy ideas, thereby rendering the president less knowledgeable. Such a development might render the president excessively dependent on the supposed assistant!

Other schemes have been proposed to provide greater unity and control over the nation's foreign policy. Some have suggested that the vice president take charge of foreign policy, or that the special assistant for national security affairs do so. Most of the advantages and drawbacks of the Brookings plan also apply to these recommendations.

On reflection, it appears unlikely that any re-tooling of the foreign policy-making process will work much better than the present machinery. At least the existing setup allows the apparatus to be designed according to each president's own operating style. Kennedy could guide foreign policy with his own hand; Reagan could place that responsibility in the secretary of state; Nixon could entrust foreign policy to the special assistant for national security affairs; and Eisenhower could rely on the secretary of state and an elaborate NSC structure. To be sure, all these variations come with their own advantages and drawbacks. After all is said and done, it probably makes more sense to allow presidents the freedom to design a system that works best for them, rather than force them to fit their distinctive operating styles into a preordained mold.

FOR DISCUSSION

What factors in non-crisis decision making situations give rise to bureaucratic politics?

What are some of the strong points and drawbacks of bureaucratic politics?

Compare the influence of personality, organization and role upon decision makers.

In what sense is it appropriate to speak of the bureaucracy *versus* the president?

Explain how internal conditions at the State Department have weakened the organization. What reforms would you recommend? Why might such reforms have trouble being accepted?

Would you favor a reform of the foreign policy-making structure along the lines of the Brookings Institution proposal? Why or why not?

READING SUGGESTIONS

Allison, Graham T. *Essense of Decision: Explaining the Cuban Missile Crisis*. Boston: Little, Brown, 1971.

Barnet, Richard J. *Roots of War*. Baltimore: Penguin, 1971.

Brenner, Michael J. *Nuclear Power and Non-Proliferation: The Remaking of U.S. Policy*. New York: Cambridge University Press, 1981.

Commission on the Organization of the Government for the Conduct of Foreign Affairs. Washington: GPO, 1975.

Destler, I. M. *Presidents, Bureaucrats, and Foreign Policy*. Princeton: Princeton University Press, 1974.

Etheredge, Lloyd S. *A World of Men: The Private Sources of American Foreign Policy.* Cambridge, Mass.: The MIT Press, 1978.

Halperin, Morton H. *Bureaucratic Politics and Foreign Policy.* Washington, D.C.: Brookings Institution, 1974.

Hilsman, Roger. *The Politics of Policy Making in Defense and Foreign Affairs.* New York: Harper and Row, 1971.

Neustadt, Richard E. *Presidential Power.* New York: John Wiley and Son, 1960.

Pringle, Robert. "Creeping Irrelevance at Foggy Bottom," *Foreign Policy,* No. 29 (Winter 1977–78): 128–39.

NOTES

1. The models described here are based on Graham T. Allison, *Essence of Decision: Explaining the Cuban Missile Crisis* (Boston: Little, Brown and Company, 1971). Allison identifies a third model of decision making, which he calls the Organizational Processes Model. We shall not concern ourselves with this model here.

2. Ibid., p. 18.

3. Some classic studies of bureaucratic politics include Morton H. Halperin, *Bureaucratic Politics and Foreign Policy* (Washington, D.C.: Brookings Institution, 1974); Roger Hilsman, *To Move A Nation* (New York: Doubleday, 1967); Samuel P. Huntington, *The Common Defense* (New York, 1961); Richard E. Neustadt, *Presidential Power* (New York: John Wiley and Son, 1960); and Warner R. Schilling, "The Politics of National Defense: Fiscal 1950," in W. R. Schilling, P. T. Hammond, and G. H. Snyder, *Strategy, Politics, and Defense Budgets* (New York: Columbia University Press, 1962).

4. I. M. Destler, *Presidents, Bureaucrats, and Foreign Policy* (Princeton: Princeton University Press, 1974), p. 52. A highly recommended study of bureaucratic politics.

5. Hilsman, pp. 554–55.

6. Richard J. Barnet, *Roots of War* (Baltimore: Penguin, 1971).

7. See, for example, Bruce Mazlish, *In Search of Nixon: A Psychohistorical Inquiry* (New York: Basic Books, 1972); Arthur Woodstone, *Nixon's Head* (New York: St. Martin's, 1972); Dana Ward, "Kissinger: A Psychohistory," *History of Childhood Quarterly: The Journal of Psychohistory* (Winter 1975).

8. Alexander L. and Juliette L. George, *Woodrow Wilson and Colonel House: A Personality Study* (New York: Dover, 1964).

9. Barnet, especially Chapter 5.

10. Lloyd S. Etheredge, *A World of Men: The Private Sources of American Foreign Policy* (Cambridge: The MIT Press, 1978).

11. Richard E. Neustadt, "Whitehouse and Whitehall," *The Public Interest,* No. 2 (Winter 1966): 64.

12. Allison, p. 148.

13. Quoted in Allison, pp. 172–73.
14. Neustadt, *Presidential Power*, p. 10.
15. Destler, Chapter 6.
16. Robert Pringle, "Creeping Irrelevance at Foggy Bottom," *Foreign Policy*, No. 29 (Winter 1977–78): 128–39.
17. US Department of State, *Diplomacy for the 1970s* (Washington: GPO, 1970), p. 5.
18. This description, however, would not apply to William P. Clark, nominated in 1981 by President Reagan to be deputy secretary of state and shifted the following year to the post of national security adviser. In his confirmation hearing before the Senate Foreign Relations Committee, Clark was unable to name the prime minister of South Africa, the leader of Zimbabwe, the precise NATO countries that were balking at providing bases for US tactical nuclear weapons, and recent developments in British politics. All these topics had received extensive press coverage at the time of the hearings. *Philadelphia Inquirer*, February 3, 1981.
19. In October 1980, Congress created a Senior Foreign Service as part of the Foreign Service Act of 1980. Members are to be chosen for this group on the basis of outstanding performance as opposed to seniority. As part of this reward for excellence, those admitted to the Senior Foreign Service are eligible for bonuses up to 20 percent of their basic pay.
20. Quoted in Destler, p. 32.
21. Alexander M. Haig, Jr., confirmation testimony before the Senate Foreign Relations Committee, January 9, 1981, reprinted in the *New York Times*, January 10, 1981.
22. Hodding Carter III, "State Department—Memoir," *Playboy*, XXVIII (February 1981): 214.
23. US Department of State, *Diplomacy for the 1970s*.
24. Destler, *Presidents, Bureaucrats, and Foreign Policy*.
25. According to former ambassador to Chile Edward M. Korry, AID provided funds to anti-Communist Roman Catholic groups in Chile as well as to the 1964 presidential campaign of Eduardo Frei (the victorious candidate). *New York Times*, February 9, 1981.
26. Bayless Manning, "The Congress, The Executive and Intermestic Affairs: Three Proposals," *Foreign Affairs*, LV (January 1977): 306–24.
27. The drawbacks and advantages of the policy-making process are skillfully treated in Roger Hilsman, *The Politics of Policy Making in Defense and Foreign Affairs* (New York: Harper and Row, 1971), Chapter 7.
28. US Department of State, *Diplomacy for the 1970s*, p. 11.
29. Destler, *Presidents, Bureaucrats and Foreign Policy*, p. 11. DOD has approximately the same proportion of overseas staffers.

Chapter 9
Intelligence

And ye shall know the truth
And the truth shall make you free

John, VIII:32 (inscribed on the lobby
at CIA headquarters, Langley, Virginia)

In 1978 a singular gathering took place in West Germany.[1] There, Allied code-breakers from World War II met with their Axis adversaries, German cryptographers who had worked for Hitler. Under discussion was one of the greatest intelligence coups in history, called Ultra. Thanks to the efforts of British code-breakers, the Allies were privy to high-level German communications, including those between Hitler and his generals. Due to this intelligence breakthrough, Allied convoys were able to steer around U-boat wolfpacks, helping to win the Battle of the Atlantic. Early knowledge of Germany's V-rockets alerted Allied air forces to bomb a key research center at Peenemunde and launching sites in France. By reading what the Japanese ambassador in Berlin was reporting back to Tokyo, the Allies learned Hitler's intentions toward Europe.

By most accounts, Ultra shortened the war and saved many lives. While the consequences of most intelligence operations are less dramatic, Ultra demonstrates that an effective intelligence arm can contribute significantly to a government's foreign policy.

Strictly speaking, the agencies and departments engaged in intelligence are not part of the policy-making model described in

309

Chapter One. In a technical sense, intelligence organizations do not formulate policy. Rather, they provide the information that others utilize in making policy decisions. As we shall see, however, this distinction does not always coincide with reality. So long as knowledge is power, those agencies that possess knowledge will have influence over policy. We include intelligence organizations here for yet another reason. The quality of a government's foreign policy is largely dependent on the information upon which it acts. If we are to understand American foreign policy, we must comprehend the processes by which information is gathered and communicated to those who set policy. Clandestine operations, sometimes known as "dirty tricks," also pose questions for the understanding of foreign policy.

Some of the more spectacular successes and failures of recent American foreign policy are closely linked with intelligence operations. Perhaps the most stunning intelligence success occurred in 1961, when U-2 spy planes confirmed the existence of Soviet missiles in Cuba in time for Washington to have them removed. One year later a dismal failure occurred, as a CIA-sponsored invasion of Cuba sputtered to a bloody end on the beach at the Bay of Pigs.

Other episodes are less well known. Shortly after World War II, the United States secretly channeled money and advice to nonleftist political parties in Italy and thereby helped prevent the formation of a Communist government. In 1953 the CIA helped topple Premier Mohammed Mossadegh of Iran, after he had nationalized the British-owned Anglo-Iranian Oil Company. One year later the CIA formed a military force that overthrew President Jacobo Arbenz of Guatemala, who had raised fears of planting communism in the Western Hemisphere, where he invited Communists to join his cabinet and expropriated 400 thousand acres of land owned by the United Fruit Company.

The development of photo-reconnaissance satellites in the 1960s was one of the major intelligence triumphs in recent decades. These "spies in the skies" take high-resolution photographs of the earth's surface from many miles up. Such photography has made possible the SALT agreements, for satellites can spot the construction of missile silos. Today, satellites account for more intelligence on the Soviet Union than any other method of collection. The Soviet Union too has satellites. The capacity of such devices is illustrated by the following episode.[2] In 1970, special Army units were training to raid a North Vietnamese compound at Son Tay in order to free American prisoners. For training purposes, the Army constructed a mock-up of the prison at Eglin Air Force Base in Florida. In order to escape detection by the Russian Cosmos satellite that passed 70 miles overhead every day, the Army dismantled the model each dawn and even covered over post-holes for the two-by-fours that held it up. Nevertheless, when the Army carried out the raid in November 1970, it found the prison compound deserted.

American intelligence has had its share of failures. After World War II the United States sought to establish networks of agents throughout Communist Eastern Europe. These agents, it was hoped, would carry out general disruption and would act as fifth columns in case of war with Russia. Instead, the Soviet Union penetrated the networks and all but eliminated them. In 1958, rebel troops supported by the CIA failed to overthrow President Sukarno of Indonesia; the CIA's denial of involvement collapsed when one of its American pilots was shot down. Throughout the 1970s, the CIA supplied estimates of Soviet military spending that are now considered low. In 1980 the agency suddenly doubled the proportion of GNP it estimated the Soviets had been spending on the military—from about 5-7 percent to about 11-13 percent. Despite a pervasive CIA presence in Iran, the overthrow of the shah in 1979 caught the agency by surprise.

A full 60 minutes after President Sadat of Egypt died of gunshot wounds in 1981, President Reagan sent him a get-well message.

Of course, the above list of successes and failures is far from complete. It must be borne in mind that intelligence organizations generally operate in secret. Years often pass before their exploits become known, if they ever do. On the other hand, congressional and executive investigations in the 1970s of America's intelligence operations and organizations have made them the most widely known about in the world (to the dismay of many intelligence operatives). Therefore, while we must hedge our conclusions with the realization that we may not know all there is to know, enough has been revealed to warrant some judgments.

Before proceeding to analyze the intelligence component of American foreign policy, we should pause to define what we mean by intelligence. Intelligence may be defined as "knowledge, organization, and activity that results in (1) the collection, analysis, production, dissemination and use of information which relates to any other government, political group, party, military force, movement or other association which is believed to relate to the group's or the government's security; (2) countering similar activities by other groups, governments, or movements; and (3) activities undertaken to affect the composition and behavior of such groups or governments."[3] This definition helps us perceive an important distinction between intelligence and the mere accumulation of information. Intelligence concerns the collector's security, which may be defined in military, political or economic terms. Intelligence also embraces the steps a government takes to prevent the collection of information about itself; this is called counterintelligence. Intelligence also includes actions designed to affect other governments or political groups. When done secretly and/or illegally, these measures are referred to as clandestine or covert.

Revelations of the activities of American intelligence organizations, which came to light after the 1972 Watergate break-in, compelled Americans to ask some hard questions. Under what circumstances, if any, should the United States resort to illegal actions in pursuit of the national interest? Is American foreign policy democratic if the government conceals some of its activities from the people? Do the president and the president's chief assistants control intelligence agencies, or do they simply do as they please? What role does Congress deserve in oversight of intelligence activities? Do intelligence agencies threaten the civil liberties of the American citizens they are sworn to defend? Do covert actions against other governments, even when they succeed, advance or retard America's standing in the world? We shall examine these and other issues in the following pages.

FUNCTIONS OF INTELLIGENCE

Intelligence organizations are the eyes and ears of government. To be more specific, intelligence organizations perform five principal functions: collect data, analyze data, distribute information, undertake covert operations, and suggest policy. To protect themselves, intelligence agencies also engage in counterintelligence. We shall examine these functions in turn.

Collect Data

The first stage in policy planning is, or should be, the collection of data about the target. American intelligence agencies gather enormous amounts of information about a seemingly limitless number of topics on every country in the world. While American intelligence concentrates on Communist regimes, especially the Soviet Union, Washington acquires significant information about all countries, both friends and foes. Naturally, policymakers seek information about a hostile country's military forces. This may include not only the number of men in uniform but also the location of missile sites and technological breakthroughs the other side is about to achieve. American policymakers are vitally interested in other countries' industrial production as well as their rates of economic growth. Views on leading political figures—both in the government and out—are important. Awareness of energy scarcity has elevated the importance of knowing about energy production and consumption patterns in various countries. Seemingly trivial information can assume importance in certain circumstances. For example, the distance between trees across a road may determine which armored vehicles can be deployed in a military emergency.

Like other advanced countries, the United States uses a variety of techniques to collect data. A great deal of material (particularly about the United States) is available from open sources—newspapers, public opinion surveys, trade journals, government publications (in open societies), and the like. The most familiar intelligence collection method is spying, known as human intelligence or HUMINT among intelligence practitioners. Spies always work under "cover." Some American intelligence agents overseas operate under diplomatic cover, such as political adviser to the ambassador or commercial attaché; these persons are generally known to be intelligence agents by other members of that country's diplomatic community. (The fictional character James Bond was well known to friend and foes as an agent of British intelligence, for example.) Other agents work under "deep cover." Such individuals may pose as businessmen, journalists or travelers, and their actual identity is known to only a very few. Today, human intelligence is responsible for only a small amount of the total data collected by intelligence agencies. There is no substitute for human intelligence when it is necessary to know the intentions and opinions of foreign government officials, military figures and prominent dissidents. Without human contact, it is difficult to tell how strongly a minister espouses views announced in a public speech. Spies provide the best clues about the forward planning of other governments. By most accounts, neither the United States nor the Soviet Union has been notably successful in placing spies in the other's government. The Russians, however, have planted various "moles" such as Kim Philby in the British government, and some of these agents have transmitted information about American policies and practices.

As a source of foreign intelligence, spying has largely given way to signal intelligence (SIGINT) and photographic intelligence (PHOTINT). SIGINT refers to obtaining information from transmissions. It is divided into two categories. COMINT, or communications intelligence, concerns the interception of communications. This may include telephone calls, messages between a military headquarters and a unit in the field, transmissions between a submarine and fleet command at home, or messages between a bomber pilot and a control tower. For several years up to 1971, the CIA was able to intercept telephone messages to and from top Soviet officials in their limousines as they drove around Moscow. The Soviets, for their part, managed to place a "bug" in the American eagle at the Moscow embassy. In order to protect sensitive communications, governments usually send them in code. Thus, there is a constant battle going on between the world's code-makers and code-breakers. The other form of SIGINT is ELINT, or electronic intelligence. In contrast to COMINT, ELINT refers to impulses emitted not by persons but by machines. By "reading" radar impulses, for instance, one can gauge a radar system's capabilities. Through intercepting electronic impulses transmitted to missiles in flight tests it is possible to gain some knowledge about a missile's range, altitude, accuracy, MIRV capabilities, and so on. Photographic intelligence is carried out mostly by satellites, and photo-reconnaissance aircraft. The U-2 airplane that photographed Soviet missile emplacements in Cuba in 1961 was engaged in PHOTINT.

How do American intelligence agencies determine what data to collect? On a routine basis, enormous quantities of data on every country are stored and updated in data banks maintained by the CIA. These country profiles typically include information on the economy, the military, population trends, transportation and communication facilities, key political figures, and so on. Additional intelligence is gathered in response to specific demands from high officials. For example, the special assistant for national security may want information about the leaders of a dissident movement in Central America. Or, the secretary of defense may request information about alternative sources of chromium or the capabilities of a new Russian tank.

Two former CIA agents, Victor Marchetti and John D. Marks, suggest that it is possible to collect too much information. "Clearly, the prevailing theology in the US intelligence community calls for the collection of as much information as possible. Little careful consideration is given to the utility of the huge amounts of material so acquired. The attitude of 'collection for collection's sake' has resulted in mountains of information which can only overwhelm intelligence analysts charged with interpreting it."[4] Streamlining data collection to avoid a glut remains a problem in the intelligence community.

Analyze Data

Once data are accumulated by the several means described above, they must be turned into finished intelligence products. Busy government officials are not going to plow through reams of facts and figures in search of patterns and conclusions. This is the task, and a very difficult one, of the intelligence analyst. It is one thing, for instance, to assemble figures on numbers and types of Soviet forces in Afghanistan. It is quite another to predict whether the Soviets will use these forces to seize the Persian Gulf. Similarly, one can gain a fairly accurate count of Soviet strategic missiles, but it is far more difficult to gauge how the Kremlin will use this power to extract political concessions from Western Europe. Analysts may be asked to produce papers on all types of questions. Would a black-ruled South Africa welcome a Cuban military presence? What is the strength of communism in Central America? What steps should the United States avoid in order to prevent a reconciliation between Russia and China? How stable is the Saudi monarchy? Which countries are most likely to construct nuclear weapons, and how might the United States prevent this? What progress are the Soviets making in being able to detect the whereabouts of American submarines? What regions of the world seem destined to experience famine in the next decade?

Answering such questions is made more difficult by the fact that the analyst rarely has all the information he or she needs. Furthermore, the information that is available may be incorrect or incomplete, although the analyst may not know that. Let us remember that governments seek to conceal the very information that intelligence analysts desire. Occasionally, governments offer "disinformation" to rival intelligence organizations.

Like data collection, some analyses are performed on a routine basis, while others are completed in response to special requests from high officials. Illustrative of the first type, the CIA produces a National Intelligence Daily (much like a newspaper), as does the Defense Intelligence Agency. The CIA also prepares a daily report for the president. These analyses are short and descriptive, based on the events of the day. Intelligence agencies also produce in-depth studies on a regular basis, such as the annual assessment of Soviet strategic forces. The studies produced in response to requests by policymakers may have a deadline of a few hours, a week, or several months. The most important such studies are called National Intelligence Estimates. In the preparation of a National Intelligence Estimate, all the intelligence organizations with expertise on the particular topic pool their information and seek to reach an agreed analysis of the issue at hand. Should agreement prove impossible, dissenting footnotes are appended to the study. The finished product thus represents the best thinking of the entire intelligence community on a particular subject.

Of course, unforeseen events and hidden facts routinely defy the most thorough efforts to analyze a situation. Most British analysts were surprised by Argentina's attempt to seize the Falkland Islands in 1982. Soviet policymakers hardly planned for the Sino-Soviet split. Despite the pervasive presence of American officials throughout Iran during the shah's tenure, the religious revolution that overthrew him caught the United States by surprise. While one should constantly seek to upgrade the performance of intelligence agencies, one should also recognize that intelligence analysis is a task fraught with difficulties.

Distribute Information

As intelligence organizations generally do not determine foreign policy, it is essential that the data and analyses they produce reach important policymakers. This is accomplished through elaborate routing channels, based on the concept of "need to know." This concept is designed to minimize leaks of classified information. Intelligence organizations operate in constant fear of leaks, largely because a leak often reveals the source of information. A large number of leaks rapidly dries up sources. Therefore, intelligence agencies seek to put information in the hands of officials who need to know it, while at the same time denying the information to others.

Of course, getting information to the right people does not necessarily mean they will make use of it. For years the CIA expressed doubts that North Vietnam would succumb to American military pressure. However, no American president cared to go down in history as giving up a struggle, and so the United States pressed on until the final debacle. Harry Howe Ransom, a long-time student of American intelligence, hypothesizes that "intelligence systems tend to report what they think the political leadership wants to hear, and whatever is reported, leaders often take actions without regard for the intelligence reports. If it is true, intelligence makes little difference in policy formation. . . . Intelligence may be less a policy determinant and more an ingredient to be manipulated by policy makers."[5] Should Ransom's hypothesis prove valid, the implications are disturbing, to say the least.

Covert Operations

Of all the functions that intelligence agencies perform, covert operations are the most controversial by far. Covert operations may be defined as "an attempt to influence politics and events in other states without revealing involvement."[6] In a talk before the Council on Foreign Relations in 1968, Richard Bissell, a former covert operator for the CIA, listed nine types of covert operations:

(1) secret political advice and counseling to foreign governments, political candidates, and intelligence organizations;
(2) payoffs to foreign individuals, such as cabinet ministers, police chiefs, newspaper editors, and military generals; in return these persons supply information or take action favorable to the United States;
(3) financial support or technical assistance to foreign political parties; the United States secretly provided help in the election campaigns of Ramon Magsaysay of the Philippines, Eduardo Frei of Chile, and numerous non-leftist candidates in Italy;
(4) the support of private organizations overseas, such as labor unions, farm cooperatives, business firms, and the like; by secretly funneling money to the striking trucking union in Chile in the 1970s, the United States prolonged the walk-out and helped bring down the government of leftist Salvador Allende;

"If the U.S. is to survive, long-standing American concepts of 'fair play' must be reconsidered. We must develop effective espionage and counterespionage services. We must learn to subvert, sabotage, and destroy our enemies by more clever, more sophisticated and more effective methods than those used against us."
Doolittle Report on government operations, 1954

---

(5) propaganda; the United States prepared radio broadcasts in foreign languages to support nation-building efforts of Third World allies;

(6) training of individuals and exchange of persons; the United States trained the shah's secret police *Savak* as well as numerous internal security forces in Latin America;

(7) economic activities; this can involve a wide range of actions from sabotage to secret economic development aid;

(8) paramilitary operations to overthrow or support foreign governments; the United States has assisted in the overthrow or attempted overthrow of governments in Iran (1953), Guatemala (1954), Indonesia (1958), Cuba (1961) and Chile (1970s); during the 1960s the CIA covertly supported an army of approximately 300 thousand Meo tribesman in Laos who were fighting the Communists;

(9) counterinsurgency training, guidance and advice; Bolivian counterinsurgency forces trained by the CIA captured and killed Che Guevara.

As we shall see later, excessive zeal in conducting covert operations aroused the American public and led to several investigations of the intelligence establishment.

Propose Policy

While intelligence organizations are not charged with responsibility for proposing policy, quite often they do so. The most oft-quoted cliché in Washington says that knowledge is power, and intelligence organizations generally have more knowledge than anyone else.

Whether or not the intelligence community plays a significant policy-making role depends on a number of factors. Most important is the relationship between the president and the director of central intelligence. If the president looks to the director for advice, the director is bound to carry influence. This was the case with President Eisenhower and Allen Dulles, and with President Kennedy and John McCone. As former CIA director John McCone said, "Mine is not a policy job, but when asked I'll give my opinion."[7] Presidents Johnson, Nixon, Ford and Carter did not include their intelligence chiefs within their inner circles.

As former CIA director Allen Dulles himself warned, there is a danger in allowing an intelligence organization to take a hand in formulating policy. The following passage is worth pondering.

> For the proper judging of the situation in any foreign country it is important that information should be processed by an agency whose duty it is to weigh facts, and to draw conclusions from those facts,

without having either the facts or the conclusions warped by the inevitable and even proper prejudices of the men whose duty it is to determine policy and who, having once determined a policy, are too likely to be blind to any facts which might tend to prove the policy to be faulty. The Central Intelligence Agency should have nothing to do with policy. It should try to get at the hard facts on which others must determine policy. The warnings which might well have pointed to the attack on Pearl Harbor were largely discounted by those who had already concluded that the Japanese must inevitably strike elsewhere. The warnings which reportedly came to Hitler of our invasion of North Africa were laughed aside. Hitler thought he knew we didn't have the ships to do it.[8]

More recently, the House Committee on Intelligence found that Dulles's advice has not always been heeded. In seeking to explain why the overthrow of the shah of Iran in 1979 caught the United States by surprise, the committee said:

> In the case of Iran, longstanding United States attitudes toward the Shah inhibited intelligence collection, dampened policy makers' appetite for analysis of the Shah's position and deafened policy makers to the warning *implicit in available current intelligence.*[9] (emphasis added)

Counterintelligence

Counterintelligence is "the identification, neutralization and manipulation of other states' intelligence services."[10] Counterintelligence is not an end in itself, but it is necessary if an intelligence organization is to perform its other functions well. The importance of counterintelligence can be illustrated by the case of Kim Philby. Over the course of many years, Philby rose to one of the highest positions in British intelligence. In this elevated post, he was privy to numerous secrets concerning the NATO alliance. For a time he was also in charge of British liaison with the CIA; hence he was able to gauge the extent of CIA knowledge on many subjects. Philby also was chief of British counterintelligence, particularly British efforts to prevent Soviet penetration. In 1963, Philby turned up in Moscow and triumphantly announced that he had been a Soviet double agent all along. While with the British, Philby's access to classified information enabled him to pass many secrets to the Kremlin. As chief of British counterintelligence, he was in a position to protect other Soviet spies. Philby also passed to the Russians much information about the CIA.

It is the function of counterintelligence to prevent someone like Kim Philby from succeeding. Without counterintelligence, an intelligence organization can be manipulated by a hostile power. By a clever ruse, Allied intelligence in World War II misled Axis intelligence about the invasion of Sicily and contributed greatly to the success of that operation.[11] Aware of such possibilities, the CIA carefully checks Eastern bloc defectors to make sure they are not deliberately feeding false information to their adopted country.

Investigations of intelligence agencies in the 1970s revealed that the CIA and the FBI resorted to illegal methods in their efforts to root out agents of foreign powers. These methods included telephone wiretaps, mail openings, and breaking and entering. We shall discuss the implications of these activities later in this chapter.

In practice, the functions of intelligence are more interrelated than expressed here. An organization that collects incomplete or erroneous information is unlikely to produce helpful analyses for policymakers. Covert operations based upon faulty data are not likely to succeed, as the planners of the Bay of Pigs landing learned. Without proper distribution, the most polished analyses will languish in the in-baskets of officials who lack reason to read them. And, failing successful counterintelligence, an intelligence agency may be working unwittingly for an unfriendly power.

THE INTELLIGENCE COMMUNITY

Thus far we have referred to intelligence organizations in a rather general way. It is now time to turn our attention to the specific departments and agencies that conduct intelligence for the United States. The collectivity of these organizations is referred to as the "intelligence community," which is depicted in Figure 9–1. As Figure 9–1 reveals, the intelligence community consists of a number of elements besides the CIA. While the manpower and budgets of these organizations are classified, Marchetti and Marks offered estimates in the early 1970s (see Table 9–1).

We shall examine the components of the intelligence community separately and then explore relationships among them.

Central Intelligence Agency

The CIA is perhaps the most well-known US government agency in the world. Whenever calamity strikes abroad the CIA is routinely blamed. Standard agency practice of neither confirming nor denying involvement in particular incidents enhances the agency's reputation for bravado.

FIGURE 9–1: THE INTELLIGENCE COMMUNITY

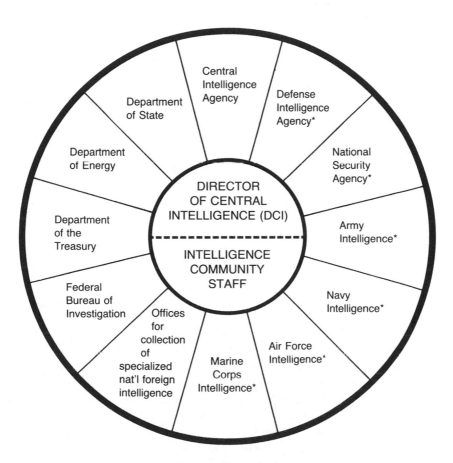

*Department of Defense Elements

Source: Central Intelligence Agency, *Fact Book*, January, 1982.

TABLE 9–1: SIZE AND COST OF INTELLIGENCE COMMUNITY

ORGANIZATION	PERSONNEL	ANNUAL BUDGET
Central Intelligence Agency	16,500	$750,000,000
National Security Agency*	24,000	$1,200,000,000
Defense Intelligence Agency*	5,000	$200,000,000
Army Intelligence*	35,000	$700,000,000
Naval Intelligence*	15,000	$600,000,000
Air Force Intelligence* (Including the National Reconnaissance Office)	56,000	$2,700,000,000
State Department (Bureau of Intelligence and Research)	350	$8,000,000
Federal Bureau of Investigation (Internal Security Division)	800	$40,000,000
Atomic Energy Commission[1] (Division of Intelligence)	300	$20,000,000
Treasury Department	300	$10,000,000
TOTAL	153,250	$6,228,000,000

*Department of Defense agency.
[1]AEC abolished 1974; functions performed by Department of Energy.

Source: Victor Marchetti and John D. Marks, *CIA and the Cult of Intelligence.* Copyright © 1974 by Alfred A. Knopf, Inc. Reprinted by permission of Alfred A. Knopf, Inc.

The CIA occupies two roles in the intelligence community. The agency's notoriety derives from its actions as an operating agency, that is, an organization that employs spies, gathers information, conducts clandestine operations, and the like. At its inception, however, the CIA was assigned a coordinating function, which it continues to fulfill with varying degrees of success. The word "central" in the organization's title expresses this second role. The men who conceived the CIA had in the backs of their minds America's most tragic intelligence failure, Pearl Harbor. Retrospective studies[12] revealed the existence of ample evidence that an attack was coming. However, these bits of evidence lay scattered in various government offices, including the different branches of military intelligence. Had an intelligence organization existed to pull together these pieces of information, the United States might have had sufficient warning of the Japanese attack to have averted destruction of the fleet. The official title of the CIA's head, Director of Central Intelligence (DCI), mirrors the agency's dual role. The DCI not only supervises the CIA's activities, but is also responsible, at least on paper, for coordinating and monitoring all components of the intelligence community. The DCI's hub position in Figure 9–1 reflects this latter assignment.

The CIA was created by the National Security Act of 1947. That legislation, passed just as the United States was entering the containment era, assigned the CIA five functions:

(1) advise the NSC on intelligence matters relating to national security;
(2) make recommendations to the NSC for coordinating the intelligence activities of other departments and agencies;
(3) correlate and evaluate intelligence and disseminate it throughout the government;
(4) perform for the benefit of existing intelligence agencies such additional services as the NSC directs (such as a biographical data bank and an aerial photo interpretation center);
(5) and to perform "such other functions and duties related to intelligence affecting the national security as the NSC may from time to time direct." (This is the catch-all used to justify covert operations, which are not mentioned explicitly in the National Security Act.)

The law placed the CIA under the NSC, which is responsible for giving direction to the CIA.

In 1949, the Central Intelligence Agency Act was passed supplementing the 1947 law. Congress enacted additional provisions permitting the agency to use confidential fiscal and administrative procedures and exempting the CIA from many of the usual limitations on the expenditure of federal funds. It provided that CIA funds could be included in the budgets of other departments and then transferred to the agency without regard to the restrictions placed on the initial appropriation. This act is the statutory authority for the secrecy of the agency's budget.

In order to further protect intelligence sources and methods from disclosure, the 1949 act further exempted the CIA from having to disclose its "organization, functions, names, officials, titles, salaries, or numbers of personnel employed."

As the CIA expanded to its present size of 16,500 persons and a budget approaching $1 billion, the agency assumed the structure shown in Figure 9–2. The DCI is appointed by the president and is responsible for overseeing the CIA and all other elements in the intelligence community. The deputy director has traditionally been a military person charged with liaison with the Defense Department. Four directorates carry out the agency's programs and activities. The directorate of intelligence produces intelligence reports

FIGURE 9–2: THE CENTRAL INTELLIGENCE AGENCY

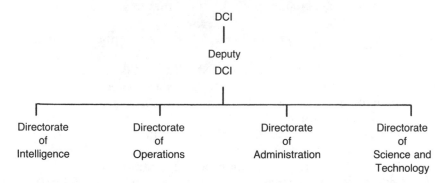

based on information collected from open and secret sources. Open sources, which provide the bulk of raw intelligence data, include foreign newspapers and periodicals, radio broadcasts, and interviews with foreign officials. Secret information is gathered by covert agents operating overseas as well as by SIGINT and PHOTINT. The intelligence directorate also performs some services for the entire intelligence community, such as the production of transcripts of foreign radio broadcasts, a computerized data bank on foreign personages, and a facility that interprets PHOTINT. The directorate of operations is the agency's "department of dirty tricks." Formerly given the purposely misleading label directorate of plans, this element is responsible for covert operations and counterintelligence. The administration directorate performs housekeeping tasks, such as providing supplies and maintaining "safe houses" and other facilities. Finally, the directorate of science and technology conducts research and development of technologies in the areas of SIGINT and PHOTINT for gathering information. This directorate developed photographic satellites in the 1960s.

While the CIA started life as a coordinating agency, it rapidly began to give top priority to covert operations. This was due in part to the individuals who first occupied the agency's high posts— adventurers from the Office of Strategic Services, which engaged in all manner of secret exploits in World War II. The climate of the times also affected the CIA; many Americans in and out of government agreed that any means were justified to halt communism. Between 1962 and 1970, the operations directorate absorbed an average of 52 percent of the CIA's budget and employed 55 percent of the organization's personnel.[13] Furthermore, the clandestine operators received promotions and rewards more quickly than the people who staffed the intelligence directorate.[14] A series of DCIs, from Allen Dulles to Richard Helms and William Colby, themselves rose up in the operations directorate and tended to favor it over other branches of the agency. Finally, as the Church Committee observed in its investigation of the CIA in the 1970s, the ethos of secrecy within the agency contributed to the operations directorate's dominance by freeing it from accountability.

By the early 1970s, covert operations had risen to an unchallenged position in the CIA, overshadowing both intelligence collection and management of the intelligence community. The Church Committee observed that the intelligence and operations directorates drew so far apart that the analysts lacked knowledge of the covert operations being planned, and the operations officers were cut off from the analysts' reports. The committee speculated that had the planners of the Bay of Pigs invasion seen the analysts' reports of strong support for Castro, they might have altered or called off the ill-fated landing.[15]

"The necessity of procuring good Intelligence is apparent and need not be further urged. All that remains for me to add is, that you keep the whole matter as secret as possible. For upon such secrecy, success depends in most Enterprises of the kind, and for want of it, they are generally defeated however well planned and promising a favourable issue."

George Washington, quoted in Cline,
The CIA under Reagan, Bush and Casey,
p. 300

"If this Government is one truly based upon the consent of the governed; if it is to function as the people's servant rather than their master, a proper measure of accurate information is essential for the people to determine whether their Government is wise and right in its response to their needs."

Senator Stuart Symington, 1970

The privileged position of the operations directorate no doubt contributed to the attitude that the agency could flout the law in the performance of its duties. When these violations came to light in the mid-1970s, the operations directorate came under severe attack. President Carter's DCI, Admiral Stansfield Turner, eliminated many positions in the operations directorate. Hundreds of clandestine operators were either forced to retire early or were simply fired. President Carter's intention to get along with the Soviets left little room for a service that took a highly confrontational view of US-Soviet relations. By the end of Jimmy Carter's presidency, the operations directorate was almost out of the covert operations business. The departure of so many of the most experienced clandestine officers left the agency with a severely reduced capacity to engage in such activities.

President Reagan and his DCI, William Casey, came into office determined to counter the Soviets across a global front. One of the instruments they intended to rely upon was the CIA and its clandestine service. Consequently, DCI Casey proceeded to rebuild the directorate of operations as the 1980s began.

The Defense Department

As Table 9–1 shows, the Department of Defense expends more money and employs more people in intelligence than any other department or agency. Each of the military services fields an intelligence arm, and both the National Security Agency and the Defense Intelligence Agency contribute to DOD's intelligence effort. DOD's intelligence units together dwarf the CIA in terms of both money and personnel.

The largest intelligence organization in the US government is run by the Air Force. Air Force intelligence employed 56 thousand people and spent $2.7 billion in the mid-1970s (see Table 9–1). Extremely costly photo-satellites, developed by CIA but now operated by the Air Force, absorb the bulk of these resources. The super-secret National Reconnaissance Office, an Air Force unit, dispatches the rockets that place these satellites in orbit and monitors the satellite program.

Each of the military services collects intelligence relating to its specific missions. Thus, naval intelligence tracks the movement of ships from the world's navies and keeps abreast of shipbuilding and new naval technologies being developed by other countries. With each service gathering data on the military capabilities of other countries, wasteful duplication has always been a problem. In order to minimize this, Secretary of Defense McNamara created the Defense Intelligence Agency (DIA) in 1961. The DIA was supposed to coordinate the intelligence activities of the separate services. However, strong service loyalty has largely crippled DIA's efforts to assign tasks and consolidate the views of the various services. Few intelligence officers deem it worthwhile to jeopardize their careers by offending superior officers in their own service, in order to facilitate DIA's coordinating role. Each service intelligence unit tends to find information that supports the perceptions and budgetary needs of that service. The Air Force always manages to find an alarming number of enemy airplanes, just as the Army generally manages to turn up a disturbing number of enemy tanks. The DIA, with fewer personnel than any one of the military intelligence units, today has become another advocacy unit within DOD rather than a coordinating agency.[16] The DIA's intelligence reports tend to represent the views of the Joint Chiefs of Staff. These reports are based on raw data collected by the service intelligence units, as the DIA collects little information on its own. DIA also manages the military attaché system.

"Gentlemen do not read other people's mail."
—Henry L. Stimson, Secretary of War, 1929,
upon learning of and closing down
a State Department—War Department Cipher Bureau

Headquartered at Fort Meade, Maryland, DOD's National Security Agency (NSA) is one of the nation's largest intelligence organizations. NSA's mission is to crack the codes of other countries—friend and foe alike—and to protect America's codes. To accomplish this task, NSA uses some of the most advanced mathematical and computer techniques in the world. NSA also records, translates and distributes to appropriate government officials messages among foreign nations, selected foreign citizens and corporations. These communications are picked up all over the world by ships, planes, satellites and ground receivers operated by NSA. In the 1960s and 1970s, the government used NSA's eavesdropping capabilities to obtain data on antiwar activists, a practice that President Ford halted. Still, the existence of NSA represents for some the threat of "Big Brother" in the United States.

The enormous intelligence operations of the DOD inevitably give the Pentagon a commanding voice in the intelligence community and complicate the CIA's attempts to direct the government's overall intelligence efforts.

Other Intelligence Organizations

The other intelligence organizations represented in Figure 9–1 are rather minor producers and consumers of foreign intelligence. The State Department's Bureau of Intelligence and Research has no overseas agents of its own. It produces analyses based on information it receives from other intelligence organizations and the voluminous reports sent to Washington every day by Foreign Service officers posted abroad, who thereby assist in intelligence gathering. The bureau's small staff and budget severely limit its range of activities. The FBI, primarily a domestic agency, is responsible for domestic counterintelligence and for investigating and preventing espionage, treason and sabotage in the United States. The Drug Enforcement Administration, under the Justice Department, collects information on illegal drug transactions both at home and abroad. The Treasury Department conducts intelligence to control illegal traffic in alcohol, tobacco, firearms and other controlled items. The Treasury's Secret Service also relies on intelligence to help protect the president, presidential candidates and foreign officials who visit the United States. The Department of Energy, successor to the Atomic Energy Commission, operates a worldwide system for detecting and measuring nuclear explosions, mostly by measuring radioactivity in the atmosphere. The Energy Department also tracks and reports on foreign advances in nuclear weaponry as well as developments in the energy area that could affect the United States.

Evaluating the Intelligence Community

As Table 9–1 reveals, the United States spends over $6 billion annually and employs over 150 thousand men and women to conduct its worldwide intelligence activities. How efficiently does this apparatus work? Does a rational system of assigning tasks exist? Is duplication at an acceptable level? Is intelligence collected on all necessary topics? Does information get to the right policymakers? In short, is America getting its money's worth from its intelligence community? Since the responsibility for managing and coordinating the intelligence community falls upon the CIA and its director, the DCI, we shall focus most of our attention here.

Practically every recent president has been exasperated with the intelligence services and has vowed to refashion the intelligence community. After the Bay of Pigs, President Kennedy threatened to "scatter the CIA to the winds." The persistence of such high-level dissatisfaction suggests that the intelligence community, despite a number of stunning successes, has considerable room for improvement.

The most commonly heard criticism of the intelligence community is that it lacks management. Each intelligence organization performs its mission with little regard for what other intelligence organizations are doing. Duplication is the order of the day. Little sense of priority exists. In the classical manner of bureaucratic politics, each intelligence organization seeks to expand its program, personnel and budgets, regardless of national needs. The CIA, charged by law with overseeing the community, is simply another competitor in the bureaucratic tug-of-war.

> The Agency was created in part to rectify the problem of duplication among the departmental intelligence services. Rather than minimizing the problem the Agency has contributed to it by becoming yet another source of intelligence production.[17]

In light of the explicit purpose of the 1947 National Security Act to coordinate and integrate intelligence, how has this fragmentation come about? Several factors seem to be relevant. The Church Committee found that those who charged the CIA with coordination failed to take into account institutional obstacles.

> From the outset no Department was willing to concede a centralized intelligence function to the CIA. Each insisted on the maintenance of its independent capabilities to support its policy role. With budgeting and management authority vested in the Departments, the Agency was left powerless in the execution of interdepartmental coordination.[18]

Marchetti and Marks observe that "each of the many agencies which carry out such programs has a vested bureaucratic interest in keeping its particular system in being, and the extreme compartmentalization of the operations has made it almost impossible for the programs to be evaluated as a whole. . . . No CIA Director has ever been able to manage the intelligence community."[19]

The Church Committee stressed the outlooks of the president and secretary of defense. If they back the DCI as an intelligence commander, as President Kennedy and Secretary McNamara supported DCI McCone, then the DCI has a good chance of managing the intelligence community, the committee found. In most cases, however, presidents have given their DCIs only lukewarm support and defense secretaries have regarded them as trespassers on their intelligence turf. The personal predilections of the DCI are also significant. Most DCIs, particularly Allen Dulles and Richard Helms, have displayed more interest in supervising the CIA and running covert operations than in coordinating the intelligence community. The rapid turnover of DCIs following Helms's departure in 1972—Helms was followed by James Schlesinger, William Colby, George Bush, Stansfield Turner and William Casey—has also made it difficult to establish overall control. Another impediment to effective coordination has been the DCI's lack of authority over the budgets and personnel of other intelligence agencies. For most of the CIA's existence, the DCI exercised control over only that agency's budget; most of the balance of the intelligence community's budget was controlled by the secretary of defense. The DCI also lacked appreciable effect on the careers of people outside CIA, so these people naturally paid heed to their own bosses. In brief, the DCI had the responsibility but not the authority to command the nation's intelligence resources.

Dissatisfied with the intelligence product and the management of the intelligence community, President Nixon by a 1971 executive order gave the DCI "an enhanced leadership role . . . in planning, reviewing, coordinating, and evaluating all intelligence programs and activities, and in the production of national intelligence." While Nixon gave the DCI authority to review the budgets of other intelligence agencies, the DCI still could not set their budget totals. Nixon also appointed the DCI chairman of a new inter-agency intelligence committee, the Intelligence Resources Advisory Committee (IRAC). Other departments represented on IRAC were State, DOD and OMB. (Since the DCI was chairman, the CIA had another representative to speak for the agency on IRAC.) IRAC's function was to set priorities among intelligence missions and assign budgets to various intelligence organizations. This gave the DCI the sort of authority needed to supervise the intelligence community. The DCI remained chairman of yet another organization, the US Intelligence Board (USIB). Among its other duties, the USIB lists targets for intelligence collection and sets priorities among them. President Carter further strengthened the position of the DCI by a 1978 executive order that gives the DCI authority to approve the budgets of all foreign intelligence units, including those in the Defense Department.

While the DCI is currently in a stronger position than previously to manage the intelligence community effectively, problems remain. Other departments and agencies have powerful allies and are thus able to limit the DCI's control. The sheer size of the Defense Department's intelligence effort affords it leverage against the DCI's authority. An excess of duplication persists, as intelligence organizations cling to tasks they have become accustomed to performing. The persistence of these intelligence problems has led one retired

CIA official, Theodore Shackley, to propose that the duties of the DCI be split into two offices.[20] The CIA director would run the agency with no responsibility for the rest of the intelligence community. This concern would fall to a new director of national intelligence (DNI), who would occupy a post analogous to the president's special assistant for national security. As the president's designated intelligence chief, with an office in the White House, the DNI would seek to direct the nation's foreign intelligence organizations. Such an arrangement might also improve the nation's intelligence product. The DNI, not bound by loyalty to one particular intelligence organization and its views, could take a more national perspective. Thus liberated, the DNI would be in a position to lay before the president, in an unbiased manner, the various assessments of the separate intelligence components. As yet, Shackley's idea appears to enjoy insufficient support for implementation.

Other difficulties continue to affect the intelligence community. Marchetti and Marks observe that some intelligence agencies, particularly the armed services, occasionally inflate estimates so as to obtain larger appropriations. In 1963–65, for example, the military intelligence services collaborated in promoting the idea that the Soviets were deploying an ABM system capable of nullifying America's strategic forces.[21] Had the military succeeded in persuading CIA and State, the armed services stood to gain much. The Air Force might receive permission to construct more ICBMs; the Navy, more SLBMs; and the Army might get the go-ahead to build an ABM for the United States. As it turned out, the military view did not prevail.

Graham Allison, dean of the Kennedy School of Government at Harvard, has scored American intelligence for generating too few area experts. Allison has written,

> The central test of a national intelligence service is how well its analyses and estimates inform policymakers of probable developments abroad. More than any other, it is this test that the United States intelligence community is failing today.[22]

Citing the misassessment of the forces that overthrew the shah of Iran, Allison argues the need for more intelligence professionals with a deep understanding of particular societies. The CIA, like the Foreign Service, currently assigns agents to a particular foreign post for two or three years at a time.

Despite evident failings in the organizational structure of the intelligence community, the intelligence services have done a creditable job in their most important task, tracking Soviet military developments. Policymakers have yet to be surprised by a new Soviet capability that leaves the United States far behind. Even the Soviet Union's boldest initiative, the placement of missiles in Cuba, was discovered soon enough for the United States to respond satisfactorily.

In William Casey, President Reagan has found a DCI who is less enamored of covert operations—although he served in OSS— and is more interested in community management than most of his predecessors. It is still too early to tell whether he will be the first DCI to manage the intelligence community effectively.

SOME ISSUES

Having examined the functions of intelligence and the intelligence community, we now turn to some issues raised by the presence of a secret intelligence service in a democratic society. These issues were catapulted to America's political consciousness by three highly publicized investigations of the intelligence community in the 1970s. These were conducted by the Senate Select Committee on Intelligence (Church Committee), the House Select Committee on Intelligence (Pike Committee), and an executive branch commission (Rockefeller Commission). The investigations were prompted by the discovery that some of the Watergate burglars had formerly been in the employ of the CIA and by a *New York Times* story by Seymour Hersch, alleging that the CIA and FBI had been illegally opening American mail for 20 years. The probes that followed these exposés brought to light a host of other practices of questionable legality. Some of these actions underline the connection between foreign policy and domestic affairs and reveal how external intelligence-related efforts can lead to domestic abuse. We shall cite the most serious of these activities in the pages that follow.

The issues we are about to raise pierce to the heart of the democratic polity and hardly lend themselves to easy answers. We shall seek less to take a stance on these issues than to provide information that will help the reader make up his or her mind.

Should the CIA Undertake Covert Operations Abroad?

America prides itself on standing for certain moral principles, such as a belief in self-determination and noninterference in the affairs of other states. These principles, it is believed, set the United States apart from other nations who will use any means to achieve their selfish aims.

Are covert operations consistent with this image of America? Consider some of the covert operations mounted by the CIA in recent decades. The CIA secretly financed and trained military forces in Laos and Angola. In Italy, the Philippines and Chile, the CIA attempted to manipulate elections by helping some candidates and hindering others. The CIA routinely bribes foreign officials in return for information and/or behavior favorable to the US. The CIA has secretly trained the police forces of numerous dictatorial regimes; in such cases as Iran and Uruguay, the government has turned the police against its political opponents. In the quest for "stability" the CIA secretly assists friendly governments in conducting propaganda campaigns against their internal political rivals.

"It is a multi-purpose clandestine arm of power . . . more than an intelligence or counterintelligence organization. It is an instrument for subversion, manipulation, and violence, for the secret intervention in the affairs of other countries." Allen Dulles wrote those words about the KGB in 1963 . . . but he could—just as accurately— have used the same terms to describe his own CIA."
Marchetti and Marks, p. 347

One of the most startling revelations to emerge from the Church Committee's probe concerned the CIA's attempt to assassinate foreign leaders. The committee found that the CIA attempted, without success, to murder Fidel Castro of Cuba and Patrice Lumumba of the Belgian Congo (now Zaire). Having failed to overthrow Castro through the Bay of Pigs invasion, the CIA in the early 1960s made several attempts on his life. In one effort, the CIA arranged for the Mafia to do the job. When this failed, the CIA tried to place poisoned pills in his food. The agency even considered planting an exploding seashell in the waters where he liked to skin-dive.[23] In the case of Patrice Lumumba, the CIA was beaten to the task by Congolese soldiers during a civil war in the 1960s. The Church Committee also established that the CIA knew of South Vietnamese plans to overthrow President Ngo Dinh Diem in 1963 but did not try to block the coup. During the changeover Diem and his notorious brother were killed, but the CIA was not charged with complicity in these murders.

We return to the question whether the United States should engage in covert activities. The case for doing so has often been made. In the jungle of international relations, the only law is that of survival. So long as other states use gangster methods the US must do the same, however reluctantly. Should Washington set an example by renouncing covert actions, other countries will only see this as a lack of resolve and fill the breach with their own clandestine operators; only the US would suffer. Perhaps some day, when international anarchy gives way to an orderly global society, the United States will be able to dismantle the CIA. Until that distant time, however, America must fight fire with fire.

Opponents of this view insist that when one fights fire with fire, everyone gets burnt. Those who would eliminate or drastically curtail covert operations offer two arguments, one pragmatic and the other moral. In pragmatic terms, they say, covert operations have resulted in more harm than good for the United States. Despite occasional successes, these forays have blighted the image of America all over the world. Wherever calamity strikes the CIA is blamed, and the people dwelling in the world's huts and villages are prepared to believe the charge. It will take decades for the United States to alter its reputation as an uncaring manipulator of less powerful countries, countries that today control strategic resources. Furthermore, opponents of covert actions insist, all the covert successes added up together have made very little difference for American foreign policy. The Soviet Union proving impenetrable, the CIA has mounted its covert assaults against Third World countries that are miniscule quantities in the equations of world politics. Castro has been at most no more than a nuisance to America. The Communist victory in Indochina, site of numerous covert actions, has resulted in no great loss for American interests, proving that CIA operations there mattered little one way or the other. In sum, opponents say, covert operations have tarnished America's name without producing anything of significance in return.

In its simplest form, the moral argument against covert operations states that such actions are wrong. If the United States stuffs ballot boxes, bribes foreign officials, and tries to murder foreign heads of state, then how can America claim to represent a morality superior to that of America's foes? If America adopts the most despicable methods of its adversaries, then is America truly different from them? In fighting fire with fire, the United States risks consuming the very values it seeks to defend.

Do Intelligence Organizations Endanger the Civil Liberties of Americans?

As defenders of the US Constitution and statutes, intelligence agencies are pledged to protect the values by which Americans live. Among these cherished values is the right of privacy expressed in the Fourth Amendment, which guarantees "the right of the people to be secure in their persons, houses, papers, and effects, and against unreasonable searches and seizures. . . ." Americans live in one of the few countries where citizens can expect that their homes will be secure from government intrusion, and that their letters and telephone calls will remain private. The law enjoins the CIA in particular from engaging in domestic surveillance.

The Rockefeller Commission probe, however, revealed that:

the CIA opened over 215 thousand letters between 1953–73, and the FBI opened others;

the National Security Agency scanned virtually every overseas telephone call and cable from 1967–73 to intercept communications of 1,680 American political dissenters, those suspected of representing a physical threat to the president, and narcotics traffickers; the NSA was probing for links between these individuals and hostile foreign governments (none was found);

to discover the effects of mind-control drugs possibly being used by Russia, the CIA administered LSD to unwitting subjects, one of whom plunged out of a window to his death;

the FBI committed numerous illegal break-ins in 1972–73 of the homes of political dissidents;

in Operation COINTELPRO, the FBI used forged letters, anonymous telephone calls and *agents provocateurs* to disrupt militant antiwar and civil rights groups by spreading rumors about leading members (including bogus sexual liaisons);

from 1952–67, the CIA secretly gave $3 million to the National Student Association, so it could afford to send delegates to voice American viewpoints at international student congresses dominated by Communists;

the CIA secretly bought thousands of subscriptions to the Communist newspaper *Daily Worker*, to demonstrate the magnitude of the Communist threat;

Army Intelligence maintained dossiers on approximately 18 thousand American political dissidents and black militants from 1967–70, including members of the Ku Klux Klan, NAACP, John Birch Society, the Black Panthers, and the DAR;

"plumbers" hired by the Nixon White House illegally burglar-
ized the office of the psychiatrist of Daniel Ellsberg, who had leaked
the Pentagon Papers, in a search for damaging evidence about his
character;

under White House pressure, the CIA gave a wig and voice
disguise device to "plumber" Howard Hunt, a former CIA employee,
and developed Hunt's films of the building where Ellsberg's psychiatrist maintained his office;

the Internal Revenue Service set up special files on over 8 thousand political activists and nearly 3 thousand political organizations, and it supplied supposedly confidential tax information to
the CIA and the FBI.

What accounted for such widespread domestic surveillance of
American citizens? Many officials were convinced foreign powers
were behind the antiwar demonstrations and civil rights marches
of the 1960s and 1970s. Wasn't disruption of American society
precisely what hostile governments could be expected to do? Chants
of "Ho, Ho, Ho Chi Minh" and brandishing Viet Cong flags at
antiwar rallies only confirmed these suspicions.

In fact, the surveillance never uncovered such links to foreign
regimes. Supposedly, illegal domestic spying ended after President
Nixon resigned in 1974. By a 1978 executive order, President Carter
limited the physical surveillance of Americans to those suspected
of being foreign agents, terrorists, narcotics traffickers, or current
or past American intelligence agents believed to endanger secret
intelligence sources and methods. Carter also barred electronic surveillance, television monitoring, physical searches and mail openings of all Americans, unless the president approved a technique
and the attorney general authorized a specific application. President
Reagan, discomfited by these limitations, issued Executive Order
12333 in December 1981, which permitted electronic surveillance,
unconsented physical searches, mail openings, physical surveillance, and monitoring devices to be used against Americans under
certain circumstances. The Reagan order also authorized the CIA
to conduct domestic and foreign operations if approved by the
president, and if undertaken to further "national foreign policy
objectives abroad."

From today's perspective, it is difficult to justify the violations
of American civil liberties catalogued above. At the time, however,
many well-meaning Americans believed the country to be the target
of subversion by foreign powers. In their view, a nonshooting war
was in progress to complement the very lethal war in Vietnam.

Under such circumstances, isn't a government entitled to, or even obliged to, set aside statutory niceties to protect its citizens?

Such reasoning may at least explain, if not fully justify, the search for links between American militants and foreign powers. On the other hand, there is no excuse whatever for using intelligence services solely to maim one's political opponents, as Johnson and Nixon were accused of doing. Such conduct is incompatible with a democratic society.

To conclude, the words of Harry Howe Ransom are worth considering.

> One of the greatest dangers of the cold war mentality is that it tends to ape the adversary. . . . The waters of American free institutions have already been muddied by these ill-advised experiments of 1947–1967. It would be hard to demonstrate that the national security would have been seriously endangered had such programs not been undertaken. It is somewhat easier to demonstrate that the American free society has been injured by what was done.[24]

Is the CIA a State within a State?

Exposure of the above abuses led the American citizenry to ask, who authorized such transgressions? Did the president send assassination teams to Havana and the Congo? Did Congress authorize the overthrow of foreign governments? Did the attorney general know about unlawful break-ins and mail openings? Or, did the CIA (and other intelligence organizations) simply act without consulting higher authority?

The Church Committee hunted in vain for a document that would demonstrate that the president either commanded or knew about the attempted assassinations of Fidel Castro and Patrice Lumumba. What the committee found instead was the doctrine of "plausible denial." This concept calls for the dissolution of some of the links in the chain of authority, so that denial of responsibility cannot be disproven. Written authorizations are avoided. Euphemisms such as "highest authority" are used to conceal identities. Files are purged of the names of individuals who issue orders. Thus, in the absence of incontrovertible evidence to the contrary, the Church Committee was unable to prove that the chief executive knew of or initiated assassination orders. At the same time, the committee could not establish that the president did not know about these attempts. Based on usual clearance procedures for operations of such consequence, it seems reasonable to suppose that the president did know of the assassination efforts.

The Church Committee learned that plausible denial was structured into many covert operations, in order to protect officials in case the operations went sour. The committee strongly condemned this decision-making procedure which, it said, created an environment of "blurred accountability which allowed consideration of actions without the constraints of individual responsibility."[25] The committee recommended that henceforth all covert operations be authorized in writing.

The question of whether the CIA is a state within a state is best discussed by considering executive and congressional oversight separately.

Executive Oversight

From the beginning it was recognized that the CIA required executive supervision, in order to ensure that the agency acted in conformity with the nation's broad foreign policy objectives. The National Security Act of 1947 directed the CIA to report to the NSC, and an NSC committee has generally been responsible for overseeing the CIA and approving covert operations. This committee has had different names—the 54–12 Committee, 40 Committee, the Special Coordinating Committee, and, in the Reagan administration, the Senior Interagency Group, Intelligence. Generally, the president's special assistant for national security has chaired the committee. The DCI sits on the committee, as do the secretaries of state and defense, the chairman of the Joint Chiefs of Staff, the attorney general, and the director of OMB. The exact membership has fluctuated somewhat over the years.

The deliberations of this committee are highly secret, and this has contributed to questions about its effectiveness. Marchetti and Marks claim that under President Nixon the 40 Committee was little more than a conduit between the president or secretary of state and the CIA.[26] The committee rarely rejected a proposal for a covert operation and often initiated proposals of its own, Marchetti and Marks said. They added that certain institutional features limit the stringency of NSC control. 40 Committee (and its successors) members are too busy to meet regularly. When they do gather, the meeting is stacked in favor of the CIA. The agency usually presents its proposals, thereby setting the framework for discussion. To preserve secrecy, committee members limit their own staff studies of the proposals; therefore, they lack a non-CIA perspective on the matter under review. They may also be unable to establish whether CIA assumptions are valid or self-serving. The members themselves lack time to study the issues thoroughly and tend to defer to CIA experts, Marchetti and Marks claim. If the covert operation under discussion is sensitive, the NSC committee's decision is communicated to the president for approval. This includes interventions in the affairs of other countries. Less controversial items are often passed without bothering the chief executive. In any event, the president does not sign anything, so as to maintain plausible denial. As with so many aspects of government, the effectiveness of the NSC committee as a watchdog depends on how rigorously the president wishes it to ride herd on the CIA.

The president has other organizations to help direct the nation's foreign intelligence. The following organizations are less watchdogs than coordinating and planning bodies, although in recent years they have shown sensitivity to the need for preventing abuses. The National Foreign Intelligence Board, formerly the US Intelligence Board, is composed of the heads of the departments and agencies that make up the intelligence community. With the DCI as chairman, the board is charged with setting intelligence priorities and assigning the various components to carry them out. Our previous discussion has revealed how difficult it has been to translate such a calculated division of labor into practice. The President's Foreign Intelligence Advisory Board is composed of 19 distinguished citizens outside government who are appointed by the president. The board meets several times a year to review the performance of the intelligence community and make recommendations for improvement. Like the National Foreign Intelligence Board, this group is more concerned with efficiency and performance than the propriety of intelligence operations. The Intelligence Oversight Board, by contrast, is directly charged with discovering and reporting to the president any intelligence activities that might be of questionable legality or propriety. Composed of three persons from outside government who are appointed by the president, the board's effectiveness as a sentinel has yet to be confirmed. An inherent limitation lies in the fact that the president may approve a covert operation even if it has been determined to be illegal and/or improper. These advisory groups merely help the president decide.

Congressional Control

As we have seen, within the executive branch an NSC committee is charged with oversight of the intelligence community. Nonetheless, a large number of abuses occurred. This indisputable fact led many members of Congress to believe that additional sentries were needed to stand guard over the nation's intelligence organizations. As part of the resurgence of Congress in foreign policy, described in Chapter 10, the youthful, brash legislators who took their posts following Watergate determined to take an active role in overseeing intelligence operations.

Up to that point, the attitude taken by most legislators toward the intelligence community was expressed by Senator John Stennis (D-MS), one of those charged with intelligence oversight. "You have to make up your mind that you are going to have an intelligence agency and protect it as such and shut your eyes some and take what is coming." Indeed, the subcommittees of the House and Senate committees on appropriations and armed services, assigned to examine American intelligence, seemed more interested in protecting intelligence organizations than in calling them to account. These subcommittees met irregularly, when they met at all, and many members declined to be informed about unsavory operations.

Watergate dissipated Congress's willingness to trust in executive omniscience. Just as Congress passed the War Powers Act to gain a larger role in using military force, so the legislature passed the Hughes-Ryan Amendment to the 1974 Foreign Assistance Act to widen its surveillance of intelligence. The amendment designated eight committees as entitled to information about the CIA's covert operations: the appropriations, armed services, intelligence (a new committee), and foreign affairs committees in each house. The law required the president to approve in writing all important covert actions—thereby nullifying "plausible denial"—and report them in "timely fashion" to these eight committees. Intelligence professionals were aghast. Disclosing secret information to eight committees was like broadcasting it to the world, they cried. Besides, they lamented, how could intelligence professionals carry out their duties if they had to spend all their time testifying on Capitol Hill?

In time, the cry for such widespread congressional oversight became muted. The mass firings and forced retirement of many clandestine officers in the 1970s nearly put the CIA out of the covert operations business, anyway. The deterioration of US-Soviet relations led numerous legislators to call for the unleashing of the CIA, despite the fact that many of its teeth were drawn. In 1980

Congress passed a new law, the Intelligence Oversight Act, which superseded the Hughes-Ryan Amendment. The new law reduced to two the number of committees to be informed about intelligence activities—the now permanent intelligence committee in each house. At the same time, the bill widened the scope of intelligence activities that must be reported. Hughes-Ryan called for information only about covert activities undertaken by the CIA. The later act requires that the intelligence committees be "fully and currently" informed about the full range of intelligence activities being conducted by every component of the intelligence community. These committees also annually authorize appropriations for all intelligence agencies, providing another measure of congressional control.

The Intelligence Oversight Act did not satisfy the most vehement critics of the CIA. They were displeased in that the bill did not give Congress the right to veto intelligence operations, although the intelligence committees may suggest alterations. Timely information does not require that Congress be informed before an operation is in progress. Thus, the CIA notified congressional intelligence committees that it was supervising mine laying in Nicaragua's harbors in early 1984 only after the operation had begun. The CIA need not report a specific action if it believes, and the NSC agrees, that it has already been covered by a larger category of previously reported activities. "In extraordinary circumstances," the president can withhold information from the committees, but then must report it to the two top party leaders in each house as well as the chairman and ranking minority party member of each intelligence committee (eight individuals in all). A somewhat ambiguous section of the law allows the president to remain silent on operations "intended solely for obtaining necessary intelligence," although another section requires a presidential report on "all intelligence activity." Some CIA critics were also unhappy because the act says nothing about what circumstances justify covert operations. The bill certainly did not satisfy those who called for an elaborate intelligence charter, which would spell out criteria for allowing a variety of intelligence operations and impose strict limits on what intelligence organizations may do. However, it must be said that the 1980 law did require that Congress be informed about intelligence activities. Whether Congress will seize upon the law and demand complete and timely information will depend more on the insistence of Congress than the letter of the law. Furthermore, by establishing legislative accountability for intelligence organizations, the law is likely to discourage the kinds of improper activities that occurred in the past.

INTELLIGENCE IDENTITIES PROTECTION ACT

In the early 1980s, the question of publicly identifying CIA agents raised some First Amendment difficulties. The matter arose after some former CIA agents, joined by other foes of the intelligence agency, deliberately released in a series of newsletters and books the names of some 2 thousand former and (mostly) current CIA operatives. There can be little doubt that the purpose of these exposures was to cripple the CIA. The perpetrators argued that this disability would be healthy for American foreign policy, as (in their view) the CIA had generated more harm than good for the United States. The issues gained urgency when one exposed agent was gunned down in Athens in 1975 and another's home was machine-gunned in Jamaica in 1980 at a time when he happened to be out.

Legislation was introduced making it a crime to name publicly an undercover intelligence agent. Few disputed the propriety of such a law as applied to present or former officials who had access to classified information. But should the law apply to a journalist who learns the identities of secret agents and publishes them? And if so, should the reporter be penalized if he or she "intended to impair or impede" American intelligence activities, or if the journalist only "had reason to believe" the exposure would have such an effect? CIA director Casey, supported by President Reagan, urged the "reason to believe" test as the best way to protect America's intelligence operations. The American Civil Liberties Union and the American Newspaper Publishers Association insisted that the "reason to believe" test was too easy to prove. They claimed that such a test not only violated the spirit of the First Amendment but would also have a "chilling effect" on the reporting of intelligence abuses. Had such a law been on the books, they said, newspapers might have shied away from reporting on CIA ties to Watergate and on the alleged assistance to Libyan terrorists by former CIA agents.

In 1982 Congress settled the issue by passing the Intelligence Identities Protection Act. The legislation provided a fine up to $15 thousand and/or a prison term up to three years for anyone without access to classified information who disclosed the identity of a covert agent after engaging in "a pattern of activities intended to identify and expose covert agents" and "with reason to believe" the disclosure would "impair or impede the foreign intelligence activities of the United States." Whether this law violates the First Amendment will be up to the courts to decide.

FOR DISCUSSION

Identify the principal components of the intelligence community and describe their missions.

What obstacles block effective management of the intelligence community?

Under what circumstances, if any, should the CIA use illegal methods? Should the CIA seek to assassinate the Soviet party chief?

How effectively is the CIA supervised by the executive branch? by Congress?

Should the CIA renounce covert activities and concentrate solely on intelligence collection and analysis?

On balance, has the CIA been an asset or a liability for the United States?

READING SUGGESTIONS

Agee, Philip. *Inside the Company: CIA Diary.* New York: Stonehill, 1975.

Cline, Ray S. *The CIA under Reagan, Bush, and Casey.* Washington, D.C.: Acropolis Books, 1981.

Colby, William E., and Peter Forbath. *Honorable Men: My Life In the CIA.* New York: Simon and Schuster, 1978.

Marchetti, Victor, and John D. Marks. *The CIA and the Cult of Intelligence.* New York: Dell, 1975.

Powers, Thomas. *The Man Who Kept the Secrets: Richard Helms and the CIA.* New York: Alfred A. Knopf, 1979.

Rositzke, Harry. *The CIA's Secret Operations: Espionage, Counterespionage, and Covert Action.* New York: Reader's Digest Press, 1977.

Stockwell, John. *In Search of Enemies: A CIA Story.* New York: Norton, 1977.

United States Senate, Select Committee to Study Governmental Operations with Respect to Intelligence Activities. *Final Report,* 1976. (The Church Committee)

United States, *Report to the President by the Commission on CIA Activities within the United States.* 1975. (The Rockefeller Report)

NOTES

1. This meeting is described in David Kahn, "Cryptology Goes Public," *Foreign Affairs,* LVIII (Fall 1979): 141–59.
2. Recounted in Thomas Powers, *The Man Who Kept the Secrets: Richard Helms and the CIA* (New York: Alfred A. Knopf, 1979).

 3. Roy Godson and Richard Shultz, "Foreign Intelligence: A Course Syllabus," *International Studies Notes*, VIII (Fall/Winter 1981–82): 5.
 4. Victor Marchetti and John D. Marks, *The CIA and the Cult of Intelligence* (New York: Dell Publishing Company, 1975), p. 204.
 5. Harry Howe Ransom, "Being Intelligent about Secret Intelligence Agencies," *American Political Science Review*, LXXIV (March 1980): 147.
 6. Godson and Shultz, p. 5.
 7. Powers, pp. 162–63. William Colby, DCI under Nixon and Ford, also states that the DCI is more effective to the extent that the president relies on the DCI's counsel (a position in which Colby rarely found himself). Colby cautions, however, that too close a contact between the White House and the DCI has its dangers. "The Director is likely to be sucked into the President's orbit and feel obliged to look not only for how intelligence can help a President to choose policies but how it can justify his choices." William Colby and Peter Forbath, *Honorable Men: My Life in the CIA* (New York: Simon and Schuster, 1978), p. 375.
 8. US, Congress, Senate, Committee on Armed Services, Hearings, *National Defense Establishment*, 1947.
 9. *New York Times*, January 25, 1979.
10. Godson and Shultz, p. 5.
11. See Ewen Montagu, *The Man Who Never Was* (Philadelphia: Lippincott, 1965).
12. See, for example, Roberta Wohlstetter, *Pearl Harbor: Warning and Decision* (Stanford: Stanford University Press, 1962).
13. US, Congress, Senate, Select Committee to Study Governmental Operations with Respect to Intelligence Activities, *Final Report*, Book I, 94th Cong., 2nd sess., 1976, p. 82. Hereafter, *Final Report*. This committee, sometimes known as the Church Committee after its chairman Senator Frank Church, conducted one of the most exhaustive studies of US intelligence operations ever undertaken. The committee's findings, published in five books, contain a wealth of information on the intelligence community.
14. Ibid., pp. 92–93.
15. Ibid., p. 94.
16. Marchetti and Marks, pp. 103–04.
17. *Final Report*, Book IV, p. 94.
18. Ibid., p. 91.
19. Marchetti and Marks, p. 205.
20. Theodore Shackley, *The Third Option: An American View of Counterinsurgency Operations* (New York: Reader's Digest/McGraw Hill, 1981), pp. 165–66. This volume offers an excellent systematic concept of counterinsurgency by an experienced practitioner. Shackley would also change the CIA's name, arguing that CIA has a tarnished image throughout the world.
21. Marchetti and Marks, p. 299.
22. *New York Times*, December 21, 1980, Op-Ed page.
23. Powers, pp. 132–48.
24. Harry Howe Ransom, *The Intelligence Establishment* (Cambridge: Harvard University Press, 1970), p. 244.
25. *Final Report*, Book IV, p. 93.
26. Marchetti and Marks, pp. 308–15.

Chapter 10
Congress

Like the executive branch, the legislature is a participant in the political process (see Fig. 1–1). Congress engages in various activities that have an important bearing upon the formulation and conduct of United States foreign policy.

THE FOREIGN POLICY POWERS OF CONGRESS

The constitutional basis of this role of Congress has already been reviewed in Chapter 7. It is rooted in the overall separation of powers between executive, legislative, and judicial branches of the government.

Most of the powers of Congress are listed in Article I, Section 8 of the Constitution. Those relevant to foreign policy include: raising revenue to provide for the common defense and general welfare of the United States; regulating commerce with foreign nations and with the Indian tribes; establishing a uniform rule of naturalization; regulating the value of foreign coin; defining and punishing piracy and felonies committed on the high seas and offenses against international law; declaring war, granting letters of marque and reprisal, and making rules concerning capture; raising and supporting armies; providing and maintaining a navy; regulating the land and naval forces; calling out the militia to repel invasions; organizing, arming, and disciplining the militia; exercising exclusive legislation over the territories used for the seat of government and for military installations; and making laws necessary for carrying out these functions.

Additional powers pertaining to foreign relations derive from various requirements that Congress (or at least the Senate) must give advice and/or consent before certain actions may be taken. US officials must have the consent of Congress before accepting any gifts, offices, or titles from kings, princes, or foreign states (Article I, Section 9). US states may not levy import-export duties, keep armies, make agreements with foreign powers, or engage in wars (except in emergencies) without the consent and supervision of the Congress (Article I, Section 10). Treaties signed by the president are subject to ratification by a two-thirds majority of the Senate, which must also approve the appointment of ambassadors, other public ministers and consuls, and other public officials whose appointment is not otherwise provided for in the Constitution (Article II, Section 2). Finally, Congress may admit new states to the Union (Article IV, Section 3).

In essence, these powers define the rights and duties of the Congress in relation to foreign policy. As in the case of the executive branch, both time and custom have shaped the manner in which the Congress carries out these functions in actual practice. To illustrate the processes involved, the present discussion will focus on the influence of the legislature vis-à-vis the executive branch. This balance has shifted back and forth over time. During the 1930s, for instance, Congress wielded a potent club in passing various neutrality acts designed to keep the United States out of the war that threatened to engulf Europe. In the two and a half decades after that global conflict, the executive branch reigned supreme. Since the early 1970s, Congress has once again flexed its foreign policy muscles, leading a succession of presidents to lament undue legislative "interference" in foreign policy. The struggle can be seen in the areas of authority over the armed forces, appointments, treaty making, and appropriations and legislation.

Authority over the Armed Forces

In the two decades following World War II, presidential authority over the armed forces clearly overshadowed that of Congress, largely due to a consensus among the public that vigorous prosecution of containment required the capacity to deploy military force with dispatch. Thus, in Korea, Lebanon, the Dominican Republic, Cuba and Vietnam, chief executives sent military forces abroad without first obtaining congressional approval. Furthermore, military spending requests by the executive regularly sailed through Congress practically unchanged. In some years Congress actually increased the level of spending requested by the executive!

Congressional passivity gave way in the 1970s to assertiveness regarding authority over the armed forces. The War Powers Act of 1973, passed over President Nixon's veto, represented Congress's high water mark in this area.

Confirming Appointments

In accordance with the Constitution, the Senate has authority to approve or disapprove—and sometimes offer advice about—the appointment of a wide range of presidential appointees, including members of the Cabinet, ambassadors, Foreign Service officers, military officers, and a host of officials in the executive branch that enter and leave their posts with the president who appointed them.

In theory, this power enables Congress to exert considerable influence over foreign policy, by deciding upon many of those individuals in the executive branch with the discretion to make important foreign policy decisions.

However, the Senate has only rarely challenged presidential appointees, especially in the foreign policy sphere. In most cases the Senate has acted on the belief that the president, elected by the entire nation, is entitled to select a team that will implement the president's policies. The Senate has rejected only eight Cabinet nominees (unless one counts twice the individual President Coolidge nominated on two occasions), and it rarely turns down other presidential appointees. A president who fears a senatorial rejection can always appoint that endangered person as a personal representative or make him or her a member of the White House Staff. Since this group of individuals is considered an extension of the president, White House staffers are not subject to confirmation by the Senate. This immunity has sparked considerable controversy with regard to the special assistant for national security, who need not be confirmed by the Senate but who may have more influence over foreign policy than the secretary of state (or, as was sometimes the case with Henry Kissinger, even than the president).

While Congress has grown accustomed to letting the president select a compatible team, the appointment process does permit a certain degree of congressional input into foreign policy. During confirmation hearings and floor debates, legislators have the opportunity to send messages to the executive branch, elicit responses from nominees (which then become policy commitments), debate controversial foreign policy issues, and reassert the prerogatives of Congress in the foreign policy process. During the 1981 confirmation hearings of Secretary of State Haig, for example, the Senate extracted promises to abide by the 1973 War Powers Act and the Intelligence Oversight Act and to seek arms reductions with the Soviet Union.[1] Senator Jesse Helms (R-NC) put Secretary of Defense Weinberger on notice that he must make a strong commitment to boost military spending if he expected support from the conservative wing of the Republican party.

Treaties

Article II, Section 2 of the Constitution states that the president has the power, "by and with the Advice and Consent of the Senate, to make treaties, provided two thirds of the Senators present concur." This provision raises many questions bearing on executive-legislative relations. What, for instance, does the word "make" mean? Does it refer to the negotiating process, the final approval of the treaty, or both? Is the Senate entitled—or obligated—to provide advice and consent during the negotiating stage or only at the point at which the treaty is approved or rejected? If the latter, then what does the term "advice" mean? Must a president who disagrees with the Senate's advice abide by it anyway?

In most cases, the executive branch has negotiated treaties and then submitted them to the Senate for approval. Senatorial advice has only infrequently been sought during the negotiating phase. On occasion, the executive has included senators on the negotiating team, but this practice has been the exception.

Once the executive submits a treaty to the Senate, the latter has the choice of accepting it as is, amending it, rejecting it, or attaching reservations and understandings concerning the meaning of certain provisions. The addition of amendments, reservations or understandings may require renegotiation of the treaty. Once the Senate approves a treaty, the president must sign it to complete the ratification process.

At the turn of the century, Secretary of State John Hay, in reaction to senatorial fiddling with some arbitration conventions, wrote that a "treaty entering the Senate is like a bull going into the arena; no one can say just how or when the blow will fall—but one thing is certain—it will never leave the arena alive."[2] Times have certainly changed. In Chapter 7 we saw how a succession of presidents has evaded the requirement of Senate approval by concluding executive agreements. According to the study by Johnson and McCormick cited in that chapter, the United States concluded 7,201 agreements with other nations between January 1, 1946, and December 31, 1976.[3] Of these, only 6 percent were treaties requiring Senate consent. In the eyes of more than one senator, such a ratio represented a consistent and deliberate evasion of the president's constitutional obligation to cooperate with the Senate on reaching agreement with other powers. Congressional ire was further inflamed as the result of an investigation conducted in the 1960s by a Senate Foreign Relations subcommittee, headed by Stuart Symington (D-MO). This inquiry into American commitments abroad astonished many senators by uncovering several commitments presidents had made to other countries that had remained secret (even to members of the Senate Foreign Relations Committee)! Such agreements included annexes to the Spanish Bases Agreement (1953) and commitments to help defend Ethiopia (1960), Laos (1963), Thailand (1964 and 1967) and South Korea (1966).[4] Furthermore, the executive branch, on its own authority, has pledged military support to Pakistan, Turkey and Iran; and it has contracted for military bases in—implying an affinity for if not a specific military commitment to—such places as the Philippines, Bahrein, Diego Garcia, and Portugal.[5] These findings seemed to lend support to a statement made by Senator Fulbright at the time he headed the Foreign Relations Committee: "The Senate is asked to convene solemnly to approve by a two-thirds vote a treaty to preserve cultural artifacts in a friendly neighboring country. At the same time, the chief executive is moving military men and material around the globe like so many pawns in a chess game."[6]

Congressional outrage at perceived executive high-handedness led in 1972 to passage of the Case-Zablocki Act. This piece of legislation requires the secretary of state to report to Congress within 60 days "the text of any international agreement, other than a treaty, to which the United States is a party. . . ." Secret agreements are to be transmitted to the Senate Foreign Relations Committee and the House Foreign Affairs Committee. The Case-Zablocki Act does not require Congress to approve executive actions before they can take effect. However, the law does make it likely that Congress will at least know the extent of American commitments and be in a position to challenge them either at the time or later.[7]

Legislation and Appropriations

Through the passage of laws and the raising (or refusal to raise) of money, Congress has additional powers assigned by the Constitution to affect foreign policy. As we shall see later, Congress has in recent years made substantial use of its legislative prerogative to influence foreign policy. One reason for the growing use of this instrument concerns the increased blending of foreign and domestic matters, as occurs in the areas of food and energy. Many of the laws that traditionally affected only domestic matters now have an impact upon foreign policy as well.

Congressman Les Aspin (D-WI) has suggested that Congress can best shape foreign policy not so much by setting foreign policy objectives as by passing legislation that determines how foreign policy will be made.[8] By establishing or abolishing certain organizations or offices, such as the Central Intelligence Agency or the Assistant Secretary of State for Human Rights and Humanitarian Affairs, Congress can mandate that the executive will perform— or will cease to perform—certain functions. Because certain bureaucratic organizations have relatively predictable positions on various matters, Congress can affect policy by assigning a function to one organization rather than another. In the early 1970s, for example, Congress transferred authority to approve military aid to South Vietnam from the Armed Services Committee to the Foreign Relations Committee, in the knowledge that the latter would be more reluctant to authorize such funds.

While the "power of the purse" is a classic instrument of legislative control over the executive branch, such usage has been uncommon in American foreign policy. Until the recent resurgence of Congress in the foreign policy field, the legislature had generally provided the means requested by the president to conduct foreign policy. Such generosity even extended to military appropriations bills, among the largest of government expenditures in the period since World War II. On the other hand, the minor annual expenditure on foreign aid never seems to escape an intensity of scrutinization that would make Sherlock Holmes proud.

Until the recent revival of congressional participation in foreign policy, neither the legislative nor the appropriations power was regularly used by Congress to exert a significant degree of control over foreign policy.

Other Powers

The Constitution assigns additional powers to Congress in the foreign policy field. Congress has the power to regulate foreign commerce, make rules for governance of the armed forces, and establish immigration and naturalization policy. At times these responsibilities embroil the nation in serious disputes with other countries, as illustrated by the strained relations today with Mexico and Haiti over immigration. In view of the desire of poor countries throughout the world to gain a larger share of the planet's wealth, the legislature's voice in foreign commerce is often a strong determinant of America's relations with the Third World, a topic to which we shall return in Chapter 13.

THE DECLINE AND RESURGENCE OF CONGRESSIONAL INFLUENCE

Between 1945 and approximately 1970, Congress displayed a marked tendency to follow the president's lead in foreign policy. Among the numerous explanations for this surrender of power by Congress, perhaps the most compelling consists of the general agreement throughout the nation on the country's foreign policy priorities. Most Americans accepted the need to restrain what was perceived as an aggressive Soviet monolith that sought to dominate the globe. Whatever steps the president took toward this goal the majority of Americans both in and out of Congress was likely to accept.

As the decade of the 1960s came to an end, marked by a grim procession of American bodies returning in coffins from the battlefields of Southeast Asia, Congress began to reassert itself in the foreign policy field. It is to that development that we now turn.

Evidence

Congressional initiative in foreign policy is not without precedent. In the 1930s the legislature passed a series of neutrality acts designed to keep the United States out of the brewing war in Europe. Following World War II, Congress took the lead in establishing educational and cultural exchange programs with other countries, creating the Food for Peace program, setting up an arms control agency (ACDA) separate from the State Department, and bringing about the Peace Corps. Such initiatives occurred at widely separated intervals, however, and they generally enjoyed the support of the executive branch. Beginning in the 1970s, in contrast, Congress took several actions strongly opposed by a succession of presidents, who complained of congressional "handcuffing" of the executive in carrying out its foreign policy responsibilities. Some of the major congressional actions in recent years include:

Case-Zablocki Act (1972). Required secretary of state to report to Congress within 60 days of execution the text of any international agreement other than a treaty to which the US is a party (aimed at excessive use of secret executive agreements);

War Powers Act (1973). See Chapter 7;

Cooper-Church Amendment (1973). Prohibited US combat activity in Indochina;

Jackson-Vanik Amendment (1974). Conditioned extension of credits and most-favored-nation status to Russia on that country's explicit assurance that it would remove emigration restrictions;

Foreign Assistance Act (1974). Required that any intended sale of defense articles or services worth $25 million or more, or of major defense equipment costing $7 million or more, be reported to Congress. Congress then has 30 days to disallow the sale by a majority vote in both chambers;

Ban on military aid to Turkey (1974). Repealed in 1978;

Hughes-Ryan Amendment (1974). Required that CIA covert activities be reported to "the appropriate committees of the Congress" (held at the time to include eight committees but presently reduced to two);

Clark Amendment (1975). Prohibited US military operations in Angola;

Series of congressional investigations of intelligence agencies (1975–76) followed by creation of a permanent intelligence oversight committee in each house;

Amendment to Foreign Assistance Act of 1974, declaring "a principal goal of the foreign policy of the US shall be to promote the increased observance of internationally recognized human rights by all countries." Congress further required the president to submit an annual report on the human rights practices of each country for which security assistance was requested (1976);

Prohibition of any kind of military assistance, sales, exports or training to Chile (1976);

Nuclear Non-Proliferation Act (1978). Prohibited the export of nuclear materials to countries that refused to accept comprehensive international safeguards on all their nuclear facilities. The president may waive this ban, but a concurrent resolution can override the waiver. (President Carter successfully waived the ban in the case of India);

Requirement that the executive branch provide an annual human rights observance report on all members of the United Nations (1979).

Several of the above measures include what is known as a "legislative veto." This refers to the capacity of one or both houses of Congress to block executive branch action (such as the sale to another country of military equipment costing $7 million or more) within a specified period of time, usually 30 or 60 days. In 1983 the Supreme Court declared legislative vetos in violation of the Constitution.

The Panama Canal Treaty negotiations of 1977–78 provide an illuminating instance of congressional resurgence in the foreign policy field. Ever since the 1903 treaty giving the United States the right to build a canal across Panama, Panamanians—and many other Latin Americans—resented what they perceived to be an infringement of their sovereignty. When, in 1964, these feelings came to a head in the form of violent Panamanian demonstrations against the United States (over the right to fly the Panamanian flag in the American-controlled Canal Zone), Washington agreed to renegotiate its canal rights with Panama. These tortuous negotiations proceeded from 1964 to 1977. Finally, in September 1977, President Carter and Brig. Gen. Omar Torrijos Herrera of Panama initialed two new treaties at an elaborate ceremony attended by representatives of 26 Western Hemisphere nations.[9] The first of these treaties terminated and superseded the 1903 treaty and its later modifications. In abolishing this agreement, the new treaty also abolished the US Canal Zone. Under the new pact, the United States retained until 1999 the right to manage, operate and maintain the Canal; this was to be done under the auspices of a new organization, the Panama Canal Commission, which has a board of nine members (4 Panamanians and 5 Americans). After 1999 the Canal in its entirety will pass under exclusive control of Panama. Until that time, the United States will retain base rights in Panama and also hold primary responsibility for defending the waterway. The United States also agreed to make annual financial payments to Panama.

The second agreement, called the Neutrality Treaty, established a permanent regime of neutrality for the Canal. This meant that in time of peace and war the ships of all nations could pass through the Canal.

Shortly after signing these treaties, President Carter submitted them to the Senate, whereupon that body engaged in the most exhaustive examination of any treaty in the nation's history. Conservatives in particular railed against the agreements, calling them a giveaway and a surrender of American sovereignty in Panama (which liberals countered the United States never possessed in the first place). In an unprecedented fashion, nearly half of the American Senate journeyed to Panama during the period of debate on the treaties. Several of these visitors held lengthy substantive discussions with Panamanian leaders, including the head of state. Such meticulous first-hand investigation by legislators led some people to question whether the Senate was not overstepping its bounds. Must foreign governments negotiate first with the president or the president's representative and then engage in a subsequent round of discussions with the Senate? If so, then who negotiates on behalf of the United States? Could a foreign government be blamed for withholding its maximum concessions from the talks with the president, for fear of having nothing to bargain with in negotiating with the Senate? Might not such extensive Senate participation in the treaty process undermine the president as the chief diplomat of the United States? That such questions did not trouble all members of the Senate is evident from the fact that a similar (though less extensive) parade of senatorial diplomats journeyed to the Kremlin when the Senate began consideration of the SALT II treaty (withdrawn from Senate consideration at President Carter's request in 1980).

By the time the Senate had concluded its debate on the Panama treaties, various senators had offered 145 amendments, 26 reservations, 18 understandings and 3 declarations. The full body passed 88 of the these modifications. All changes enacted by the Senate were accepted by President Carter (though with varying degrees of enthusiasm). At least two of these legislative modifications were quite significant. One gave the United States, along with Panama, "the right to act against any aggression or threat directed against the Canal or against the peaceful transit of vessels through the Canal." The other ensured the United States, in case of need, the right of expeditious passage through the waterway. In 1978 the Senate passed the treaties.

While the Senate became involved in the Panama episode through its constitutional duty to provide advice and consent on treaties, the House became a party through the necessity to enact certain implementing legislation so that the treaties could take effect. Four House committees became embroiled in the Panama situation: Foreign Affairs, Merchant Marine and Fisheries, Post Office and Civil Service, and Judiciary. The Senate counterparts of these committees had also to approve the implementing legislation.

If the Panama Canal treaties provide one form of evidence of Congress's revival, then another may be found in the increased efforts of foreign governments to affect legislative opinion. Some foreign governments sponsor trade groups, such as the US-Japan Trade Council, that finance trips abroad for members of Congress. More direct action sometimes occurs. In the late 1970s, when Congress was deliberating an arms embargo against Turkey, the prime ministers of both Greece and Turkey met with members of the House International Relations Committee. In 1975, amidst congressional opposition to the proposed sale of 14 Hawk missile batteries to Jordan, King Hussein sent letters directly to all 100 senators and 50 key representatives arguing for the sale (which Congress eventually approved). In 1978 Indian Prime Minister Morarji Desai appeared before committees in the House and Senate to persuade them—successfully—not to veto President Carter's decision to sell India enriched nuclear fuel.[10]

On the basis of the evidence, it seems clear that Congress has reasserted itself in the foreign policy sphere. No longer can presidents count on a compliant Congress to do their bidding.

Explanation

What has led Congress to such a reawakened interest in overseeing the country's foreign relations after two and a half decades of slumber following World War II? Several factors would seem relevant. First and foremost was the war in Vietnam. By the early 1970s, there was no denying the fact that the very best advice of the experts in the executive branch had drawn the United States into a war that seemed unwinnable (at prices the country was willing to pay) and was grievously dividing the population.

Coming on top of the Vietnam debacle, the Watergate fiasco drove another nail into the coffin of executive authority. After the revelations of wrongdoing by the president and many presidential assistants, few members of Congress remained in awe of the presidency. For a time, congressional reputations could be made by staunchly opposing requests that came from the occupant of the Oval Office. In both foreign and domestic matters, the chief executive was in retreat before a Congress that correctly sensed an opportunity to reverse executive dominance.

One of the most important spurs to congressional challenge of the executive branch was the gradual erosion of the Cold War consensus that had supported the containment policy.[11] During the 1940s and 1950s, practically any step the president took to counter the Soviet Union was applauded in and out of Congress. But in the 1960s the unmitigated rivalry between the two superpowers began to fade. The Communist bloc showed signs of decay. In 1948 Yugoslavia, under Tito's leadership, broke with Moscow. East Germany, Hungary and Czechoslovakia attempted to do the same, but without success; nonetheless, these efforts in themselves evidenced disarray in the Communist camp. Rumania challenged the Soviet Union in numerous foreign policy issues. China did make a clear break with Moscow and later gained the support of Albania. The rift between Russia and China led some strategists to suggest that Washington could play off one of these Communist giants against the other. Many Third World countries that had dallied with the Soviet Union upon achieving independence later warded off the Kremlin's advances and began to flirt with the West. This development led many observers to question the permanence of Communist inroads into emerging nations, as well as the necessity for the United States to counter every such penetration. The upshot of these considerations was the breakdown of the rarely challenged belief that the United States had to oppose the Soviet Union at every turn. Once foreign policy became open to question, it was only natural that the legislature should assume the role of questioner.

The changing nature of the foreign policy agenda also helps explain the rejuvenation of congressional activity in foreign policy. Such issues as food, energy, resource depletion, seabed mining and import restrictions have begun to supplement traditional security concerns to an increasingly large extent. Since the outcomes of such issues have highly visible domestic consequences, Congress is drawn ever more deeply into the foreign policy process. To illustrate, grain sales abroad have a decided impact upon the price Americans pay for bread, just as Japanese auto exports affect unemployment rates in Detroit. Put simply, Congress has become more involved in foreign policy because foreign policy has a larger effect on the American citizen than at any previous time in the country's history.

Dramatic increases in the size of congressional staffs, which afford the legislature more expertise, and the arrival of a "new breed" of legislator unwilling to defer to executive leadership, have also boosted congressional participation in foreign policy.

Consequences

What consequences can we expect from the heightened participation of Congress in foreign policy? Is Congress's new role likely to improve or weaken American foreign policy? Will the additional voice or voices from Congress lend wisdom to American actions, or will they merely confuse our friends and encourage our foes? Is Congress's strengthened role a transitory phenomenon, or is it likely to persist for years to come?

It is far too early to provide definitive answers to these questions. Clear-cut patterns have yet to emerge. The following discussion must therefore be regarded as no more than speculation.

Given the breakdown of consensus about the goals of American foreign policy, a fortified congressional voice may well be an obstacle in the path of decisive foreign policy action. Seen in this light, Congress represents yet another element that the president must bring along before taking action. Signs of this trend have already appeared. In early 1981, Congress refused President Reagan's request to repeal the Clark Amendment, which forbids American military assistance to any of the factions fighting for power in Angola. In 1984 as President Reagan withdrew American Marines from Lebanon, he denounced Congress for interfering in Middle East foreign policy, saying, ". . . the subsequent second-guessing about whether to keep our men there [Lebanon] severely undermined our policy. It hindered the ability of our diplomats to negotiate, encouraged more intransigence from the Syrians and prolonged the violence."[12] Should Congress resist many other presidential initiatives, the resulting paralysis in American foreign policy could only discourage America's allies and give heart to those who do not wish America well.

In a more positive vein, active involvement by Congress represents a victory for the democratic process. The House of Representatives, which stands for election every two years, reflects more closely than any other national institution the wishes of the American public. If America professes to be a democracy, should not congressmen and congresswomen have a major say in the nation's foreign policy?

Skeptics might observe, however, that a victory for democratic foreign policy is not necessarily a victory for prudent foreign policy. How well-versed are members of Congress in foreign affairs? Does the American electoral system give legislators incentives to steep themselves in foreign policy, or do voters care more about domestic and particularly local matters? In short, how well-suited is Congress to make important foreign policy decisions?

Some analysts argue that the quality of Congress's input to foreign policy almost hardly matters. There is no point, these advocates maintain, in pursuing *any* foreign policy course, no matter how brilliant, if Congress and the public do not go along. As American policy in Vietnam revealed, no policy can succeed over a sustained interval without domestic support. (The almost exclusive reliance on this single episode weakens the arguments of those who take this point of view, however.) Therefore, it is better to screen policies by subjecting them to the test of congressional approval than to embark upon policies that will only have to be aborted before fruition.

The heightened role of Congress in foreign policy may have the indirect effect of boosting public support for the nation's foreign policy. This argument presumes that congressional participation will force the executive, and especially the president, to articulate publicly the goals of American policy and to persuade the country to accept them. Such an airing of foreign policy options should help educate the public and perhaps also lead to better policy.

SUITABILITY OF CONGRESS
FOR MAKING FOREIGN POLICY

It is indisputable, as we have seen, that Congress now plays a very prominent role in the formulation of American foreign policy. While often hailing Congress's newly rediscovered sense of responsibility, not all observers are persuaded that Congress is well-suited to play a constructive part in making foreign policy. This doubt has nothing to do with the capabilities of particular representatives and senators. Instead, it stems from an appraisal of the operating procedures of the legislature as well as the rewards that the country's electoral system imposes upon the nation's lawmakers. The major drawbacks which have been cited include the domestic bias in the representative's role, the diffusion of power in Congress, the nature of the budget-making process, lack of information, slowness of congressional action, and the danger of information leaks. These weaknesses are discussed below, followed by some comments on the strengths of Congress in making foreign policy.

Domestic Bias in the Legislator's Role

Franklin D. Roosevelt once said that the first duty of a president is to get elected. Most representatives and senators would agree with this statement as it applies to themselves. Getting elected means appealing to the interests of voters and groups within one's constituency. Since most electors are far more concerned about national and local matters than international affairs (see Chapter 5), legislators who wish to retain their jobs have strong incentives to immerse themselves in domestic matters. In the words of one commentator from Philadelphia, "In voting on Congressional races, people here don't vote for national issues, they vote for constituent services. They vote on who can get their potholes fixed."[13] A legislative candidate who adopts a broad national perspective at the expense of local interests is likely to suffer defeat. All Americans may agree to cut fat out of the military budget, but woe unto the congressional candidate who advocates the closing of the local military base. Lower trade barriers may lead to more efficient production of goods and services, but the candidate from a textile-producing region who favors reduction of tariffs on textile imports might just as well plan on staying home.

Under the conception of pluralism, it is presumed (or perhaps wished) that these local interests balance each other, yielding what is best for the national interest. There is no guarantee that such will be the case, however. Former House Foreign Affairs Committee Chairman Clement J. Zablocki candidly admitted as much when he said, "Congress is too responsive to the lobbies of ethnic and special interests in the US to be able to take the lead in foreign policymaking without endangering the national interest."[14]

Because most voters choose congressional candidates on the basis of local and national issues, legislators have little incentive to steep themselves in knowledge of foreign policy. Legislators gain minimal electoral advantage by participating in such issues as arms control, helping the needy people of other countries, and intelligence oversight (which is concealed from public knowledge). Voters are much more responsive if the legislator obtains a federal grant for the local school system, secures the location of a large corporate production plant in the home district, or keeps open a military installation that provides substantial employment. It may be true that a minority of senators and representatives, through long service on committees that treat foreign policy, possess considerable foreign policy expertise. But this must be viewed as the exception rather than the rule. Like bees in a flowerbed, most legislators flit from one foreign policy question to the next, with a minimum of sustained interest or competence in any of them.

Diffusion of Power

The diffusion of power is another characteristic of Congress that gives pause to some who note Congress's growing role in foreign policy. In the legislative branch power is dispersed. No individual or group of individuals has strong control over others. Thus, the speaker of the house cannot fire a member who refuses to vote along with the majority of the chamber. Party leaders can suggest that legislators vote according to party lines, but they have little leverage to compel them to do so. A legislator who has the support of the voters back home is practically immune from punishment by legislative or party leaders. To be sure, such immunity, like most things in Washington, is not absolute. With the passing of the seniority system, party leaders have more leeway than previously to offer favored committee assignments and chairs to loyal party followers. Still, the American legislator is largely independent when it comes to voting on the issues.

The committee system in Congress reinforces the diffusion of power. As has often been observed, the work of Congress is done in committees. Here, legislators summon experts and debate issues. Through years of service on the same committee, a legislator may accumulate significant expertise on certain matters, including foreign policy. Both logic and the pressure of time suggest that, once a committee has examined an issue and reached a conclusion, there is little purpose in having the entire chamber reexamine the issue from square one, especially since few if any members will have more knowledge about the subject than committee members. Consequently, with numerous and significant exceptions, the entire house usually accepts the recommendations of its committees. It is the independence of most committees—and even of some sub-committees—that heightens the dispersal of power in Congress. Committees not infrequently operate in secret. Although forced to consult committee members more frequently than before, committee chairs continue to have the dominant voice in setting agendas and deciding which expert witnesses to summon. Party and chamber leaders exert minimal influence over committee chairs. Committee chairs do not meet on a regular basis to coordinate various aspects of foreign or domestic policy. The multiplicity of legislative committees that handle foreign policy matters only compounds the fractionization of power in Congress. These committees are depicted in Table 10–1. In 1977, a typical year, approximately 56 House committees and subcommittees were active in foreign policy. Sometimes as many as three or four different committees in each house may be concerned with different aspects of American relations with a single country.

In a sense, the House Foreign Affairs Committee and the Senate Foreign Relations Committee face a problem not unlike that confronting the State Department. As observed in Chapter 7, the State Department shares jurisdiction over various aspects of foreign policy with other departments and agencies. The two congressional committees nominally charged with overseeing the nation's foreign policy (from the legislative standpoint) similarly find themselves unable to control the entire foreign policy agenda. Such matters as appropriations, military affairs, intelligence, international energy policy, international trade, refugees, immigration, distribution of surplus food overseas, American policy toward international financial institutions, and nuclear proliferation fall under the jurisdiction of other committees. In 1981, for example, it was not the House Foreign Affairs Committee, but rather a subcommittee on public lands and national parks, that held hearings on alternative basing systems for the proposed MX missile system. (The rationale: this subcommittee was authorized to rule on the use of public lands the Air Force might require for a land-based system.) If the legislature's foreign policy experts are excluded from the handling of important foreign policy problems, there is no good reason why the entire chamber should accept the recommendations of committees with questionable foreign policy credentials. It is this reasoning, no doubt, that has led to the proliferation of foreign policy amendments proffered from the floors of both houses, a further sign of diffused power.

The dispersal of power in Congress means the president cannot go to an individual or leadership body in Congress and expect the latter to bring the remainder of Congress along. It is difficult enough to bring some level of policy coordination and consistency to a single house of Congress. The problems grow immensely when one seeks to accomplish the same task across both houses. Just as each congressional committee jealously guards its privileges, so does each

TABLE 10–1. CONGRESSIONAL COMMITTEES AND SUBCOMMIT-
TEES INVOLVED IN FOREIGN POLICY, 1980

House	Senate
Foreign Affairs (subcommittees: Africa; Asian and Pacific Affairs; Europe and the Middle East; Inter-American Affairs; International Economic Policy and Trade; International Operations; International Organizations; International Security and Scientific Affairs)	Foreign Relations (subcommittees: Arms Control, Oceans, International Operations and Environment; International Economic Policy; African Affairs; East Asian and Pacific Affairs; European Affairs; Near Eastern and South Asian Affairs; Western Hemisphere Affairs)
Armed Services (8 subcommittees)	Armed Services (6 subcommitteees)
Intelligence (4 subcommittees)	Intelligence (4 subcommittees)
Appropriations (subcommittees: Defense; Foreign Operations; Military Construction; State, Justice, Commerce and Judiciary)	Appropriations (subcommittees: Defense; Foreign Operations; Military Construction; State, Justice, Commerce and Judiciary)
Budget (Defense and Intelligence Affairs Task Force)	Budget
Ways and Means (subcommittee: Trade)	Finance (subcommittees: International Trade, Terrorism and Sugar)
Interstate and Foreign Commerce (3 subcommittees)	Commerce, Science and Transportation (5 subcommittees)
Banking, Finance and Urban Affairs (subcommittees: International Development Institutions and Finance; International Trade; Investment and Monetary Policy)	Banking, Housing and Urban Affairs (subcommittee: International Finance)
Agriculture	Agriculture, Nutrition and Forestry (subcommittee: Foreign Agriculture Policy)
Government Operations (subcommittee: Legislation and National Security)	Government Operations (subcommittee: Energy, Nuclear Proliferation and Federal Services)
Judiciary (subcommittee: Immigration, Refugees and International Law)	Judiciary
Science and Technology	Energy and Natural Resources
Interior and Insular Affairs	Environment and Public Works (subcommittees: Environmental Pollution; Nuclear Regulation)
Merchant Marine and Fisheries (5 subcommittees)	

House-Senate Bodies

Joint Economic Committee (subcommittees: Energy; International Economics)
Commission on Security and Cooperation in Europe (includes members from executive branch)
Select Commission on Immigration and Refugee Policy
Japan-US Friendship Commission

Source: *Congressional Staff Directory*, 1980.

of the two houses against the other. Thus, talk of a "congressional foreign policy" is mostly just talk. It is virtually impossible to bring about the level of compromise and coordination that would yield an internally consistent congressional foreign policy.

In the executive branch, by contrast, at least the possibility of consistency exists. There, power is concentrated. Unlike Congress, where there is no locus of ultimate authority, the executive branch culminates in the Oval Office. The president can fire or at least reassign uncooperative individuals in the executive branch. We have seen in Chapter 7 that even the president cannot always act in disregard of the wishes of those in subordinate positions. However, there is no question that the president has far more leverage over these people than do the leaders of Congress over their charges. The president is in a position to decide, should different bureaucratic organizations produce conflicting policy recommendations. Thus the president can impose a particular view of foreign policy upon the executive branch.

The structure of American political parties aggravates the dispersal of legislative power. American political parties are essentially a collection of state and local party organizations that come together every four years to try and elect a candidate for president. Once the election is over, national political parties fragment once again. State and local party organizations, not national party headquarters, select candidates for various offices, or, mavericks can become party candidates through primaries. Most fund-raising is conducted by state and local party organizations. Thus, office holders do not suffer if they violate national party positions on the issues. In the British system, by way of contrast, national party discipline remains strong. Since national party organizations screen local party candidates, lawmakers who veer too far from the national party platform find their political careers at an end. Members of Parliament who refuse to vote the party line, except on rare matters declared to be issues of conscience, are barred from running on the party's ticket in the next election. As a result, party leaders in Great Britain are usually able to deliver their party's vote. Leaders of the majority party, joined in the Cabinet, are in a position to design a consistent foreign policy, which followers in Parliament then support.

Budget-Making

The budgetary process provides one means of coordinating foreign policy, by forcing policymakers to determine foreign policy priorities. There is never enough money to fund every foreign policy objective that the government would like to pursue. Therefore, government must select those goals it believes most important and devote the bulk of available funds to them. Lesser objectives receive lower levels of monetary support.

The Constitution confers the appropriations power upon Congress. In 1974, Congress made significant strides toward rationalizing the budgetary process with passage of the Budget and Impoundment Control Act. To understand the degree of progress made, it is necessary to glimpse briefly at budgetary procedures before these healthy reforms.

Prior to 1974, making the congressional budget was a three-stage process. In stage 1 the president, working with officials at the Office of Management and Budget (OMB), previously known as the Budget Bureau, formulated a budget for the coming fiscal year (which now begins October 1). This budget was a very long and complicated document. In it, the president indicated how much money was proposed for hundreds of domestic and foreign policy programs. Each program was listed separately with a dollar figure beside it; these are called "line items." Each program was further broken down into various components, with a dollar figure accompanying each one. Thus, "military forces" is a major program that is broken down into such components as personnel, strategic weapons, and tactical weapons. In actuality, these breakdowns are much more detailed than we have indicated.

The presidential budget is in actuality a request to Congress for funds, as only the latter can appropriate money. Stage 2 began with Congress's consideration of the budget, which commenced with the parceling out of each major program request to the House committee that normally handled that topic. Thus, the military forces request would go to the Armed Services Committee; requests for international trade matters would be sent to the Interstate and Foreign Commerce Committee; funding for the corps of agricultural attachés at overseas posts would receive consideration by the Agricultural Committee. Each committee, operating largely in isolation from the others, would then use the presidential request as a basis for setting a spending target. These targets did not constitute actual appropriations. Rather, they represented the best judgments about spending levels from those committees that presumably had the best knowledge about the substantive matters at issue. Sometimes these targets, known as "authorizations," met the president's request, while at other times they exceeded or fell below it. Senate committees likewise determined authorizations. Each house then passed authorization bills, differences being resolved in conference committees.

The actual raising of money did not occur until the third stage of the budgetary process. The various authorizations were funneled to the House Appropriations Committee, which was (and is) divided into several subcommittees. A subcommittee exists for practically each program area for which a substantive committee exists. These subcommittees, again acting for the most part in isolation, would make the actual appropriation, which then needed approval from the Appropriations Committee and the full House. The same procedure was then repeated in the Senate, with differences being resolved through conference committees.

Outside specialists had long criticized this process for its lack of coordination. Once the president's budget request reached Congress, no office equivalent to OMB existed to set spending priorities on behalf of the legislature. Since each authorizing committee reached its decision without reference to the others, Congress lacked a mechanism to set priorities. Similarly, the subcommittee of the Appropriations Committee consulted only sporadically. The resulting budget therefore consisted of a hodgepodge of appropriations with little rational planning behind them. No congressional body was charged with the task of dividing funds between domestic and foreign concerns or of setting spending priorities within each of these categories.

The reform-minded legislators elected to Congress in the aftermath of Watergate set out to improve the budgetary process. In essence, what they did was to insert an additional stage between the submission of the president's request and its consideration by the various substantive committees. To handle the activities involved in this additional stage, the Budget and Impoundment Control Act of 1974 established a Congressional Budget Office (CBO) as well as a Budget Committee in each house. After receiving the president's budget request (target date January 1 for the fiscal year beginning the following October 1), the CBO takes these figures and prepares its own tentative budget. While the CBO uses the president's spending proposals as a starting point, it may modify them as it wishes. The new Budget Committee in each house then takes the recommendations of the CBO, holds hearings, and produces a budget of its own. This budget then goes to the full house, where it is voted upon, usually after some modifications. A House-Senate conference works out a common congressional budget, which then must be adopted by each house in the form of a concurrent resolution. The target for this stage is May 15. While not binding, this concurrent resolution serves as a guideline for the authorizing and appropriating committees, which continue to perform the same functions as before the budgetary reforms.

The new procedures incorporate a certain degree of planning and coordination into the appropriations process. In a sense, the new Congressional Budget Office performs a similar function as OMB: both organizations set priorities among various governmental programs, and they suggest funding levels for each program. There now appears to be a sense of order and rationality to the operation. Under the old system, Congress never started with an overall spending ceiling and allocated portions of it to various programs; now it does.

However, one might ask, what is the purpose of retaining a separate appropriations process, now that a budget committee exists to set spending ceilings? Would it not make sense to merge the authorization and appropriation steps in the authorizing committee and abolish the appropriations committee entirely? Such a measure was recommended in 1973 by the Bolling Commission, set up to study the organization of Congress. Retention of the appropriations committees proves frustrating to the members and staff of the House Foreign Affairs and Senate Foreign Relations committees. With a staff of several dozen professionals each, these committees meticulously study a wide range of foreign policy issues and draft legislation and issue recommendations. But as often as not the executive agencies in charge of foreign policy remain in awe not of these committees but rather of the appropriations committees, which detail one or two professionals to foreign policy issues. Control over the purse amounts in practice to annual reviews of each department and its activities. In hearings, appropriations committee members put questions to agency heads that reveal the committee's preferences and priorities. Agency heads who desire adequate funding have learned to listen well and consider these recommendations. Thus, the appropriations committees, which possess limited expertise in foreign policy, often have a greater input into executive decision making than the very committees blessed with expert knowledge of foreign policy! It remains unlikely, however, that the entrenched members of the appropriations committees will yield their central position in the policy-making process, and so the anomaly is likely to continue.

Lack of Information

It has often been said that inadequate information hinders Congress's ability to exert vigorous and creative leadership in foreign policy. In contrast to domestic policy making, few legislators have direct experience with problems of foreign policy. In the former area, many lawmakers have served on school or zoning boards or have participated in the establishment or operation of corporations. Legislators from the farm states have often spent many afternoons behind a plow. Those from urban districts know about the problems of large cities. By contrast, few legislators have participated in the management of a military alliance, in the operations of a foreign assistance program, or in the clandestine activities of an intelligence organization. Few have gained familiarity, through direct experience, with such activities as nuclear testing, the law of the sea, international modification of the environment, or joint space exploration. The point is, that whereas most legislators may gain, through direct experience, some knowledge of the domestic affairs over which they have charge, they rarely do so in matters of foreign policy. Therefore, lawmakers must rely on outside expertise to understand foreign policy to a much greater extent than in the case of domestic policy.

The same limitations on direct experience in foreign policy also apply to most presidents. Few chief executives have had extensive experience with foreign policy before arriving at the White House. However, the informational resources available to the president dwarf those that serve Congress. The president stands at the apex of several massive reporting systems, including the Departments of State and Defense and the intelligence services. In all, thousands of persons feed information into the executive branch, the most important of which—in theory—reaches the president or top presidential aides. Should the president need information or an analytic study on any topic, these same networks are in a position to supply it rapidly.

While better served than in the past, Congress has nowhere near the same resources as the executive branch for obtaining information and analysis. Therefore, it is often argued, Congress is hardly in a position to exercise creativity and leadership in foreign policy. Indeed, Congress must often rely upon the executive branch for information. The executive's advantage in this respect places it in a position to frame foreign policy issues for discussion. Congress therefore finds itself debating executive initiatives, adding here and trimming there like a busy gardener tending a flower bed. Oftentimes Congress finds itself handicapped in evaluating executive actions because of its reliance upon information from the executive. By stressing some facts and perhaps concealing others—unless Congress directly asks for them—executive officials can often make actions under discussion appear advisable. In trying to appraise an executive proposal, a legislator is often in the same position as an individual who receives a medical report from a doctor. Incapable of challenging the physician's findings, the most the patient can do is seek another opinion.

In recent years Congress has taken some steps to render itself less helpless in the face of executive expertise. The legislature has increased the size of personal and committee staffs, and it has enlarged various congressional reference units. Personal and committee staffs can provide enormous assistance to the harried legislator with a modicum of specialized knowledge. Franck and Weisband offer a vivid glimpse of the service performed by a personal staff member.

> The power of staff in relation to their member becomes particularly obvious when the buzzer sounds to call members to the floor for a vote. During such a vote call, staffers can be seen milling about the doors of nearby elevators waiting to meet their principals. In the thirty seconds it takes to sprint from the banks of elevators to the floor of the chamber, the staffer delivers a rapid-fire summary of the issue in an upcoming vote. How he characterizes that issue and the recommendations he makes frequently determine the member's vote. If the issue is not one of profound interest or concern to the legislator, this briefing may be the first and only time the member focuses on that subject.[15]

Competent staff members can develop independent sources of information (journalists, colleagues, their own expertise, disgruntled executive officials who wish to leak data), challenge policy analyses set forth by the executive, be aware of expert witnesses capable of disputing executive experts, propose probing questions for legislators to put to executive officials arguing for a particular policy or appropriation, and draft legislation. Thus, an enlarged and capable staff can render Congress less dependent on the executive branch for information and analysis. This is not to say that the executive branch regularly employs deception, spreads half-truths, or proposes policies that conflict with the national interest. Quite the opposite is the case. However, if the legislature is to carry out its responsibility of challenging the executive, it must be in a position to compel the latter to justify its actions.

The increase in legislative staff has been dramatic. Between 1950 and 1980, the staff serving Congress has increased five times. During the 1970s alone, the congressional staff grew from 10,700 to 18,400.[16] In 1965 the staff of the Senate Foreign Relations Committee equaled 9; as of 1980 it numbered approximately 30. The

House Foreign Affairs Committee staff grew in the same period from 9 to 50. In 1969, the average number of Senate staff employees per senator equaled 34; by 1980 the number was close to 80.

Aside from their personal and committee staffs, legislators receive help from research units attached to Congress. The principal units that perform this function are the Congressional Research Service, the General Accounting Office (GAO), the Congressional Budget Office, and the Office of Technology Assessment. The last-mentioned organization conducts studies of technical issues, such as alternative energy futures, the number of deaths that would result from a nuclear exchange, or alternative basing systems for the MX missile system. The staffs of these organizations have also increased. As of 1980, the GAO's staff numbered over 4 thousand professionals, while the Congressional Research Service employed approximately 550 professionals. Naturally, the cost of maintaining the legislative staff has increased along with its numbers. In 1980, the cost of the staff approximated $550 million annually.

The growth in the legislative staff has unquestionably augmented the legislature's capacity to challenge the executive branch and occasionally to propose foreign policy initiatives of its own. It bears mentioning, at the same time, that one by-product of the larger staff is increased diffusion of legislative power. As each representative and senator, and each committee and subcommittee, enjoys the benefit of its own expertise, it becomes less amenable to persuasion from the leaders of Congress.

Need for Speed

The requirement to make foreign policy decisions in a hurry is often cited as a factor that makes Congress fundamentally unfit to play a leading role in making foreign policy. Those who take this position ask how Congress can respond if America's distant radars detect a flight of missiles coming across the North Pole, giving the government only 15 minutes to react. Or, they say, suppose hostile military forces invade a country friendly to America (often Korea or Israel is named); unless Washington takes action within 24 hours, these forces may well conquer the country. In neither such case, it is argued, is Congress capable of responding in a timely manner. Even when there is plenty of time to act, Congress may not meet deadlines. Warren Christopher, deputy secretary of state in the Carter administration, observes that

> In the case of Nicaragua in 1979, when there was still a chance that
> we could influence the direction of the Sandinista government, it took
> months to gain authority from the Congress for a modest aid program,
> and even then it was hedged with debilitating conditions. Educators,
> medical personnel and others from Cuba, meanwhile, were on the
> scene within hours.[17]

The necessity for speedy action as an impediment to congressional participation in foreign policy is largely overdrawn. Obviously, the 535 members of the legislature could not assemble and make a decision instantaneously. But, one must ask, how frequently is the government called upon to make such rapid decisions? In reality, the occasions for such immediate action are extremely rare. Of all the foreign policy crises facing the United States since World War II, only the 1950 North Korean invasion required such a speedy response. Certainly Vietnam did not necessitate immediate decisions; America's involvement in that struggle was the result of a series of decisions no one of which was made under extraordinary pressure of time. Even during the Cuban missile crisis, President Kennedy's hand-picked team of advisers—called EXCOMM—took approximately ten days to decide on a blockade.

While instantaneous decisions are the exception, it cannot be denied that when they arise, the stakes could involve the survival of the nation. Therefore, it would not be appropriate to place such decisions in the hands of Congress. The authors of the War Powers Act of 1973 recognized this fact, which is why they gave the president leeway to deploy American forces overseas for 60 days without first seeking permission from Congress. The proper role for Congress is not to determine America's reaction in a crisis, but rather to determine in advance who is authorized to make such decisions and what guidelines that person or persons should follow. Congress is eminently suited for this task.

We must recall that the great majority of foreign policy decisions are not taken in times of crisis. To deny Congress a role in these decisions, because the legislature is not suited to react in an emergency, is like keeping a swift and cunning runner off the basepaths for failing to hit home runs.

Leaks

It is also alleged from time to time that Congress is unsuited to play a vigorous part in foreign policy because it is too prone to leaks. Foreign policy, it is asserted, deals with sensitive information.

If Congress resembles a sieve, then it should not be made privy to classified information, and without it the legislature is not in a position to make foreign policy.

There is no doubt that secret information given to 435 representatives and 100 senators risks some chance of being disclosed. A lawmaker up for reelection may be tempted to expose startling information in order to gain public attention. A legislator might be tempted to release information, if he or she felt it would result in an alteration of a policy he or she deemed harmful to the nation. A representative or senator might feel little hesitation in revealing classified information that he or she doesn't believe should be classified in the first place. To guard against such risks of disclosure, not all information need be released to the entire membership of Congress. Information concerning the covert operations of intelligence agencies is uncovered only to members of the intelligence committees in each house. Certain classified executive agreements are made known only to members of the Senate Foreign Relations and the House Foreign Affairs committees. This practice could be extended to other areas.

Before saddling Congress with a host of new restrictions, however, one should examine the record of congressional revelations of classified material. For the most part, Congress has been extremely careful in its handling of classified information. In fact, one can make a strong case that the executive branch is far more guilty than the legislature in making unauthorized disclosures of secret information. At the very least, Congress's record in this regard is no worse than that of the executive branch. Thus, the fear of leaks, like the need for rapid action, is not a very persuasive reason for denying Congress a role in foreign policy.

Strengths of Congress

This review of Congress's actual or supposed weaknesses in the foreign policy field should not blind us to the very real strengths that Congress can bring to the foreign policy process. Furthermore, it would be a mistake to assume that the executive has always been correct in its decision. Recognizing the room for more than one view on these matters, one might suggest serious errors on the part of executive decision makers with regard to Vietnam, illegal operations of intelligence services, the 1956 decision to intervene at Suez on the side of Egypt instead of Britain and Israel and France, delayed recognition of mainland China, and security of the American embassy in Teheran in 1979–80.

What are some of the strengths that Congress can bring to the making of foreign policy? At least some members of Congress have amassed considerable expertise concerning foreign policy. Normally, it is assumed that the executive branch holds the repository of government expertise on foreign policy, since it houses the career professionals who devote their working lives to foreign policy questions. These civil servants need not divide their time among constituents and special interest groups, nor need they engage in immensely time-consuming electoral campaigns. Yet through long years of service on the same committee, certain representatives and senators have gained significant expertise in foreign affairs. Senators Jackson, Nunn, Fulbright and Church have distinguished themselves in the foreign policy field, as has Representative Aspin on defense matters. Many legislators have had more exposure to foreign affairs than some of the presidential appointees assigned to top foreign policy posts. The increase in legislative staff has also contributed to more congressional awareness in the foreign policy realm. Many congressional staffers formerly served at State, Defense, or the intelligence services.

The oft-lamented delay that congresssional consideration builds into the foreign policy process has its advantageous side. By blocking hasty unconsidered actions, Congress can impose a sobering interval upon the conduct of government.

Perhaps the major strength that Congress brings to governmental activity is one that pierces to the heart of the American political system. This system rests on a belief in representative government. The majority of Americans have rejected the idea that a cadre of technical wizards or enlightened philosophers can govern the nation better than the people themselves. Elected every two years, the House of Representatives offers the most accurate reflection of public opinion of any institution in the federal government. To ignore congressional positions verges on tampering with the process of democratic government. As the Nixon administration revealed, it is possible for the chief executive and top assistants to lose touch with the people—their doubts, their fears, and their aspirations. Sealed off in the world of official Washington, officials in the executive bureaucracy sometimes forget they exist to serve the public rather than to direct it.

But there is an other than philosophical reason to heed public opinion. The Vietnam experience showed that there are definite limits to how far the public will undergird a policy with which it disagrees. Any administration that sets aside public opinion in order to carry out its own policies, however well-meaning they may be, does so at the peril of having to cut short those policy actions before they bear fruit.

IMPROVING CONGRESS'S FOREIGN POLICY CAPABILITIES

To identify Congress's strengths is not to deny that the legislature would benefit from an enhancement of its capabilities. In this section we shall explore some possibilities for improving Congress's foreign policy capacities.

It is generally recognized that the diffusion of congressional power detracts from Congress's ability to exercise creative leadership in foreign policy. In establishing a permanent budget committee in each house, as well as a Congressional Budget Office, the legislature has made an effort to bring more coordination into the policy process. Some experts have recommended a tightening of party discipline, along the lines of British parties, as a way of enhancing control by congressional leaders. Presumably, this would permit them to formulate a "congressional" foreign policy that would enjoy the backing of the majority party in each house. To be sure, serious problems would arise if each house were controlled by a different party, or one party controlled both houses but the president came from the other party. In any event, given the American preference for independence for their representatives, such a reform of parties does not seem likely.

A more practical means of enhancing Congress's capability in foreign policy was suggested by former Vice President Hubert Humphrey in 1959, while he was serving in the Senate. Humphrey proposed the creation of a joint committee on foreign policy. Numerous variations of this scheme have surfaced since then. In Bayless Manning's conception,[18] membership on such a committee would be composed of the chair and ranking minority member of each committee that regularly deals with foreign policy issues in each house. A staff of professionals would be available to perform research and other tasks. The new committee would serve as the entry point for foreign policy matters into the Congress; that is, a foreign policy issue would be discussed for the first time in Congress in the joint committee. Such deliberation would allow committee members to place the issue in an overall foreign policy context. As opposed to the current practice of sending bills immediately to substantive committees, where they are examined separately with little or no reference to other foreign policy proposals, the new committee would allow influential members of these substantive committees to consider each bill in the total context of American foreign policy objectives.

Following its consideration in the joint committee on foreign policy, a bill would be forwarded to the appropriate substantive committee for approval, rejection or amendment. During this stage, leading committee members, benefiting from previous discussion at the joint committee level, would be in a position to explain the significance of the bill in terms of the grand fabric of foreign policy objectives. Before going to the full house for final action, the bill would return once again to the joint committee. Here, members could review the work of the substantive committees to see if their final product was consistent with the goals of American foreign policy. If so, the joint committee would forward the legislation to each house for final action. If the joint committee felt that the substantive committee's work was not in keeping with the national interest, it could return the bill to the substantive committee in each house with recommended alterations. Such recommendations would not be binding, however; whatever action the substantive committees took—including affirmation of the bill exactly as originally reported out—would go to each house for final action.

Proponents of a joint committee argue that it will help Congress fashion a coherent and consistent foreign policy. In their view, the present system of farming out different foreign policy bills to various committees prevents Congress from ever considering any single bill in terms of an entire foreign policy program. Like practically all proposals, this one is not without its drawbacks. Would not an additional level of consideration result in even more obstructionism and delay, not to mention bureaucratic red tape? Would not substantive committee chairmen jealously guard their prerogatives against the "trespasses" of the joint committee? Given the dependence of electoral success on the satisfaction of local interests, is it not simply futile to create a body whose main purpose will be to persuade lawmakers to take the broad national view? Advocates of the joint committee approach do not deny these negative factors, but they insist that the benefits, in terms of coordination and consistency, outweigh them.

A third suggestion for enhancing the role of Congress in foreign policy derives, like the first, from governmental practice in Great Britain. One of the highlights of every parliamentary session in Great Britain is the Question Period. At least once a week (usually on Fridays), the full Parliament meets so members may pose questions to the prime minister and cabinet. Given the absence of separation of powers in Britain, ministers may not claim immunity from responding on the basis of executive privilege. Often these questions are controversial, not to mention politically embarrassing. A member of Parliament might inquire why a particular decision was taken, why a particular policy was not working better, or why a particular individual was behaving incompetently. Knowing that their misdeeds are likely to be exposed in the Question Period, where press coverage is substantial, those in positions of authority have every incentive to govern properly. A secondary purpose of the practice, however, is to provide lawmakers and the public an explanation of the purposes underlying government policy. The separate patches that constitute policy are here woven together into a pattern for all to see.

Institution of a question period has been proposed for the United States. As in Great Britain, the chief executive and the Cabinet would appear before a joint session of Congress to answer questions. A question period might occur once a week whenever Congress was in session. There would be no air of impeachment or criminal activity in these meetings. Rather, the government's judgment would be on trial. An American question period, it is argued, would help offset the diffusion of power that presently characterizes Congress. Legislators who normally consider bills in the compartmentalized setting of committee rooms would have the opportunity to have explained to them the overall pattern of policy. Having digested the larger picture, it is alleged, these lawmakers would be better able to fashion a coherent and consistent foreign policy when they return to their committee chambers. To be sure, opponents of a question period would raise the constitutional issues of separation of powers and executive privilege. While requiring special attention, these problems are not necessarily insurmountable.

CONCLUSIONS

We have seen in this chapter how Congress has begun to play a forceful role in foreign policy. In many respects, Congress insists on being a co-equal partner with the executive branch; the legislature is no longer content with simply being informed after the fact about executive foreign policy decisions.

We have also inquired into the suitability of Congress for playing an active foreign policy role. Although additional staff provides Congress with more information than in the past, and although new budgetary procedures have helped to rationalize the spending process, Congress continues to suffer from some institutional deficiencies that detract from its capacity to make constructive contributions to foreign policy. Congressional power remains diffused despite the noteworthy reforms of the 1970s. Most members continue to invest the bulk of their time in domestic concerns, for this is what the voter appears to demand and is the type of behavior the voter rewards at election time. The legislature is unable to act with great speed, and, like the executive branch, its record in preserving secret information is not without flaws.

One issue that would seem to merit some thought centers around the permanence of the congressional resurgence. Is the new congressional activism a flash in the pan, a short-lived reaction to executive excesses and mistakes associated with Watergate and Vietnam? Or does the revival of congressional interest in foreign policy signal a new and enduring departure in American political practice? Only time will reveal the answers to these questions. However, there are reasons to suspect that the resurgence of Congress will be more than transitory. In the first place, foreign policy is becoming increasingly meshed with domestic policy, traditionally an area of great concern to legislators. So long as agricultural assistance to other countries affects prices in the American supermarket, military policy in the Middle East influences gasoline prices at the American service station, and the availability of scarce minerals is dependent upon maintaining cordial relations with Third World states, Congress is bound to take a strong interest in such matters. In the second place, Congress has legislated for itself a role in the policy process. For example, the executive must now submit to Congress any proposal to sell a sizable quantity of military goods to another country; Congress has 30 days to veto the sale by joint resolution. Thus, either by an act of commission or omission, Congress is involved in the policy decision. The 1973 War Powers Act contains a similar provision with respect to the deployment of military force abroad. As Franck and Weisband point out,[19] this type of congressional activity differs from the more traditional investigative powers of the legislature. In the latter case, Congress inquires into executive performance after the executive has acted. Several of the laws passed by Congress in the 1970s require the executive to consult with Congress before final decisions are taken. The object is decision-sharing. With respect to such issues as human rights, arms exports and nuclear sales, Congress has won the right to be consulted before the government acts. As a result of its own decisions, Congress no longer enjoys the luxury of ignoring foreign policy even if it chooses to do so. A third reason why Congress is likely to continue to play a significant role in foreign policy concerns the legislature's new capability to obtain and analyze information independent of the executive branch. Eager staffers, as well as legislators with a strong interest in foreign affairs, are not likely to let this asset atrophy. They will want to capitalize on their knowledge capabilities to make an impact on the nation's foreign policy. It thus appears that Congress will play an active part in formulating the nation's foreign policy for years to come.

If Congress is likely to play a vigorous role in foreign policy, then it seems appropriate to inquire into what that role should be. Should Congress take a hand in the day-to-day foreign policy decisions of the government, or should the legislature confine itself to setting broad foreign policy guidelines? Most investigators recommend the latter role for Congress, a determination based on the nature of both diplomacy and Congress itself. Few legislators have the time or inclination to oversee the myriad daily foreign policy operations of the government, nor do many have the breadth of knowledge that such oversight requires. Furthermore, successful diplomacy requires a certain degree of ambiguity and flexibility. A government must have room to maneuver, to offer threats and hold out rewards as each situation requires. In contrast, legislation, the output of Congress, is inherently absolute and inflexible. Laws state who must do what and under what conditions. A diplomacy constricted by a corset of legislation would find itself unable to employ uncertainty and surprise to the nation's benefit.

In sum, Congress best contributes to foreign policy when it sets forth broad foreign policy goals that the nation should pursue. Crabb and Holt propose that the legislature is particularly well suited to performing the following tasks:

> granting or withholding funds for foreign policy purposes;
> overseeing executive performance, as in the case of congressional scrutiny of the intelligence agencies;
> prescribing limits to the presidential use of military force, as Congress did in the case of the 1973 War Powers Act;
> supplying a base of constitutional legitimacy to foreign policy.[20]

The last-mentioned activity refers to Congress's capacity to persuade the American people to accept the government's foreign policy, as the result of a congressional airing and concurrence in that policy.

The nation's foreign policy enjoys the greatest likelihood of success when the executive and legislative branches act in harmony. In that situation, the nation's allies can remain confident that the United States will carry out its commitments to them, and the nation's foes will suffer minimal temptation to test America's will. In recent times, the nadir of executive-legislative concord occurred in the late 1960s and early 1970s, spurred by Vietnam and Watergate. Today, the situation is much improved, with both branches cooperating in what might be called a vigorous partnership.

This examination of the role of Congress in foreign policy concludes our investigation of the foreign policy-making process in the United States. In the course of this investigation, we have studied the interacting roles of the public, the media, the various units of the executive branch, and finally the legislature. These interactions are colored by the nation's values, traditions and beliefs, as well as the consequences or feedback from foreign policy itself. We turn in the next three chapters to specific elements of that foreign policy. In particular, we shall examine military policy, arms control, and the diplomacy of food, minerals, and energy.

FOR DISCUSSION

What strengths and weaknesses does Congress bring to the formulation of foreign policy? Based on this assessment, would you favor a stronger or weaker role for Congress in this area?

On balance, has the resurgence of congressional participation in foreign policy been helpful or harmful to American foreign policy thus far?

What alterations of congressional practices and procedures would you recommend to enhance the legislature's capacity to play a constructive role in making foreign policy?

READING SUGGESTIONS

Bennet, Douglas J., Jr. "Congress in Foreign Policy: Who Needs It?" *Foreign Affairs*, XVII (Fall 1978): 40–50.
Christopher, Warren. "Ceasefire between the Branches: A Compact in Foreign Affairs," *Foreign Affairs*, LX (Summer 1982): 989–1005.

Cohen, Richard E. *Congressional Leadership Seeking a New Role*. The Washington Papers, Vol. VIII, No. 79. Beverly Hills: Sage Publications, 1980.

Crabb, Cecil V., Jr., and Holt, Pat M. *Invitation to Struggle: Congress, the President and Foreign Policy*. Washington: Congressional Quarterly Press, 1980.

Cutler, Lloyd N. "To Form a Government," *Foreign Affairs*, LIX (Fall 1980): 126–43.

Franck, Thomas M., and Weisband, Edward. *Foreign Policy by Congress*. New York: Oxford University Press, 1979.

Manning, Bayless. "The Congress, the Executive and Intermestic Affairs: Three Proposals," *Foreign Affairs*, LV (January 1977): 306–24.

Muravchik, Joshua. *The Senate and National Security: A New Mood*. The Washington Papers, Vol. III, No. 80. Beverly Hills: Sage Publications, 1980.

Spanier, John, and Nogee, Joseph, eds. *Congress, the Presidency and American Foreign Policy*. New York: Pergamon Press, 1981.

NOTES

1. *New York Times*, January 24, 1981.
2. Quoted in Thomas M. Franck and Edward Weisband, *Foreign Policy by Congress* (New York: Oxford University Press, 1979), p. 137.
3. Loch Johnson and James M. McCormick, "Foreign Policy by Executive Fiat," *Foreign Policy*, XXVIII (Fall 1977): 117–38.
4. The Symington investigation may be found in US, Senate, Committee on Foreign Relations, *U.S. Security Agreements and Commitments Abroad*, Hearings before the Subcommittee on United States Security Agreements and Committees Abroad, volumes I and II (91st Congress, 1st session) 1978
5. Johnson and McCormick, p. 117.
6. Ibid., p. 118.
7. However, there is evidence that on occasion State sends these agreements to Congress weeks or even months after their conclusion. Furthermore, Congress is not in a position to know if it has received the texts of all executive agreements. Finally, the law does not require the executive branch to transmit informal verbal understandings, which other governments view as binding as treaties. Examples include President Nixon's 1973 promise to North Vietnamese Premier Pham Van Dong to provide reconstruction aid and Secretary Kissinger's 1975 understanding with Israel and Egypt to use Americans to monitor the Sinai disengagement.
8. Les Aspin, "Why Doesn't Congress Do Something?" *Foreign Policy* (Summer 1974): 70–82.
9. The following account is based upon Cecil V. Crabb, Jr., and Pat M. Holt, *Invitation to Struggle: Congress, the President and Foreign Policy* (Washington: Congressional Quarterly Press, 1980), chapter 3.
10. These episodes are recounted in Franck and Weisband, pp. 180–86.

11. For further discussion of the end of consensus (and the unlikelihood of fashioning a new one), see Ole R. Holsti and James N. Rosenau, "Vietnam, Consensus, and the Belief Systems of American Leaders," *World Politics*, XXXII (October 1979): 1–56.

12. Speech at Georgetown University Center for Strategic and International Studies, April 6, 1984, quoted in *New York Times*, April 7, 1984.

13. *New York Times*, July 23, 1981.

14. Quoted in Franck and Weisband, p. 165.

15. Franck and Weisband, p. 235.

16. Various authorities supply different figures on the size of the staff, reflecting different methods of counting. The figures supplied here come from Crabb and Holt, pp. 190–92, and John Spanier and Joseph Nogee, eds., *Congress, the Presidency and American Foreign Policy* (New York: Pergamon Press, 1981), p. xxvii.

17. Warren Christopher, "Ceasefire between the Branches: A Compact in Foreign Affairs," *Foreign Affairs*, LX (Summer 1982): 998.

18. Bayless Manning, "The Congress, the Executive and Intermestic Affairs: Three Proposals," *Foreign Affairs*, LV (January 1977): 306–24.

19. Franck and Weisband, p. 62.

20. Crabb and Holt, pp. 217–18.

Chapter 11
Military Policy

The lamb may lie down next to the lion, but the lamb won't get much sleep.

Woody Allen

The previous chapters of this volume have explored the policy-making process within the United States. This chapter and the two that follow shift focus to the substance of American foreign policy. While it is possible for purposes of analysis to differentiate between policy formulation and policy itself, one must always keep in mind the symbiotic connection between the two. The way in which policy is made affects that policy, just as the substance of policy bears upon the policy-making process. For example, had not Congress had a role to play in the decision about whether to intervene in the civil war in Angola, it is likely that the United States would have become involved on a large scale. Similarly, America's extensive involvement in international trade led to the establishment of the president's special representative for trade.

The present chapter attempts to analyze America's military policy. It begins with a survey of military doctrines followed by the United States since World War II. The next section examines the military balance between the United States and its principal military rival, the Soviet Union. The discussion then broadens to explore the military situation between NATO and the Warsaw Pact. The chapter ends with a discussion of readiness and arms transfers.

381

AMERICAN MILITARY DOCTRINE

The United States is a nation with global interests and a wide range of military capabilities and objectives. According to a recent Defense Department document, America's three highest military priorities are: (1) to deter nuclear war; (2) to deter or defeat any attack upon the United States or its allies; (3) to deter or defeat any other attack upon America's vital interests.[1] To carry out these objectives, the nation follows a military doctrine. The Defense Department defines military doctrine as "fundamental principles by which the military forces or elements thereof guide their actions." Military doctrines do not spell out how field commanders will deploy their forces. Rather, doctrine lays out a broad strategy that the nation will follow to achieve its political objectives. Since World War II, the United States has followed a number of military doctrines, which we shall examine in the pages that follow.

Eisenhower: Massive Retaliation and Brinkmanship

Massive retaliation is the label given to American military doctrine during much of the period of decisive American strategic superiority over the Soviet Union (approximately 1945–1965). This doctrine flowed from the broad objective of "containment." As explained more fully in Chapter 2, containment signified United States determination to prevent the extension of world communism, especially Soviet communism. Under the Truman administration, the containment policy included aid to Greece and Turkey (threatened by Communist subversion), Marshall Plan assistance to Europe, the formation of NATO, and intervention in Korea. By the time of the 1952 election, the Korean War had resulted in a military stalemate frustrating to Americans who were used to winning wars. In his election campaign, Eisenhower vowed to end the war and reduce defense spending, a measure deemed essential to balance the budget (a traditional GOP objective). In 1953, just after Eisenhower's election, a Korean armistice was signed. At the same time the Eisenhower administration unveiled its plan for reducing defense expenditures, namely, the doctrine of massive retaliation.

Massive retaliation relied upon the threat of nuclear destruction to dissuade the Soviet Union from expanding. According to the doctrine, the United States would not meet Soviet forces at the location of aggression (as occurred in Korea) but would instead respond by reducing Soviet cities to rubble with nuclear weapons.

In T. H. White's words, massive retaliation meant, "You step on my toe and I'll bash in your skull."[2] Presumably, the Soviets would not regard any expansion of power as worth such a price and thus would be "contained." On the economic side, the Republicans touted the new doctrine as providing "more bang for the buck." Surely, they said, it was cheaper to maintain a small force of nuclear weapons than large armies and navies. Nuclear weapons need not be fed, clothed and sheltered, nor do they require spending money and pensions. Massive retaliation, the new administration averred, would not only contain the Soviet Union, but it would do so at a lower cost than the methods of the Truman administration.

As a corollary of massive retaliation, the United States embarked upon a program of military and economic assistance to friendly countries and signed security agreements with over 40 nations. The signing of these security agreements, which included NATO, SEATO, ANZUS, the Rio Pact and others, has been dubbed "pactomania." Washington envisaged a division of labor with its allies. While the United States would provide a nuclear shield against direct Soviet or Chinese attack, local forces would use American aid to combat insurgency and subversion.

The people in the front lines today are the women and the children. Every man goes to war this time with his family strapped to his back.

Jerome B. Wiesner, former
presidential science adviser, 1982

In line with massive retaliation, the Eisenhower administration severely reduced the size of the country's conventional forces while building up the Strategic Air Command (SAC), which would carry atomic bombs to the Soviet heartland in case of aggression.

Emboldened by nuclear superiority, the Eisenhower administration engaged in the tactics of "brinkmanship." This term is associated with Eisenhower's secretary of state, John Foster Dulles, who had a large hand in shaping the military and political policies of the Eisenhower years. Voicing the frustrations of many Americans with containment, Dulles argued that the policy held out no hope of ultimate victory over the Communist foe. Furthermore, containment gave the initiative to the enemy; they could choose where confrontations would occur. Brinkmanship offered the possibility of victory. Thanks to American nuclear superiority, America could drive the Soviets to the "brink" of war and then force them to back down. As part of this strategy, Dulles urged the populations in the East European satellites of the Soviet Union to revolt, and he implied—without ever promising—that they would be sheltered by the protective umbrella of America's nuclear weapons. Ultimately, Dulles hoped to "roll back" and eliminate Soviet power.

The doctrine of massive retaliation contained one fatal flaw—the Russians didn't believe it. The Kremlin couldn't conceive that the Americans would be willing to risk total war over small Soviet incursions on the periphery of the Communist bloc—and events proved them right. So long as the Communists confined their expansionary efforts to insurgencies, coups and subversion, the United States might threaten mightily, but it would not unleash its nuclear arsenal. Thus, Washington extended little more than moral support when East Germans in 1953 and Hungarians in 1956 rose up against their Soviet masters.

It soon became clear that the Russians were not cowed by America's threats of nuclear destruction. Ironically, massive retaliation permitted the weaker power (Russia) to take the offensive against the stronger.

As the weaknesses of massive retaliation became apparent, critics began to attack the doctrine. Some, like Henry Kissinger in his book, *Necessity for Choice*, argued that the United States needed a varied arsenal of weapons that would give the country a choice between nuclear war and doing nothing; he urged a buildup of the country's conventional and counterinsurgency forces. Other skeptics saw difficulties in the division-of-labor concept. It appeared that a number of countries on the Communist periphery were so weak and unstable that no amount of American aid could enable them to withstand subversion and insurgency. America would have to intervene militarily—as it did in Vietnam—if these countries were to be salvaged. Furthermore, a number of such states, like India, elected to become neutrals rather than join with the United States against Soviet communism. Within NATO, massive retaliation was causing strains. Several European statesmen voiced the fear that if America responded to a Soviet invasion with its only option, nuclear weapons, the continent would be reduced to a pile of rocks. Finally, the doctrine had unintended and harmful effects upon Soviet strategic thinking, as Jerome Kahan has observed.[3] Cognizant that the Americans were far ahead militarily, the Russians viewed the building up of SAC as provocative. Coupled with calls by SAC's commander, General Curtis E. LeMay, for nuclear destruction of the Soviet Union, SAC's growth appeared in Moscow as the prelude to an offensive strike. The Russians responded by redoubling their military efforts and by emplacing medium-range missiles in Europe. These steps represented a significant acceleration of the arms race. When the Soviets launched Sputnik in 1957, and thereby demonstrated that they could land nuclear warheads upon American soil, massive retaliation lost whatever feasibility it might have had. It was time for a new military doctrine.

Kennedy: Flexible Response and Globalism

President Kennedy and his defense chief, Secretary Robert McNamara, determined that the United States needed options between nuclear war and inaction. Jettisoning massive retaliation, the new administration devised a new military doctrine that came to be known as "flexible response." Flexible response marked a return to the very strategy that Eisenhower and Dulles had sought to bury. According to the new doctrine, the United States, assisted if possible by its allies, would challenge Communist aggression where it occurred. Furthermore, America would meet such aggression with approximately the same level and type of force as used by the aggressors. In other words, should the Communists send a column of tanks and infantry into a neighboring country, the United States would respond with antitank weapons and infantry of its own. Should the Communists mount guerrilla warfare abroad, the United States would react by sending in counterguerrilla forces. Naturally, in order to win, the West might have to deploy a somewhat more lethal amount of force than the enemy. However, according to flexible response, this reaction would not entail a dramatic escalation to a new level of warfare, such as the introduction of nuclear weapons against guerrilla forces. Nor would the United States respond to aggression immediately by attacking the Soviet (or, as later became appropriate, the Chinese) heartland. Thus, the two principal differences between massive retaliation and flexible response concerned the level of retaliatory force and the place where that force would be exerted. Figure 11–1 illustrates these differences.

Flexible response demanded that a practically infinite supply of military hardware and personnel be kept on hand, available for use in different situations. While Eisenhower might have offered the country more bang for the buck, Kennedy was clearly providing more bangs. Under Kennedy and his successor Johnson (who continued the doctrine of flexible response), the number of combat-ready divisions in the nation's armed forces rose from 11 to 16.[4] Kennedy also took special interest in the Special Forces—known as "Green Berets"—and other counterinsurgency capabilities. In

FIGURE 11–1: MASSIVE RETALIATION COMPARED WITH FLEXI-
BLE RESPONSE

MASSIVE RETALIATION

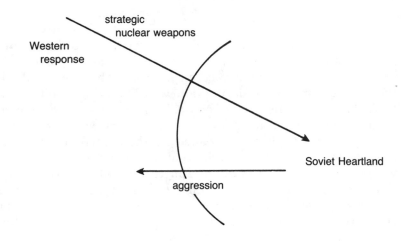

FLEXIBLE RESPONSE

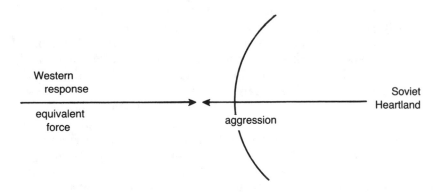

order to place troops and equipment on battlefields quickly, Kennedy expanded the country's airlift and other transportation capabilities.

There can be little doubt that the new doctrine, and its attendant accumulation of conventional military forces, gave the American government a host of options between doing nothing and waging unrestrained nuclear war. Indeed, it was the presence of these intermediate options that allowed the Kennedy and Johnson administrations to carry out containment on many fronts throughout the globe. In terms of military opposition to Communist expansion, the Kennedy and Johnson administrations were actually more active than the supposedly more anti-Communist Eisenhower administration. When Soviet Premier Khrushchev threatened to recognize unilaterally East Germany, and thereby turn over control of West Berlin to the East German Communists, Kennedy called up the Reserves and threatened to resist any efforts to isolate West Berlin. Eventually, Khrushchev backed down. It was in Southeast Asia that the new capabilities associated with flexible response received their fullest test. Kennedy sent up to 16 thousand American military advisers to South Vietnam. In Laos, under siege by North Vietnamese regular forces, Kennedy sent his counterinsurgency teams to stiffen loyalist resistance. When Thailand grew nervous about North Vietnamese expansion, Kennedy mounted an aid and counterinsurgency effort there.

While Kennedy and Johnson were concerned with defeating what Communists called "wars of national liberation," they also took steps to implement "assured destruction." As defined by Defense Secretary McNamara, assured destruction means "to deter a deliberate nuclear attack upon the United States and its allies by maintaining a clear and convincing capability to inflict unacceptable damage on an attacker."[5] Concern for assured destruction arose because by the mid-1960s the Soviet Union had gained the capability of striking American cities and military facilities with nuclear warheads. The United States sought to preserve the capacity to inflict unacceptable damage upon the Soviet Union even after all the latter's weapons had landed upon the United States. The capacity to retaliate and produce unacceptable damage after absorbing a first strike is referred to as "second-strike capability."

But how much weaponry was required to achieve second-strike capability? McNamara judged that the United States needed sufficient firepower to destroy 25–30 percent of the Russian population and two-thirds of its industrial capacity.[6] Such casualties would amount to over twice the number of Russians killed in World War II (estimated at 20 million). By the middle of the 1960s, the United States was on the verge of acquiring sufficient forces for such assured destruction. These forces included 1 thousand Minuteman intercontinental ballistic missiles (ICBMs), 54 Titan ICBMs, 41 Polaris submarines armed with nuclear missiles, and over 600 B–52 bombers. The Soviet Union too was seeking assured destruction against the United States. By the 1970s both sides had achieved second-strike capability. This resulted in a situation of mutual assured destruction, which skeptics have dubbed MAD.

Nixon: The Guam Doctrine and Sufficiency

As the decade of the 1960s drew to a close, the American public had grown disenchanted with a seemingly endless war that (in 1968) saw half a million American troops fruitlessly slogging through the rice paddies of Southeast Asia. The cry "No more Vietnams" mirrored the public determination to avoid future such entanglements. Many Americans also demanded a reallocation of resources away from military spending and in the direction of such domestic programs as energy, health, urban renewal, and the like. Always with a keen ear placed against the ground of public opinion, Nixon responded to these twin concerns in a press conference held in 1969 on Guam, where he stopped after witnessing the splashdown of the first men to land on the moon. After affirming that "the United States will keep all of its treaty commitments," Nixon went on to say that the United States "shall provide a shield if a nuclear power threatens the freedom of a nation allied with us or of a nation whose survival we consider vital to our security." It was the third element in Nixon's announcement that the press and public seized upon, however. Referring to future outbreaks of insurgency, limited war and other forms of indirect aggression, Nixon declared that the United States "shall furnish military and economic assistance when requested in accordance with our treaty commitments. But we shall look to the nation directly threatened to assume the primary responsibility of providing the manpower for its defense."

As these words make clear, the United States was returning to the division of labor between itself and its allies that had existed in the era of massive retaliation. The United States would continue to provide a strategic shield against direct attack by a nuclear power. However, American allies must take responsibility for local defense against infiltration and subversion. While America would supply the wherewithal for allies to defend themselves, they would have to send their own men into battle and bear the casualties. America would no longer do their fighting for them.

While responding to the public yearning for assurances against American involvement in future limited wars, the Guam Doctrine gives rise to a dilemma that the country may one day have to face. Suppose an ally, even with the provision of American aid, is unable to protect itself. In that case, would American troops once again don combat gear and intervene? Indeed, is not the Central Command (to be described forthwith) designed for exactly such a mission?

In the area of strategic weaponry, Nixon formulated the concept of "sufficiency." As Jerome Kahan has observed, Nixon was the first American president to enter office under conditions of military parity with the Soviet Union.[7] Early in 1969 Nixon formally stated that America's strategic goal vis-à-vis the Soviet Union was "sufficiency," as opposed to the previous objective of superiority. According to the concept of sufficiency, the United States would maintain sufficient forces to dissuade the Soviet Union from attacking the United States or its allies (assured destruction), and it would retain a variety of military responses so as to be able to deter or overcome lower levels of military aggression (flexible response). The latter requirement had become more important than ever, since the use of nuclear weapons against an equally powerful Soviet Union was no longer feasible for any purpose other than national survival.

Some strategists challenged the need even to maintain military parity with the Soviet Union and instead called for a strategy of "minimum deterrence." According to this concept, the nation need maintain no more weapons than necessary to inflict unacceptable damage upon the Soviet Union after the latter has launched an attack upon the United States. Any further military spending would be wasteful, they argued, because it would not exert any additional deterrent effect upon the Soviet Union. After destroying Russia, further military action would only "bounce the rubble," to use Winston Churchill's phrase. Let the Soviet Union build unneeded weaponry; the United States can find better things to do with its money.

The Nixon administration refused to accept this argument. In its view, appearance was of enormous significance. If American allies perceived the United States to be in a position of military inferiority to the Soviet Union, those allies might lose heart and perhaps bend to Moscow's will. Also, neutral countries might feel they could no longer count on America in a crisis, and they might do the same. Further, America's foes might become emboldened.

As Admiral Thomas Moorer, chairman of the Joint Chiefs of Staff, said, "The mere appearance of Soviet strategic superiority could have a debilitating effect on our foreign policy and our negotiating posture . . . even if that superiority would have no practical effect on the outcome of an all-out nuclear exchange."[8] Foes of minimum deterrence cited the leverage afforded to the United States by its military superiority at the time of the Cuban missile crisis. In consequence, the Nixon administration included the notion of "parity" in the concept of sufficiency. While the United States need not match the Soviet Union weapon for weapon, America had to maintain overall military equality with that country. The United States might no longer be able to "negotiate from strength," but it could not allow itself to get into a position where it would have to negotiate from weakness.

Carter: Countervailing Strategy and Rapid Deployment

The administration of Jimmy Carter did not make any fundamental alterations of American strategic doctrine. However, it did fine-tune America's assured destruction capability by stressing the intention to eliminate, in case of war, not primarily Soviet cities but rather those facilities needed to sustain combat. These facilities included troop concentrations, staging points, transportation centers, supply depots, military and civilian communications centers, industrial plants, and military and political command posts. The Carter administration gave the name "countervailing strategy" to this concept.

As a military doctrine, countervailing strategy was not novel. Previous administrations had not ruled out destruction of war-fighting facilities in their interpretations of assured destruction. However, the degree of accuracy possessed by strategic weapons had always limited the surgical precision with which military attacks could be conducted. By the time the Carter administration left office, however, several of these weapons had become sufficiently accurate to render a countervailing strategy feasible. This strategy, it should be noted, did not proscribe the destruction of cities; it merely stressed the capability and intention to strike other targets in the opening phase of a strategic exchange.

President Carter's principal contribution to America's military posture lay with the creation of the Rapid Deployment Force (presently called the Central Command). The Carter administration came to power on the heels of a long and costly American military intervention in Vietnam. The Democratic president shared the view of most Americans that the United States should not plunge into another foreign military venture without great deliberation. Whereas some of Carter's predecessors, unchastened by Vietnam, might have dispatched American forces to the Horn of Africa, Angola, Zimbabwe (formerly Rhodesia), Nicaragua, Iran and Afghanistan, Carter showed no inclination to "Americanize" any of these struggles. At the same time, the entire Western world realized how fragile its oil lifeline had become. Reflecting this awareness, President Carter made the following statement in his 1980 State of the Union address. "An attempt by any outside force to gain control of the Persian Gulf region will be regarded as an assault on the vital interests of the United States of America and such an assault will be repelled by any means necessary including military force." The president singled out the Persian Gulf, because it is the principal source of American, European and Japanese oil imports. In the context of the speech, "outside force" clearly referred to the Soviet Union, which had just invaded Afghanistan. In order to supply muscle to these words, Carter ordered the creation of a Rapid Deployment Force (RDF).[9]

The RDF came into being in 1980 with the establishment of a headquarters at MacDill Air Force Base in Florida. As soon as a crisis occurred, RDF headquarters would call upon designated units from all four services. Depending on the situation, the RDF could call into action any level of force ranging from a small Ranger unit to several Army and Marine divisions. The RDF might be called upon to face a variety of threats, such as Soviet invasion of the Gulf, military aggression by one Gulf state against another, civil war in an oil-producing state, or terrorist attacks against oil wells or pipelines.

Practically all observers agree that actual deployment of the RDF would pose enormous difficulties, mostly of a logistical nature. By air, the Persian Gulf lies at a distance of 7 thousand miles from the United States. Passing through the Suez Canal, ships would have to travel 8 thousand miles to reach the Gulf from American ports. If Suez were closed, ships would have to steam 4 thousand additional miles around the southern tip of Africa. Supplying troops and repairing equipment would pose enormous difficulties, as the US has access to only a few ports and airfields in the Indian Ocean region—specifically the British-owned island of Diego Garcia and facilities at Mombasa in Kenya, Ras Banas in Egypt, Berbera in Somalia, and in Oman. The United States continues to seek additional footholds in the area. Even should Washington succeed in this regard, it would still face huge problems in getting a sizable force to the Persian Gulf in time to have any effect. Hostile forces, with much shorter supply lines than the United States, will be in position to interdict the movement of American troops and supplies. If the Soviet Union, with staging bases in nearby Afghanistan, becomes actively involved, the hazards to the RDF will increase dramatically. Should the RDF be deployed against Moslem governments or Palestinian "freedom fighters," local governments might refuse the United States permission to use their promised facilities. The abortive American effort in 1980 to rescue the hostages held by Iran offers an indication of the difficulties involved.

American attempts to preserve the security of the Persian Gulf also include strengthening indigenous forces, by providing military and economic assistance, and persuading the NATO powers to contribute to the defense of the area.

Maintaining Assured Destruction

As the decade of the 1980s opened, American policymakers voiced concern about maintaining assured destruction of the Soviet Union. Advances in military technology, some feared, stood to render the United States unable to discourage a Soviet attack by the threat of effective retaliation—referred to earlier as second-strike capability. To understand this concern, we must take ourselves back to military developments in the 1960s.

America's strategic forces are composed of three legs. One leg consists of land-based intercontinental missiles (ICBMs). The second leg is represented by submarine-launched ballistic missiles (SLBMs), and the third by long-range nuclear bombers.

By permission of Johnny Hart and Field Enterprises, Inc.

In order to protect itself against America's strategic arsenal, the Soviet Union began to develop antiballistic missiles (ABMs). In 1964 the Kremlin unveiled its Galosh missile, designed to intercept incoming American missiles. American military planners feared

FIGURE 11–2: AREA OF THE ARABIAN SEA AND PERSIAN GULF

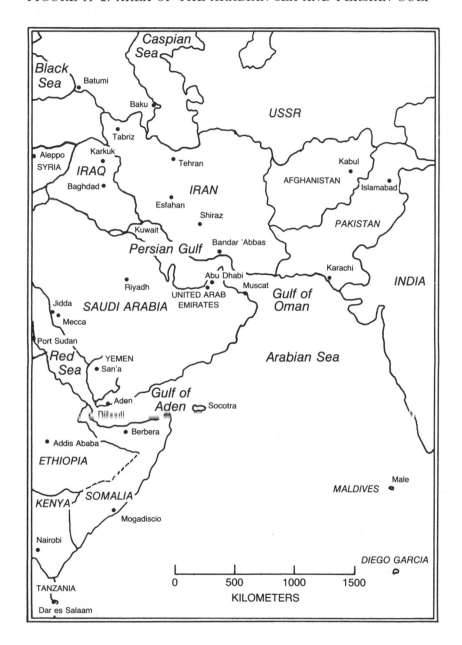

that wide-scale ABM deployment by the Soviet Union would neutralize America's assured destruction capability. Consequently, the United States decided to overwhelm any ABM system the Soviets could build through a new military technology, multiple, independently targeted re-entry vehicles, more commonly known as MIRV. MIRV technology allowed the United States to mount more than one warhead upon a single missile. Furthermore, each warhead could be aimed at a different target. Thus, by MIRVing its missiles, the United States could launch so many warheads that no Soviet ABM system could prevent an unacceptable degree of damage. Assured destruction would be maintained.

It so happened, however, that the Soviet Union never constructed the vast number of ABMs that American military planners had feared. Indeed, as part of the SALT I accords, concluded in 1969, each side agreed to build ABMs at no more than two sites; in 1974 at Vladivostok this number was reduced to one. (The Soviet Union has ringed Moscow with ABMs; the United States has dismantled its entire ABM system except for radar stations.) But, as so often occurs in the arms race, one side could not let its rival get too far ahead in an important technology. The Soviets decided to MIRV their own missiles. By the early 1980s, many American military planners voiced fears that Soviet warheads could take out enough land-based ICBMs to undercut assured destruction. MIRV technology, developed by the United States, had been turned by the Russians against American missiles.

In retrospect, it can be asked whether the United States was wise in developing MIRV in the first place. At the time, several scientists warned that MIRV would carry the arms race to a much higher level. Jerome Kahan argues that Washington should have MIRVed its forces at the same rate that the Soviets built their ABMs. At that pace, both American and Soviet missiles would have remained un-MIRVed, and the United States would not need to fear today that the Soviets could eliminate American ICBMs.[10]

The Reagan administration entered office persuaded that two measures were needed to maintain assured destruction. The first initiative sprang from fear that Soviet missiles could eliminate America's land-based ICBMs. To counter this, Reagan accepted his predecessor's decision to build a new ICBM that would remain impervious to Soviet attack. This new missile, designated MX, would be more powerful and accurate than existing ICBMs. To withstand a Soviet strike, several deployment schemes were considered, including placement of the missiles on underground tracks in the Southwest, on trucks, railroad cars, and airplanes, and stationing them in super-hardened underground silos. While the last mentioned basing mode was finally chosen, none of these plans appeared ideal.

The second measure addressed itself to concern about the ability of the B–52 bomber to penetrate increasingly sophisticated Soviet air defenses. As of 1980, the Soviets had 10 thousand surface-to-air missiles deployed at 1 thousand sites throughout the Soviet Union. Some strategists were already arguing that huge intercontinental bombers were obsolete, as they presented easy targets for highly accurate surface-to-air missiles. President Reagan rejected Carter's decision to retain the B–52 but equip it with cruise missiles. This plan would allow the B–52 to fly along the edge of Soviet airspace and release cruise missiles against targets inside the Soviet Union. The bomber would remain at a safe distance from Soviet anti-aircraft batteries; each B–52 would carry up to 20 nuclear-tipped cruise missiles which could fly below enemy radar. Instead, Reagan elected to replace the B–52 with a new bomber, the B–1, which would be equipped with electronic devices to evade surface-to-air missiles. By 1990, the B–1 was scheduled to be replaced by still another bomber, equipped with "stealth" technology to make it invisible to Soviet radar.

THE UNITED STATES-SOVIET STRATEGIC BALANCE

The importance of the US-Soviet strategic balance lies in its role in deterring nuclear war. Should that deterrence fail and all-out nuclear war result, it is possible that both sides would unleash a total of 16 thousand nuclear warheads and bombs. The consequences of such an exchange challenge the human imagination. Consider the following estimate of the effect of a single nuclear warhead, measuring one megaton (or the equivalent of one million tons of TNT) detonated upon a typical major American city:

All reinforced concrete structures within a radius of 0.8 miles from the impact point would be completely destroyed, as would all wood-frame and brick residences within three miles, and all lightly constructed commercial buildings and typical residences within 4.4 miles;

Everyone within a 1.7 mile radius would be killed instantly, as would half of those within a 2.7 mile radius, making a total of about one-quarter million fatalities;

Up to 200 thousand additional people would die eventually from severe burns;

Several hundred thousand others would suffer injuries.

In the event of a full-scale nuclear attack on the United States, the Defense Department estimates that the number of fatalities would range from a low of 20–55 million to a high of 155–165 million. For the Soviet Union, the corresponding figures would run from 23–34 million to 64–100 million. These numbers would increase from longer-term fallout and other indirect causes of death.[11] It is in the hope of avoiding such an immeasurable catastrophe that the United States and the Soviet Union seek to maintain mutual deterrence.

Success in this effort depends to a certain degree upon maintaining equivalence in strategic weapons. Should either side feel confident that it could attack its rival and fend off or comfortably survive retaliation, it might be tempted to do so. Even if it were not so tempted, the other side might believe it to be so and might strike a pre-emptive blow. While no one can say that either government would yield to such temptations, most observers agree that strategic parity is a more stable condition than the superiority of one side over the other.

Table 11–1 describes the US-Soviet strategic balance at the beginning of the 1980s. America's ICBMs included 54 single-warhead Titan IIs, 450 single-warhead Minuteman IIs (more accurate and destructive), and 550 MIRVed Minuteman IIIs (still more accurate and powerful). The SLBM force includes a mix of Polaris, Poseidon and Trident missiles. The Trident, America's newest submarine, is quieter and can remain at sea longer than the other two

TABLE 11–1: US AND SOVIET STRATEGIC FORCE LEVELS, JANUARY 1, 1981

	US	USSR
ICBM launchers	1,054	1,398
SLBM launchers	576	950
Long-range bombers	570	156
Total warheads and bombs[a]	9,000	7,000

[a]Reflects total warheads and bombs deliverable by above launchers and aircraft, taking account of MIRV technology and the capacity of bombers to carry several bombs.

Source: DOD, Annual Report, Fiscal 1982, p. 53.

types. Furthermore, its missiles are more powerful and accurate than the weapons carried by the older boats. The longer range of the Trident missile enables these ships to cruise in a wider body of water than the other kinds of vessels.

In an all-out nuclear war, more destructive power than in all of World War II would be unleashed every second for the long afternoon it would take for all the missiles and bombs to fall. A World War II every second—more people killed in the first few hours than all of the wars of history put together. The survivors, if any, would live in despair amid the poisoned ruins of the civilization that had committed suicide.

Jimmy Carter, Farewell Address, 1981

While the above figures are helpful in calculating the US-Soviet strategic relationship, one must be careful in interpreting them. For example, the data reveal that the Soviet Union has a larger number of missile launchers and bombers (combined) than the United States. However, due to MIRV technology, the latter has a higher total of deliverable weapons (9 thousand versus 7 thousand). These weapons, however, reflect only those forces designated "strategic"; that is, those whose main purpose is to cause destruction on the other's territory. The United States has many land- and carrier-based nuclear-capable bombers in and around Europe that could strike targets inside the Soviet Union. These weapons are not included in Table 11–1 because their primary mission relates to the European theater. The Soviets, for their part, have a much smaller number of bombers—named Backfire—that could release bombs over the United States if they could then land somewhere near American territory, such as Cuba. These also are not included in Table 11–1. Furthermore, Table 11–1 does not include the nuclear forces of France and the United Kingdom, which would presumably play a role in an all-out war. Geographical considerations also complicate calculations of relative military might. Except for Cuba, the Soviet Union lacks bases in the vicinity of the United States. The latter, however, possesses military bases in Europe along Russia's western border, in the Pacific to Russia's east, and in the Mediterranean Sea. In case of strategic war, no one knows what actions China might take, but such possibilities leave Soviet planners unnerved, as the two countries share a 4,500 mile border. Also, would the armies of Eastern Europe fight alongside the Soviet

Union, or would they use the conflict as an opportunity to break free of Soviet domination?

Technological factors add additional complications. No one knows for sure how well existing weapons systems would work in actual combat. Practically all testing is performed with individual weapons systems. In war, would the effects of earlier nuclear explosions have any impact on the guidance systems of incoming warheads? How well would military command communications systems work? Would orders be transmitted clearly and in a timely fashion, or might they get lost in damaged communications systems? Finally, little thought has been given to who would do what once the firing stops.

One can readily see how difficult it is to measure the relative military power of the US and the Soviet Union. The inexactness of these measurements allows for considerable differences in estimating the US-Soviet military balance. This issue attained importance when President Reagan assumed office in 1981. Reagan had campaigned on the premise that the United States was falling behind the Soviet Union in terms of military power, and he vowed that if elected he would take steps to right the balance. The outgoing Carter administration disputed Reagan's claims. Shortly before leaving office, Secretary of Defense Harold Brown wrote, "As for the overall strategic balance, it is my judgment that the United States and the Soviet Union remain essentially equivalent."[12] When Reagan took office, he promised to increase military spending by 7 percent annually, after accounting for inflation. He also determined, as we have seen, to construct 100 MX missiles, deploy the B–1 bomber, and develop stealth technology. In addition, he allocated funds to build up the nation's conventional forces, including airlift and sealift capabilities.

Whether or not Reagan was correct in assuming that the United States had fallen behind the Soviet Union, few analysts doubted that the latter had engaged in a major military buildup during the previous decade. If it had taught the Russians nothing else, the Cuban missile crisis of 1962 convinced them of the coercive value of strategic superiority, or at least the importance of not being inferior. It was America's strategic superiority that enabled it to pry Soviet missiles out of Cuba. Following this incident, the Soviets began to build up their forces with the intention of at least matching those of the United States. The Soviets increased their ICBM force from 200 in 1964 to a number equaling those of the United States by 1970 and surpassing it soon thereafter. Similarly, they built up their fleet of missile-launching submarines so as to exceed the American total by 1972. One year later they began flight testing

MIRVed missiles.[13] Soviet armed forces personnel today total 3.6 million, compared with 2.0 million for the United States.

Viewing their own forces as strictly defensive, American planners questioned the motives behind the immense Soviet construction program. Were the Soviets simply seeking to erase America's strategic lead, so as to avoid future humiliations such as the one in Cuba? Or, were the Soviets striving for military superiority? Such questions are still being asked today, and the answers remain elusive. Obviously, Soviet leaders are not going to reveal their ultimate intentions, and there is no way they could convince others that they were telling the truth anyway. (The same obviously applies to the United States.) It is even possible that some Soviet leaders aim at parity while others seek superiority, and that military spending varies from time to time depending upon which group is ascendant.

While "Kremlinologists" may not concur on exact figures, most agree that Soviet military spending has been trending steadily upward. According to the Defense Department, Soviet military spending has increased 4–5 percent for each year between 1960 and 1980, while American defense spending has risen and fallen during that interval.[14] Furthermore, much of American military spending during this period was absorbed by the Vietnamese war, while the Soviets were acquiring weapons and ammunition that was not expended. The CIA has estimated that in recent years the Soviets have been spending 12–14 percent of GNP on defense, while the United States has spent 5 percent.[15] However, when one realizes that America's GNP is about twice as large as Russia's, the total sums spent on defense may not differ vastly. Furthermore, it has been estimated that as much as one-fifth of Soviet military spending is directed not against the West but against China. It must also be remembered that Soviet forces in Europe have an important auxiliary function, keeping Eastern Europe in line, and that this absorbs certain funds. When one compares the military spending by the Soviet Union and its East European allies to that of the United States, Western Europe, China and Japan, one discovers the latter total to be greater.

In the Defense Department's eyes, the Soviet military buildup has had the following consequences:

Highly accurate and destructive Soviet ICBMs pose a threat to America's land-based missiles;

The Soviets now have a substantial arsenal of intermediate-range theater nuclear weapons in Europe, including the SS-20 mobile missile (with three warheads of high accuracy) and the Backfire bomber;

Postal Service Plan Covers Snow, Sleet and Atom War

WASHINGTON, Aug. 12—Neither snow nor rain nor heat nor gloom of night used to prevent the postal couriers from delivering the mail, and now the Postal Service says it will not be deterred on its appointed rounds by a nuclear war either.

But a 300-page plan for continued mail deliveries after an atomic war or other national emergency was ridiculed today by members of a House Subcommittee on Postal Personnel and Modernization and by others who called the plans "idiotic," "deceitful" and "futile."

The officials described an elaborate chain of command under which one of the five regional postmasters general would assume control if Washington was destroyed. The headquarters would shift first to Memphis and then, if Memphis was devastated, to San Bruno, Calif.

The officials also said about 2,000 emergency change-of-address forms had been stocked in each post office except very small ones.

"What good will that do?" said Representative Edward J. Markey, Democrat of Massachusetts. "There will be no addresses, no streets, no blocks, no houses."

Mr. Markey also questioned the plan's goal of continuing to deliver first-class letters. "There won't be a lot of people left to read and write those letters," he said.

"But those that are will get their mail," Mr. Jusell replied.

New York Times, August 13, 1982.
© 1982 by the New York Times Company. Reprinted by permission.

The Soviet navy need no longer confine itself to coastal defense but is now capable of projecting Soviet power long distances;

The Soviets have a respectable capacity to wage chemical warfare.[16]

In light of the above information, what conclusions can we draw about the strategic relationship between the United States and the Soviet Union? It is clear that the Soviet Union has engaged in a determined effort to redress a balance that in the 1960s was decidedly in America's favor. In the view of most analysts, the Kremlin has succeeded in this drive. Some writers go so far as to assert that the Soviet Union has already surpassed the United States and seeks decided military superiority. Secretary of Defense Caspar W. Weinberger has said, for example, that the United States is in "a position of dangerous imbalance with the Soviet Union."[17] The complexity of military technology, together with the hazards of evaluating the combined effects of various weapons systems, makes precise comparisons extremely difficult to verify. For the time being, it seems safe to conclude that the Soviets are ahead in some military sectors, while the United States is ahead in others. Overall, the military relationship between the two nations seems best characterized by parity. Based on rational calculation, neither side is justified in believing it can escape catastrophic destruction should a nuclear war occur.

NATO AND THE WARSAW PACT

The US-Soviet balance is only one phase of the overall East-West military relationship. The military balance in Europe must also be considered.

In 1949, the North Atlantic Treaty Organization (NATO) was formed by the United States, Canada and most of the states of Western Europe. Today, this alliance includes 16 countries. Alliance members have pledged to come to one another's assistance in case of attack. The Warsaw Pact was formed in 1955 largely in response to the creation of NATO and the inclusion of West Germany therein. More an appendage of Soviet military might than an alliance of freely consenting states, the Pact embraces the Soviet Union and its six East European satellites. In Europe today, these two alliances glare at each other across the "iron curtain."

NATO's fundamental military purpose is deterrence of a Warsaw Pact attack upon Western Europe. Should deterrence fail, NATO is designed to defend its member states. In order to achieve deterrence, NATO must ensure that the Soviet Union and its allies perceive no advantage in attacking. To sustain such an impression, NATO fields an array of tactical nuclear weapons as well as an assortment of conventional land, air, naval and chemical weapons. The Warsaw Pact deploys a similar arsenal.

Theater Nuclear Forces

As opposed to strategic weapons, theater or tactical weapons are designed for battlefield use. Although theater weapons are generally less powerful than their strategic counterparts, that need not necessarily be the case. Many weapons can be used for either strategic or tactical purposes. As employed against infiltration routes in Vietnam, B–52 bombers served a tactical mission. When targeted against Hanoi, however, they were performing a strategic role. It is the mission, not the inherent characteristic of a weapon, which determines whether it is strategic or tactical.

Like the Warsaw Pact, NATO deploys an impressive array of theater nuclear forces (TNF). These weapons include air-to-surface missiles, air-to-air missiles, artillery rounds, depth charges, torpedoes, land mines, ocean mines and aircraft capable of delivering nuclear bombs and missiles. Some of these weapons are more destructive than the bomb that leveled Hiroshima. In all, the United States deploys approximately 7 thousand tactical nuclear weapons in Europe.[18] France and the United Kingdom add to this arsenal. The Soviet Union stations approximately 3,500 theater nuclear weapons in Eastern Europe,[19] mostly of the same type as those possessed by NATO. Primary Soviet TNF included, as of January 1, 1981, 65–70 Backfire bombers, 450 older Badger and Blinder bombers, and approximately 500 medium-range nuclear missiles (SS–4, SS–5, SS–20).[20] Both Soviet and American SLBMs in the Baltic and the Mediterranean are likely to be used for tactical purposes in case of a European war.

The United States began to introduce small numbers of theater nuclear weapons in Europe in 1952.[21] The rationale then as now is that the Warsaw Pact enjoys numerical superiority over NATO in both military manpower and conventional weapons, especially tanks and other types of armor.

Former Secretary of Defense James Schlesinger spelled out the rationale for theater nuclear weapons as follows:

> We deploy nuclear weapons to Europe for three major reasons:
>   First, maintaining nuclear capabilities is essential to deterrence as long as the Warsaw Pact maintains roughly comparable theater nuclear capabilities. These weapons help to deter use of nuclear weapons by the Warsaw Pact and, along with the conventional and strategic nuclear forces, provide a general deterrent across the entire spectrum of possible aggression.

Second, should deterrence fail, our tactical nuclear capabilities provide a source of nuclear options for defense other than the use of strategic forces.

Third, in keeping with the flexible response strategy, we do not rule out the use of nuclear weapons by the U.S. and its Allies if necessary to contain and halt major conventional aggression.[22]

NATO apprehensions were fueled in the late 1970s, when the Soviet Union began to replace its SS–4 and SS–5 rockets with a new medium-range nuclear missile, the SS–20. These newer, more accurate and destructive weapons are deployed in Eastern Europe and the western sector of the Soviet Union. By the middle of 1984, the Soviets had deployed over 300 SS–20 launchers, two-thirds of them in Europe and the remainder near the Chinese border. The SS–20 is a two-stage, solid-fuel ballistic missile which can be launched from mobile platforms, making it practically invulnerable to destruction. The missile comes in three versions. One version is capable of propelling a single 1.5 megaton nuclear warhead 3,500 miles. A second is able to carry three smaller warheads shorter distances to three separate targets. The third can carry a smaller 50 kiloton warhead 4,600 miles. (By way of contrast, the Hiroshima bomb measured 12–15 kilotons; one thousand kilotons equals one megaton.) When fully deployed in the mid-1980s, the SS–20 will allow the Soviet Union to destroy almost every military target in Western Europe from deep inside Soviet territory (see Fig. 11–3). As a prelude to a Warsaw Pact attack, the Soviets could thereby destroy much of Western Europe's retaliatory forces. Unless American power based outside Europe were called in, the Pact armies would be assured of victory.

In response to Soviet deployment of the SS–20, NATO decided in December 1979 to strengthen its own theater nuclear forces. At that time none of NATO's TNF missiles—Pershing, Honest John or Lance—had a range exceeding 450 miles. In order to restore a balance in the theater nuclear weaponry, NATO decided that starting in 1983 the Alliance would deploy 108 Pershing II missiles and 464 ground launched cruise missiles in selected European countries. As Fig. 11–3 shows, these weapons will be able to destroy targets in Eastern Europe and western sectors of the Soviet Union. NATO also determined to seek an arms control agreement with the Soviets to limit deployment of the SS–20. A successful agreement might make NATO deployment of offsetting missiles unnecessary.

*FIGURE 11–3: RANGES OF TACTICAL NUCLEAR WEAPONS IN
EUROPE*

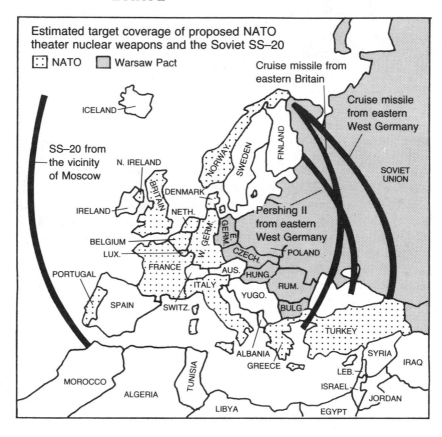

Source: Stockholm International Peace Research Institute.

NATO's decision to modernize its TNF sparked large-scale citizen demonstrations against the deployment of new NATO missiles. Advocates of emplacing new missiles say that without them, European defense must rest upon American strategic weapons, because the SS–20 can knock out existing TNF in Europe. Furthermore, these weapons lack the range to strike targets inside the Soviet Union, as the new missiles will be able to do.

Some Europeans ask, what is so bad about relying upon America's strategic arsenal to deter an attack upon Western Europe? One reply is that, in order to avoid a strategic exchange, the United

States might prefer to negotiate a European settlement favorable to Russia. Western Europe would then fall to the Warsaw Pact without a shot being fired. Alternatively, the Soviets might erroneously assume that America would refrain from resisting aggression in Europe, when in fact America was prepared to defend her allies. In that case, the two superpowers would find themselves in a nuclear war that neither of them intended. It is far safer, assert advocates of the new missiles, for NATO to be able to defend itself in Europe. Besides, they add, the existence of TNF capable of destroying targets in the Soviet Union might deter a Warsaw Pact attack in the first place.

Some opponents of the new missiles question the basic rationality of defending Europe with nuclear weapons. These people note Europe's population density and the proximity to residential areas of military targets—communications centers, government and military command centers, harbors and railyards, industrial plants, and airports. Would not a nuclear war to defend Europe, they ask, destroy the continent in the process? Such fears cannot be lightly dismissed. War games and studies undertaken as far back as the 1960s indicate that between 2–20 million Europeans would be killed during a nuclear defense of Western Europe.[23]

Conventional Forces

While of undoubted importance, nuclear forces are not the only ones deployed by NATO and the Warsaw Pact. Each alliance also fields an enormous arsenal of non-nuclear or conventional weapons.[24] There can be no assurance that in time of war each side will use up its conventional weapons before resorting to nuclear war. In fact, quite the opposite is more likely; that is, each side will employ from the outset a combination of conventional and nuclear weapons. Nonetheless, for analytical purposes it makes some sense to try to evaluate the balance of conventional forces possessed by the two alliances.

Most analysts are in agreement that the Warsaw Pact is ahead in some categories, while NATO leads in others. The Warsaw Pact fields about twice as many divisions in Europe as NATO, but because Pact divisions have fewer personnel, Pact manpower outnumbers NATO's by only a 1.2:1 ratio. In air power, NATO holds a slim qualitative edge, while the Pact has more airplanes (5 thousand versus 3 thousand). In case of war, NATO will rely more than the Pact on air power to make up for NATO's inferiority in manpower and tanks. The latter presents a particular problem for NATO. Many analysts believe that if the Pact were to attack, it would rely on its 3:1 advantage in armor to spearhead the assault. Halting this tank advance would become the responsibility of NATO air power and antitank forces. The Pact outnumbers NATO not only in tanks but also in armored personnel carriers, artillery, fighting vehicles, and air defense systems. NATO is ahead in air support for ground forces, the range and quality (but not quantity) of logistical support services, and antiarmor systems.

On the sea, Pact navies including the Soviet navy could place into action a greater number of warships than NATO. The picture turns even bleaker for NATO naval forces when one realizes that their mission will be more demanding than that of the Pact. NATO navies will have to keep open the sea lanes linking the United States to Europe. The Pact's primary mission will be to deny NATO use of the seas around Europe long enough for Pact armies to seize Western Europe before reinforcements arrive. NATO's requirement of assuring the sea-borne flow of oil from the Middle East will place a further drain on its naval power.

Total victory by military means has become a formula for mutual catastrophe. Even the use of conventional force risks unpredictable consequences.
Secretary of State Alexander M. Haig, Jr., 1982

Having noted areas where the Pact and NATO are ahead of each other, in both nuclear and conventional forces, we have only begun to form the basis for a conclusion about which side is stronger militarily. Before reaching such a determination, we must consider some of the complicating factors that must be taken into account.

Counting weapons can yield misleading conclusions. In time of war, soldiers will not be facing each other unassisted, nor will tank battles be restricted to 1-on-1 tank duels. Elaborate combinations of weapons will face offsetting combinations. Thus, it makes more sense to evaluate forces on the basis of how well they are likely to perform their missions. In the case of NATO, that mission is first deterrence, and second, should deterrence fail, forward defense and defeat of a Pact attack. Forward defense refers to the capacity to meet and overcome an attack at the point of assault (presumably along the eastern borders of West Germany) rather than deep inside

Western Europe. Seen from this perspective, the Pact's 1.2:1 numerical advantage in manpower does not seem quite so serious, since military planners estimate an attacker needs a 2:1 or 3:1 advantage to overcome defenders. Furthermore, the reliability of East European divisions is open to question. Might they not turn against their Soviet overseers instead of fighting alongside them? NATO enjoys the advantage of training on the very ground it must defend. Military commanders can walk and survey probable lines of attack, determine fields of fire, reserve areas for mines and other obstacles, set lines of sight, and locate cover and concealment. Defending one's homeland provides an extra incentive to fight, compared with seizing another's territory.

The Pact's decisive advantage in armor is bound to cause NATO problems. NATO commanders fear Soviet tank columns will be able to make quick and deep penetrations. To counter this, NATO is developing increasingly accurate antitank weapons, known as precision-guided munitions. President Reagan's decision to deploy the neutron bomb in Europe will also limit the Pact's advantage in tanks. By killing through radiation rather than blast, neutron weapons are designed to kill Soviet tank crews without obliterating surrounding structures. NATO would also use highly accurate air-to-ground missiles (called "smart bombs") against Pact armor. Soviet planners will have to contend with the possibility of Chinese efforts to retake land that Beijing claims Russia stole from them in the previous century. NATO forces are likely to suffer from the lack of standardized equipment and a serious imbalance in chemical warfare capabilities, two issues to be examined later in this chapter.

The foregoing suggests how difficult it is to calculate the East-West military balance. We have not even addressed ourselves to the issues of morale and training. The only thing we can say with some certainty is that neither side can feel hopeful of winning a European war without absorbing enormous casualties. Furthermore, the probable condition of Europe after a major war might not make it worthwhile for either side to launch an aggressive war there. Another dimension remains to be considered. Just as there can be no guarantee that a European war will remain conventional, there can be no assurance that a limited nuclear war will remain limited. Fear of escalation acts as a brake on superpower aggression, so long as each remains persuaded the other will resist. Should either side convince itself that it could win a European war, or that the other side would refuse to fight, it might well attempt such an initiative. The result could be a historic victory or a suicidal nuclear exchange. The balance of terror is aptly described as "delicate."

Chemical Warfare

Americans do not like to think about chemical weapons (CW). The following poem written about a gas attack in World War I evokes a common attitude toward chemical implements of war.

> Gas! GAS! Quick, boys!—An ecstasy of fumbling,
> Fitting the clumsy helmets just in time,
> But someone still was yelling out and stumbling
> And floundering like a man in fire or lime.—
> Dim through the misty panes and thick green light,
> As under a green sea, I saw him drowning.
> In all my dreams before my helpless sight
> He plunges at me, guttering, choking, drowning.
>
> If in some smothering dreams, you too could pace
> Behind the wagon that we flung him in,
> And watch the white eyes writhing in his face,
> His hanging face, like a devil's sick of sin;
> If you could hear, at every jolt, the blood
> Come gargling from the froth-corrupted lungs,
> Bitter as the cud
> Of vile, incurable sores on innocent tongues,—
> My friend, you would not tell with such high zest
> To children ardent for some desperate glory,
> The old Lie: *Dulce et decorum est*
> *Pro patria mori.*
>
> Wilfred Owen, "Dulce Et Decorum Est"

Nevertheless, the realities of the East-West struggle compel American military planners to worry about CW.

Chemical weapons were last used in protracted warfare in World War I, when they caused 1.3 million casualties, including 91 thousand deaths.[25] Horrified by the results of CW, the nations of the world drafted the Geneva Protocol in 1925 prohibiting the use of chemical weapons. The United States did not sign it until 1975 and then did so with the stipulation that it would reply in kind if "an enemy state or any of its allies" initiated CW. Although it took the United States 50 years to sign the Geneva Protocol, America had never been enthusiastic about the use of chemical weapons. When, in 1968, several thousand sheep in Utah were killed by some nerve gas that drifted off an Army test site, President Nixon renounced the first use of CW and Congress imposed a ban on testing. American CW capabilities, never formidable, began to decline. The 1973 Middle East war revived American interest in

CW, however. Captured Soviet armored vehicles were shown to contain air filtration systems to protect crews against CW. This equipment confirmed American suspicions that the Soviets were training their troops to fight on a battlefield following a Soviet CW attack, most likely in Europe.

American apprehensions appear to be well-founded. According to Julian Perry Robinson, the Soviet Union has made a determined effort to incorporate chemical weapons into its military forces.[26] In Robinson's estimation, Soviet ground forces are capable of operating efficiently in a CW environment. This conclusion is based upon the amount of time Soviet troops spend training (sometimes with live CW ammunition), the existence of some 80 thousand Chemical Defense Troops as a separate combat-arms unit,[27] the quantity and variety of protective equipment in general issue, the presence of built-in air-filtration units on Soviet armored vehicles, and the close attention to CW in Soviet military and defense-related literature. In contrast, the US Defense Department has stated recently that NATO forces "lack the capability to defend adequately against the Pact chemical threat."[28] Inconclusive reports have indicated that Soviet troops and their allies used CW in Afghanistan and Southeast Asia.[29] American intelligence reports have said that one-third of the Soviet Union's artillery shells, warheads and bombs in Eastern Europe contain lethal chemical agents.[30]

In reaction to such disturbing information, the United States has begun to rejuvenate its CW arsenal. American spending for CW research increased from $29 million in 1976 to $106 million in 1981.[31] In 1981 Congress voted $3.15 million to begin construction of a plant at Pine Bluff, Arkansas, for manufacturing nerve gas shells and bombs. No chemical weapons have been fabricated by the United States since 1969.

Estimates of CW stocks held by the United States and the Soviet Union are very difficult to reach, since both countries cloak CW activities in strict secrecy. A report in the *New York Times* of December 10, 1980, said the Soviets have an 8:1 lead over the United States in chemical weapons, and that the Russians currently have 14 production facilities in operation (compared to none for the United States). The same report said that the United States had 150 thousand tons of CW, mostly left over from World War II. Many observers maintain that these stocks are badly deteriorated.

Before considering how each side might make use of CW, we should perhaps pause to examine the varieties of chemical weapons that now exist. All of the agents described below can be delivered by bombs, missiles or artillery shells. Poison gases are liquids that vaporize when dispersed, forming a cloud. Phosgene and chlorine cause choking; mustard gas burns and blisters; other gases induce psychological disorientation. Tear gas and other riot control agents irritate the eyes and the respiratory tract. The principal chemical agent today is nerve gas, a substance which is colorless and odorless. Entering the body either through the skin or the lungs, nerve gas kills or disables by disrupting the central nervous system. Depending upon the type of gas absorbed and the dosage, death may take minutes or hours. The victim is likely to suffer convulsions, uncontrollable vomiting and diarrhea, dimming of vision and eventual asphyxiation. Those who do not die are likely to suffer permanent neurological or psychiatric disorders. Regardless of the ultimate effect, the symptoms are extremely painful. Like all chemical weapons, nerve gas can be delivered by bombs, missiles or artillery shells.

While the effects of chemical weapons are undeniably horrendous, defense against CW is a relatively simple matter. Ponchos can prevent contact with the skin, and masks can filter out gas. The trick is to don protective gear in time. As in offensive chemical warfare, the Soviets are far ahead of NATO in training for protection during a chemical attack.

What should America's policy be with regard to CW? Should the United States seek to match the Soviet Union's present superiority? Or, should the United States follow the advice of James F. Finan, a scientist with the Canadian Department of National Defense: "Reliance on the existing system of nuclear deterrence rather than attempting to elaborate some parallel system of chemical deterrence appears to offer a greater chance of preventing the initiation of chemical warfare by the Warsaw Pact."[32] One argument in favor of an American CW buildup cites the secondary effects of fighting in a chemical environment. This argument states that the masks, bulky protective gear and decontamination devices used by armies in a chemical environment can impede fighting effectiveness, particularly speed and mobility, and that this reduced measure of combat capability justifies an American CW buildup. As matters presently stand, the Soviet Union is in a much better position than the United States to force its foe to fight with such impediments. Opponents of CW draw attention to the unpredictability of chemical weapons. A shift in wind direction can have disastrous effects upon the users. Therefore, they argue, it makes much more sense for NATO to continue relying on conventional and especially nuclear weapons to deter a Warsaw Pact chemical attack. NATO can make known that it will not hesitate to respond to a chemical attack with nuclear weapons.[33] If the nuclear deterrent suffices to forestall a Warsaw Pact assault at present, the addition of chemical weapons to NATO's arsenal will add nothing to the deterrent, argue these proponents. Furthermore, they assert, it would do little good to match Pact chemical capabilities, unless NATO is prepared to use CW first, which seems unlikely given attitudes prevalent in Western Europe. Experience with CW in World War I revealed that surprise is of the essence. Military forces that are expecting a chemical attack can defend themselves adequately by wearing protective gear. Should Pact forces advance under a chemical barrage, they would be ready for a riposte in kind, which would then have little effect. Besides, it is sometimes argued, the use of chemical weapons in densely populated Europe would produce enormous numbers of casualties among civilians, who would lack any protective equipment.

Alliance Problems

Any coalition of states is bound to experience strains, and NATO is no exception.

Burden-sharing.

Throughout the thirty-plus years of NATO's existence, the United States has complained that its European allies have not contributed their fair share of defense expenditures. The United States has devoted a higher proportion of GNP to defense than the European members of NATO. When the latter object that much of this spending is directed toward non-European areas (especially during the time of the Vietnam War), American policymakers counter that such efforts benefit Europe nonetheless. Thus, Washington maintains, American attempts to contain Soviet expansion in Southwest Asia or the Caribbean indirectly benefit Western Europe, by preventing Moscow from increasing its overall power. A recent Defense Department document takes note of the new importance of the Persian Gulf region and recognizes that only the United States has the capability to maintain the flow of oil to the Western world. As a result, the document states, "The Allies must do more to maintain and improve Western defenses in Europe, to accommodate augmented infrastructure requirements, and to meet the increased host nation support needs of US military forces, so that NATO's ability to contain the increasing Warsaw Pact threat is not eroded."[34] In addition, American strategists observe that the country's strategic arsenal, though not restricted to Europe's defense, helps deter the Warsaw Pact from attacking Western Europe. More directly related to European defense, the United States maintains over 300 thousand troops in Western Europe—mostly in West Germany—along with an arsenal of conventional and tactical nuclear weapons.

In return for its contribution to Western defense, Washington would like European governments to provide more military manpower and contribute a larger share of the expense of maintaining American troops in Europe. West Germany already helps to defray these expenses, but Washington would like to see Bonn do more. In the eyes of many Americans, it is not fair that their country should contribute 55 percent of NATO's annual military spending (down from 65 percent in the early 1970s),[35] while the other 15 members donate the remainder.

European leaders note that the countries of Western Europe provide the bulk of NATO's troops, and they insist that their populations refuse to make any greater sacrifices for their own defense. Particularly during a period of stagflation, government leaders maintain, Europeans seek to preserve state-provided social services without raising taxes. The impasse over burden-sharing seems likely to continue and perhaps even worsen, as weapons grow ever more costly.

Standardization and Interoperability.
NATO has been described as a "military museum" as opposed to an integrated alliance. This description underlines the fact that, despite a certain degree of strategic coordination at the top, NATO remains an alliance of separate military forces that carry different weapons. An integrated military alliance would deploy a single rifle, for instance, or a standard-size nozzle for oil refueling operations. Instead, NATO deploys numerous guns of varying calibers, over seven different main battle tanks, 23 different types of combat aircraft, and over 100 different types of tactical missile systems.[36]

Two measures often recommended to reduce the inefficiency caused by incompatible weapons are standardization and interoperability. As explained by Eliot Cohen, standardization refers to the adoption by two or more countries of the same make of one type of weapon, while interoperability describes military systems of similar types but different makes which nevertheless use identical consumables, such as ammunition or fuel.[37] Different rifles that all make use of the same caliber ammunition would be interoperable.

The military arguments for standardization are rather compelling. Nonstandardized armies require separate supply lines. Each such army must stock its own spare parts and operate its own system of logistics. Troops from countries fighting side by side would not be able to supply each other with spare parts and supplies.

The economic arguments for standardization are no less persuasive. Such a step would eliminate duplication in R & D.[38] The per-unit cost of NATO's weaponry could be reduced by taking advantage of the economy of large-scale production.

Coproduction is a promising means to bring about standardization. NATO has experimented with this technique. West Germany, Italy and Great Britain jointly produce the multi-role combat airplanes designated Tornado. The United States is producing, along with European countries, the Roland II antiaircraft missile system developed by France and West Germany. Europeans are producing the F-16 fighter plane under license from the United States. The most ambitious NATO joint project thus far is an airborne early warning and control system. The alliance plans to acquire 18 American-made E-3A AWACS aircraft and 11 British-made Nimrod aircraft. These airplanes will be integrated with ground communication and radar sites in Europe. Thirteen NATO states are cooperating in the deployment of this system, which will enhance the alliance's detection, warning and control capabilities to defend against low-altitude air attacks. Other coproduction arrangements include the AIM-9L Sidewinder air-to-air missile and the American XM-1 tank, which will mount a 120-mm gun developed by West Germany. Five NATO countries are collaborating with West Germany on the production of the Leopard II tank, one of the world's most advanced.

Yet, coproduction is not without drawbacks. Warplanes and missile systems are difficult enough to produce without introducing such complications as language differences and incompatible production techniques. Believing its weapons to be generally superior to those of its alliance partners, the United States remains reluctant to deploy weapons designed and manufactured elsewhere.[39] Coproduced weapons often cost more and take longer to produce than weapons fabricated by a single country. Governments are wary about the release of military and industrial secrets through joint ventures.

On the other side of the coin, weapons diversity is not without some advantages. The adversary of an alliance that fields a multitude of weapons must plan to defend against a wider variety of threat. During World War II, nonstandardized armies fought well side by side. In a war of short duration, as many strategists believe a future European war will be, the drawbacks of several separate supply lines might not be significant.

Nuclear Sharing.
Once a major source of contention in NATO, the problem of nuclear-sharing has been solved to a large degree. For many years, the European members of NATO felt that they had too little say about the conditions that would trigger the launching of NATO's nuclear weapons, most of which were controlled by the United States. Accusations of American "hegemony" were not uncommon. More recently, however, the United States has shown itself amenable to frequent and regular consultation with its European partners concerning nuclear matters. These include target selection and the conditions under which nuclear war will be initiated.

Figure 11–4 illustrates some of the consultative machinery established by NATO. The highest decision-making body and forum for consultations within the alliance is the North Atlantic Council, composed of permanent representatives from each of the 16 member nations. These representatives meet at least once a week. Twice a year the ministers of foreign affairs of these governments convene, and the heads of state gather as the occasion warrants. More specifically focused on military concerns than the council, the Defense Planning Committee (DPC) is also represented by permanent members from each NATO partner. Supplementing regular meetings of these representatives, the defense ministers of NATO countries meet twice a year. Nuclear consultations are conducted by the Nuclear Planning Group, in which 12 countries now participate. It meets regularly at the level of permanent representative and twice a year at the level of defense ministers. The highest military body in the alliance is the Military Committee. This committee is responsible for making recommendations to the council and the DPC on military matters and for supplying guidance on military questions to allied commanders and subordinate military authorities. It is composed of the chiefs of staff of all member countries except France, which has withdrawn from the committee, and Iceland, which has no military forces. These chiefs meet three times a year and whenever else it may be necessary. In between these meetings, permanent representatives gather on a regular basis. This rather elaborate structure for joint planning is highly conducive to

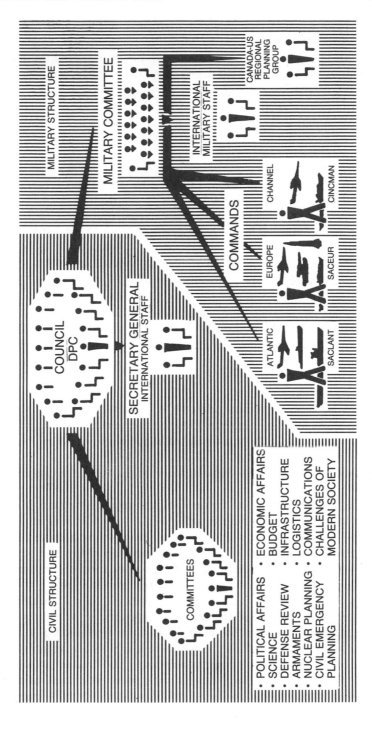

FIGURE 11-4: NATO'S CIVIL AND MILITARY STRUCTURE

Source: NATO Information Service, *NATO Handbook.*

the type of consultation that the European members of the alliance seek. American willingness to bring its allies into the nuclear planning process has substantially stilled European complaints about Washington's tendency to make unilateral decisions on nuclear matters.

READINESS

It is one thing for a government to have plans for worldwide military operations, and it is quite another to be able to implement them. The capacity to do so is referred to as readiness.

The readiness of the American armed forces has been called into question lately, both in terms of manpower and material.[40] Experts have questioned whether the United States would be able to place reinforcements in Europe in time to block a Soviet advance or to get enough troops to the Persian Gulf to prevent hostile forces from seizing it. In November 1980, for example, the United States conducted an elaborate simulation of mobilization for a major war.[41] The simulation, code-named "Proud Spirit," embraced the activities of the Pentagon and 35 other federal agencies that would participate in wartime mobilization. The results proved disturbing due to:

a failure of the computerized Worldwide Military Command and Control system that left military commanders without essential information about the readiness of their units for 12 hours during the height of the "crisis";

shortages of 350 thousand trained soldiers to fill units departing the US;

the inability to bring front-line American Army units in West Germany up to wartime strength;

the shortage of one million tons of ammunition and military equipment supposedly in war reserve stocks in Europe;

industry's inability to resupply the armed forces with basic items of military hardware, such as tanks and ammunition.

The purpose of conducting such simulations is to uncover shortcomings before a real crisis actually occurs. However, governments rarely are able to schedule crises for their convenience; governments must be prepared. How well prepared is the United States?

According to the Defense Department itself, the most severe readiness problem lies in shortages of key personnel.[42] Specifically, the armed forces lack a sufficient number of senior enlisted personnel—the sergeants and petty officers who provide leadership, experience and training to mold new recruits into an effective fighting force. There has been an exodus of such people from the armed forces, in large part due to gaps between military and civilian salaries. New enlistees cannot fill the boots of these seasoned veterans. Highly skilled technical specialists are also in short supply. Pilots, skilled technicians and weapons specialists are needed in greater numbers in all the services. The Air Force lacks the needed number of electricians, engine mechanics, and specialists in radar and avionics.

The Navy estimates that it is short 20 thousand petty officers. Many specialists with 8–10 years of experience are leaving the fleet. As in the case of Air Force personnel, Navy people are leaving because of higher pay and allowances in civilian industry. The Navy also has to contend with disgruntlement caused by long deployments at sea and resulting family strains. The Army too suffers from retention of technical specialists. Furthermore, under the all-volunteer army, that branch is not getting enough well-educated recruits to fight on the electronic and mechanized battlefield of the 1980s. In fiscal 1980, for example, the proportion of Army recruits who completed high school dropped to 54 percent, and the fraction of recruits in the lowest and next to lowest aptitude categories amounted to nearly 50 percent.[43] Since then, education levels have risen somewhat.

If the armed services are in difficulty on account of manpower, no less is the case with regard to equipment. The nation's fleet of B–52 bombers is over 20 years old, as are the 53 strategic Titan II missiles. Defense Department planners are worried about the vulnerability of all the nation's 1053 land-based strategic missiles to the Soviet Union's growingly accurate strategic missiles. Malfunctions plague the country's strategic early warning and communications system, triggering false alarms and sending bomber crews into their airplanes for takeoffs. A shortage of over $2 billion in spare parts has idled many planes, some by as long as nine months. Inspectors at Langley Air Force Base in Virginia in 1980 found only 23 of 66 F-15s "mission capable."[44] Delivery lags of 2–3 years for radar equipment are not uncommon. Rising fuel prices are reducing practice flight hours for pilots and steaming time for the Navy. Inventories of weapons and spare parts are low.

A major problem concerns transport. To emerge victorious, nations must be able to move large amounts of heavy equipment and personnel swiftly. Earlier in this chapter we commented upon the nation's shortcomings in this regard, when we examined prospects for the Rapid Deployment Force.

ARMS TRANSFERS

An implement of growing importance in the foreign policy toolbox is the sale or grant of arms to other countries. Such transactions are known collectively as arms transfers.

As Figure 11–5 shows, the United States is the world's leading arms supplier, with the Soviet Union coming in second. Figure 11–5 also reveals the destination of these arms. Awash in petro-dollars, the Middle East is the leading importer of weapons.

There have been several changes in the arms trade in the last 35 years. Just after World War II, most arms being transferred were on the verge of obsolescence. The bulk of transfers took the form of gifts, particularly from the United States and the Soviet Union to their European allies. Today, buyers want—and are getting—the very latest armaments that roll off the assembly lines: laser-guided bombs, missiles, communications gear, radar, supersonic jet fighters, and the like. Almost all transfers today take the form of sales. Finally, the majority of arms transfers are now between developed states and the developing world, particularly the Middle East. An important feature of many arms transfer agreements is the inclusion of troop training and maintenance assistance.

Recipients of American Arms

Since 1950, the United States has transferred abroad approximately $160 billion in arms and related military services (see Fig. 11–5). In recent years, approximately 60 percent of American arms transfers have gone to the Middle East, especially Saudi Arabia, Iran (before the overthrow of the shah), Israel and Egypt. (The bulk of Soviet arms sales also go to this region, with emphasis on Iraq, Syria, Algeria and South Yemen.) Another one-third of American arms exports goes to Japan, NATO, and South Korea. The remainder is allocated among several other non-Communist countries. (The United States may be sending arms to China in the near future.)

FIGURE 11–5: WEAPONS EXPORTERS AND IMPORTERS, 1977–1980

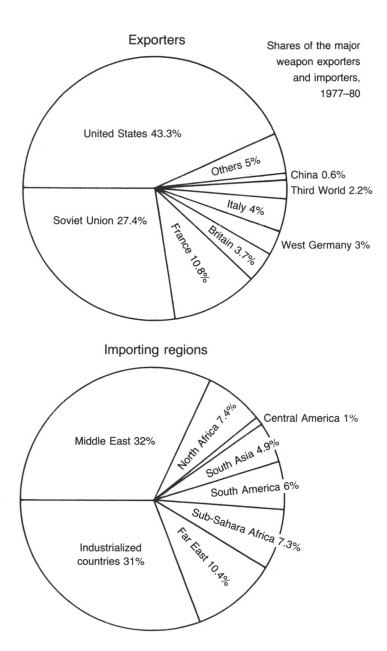

Source: Stockholm International Peace Research Institute.

FIGURE 11–6: UNITED STATES ARMS SALES, 1970–1980

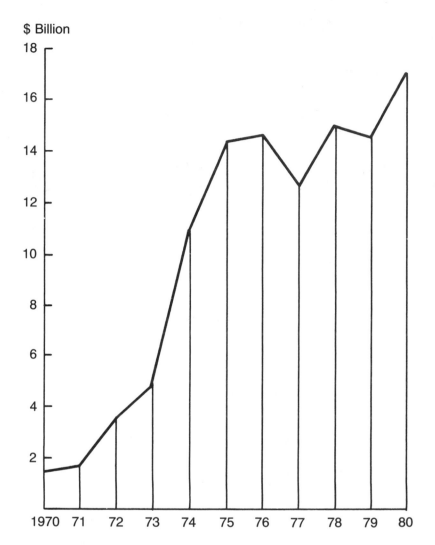

U.S. government-to-government sales agreements
and commercial arms exports (in billion current dollars)

Source: Andrew J. Pierre, *The Global Politics of Arms Sales*. Copyright © 1982 by Princeton University Press. Graph, p. 47, reprinted by permission of Princeton University Press.

Mechanisms of Arms Transfers

American transfers of arms and military services are accomplished in three ways. Formerly the principal means of transfers, the Military Assistance Program provided for defense articles and services on a grant basis. This program was phased out entirely in fiscal year 1981. Approximately 10 percent of American arms exports take place through commercial sales, that is, sales by American corporations to other governments. The International Military Education and Training Program provides for the training of foreign military personnel on a grant basis. By far the largest arms transfer program falls under the category of Foreign Military Sales (FMS), that is, sales by the US government directly to foreign governments. These sales may be for cash or credit. In fiscal 1980, the FMS program accounted for over $15 billion in sales agreements or about 90 percent of American arms transfer agreements during that year.[45] Under the Arms Export Control Act, a majority vote by both houses of Congress within 30 days from the executive branch's formal announcement of a sales agreement can block the sale. Thus far, Congress has not blocked any such sale.

Benefits to the United States

Like other suppliers, the United States transfers arms abroad in support of its own national interest. Presumably, the receiving country also perceives benefits from acquiring arms.

Among us, the giant arms dealers of the world—the U.S., the U.S.S.R., the U.K., France, West Germany and Israel—have armed the world's thugs, blunderers and psychopaths. Among us, we have given or sold ... the wherewithal to destroy major cities and small nations.
Professor Robert J. Wolfson, 1982

Those who support the sale of arms abroad cite numerous advantages to be gained. A recent Defense Department document states:

> Security assistance serves U.S. interests by strengthening the ability of our allies and friends to defend themselves against threats to their national security. By assisting other nations in meeting their defense needs, we, in turn, strengthen our own security.[46]

Among the many benefits that the United States expects to derive from arms transfers are the following:

access to military bases and repair facilities, as in Oman and Somalia;

relief from balance of payments deficits;

strengthening of allied and friendly governments against internal foes, as in Saudi Arabia and El Salvador;

reinforcement of friendly governments against outside predators, as in Israel and NATO;

increase in American influence in recipient governments, especially military regimes, through personal contacts and reliance on America for spare parts and training;

reduced likelihood of American involvement in foreign wars by helping allies to defend themselves, as in Israel and South Korea;

limitation of Soviet influence;

providing a symbol of American commitment or expression of concern toward a friendly state, as in Egypt or Japan;

discouragement of a state from seeking to acquire nuclear weapons, by providing adequate conventional means of defense, as in Pakistan;

maintenance of employment in American defense industries;

fostering of regional stability by maintaining a balance of arms, as in the Middle East or the Greek-Turkish dispute;

lowering the per-unit cost of weapons provided to American forces by taking advantage of the economies of large-scale production;

testing new weapons in battle conditions, as in the Middle East.

Finally, there is the argument that "if we don't sell them arms, someone else will."

Criticisms of Arms Transfers

Although arms transfers have become a diplomatic tool of growing importance, many observers criticize them both for failing to yield their promised results and for the negative side effects they are alleged to produce.[47] During his 1976 presidential campaign, Jimmy Carter scored the United States for being the "arms merchant to the world."

It is alleged by some that arms transfers give rise to arms races and aggravate tensions between rival states. Proponents of this view cite spiraling hostility between Greece and Turkey, between India and Pakistan, and between Israel and the Arabs, all major buyers of arms.

Arms transfers also greatly increase the destructiveness of war in regions whose own arms production is fairly rudimentary. The largest tank battles in the history of warfare occurred not during World War II but in the course of the 1973 Middle East war. The plentitude of military hardware in the arsenals of so many countries may in itself encourage recourse to war as a means of settling disputes.

The United States is often condemned for selling arms to authoritarian regimes, on the ground that such military equipment strengthens the hands of dictators. Helicopters, rifles, side arms and communications gear that can be fielded against a foreign army can also be used against internal critics. Indeed, one might argue that the ready availability of such military items discourages dictators from enacting the very reforms that are necessary to gain popular support. Sales of arms to regimes that regularly violate human rights make the United States appear hypocritical in the eyes of many.

Other critics of arms transfers question the assertion that arms buy friends. Citing the Soviet experience in Egypt and Indonesia and the American experience in Iran, these observers insist that the arms recipient tail often wags the arms supplier dog. In international politics influence rarely flows in just one direction. More usually, the arms recipient controls something the supplier wants, such as resources or harbors or land areas for military bases. Thus, Turkey exerts some leverage over the United States, its major arms supplier, because it houses important listening posts near the Soviet Union. After the United States placed a ban on military aid to Turkey in 1974 (since lifted), Turkey closed down these American intelligence and surveillance facilities along the Turkish-Soviet frontier. William H. Lewis theorizes that military assistance is likely to translate into influence when it helps the recipient do something it wants to do.[48] But the use of aid to persuade a government to take actions it opposes, or for the purposes of blackmail, is much less likely to succeed. Thus, the United States has had little success in persuading Israel to dismantle settlements in the West Bank by threatening to withhold military assistance. Aid is also not so likely to result in influence if the donor asks the recipient to take actions that involve high political costs.

Do arms transfers make American intervention in foreign wars less likely, as proponents claim? While not denying that arms may sometimes have this effect, by enabling allies to defend themselves, some critics of arms transfers believe military aid tightens Washington's commitment to other regimes.

> Arms transfers, rightly or wrongly, are often viewed as barometers of the state of political relationships, aside from their impact on the security of a given recipient or stability in a region. They convey a political message and are often perceived to create a bond between the seller and purchaser in a way civilian exports do not.[49]

Can there be any doubt that American arms transfers to Israel have helped to confirm Washington's commitment to that state in the eyes of the world, despite the absence of any formal treaty between the two states? Of course, not all commitments are to be avoided. Sometimes, it is desirable to put others on notice that one is willing to defend another state.

Some critics of arms transfers have questioned the wisdom of placing the world's most advanced weapons in the hands of regimes whose stability is at best dubious. Today's friends could become tomorrow's well-armed foes. Should a recipient switch sides in the Cold War, advanced American weapons could fall into Soviet hands. Such reservations were raised (to no avail) in the case of American arms transfers to Iran, and they are being voiced again with regard to Saudi Arabia. In the early 1980s Saudi Arabia emerged as the largest single purchaser of American military supplies. Between 1970 and 1980, Riyadh bought $18.7 billion worth of American military equipment.[50] The Saudis have added to their arsenal some of the most sophisticated military equipment that America produces, including F-15 fighter planes, AWACS surveillance aircraft, laser-guided bombs, and Sidewinder and Maverick missiles. Should the authority of the 4 thousand princes who rule Saudi Arabia become seriously weakened, American-supplied weapons could fall into the hands of Arab regimes opposed to American interests or even into the hands of the Soviets.

Finally, a number of writers have lamented the enormous expenditures by relatively poor countries on elaborate weapons instead of economic development. It often seems as though the countries least able to afford weapons are the ones most anxious to buy them. Unlike capital goods such as tractors or steel mills, weapons do not create additional wealth and hence do not generate economic development. Therefore, some allege, arms sales have the effect of impeding the economic development of poorer lands. Underlying this argument is the assumption that the money spent on arms would otherwise be spent for economic development. There is no way of proving that this would indeed be the case. What makes this situation so deplorable, in the eyes of some, is that many impoverished arms recipients face no outside threat that warrants such expenditures on weapons.

Curbing the Arms Trade

Over the years there have been many calls for reducing and hopefully eliminating the sale of arms abroad. Yet, in recent years sales have been increasing, not diminishing. This pattern indicates the existence of severe obstacles lying in the path of reducing the traffic in arms.

To comprehend these impediments, we must first recall the identities of the principal buyers and sellers of arms. As Figure 11–5 reveals, the United States and the Soviet Union are the primary sellers, followed by France, Italy, West Germany and Great Britain. Other significant purveyors are Israel and Sweden. Figure 11–5 also shows that the largest buyers are the relatively prosperous developed states in Europe and Japan and the Middle East. The remainder of the market is shared more or less equally by the other regions of the world. The picture that emerges from this examination is a market with many buyers and sellers. Such a market structure complicates the task of those who would limit arms transfers. The existence of several sellers heightens the likelihood that if one were to restrain its arms exports, the others would race to get additional orders.[51] The deep-seated rivalry between the United States and the Soviet Union minimizes the chances that these two major suppliers could agree to refrain from seeking the political advantages that arms transfers are believed to confer. The other arms suppliers often cite economic reasons for their reluctance to curb arms exports. The small size of their armed forces keeps the per-unit cost of arms production high. By selling abroad, these countries can significantly reduce the cost of arms to their own military forces. Furthermore, arms sales generate foreign exchange needed to pay for energy imports. Arms exporting nations also hope to cement friendly ties with oil-exporting nations, who are among the largest arms importers. During the current extended period of stagflation in the West, arms exports provide jobs to domestic workers and keep open production lines.

On the demand side, the appetite for state-of-the-art weaponry seems insatiable. Despite the logic inherent in the argument that

arms purchases retard economic development, the facts clearly substantiate the conclusion that developing states seek large quantities
of arms. If one supplier were to restrict its sales, buyers would look
elsewhere. Since there are a number of willing sellers, buyers would
have no trouble in locating sources of arms.

The preceding analysis suggests that the prospects for curbing
the arms trade are dim. One suggestion that offers at least limited
promise is an arrangement between the United States and Western
Europe. The latter complains that one reason why it must export
arms is that the United States refuses to buy European arms. Should
Washington do so in significant quantity, West European arms
suppliers could obtain most of the advantages of arms exports
without selling to the Third World, which currently accounts for
two-thirds of the world's arms purchases. As we observed in examining the issue of NATO standardization, however, the United
States thus far has shown little enthusiasm for purchasing European
weapons. The dominant position of the United States and the Soviet
Union in the arms trade—together they account for nearly three-
fourths of arms sales—suggests that if these two states could agree
on limiting arms sales, the worldwide traffic in arms would diminish
significantly. To state this likely proposition is hardly to bring it
about, however. During the Carter administration, both powers
engaged in talks aimed at limiting arms sales. These negotiations
proved fruitless, however, and the deterioration of US-Soviet relations in the early 1980s holds little immediate hope for the success
of such endeavors. We are left with the conclusion, therefore, that
the sale of lethal military equipment abroad is likely to continue
if not accelerate.

FOR DISCUSSION

Explain and evaluate the concept of "minimum deterrence."

Does the US-Soviet military balance seem to favor Washington
or Moscow?

Which type of military spending seems most urgent for the US—
strategic weapons, tactical nuclear weapons, conventional weapons,
manpower augmentation, airlift and sealift, or readiness?

Would you favor an immediate US freeze on new strategic
weapons, while efforts are undertaken with the Soviet Union to
reduce arms?

What strategy would you recommend to counter the Warsaw Pact's advantages in armor and manpower in Europe?

Can a limited nuclear war in Europe remain limited? What factors might help keep the fighting within bounds? What factors might cause the fighting to escalate?

In order to have larger numbers of capable people in the armed services, should the US reinstitute the draft?

In order to offset the Warsaw Pact's advantage in chemical weapons, should the US resume production of CW?

Have arms transfers been a successful instrument of policy for the US? Should Washington continue to ship large quantities of arms abroad? Which countries, if any, should not be permitted to buy American arms?

READING SUGGESTIONS

Barnet, Richard J. *Real Security: Restoring American Power in a Dangerous Decade*. New York: Simon & Schuster, 1981.

Carnegie Endowment for International Peace. *Chemical Weapons and Chemical Arms Control*. New York: Carnegie Endowment, 1978.

Fallows, James. *National Defense*. New York: Random House, 1981.

Kahan, James H. *Security in the Nuclear Age*. Washington: The Brookings Institution, 1975.

Kaplan, Stephen S., et al. *Diplomacy of Power: Soviet Armed Forces as a Political Instrument*. Washington: The Brookings Institution, 1981.

Neuman, Stephanie G., and Harkavy, Robert E., eds. *Arms Transfers in the Modern World*. New York: Praeger, 1979.

Pierre, Andrew J. *The Global Politics of Arms Sales*. Princeton: Princeton University Press, 1982.

Record, Jeffrey. *The Rapid Deployment Force and U.S. Military Intervention in the Persian Gulf*. Cambridge: Institute for Foreign Policy Analysis, 1981.

Stockholm International Peace Research Institute. *Tactical Nuclear Weapons: European Perspectives*. New York: Crane, Russak and Company, 1978.

NOTES

1. United States, Department of Defense, *Report of Secretary of Defense Harold Brown to the Congress on the Fiscal Year 1982 Budget, Fiscal Year 1983 Authorization Request and Fiscal Year 1982–1986 Defense Programs*, January 19, 1981 (Washington: GPO, 1981), p. 4. Hereafter cited as DOD, *Annual Report, FY 1982*.

2. T. H. White, "Weinberger on the Ramparts," *New York Times Magazine*, February 6, 1983, p. 19.

3. Jerome H. Kahan, *Security in the Nuclear Age* (Washington: The Brookings Institution, 1975), Chapter 1.

4. Ibid., p. 75.

5. Ibid., p. 94.

6. Ibid., p. 96. Later McNamara reduced these requirements to 20–25 percent of the population and one-half of Russia's industrial capacity.

7. Kahan. Much of the following analysis of "sufficiency" is based on Kahan, pp. 142–64.

8. Quoted in Kahan, p. 163.

9. For a thorough description of the Rapid Deployment Force and the problems it faces, see David D. Newsom, "America Engulfed," *Foreign Policy* (Summer 1981): 17–32. Mr. Newsom was undersecretary of state for political affairs from 1978 to 1981.

10. Kahan, pp. 94–109.

11. The above figures were reported in DOD, *Annual Report, FY 1982*, pp. 37–38. The wide variations in the figures cited reflect different possible types of weapon combinations, different types of explosions (above-ground or below), wind direction, etc.

12. Ibid., p. 5.

13. Kahan, pp. 165–69.

14. DOD, *Annual Report, FY 1982*, pp. 15–20.

15. Ibid.

16. Ibid.

17. Quoted in *New York Times*, September 27, 1981. In the fall of 1981 the Defense Department published a report entitled "Soviet Military Power," that details recent Soviet military efforts and supports the conclusion that the Russians have achieved military superiority. However, because the report does not describe American efforts, this conclusion is open to challenge.

18. M. Leitenberg, "Background Materials in Tactical Nuclear Weapons," in Stockholm International Peace Research Institute, *Tactical Nuclear Weapons: European Perspectives* (New York: Crane, Russak and Company, 1978), p. 17.

19. O. Sukovic, "Tactical Nuclear Weapons in Europe," in SIPRI, *Tactical Nuclear Weapons*, p. 151.

20. DOD, *Annual Report, FY 1982*, p. 66.

21. Leitenberg in SIPRI, *Tactical Nuclear Weapons*, p. 12.

22. Ibid., pp. 32–33.

23. Alain C. Einthoven, "U.S. Forces in Europe: How Many? Doing What?" *Foreign Affairs*, LIII (April 1975): 514.

24. The following analysis relies largely on DOD, *Annual Report, FY 1982*, pp. 72–80.

25. Wayne Biddle, "Restocking the Chemical Arsenal," *New York Times Magazine*, Summer 1981 (no date provided).

26. Julian Perry Robinson, "Chemical Weapons for NATO?" in Carnegie Endowment for International Peace, *Chemical Weapons and Chemical Arms Control* (New York, 1978), pp. 28–33. Hereafter: Carnegie Endowment, *Chemical Weapons*.

27. This estimate was reported in Carnegie Endowment, *Chemical Weapons*, p. 59.

28. DOD, *Annual Report, FY 1982*, p. 72.
29. See, for example, the allegations by a State Department official reported in *New York Times*, November 11, 1981. The State Department claimed to have found traces of chemicals used in chemical weapons on rocks and leaves.
30. *New York Times*, December 7, 1980.
31. Biddle, "Restocking the Chemical Arsenal."
32. "Communication of James F. Finan," in Carnegie Endowment, *Chemical Weapons*, pp. 98–99.
33. Finan has proposed that NATO explicitly enunciate such a policy. Ibid.
34. DOD, *Annual Report, FY 1982*, p. 220.
35. Ibid., p. 218.
36. Senator John Culver (D–IA), cited by Anne Hessing Cahn, "Economics of Arms Transfers," in Stephanie G. Neuman and Robert E. Harkavy, *Arms Transfers in the Modern World* (New York: Praeger, 1979), pp. 173–83.
37. Eliot Cohen, "NATO Standardization: The Perils of Common Sense," *Foreign Policy*, XXXI (Summer 1978). 72–90. The analysis that follows is based largely upon this article.
38. The Defense Department estimates that, on account of duplication, NATO derives only $15–$16 billion in value from the $20 billion it invests annually in R & D. DOD, *Annual Report, FY 1981*, p. 48.
39. As of 1980, the United States sold to other NATO countries ten times the value of the military goods it purchased from them. Cahn, "Economics of Arms Transfers."
40. Beginning September 21, 1980, the *New York Times* ran a series of seven articles on the topic of readiness. Much of the following analysis is based on this reporting.
41. This simulation was reported in *New York Times*, December 22, 1980.
42. DOD, *Annual Report, FY 1982*, p. viii.
43. DOD, *Annual Report, FY 1982*.
44. *New York Times*, September 23, 1980. The *Times* further reported that on any given day 32–65 percent of the Air Force's tactical aircraft are incapable of carrying out their missions.
45. DOD, *Annual Report, FY 1982*, p. 221.
46. Ibid.
47. For a thoughtful essay on the limits of influence generated by arms transfers, see William B. Quandt, "Influence through Arms Supply: The U.S. Experience in the Middle East," in Uri Ra'anan, Robert L. Pfaltzgraff, Jr., and Geoffrey Kemp, eds., *Arms Transfers to the Third World: The Military Buildup in Less Developed Countries* (Boulder, CO: Westview Press, 1978), pp. 121–30.
48. William H. Lewis, "Political Influence: The Diminished Capacity," in Neuman and Harkavy, p. 196.
49. Statement by Matthew Nimitz, Undersecretary of State for Security Assistance, Science and Technology, before the Senate Committee on Foreign Relations, March 6, 1980, in US Department of State, Current Policy #145, March 1980.
50. *New York Times*, June 14, 1981.
51. This is precisely what occurred after Congress in 1961 imposed a $55 million limit (later raised to $100 million) on arms sales to Latin America. Unable

to make purchases in the United States, Chile bought Hawker-Hunter airplanes from Great Britain, and Peru purchased Mirage airplanes from France. Later, when President Carter sought to encourage other arms suppliers to reduce sales, by force of unilateral American restraint, the other suppliers eagerly sought opportunities to pick up the slack. Eventually Carter gave up on his efforts to curb arms transfers.

Chapter 12
Arms Control

Today, every inhabitant of the planet must contemplate the day when this planet may no longer be habitable. Every man, woman and child lives under a nuclear sword of Damocles, hanging by the slenderest of threads, capable of being cut at any moment by accident, or miscalculation or by madness. The weapons of war must be abolished before they abolish us.

John F. Kennedy, 1961

The untold destruction of nuclear weapons has raised the world's consciousness about the need for arms control. President Kennedy's words printed above etch in stark terms the stakes involved.

Concern about abolishing the weapons of war dates as far back as warfare itself. For the most part, this concern has been voiced by people who longed for a world without war. In their view, arms cause war; therefore, disarmament would eliminate violent disputes between states. Without seeking to pass judgment on such opinions, we shall focus on arms control less as a pathway to peace than as an instrument of foreign policy. Like other such instruments, arms control can be used by governments to advance their own interests. Sometimes this occurs at the expense of other states; sometimes, to their benefit.

ARMS CONTROL AND DISARMAMENT

Before proceeding further, it would be well to explain what arms control means and particularly to distinguish it from disarmament. As the more familiar term, disarmament refers to the elimination of weapons. "General and complete disarmament" describes a state of affairs in which the nations of the world destroy all their weaponry.

The inability to bring about disarmament has led to a less ambitious if not more feasible objective, arms control. According to one definition, arms control "includes all those actions, unilateral as well as multilateral, by which we *regulate* the levels and kinds of armaments in order to reduce the likelihood of armed conflicts, their severity and violence if they should occur, and the economic burden of military programs."[1] It will be noted that the emphasis here rests not on dumping weapons into the sea but on controlling their growth and use. Arms control reflects a recognition that the arms race is here to stay, but that it is subject to some measure of regulation. Indeed, while advocates of disarmament seek to eliminate the arms race, arms controllers seem more intent on making more *stable* an arms race they accept as a permanent feature of international affairs. Arms control theory rests on the notion that decisions to acquire certain types and quantities of weapons can aggravate political conflict and lead to war. It is therefore possible to heighten stability and lower tensions by refraining from the deployment of "destabilizing" weapons. Some arms controllers go so far as to oppose general and complete disarmament on the grounds of instability. Such an environment, they maintain, would provide an irresistible temptation to cheat, since the successful cheater would be in a position to coerce defenseless (though law-abiding) states. In this view, stability is enhanced when every state has a small number of weapons sufficient to deter attack.

As paradoxical as it may seem, the construction of more weapons, *of a certain type*, may actually improve stability. For example, fighter planes with a short range and no in-flight refueling capability may help deter attack but be practically useless for offensive purposes (due to short range). Similarly, tight command and control systems can contribute to stability by minimizing the likelihood that a military officer with access to nuclear weapons will fire them without authorization. The Strategic Arms Limitation Talks (SALT) represent a facet of arms control, in that they place ceilings on various categories of arms. Such upper limits restrict the number of weapons each superpower must build to offset its adversary. We shall explore additional facets of arms control in the remainder of this chapter.

Arms control, then, accepts the existence of international conflict and military arsenals and tries to make the best of the situation by enhancing stability. Other objectives of arms control include minimizing destruction in case war does occur and lowering expenditures on armaments.

In contrast to some proponents of arms control, who view it as a means to fashion a "new Jerusalem" on earth, former Secretary of Defense Harold Brown deems arms control as no less self-interested or "hard-headed" than other tools of diplomacy.

> Equitable and verifiable international agreements that limit the size and capability of military arsenals can enhance our security by reducing the military threat arrayed against us, thus helping to reduce the chances of war. They can contribute to improved East-West relations by stabilizing the most dangerous aspects of that competition. And multilateral arms control agreements, such as the Non-Proliferation Treaty, can help avoid regional developments that could threaten US interests.[2]

Arms control can also serve American interests by preventing the development of new weapons that could destabilize the military balance and thereby jeopardize American security.

A fable by the Spanish philosopher Salvador de Madariaga suggests another way in which arms control can serve the national interest. Madariaga compares arms control negotiations to an imaginary gathering of animals who seek to "humanize" the law of the jungle. The lion proposes elimination of all weapons but claws and jaws; the eagle, all but talons and beaks; and the bear, all but all-embracing hugs. Translated into human terms, this approach might be termed "let's you control the arms in which you are strongest." While other motivations may have been involved, President Reagan's strategic arms proposal of May 1982 suggests a parallel to Madariaga's tale. The president proposed, among other things, that each superpower be limited to 850 intercontinental land-based and sea-based missiles. By US count, the Soviet Union had 2,400 such missiles, while the US had 1,700. To fall within the proposed limit, Moscow would have to eliminate nearly twice as many missiles as Washington would. Another part of the package called for a ceiling of 5 thousand missile warheads to be allowed on the 850 missiles. Within this total, only 2,500 could be placed on land-based missiles.

This limitation would also affect the Soviet Union more than the United States, since the former has about 70 percent of its warheads on land-based missiles. (The corresponding figure for the United States is 20 percent.) Since the Soviets had 5,500 warheads on land-based missiles, while the United States had only 2,152, the Soviets would have to cut nearly half of their land-based warheads. The United States, by contrast, could construct 348 more and still not exceed the limit. The Reagan proposal would severely reduce what the United States deems Russia's primary threat, the highly accurate and enormously powerful land-based missile. The proposal would not curtail American plans to proceed with a new generation of strategic weapons, including the MX missile, the Trident nuclear submarine, the B–1 bomber, and cruise missiles. Not surprisingly, the Soviets rejected the president's offer.[3] (The United States subsequently modified its position, as will be discussed below.)

FORMULATING ARMS CONTROL POLICY

While the primary purpose of this chapter is not to examine the policy-making process, a few words about the formulation of arms control policy will help us understand the policy itself.[4]

In most countries, arms control policy is set by the military. This fact alone may account for the limited extent and nature of arms control progress worldwide. The same arrangement held true for the United States—although State had a decided input—until the creation in 1961 of the Arms Control and Disarmament Agency (ACDA). The Arms Control and Disarmament Act, which established the agency, also made its director "the principal advisor to the Secretary of State and the President on arms control matters." At the same time, the law placed the director "under the direction of the Secretary of State." Today, ACDA is a quasi-independent agency that takes direction from but is not subordinate to the Department of State. The actual influence of ACDA and its director depends more than anything else on the president. If the latter deems arms control important and has cordial relations with ACDA's director, then the agency is likely to enjoy considerable influence in Washington. Such was the case during President Carter's administration, particularly when Paul Warnke served as ACDA's director, but this has generally not been true under President Reagan.

While ACDA "has generally been the point man for arms control,"[5] the organization shares policy-making responsibility with State, Defense, the Joint Chiefs, the Energy Department and the

White House. Congress also participates, particularly if negotiations lead to a treaty that the Senate must approve. Regarding the bureaucratic wrangling that accompanies arms control policy making, Jerome Wiesner, science advisor to President Kennedy, said:

> I have seen more arms limitations proposals destroyed by the compromises that had to be made to get them agreed to by everyone who had to agree to [them] in the Government, and very many times what one does in this process is to make a sort of treaty.
>
> I used to say when I was working in the White House that we were fighting a four-front war when we tried to do something about arms limitation.
>
> We had to deal with the Pentagon, we had to deal with the Congress, we had to deal with the public; and I was never certain which of these groups gave us more problems because we rarely got to deal with the Russians.[6]

As in other types of policy battles, the bureaucratic agencies involved seek to advance their own interests as well as what they perceive to be the national interest. Arms control very often appears as a threat to the Pentagon, since most international negotiations are aimed at limiting or reducing weapons. As seen by the military services, such agreements endanger military budgets, manpower levels, and task assignments.

Reprinted by permission of Tony Auth.

How effective has ACDA been in the policy arena? According to Duncan L. Clarke, for most of its existence ACDA's effectiveness has been limited by the absence of good rapport between the agency's director and the president. Several presidents have looked to State, DOD or the special assistant as the prime source of advice on arms control. President Nixon in particular distrusted ACDA, viewing its staffers as "woolly-headed" and lacking in toughness. Under Jimmy Carter, ACDA's director for the first time had the president's ear on a regular basis. Nevertheless, President Carter's arms control accomplishments were few. It was Nixon, not Carter, who successfully marshalled a SALT agreement through the Senate. ACDA played a major role in drafting the Limited Test Ban Treaty, signed in 1963, and the agency displayed initiative in proposing a nonproliferation treaty (finalized in 1968). While ACDA has had a significant voice in the SALT process, the special assistant and the Defense Department (particularly under Nixon) have often drowned out the agency. Two ACDA directors, Gerard C. Smith and Paul Warnke, also acted as the nation's chief negotiator at SALT. While this position guarantees the agency an input into the negotiations, it does not necessarily amount to control. With Nixon's approval, Kissinger on occasion bypassed Smith and negotiated directly with the Russians on difficult SALT issues.

ACDA's bureaucratic clout is affected by its small size. The agency employs about 250 people, including clericals, of whom approximately one-fifth are on loan from State and the military. The agency suffers from high turnover, as more ambitious people seek jobs in other agencies that have a more central role in setting the overall direction of foreign policy. In fiscal 1984, Congress authorized $18.5 million for ACDA.

ACDA is a bureaucratic midget, particularly when compared with the military. For every civilian employee in ACDA and State combined, DOD employs 30. For every dollar spent by ACDA and State together, DOD spends 150.[7]

ACDA's influence is also restricted by the absence of an outside constituency. Whereas farmers support the Agriculture Department and veterans support Defense, ACDA finds no comparable group to lobby for higher budgets, more task assignments, and additional personnel. While scores of senators and representatives are veterans of the armed services (and offer them some measure of support), practically none has served in ACDA.

Along with its reviving interest in foreign policy in the 1970s, Congress has taken an increasingly active part in arms control. Of course, Congress had not been totally divorced from such activities in earlier years. It was the legislature (and particularly Senator Hubert Humphrey) that created ACDA, largely to ensure an advocate for arms control within the corridors of the executive branch. In 1967 Senator Claiborne Pell, a long-time proponent of arms control, introduced a resolution calling for the commencement of international negotiations to prevent the stationing of nuclear weapons and other weapons of mass destruction on the ocean floor. Thus was born the Seabed Treaty of 1971. In 1971 the same senator, alarmed by reports of military uses of the environment (such as rainmaking), introduced a resolution declaring it to be the sense of the Senate that there be a "complete cessation of research, experimentation, and use of environmental and geophysical modification activities as weapons of war." This initiative culminated in the Environmental Modification Convention, signed by the United States in 1977. In 1975 Congress amended the Arms Control and Disarmament Act so as to give ACDA a say in the development of new weapons. Previously, little attention was paid to the arms control implications of new weapons systems. The 1975 amendment called for "arms control impact statements" to be appended to requests for new weapons. While the effect of these statements remains open to question thus far, Congress at least required that the arms control fallout of new weapons be considered as a regular part of the arms acquisition process. In 1976 Congress, in passing the International Security Assistance and Arms Export Control Act, ordered that requests to Congress for security assistance be accompanied by an arms control impact statement for each purchasing country. ACDA plays a major role in writing both types of these impact statements. Congress also enacted a law requiring the president to notify Congress of any proposed foreign arms sale exceeding $25 million; Congress then had 20 days to overrule the sale by concurrent resolution (not subject to a veto). In 1976 these provisions were narrowed by the International Security Assistance and Arms Export Control Act; the new law stipulated that the president must notify Congress of sales over $7 million, and that Congress has 30 days to object. While Congress has yet to prohibit a sale, some of the votes concerning arms sales to Arab countries have been very close. In 1984 President Reagan withdrew an offer to sell shoulder-fired antiaircraft missiles to Jordan for fear Congress would reject the sale. Congress further legislated for itself a significant role in the sale of civilian nuclear technology in passing the Nuclear Non-Proliferation Act of 1978. This law sets definite limits to the export of civilian nuclear technology abroad.

ARMS CONTROL BEFORE WORLD WAR II

Although the urge to restrict the implements of warfare goes back to time immemorial, there were few concrete efforts to do so until the present century. The Hague Conferences of 1899 and 1907 placed some restrictions on the conduct of warfare, such as prohibiting asphyxiating gases and expanding bullets (dum-dum bullets). Following World War I, the League of Nations was created to control aggression. At the Washington Naval Conference in 1921–1922, the United States, United Kingdom, Japan, France and Italy agreed to place a lid on naval competition. Interestingly, the powers did not feel the need to regulate air power, which was to play a

---

I am skeptical of peace. . . . It is the most talked of and least practiced of all social endeavors. . . . Historians have estimated that society has spent more time fighting than in any other activity except agriculture.
Historian Barbara W. Tuchman, 1982

---

crucial role in the next war, nor did they regulate submarines. The Geneva Protocol, which outlawed chemical and biological warfare, was issued in 1924. Four years later the majority of nations signed the Kellogg-Briand Pact, which called upon states to renounce war as an instrument of national policy. Stimulated by naval arms building, several conferences were held to curtail the construction of warships, including the Geneva Three-Power Naval Conference of 1927, the London Naval Conference of 1930, and the London Naval Conference of 1935. Despite the fanfare that accompanied all of these accords, the guns of World War II left them in shreds upon the scrapheap of history.

THE BARUCH PLAN

In the closing days of World War II, the United States employed a new and terrible weapon that ushered in the atomic age. When the smoke of World War II cleared, the people of the world were more determined than ever before to bring about disarmament. It is perhaps understandable that atomic weaponry was the first target of this resolve. There was actually substantial optimism that such an effort could succeed. The global war had seemingly settled all major outstanding issues of world politics. The two main threats to world peace, Germany and Japan, lay in smoldering ruins. The victorious powers seemed in agreement on many aspects of the new international order, although some differences between Russia and the West over Europe appeared on the horizon. A new international organization, the United Nations, had taken its place for the purpose of keeping the peace.

One of the first issues to be discussed by the new international body was a disarmament proposal tabled by the United States. Introduced in June 1946, the Baruch Plan represented an effort to halt the spread of atomic weapons. At the time, America was the sole possessor of such weaponry. The nuclear genie had one leg out of the bottle, but it still seemed possible to put it back and replace the stopper.

In essence, the Baruch Plan called for the establishment of a new international agency that would own or control all nuclear facilities. Through a system of licenses and inspections, the agency would ensure that no country diverted nuclear knowledge to the construction of weapons. The agency would also sponsor research and development in the nuclear field, and it would seek to foster the use of atomic energy for the benefit of all. In order to carry out the plan, the United States offered to transfer to the new agency all its nuclear knowledge and facilities.

Considering the hazards that nuclear proliferation poses today, one cannot help but wonder "what if" the Baruch Plan had taken effect. Would we be living with the "balance of terror" and all its consequences? Would nuclear terrorism and the prospect of global nuclear war have remained the province of science fiction writers instead of news journalists? What other—possibly worse—military technology would be with us today?

In American eyes, the Baruch Plan was an extraordinarily generous offer. America was willing to yield its highest diplomatic trump card for the sake of world peace. Why did not the plan become a reality? The answer is to be found in the lowering clouds of the Cold War that were beginning to block out the sunshine of the postwar peace. Given fundamental Soviet distrust of the West, as well as Stalin's tendency toward paranoia, the Baruch Plan contained several features Moscow found unacceptable. Could the Americans be trusted to destroy all of their atomic weapons or would they reserve a few for Moscow and Leningrad? Regardless of the answer to that question, could not the Americans build nuclear weapons someday with the knowledge they already possessed?

Reflecting its traditional suspicion of outsiders, Russia objected to the presence of foreign inspectors at its nuclear facilities. Were not such inspectors Western spies or agitators? Although the global agency proposed by the United States was to be controlled by the world community, would it not in reality fall under Western dominance, as had the United Nations? And if the Baruch Plan collapsed in midstream, the United States would retain its nuclear monopoly while the Soviets would be left with nothing. Since the Russians themselves were working on an atomic bomb, which they successfully exploded in 1949, might not such a program better serve Soviet security interests than internationalization of the atom? The Russians rejected America's proposal.

Six days after Washington floated the Baruch Plan, the Soviets issued a plan of their own. The Kremlin proposal called for pledges to refrain from using nuclear weapons, the destruction of stockpiles, and the establishment of an international agency with very limited powers. This agency would report to the United Nations Security Council, where permanent members could exercise a veto over its activities. Since the Soviet initiative included no dependable inspection and verification arrangements and rested almost entirely on the promises of states, the United States refused to accept it.

NEGOTIATIONS AFTER THE BARUCH PLAN

Not long after these abortive disarmament efforts the Cold War crystallized. As explained in Chapter 2, the United States adopted the policy of containment in 1947. Arms control as a national objective was displaced by military construction, as each superpower sought to counter the perceived threat from the other.

While the prospects for arms control appeared dim, hardly a year passed when one side or the other did not suggest an idea for limiting the weapons of war. Two notable American proposals were the Atoms for Peace Plan (1953) and the Open Skies concept (1955). The formal proposal, enunciated by President Eisenhower before the United Nations General Assembly, called for the creation of an International Atomic Energy Agency (subsequently established), which would serve as a depository for nuclear fuel contributed by the United States and the Soviet Union. The United States achieved a propaganda victory by then contributing nuclear fuel to the new organization, while the Soviets at first refused to do so. In his Open Skies plan, Eisenhower proposed that the United

States and the Soviet Union each be permitted to make aerial surveys of large areas of the other's territory, and that they exchange maps of military installations. With more to hide than the United States, the Soviet Union rejected this proposal, again appearing before the eyes of the world intransigent about arms control.

As each side placed increased reliance upon arms acquisition rather than arms control, each routinely structured its arms control initiatives in such a way that it knew the other would find them unacceptable. The United States invariably insisted on inspection of Soviet territory, knowing that the Russians would not agree. The latter continually called for drastic cuts in armaments without verification, an arrangement Moscow knew Washington found intolerable. Meanwhile, military production kept steadily on.

The Cuban missile crisis marked a turning point in arms control negotiations. As Soviet ships steamed toward the blockade imposed by America around Cuba, the reality of nuclear war was driven home as never before. Up to that point, most people had grown accustomed to living with the prospect of nuclear holocaust, just as one's eyes grow accustomed to the dark. But the "eyeball-to-eyeball" confrontation over Cuba made people everywhere see that a world on the brink of nuclear war was too dangerous a place in which to live. The Cuban missile crisis, the closest the world has yet come to nuclear war, infused new urgency into arms control.

One notable feature of the diplomacy that resolved the missile crisis was direct contact between the two principals, President Kennedy and Chairman Khrushchev. As a result of their mutual trial, the two leaders seemed to develop a certain sympathy for each other. Each realized the necessity of seeing things from the other's perspective. The two leaders also realized how easily a misunderstanding or accident could upset the most carefully contrived agreement. To ensure instant communication in the event of future crisis, the United States and Russia agreed in 1963 to install a "hot line" between the White House and the Kremlin.

The hot line accord was among the first of numerous arms control agreements concluded in the 1960s and 1970s. There were at least three reasons for this unprecedented progress in arms control. The Cuban missile crisis had driven home the need to restrain US-Soviet competition because of the danger of nuclear calamity. Resolution of the missile crisis in itself helped build a certain amount of trust between the superpowers. Scientists achieved breakthroughs in the techniques of verification. Due to advances in aerial photography, satellite surveillance, electronic monitoring and

"SOMEDAY, SON, THIS WILL ALL BE YOURS!"

Paul Conrad, 1982, Los Angeles Times. Reprinted by permission.

seismology, certain kinds of violations could be identified without on-site inspection. For example, the above methods enabled officials to spot craters for new missile silos and detect large nuclear tests without having to be on the scene. Consequently, it became possible to conclude some types of agreements with full confidence that cheating could not go undetected. In the pages that follow, we shall examine some of the agreements concluded as well as those areas of arms control where negotiations remain in progress.

THE PREVENTIVE TREATIES

A number of treaties have been signed with the purpose of preventing arms competition where none presently exists. In addition to insulating these areas from military competition, the treaties have established expectations and prohibitions regarding future conduct.

The first arms control treaty concluded after World War II was the Antarctic Treaty. By the early 1950s some 15 countries were exploring this glacial continent; several had claimed sovereignty over portions of it. Some observers feared that at some time in the future, governments might deem Antarctica suitable for emplacing nuclear weapons. In order to avoid the militarization of Antarctica, the United States in 1959 invited various countries to an international conference. By the end of that year, the delegates had drafted the Antarctic Treaty.

The treaty provides that Antarctica shall be used for peaceful purposes only. It specifically prohibits "any measures of a military nature, such as the establishment of military bases and fortifications, the carrying out of military maneuvers, as well as the testing of any types of weapons." Also prohibited are nuclear explosions and the deposit of nuclear wastes. All parties to the treaty—there are 12 in all, including the United States—may have access at any time to all parts of the continent for peaceful purposes. Furthermore, any party may inspect the installations of any other party, a right the United States has exercised with regard to Soviet and some other stations. No violations of the treaty have been reported.

In the interval between Russia's success in launching the first satellite (Sputnik) in 1957 and America's landing on the moon in 1969, the space age had its origin. The new era brought with it concern that outer space might become the battlefield of the future. In September 1960, President Eisenhower, in a speech delivered at the United Nations, proposed the demilitarization of outer space, modeled on the Antarctic Treaty. After a series of tortuous negotiations, the Outer Space Treaty was concluded in 1967.[8] Over 90 nations, including the United States and the Soviet Union, have signed it.

According to the treaty, signatories agree not to place in orbit around the earth, install on the moon or any other celestial body, or otherwise station in outer space nuclear or any other "weapons of mass destruction." The agreement also limits the use of the moon and other celestial bodies to peaceful purposes.

By proscribing only weapons of mass destruction, as opposed to weapons of any type, the treaty does not totally foreclose the use of outer space for military purposes. Antisatellite satellites, or "killer satellites," do not qualify as weapons of mass destruction, nor do lasers capable of shooting down ballistic missiles. Military communication and reconnaissance satellites revolve in outer space; the treaty does not outlaw them. Should the American space shuttle carry military equipment, as more than one government official has stated would be the case, this type of military activity will not be banned. As one can easily see, the Outer Space Treaty hardly forbids all military activity in outer space.

Like the Antarctic Treaty and the Outer Space Treaty, the Treaty for the Prohibition of Nuclear Weapons in Latin America seeks to prevent the spread of nuclear weapons to an area where they are not located. As opposed to the other two treaties, the Latin American treaty—often termed the Treaty of Tlatelolco after the section of Mexico City where it was finalized in 1967—applies to a populated region.

The parties to the treaty—Cuba and Argentina have yet to sign—agree to use their nuclear facilities exclusively for peaceful purposes. The agreement further obliges them not to receive, produce, store, test or use nuclear weapons. The parties agree to arrange with the International Atomic Energy Agency (IAEA) for application of its safeguards to their peaceful nuclear activities, such as nuclear reactors for electric power. The treaty also establishes an organization to assure compliance and to undertake inspections under special circumstances.

Two protocols accompany the treaty. These regulate the activities of nuclear weapons states, which are all located outside Latin America. Protocol I calls on nations outside the treaty zone to apply the denuclearization provisions of the treaty to their possessions inside the zone. The United States, whose possessions include the Canal Zone, the Guantanamo Naval Base in Cuba, the Virgin Islands, and Puerto Rico, signed Protocol I in 1977.

In Protocol II, nuclear-weapons states agree to respect the denuclearized status of the zone, to refrain from encouraging signatories to violate the treaty, and to refrain from using or threatening to use nuclear weapons against the contracting parties. France, the United Kingdom, the United States and China have consented to Protocol II; the Soviet Union has not.

On balance, the Treaty of Tlatelolco appears to advance the security interests of the United States. It prohibits Latin American states, with the important exception of Cuba, from inviting outside powers to deploy nuclear weapons in their territories. The treaty also contributes to halting the spread of nuclear weapons by requiring IAEA safeguards on all nuclear materials and facilities belonging to the contracting parties. While it has yet to occur, some persons are hopeful that the Latin America treaty can serve as a model for the creation of other nuclear weapons free zones, particularly in Africa and the Indian Ocean.

The fourth preventive treaty concerns the seabed. Oceanographic advances in the 1960s promised to make available the vast untapped resources of the ocean floor. These developments also aroused fears that some nations might use the seabed for military purposes. International regulation of the seabed was called for, as many people proclaimed that the seas were the common heritage of all humankind.

In 1969 the Soviet Union presented a draft treaty to the United Nations General Assembly, which had established an *ad hoc* committee to consider the reservation of the seabed for peaceful purposes. This draft called for the complete demilitarization of the seabed beyond a 12-mile limit. The United States found a total demilitarization of the seabed objectionable, as it would preclude submarine surveillance systems affixed to the ocean floor. Washington submitted a draft of its own, following which there were intensive negotiations by many states for two years. Finally, in 1971 an acceptable treaty emerged.

The Seabed Arms Control Treaty of 1971 prohibits the signatories from emplacing nuclear weapons and other weapons of mass destruction on the seabed and ocean floor beyond a 12-mile coastal zone. Inside 12 miles nations may do as they please. Like the Outer Space Treaty, the Seabed Treaty allows for military uses of the seabed that do not involve weapons of mass destruction. The United States ratified the Seabed Treaty in 1972.

NUCLEAR TESTING

The control and elimination of nuclear testing has been an objective of arms control since the 1950s. During that decade the United States and the Soviet Union developed hydrogen bombs with yields in the millions of tons of TNT. Radioactive fallout from the explosions of such weapons threatened whoever happened to lie in the direction of the winds prevailing at the time. Many scientists sounded alarms about the cumulative efforts of nuclear tests upon the environment. Another motive for restricting nuclear testing has to do with a long-standing objective of American policy, halting the spread of nuclear weapons.

A treaty prohibiting nuclear tests would exert substantial pressure on all nations, including nonsignatories, against such tests. Since any nation would be extremely reluctant to base its security upon untested weapons, a test ban would help curb the spread of nuclear weapons.

During the 1950s the United States and the Soviet Union began to discuss a nuclear test ban. From the start, however, the negotiations foundered on a recurrent obstacle in US-Russian arms control talks, namely, verification. Soviet proposals generally lacked verification provisions acceptable to Washington, particularly on-site inspection. The United States continued to believe that, as an open society, it would have trouble cheating, but that the Soviets were under no comparable restraint. No technology existed for distinguishing between earthquakes and nuclear tests that registered below 4.75 on the Richter scale. Finally, in 1963, the United States, the United Kingdom and the Soviet Union agreed upon a treaty that would ban nuclear tests in the atmosphere, under water and in outer space, three environments where existing technology permitted unambiguous identification of nuclear explosions without on-site inspection. This accord is known as the Limited Test Ban Treaty (LTBT). The LTBT is "limited" in that it does not ban tests underground. Over 100 countries have ratified the accord, important exceptions being China and France.

At the time of its signing, the LTBT was hailed worldwide as a milestone in the effort to control the spread of nuclear weapons and as a safeguard to the environment. From today's vantage point, the second accomplishment appears much more substantial than the first. It can be argued that the LTBT achieved little more than to drive tests underground. Indeed, more tests have been conducted underground since 1963 than were previously carried out above ground.

Recognizing the limitations of the LTBT, the parties to the agreement stated their intention to pursue a comprehensive test ban. Few achievements were recorded until 1974, when the United States and the Soviet Union negotiated the Threshold Test Ban Treaty (TTBT). This agreement is so named because it establishes a threshold by prohibiting tests having a yield exceeding 150 kilotons (equivalent to 150 thousand tons of TNT).

The Threshold Test Ban Treaty is notable, because for the first time each party agreed to make available to the other important scientific information to assist in verification. The treaty limits testing to certain designated sites. The data to be exchanged include information on the geology of these sites, including density of rock formations, water saturation, and depth of the water table. This information helps in verifying test yields, because the seismic signal produced by an underground explosion varies with these factors. The treaty also provides that the two governments will exchange data on a certain number of tests for calibration purposes. By establishing correlations between yields and seismic signals produced at specific sites, the two governments can gain confidence in being able to tell from seismic monitoring stations the size of nuclear explosions. Washington, however, remains unsatisfied that these arrangements suffice to detect violations of the 150 kiloton limit and so has yet to ratify the treaty.

In negotiating the TTBT, both parties recognized the difficulties in distinguishing between weapons tests and a series of peaceful nuclear explosions in rapid succession, such as might be required for digging a river channel or reservoir. Two years of negotiations on this subject resulted in the Treaty on Underground Nuclear Explosions for Peaceful Purposes (PNET). This agreement was signed in 1976 but has yet to be ratified by the United States, again for reasons of verification.

The PNET places an aggregate ceiling of 1,500 kilotons on a group of peaceful nuclear explosions, that is, two or more explosions within five seconds for nonmilitary purposes. The central verification problem of a series of explosions is insurance that no single explosion exceeds the 150 kiloton limit set in the Threshold Test Ban Treaty. This is to be accomplished through the exchange of data and also by permitting observers on the scene. For the first time, the PNET provides for on-site inspection, albeit within very narrow limits. The PNET, together with the TTBT, establishes a comprehensive system of regulations to govern underground nuclear explosions by the United States and the Soviet Union.

While the three treaties described thus far—the LTBT, TTBT, and PNET—set boundaries for nuclear testing, they still permit nuclear tests underground below 150 kilotons. This permits the nuclear nations to test new and improved weapons, thus accelerating the arms race. It also allows nations presently without nuclear weapons to develop and test them. These treaties, for all the good they accomplish, still do not bar the door to nuclear weapons proliferation. It is for this reason that some arms control specialists assert the need for a comprehensive test ban (CTB) that would prohibit all nuclear tests.

Not everyone is enthusiastic about a CTB, however.[9] Particularly in the Pentagon, there is a strong feeling that a CTB would not serve American interests. Without periodic tests, some weapons experts feel, the United States could not be confident in the reliability of its weapons stockpile. In the absence of tests, there

---

The negotiation and implementation aspects of arms control agreements, because of their potential for promoting and institutionalizing relationships of trust, are equally important to, if not more important than, the military weaponry and force-level features of these agreements.

R. Goldman, *Arms Control and Peacekeeping*, page 230

---

would be no reliable way to develop improved warheads for use in such systems as the MX and Trident strategic missiles and various tactical nuclear systems slated for deployment in Europe. (This is one of the reasons why arms controllers support a CTB.) CTB opponents further assert that it would be difficult to maintain America's scientific-technical capabilities in weapons design if tests could not be conducted. Weapons scientists would switch to other fields where their research could be validated. Should the Soviets achieve a technical breakthrough, the departure of American scientists from weapons design would compound the task of catching up. Other opponents of a CTB worry about verification. While opinion is not united, some weapons experts aver that it is possible to "hide" an underground explosion up to 10 kilotons (nearly the size of the Hiroshima bomb) within an earthquake. Some writers have gone so far as to state that tests up to 100 kilotons could be conducted clandestinely and be made to look like an earthquake.[10] CTB advocates acknowledge the possibility of cheating, but they ask whether the deceiver could learn enough from testing before discovery and equivalent tests by the other side.

To meet the above objections to a CTB, some specialists have proposed a treaty that would permit a certain number of tests annually with low yields.[11] Such a treaty would permit verification of weapons reliability, allow for the improvement of warheads, keep scientists in weapons design, and prevent either side from achieving a destabilizing technical breakthrough while the other refrains from testing. If the number of tests permitted were very low, say two or three each year, significant improvement in weapons would be impeded, one of the objectives of arms control.

Despite objections from the Pentagon and the Department of Energy (which conducts nuclear weapons tests for the US government), the United States in 1977 entered into negotiations with the

Soviet Union and the United Kingdom for a comprehensive test ban. By 1980, when the talks were suspended so the Reagan administration could formulate its own position, the parties had agreed on several points. Ten seismic monitors would be placed in both the United States and the Soviet Union. In a major concession, the Soviets agreed to forego peaceful nuclear explosions in return for American consent to conduct joint studies on the possibility of staging peaceful nuclear explosions without serving arms developments. The Soviets also accepted on-site inspection in the event that seismic stations provided strong evidence of a treaty violation. Dissatisfied by these verification provisions, the Reagan administration had not resumed CTB negotiations as of late 1984.

PROLIFERATION OF NUCLEAR WEAPONS

Virtually every presidential administration since the dawn of the atomic age has sought to restrict the number of states that possess nuclear weapons. Today, five nations besides the United States have conducted nuclear explosions: China, France, India, the Soviet Union and the United Kingdom. The American intelligence community believes Israel has the capacity to build nuclear weapons and has either assembled some or is "within a screwdriver's turn" of doing so.[12] Scientists have also identified about a dozen "threshold states," that is, states with the technology to build a nuclear bomb in the near future. States normally included in this category are Canada, Italy, South Africa, South Korea, Taiwan, Japan, Iran, Brazil, Iraq, Pakistan, Australia, Syria, Egypt, Argentina, Sweden, Switzerland and West Germany. The day may not be far off when terrorist groups and organized criminal gangs are able to obtain nuclear bombs, either through purchase or stealth or even as a gift from a government sympathetic to their aims. There are, of course, many reasons why a state might want to acquire nuclear weapons. A study prepared by the Hudson Institute in 1976 categorized these reasons as follows:

Security
deterrence of nuclear rival
defense against invasion
weapon of last resort
intimidation of nonnuclear rival(s)
buttress of bargaining position

Status or Influence
quest for regional or international status
demonstrate national viability
fashion

Bureaucratic Factors
strengthen military, scientific and/or bureaucratic morale
scientific-bureaucratic momentum
pressures from a military-industrial complex
bureaucratic politics within governments and/or armed services

Domestic Politics
strengthen domestic morale
divert domestic attention away from foreign or internal problems

The study also cited constraints on the decision to go nuclear, such as cost, a limited technological and industrial base, unwanted dependence upon foreign nuclear assistance, domestic public opposition, the risk of unauthorized seizure of weapons, difficulty in developing a credible nuclear strategy, and the reactions of regional opponents and allies.[13] Only time will reveal which will prevail, incentives or constraints, for those nations capable of building nuclear weapons.

A government may obtain a weapon either by purchase, grant or stealth, or it can acquire the technology and material to build a bomb of its own. Each method suggests different safeguards to be taken by those who seek to prevent the spread of nuclear weapons.

The Nuclear Fuel Cycle

Building a nuclear bomb requires two elements, the technology to construct a nuclear device and the "fuel" or explosive material that produces a nuclear reaction. The first of these is now in the public domain, as demonstrated by a Princeton University undergraduate who designed an atomic bomb based on open sources. (His design was subsequently classified.) For the second ingredient, either "enriched" uranium or plutonium may be used. As neither of these substances is found in nature, each must be manufactured. Natural uranium may be enriched in special enrichment plants. Plutonium, as well as unenriched uranium, may be recovered from the "ashes" of spent fuel burned in reactors. This can be accomplished in expensive units known as reprocessing plants. Approximately 10 kilograms of plutonium or 20 kilograms of highly enriched uranium are needed to build an atomic bomb. A kilogram equals 2.2046 pounds.

After the oil shortages and fuel price increases of the 1970s, more and more countries have decided to free themselves from oil dependence by turning to nuclear energy. As more countries take this route, the likelihood of nuclear proliferation is bound to rise.

The problem is further compounded by a new type of reactor known as the breeder reactor. The reactor is so-called because while consuming fuel it "breeds" or creates useable fuel as it operates, as though an automobile engine were to manufacture more gasoline as it continued to run. The breeder reactor accomplishes this by "breeding" plutonium from the nonfissionable (nonexplosive) U–238 isotope of uranium that comprises 99 percent of uranium in its natural form. This plutonium can then be used as additional fuel for the reactor. It is estimated that the breeder reactor can increase the energy output of natural uranium by 20 or 30 times. Breeder technology has obvious appeal in a world of energy scarcity. This appeal is further enhanced when one takes into account the fact that uranium, like oil, is in finite supply. As appealing as the breeder reactor might be from an energy standpoint, it is no less frightful in the context of nuclear proliferation. The plutonium bred by the reactor is eminently appropriate for making atomic bombs. It is for this reason that President Carter announced that the United States would not build a breeder reactor and would urge other countries not to do so. (None has been built yet.) Certain European countries who are less energy sufficient than the United States have stated, however, that they planned to go ahead and build breeder reactors. The dispute has yet to be resolved.

American Policy

As stated above, the United States opposes the proliferation of nuclear weapons. This opposition has usually taken the form of curbs on the transfer of weapons themselves.[14] For many years, the United States has been the foremost exporter of nuclear technology for "peaceful purposes." The United States has trained over 13 thousand foreign scientists in atomic energy. America supplies nearly all the non-Communist world's uranium for use in reactors. While exports of nuclear reactors have slowed in recent years, the United States has been the world's leading supplier of these power plants. Approximately 250 nuclear reactors were in operation worldwide in 1980. In 1976, ACDA estimated that a 1,000 megawatt nuclear reactor could produce material for 10–100 nuclear weapons annually, depending on the type of reactor and assuming the use of enrichment and reprocessing.[15] With so many nuclear reactors, the possibilities for diversion of material to weapons is alarmingly high. The United States clearly bears much of the responsibility for this situation. The Soviet Union, by contrast, has been extremely cautious in exporting nuclear technology and materials. How did the current situation come about?

By 1950 nuclear power appeared to be a feasible supplement to existing forms of energy. Despite admonitions to the contrary, the United States acted on the premise that it was possible to promote nuclear technology for peaceful purposes while preventing the diversion of nuclear material to weapons construction. In 1953 President Eisenhower announced the Atoms for Peace program, a design to disseminate peaceful nuclear knowledge worldwide. Toward this end, the United States trained foreign scientists in nuclear technology and sold or gave nuclear reactors to other countries. In return, the United States insisted the recipients promise to use this technology for peaceful purposes only. As the sole nuclear

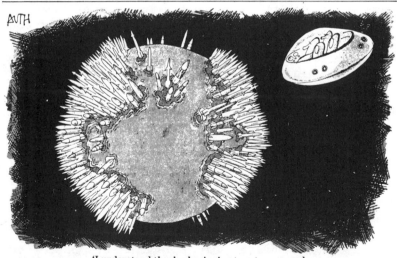

'I understand they're beginning to get concerned
about nuclear proliferation.'

Reprinted by permission of Tony Auth.

exporter, Washington was in a position to enforce this demand. In order to ensure that governments were keeping their pledges, the International Atomic Energy Agency (IAEA) was created in 1957 under the United Nations to inspect nuclear facilities. The IAEA also helped diffuse nuclear technology through training programs, conferences and publications.

By the early 1960s an international nuclear regime was taking shape. Nonweapons states appealed for technological assistance and nuclear fuel in return for pledges not to build weapons. This arrangement was codified in the Non-Proliferation Treaty (NPT), opened for signature in 1968. Under this accord, to be described in more detail later, nuclear-weapons states promised not to provide weapons or the know-how to build them to nonweapons states. The latter agreed not to acquire nuclear weapons. Adherence to the treaty has been far from universal. On the supplier side, France and China have not signed. Numerous threshold states too have not signed, including Israel, Brazil, South Africa, Pakistan, and Argentina. The IAEA was designated to police the NPT. The agency has developed safeguards and inspection schedules to apply to the nuclear facilities of nonweapons signatories. The adequacy of the IAEA's performance will be discussed henceforth.

The diversion of nuclear material for military purposes was little discussed outside specialist circles until India exploded a nuclear device in 1974. The Indian explosion highlighted the inadequacies of an international nuclear regime in which the suppliers acted largely without coordination. The Indian reactor that produced the explosive material had been supplied by Canada, but the heavy water required for its operation came from the United States. The reprocessing plant used to separate the spent fuel was built by the Indians themselves. Like other importers, India had pledged to use its nuclear facilities only for peaceful purposes. Indeed, India defended its nuclear explosion by contending that it merely wanted to perfect the technique in case of future need for nonmilitary purposes. The United States was incensed. In the American view, a nuclear explosion is a nuclear explosion, and it hardly matters whether it be used to build a reservoir or level a city.

Since the Indian episode, the number of nuclear suppliers has grown. France, West Germany, Great Britain and Japan are now in a position to export reactors, reprocessing and enrichment plants. There are ready markets for these items, as countries wish to free themselves from reliance on foreign sources for nuclear fuel. France arranged to sell reprocessing plants to South Korea and Pakistan, although American pressure led to renunciation of the deals. West Germany has sold an enrichment and a reprocessing plant to Brazil.

As more sellers and buyers entered the international nuclear trade, the likelihood of imposing controls was diminishing. In response to this situation, the primary suppliers of nuclear technology began meeting in 1975 as the Nuclear Suppliers Group. The key members among this group of 15 states are the United Kingdom, France, West Germany, Japan and the United States. The Nuclear Suppliers Group has tried to evolve common policies governing the export of nuclear materials, with a view toward curbing nuclear weapons proliferation. These countries have agreed to impose stricter safeguards and exercise some restraint in exporting equipment that can be used to make weapons. While all the members are in accord on this objective, they have not always been able to agree on common actions. One proposal that was not accepted was a requirement that importers accept full-scope IAEA safeguards on all their nuclear facilities. Lacking sizable domestic markets, some of the Europeans, France in particular, insist they need to export in order for their nuclear industry just to break even. Accordingly, they have resisted American calls for tighter restraints. The Nuclear Suppliers Group continues to meet about once a year in the hope of concerting its policies.

Even the United States has not found it easy to apply nuclear restraints. In 1978 Congress passed the Nuclear Non-Proliferation Act. This legislation requires the cutoff, after 24 months, of all nuclear exports—materials, facilities and technology—to non-weapons states that refuse to permit IAEA monitoring of all their nuclear facilities. The act further provides that, subject to congressional veto, the president can waive these restrictions in particular cases. An opportunity to apply the policy arose in respect to India.

In 1963 the United States agreed to supply enriched uranium to India's nuclear reactor at Tarapur for 30 years. For its part, India agreed to open the Tarapur reactor to international inspection and not to reprocess spent fuel from that reactor. India has abided by this agreement. However, India has never agreed to admit IAEA inspectors to all its nuclear facilities, and it has refused to promise not to manufacture nuclear weapons (on the ground that such a pledge is unfair so long as other states have such weapons). In 1980 India applied for another fuel shipment under the 1963 agreement. The Nuclear Regulatory Commission, which passes on such applications, refused to approve the Indian request, citing the Non-Proliferation Act. President Carter, however, asserted that other foreign policy factors outweighed the nonproliferation issue and he overruled the NRC. Congress failed to overturn the president's decision by only two votes. President Carter, one of the most ardent advocates of arms control to occupy the White House, pointed out the need to avoid antagonizing India at a time when Soviet troops were occupying India's neighbor Afghanistan. Furthermore, Carter said, cutting off American nuclear aid to India would eliminate whatever leverage Washington possessed over India's nuclear power industry. Finally, the president averred, halting the fuel shipment would free India from its obligations to admit IAEA inspectors to the Tarapur facility and refrain from reprocessing Tarapur's spent fuel. President Carter allowed the sale, and the United States shipped 38 tons of enriched uranium to Tarapur. The incident starkly reveals the competing nature of foreign policy objectives, even when one of them is limiting the spread of nuclear weapons.

President Reagan announced his policy toward nuclear proliferation in July 1981.[16] This statement differed sharply from the stance taken by candidate Ronald Reagan. At a campaign news conference in January 1980, he said the United States should not stand in the way of countries that sought to acquire nuclear weapons. "I just don't think it's any of our business," Mr. Reagan declared.[17] After six months in office, however, President Reagan declared himself opposed to the spread of nuclear weapons. His strategy for accomplishing this objective differs somewhat from that of Jimmy Carter. President Reagan said that in order to reduce the incentive to go nuclear, the United States would take a sympathetic view toward selling conventional arms to states that feel threatened, such as Pakistan. President Carter, it will be recalled, declared that the United States already was too generous an arms supplier. The Reagan announcement also said that the United States must be a reliable nuclear supplier to countries who observe international safeguards. By being able to count on American supplies, these countries will not have to engage in enrichment or reprocessing. Like Jimmy Carter, President Reagan mentioned the need to cooperate with other suppliers to prevent the transfer of technology and material where such transfer carries the risk of conversion to nuclear weapons; we have already seen how difficult it is to obtain such cooperation. The new president also called for heightened intelligence to detect weapons-related activity and more support for the IAEA. President Reagan also relaxed American opposition to the breeder reactor, saying that Washington would not object to its use in Europe, where the danger of weapons diversion is low.

The Non-Proliferation Treaty

The principal document that codifies global nuclear transfers is the previously mentioned Non-Proliferation Treaty (NPT) concluded in 1968. As of 1981, 115 nations had signed the NPT. Among nuclear-weapons states, China, India and France refuse to sign. Certain threshold states also have not signed, including Argentina, Brazil, Israel, Pakistan and South Africa.

The NPT directs states possessing nuclear weapons not to provide them to nonweapons states. The latter agree not to acquire nuclear weapons. To meet complaints voiced by some nonweapons states that the treaty requires the nuclear-weapons states to give up nothing, while depriving other states from developing nuclear weapons, Article VI obliges the nuclear-weapons states to negotiate an end to the nuclear arms race and strive for general and complete disarmament. Considering the pace of the nuclear arms race since 1968, is it any wonder that some nonweapons states feel bitter about the NPT?

The IAEA, which was given responsibility for policing the treaty, is a source of some controversy concerning its capacity to detect the diversion of nuclear material to weapons construction. The organization relies on approximately 140 inspectors from different nations. These investigators periodically visit nuclear plants, audit their records to make certain all materials are accounted for, and make their own measurements of material to see that these records are accurate. The IAEA also uses cameras and seals to detect the removal of material between inspections or the introduction of unauthorized material. What unsettles some proliferation specialists are the limitations placed upon the IAEA. The organization's inspectors may examine only those facilities a country agrees to open. The inspectors have no authority to search a country for hidden weapons or assembly plants. In accordance with the concept of national sovereignty, the IAEA normally gives advance notice of an inspection. Governments even have the right to request inspectors from certain countries. Should the IAEA uncover violations, it has no power to enforce compliance or carry out punishment. It can do no more than bring infractions to the attention of the world public.

These restrictions have led some critics to describe the IAEA as more of an accounting agency than a policing agency. A 1981 study by the US Nuclear Regulatory Commission, written by a former IAEA inspector, concludes that the IAEA is "incapable of detecting the diversion of a significant quantity" of nuclear fuel "in any state with a moderate to large nuclear energy establishment."[18] The report maintains that the international agency does not regularly and promptly compare shipments of nuclear fuel on arrival and departure; that some of the seals are fabricated of paper and are easily counterfeited or duplicated; that cameras occasionally malfunction; and that the photographs are sometimes blurry. In bombing Iraq's Osirik nuclear reactor in 1981, Israel unequivocally expressed its lack of faith in the IAEA.

Controlling Proliferation

Concern about nuclear proliferation has led to numerous proposals for preventing the further spread of nuclear weapons. Most of these suggestions aim at precluding the diversion of nuclear material from peaceful uses, as this is the most likely source of proliferation.

Since enrichment and reprocessing represent stages in the fuel cycle where diversion is most easily accomplished, some specialists have suggested internationalization of these activities. In other words, an international authority, operating under rigid safeguards, would enrich and reprocess fuel for individual countries, for a fee. A recurrent problem with such schemes is establishing a nonpolitical international body to conduct the operations. Opponents of an international nuclear regime cite the United Nations and its alleged prejudice against Western nations and such states as Israel and South Africa in arguing that an unbiased organization lies beyond the realm of possibility.

Not all spent reactor fuel is reprocessed. Some of it is just stored away. Here lies another danger point in the nuclear fuel cycle. The hazard lies not just in the extreme radioactivity of the spent fuel, but in the possibility that it could be stolen, reprocessed, and used in a bomb. To meet this contingency, some specialists have proposed international storage of spent fuel, again under rigid safeguards.

Another approach to curbing proliferation concerns incentives rather than capabilities. Might it not be possible to alter the conviction of states that they must have nuclear weapons in order to accomplish their international objectives? A number of measures have been proposed. One envisions guarantees by nuclear-weapons states of the integrity of nonweapons states against attack. Armed with such guarantees, a state might forego acquisition of nuclear weapons of its own. Another proposal calls for severe punishment

By permission of Johnny Hart and Field Enterprises, Inc.

of a state that employs nuclear weapons for aggressive purposes. Should the offending state possess a large nuclear arsenal, such punishment might entail unacceptable costs. Furthermore, few states would be eager for the opportunity to inflict penalties, especially of a military nature. Both of these schemes would seem to require far more cooperation in the international community than is presently found. Furthermore, so long as current nuclear-weapons states continue to prize their atomic arsenals, why should nonweapons states be expected to lack motivation for acquiring nuclear weapons?

To conclude, the prospects for halting the spread of nuclear weapons do not seem bright. Occasionally, an influential state like America might be able to dissuade a government from building an enrichment plant or reprocessing facility, as was the case with South Korea. Washington threatened to cut off military assistance if South

Korea went ahead. But international governance of nuclear affairs seems no more likely than international regulation of the arms trade. Between Hiroshima and the Indian nuclear explosion of 1974, a new nuclear state came into being every five years, on average. There is little reason to believe that this rate will decline.

CONTROLLING CHEMICAL AND BIOLOGICAL WEAPONS

Since World War I, chemical and biological weapons have been joined in the public mind. This is due to the widespread and acute suffering that each causes. In reality, the two types of weapons are not identical. Biological weapons disperse living organisms, usually bacteria or viruses, and produce casualties by spreading disease. Biological weapons can be targeted against people, vegetation, animals, and water supplies. Chemical weapons cause casualties by contact with deadly chemicals, usually nerve gas. Chemical weapons do not produce epidemics; only persons who come in contact with the chemicals are affected. Chemical weapons may also be targeted against vegetation, as illustrated by American defoliation strikes in Vietnam. The Geneva Protocol of 1925 prohibited both types of warfare. In the 1960s, several proposals were introduced at the United Nations Eighteen Nation Disarmament Commission and its successor, the Conference of the Committee on Disarmament, to ban chemical and biological weapons. None of these initiatives led to any agreements, however.

While chemical weapons have been used in modern warfare, biological weapons have not. The United States used biological warfare during the nineteenth century in trading infected blankets to Indian tribes. A number of armies possess chemical warfare stocks as well as doctrines for their use. In contrast, few military establishments store biological weapons.

Biological warfare never gained as many adherents as did chemical warfare. This is because epidemics are hard to control; they do not respect the political formalities that prevail at border crossings. As there are few defenses against biological warfare, the initiator may expect to suffer as grievously as the target. While the effects of chemical weapons can be largely confined to the battlefield, biological weapons strike combatants and civilians alike.

Shortly after taking office, President Nixon ordered a review of American chemical and biological warfare policies. On

November 25, 1969, the president renounced the first use of lethal or incapacitating chemical agents and all forms of biological warfare.

In 1972, US-Soviet talks yielded the Biological Weapons Convention, which has been signed by nearly 120 nations. The Biological Weapons Convention prohibits the development, production, stockpiling or acquisition of biological weapons. It also requires the destruction of existing stocks, a measure Washington has taken. Under Article 9 of the Biological Weapons Convention, each party recognized the desirability of negotiating an accord limiting chemical weapons and pledged to work toward this goal. In 1976 negotiations began.

Among the various problems associated with a chemical arms control agreement, verification looms largest. Many chemicals, such as chlorine and phosgene, have nonmilitary as well as weapons uses. Consequently, it is not desirable to ban the production of such chemicals but only their use in weapons. Without constant surveillance of chemical stocks, it is virtually impossible to be certain of their disposition, and no country is receptive to the presence of inspectors at all its chemical plants and storage facilities. Satellite photography cannot reveal what is being made inside chemical plants the way such reconnaissance can spot missile silos.

Should countries agree to destroy their chemical weapons stockpiles, verification would be no easy task. It is far easier to conceal chemical weapons than to hide nuclear submarines. The precise extent of each nation's stockpile is not known, so even destruction in the presence of inspectors would not guarantee total elimination of chemical weapons. Since it is relatively simple and quick to insert chemicals into bombs and artillery shells, even the elimination of existing chemical weapons would not ensure against the fabrication of new ones.

However, as Herbert Scoville, Jr., has pointed out, even a partially verifiable agreement may be useful.[19] While such an accord may not provide fool-proof guarantees against cheating, it would probably deter deception on the large scale required to produce a significant margin in warfare. Scoville maintains that intelligence would probably be able to detect a major buildup of chemical weapons.

A partially verifiable accord could inspire more confidence if accompanied by certain confidence-building measures. For example, states that presently conduct troop training in chemical warfare attacks could abolish such exercises. They could also eliminate training with protective clothing and masks and disband separate chemical corps. The mothballing of detoxification equipment might also generate confidence that said country no longer planned to use chemical weapons.

Another difficulty in US-Soviet chemical warfare negotiations concerns incentives. The United States, it would seem, has more to gain from a chemical arms control agreement than the Soviets. This asymmetry can be traced to a far greater integration of chemical warfare into Soviet military training and doctrine. As described in the previous chapter, Soviet forces have much larger chemical weapons stocks and conduct far more extensive chemical warfare training than American soldiers. Accordingly, the Soviets would have much more to give up in the case of an agreement. Psychological factors further complicate the issue. By most accounts, the West feels more constrained than the Soviets about using chemical weapons, especially if they are to be employed in highly urbanized Western Europe. Western Europe's reluctance even to store chemical weapons further diminishes Moscow's desire to sign an arms accord. For all practical purposes the West, particularly Western Europe, has unilaterally disarmed in the chemical arena. Why should Moscow yield its advantage by signing a treaty?

Partly to alter the Kremlin's outlook, the United States has taken steps toward resuming production of chemical weapons, after a lapse dating back to 1969. In 1980, Congress voted $3.15 million for a plant, now under construction, designed to produce a new generation of nerve gas. Only the president is empowered to give the order to actually produce chemical weapons, and no such directive has been issued as yet. Proponents of renewing production maintain that Russia has an 8:1 lead over the United States in chemical munitions, that Soviet weapons are newer and more sophisticated than American weapons, and that the American stockpile—estimated at 150 thousand tons, two-thirds of which is nerve gas placed in three million artillery shells[20]—will seriously deteriorate by 1990. US-Soviet discussions on banning chemical weapons are currently taking place in the Geneva-based United Nations Committee on Disarmament. Verification difficulties have so far prevented this 40-member body from completing an agreement.

ARMS CONTROL IN EUROPE

As the central theater in the East-West contest, Europe has been the subject of numerous arms control initiatives. Two in particular merit consideration.

Mutual and Balanced Force Reductions (MBFR)

East-West negotiations to reduce troop strength in Central Europe have been going on since 1973, with agreement yet to be reached.[21] From the outset, two issues have beleaguered these discussions, known as Mutual and Balanced Force Reductions talks (MBFR). Most important, the two sides have been unable to agree on the number of troops currently stationed in the area of deployment (see Fig. 12–1). Failing such consensus, it has been impossible to move toward force reductions. The East claims to have 805 thousand active duty troops in Central Europe; the West insists the correct figure is 962 thousand, based on intelligence reports. Both sides accept a count of 791 thousand for Western troop strength. The disparity over Eastern troop counts has prevented progress on force reductions to reach the agreed ceiling of 700 thousand troops for each side. Using Western figures, the East would have to reduce its forces by 262 thousand; using Eastern data, the required cut would be only 105 thousand. Put differently, the West wants the East to draw down by 262 thousand, while the West is willing to reduce by 91 thousand. The Soviets insist on equal cuts. No resolution of this impasse appears in sight.

The second issue impeding agreement concerns various asymmetries between Eastern and Western force compositions and objectives. Geography accounts for some of these imbalances. Russia lies on the periphery of Central Europe, while America sits across an ocean. In consequence, Moscow could bring its withdrawn forces to bear much quicker than Washington in case of a flare-up in Europe. When this fact is coupled with Western perceptions of Eastern numerical superiority, it is easy to understand the West's fear of surprise attack. This uneasiness explains why the West refuses to accept the East's proposals for equal troop cuts and demands greater reductions by the East. Western anxiety is further fueled by Eastern superiority in tanks, tactical aircraft and, now, intermediate-range nuclear missiles such as the SS–20. In Western eyes, a major accomplishment of MBFR should be to eliminate the East's advantage so as to reduce the likelihood of surprise attack. To the East, of course, things look different. Taking into account NATO's forces both in and around Central Europe—including the American Sixth Fleet in the Mediterranean—the East insists that parity exists, and that this parity has preserved the peace. To reduce its forces by as much as the West demands, Moscow claims, would only tempt the West to launch an attack on Communist Europe.

FIGURE 12-1: REDUCTION OF GROUND TROOP LEVELS IN EUROPE

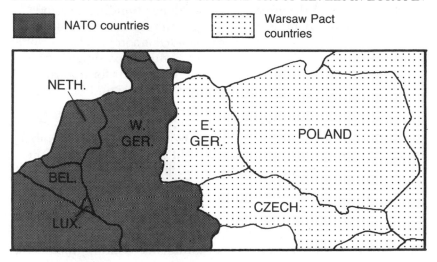

	NATO COUNTRIES	WARSAW PACT COUNTRIES	
		U.S. Count:	Soviet Count:
1982 Levels	**791,000**	**962,000**	**805,000**
Reagan Proposal	**—Reduce to common ceiling of 700,000**		

Citing the seemingly insurmountable obstacles to force reductions, Leslie Gelb, a high State Department official in the Carter administration, has suggested a shift of emphasis away from troop withdrawals and in the direction of confidence-building measures.[22] Confidence-building measures enhance stability by reducing fears of surprise attack and risks of other misunderstandings. They include prior notification of large troop movements (exceeding 25 thousand); designation of specified entry and exit points for troops, with inspectors present to check on numbers entering and leaving the MBFR zone; and exchange visits of military personnel.

John G. Keliher suggests force realignments instead of reductions.[23] Troops in the MBFR area, regardless of their number, would be configured for defense only, in Keliher's proposal. Permitted forces would include lightly armed border guards, mechanized (as opposed to armored) reconnaissance units, and motorized infantry equipped with portable antitank weapons. No units equipped with tanks, armored personnel carriers, artillery, armed helicopters or other primarily offensive weapons would be allowed. These restrictions, combined with confidence-building measures, would eliminate the fear of surprise attack and might pave the way for future troop cuts, Keliher believes.

The prospects for progress on MBFR continue to appear dim.

Nuclear Arms Control in Europe

The second major European arms control negotiations concern tactical nuclear forces. These weapons fall between strategic nuclear weapons, already covered in SALT, and the conventional forces that are the subject of MBFR. Current emphasis focuses upon immediate-range (1–4 thousand miles) nuclear missiles and aircraft capable of delivering nuclear bombs and missiles. The United States and the Soviet Union entered into negotiations to limit these weapons in November 1981.

As in the case of MBFR, the primary stumbling block to an accord lies in failure to agree on existing force levels. Table 12–1 reveals these discrepancies. According to American tallies, the Warsaw Pact fields 2,537 launchers and 3,787 warheads. The East says it has 1,055 launchers and 2,035 warheads. Taking the Soviet tally as shown in Table 12–1, the two sides are essentially equal in terms of launchers, while the East has more warheads. Using this data, the East insists that the two sides have approximate parity in TNF and should proceed to negotiate equal cuts. Citing the US tally in

TABLE 12-1: TWO VIEWS OF THEATER NUCLEAR FORCES IN EUROPE

US Tally

WESTERN ALLIES		WARSAW PACT	
American			
F-111 fighter-bombers	156	Backfire bombers	65
FB-111A fighter-bombers*	60	Badger bombers	310
F-4 fighter-bombers	244	Blinder bombers	125
A-6/A-7 fighter-bombers	33	Fencer fighter-bombers	480
Pershing-1 missiles	108	Flogger-D fighter-bombers	500
Subtotal	601	SS-20 missiles	270
		SS-4 missiles	340
Allied		SS-5 missiles	40
British Polaris missiles	64	SS-12 missiles	350
French submarine missiles	80	SS-N-5 missiles	57
French land-based missiles	18	**Total**	2,537
British Vulcan bombers	56		
French Mirage-4 bombers	33		
German Pershing-1 missiles	72		
Subtotal	323		
Total launchers	924		2,537
Approximate total warheads	1,229		3,737

Soviet Tally

American			
F-111 fighter-bombers	156	Backfire bombers	65
FB-111A fighter-bombers*	60	Badger bombers	310
F-4 fighter-bombers	324	Blinder bombers	125
A-6/A-7 fighter-bombers	60	SS-20 missiles	175
Pershing-1 missiles	103	SS-4 missiles	340
Subtotal	708	SS-5 missiles	40
		Total	1,055
Allied			
British Polaris missiles	64		
French submarine missiles	80		
French land-based missiles	18		
British Vulcan bombers	56		
French Mirage-4 bombers	33		
German Pershing-1 missiles	72		
Subtotal	323		
Total launchers	1,031		1,055
Approximate total warheads	1,483		2,035

*US-based but for European theater use

Source: Congressional Research Service.

the table, the West maintains the East has an advantage of approximately 3:1 in launchers as well as warheads. Consequently, the West maintains, either the East should make drastic cuts while the West holds fast, or the West must build to parity before meaningful negotiations can occur.

The conflicting figures reflect in part different intelligence estimates of the same items. But they are also due to separate judgments about what should be counted. The United States insists that only those launchers based on European soil should be counted. The East argues that any nonstrategic weapon that can hit Eastern Europe deserves to be included, whether it be based on European soil or on a ship in the Mediterranean Sea or the Atlantic Ocean.

These conflicting data bases provide the foundations for the negotiating positions put forth by both sides at the TNF talks in Geneva. Persuaded that the East enjoys a significant edge in TNF, President Reagan set forth his "zero option" proposal in November 1981, in a speech given before the National Press Club. The president offered to cancel plans to deploy 108 Pershing II and 464 ground-launched cruise missiles in Europe, if the Soviets would dismantle their approximately 600 SS–4, SS–5, and SS–20 medium-range missiles. The SS–20 is a highly accurate missile that carries nuclear warheads and can reach most of Western Europe from launching pads inside the Soviet Union. In arguing for his proposal, the president claimed the Soviets enjoyed a 6:1 lead over the West in medium-range missile warheads.

The Soviets immediately retorted that President Reagan was being extremely selective in his figures. If one counts all TNF, including American and allied planes and missiles at sea, the Soviets said, the two sides enjoy rough parity. This is reflected in the Soviet count in Table 12–1. In rejecting the American offer, Moscow claimed that the United States was simply engaging in propaganda and was appealing to Western European sentiment in favor of disarmament. In addition, the Soviets claimed that the president was seeking to justify the deployment of new missiles, on the trumped-up charge that the Soviets refused to negotiate a good-faith offer.

The TNF talks took a turn for the worse in November 1983, when the Soviets walked out of the negotiations in response to deployment of the first of the Pershing IIs and ground-launched cruise missiles by the West. With the two sides so far apart on weapons counts, one can expect TNF negotiations to drag on for years. Let us recall that the MBFR talks have been in session since

1973 with no agreement yet on troop counts, let alone measures to reduce forces.

STRATEGIC ARMS LIMITATION TALKS

The most important arms control negotiations since World War II are the Strategic Arms Limitation Talks, known as SALT. Three series of discussions have been held under the SALT framework. In 1972 the United States and the Soviet Union signed the SALT I accords. Two years later, President Ford and Chairman Brezhnev concluded an interim agreement at Vladivostok. In 1979 the SALT II Treaty was drawn up between President Carter and Secretary Brezhnev, but the Senate never voted on this treaty. Displeased by SALT II, President Reagan set it aside and reopened negotiations with the Soviets in mid-1982. In so doing, President Reagan decided to rename the discussions START—Strategic Arms Reduction Talks.

SALT I

The SALT agreements acquire their significance from the fact that they concern the world's most lethal weapons. These are the super-powerful nuclear missiles and bombs with intercontinental range targeted on the cities, military installations, transportation centers and communications hubs in each adversary's homeland. For the most part, SALT has sought to limit three types of weapons, all nuclear: long-range bombers, land-based intercontinental ballistic missiles (ICBMs), and submarine-launched ballistic missiles (SLBMs).

The motivations leading up to SALT were expressed by Chairman Khrushchev in an address to the East German Communist Party Congress in 1963:

> There is no doubt that if a thermonuclear war were unleashed by the imperialist maniacs, the capitalist system that gave rise to the war would perish in it. But would the socialist countries and the cause of the struggle for socialism throughout the world gain from a world thermonuclear catastrophe? Only people who deliberately close their eyes to the facts can think this.[24]

If nuclear war were mutually suicidal, then it was imperative to control the instruments of nuclear annihilation. This effort had to await a propitious moment for negotiations, namely, the achievement of superpower parity in strategic weaponry. By the late 1960s this interval had arrived. In 1969 American and Soviet negotiators sat down to discuss strategic arms limitations. Three years later President Nixon and Secretary Brezhnev, meeting in Moscow, put their signatures on SALT I.

SALT I embraces two separate treaties. The first, known as the ABM Treaty, limited each state to two sites for the stationing of antiballistic missiles (ABMs). A protocol signed in 1974 reduced this number by half. Today, Moscow is ringed by ABM batteries, while the United States has elected to forego the construction of ABMs. In effect, both sides agreed to a mutual baring of throats.

The second treaty covered strategic nuclear weapons. This accord was intended as an interim measure until more comprehensive limitations could be negotiated; SALT II thus represents the continuation of a process that has yet to run its entire course. SALT I imposed certain limits on various types of strategic weapons for five years. Table 12–2 describes these restrictions.

These figures reflect the number of weapons systems in operation or under construction at the time of the agreement. In essence, therefore, SALT I froze the number of weapons on each side; it did not call for reductions. The agreement allowed the United States to expand its SLBM forces to 710 and the Soviet Union to 950, but only by dismantling an equal number of older ICBM launchers or SLBM launchers on older submarines. There were also prohibitions against converting launchers for light ICBMs or older heavy ICBMs into launchers for modern heavy ICBMs.[25] The parties agreed not to interfere with each other's satellite surveillance, expressed in the euphemism "national technical means." Finally, the parties established a Standing Consultative Commission to consider complaints about violations of the agreement.

TABLE 12–2: SALT I LIMITATIONS (LAUNCHERS)

	ICBMs	SLBMs	Missile-Firing Submarines
United States	1,054	656	44
Soviet Union	1,618	740	62

It will be noticed that SALT I allowed the Soviets more missiles than the United States. Several reasons accounted for this imbalance. An accord seemed possible only if it accepted the existing asymmetry in ICBMs and SLBMs. The inequality was offset, however, by American numerical superiority in long-range bombers and the superior quality of all American strategic systems. The United States also led in MIRV technology, so it could mount more warheads than the Soviets on its launchers. At the time SALT I was concluded, American launchers could deliver 5,900 nuclear warheads and bombs, while Soviet launchers could deliver 2,200 such weapons.

Many proponents of arms control hailed SALT I as an historic milestone in the age-old attempt to control armaments. By placing ceilings on certain weapons, the agreement capped the arms spiral. No longer was it necessary for each superpower to prepare against the worst that its adversary could inflict, for now there were known limits to the number of weapons on each side.

Not everyone was so enthusiastic about SALT I, however. Senator Henry Jackson criticized the agreement because it allowed the Soviets to continue deployment of "super" warheads far more powerful than anything in America's arsenal.[26] Others lamented that the ceilings were far too high; that the agreement reduced no weapons; and that no constraints were placed on the development of new technologies, MIRV in particular.

The Senate approved both SALT I treaties by wide margins. In doing so, however, it also passed a resolution urging that future SALT agreements provide for equal US and Soviet limits on launchers.

Vladivostok

Not long after the signing of SALT I, it became apparent that America's qualitative edge in weaponry and numerical lead in bombs and warheads was no longer sufficient to offset Moscow's quantitative advantage in launchers. The Soviets were also making big strides in MIRV technology, foreshadowing numerical superiority in warheads. These unsettling trends led the United States to press for a new accord. In 1974, President Ford met with Chairman Brezhnev at the Soviet port city of Vladivostok and signed a new interim measure that was to provide guidelines for a second SALT treaty.

The Vladivostok accord allowed each side a total of 2,400 strategic launchers. These included ICBMs, SLBMs, and heavy bombers (not included in SALT I). Each side could select its own mix of launchers, so long as the total did not exceed 2,400. Within this total, each side could MIRV no more than 1,320 launchers. The Soviets were also limited to about 300 "heavy" missiles, an imprecise term that described missiles capable of carrying much heavier payloads than America's Minuteman ICBMs.

In many ways, Vladivostok represented an attempt to placate some of the critics of SALT I. Now both sides operated under identical ceilings. Defenders of the accord cited two points said to favor American interests. First, America was still ahead in MIRV capabilities, so the United States could place more warheads than the Soviets atop its missile launchers. Second, the United States persuaded the Soviets to drop their demand that Western tactical nuclear forces capable of striking Soviet territory from launching sites in Europe be included in the totals. In terms of warheads capable of striking the homelands of the superpowers, this omission placed the Soviet Union at a distinct disadvantage compared to the United States.

The Vladivostok agreement had an expiration date of 1985, by which time it was hoped a new SALT agreement would be in place.

SALT II

Both SALT I and Vladivostok were intended as interim accords only. Before they expired, the superpowers expected to draw up a more comprehensive agreement with a much longer lifetime. SALT II was to fulfill that purpose.

More enthusiastic about arms control than most of his predecessors, President Carter early in his administration proposed deep cuts in both Soviet and American strategic weapons. The Soviets promptly and angrily rejected this idea, arguing that the Vladivostok agreement should provide the framework for future and gradual reductions. The Soviets also took exception to the Carter proposal's sharp cutbacks of land-based missiles, the mainstay of Soviet strategic forces.

Soviet and American negotiators went back to the drawing boards, and in early 1979 they emerged with the SALT II Treaty. The SALT II package is illustrated in Figure 12–2.

The SALT II Treaty provided for:

FIGURE 12–2: SALT II LIMITATIONS (1979)—LAUNCHERS

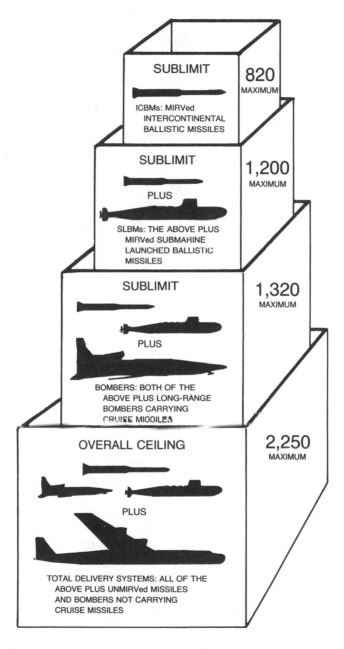

SUBLIMIT 820 MAXIMUM

ICBMs: MIRVed INTERCONTINENTAL BALLISTIC MISSILES

SUBLIMIT 1,200 MAXIMUM

PLUS

SLBMs: THE ABOVE PLUS MIRVed SUBMARINE LAUNCHED BALLISTIC MISSILES

SUBLIMIT 1,320 MAXIMUM

PLUS

BOMBERS: BOTH OF THE ABOVE PLUS LONG-RANGE BOMBERS CARRYING CRUISE MISSILES

OVERALL CEILING 2,250 MAXIMUM

PLUS

TOTAL DELIVERY SYSTEMS: ALL OF THE ABOVE PLUS UNMIRVed MISSILES AND BOMBERS NOT CARRYING CRUISE MISSILES

Source: US Department of State, *SALT and American Security*, 1978.

an equal aggregate limit on the number of MIRVed and unMIRVed strategic launchers—ICBMs, SLBMs, and heavy bombers. Initially, this ceiling will be 2,400, as agreed at Vladivostok; eventually it will be lowered to 2,250;

an equal aggregate limit of 1,320 on the total number of MIRVed ballistic missiles, MIRVed submarine-launched ballistic missiles, and heavy bombers with long-range cruise missiles;

a limit of 1,200 on the total number of MIRVed ballistic missiles (ICBMs and SLBMs);

a limit of 820 on MIRVed ICBMs;

a ban on construction of additional fixed ICBM launchers, and on any increase in the number of fixed heavy ICBM launchers;

a ban on certain new types of strategic offensive systems such as ballistic missiles on surface ships;

a limit of one new type of ICBM for each side; and

advance notification of certain ICBM test launches.

The treaty was to last through 1985.

President Carter submitted the treaty to the Senate. After the Foreign Relations Committee approved the document by a 9–7 vote, however, the president withdrew it from full Senate consideration on account of the Soviet invasion of Afghanistan in late 1979. The Reagan administration found the treaty unacceptable; in June 1982, renewed SALT negotiations began under the name START. Meanwhile, both sides promised to abide by the restrictions of the 1979 treaty for the immediate future.

In arguing for the treaty, backers such as former Secretary of State Vance and former Secretary of Defense Brown noted that it would require the Soviets to dismantle 250–300 strategic launchers presently deployed. The agreement would also place a ceiling on Soviet MIRVed ICBMs, where the Soviets are most formidable, far below what it might otherwise be. Proponents further stated the accord would hold down the total number of Soviet warheads and the throw weight of their strategic forces to a level well below what they would build in the absence of an agreement. In reducing uncertainty about Soviet forces, the treaty simplifies American military planning and lowers American military expenditures. The treaty would have less of an impact on American forces, backers pointed out. No existing weapons would have to be dismantled. The United States could proceed with its planned new MX mobile missile. Programs to modernize the Minuteman ICBM force and test and develop cruise missiles were permitted, as was deployment of the Trident submarine. Finally, treaty supporters said, failure to ratify SALT II would have disastrous consequences for the entire US-Soviet relationship.

Why has the Reagan administration found SALT II objectionable? Paul N. Nitze objects to the treaty's failure to compel the Soviets to dismantle their 308 "heavy" SS–18 missiles. Each of these can carry up to ten nuclear warheads, and each of these is more powerful than any American warhead. Former Senator Henry Jackson pointed out that these missiles alone give the Soviet Union more nuclear firepower than the entire force of America's 1,054 ICBMs. It is the SS–18 that American strategists identify as capable of destroying Minutemen in their silos. Treaty critics insist that the agreement be amended so as to allow the United States an equal number of heavy missiles or to compel the Soviets to reduce theirs. Although both sides are allowed to deploy the same number of "light" missiles, critics charge that the Soviet SS–19 light missile is able to deliver over three times the nuclear payload of its American counterpart, the Minuteman ICBM. Furthermore, the SS–19 can carry up to six warheads, while the Minuteman can shoulder only three. In all, the treaty allows the Soviets a total throw weight of 11.2 million pounds, compared to an American throw weight of 4 million pounds. Critics are also unhappy because Washington would have to phase out well over a hundred B–52 heavy bombers, in order to come in under the limit on missiles and bombers. Treaty foes are further disturbed by omission of limits on the Soviet TU–22M bomber, known in the West as the Backfire. American negotiators accepted Moscow's claim that this high-performance nuclear bomber was designed for medium-range missions and therefore should not be included as a strategic weapon. Critics argue that, if the airplane flies at subsonic speeds, it could deliver a nuclear payload against America and land in Cuba— a strategic mission. Critics also question whether the United States could properly monitor treaty restrictions on upgrading existing missile systems, since the loss of electronic listening posts in Iran following the shah's overthrow. Without these stations, they suggest, Moscow could increase the thrust and payload of current missiles without America's knowledge. In sum, opponents of the treaty maintain that SALT II would leave the Soviets far superior to the United States in nuclear firepower. In an international crisis, the Soviet Union could call upon this advantage to bully the United States into accepting Soviet outcomes (a Cuban missile crisis in reverse).

In facing these arguments, treaty proponents say that the United States does not need heavy missiles like the SS–18, because American missiles are more accurate than Soviet ones. Furthermore, they maintain, the United States still has a decided edge over the Soviets in numbers of warheads; the United States could destroy Soviet targets several times over already. There is no need, treaty supporters insist, for the United States to match Soviet excess destructive capacity. While treaty proponents concede that SALT II would leave the Soviets with an advantage in throw weight, or deliverable destructive power, they counter that the Soviets would be unable to make political capital out of this edge. The United States has too much destructive punch for the Soviets to risk blackmail; a single Trident submarine, for instance, could fire 160 nuclear warheads at various Soviet targets. In discussing the Backfire bomber, treaty advocates state that the Soviets would be reluctant to use the airplane against American territory if it had to fly at subsonic speeds, because American interceptor aircraft could shoot it down. Treaty backers further maintain that experience in monitoring SALT I reveals that Washington is capable of detecting violations. Perhaps the Soviets could get away with small infractions, but not enough to make a real difference. Finally, treaty supporters say the Soviets would be free to build many more heavy missiles and MIRVs in the absence of SALT II.[27]

There is still another series of issues, less dependent on the provisions of SALT II, that treaty opponents cite. These issues relate to the overall record of Soviet policy since SALT I was concluded in 1972. At that time, critics observe, many supporters of SALT hailed it as a symbol of a new cooperative era in US-Soviet relations. Henceforth, they said, the Soviet Union would follow America's lead in demonstrating restraint in foreign policy. Instead, critics go on to say, the Soviets have behaved in exactly the opposite manner. Right after SALT I, the Soviets made available to the Arabs weapons needed for the 1973 Middle East war, and then the Kremlin threatened to intervene militarily when Israel was on the verge of victory. This threat prompted the United States to issue a "red alert" to its forces, a signal that dissuaded the Soviets from military involvement. Thereafter, Moscow urged OPEC to use oil as a weapon against the West. The Soviets also supplied arms to North Vietnam to help it conquer the South. In Africa, the Soviet Union, with the aid of its Cuban proxy, intervened in Angola and Ethiopia. In 1979 Russia invaded Afghanistan. The Kremlin has also menaced Poland and induced authorities there to impose martial law. As grievous as any of these moves on the global political front has been the steady Soviet military buildup during the era of SALT. If SALT truly signified a "generation of peace," to use President Nixon's term, then why have the Soviets acted as though a war were imminent, critics ask. During SALT, the Soviets have constructed numerous new types of missiles and have built up a blue-water navy. At the same time, a naive America abided by the spirit of SALT and allowed itself to fall behind the Soviets in military power, foes of the treaty complain. In short, critics assert that while the United States regarded SALT as a path to a more peaceful and stable world, the Soviets used it as a license to build new weapons and intervene militarily. Instead of forging a new arms limitation agreement with the Soviet Union, these critics insist, the United States should drive forward with new military programs.

Persuaded by many of the arguments advanced by SALT II opponents, the Reagan administration elected to renegotiate a strategic arms pact, while at the same time respecting the provisions of SALT II. The START negotiations began in June 1982, and proceeded at a glacial pace. During 1983, Washington proposed that both sides reduce their strategic missile launchers to 850 each and limit their strategic nuclear warheads to 5,000 for each side; no more than half of these warheads could be installed on land-based missiles. If accepted, this provision would force the Soviets to dismantle a hefty proportion of their massive ICBMs, the core of their strategic arsenal. The United States also put forth a build-down proposal: each side would destroy a certain number of existing weapons for every new one built. Under this concept, newer meant fewer.

The Soviets showed little interest in these proposals. Instead, the Soviets proposed a 25 percent cut in all strategic delivery systems. As the middle of the 1980s approached, the two sides remained wide apart in their positions on strategic weapons reductions.

FOR DISCUSSION

Comment on the following appraisal of arms control efforts by Leslie Gelb: "Arms control has essentially failed. Three decades of US-Soviet negotiations to limit arms competition have done little more than to codify the arms race."

What steps should the United States take in order to counter the Soviet Union's advantage in chemical weapons?

Would a comprehensive test ban serve American interests?

What measures should the United States adopt to curb the spread of nuclear weapons?

Should Washington condition SALT policy on Russian "good behavior"? In other words, should the United States link willingness to negotiate a new SALT agreement with Moscow's international conduct?

READING SUGGESTIONS

Carnegie Endowment for International Peace. *Chemical Weapons and Chemical Arms Control*. New York: Carnegie Endowment, 1978.

Clarke, Duncan L. *Politics of Arms Control: The Role and Effectiveness of the U.S. Arms Control and Disarmament Agency*. New York: The Free Press, 1979.

Dunn, Lewis A. *Controlling the Bomb: Nuclear Proliferation in the 1980s*. New Haven: Yale University Press, 1982.

Keliher, John G. *The Negotiations on Mutual and Balanced Force Reductions: The Search for Arms Control in Central Europe*. New York: Pergamon Press, 1980.

Nincic, Miroslav. *The Arms Race: The Political Economy of Military Growth*. New York: Praeger, 1982.

Osgood, Charles E. *An Alternative to War or Surrender*. Urbana, IL: University of Illinois Press, 1962.

Seagrave, Sterling. *Yellow Rain: A Journey through the Terror of Chemical Warfare*. New York: M. Evans, 1981.

Talbott, Strobe. *Endgame: The Inside Story of SALT II*. New York: Harper, 1979.

United States Congress, Office of Technology Assessment. *The Effects of Nuclear War*. Montclair, NJ: Allanheld, Osmun, 1980.

Yager, Joseph A., ed. *Nonproliferation and U.S. Foreign Policy*. Washington: The Brookings Institution, 1980.

NOTES

1. United States, Arms Control and Disarmament Agency, *Arms Control Report* (Washington: GPO, 1976), p. 3.

2. United States, Department of Defense, *Annual Report, Fiscal Year 1982* (Washington: GPO, 1981), p. 27.

3. The figures in this account are based on a dispatch by Leslie H. Gelb in *New York Times*, May 11, 1982.

4. Much of the material in this section is drawn from Duncan L. Clarke, *Politics of Arms Control: The Role and Effectiveness of the U.S. Arms Control and Disarmament Agency* (New York: The Free Press, 1979).

5. Ibid., p. 28.
6. Quoted in John H. Barton and Lawrence D. Weiler, *International Arms Control* (Stanford: Stanford University Press, 1976), p. 152.
7. Clarke, p. 154.
8. For an illuminating insider's account of policy making with regard to the Outer Space Treaty, see Raymond L. Garthoff, "Banning the Bomb in Outer Space," *International Security*, V (Winter 1980–81): 25–40.
9. For the argument against a CTB, see for example Robert L. Pfaltzgraff, Jr., "The Proposed Comprehensive Test Ban Treaty: A Means Toward What Objectives?" *Commonsense* (Fall 1978): 44–56.
10. Ibid., p. 48.
11. See, for example, Peter Zimmerman, "Quota Testing," *Foreign Policy* (Fall 1981): 82–93. Zimmerman suggests 2–3 tests per country annually with a ceiling of 10 kilotons per test.
12. Moshe Dayan, former defense and foreign minister of Israel, said in 1981 that Israel has no atomic bombs but could fabricate some "in a short time." *New York Times*, June 25, 1981. Dayan, now deceased, did not elaborate on the meaning of "short."
13. The Hudson Institute study is cited in Library of Congress, Congressional Research Service, *Nuclear Proliferation Factbook*, 1980, p. 326.
14. In the 1950s the United States was prepared to share control over its nuclear weapons with NATO allies. This arrangement, known as the Multilateral Nuclear Force, died for lack of European enthusiasm.
15. Congressional Research Service, *Nuclear Proliferation Factbook*, p. 325.
16. See *New York Times*, July 8, 1981, for a complete summary of the Reagan position.
17. Ibid.
18. *New York Times*, November 16, 1981.
19. Remarks by Herbert Scoville, Jr., in Carnegie Endowment for International Peace, *Chemical Weapons and Chemical Arms Control* (New York, 1978), pp. 6–7.
20. *New York Times*, September 21, 1980.
21. An excellent account of the MBFR negotiations may be found in John G. Keliher, *The Negotiations on Mutual and Balanced Force Reductions: The Search for Arms Control in Central Europe* (New York: Pergamon Press, 1980). Much of the present section is drawn from Keliher's description.
22. Leslie H. Gelb, "A Glass Half Full," *Foreign Policy*, No. 36 (Fall 1979): 21–32.
23. Keliher, pp. 158–62.
24. *Pravda*, January 17, 1963.
25. Ambiguity about the definition of light and heavy sparked opposition to SALT by some American specialists. They contended that the Soviets stretched these definitions in replacing some of their missiles with more modern ones (SS–17, 18, 19).
26. SALT proponents countered that American missiles, enjoying more accuracy than their Soviet counterparts, did not need to be as powerful in order to get the job done. A bullet that strikes the heart need not be as large as one that hits the shoulder.

27. A national intelligence estimate completed by the CIA in 1980 concluded that the Soviet Union, in the absence of SALT II, could possess a missile arsenal in 1985 capable of delivering as many as 16 thousand nuclear warheads against the United States. With the 1979 SALT II treaty, this number would be reduced by half. See *New York Times*, May 13, 1980.

Chapter 13
Resource Diplomacy

In recent years, those who study the international state system increasingly make reference to a "new agenda." This roster of concerns reflects an awareness of the planet's finite resources and economic interdependence among all nations. In contrast to such traditional subjects as military power, warfare and treaties, the new agenda includes food, energy, minerals, population, pollution, seabed mining, and other topics related to the distribution and preservation of natural resources. The vision of earth, a bluish sphere afloat in space, from satellite cameras, has underlined the fact that all humanity dwells in a "global village." Increasing numbers of people feel it imperative that humankind protect natural resources and apportion them in a manner so as to ensure tranquillity.

This chapter concerns three selections from the menu of the new agenda: food, energy, and minerals. It will make clear how deeply enmeshed the United States finds itself in the global community. The United States is both a provider and a consumer of natural resources. As a supplier, the United States may be in a position to exert political leverage on needy countries by threatening to withhold commodities. Conversely, America as a consumer is vulnerable to similar actions taken by others. In most cases, supplier-consumer relationships entail a degree of mutual dependence.

479

FOOD DIPLOMACY

Hunger admidst Plenty

The scene is all too familiar. Squatting on a scorched dusty road, a dark-skinned girl in tattered clothes picks cream-colored lice out of her little brother's matted hair and puts them in her mouth. Occasionally she feeds some to her brother. This is the lunch hour in areas of the world stricken by hunger.

Experts are in agreement that approximately 500 million people, one-eighth of the world's population, go to bed hungry. This is roughly equivalent to the total populations of the Soviet Union and the United States, or the entire population of the world three centuries ago. According to the World Bank, 80 percent of the world's hungry are women and children, and most of them live in Africa, South Asia, the Middle East and Latin America. Two-thirds of these souls reside in nine countries: India, Bangladesh, Pakistan, Indonesia, the Philippines, Cambodia, Brazil, Zaire and Ethiopia. In India, 300–400 million people, nearly eight times the population of France, don't have enough to eat. Worst of all is the Sahel region of Africa, where 70 percent of the population is malnourished.[1] Noted nutritionist Jean Meyer testified before Congress that:

Blindness caused by lack of vitamin A occurs in 100 thousand children every year;

10–50 percent of women in Latin America, Africa and Asia suffer from iron deficiency anemia;

Up to 5 percent of the population in remote areas of Africa, Latin America and the Himalaya Mountains are affected by cretinism caused by iodine deficiencies in child-bearing women;

Chronic undernourishment accounts for listlessness and a reduced capacity for learning and activity, which perpetuate the poverty that is the source of so much hunger.[2]

The above facts gain force when set before another: enough food is produced today to provide each man, woman and child with 3 thousand calories per day, well above the minimum needed and exceeding average consumption in the United States.[3] The 137 million tons of food American wholesalers and supermarkets discard each year would feed well over half the world's starving population.[4]

If enough food is available, why do so many people suffer hunger pains? The answer is poverty. World hunger is not so much a problem of adequate supply as adequate purchasing power. Parents who urge their children not to waste food for the sake of starving people elsewhere fail to realize that what these people need is money; calories follow cash.

To overcome the poverty that is the root cause of hunger, it is necessary to stimulate economic development in poorer lands. Rural modernization is especially needed. Economic development is an extremely complex topic that goes far beyond the boundaries of this book. Suffice it to say that without economic development, chronic hunger in developing countries is likely to be a permanent if sorrowful feature of international life.

The Food-Population Balance

Since World War II, global food output has steadily increased. Between 1945 and 1975, world grain production more than doubled (see Fig. 13–1). However, the planet's population rose 80 percent during these years. Thus, per capita increase in food production has been only slight. As the compiler of these data explains, it is highly unlikely that grain production will continue to keep pace with population growth for the remainder of the century.

Population growth and rates of food production are not identical for all regions of the world. Figure 13–2 reveals the difference in per capita food production between developed and developing countries. While food production in developing countries rose 54 percent in the last decade and a half, per capita food production increased only 6 percent in the same period. Much of the food production increase can be attributed to the "Green Revolution" of the late 1960s and early 1970s. This refers to the development of dwarf varieties of wheat and rice capable of doubling or tripling yields per acre. Such breakthroughs cannot be counted on to recur regularly. The food-population gap gives every sign of widening, since world food production appears to be plateauing while population is increasing annually at the rate of nearly 2.5 percent in the developing world.

While few of us would be satisfied with a bank account that earned 2.5 percent interest, at that rate our money would double in about 35 years (assuming compounding). Most population experts estimate that between 1965 and 2000 the population of the world is likely to double. Figure 13–3 suggests that the long-term pattern of population growth resembles the progress of a passenger train leaving a downtown station. At first the engine proceeds very slowly

FIGURE 13–1: GRAIN PRODUCTION AND POPULATION GROWTH

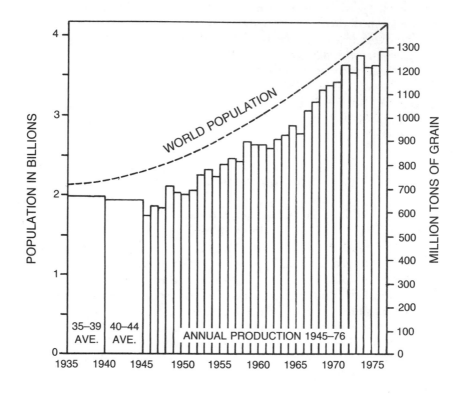

out of the station. Then it cautiously threads its way over the switches and crossovers in the freight yard. Finally it highballs along on the main line. In terms of population growth, it took 1,650 years for world population to double to 545 million by 1650. The second doubling (to 1 billion) took only another 200 years. The third doubling occurred after 75 years (reaching 2 billion in 1925). By 1980 the population stood at over 4 billion persons, three-fourths of whom lived in developing countries. According to one estimate, 9 percent of all the people who have ever lived are alive today.[5] By the year 2000, according to United Nations projections, the world population will reach approximately 7 billion persons, who will be distributed as follows:

FIGURE 13–2: TOTAL FOOD PRODUCTION AND PER CAPITA FOOD PRODUCTION IN DEVELOPED AND DEVELOPING COUNTRIES, 1955–1980 (1969–1971 = 100)

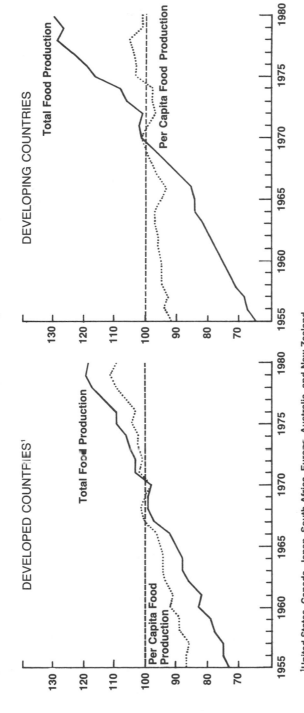

¹United States, Canada, Japan, South Africa, Europe, Australia, and New Zealand.

NOTES: Data do not include centrally planned economies; inedible fiber products such as cotton, hemp, and wool; or noncaloric products such as tobacco, coffee, tea, and spices.

Source: *U.S. Foreign Policy and the Third World: Agenda 1982* by Roger D. Hansen and Contributors for the Overseas Development Council. Copyright © 1982 by the Overseas Development Council. Reprinted by permission of Praeger Publishers and the Overseas Development Council.

FIGURE 13–3: WORLD POPULATION GROWTH

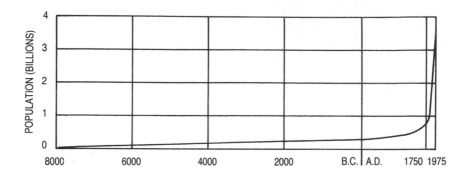

Development of agriculture (about 8000 B.C.) resulted in a modest increase in population growth, but the Industrial Revolution starting about 1750 had a much greater effect.

Source: Reprinted by permission from DIMENSIONS OF WORLD FOOD PROBLEMS edited by E. R. Duncan © 1977 by The Iowa State University Press, 2121 South State Avenue, Ames, Iowa 50010.

Asia	61.8%
Europe	15.1%
Africa	8.2%
Latin America	9.4%
North America	5.0%

Approximately 80 percent of these people will reside in non-Western poorer lands. It is staggering to contemplate the pressure these additional billions will place on natural resources, pollution control, housing, grazing lands, forests, urban crowding, clean water, employment, energy, and food.

Already food production in developing countries is falling behind population growth, even though worldwide food production is barely keeping up. As a result, food imports by developing countries have increased from 20 million tons annually in 1960 to 50 million in 1975 and nearly 80 million in 1980.[6] If present trends continue, the United Nations Food and Agriculture Organization estimates that by the year 2000 developing countries will need to import 175 million tons of food each year![7] Where will this food come from?

The previous discussion leads to the inescapable conclusion that population and food are closely related. It is nearly pointless to tackle one of these without the other. Unless unforeseen technical breakthroughs expand food production, or population growth miraculously halts, countless millions will dine no better in the future than the young girl and her brother described at the beginning of this section.

The World Food Trade

Since few countries are self-sufficient in food, there is an active market in edibles. Most discussions of the world food trade focus on grain. This is because grain, in one form or another, constitutes the primary food for most people. Between one-half and three-quarters of the world's two billion acres of cultivated land is planted with grain. Wheat and rice are the two principal grains grown and eaten worldwide; important animal feed grains include oats, barley, corn and sorghum. Soybeans are eaten by both humans and animals.

Let us see who the principal buyers and sellers of grain are.

Suppliers.

Figure 13–4 illustrates what is meant by the term "North American breadbasket." This region exports the lion's share of the grain that is shipped worldwide. The United States alone accounts for slightly more than half the world's grain exports. Aside from the United States and Canada, the only other countries that export grain in significant quantities are France, Australia and Argentina. The United States is just about the only large-scale supplier of animal feed grain.

America's farmers are truly prodigious producers. These growers harvest more grain annually than all of Latin America and sub-Saharan Africa combined. Since the United States supplies over half the world's grain exports, decisions made by American farmers and political leaders affect how hungry people will be in the huts and villages of the less developed world. Many leaders of the undernourished portion of the globe complain that these decisions are made on the basis of what is best for the farmer in Iowa or Kansas with no regard for the well-being of hungry peasants in Asia or Africa. This can have disastrous consequences, as occurred in 1972–74. For many years previously, a steady flow of American food exports had rendered the world complacent regarding adequate food supplies. Then, in the early 1970s, in order to boost incomes of American farmers, Washington authorized a reduction in grain

FIGURE 13–4: GRAIN SUPPLIERS, 1973–1978

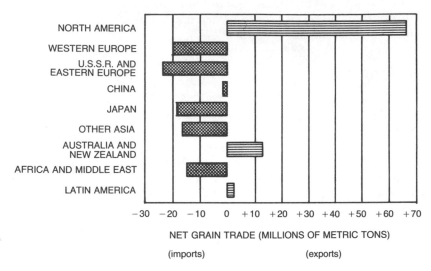

NET GRAIN TRADE (MILLIONS OF METRIC TONS)

(imports)   (exports)

Source: Raymond F. Hopkins and Donald J. Puchala, *Global Food Interdependence: Challenge to American Foreign Policy.* Copyright © 1980 by Columbia University Press. Reprinted by permission of Columbia University Press.

production. At the same time bad weather resulted in production shortfalls in several other countries. Facing a combination of lower supplies and higher prices, such countries as Bangladesh, Ethiopia, and the nations of the African Sahel suffered widespread famine. It took until the late 1970s for international reserves to build up again to a safe level. Yet, with so little worldwide coordination of food production and storage, and the decisions of the principal producer (US) so dominated by the farm vote, a recurrence of the 1972–74 crisis is not unlikely.

Consumers.

Figure 13–5 indicates which regions are importers of grain. Europe and Japan are the largest buyers, followed by the rest of Asia, Africa and the Middle East. Nearly half the world's grain exports are exchanged by the developed states belonging to the OECD. The grain that most Europeans (including Russia) buy is fed to livestock. Thus, much of the grain that enters trade enhances the diets of already well-fed people (excepting, at the moment, Poland

FIGURE 13-5: PROJECTED 1990 PRODUCTION AND CONSUMPTION OF MAJOR STAPLE FOOD CROPS IN DEVELOPING MARKET ECONOMIES, BY REGIONS (MILLION METRIC TONS CEREAL EQUIVALENT)

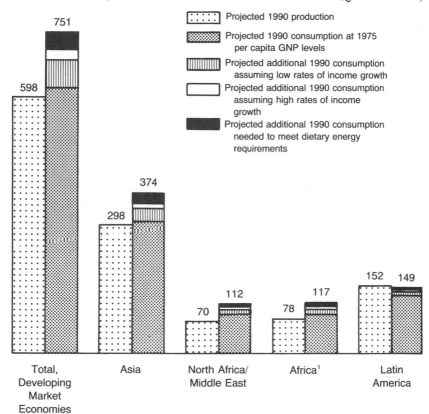

¹South of the Sahara.

NOTES: "Major staple food crops" includes cereals for all countries and root crops, pulses, and groundnuts for those countries in which these are important food sources.

"Projected 1990 consumption at 1975 per capita GNP levels" shows only the consumption attributable to population growth. "Projected additional 1990 consumption assuming low rates of income growth" shows the increased consumption resulting from slow rates of growth in per capita income. "Projected additional 1990 consumption assuming high rates of income growth" shows the increased consumption resulting from rates of growth in per capita income approximating or exceeding the historical trend in each country. "Projected additional 1990 consumption needed to meet dietary energy requirements" shows the estimated amounts required to provide enough additional food to give the underfed the minimum calories needed for an adequate diet. This is derived by taking 110 per cent of the national average dietary energy requirements provided by the Food and Agriculture Organization.

Source: *The United States and World Development: Agenda 1979* by Martin M. McLaughlin and the Staff of the Overseas Development Council. Copyright © 1979 by the Overseas Development Council. Reprinted by permission of Praeger Publishers and the Overseas Development Council.

and Russia) by supplying a tastier variety of meats and dairy products. The developing countries, in contrast, buy food so their populations will not starve; flavor and variety are luxuries few can afford.

While the industrial countries buy food at prevailing market rates, much of the food that goes to developing states is provided at substantial discount or is donated free. The latter two categories make up food aid. According to the Food and Agriculture Organization, 72 low-income countries received 8.1 million tons of food aid in 1980.[8] The United States supplied approximately two-thirds of this assistance. What these countries actually needed amounted to 27 million tons of aid, so a sizable shortfall left millions hungry. Rising affluence in some developing countries such as South Korea, Brazil, Nigeria and Middle East oil producers are beginning to drive food prices upward. As people in such countries enjoy higher incomes, one of the first things they want is better food. Middle East oil producers, for example, increased their food imports from 3.1 million metric tons in 1970 to 15 million metric tons in 1980. (A metric ton equals 2,205 pounds.) Usually the desire for better food means more meat and dairy products. Producing such items requires more grazing land, grain and labor than growing simple grain. Rising affluence is joining with population growth to increase the demand side of the world food equation. The supply side is holding relatively firm, however. Figure 13–5 reveals projected 1990 shortages in developing countries by region. What, if anything, can be done to narrow the widening gap between supply and demand?

Strategies to Overcome World Hunger

Measures to relieve world hunger can be divided into two categories. Inasmuch as poverty is the fundamental cause of undernourishment, general economic development would seem to offer much promise for reducing hunger. In addition there are many actions specific to food and agriculture that could be taken.

General economic development being too complex a topic for brief treatment, we shall avoid a detailed study of it here. We pause, however, to remind ourselves that low income, not lack of supply, is the main cause of hunger today. As indicated, however, sufficient supply may be a problem in the not-too-distant future. Economic development results in higher incomes, although this by-product is not evenly distributed throughout the population of the developing country. Rising incomes will allow more people to afford adequate diets.

There is historical reason to believe that economic development will curb a major source of rising food demand—population growth. When the industrial revolution overtook Europe, birth rates plummeted. The extra "hands" needed on the farm were merely a burden in the urban household. However, it will take decades for economic development to have such an effect, by which time the global population will more than double and perhaps even triple the current total.

The second category of steps to reduce world hunger concerns actions more directly related to malnutrition than is general economic development.

One fairly obvious idea would be to bring more acres of land under cultivation, as recommended by the 1974 World Food Conference (about which more later). Just how much land is available for such purposes is a matter of dispute. One study, considered highly optimistic by most, by the Free University at Amsterdam estimated that in 1965 only 39 percent of potential land was being used and only 3.2 percent of maximum agricultural production was being realized.[9] Another estimate held it feasible to double the planet's croplands to 4 billion acres over the next 25 years.[10]

However, broadening the amount of land under cultivation is not without its problems. Much of the available land, lying in the tropics, requires irrigation, fertilizer and pesticides beyond the means of poor countries. Many wealthy property owners, often members of the ruling elite, wish to retain their large and prestigious estates instead of converting them to farms. In many regions of the world, tradition-bound peasants resist modern agricultural technology and even rail against the idea of producing beyond one's own immediate needs. Finally environmentalists warn that bringing new areas into cultivation may destroy the ecosystem, as illustrated by efforts to cultivate portions of the Brazilian rain forest.

Practically all food experts have recommended a food reserve of one kind or another as one of the most effective measures in coping with world hunger. Such a reserve would not only provide food in case of production shortfalls, but it would also minimize food price fluctuations. Such abrupt price swings have had a disastrous impact on developing countries. During the 1950s and 1960s, food prices varied by only a few percentage points from year to year. The next decade experienced drastic price changes, however. Between 1970 and 1974, due largely to reduced supplies, the price of American wheat exports rose 400 percent. This was followed by a 200 percent decline over the next three years.[11] Such price swings wreak havoc on a poor nation's development plans. Food being a prime necessity, these governments are forced to halt long-term projects, such as roads or telecommunications, in order to purchase food. By the time food prices decline, early work on such projects often has fallen into disrepair. In effect, sudden food price variations render long-range economic development impossible.

With food problems, it appears that the creativity and dynamism spawned of crisis are ebbing rapidly, and many of the bold departures in commitment and organization taken at home in 1974 have lapsed or are bogging down in inertia. Yet it is more than likely that extraordinary food shortages will occur again long before the next decade has run its course, and it is disappointingly the case that neither the United States nor the world is presently any better prepared to deal with these than with earlier ones.

Hopkins and Puchala, *Global Food Interdependence:*
Challenge to American Foreign Policy, **p. 33.**

With such considerations in mind, UN and American food experts recommended a 30 million metric ton food reserve as necessary to provide needed food and buffer future price savings.[12] Ideally, the reserve would remain under international control and be managed for the benefit of all. The World Food Conference seconded the need for food reserves.

Years of negotiation have yielded slight progress toward such a goal, however. In 1980 a Food Aid Convention was negotiated for the purpose of stabilizing international food aid at an annual level of 10 million tons. While less than most experts deemed necessary, this figure at least seemed attainable. After Washington ratified the convention, Congress created a 4 million ton food security reserve as America's share. Reserve stocks are to remain in possession of producer countries until called upon for shipment.

International Efforts

World hunger has long been a concern of the international community. Interest in this matter came to a head in 1974 with the convening by the United Nations of a World Food Conference in Rome. Impetus for the gathering sprang from the world food shortage of 1972–1974. Not only did these years see millions suffer from starvation, but world grain reserves had declined between 1970 and 1974 from 217 million metric tons, enough for 69 days, to 90 million metric tons, adequate for only 26 days.[13]

Leaders from most of the countries of the world attended the conference. Representing the United States was Henry Kissinger, one of the prime movers of the gathering. Along with the fanfare and rhetoric that attends most large international meetings, the delegates conducted many serious debates and brought much information to light. They also created new institutions to supplement existing international organizations operating in the global food arena. All together, these bodies constitute what we might call the current world food regime.

The conference established a World Food Council to provide constant surveillance of the global food situation and monitor progress toward elimination of hunger. The International Fund for Agricultural Development, also established at Rome, was charged with funneling new resources from the industrialized North and OPEC into agricultural projects in developing countries. The conference also set up a global information and warning system to foresee major crop failures in time to mobilize food reserves and prevent famines.

The Rome gathering also spurred existing world food organizations to intensify their efforts. The most significant food organization continues to be the Food and Agriculture Organization (FAO), an autonomous body linked to the United Nations by mutual agreement. The FAO collects, analyzes and disseminates information about food and agriculture, provides an international forum for the consideration of food problems, and provides technical assistance to member countries with the ultimate objective of "ensuring humanity's freedom from hunger." Within the United Nations proper, the unit that works most closely with the FAO is the UN Development Program (UNDP), founded in 1966. The FAO carries out many UNDP projects, and the UNDP is the FAO's single largest source of revenue. The FAO also works in tandem with the World Bank, identifying and evaluating projects for funding and helping prospective loan applicants to improve their project designs. The FAO also advises the Inter-American Development Bank, the Asian Development Bank and the African Development Bank on the worthiness of loans in the area of food and agriculture. Established in 1969, the Consultative Group on International Agricultural Research supports 11 research centers specializing in the problems of food production in developing countries. Such an organization is needed, because most of the world's agricultural research is conducted by temperate-zone countries and focuses on their own problems. The ongoing UN Conference on Trade and Development (UNCTAD) often considers food problems as part of its concern with the broad area of North-South trade. The worsening terms of trade for agricultural commodities versus manufactured goods is a recurrent issue here. Finally, the General Agreement on Tariffs and Trade includes bargaining among developed states on agricultural issues, such as Common Market tariffs against American farm exports.

This catalogue of international organizations handling world food matters might leave the impression that the global community is acting with vigor and dispatch to overcome world hunger. Such complacency is hardly warranted. As Hopkins and Puchala observe in their revealing study of world food issues, international food organizations operate in a highly uncoordinated manner.[14] Duplication runs rampant. Also, "let us caution against mistaking activity for impact or accomplishment. There is a good deal of activity surrounding the international organization of food affairs, but budgets are modest, authority is limited, support from member states is tentative, and, for myriad political and bureaucratic reasons, including a strong imperative not to tamper with the sovereign integrity of any state, organizations tend to be restrained from accomplishing their mandated tasks."[15]

Obstacles to Relieving Hunger

A comprehensive account of the obstacles to relieving hunger is beyond the scope of this volume. Many of these impediments are suggested by the proposals to ease hunger discussed in the previous section. The various impediments to general economic development are among the more significant barriers to the relief of hunger. In addition, certain obstacles directly related to food production continue to slow the effort to abolish hunger.

Upon achieving independence, many developing countries followed the economic practices of their previous colonial masters. In agriculture, this meant the production of crops for export—coffee, tea, sugar, cocoa, tobacco, etc. In the quest for foreign exchange to fund industrialization, many new governments have paid minimal attention to the cultivation of crops for domestic consumption. Small farmers struggling to grow enough food for themselves and their families have received little governmental assistance, despite the fact that approximately two-thirds of the citizens in poor countries depend for their living upon agriculture. Rather, scarce funds have been channeled into industrial growth and military strength. Such patterns have been slow to change in many developing countries.

One reason for the persistence of this outlook can be traced to the availability of food aid, thanks largely to bountiful American harvests, until the early 1970s. Assured of such supplies, governments of developing countries had little incentive to transfer valuable resources to agricultural development instead of industrialization. As a result of the sudden drawdown of surplus food supplies in 1972–74, some developing countries elected to devote more resources to agricultural development. The World Bank too has recently emphasized rural modernization in its lending policies. Still, the urge to industrialize in the developing world retains a strong attraction.

Politics has also interfered with agricultural development in many poor countries. Where government leaders rode to power on the shoulders of urban political support, they sometimes fear rural development will give rise to rival power groups.

Throughout most of the developing world, agricultural modernization remains a task that has only just begun.

American Food Policy

Why should the United States concern itself with the food problems of other countries? Rather than diverting food abroad, should not the government distribute farm surpluses to America's own needy people?

Before finalizing answers to such questions, one should consider reasons for American involvement in global food affairs. These reasons fall into two groupings, one domestic and the other international.

Domestic Consequences of International Food Policy.
Assisting less fortunate nations has always appealed to Americans. After each of the world wars, America supplied large quantities of food to a Europe struggling to get back on its feet. This urge to help others is consistent with American idealism as described in Chapter 4.

There are, in addition, more self-interested reasons for providing food assistance and selling farm produce overseas. Approximately two out of every five acres harvested in the United States produce for export, 5 million acres for China alone. Farm shipments abroad provide over 20 percent of American farm income and account for some 630 thousand nonfarm jobs producing, processing, shipping and financing the export trade.[16] Over half the wheat and soybeans and nearly one-third of the corn and feed grain raised in America are destined for shipment abroad. Were America to lose these markets, US farmers would surely suffer.

Loss of such markets would also have a negative effect on the country's balance of payments. In 1978, an illustrative year, America's overall trade deficit was $47 billion. Foreign agricultural sales brought in $13.4 billion, approximately one-half the value of petroleum imports for that year.[17]

Food aid also attracts wide support in that it facilitates the disposal of surplus food and the development of overseas markets. Government purchases of agricultural production for foreign assistance help farmers by absorbing surplus production and keeping produce prices above what they would otherwise be. But the close ties between these domestic considerations and food assistance carries a complication. American enthusiasm for food aid rests more on the satisfaction of internal needs than on the welfare of aid recipients. Thus, when American farm production falls, and/or when food prices in American supermarkets rise substantially, sentiment turns against overseas food aid. This is precisely what occurred in 1973, leading the United States to suspend additional food aid commitments until food stocks accumulated.

Food aid to such countries as Japan, South Korea and Mexico illustrates the role of such assistance in developing overseas commercial markets. During the 1950s Japan received over $300 million in food aid. When Japan's postwar recovery was achieved, Tokyo began purchasing American food at commercial rates. By 1982 Japan was buying over $5 billion annually in American agricultural output. The same process has been repeated in South Korea and Mexico, which each purchased over $1 billion of American agricultural products in 1982.[18]

Not all the domestic effects of international food assistance are beneficial. Some agronomists claim that America is overfarming its land in order to ship food abroad and warn that soil depletion and erosion will result. Diversion of food overseas leads to higher food prices in America and has an inflationary effect in the price of farmland. It must be pointed out, however, that in the absence of overseas shipments some form of price support would probably take effect.

International Uses of Food Aid.

In addition to domestic goals, the United States uses food aid for international political purposes. In this sense, food aid is no different than other forms of foreign assistance.

Hopkins and Puchala have identified six overseas goals for American food aid.[19] (1) The country may use food aid for financial purposes, such as balance of payments or protecting a foreign investment. Jamaica provides an illustration. The recipient of Public Law 480 food assistance, Jamaica in 1974 abruptly raised the price of bauxite exports to the United States and threatened to expropriate American aluminum investments. Washington thereupon suspended P.L. 480 shipments, a concrete warning of harsher economic retaliation to follow. Deprived of food aid, Jamaica now had to pay market prices for food. Thus, Washington was able to manipulate food assistance both to preserve American investments and enhance the nation's balance of payments. (2) In scores of countries the United States has provided food aid to spur economic development. Undernourished people are unable to learn or apply the skills necessary to flourish in a modernizing economy. (3) Emergency relief represents another call on food assistance. The United States was a leading supplier of emergency food to northern Africa when drought struck in the 1970s. (4) America has provided aid to counter nutritional deficiencies with special programs for young school children and nursing mothers. (5) Washington has used food assistance for a wide range of political objectives, one of the primary purposes of all types of foreign aid. Washington concluded a large grain agreement with the Soviet Union in 1972, in the hope of cementing better relations with Moscow. Eight years later Jimmy Carter embargoed grain sales to Russia to display displeasure over the invasion of Afghanistan. The United States has sent large amounts of food to Egypt to encourage Cairo to make peace with Israel and agree to a Middle East settlement. (6) Finally, America sometimes provides food in return for a specific action by the recipient. In the late 1970s the United States insisted that Bangladesh cease selling jute to Cuba upon threat of losing food assistance.

One might add that the United States has used food aid to promote or maintain stability abroad. In the past, hunger has led to riots, strikes, wars of territorial expansion and large refugee flows. The troubles that led to the formation of the Solidarity Union in Poland began in 1980 with protests against higher food prices. Generally speaking, the United States finds global turmoil inimical to its interests and so uses food aid to prevent or minimize it.

While we have in this and the previous section identified various purposes for food aid, one should keep in mind that often a single assistance program serves several objectives, both foreign and domestic, simultaneously.

Food for Peace.
American food assistance on an ongoing basis began with the passage of Public Law 480 in 1954, the Agricultural Trade Development and Assistance Act. The program that took form pursuant to this legislation is known as Food for Peace. The original law provided for two types of food aid. Title I authorized sales at prices below prevailing commercial rates. Title II made available free food, generally to be supplied in emergencies. In 1977 Congress added Title III, called "Food for Development." In order to persuade recipients to undertake agricultural development, this provision authorizes writing off Title I repayments if recipients make progress in modernizing their agricultural sector. In 1975 Congress required that 75 percent of Title I sales be directed toward neediest countries, a reflection of Congress's heightened concern for human rights.

Although the State Department sought authority to administer the Food for Peace program, powerful farm interests succeeded in placing the program in the Agriculture Department. Today the department's Foreign Agriculture Service operates the program. State does have an input regarding disbursements of P.L. 480 food, as do the Departments of Commerce and Treasury.

An important impetus for the P.L. 480 program was the need to find an outlet to dispose of surplus food held by the government. These extra stocks reached their peaks in the 1950s and 1960s, when American food aid amounted to over 90 percent of all international food assistance. By the late 1970s America's share of the international effort had declined to about 60 percent, although the United States remains the largest single donor.[20]

Through 1980, P.L. 480 assistance totaled approximately $30 billion, or about 10 percent of all American food exports.[21] Figure 13.6 shows the marked decline of P.L. 480 assistance as a proportion of overall US agricultural exports—from 27 percent in 1960 to only 3 percent in 1980. The largest recipients of Food for Peace shipments have been (in descending order) India, Pakistan, South Korea, South Vietnam, Egypt, Indonesia and Yugoslavia.[22]

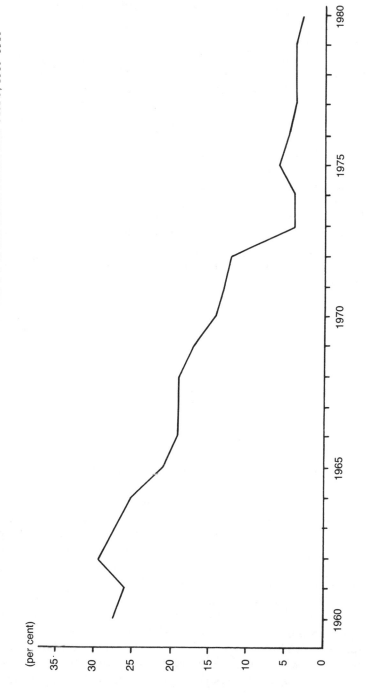

FIGURE 13–6: P.L. 480 ASSISTANCE AS PERCENTAGE OF TOTAL US AGRICULTURAL EXPORTS, 1960–1980

Source: *U.S. Foreign Policy and the Third World: Agenda 1982* by Roger D. Hansen and Contributors for the Overseas Development Council. Copyright © 1982 by the Overseas Development Council. Reprinted by permission of Praeger Publishers and the Overseas Development Council.

Food Power: A Bushel of Grain for a Barrel of Oil?

It is hardly a secret that Americans have been outraged by the quadrupled price of oil since 1973. Americans are also angered by the seeming ability of Middle Eastern shieks to manipulate oil prices and availability without reference to American wishes. Frustration over this issue has led some to propose that the United States retaliate by pegging the price of food to the price of oil. Advocates of this policy observe that food is even more essential to life than oil. Does not America's dominant position in the food market give it even more leverage in world politics than OPEC's favored energy position? Why shouldn't the United States display its "food power" the way OPEC uses oil power?

Food power proponents cite the structure of the grain market to support their position. As we have seen, five sellers—the United States, Canada, Argentina, Australia and France—clearly dominate the export of grain, with the United States and Canada accounting for approximately two-thirds of the total. No fundamental political issues divide these suppliers. All they need do is conclude a pact tying the price of grain to the price of oil.

Were this so simple, it probably would have been done already. Upon examination, it appears that the argument for food power is not nearly so strong as it may appear.

In the first place, raising food prices represents a "shotgun" rather than a "sniper rifle" approach. In other words, all importers would be hit by the blast. America's allies in Europe and Japan would resent being forced to pay more for food and would in all probability divert money from military spending to pay for it. Developing countries just barely able to afford food at current prices, and already reeling from oil price hikes, would find themselves crushed; the resulting instability would hardly serve American interests. Furthermore, the OPEC countries might well escape harm. Many of these states possess sufficient financial reserves to pay for whatever food they need; less affluent OPEC countries could curb industrial development to free funds to buy food. Besides, OPEC might ratchet up the price of oil or impose embargoes in retaliation.

In the second place, higher food prices would probably call much fallow land into cultivation, since higher prices would make such production profitable. More countries would enter the food trade as sellers, and the likelihood is strong they would sell to OPEC (perhaps in return for oil at bargain rates). Oil reserves, by contrast, are not nearly as widespread. Furthermore, there is much more latitude for expanding the export proportion of food being produced than is the case with oil. Only about 10 percent of each year's grain crop is exported, while the corresponding figure for oil is 50 percent. No doubt higher food prices would lead some governments to divert food from domestic consumption to export, and that these exports would find their way to OPEC.

Home front considerations in exporting countries present another complication. Where exports are important to the well-being of the farm community, jeopardizing sales by raising prices could be politically unwise (especially in democracies). In all the major grain exporting countries, exports represent a sizable proportion of production (see Table 13–1). Should the governments of these countries lose sales by raising prices or enacting embargoes, they would have to find some other way of compensating their farmers.

Domestic consumers represent another difficulty. If food prices rise, they too would have to pay the increased levies. Persuading American consumers to pay considerably more money for food would be a difficult task for Washington officials, especially during an inflationary period marked by high unemployment.

If an across-the-board increase in food prices incurs more penalties than gains, what about raising the price only to OPEC countries? Such a measure is likely to founder on the traditional obstacle to selective economic reprisal, namely, universal agreement. Unless all sellers cooperate, the only parties to suffer will be farmers in the countries raising prices. President Carter's attempt to punish Russia for intervening in Afghanistan is instructive. In 1980 the president suspended all grain shipments to the Soviet Union not previously arranged. Perceiving an opportunity to increase sales, Argentina increased its exports to the Soviet Union from 5.1 million

TABLE 13–1: STAKE OF MAJOR EXPORTERS IN GRAIN TRADE

Major Exporters	(by weight) Grain exports as percentage of total grain production (1973–75 average)
US	33.1
Canada	43.2
France	39.2
Australia	51.5
Argentina	41.3

Source: Adapted from Henry R. Nau, "The Diplomacy of World Food: Goals, Capabilities, Issues and Arenas," in Raymond F. Hopkins and Donald J. Puchala, eds., *The Global Political Economy of Food*. Copyright © 1978 by the University of Wisconsin Press. Reprinted by permission of the University of Wisconsin Press.

metric tons in the 1979–80 shipping year to 11.2 million in 1980–81 and 13 million in 1981–82.[23]

Even if the major suppliers agreed to penalize OPEC, what is to prevent the oil exporting countries from buying food from other customers of the principal sellers? These third parties might be more than willing to sell food in exchange for reliable oil supplies at a stable price.

Under close examination, the arguments in support of food power do not hold up very well. The only countries against whom such a policy might work are the very poorest, where higher food prices would precipitate intense suffering and starvation. The strategy of "a barrel of oil for a bushel of grain" does not seem viable.

ENERGY

A second major item on the "new agenda" is energy. Americans seem to be living in a never-ending "energy crisis." How did this impasse come about and what are its dimensions? Is the energy crisis ever likely to abate and, if so, how? Can the United States, alone or in combination with other Western powers, take any actions to mitigate dependence on the whims of Middle Eastern monarchs? Is military action in the Persian Gulf a viable policy option?

Development of Oil Dependence

The dependence of the industrialized world upon petroleum originated in the early years of this century. At that time, Western oil firms were given a virtual free hand to exploit oil reserves buried under the sands of Middle Eastern deserts. Under the concessionary system set up between 1901–1935, outside oil firms paid royalties averaging 21¢ per barrel. For the most part, the firms paid no taxes to Middle Eastern governments and were free to set production levels and prices. Dealing from a weak diplomatic hand, the Middle Eastern monarchs yielded control over their most precious resource to Western companies equipped with the technology and capital to extract oil. During this time period, Western oil companies earned handsome profits from their Middle East ventures. Since they paid so little for their oil, they were able to pass on these low prices to their customers. Thus, for decades an abundant flow of cheap oil reached Western homes and industries.

Confident that such supplies would last indefinitely, Westerners—and particularly Americans—structured their entire way of life around inexpensive and plentiful oil. Without oil, America's love affair with the automobile would not have caught fire. Americans felt no constraint to locate their homes and workplaces near each other: everyone took it for granted that long commutes by auto or train were no obstacle. America shipped large volumes of goods by trucks run on cheap diesel fuel. Instead of installing insulation in their homes, Americans just turned up their thermostats. The sight of people wearing sweaters in July in their over-air-conditioned offices was not uncommon. Without regard for energy use, middle-class Americans increasingly stocked their homes with dishwashers, clothes washers and dryers, freezers and electric ranges (not to mention electric pencil sharpeners). And why should Americans have felt concern about devouring energy? Between 1950 and 1970, the real per capita income of Americans doubled, while energy prices declined in real terms by 28 percent.[24] As America's economy burgeoned between 1950 and 1980, Americans increased their energy use at an average annual rate of 3 percent; over the thirty year span, America's energy consumption grew by 132 percent.

World War II and the postwar surge of anticolonialism shattered the timbers of the concessionary oil system.

Formation of OPEC

The inflation that accompanied the war eroded the purchasing power of the royalties Middle Eastern regimes were receiving from Western oil companies. Nationalists cried that the concessionary system was a form of colonialism. Radicals challenged the right of organizations headquartered in New York or Amsterdam to decide how much oil should come out of Middle Eastern lands.

The first break in the concessionary system came in 1945, when Venezuela persuaded outside oil companies to split profits on a 50–50 basis. By the mid-1950s, this arrangement had become the norm worldwide. Still, the oil companies continued to set production levels and prices.

Through the 1950s, the oil industry was dominated by seven major firms, known as the "Seven Sisters." These were Gulf, Texaco, Standard Oil of California, Mobil, Exxon, Royal Dutch Shell and British Petroleum. These companies cooperated so as to reduce production when the oil market became saturated, thereby maintaining prices. When demand picked up, they increased production

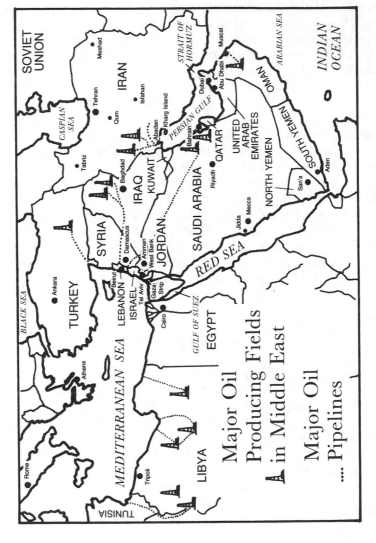

FIGURE 13-7: MIDDLE EASTERN OILFIELDS, 1981

Source: Congressional Quarterly, *Energy Policy*, 2nd ed. Copyright © 1981 by Congressional Quarterly Inc. Reprinted by permission of Congressional Quarterly Inc.

accordingly. In the 1950s, a number of other firms came onstream, including Getty, Amoco and Occidental. These new firms refused to subject themselves to the market control exerted by the Seven Sisters and sometimes charged lower prices to obtain business. In the face of oversupply, the companies refused to curb production. As a result, oil prices began to decline in the late 1950s.

In order to forestall a drop in profits, the major companies in 1959 reduced the posted price of oil. The posted price was set unilaterally by the oil companies and acted as the basis on which profits were computed for the purpose of dividing revenues with the oil producing countries and assessing taxes. While not identical to the market price, which fluctuated from day to day, the posted price was related to it. From the oil producing countries' point of view, the posted price determined the revenues they could expect to receive.

As the market price continued to diminish, the oil companies in 1960 reduced the posted price once again. To make matters worse for the oil producing countries, the United States in 1959 set quotas on imported oil. While this measure achieved its purpose of keeping out cheaper foreign oil—thereby helping domestic producers—it further reduced the revenues of oil producing countries. They now found their access to the world's thirstiest oil imbiber restricted. The quota also disturbed far-sighted critics who warned that America was depleting its own oil supplies.

In the hope of reversing their declining fortunes from oil revenue, the oil ministers from a number of oil producing countries held a meeting in Baghdad in the fall of 1960. At this gathering the Organization of Petroleum Exporting Countries (OPEC) was born. Other oil producing countries were quick to join, and the membership swelled to 13 by 1983.

At first OPEC's goal was relatively modest: move the posted price back up to previous levels and gain a right to prior consultation on future price changes. In these efforts they were largely successful. At their 1968 meeting in Vienna, the OPEC oil ministers issued an important philosophical statement that became the underpinning for future actions. The ministers declared that countries containing oil resources have the right to control production and set prices. In 1968 OPEC seemed a long way from realizing this objective.

The following year the organization got a boost toward this goal when Muammar al-Qadaffi seized control of the government of Libya and gained a higher posted price and a larger share of oil

company profits in the form of higher taxes. In 1971 Algeria nationalized the French oil company operating there. Libya followed suit,
as did Iran and Iraq. The governments of these nations found
nationalization to be good politics. By bloodying the former colonial
powers, nationalization gained popularity with the masses who
harbored much bitterness against the West. Nationalization also
tended to strengthen the stature of governments among other developing countries. Usually, the firm that had been nationalized continued doing business on a contract basis, so the oil and the money
kept flowing. During the interval 1971–1973, the oil producers also
gained a say in the determination of oil prices.

1973: War, Embargo and Price Rise

1973 proved to be a pivotal year in energy affairs. Smouldering
with humiliation after their military defeat by Israel in 1967, the
Arabs, led by Egypt, attacked the Jewish state in October 1973.
At first the Arab armies appeared to be gaining back the territory
they had lost previously. After absorbing the first blow, however,
Israeli military forces began pushing the Arab armies back to and
then beyond their jumping-off points. The Israelis surrounded a
huge Egyptian army in the Sinai and threatened to annihilate it.
Israeli forces were in position to move against Damascus. Still
another Arab military defeat appeared in the making.

Before the hostilities began, a meeting had been scheduled for
October in Vienna between OPEC oil ministers and oil company
executives to discuss price. Emboldened by Cairo's initial military
successes, the OPEC ministers asked for a posted price of $6, up
from $3. The oil executives countered with $3.50. No agreement
was reached and the meeting broke up.[25] As the fighting in the
Middle East intensifed, the oil ministers met alone and proclaimed
a new posted price of $5.12. This was the first time OPEC unilat-
erally determined oil prices and represented the realization of the
philosophy announced in 1968.

Meanwhile, on the battlefield, Israeli forces were beginning to
turn the tide. In the Arab view, Israel's military success was directly
attributable to American military assistance. OPEC decided to
deploy a weapon of its own against the supporters of Israel.

On October 18, Saudi Arabia declared it would reduce its oil
production by 10 percent and halt all oil shipments to the United
States if the latter continued to supply arms to Israel and failed to
alter its pro-Israeli policy. The very next day, President Nixon asked

Congress for an additional $2.2 billion appropriation for emergency military aid to Israel. Libya reacted quickly by imposing an embargo on oil to the United States. Most of the other Arab states, including Saudi Arabia, followed suit. OPEC also embargoed oil to other states considered friendly to Israel, namely, the Netherlands, Portugal, Rhodesia (now Zimbabwe), South Africa and Canada. The Saudis then cut their oil production by 25 percent. As other oil producers reduced their output, fears of inadequate supplies drove prices skyward. In December OPEC met in Teheran and raised the posted price to $11.65 per barrel. Thus, in the latter part of 1973 oil prices quadrupled. It is no exaggeration to say that the world has not been the same since.

Were the OPEC actions, and the embargo in particular, effective? To a certain extent the answer is yes. On November 3, 1973, representatives of the European Common Market meeting in Brussels adopted a statement calling on Israel to "end the territorial occupation which it has maintained since the conflict of 1967." The statement went on to declare that any Middle East settlement must take into account "the legitimate rights" of Palestinian refugees. Subsequently, many of the states in Western Europe began leaning more toward the Arabs than Israel. Japan also issued a statement calling on Israel to relinquish territory it had captured by war. Although the United States announced it would not be coerced, there is little doubt that OPEC's offensive was instrumental in persuading Henry Kissinger to undertake the strenuous "shuttle diplomacy" that resulted in disengagement accords between Israel and Egypt and Israel and Syria in 1974. With the cessation of military hostilities in the Middle East, OPEC lifted its embargo. Oil prices, however, remained at their lofty heights.

The 1973 OPEC measures have left oil importing countries with an unprecedented sense of vulnerability. Many fear OPEC might impose another embargo in the future, and they wonder what, if anything, they could do about it. To consider whether OPEC could at some future time reenact the events of 1973–74, let us inquire into why OPEC enjoyed such success in those years.

Worldwide Dependence on Oil

We have already seen how Americans came to base their lifestyles upon the presumption that oil would remain plentiful and cheap. Figure 13–8 shows both the dramatic increase in consumption of

FIGURE 13–8: SHARE OF US OIL CONSUMPTION SUPPLIED BY IMPORTS, 1949–1980

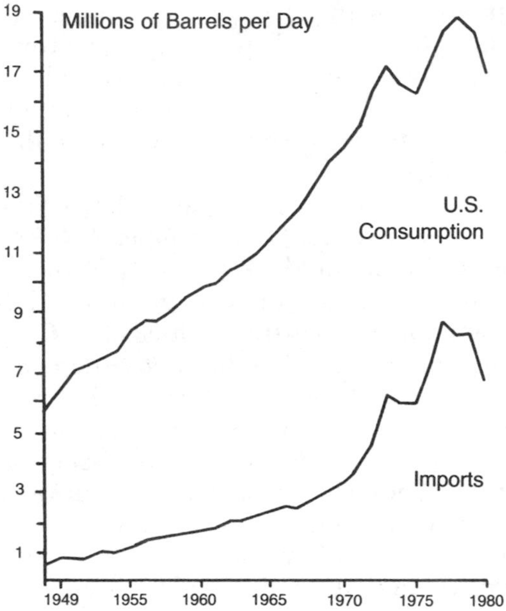

| | Millions of Barrels per Day | | |
| | | Percent | |
Year	Total Consumption	Provided by Imports	Total Imports
1949	5.76	11.3	0.65
1950	6.46	13.2	0.85
1951	7.02	12.0	0.84
1952	7.27	13.1	0.95
1953	7.60	13.6	1.03
1954	7.76	13.5	1.05
1955	8.46	14.8	1.25
1956	8.78	16.4	1.44
1957	8.81	17.8	1.57
1958	9.12	18.6	1.70
1959	9.53	18.7	1.78
1960	9.80	18.5	1.81
1961	9.98	19.2	1.92
1962	10.40	20.0	2.08
1963	10.74	19.7	2.12
1964	11.02	20.5	2.26
1965	11.51	21.4	2.47
1966	12.08	21.3	2.57
1967	12.56	20.2	2.54
1968	13.39	21.2	2.84
1969	14.14	22.4	3.17
1970	14.70	23.3	3.42
1971	15.21	25.8	3.93
1972	16.37	29.0	4.74
1973	17.31	36.2	6.26
1974	16.65	36.7	6.11
1975	16.32	37.1	6.06
1976	17.46	41.9	7.31
1977	18.43	47.8	8.81
1978	18.85	44.4	8.36
1979	18.50	43.4	8.46
1980	17.03	39.9	6.79

Source: Congressional Quarterly, *The Middle East*, 5th ed. Copyright © 1981 by Congressional Quarterly Inc. Reprinted by permission of Congressional Quarterly Inc.

oil and the increasingly important role of imported oil in the American economy following World War II. In 1949 imports made up only 11.3 percent of American petroleum consumption, but by 1980 this figure had risen to 39.9 percent. By the time of the 1973 oil embargo, petroleum supplied about half the energy used by Americans, and imports supplied just over one-third of American oil. Every sector of the American economy had grown dependent upon oil, and it has remained so to this day. The most voracious sector is transportation. In 1960 there were 74.4 million cars, trucks and buses on the road; by 1979 the number had risen to 160 million.

Meanwhile, automobiles had grown less fuel-efficient, as drivers expressed a preference for heavier cars with multiple options. As a result, fuel consumption rose from 4.11 million barrels per day (mbd) in 1960 to 8.26 mbd in 1979. In 1980, transportation accounted for 52 percent of the oil used in the United States. Industry accounted for another 20 percent, while the residential and commercial sector absorbed an additional 19 percent (mostly for heating and cooling buildings). Electric utilities, which burn mainly coal, used the remaining 9 percent.[26]

Elsewhere, oil consumption rose just as steeply as in the United States (see Table 13–2). For most other countries, however, imports constituted an even larger share of oil consumption than for the United States, as shown in Table 13–3. Japan, not shown on this table, derives over three-fourths of its energy needs from oil, practically all of it imported.

Thus, by 1973 the entire developed world had grown dependent on oil. Western Europe in 1973 used 14 times as much oil as it used in 1950, and Japan's consumption of oil rose a staggering 167 times during those years. The United States, which did not have to rebuild after the war, increased its use of oil 2.6 times during this interval, while the developing countries raised consumption four times.[27] Such reliance upon petroleum conferred enormous influence upon oil producing countries. No other fuel was readily

TABLE 13–2: WORLD OIL CONSUMPTION, 1950–1978
(thousand barrels per day)

Year	United States	Canada	Japan	Europe	Developing Countries	OPEC	Total Free World
1950	6,451	324	31	1,048	1,992	196	10,042
1955	8,458	548	152	1,960	3,116	342	14,576
1960	9,577	837	644	4,535	2,796	666	19,055
1965	11,294	1,143	1,803	8,257	3,840	840	27,177
1970	14,457	1,472	4,183	13,580	5,856	1,162	40,710
1971	14,857	1,538	4,411	14,066	6,662	1,291	42,825
1972	15,703	1,689	4,805	14,713	6,469	1,430	44,809
1973	16,971	1,867	5,207	15,153	7,784	1,925	48,907
1974	16,354	1,892	5,499	14,294	9,292	1,985	49,316
1975	15,854	1,782	5,123	12,726	7,265	2,296	45,046
1976	16,825	1,762	5,370	14,034	8,505	2,398	48,894
1977	18,428	1,928	5,731	14,013	7,918	2,637	50,655
1978	18,276	1,850	5,115	13,924	8,588	2,522	50,275

Department of Energy Figures. Amounts to 1973 estimated by DOE.

Source: Congressional Quarterly, *Energy Policy*, 2nd ed. Copyright © 1981 by Congressional Quarterly Inc. Reprinted by permission of Congressional Quarterly Inc.

TABLE 13–3: DEPENDENCE ON OIL IMPORTS (1978)

	Imports as a percentage of total oil consumption	Oil imports as a percentage of total energy
USA	46.2	22.2
France	94.8	57.1
West Germany	96.4	51.8
Italy	88.1	58.8
United Kingdom	43.0	19.6
OECD countries	64.4	33.6

Source: adapted from Robert J. Lieber, "Energy, Economics and Security in Alliance Perspective," *International Security, IV* (Spring 1980): 143. Copyright © 1980 by the President and Fellows of Harvard College and of the Massachusetts Institute of Technology. Reprinted by permission.

available or substitutable in a short time frame. Without imported oil, the economies of most industrial countries would gradually come to a silent halt.

Not only were so many nations dependent on oil, but they were dependent on OPEC oil. At the time of the embargo, OPEC produced 55 percent of the world's oil and accounted for 86 percent of oil exports. With American excess capacity gone, OPEC was the source of 37 percent of all oil consumed by the non-Communist world.[28] Furthermore, OPEC countries own approximately two-thirds of the world's proven oil reserves (Fig. 13–9). Stated quite simply, OPEC succeeded in 1973 because it owned most of the world's oil.

The above data largely explain why the oil producers have been more successful in exerting political leverage than the food producers. Although both OPEC (in oil) and North America (in food) account for a large proportion of the commodity in trade, alternative sources of food are much more available. While many countries have additional acres they can cultivate, few possess oil reserves. Whereas food importers can turn to many countries for food, oil importers have few alternatives other than OPEC. In times of food scarcity, many people can alter their diets and thus stave off starvation. In contrast, oil-burning equipment cannot utilize other fuels on a short-time basis. The proportion of the commodity in trade is also relevant. As we have seen, only about 10 percent of the world's grain is traded; the rest is consumed in the country where it is grown. A much larger percentage of the total petroleum in use is imported, and this gives the sellers considerable leverage over the buyers. In 1979, for example, OPEC supplied 32 mbd, or 48 percent of the world's total consumption of 66 mbd. (In that year, oil accounted for 22.5 percent of the world's total energy use.)[29] Of course, oil embargoes will not work if the principal suppliers fail

FIGURE 13–9: ESTIMATED CRUDE OIL PROVED RESERVES, DECEMBER 31, 1980

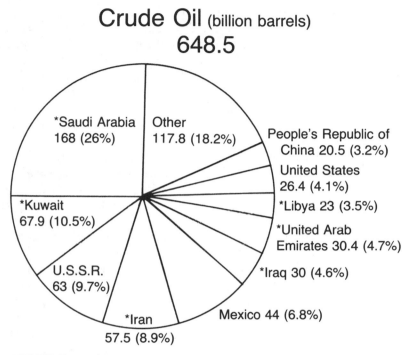

Crude Oil (billion barrels)
648.5

*Saudi Arabia 168 (26%)

Other 117.8 (18.2%)

People's Republic of China 20.5 (3.2%)

United States 26.4 (4.1%)

*Libya 23 (3.5%)

*United Arab Emirates 30.4 (4.7%)

*Iraq 30 (4.6%)

*Kuwait 67.9 (10.5%)

U.S.S.R. 63 (9.7%)

*Iran 57.5 (8.9%)

Mexico 44 (6.8%)

*OPEC Countries

Source: Congressional Quarterly, *The Middle East*, 5th ed. Copyright © 1981 by Congressional Quarterly Inc. Reprinted by permission of Congressional Quarterly Inc.

to abide by the agreement. In 1973 all the OPEC states cooperated. In the future, such tight control may be more difficult to impose, because multinational corporations acting as middlemen are increasingly able to alter the destination of oil en route. Even during the 1973–74 embargo, these firms were able to mitigate the impact by selling non-OPEC oil to embargoed countries and routing OPEC oil to countries not on the embargo list. Nonetheless, this limited capacity to disrupt future embargoes offers little ground for complacency.

In 1983, oil producing countries faced their biggest challenge to date to their ability to coordinate production and prices. This challenge was brought about by an oversupply of oil, caused by global economic recession (largely the product of rising oil prices during the previous decade), an unusually warm winter in 1982–83, conservation in oil consuming countries, and new oil discoveries in Mexico and the North Sea. In the wake of falling oil prices, OPEC oil ministers met over a period of three months in an effort to reduce overall output, assign production quotas to member countries, and reduce the price of oil. Two factors complicated OPEC's problem. Lower oil prices were preventing some OPEC countries from making payments on industrial projects already begun and financing imports; production cutbacks combined with still lower prices would further reduce revenues. Three non-OPEC oil producers, Mexico, Norway and Great Britain, already were selling oil below the OPEC price of $34 per barrel and gave no sign of willingness to reduce production. Mexico, which in 1983 owed other countries a total of $80 billion, complained that reduced oil sales would deprive the country of its principal means of paying off this enormous debt. The oil producers clearly stood at a critical crossroad. Would they succeed in reducing total production, apportioning the total agreed upon, and cutting prices? Or, would the OPEC cartel be splintered by a scramble by each member to sell as much oil as possible at whatever price the market would bear?

In March 1983, OPEC finally agreed to lower production from 18.5 to 17.5 million barrels per day and to reduce prices from $34 to $29 per barrel—the first price reduction in OPEC's history. Production costs in the Middle East ranged from $2 to $3 per barrel, leaving substantial room for further price cuts. The member states also apportioned production quotas among themselves. It remained far from clear, however, that the agreement would hold up. With the world buying (in spring 1983) only 14.5 million barrels per day of OPEC's oil, would not OPEC's target of 17.5 million barrels invite members to cheat on prices and production quotas? And if non-OPEC oil exporters refused to curb production, was not a price war even more likely? Should worldwide demand for petroleum pick up, oil prices could rise again.

While the world oil situation remains somewhat cloudy, what appears far more certain is that should OPEC at some future time agree on an oil embargo, the United States and other oil consumers will remain highly vulnerable. Figures 13–10 through 13–13 reveal why this is so. Among the ten major petroleum producing countries of the world (Fig. 13–10), seven are members of OPEC. (The USSR, US, and China are not.) Figure 13–11 shows worldwide oil supply and use. On the supply side, we can see that OPEC accounts for half the world's crude oil production. In terms of consumption, however, OPEC accounts for a negligible quantity. The OECD

FIGURE 13–10: MAJOR PETROLEUM PRODUCING COUNTRIES OF THE WORLD, 1980

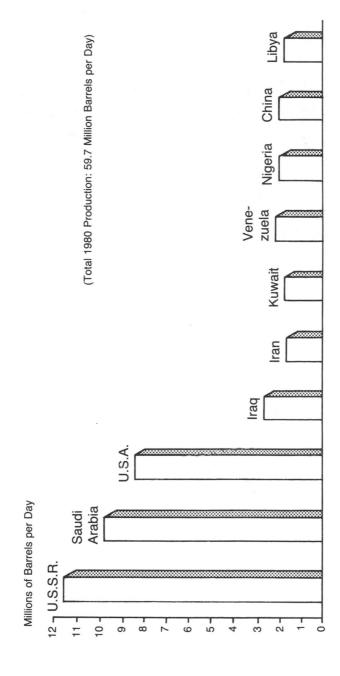

Millions of Barrels per Day

(Total 1980 Production: 59.7 Million Barrels per Day)

Source: Congressional Quarterly, *The Middle East*, 5th ed. Copyright © 1981 by Congressional Quarterly Inc. Reprinted by permission of Congressional Quarterly Inc.

FIGURE 13–11: PETROLEUM SUPPLY AND DISPOSITION, 1978

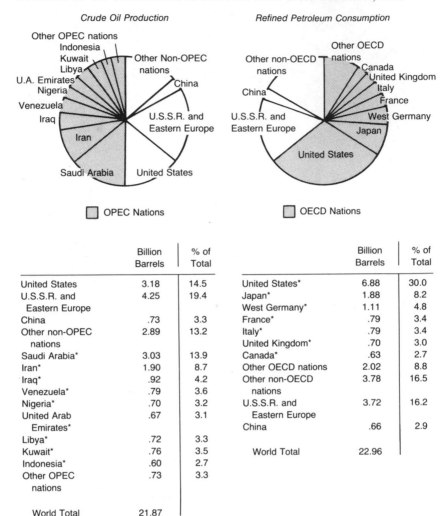

	Billion Barrels	% of Total
United States	3.18	14.5
U.S.S.R. and Eastern Europe	4.25	19.4
China	.73	3.3
Other non-OPEC nations	2.89	13.2
Saudi Arabia*	3.03	13.9
Iran*	1.90	8.7
Iraq*	.92	4.2
Venezuela*	.79	3.6
Nigeria*	.70	3.2
United Arab Emirates*	.67	3.1
Libya*	.72	3.3
Kuwait*	.76	3.5
Indonesia*	.60	2.7
Other OPEC nations	.73	3.3
World Total	21.87	

	Billion Barrels	% of Total
United States*	6.88	30.0
Japan*	1.88	8.2
West Germany*	1.11	4.8
France*	.79	3.4
Italy*	.79	3.4
United Kingdom*	.70	3.0
Canada*	.63	2.7
Other OECD nations	2.02	8.8
Other non-OECD nations	3.78	16.5
U.S.S.R. and Eastern Europe	3.72	16.2
China	.66	2.9
World Total	22.96	

*Organization of Petroleum Exporting Countries

*Organization for Economic Cooperation and Development

Source: Congressional Quarterly, *Energy Policy*, 2nd ed. Copyright © 1981 by Congressional Quarterly Inc. Reprinted by permission of Congressional Quarterly Inc.

FIGURE 13–12: SOURCES OF AMERICAN OIL, 1979

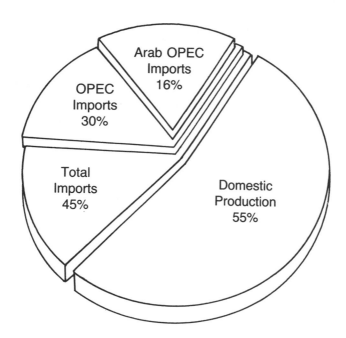

	Thousands of Barrels per Day	Percent of Total
U.S. Production	10,258	55%
Imports:	8,411	45%
OPEC Nations[1]	5,612	30%
Non-OPEC Nations	2,799	15%
Total[2]	18,669	

[1]Arab OPEC: 3,037,000, 16%.
[2]Total approximate U.S. supply in 1979. Consumption, after exports and losses, was 18,434,000 barrels per day.

Source: Congressional Quarterly, *Energy Policy*, 2nd ed. Copyright © 1981 by Congressional Quarterly Inc. Reprinted by permission of Congressional Quarterly Inc.

FIGURE 13–13: MAJOR OIL SUPPLIERS TO THE UNITED STATES,
      1979

| Country | (thousands of barrels) | | |
	Crude Oil	Petroleum Products	Total
*Saudi Arabia	488,278	3,308	491,586
*Nigeria	389,115	4,211	393,326
*Venezuela	106,554	145,680	252,234
*Libya	232,704	6,020	238,724
*Algeria	220,074	10,062	230,136
Canada	97,526	96,848	194,374
Mexico	157,795	637	158,432
Virgin Islands	—	157,486	157,486
*Indonesia	137,362	14,793	152,155
*Iran	107,811	2,839	110,650
*United Arab Emirates	102,108	—	102,108
Netherlands Antilles	—	84,428	84,428
United Kingdom	71,923	1,501	73,424
Trinidad	43,861	24,143	68,004
Bahamas	—	53,907	53,907
Puerto Rico	—	33,509	33,509
*Iraq	32,052	—	32,052
Norway	27,523	17	27,540
Malaysia	18,786	4,981	23,767
Egypt	20,205	103	20,308
Peru	14,746	1,689	16,435
Oman	13,466	2,662	16,128
*Ecuador	11,363	4,545	15,908
Angola	14,088	1,499	15,587
*Gabon	15,328	134	15,462
*Qatar	11,450	—	11,450
Total imports by U.S.	2,364,499	705,576	3,070,075
U.S. Imports from OPEC in 1979			
Thousands of barrels	1,855,713	192,677	2,048,390
Percent of Total Imports	78.5	27.3	66.7

nations are clearly the world's largest consumers of oil, with the Soviet Union and Eastern Europe a distant second. The United States, which used 30 percent of the world's oil in 1978, produced only 14.5 percent of the world's oil. Such statistics lie behind the accusation that the United States is an oil glutton. Where do America's oil supplies come from? Figure 13–12 answers this question. Thirty percent of the oil used by America in 1979 originated in OPEC lands. Figure 13–13 shows the major petroleum suppliers to the United States in 1979. It will be noted that the top five suppliers were members of OPEC.

In summary, OPEC's control of such a large proportion of the world's oil seems likely to give the organization considerable political influence for so long as oil remains an essential source of energy.

After 1973

Since OPEC lifted its embargo in 1974, the organization has undergone some strain. Certain radical states, such as Algeria, Libya and Iraq, have favored fairly steep price hikes. Others, such as Saudi Arabia, have urged more restraint. Since the Saudis account for nearly half the oil produced by Arab states, their wishes cannot be ignored.

In recent meetings, OPEC has often been unable to agree on a price for oil. In those instances, the organization has established a range of prices, with the Saudis charging the lower amount. Despite such division, oil prices continued to climb (see Table 13–4), reaching a high of $40 per barrel in 1981, until the March 1983 decision to lower prices to $29 per barrel. The rise in oil prices from $3.00 per barrel in 1973 has had drastic consequences for the oil consuming countries. The United States bill for oil imports reached $60 billion in 1979 and rose to $80 billion the following year.[30] Astronomical oil bills have contributed to inflation, stagnant economic growth and unemployment. Western Europe and Japan have been hit harder than the United States, being more dependent than the United States on imported oil. Japan imports almost all of its oil, which accounts for three-fourths of the country's energy; Western Europe gets approximately two-thirds of its oil from abroad. The developing countries suffered most of all. As Table 13–5 reveals, their bill for imported oil rose from $7.4 billion in 1973 to an estimated $98.6 billion in 1981; during the same interval, oil imports as a percentage of their total imports rose from 9 percent to 30 percent.

TABLE 13–4: PRICES PAID FOR FOREIGN OIL, 1970–1981
(In Dollars per Barrel)

Year	Saudi Arabia		Iran		Nigeria		Venezuela	
	Current	Constant[1]	Current	Constant[1]	Current	Constant[1]	Current	Constant[1]
1970	1.35	1.48	1.36	1.49	2.10	2.30	2.05	2.24
1971	1.75	1.82	1.76	1.83	2.65	2.76	2.45	2.55
1972	1.90	1.90	1.91	1.91	2.80	2.80	2.45	2.45
1973	2.10	1.99	2.11	2.00	3.10	2.93	2.60	2.46
1974	9.60	8.35	10.63	9.25	12.60	10.96	9.30	8.09
1975	10.46	8.33	10.67	8.50	11.80	9.40	11.00	8.76
1976	11.51	8.71	11.62	8.80	12.84	9.72	11.12	8.42
1977	12.09	8.65	12.81	9.16	14.33	10.25	12.72	9.09
1978	12.70	8.46	12.81	8.54	14.33	9.55	12.82	8.54
1979	13.34	8.20	13.45	8.26	14.82	9.10	13.36	8.21
1980	26.00	14.66	30.37	17.12	29.99	16.91	25.20	14.21
1981	32.00	18.04	37.00	20.86	40.02	22.56	32.88	18.53

[1]Constant 1972 dollars using GNP average annual implicit price deflator.
Source: Congressional Quarterly, *The Middle East*, 5th ed. Copyright © 1981 by Congressional Quarterly Inc. Reprinted by permission of Congressional Quarterly Inc.

TABLE 13-5: THE OIL-IMPORT BURDEN OF DEVELOPING COUNTRIES
($ billions and percentages)

Net Oil-Importing Developing Countries[1]	1973	1974	1975	1978	1979	1980	1981[2]
			($ billions)				
Oil Imports	7.4	24.0	24.4	33.6	51.9	85.0	98.6
Oil Trade Balance (Net Oil Bill)	-5.2	-17.1	-17.9	-26.0	-40.9	-66.5	-77.5
Total Imports	81.3	126.9	129.8	186.0	240.1	303.6	331.5
Oil Imports as % of Total Imports	9	19	19	18	22	28	30

[1]Excludes OPEC and such oil exporters as Oman, Bahrain, Bolivia, People's Republic of the Congo, Egypt, Malaysia, Mexico, Peru, Syrian Arab Republic, Trinidad, and Tunisia.
[2]Projections.
NOTES: Developing centrally planned economies not included.

Source: *U.S. Foreign Policy and the Third World: Agenda 1982* by Roger D. Hansen and Contributors for the Overseas Development Council. Copyright © 1982 by the Overseas Development Council. Reprinted by permission of Praeger Publishers and the Overseas Development Council.

One result of higher oil prices has been a transfer of funds unprecedented in history. By the end of 1980, the major oil producing states had accumulated some $300 billion in foreign assets. These governments have recycled their foreign exchange in three principal ways. Many countries have bought large amounts of Western consumer goods, military hardware, industrial equipment, food and other commodities. They have also invested large sums at home and abroad, especially in the West. Finally, they have lent money to some of the hard-pressed oil importing countries of the Third World.[31] The first two forms of recycling illustrate the mutual dependence between oil exporting states and the industrialized world. Were the latter to collapse, the oil suppliers would lose extensive investments and would find themselves unable to buy the goods they wanted with their excess petrodollars. As Saudi Arabian Oil Minister Sheik Ahmed Zaki al-Yamani stated, "We know that if [the West's] economy collapses, we'll collapse with you."[32]

The 1983 decline in oil prices, precipitated by oversupply, further underlined global interdependence. While many oil consumers gleefully hailed the drop in oil prices, Western bankers warned of catastrophic consequences should the price fall below $25 per barrel. Western banks had loaned so much money to the oil producers that too drastic a price decline would prevent them from paying their debts. This would throw the international monetary system into chaos and also force some Western banks to close their doors. Both the oil producers and consumers, it seemed, had become locked into a system in which oil prices could neither rise nor fall too steeply without bringing about cataclysmic results.

The 1983 oil price drop held unanticipated consequences for the oil producers. In the expectation of accumulating mountains of petrodollars for years to come, these countries had begun vast industrial undertakings and had begun to import large quantities of consumer items. Suddenly, many of these states found themselves without the funds to pay for these projects, and certain oil exporting countries even found themselves in debt! Saudi Arabia, for example, faced a $20 billion balance of payments deficit in 1983. For the time being, economic retrenchment had become the order of the day in oil exporting lands.

In the late 1970s and early 1980s turmoil continued to plague the Middle East. In 1979 young militants stormed the United States embassy in Teheran and seized hostages, demanding the return of the shah. The Soviet Union invaded Afghanistan and Iraq began a war with Iran. In 1982 Israel drove the Palestine Liberation Organization out of Lebanon. Such events bring to mind the warning of noted oil economist Walter J. Levy:

> Contingencies could arise from the Soviet threat, regional fighting, internal upheavals, terrorists, the festering Arab-Israeli issue or a sudden shift in the production and pricing policy of one or more OPEC countries. It is nearly certain that we will have to cope with one or even several of these contingencies in the years ahead.[33]

Rising oil prices and fears of future embargoes stimulated the Western industrialized states to take joint action. In 1974, 21 of the member states of the OECD, including the United States, formed the International Energy Agency (IEA). The IEA provides a framework for joint action along three lines. In the area of energy management, IEA has devised an oil-sharing scheme in case of future shortages and has encouraged member states to set lower targets for future oil consumption and imports. In December 1979, IEA states set a goal of limiting total IEA oil imports to 24.6 mbd. The following year they agreed to aim at decreasing oil consumption by 1990 to 40 percent of total energy use. IEA's research program has concentrated on ways of reducing dependence on oil by seeking new energy technologies. The long-term program sponsored by IEA has focused on developing alternative sources of energy and improving the conditions of energy investment and trade. One specific objective has been to increase reliance upon coal.

It remains to be seen whether the IEA can attain such objectives. At the very least, however, IEA represents a change from the previous pattern of competition and unilateral action by the major oil consumers. Under IEA auspices, these countries now plan and manage their energy affairs in a consultative setting. Only time will reveal whether future energy shortages, should they occur, will place an unendurable burden on such cooperative behavior.

The Future Energy Outlook

What of the future? Is there sufficient energy to sustain the economic growth of the industrial countries and to propel the developing world into the industrial age? Is the planet in danger of running out of energy? If energy may be in short supply, which countries will get it and what methods might they employ to do so?

Any attempt to foretell the future is fraught with difficulty. Who, standing on the threshold of the present century, would have predicted two world wars and the coming of the nuclear age? Unforeseen developments are bound to upset the calculations of even the most careful planners. Nonetheless, policymakers feel constrained to think ahead and to tailor national policies to outcomes that have high probabilities of occurring. Let us attempt to peer ahead into the energy future, realizing that our vision is certain to be clouded.

In 1980 the IEA published a report, *Outlook for the Eighties*, which sought to determine the adequacy of energy over the next decade.[34] The report's conclusions may be found in Table 13–6. The figures labelled "high economic growth" reflect projected economic growth rates for IEA countries of 4.1 percent from 1978–1985 and 3.7 percent from 1985–1990. The columns labelled "expected growth" assume average economic growth rates of 3–3.5 percent through the 1980s, a rate of growth the IEA deems more likely to prevail than the other set of figures. If the IEA projections prove accurate, the world will be short 3.7 or 2.1 mbd in 1985 and 8.6 or 5.7 mbd in 1990. The report assumes that OPEC is unlikely to increase significantly its oil production beyond the actual level of 31.6 mbd in 1979, as OPEC countries will wish to stretch out their oil reserves for as long as possible. Among non-OPEC developing countries, Mexico is the most likely to boost oil production; its output could reach 3.5–5.0 mbd by 1990, up from 1.2 mbd in 1978.

TABLE 13–6: GLOBAL OIL BALANCE

	1978 Actual	1985 High Economic Growth	1985 Expected Growth	1990 High Economic Growth	1990 Expected Growth
World Oil Consumption (Mbd)					
IEA Countries	38.8	43.2	41.6	45.0	42.1
Others (incl. OPEC)	12.6	17.3	17.3	22.2	22.2
World (excl. CPE)*	51.4	60.5	58.9	67.2	64.3
Non-Opec Oil Production (Mbd)					
IEA Countries	14.2	17.1	17.1	17.1	17.1
Developing Countries	4.6	8.5	8.5	11.0	11.0
Net Imports from CPE	1.3	0.4	0.4	-1.1	-1.1
TOTAL	20.1	26.0	26.0	27.0	27.0
OPEC Production (Mbd)	30.5	30.8	30.8	31.6	31.6
Additional Production or Savings Required (Mbd)	—	3.7	2.1	8.6	5.7

*CPE = centrally planned economies
Source: Adapted from International Energy Agency, *Outlook for the Eighties*. Reprinted by permission of the Organization for Economic Co-operation and Development.

The implications of this study are startlingly clear. The world must either find more oil, lower its demand for oil, or suffer deprivation. If the first two alternatives prove unattainable, economic growth will surely slow down. Clashes among countries might well result, as each nation scrambles for scarce oil supplies. Furthermore, an environment of oil scarcity is likely to heighten the diplomatic power of those countries with substantial oil reserves (see Fig. 13–9). With approximately one-fourth of the world's proven oil reserves, Saudi Arabia is bound to be a critical country. The future stability of the Saudi regime will certainly be a matter of interest to Washington as well as other oil consuming states.

Energy Alternatives

Most energy experts agree that one day in the early part of the next century, the very last drop of oil will emerge from the ground. It therefore behooves the world to search for energy alternatives. Which ones appear most feasible from today's vantage point?

Conservation.

In 1977 President Carter said, "Ours is the most wasteful nation on earth." He then called upon Americans to conserve energy. Although resentful at first, many Americans heeded the call, as much to protect their own pocketbooks as to help their country. In greater numbers than ever before, Americans began insulating, caulking windows, turning down heaters and air-conditioners, and driving more fuel-efficient cars. The government provided tax credits for the installation of energy-saving devices in buildings and set a limit of 55 miles per hour on the highways. A 1979 study by the Harvard Business School's Energy Project concluded, "The United States can use 30 to 40 percent less energy than it does, with virtually no penalty for the way Americans live."[35]

Before long these conservation efforts began paying off. Gasoline consumption declined 7 percent from 1979 to 1980. This was an important achievement, because cars and light trucks use nearly 40 percent of the oil consumed in the United States. Total American oil use in 1980 was down 8 percent from 1979, and oil imports were 18 percent less in 1980.[36] By April 1981, oil imports were down 23 percent from the same period the previous year. In 1983, the United States imported 33 percent of its oil, compared with 45 percent in 1977.

While the above figures are encouraging, many far-reaching conservation measures have already been taken. From here on the saving in oil use is likely to diminish. While conservation is a most worthwhile goal, it is unlikely to free America from reliance upon foreign oil.

Of late, many conservationists have turned their attention to the automobile, since cars are major consumers of oil. Already on the market is gasohol, a blend of 10 percent ethanol and 90 percent gasoline. Ethanol is made from grain, sugar beets or other agricultural products. Researchers are also working on an electric car to be run on a battery that could be recharged by plugging it into an electric socket. This electricity could be generated by coal, an abundant fuel popular with electric utilities. For many drivers, an electric car with a top speed of 40 miles per hour and a range of 100 miles would be adequate, especially for city dwellers or as a family's second car.

Natural gas.

Natural gas today supplies just over one-fourth of America's energy. Gas heats over half the country's homes and apartments and is the primary source of energy for industry (providing 37 percent of industry's energy compared to oil's contribution of 34 percent). Gas burns cleanly, is easy to transport and is convenient to use. America contains enough natural gas to last well into the next century. Unfortunately, it cannot be substituted for oil as a fuel for automobiles and other vehicles.

Synthetic Fuels.

In 1980 President Carter signed the Energy Security Act. This law created the Synthetic Fuels Corporation, a government-owned corporation charged with providing loans, loan guarantees, purchase agreements and price guarantees to private companies that produce synthetic fuels. Various types of synthetic fuels have potential for development. At present the main difficulty is cost; synthetic fuels are not competitive with other types of fuel. Coal, for example, can be converted into a form of oil or gas, but the process is extremely expensive. Many of the synthetic fuel proponents have focused on converting oil shale into liquid fuel. In a 16,500 square mile area straddling Colorado, Utah and Wyoming lie deposits of oil shale that the government estimates contains 400–700 billion barrels of recoverable oil, more than the oil reserves of Saudi Arabia.[37] To recover oil from shale, it is necessary to heat the shale rock to over 900 degrees Fahrenheit. A ton of good quality shale will yield up to two-thirds of a barrel of oil. Environmental considerations aside, the main barrier to commercial use of shale oil is expense. If the cost of producing a barrel of oil from shale can be brought down from the present level of $25–$35, this form of synthetic fuel could revolutionize America's energy future. Should oil prices continue the decline begun in early 1983, development of synthetic fuels would become economically unfeasible, at least in the short run.

Biomass represents another type of synthetic fuel. It is possible to convert farm and forest products and municipal solid waste into liquid fuel, such as the ethanol used in gasohol. Again, the main obstacle to commercial use is cost.

Coal.

At one time coal was the principal source of energy in America. In the nineteenth and early twentieth century, "King Coal" fueled the industrialization of the country. By the end of World War II, however, oil had surpassed coal. Today coal is responsible for about one-fifth of America's energy (see Fig. 13–14).

The United States contains enormous deposits of coal, possessing 31 percent of the world's economically recoverable coal reserves. Were America to convert from oil to coal, the country's energy problems would be largely solved.

There are reasons why this has not occurred. Chunks of coal cannot be used to power vehicles; coal seems inappropriate for the transportation sector. Coal must be moved by train or barge, a far less easy process than the movement of oil or natural gas through pipelines. Coal is much more awkward to load and unload than oil or gas. One of coal's most objectionable properties is the filth it emits while burning. (England's King Edward, who lived from 1239–1307, ordered the death penalty for anyone found guilty of burning it.) Antipollution devices known as scrubbers can remove most of this soot, but they are expensive. If not removed by these scrubbers, the sulfur given off by burning coal combines with air to form sulfur dioxide. Sulfur dioxide is the poisonous substance in "acid rain," which is harmful to crops, humans, and fish. Canada has expressed great displeasure with the United States for allegedly despoiling the Canadian environment by acid rain, produced by American plants near the Canadian border.

As homeowners and shopkeepers seem reluctant to shovel coal into furnaces, the largest hope for using more coal rests with public

FIGURE 13–14: US CONSUMPTION BY ENERGY SOURCE, 1979

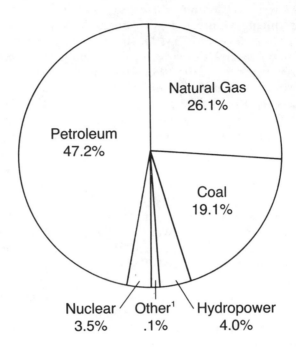

Quadrillion (10¹⁵) Btu
Coal	15.040
Gas	20.546
Petroleum	37.135
Hydro	3.163
Nuclear	2.748
Other	.089
Total	78.721

Source: Department of Energy.

Statistics reflect 1979 consumption.

[1]Other includes geothermal, wood, refuse and other vegetable fuels used by utilities to generate electricity.

utilities. Today, these electric power plants use three-fourths of the coal burned in the United States. By converting from oil or gas to coal—admittedly an expensive operation—utilities could reduce consumption of scarcer fuels.

Nuclear Power.

In the wake of the 1973–74 oil embargo, interest in nuclear energy accelerated. By the early 1980s, however, enthusiasm for nuclear power had slowed considerably. The 1979 accident at the Three Mile Island nuclear reactor in Pennsylvania probably did more to dispel interest in nuclear power than any other event. The Three Mile Island incident shattered public confidence in the safety of nuclear power. The disposal of radioactive wastes is another source of concern. Some of this material will remain radioactive for more than a thousand years. Leaks of radioactive material from storage tanks in Hanford, Washington, have called into question the adequacy of existing methods of storage. Economic stagnation has also contributed to the slowdown of the nuclear power industry. Lower levels of economic activity have reduced the demand for electricity, resulting in less demand for building electric power plants of any type. In 1980, 68 nuclear power plants were licensed to operate in the United States, excluding three shut down indefinitely for safety reasons (Three Mile Island, Humboldt Bay in California and Dresden 1 in Illinois). Another unit was licensed for testing, while construction permits had been issued for an additional 85 plants.[38] Given the disenchantment with nuclear power, however, it is far from certain that many of the unbuilt plants will be constructed.

While some people regard nuclear power as exceedingly hazardous, others regard it as one of the more promising alternatives to oil. The issue continues to arouse controversy.

Renewable Sources of Energy.

Once oil or natural gas is taken out of the ground and burned it is gone forever. In contrast, falling water that turns a turbine does not disappear; it can be used again. Such is the nature of renewable energy sources.

The principal sources of renewable energy are water, wind, sun and geothermal springs. Solar power relies on the warming rays of the sun to produce energy. Due to the large initial investment required, most homeowners are reluctant to install the necessary equipment. Should costs come down, or should government tax credits or subsidies go up, solar power may become more pacticable. Hydroelectric power already supplies approximately 4 percent of America's energy. Gigantic hydroelectric projects like Hoover Dam do not appear on the energy horizon, but more modest undertakings may prove cost effective for mid-size communities near flowing water. Like falling water, wind can be harnessed to rotate turbines that generate electricity. Thus far these devices supply only a marginal amount of energy. Finally, hot water just below the earth's surface can be used to heat buildings or turn steam-driven electrical turbines. The location of such geothermal sources is not very widespread, however; perhaps the best known examples are the geysers in California.

Once all is said and done, alternatives to oil as a source of energy do appear to hold considerable potential. However, due to high costs, conversion from oil to these alternatives is not likely to take place for some time, probably a decade or longer. In the meanwhile, the United States will remain dependent on imported oil, the bulk of which comes from the troubled region of the Persian Gulf.

Seize the Persian Gulf?

Given the continued dependence of the United States and other Western countries on Persian Gulf oil, coupled with the precarious political stability of the area, more than one observer has suggested that the United States plan to seize the Persian Gulf in case oil supplies are interrupted. As we saw in Chapter 3, President Carter declared in January 1980, that "an attempt by any outside force to gain control of the Persian Gulf region will be regarded as an assault on the vital interests of the United States. It will be repelled by use of any means necessary, including military force." President Reagan has reaffirmed this pledge. A telling argument in support of military action in the Persian Gulf is the military weakness of the Gulf states. Surely, hard-line advocates say, the small states and picturesque kingdoms of the region offer no match for the forces of the United States and its NATO allies.

Severe political upheaval that threatens to interdict oil shipments for a long interval might warrant a Western military move into the Persian Gulf. Mason Willrich cautions against taking such a decision lightly, however. Western military forces would have to consider the possibility of Soviet counteraction in an area where

FIGURE 13-15: IMPORTANCE OF THE PERSIAN GULF

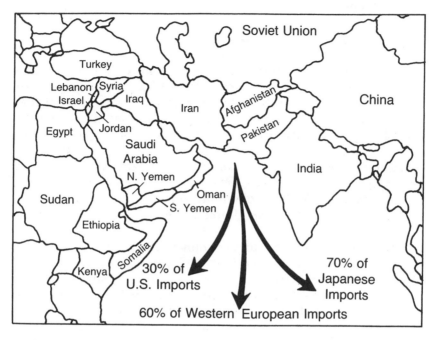

Source: Congressional Quarterly, *The Middle East*, 5th ed. Copyright © 1981 by Congressional Quarterly Inc. Reprinted by permission of Congressional Quarterly Inc.

Moscow has logistical and geographic advantages. Should the Soviets intervene, the chances of escalation to nuclear war could not be ruled out. Western military intervention would be almost certain to antagonize the Third World and might even encourage some developing countries to cut off exports in sympathy. Furthermore, it is not clear when occupying military forces could depart. Unless they remained to guard wells, pipelines, harbors and other facilities, guerrillas could easily disrupt the flow of oil. Indeed, the targets of Western military intervention could take such steps themselves once they learned attacking forces were in transit. The invaders would also have to cope with the highly sophisticated military equipment they themselves have sold to the oil producing countries, thereby increasing the monetary and manpower costs of such action. Once an invasion was begun, Western powers would encounter difficulties in supplying and reinforcing their forces across such wide distances.[39]

A military invasion of the Persian Gulf would be difficult at best and should only be contemplated under the direst of emergencies.

MINERALS

In a complex economy such as America's, almost every type of raw material has some bearing upon national security. Figure 13–16 illustrates United States dependence on mineral imports other than oil. For many of the minerals shown, American consumption derives from domestic production and imports from Canada and other non-Communist developed countries. In some cases, notably columbium, manganese, cobalt, aluminum, tin and fluorite, imports from developing countries constitute a large percentage of American consumption. Aside from platinum and chromium, Communist countries do not supply the United States with substantial quantities of minerals.

In order to have access to these minerals in time of war or other international emergency, the United States maintains a strategic stockpile of key minerals. Should the next war be a "spasm" nuclear war, whose duration lasted no more than a few hours or days, the United States would have sufficient supplies of these minerals. However, in case of a conflict that persisted for a much longer interval, the United States would be forced to import or develop substitutes. Since the latter is not always feasible, the United States seeks (primarily by naval power) to keep open shipping routes between sources of supply and the American continent. In terms of dollars, no imported mineral costs anywhere near what the United States pays for foreign oil. America's main concern is not being able to afford minerals but rather maintaining access to supplies.

Thus, in the case of minerals, as in food and energy, the United States finds its fate bound to the entire international state system.

FOR DISCUSSION

Is the alleviation of world hunger essentially an economic or a political task?

Since rapid population growth in many countries compounds the problem of overcoming hunger, should the United States condition food aid on an effective population control program in the recipient country?

FIGURE 13–16: U.S. MINERAL IMPORT DEPENDENCE, 1976

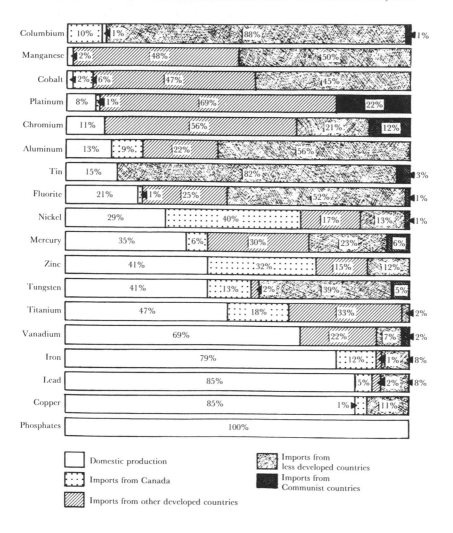

*Net imports as a percent of consumption. Figures are based on metal and metal content of ores and scrap.

Source: U.S., President, *International Economic Report of the President*, 1977, p. 12.

Should the United States give food aid to the neediest states or to those most willing to cooperate with American foreign policy?

What priorities should the United States assign to the various domestic and international objectives of food aid?

What policies should the United States adopt to reduce dependence on imported oil?

Is the United States an "energy glutton"? Should America reduce its oil consumption and let developing countries have more?

Under what conditions, if any, should the United States mount a military invasion of the Persian Gulf?

READING SUGGESTIONS

Conant, Melvin A. *The Oil Factor in U.S. Foreign Policy, 1980–1990.* Lexington, Mass.: Lexington Books, 1982.

Congressional Quarterly. *Energy Policy.* 2nd ed. Washington, D.C.: Congressional Quarterly, 1981.

Hansen, Roger D., ed. *U.S. Foreign Policy and the Third World: Agenda 1982.* New York: Praeger (for the Overseas Development Council), 1982.

Hopkins, Raymond F., and Puchala, Donald J. *Global Food Interdependence: Challenge to American Foreign Policy.* New York: Columbia University Press, 1980.

Lovins, Amory B. "Energy Strategy: The Road Not Taken?" *Foreign Affairs* (October 1976): 287–305.

Morgan, Dan. *Merchants of Grain.* New York: Viking, 1980.

Report of the Presidential Commission on World Hunger. Washington: Government Printing Office, 1980.

Willrich, Mason. *Energy and World Politics.* New York: The Free Press, 1975.

NOTES

1. Above figures from *New York Times*, August 17, 1981. This was the first of several in-depth reports on world food problems that appeared occasionally during the next several months.
2. Ibid.
3. Ibid., December 7, 1981.
4. Philadelphia *Inquirer*, July 31, 1982.
5. Estimate of Dr. Arthur H. Westing, Professor of Ecology at Hampshire College, reported in *New York Times*, October 6, 1981.
6. Sol M. Linowitz, *World Hunger: A Challenge to American Policy* (New York: Foreign Policy Association, Headline Series #252, 1980), p. 13. Linowitz was

chairman of the President's Commission on World Hunger under Jimmy Carter.

7. Ibid.

8. *New York Times*, August 16, 1981.

9. Cited in Raymond F. Hopkins and Donald J. Puchala, *Global Food Interdependence: Challenge to American Foreign Policy* (New York: Columbia University Press, 1980), pp. 25–26. A very comprehensive and lucid introduction to world food issues.

10. Louis M. Thompson, "The Food-Producing Regions of the World," in E. R. Duncan, ed., *Dimensions of World Food Problems* (Ames, Iowa: Iowa State University Press, 1977), p. 63.

11. Hopkins and Puchala, pp. 43–44.

12. Ibid., p. 56.

13. Douglas Ensminger, "Assistance to Developing Nations," in Duncan, p. 287.

14. Hopkins and Puchala, pp. 127–40, where the authors appraise the efforts of international food organizations.

15. Ibid., p. 134.

16. *New York Times*, September 1, 1981.

17. Hopkins and Puchala, p. 37.

18. According to the US Department of Agriculture, as reported in *New York Times*, February 21, 1983, America's largest customers for agricultural products in 1982 were Japan (5.5), Netherlands (3.0), Soviet Union (1.9), Canada (1.8), South Korea (1.6), China (1.5), Spain (1.5), West Germany (1.4), Mexico (1.2), and Taiwan (1.2). The figures in parentheses refer to billions of dollars of agricultural goods purchased from the United States in fiscal year 1982.

19. Hopkins and Puchala, pp. 87–92.

20. Ibid., p. 77.

21. Roger D. Hansen and Contributors for the Overseas Development Council, *U.S. Foreign Policy and the Third World: Agenda 1982* (New York, Praeger, 1982), p. 190.

22. Hopkins and Puchala, p. 81.

23. *New York Times*, August 5, 1982.

24. Congressional Quarterly, *Energy Policy*, 2nd ed. (Washington, D.C.: Congressional Quarterly, 1981), p. 7.

25. The account of this meeting and much that follows is drawn from Congressional Quarterly, *Energy Policy*, 2nd ed.

26. Ibid., p. 8.

27. Ibid., p. 16.

28. Ibid., pp. 15, 19–20.

29. *New York Times*, May 17, 1981.

30. Congressional Quarterly, *Energy Policy*, p. 23.

31. Congressional Quarterly, *The Middle East*, 5th ed. (Washington, D.C.: Congressional Quarterly, 1981), p. 82.

32. Ibid., p. 96.

33. Quoted in Congressional Quarterly, *The Middle East*, p. 98.

34. International Energy Agency, *Outlook for the Eighties* (Paris, 1980).

35. Congressional Quarterly, *Energy Policy*, p. 56.

36. Ibid., p. 23.
37. Ibid., pp. 75–79.
38. Ibid., p. 84.
39. Mason Willrich, *Energy and World Politics* (New York: The Free Press, 1975), pp. 97–101.

Index

ABMs (antiballistic missiles), 392–94, 424, 468
Acheson, Dean, 154, 244, 247, 281
Adams, John, 181
Adams, Sherman, 161
Aerospace Industries Association, 167
Afghanistan, 37, 409
    invaded by Soviet Union, 20, 25, 63, 141, 242, 245, 315, 391–92, 455, 472, 474, 495, 496, 518
AFL-CIO, 159
Africa, 12, 26, 83, 96, 112, 391
    as grain consumer, 486
    hunger in, 40, 485
    nuclear weapons freeze zone, 445
    and population growth, 484
    and Soviet Union, 474
    US food aid to, 495
African Development Bank, 491
African Development Fund, 297
Afrikaaners, 91
Agency for International Development (AID), 235, 268, 288, 298
Agricultural Committee (US Congress), 364
Agricultural Trade Development and Assistance Act, 496
Agriculture Department (Department of Agriculture), 239, 288, 300–01, 436
    and Food for Peace, 496

Air Force (US), 326–27, 331, 417
Air Force Association, 167
Albania, 356
Algeria, 281, 418, 504, 515
Allen, George, 235
Allende, Salvador, 86–88, 317
Alliance for Progress (1961), 100, 103
Allison, Graham T., 265, 275, 331
Almond, Gabriel A., 149, 153–54, 170
Alsop, Joseph, 186
Alsop, Stewart, 186
America *see* United States
American Battle Monuments Corporation, 239
American Civil Liberties Union, 342
American Council of Christian Churches, 161
American Farm Bureau Federation, 157, 160
American Footwear Manufacturers' Association, 159
American Institute of Public Opinion, 197
American Legion, 157, 166
American Medical Association, 157
American Newspaper Publishers Association, 342
American Ordnance Association, 167
American Textile Manufacturers' Association, 159
Amoco Co., 503

533

Amsterdam, 501
AMVETS, 166
Andropov, Yuri V., 26
Anglo-Iranian Oil Co., 310
Angola, 96
    Soviet intervention in, 474
    US intervention in, 112, 333, 352, 357,
        381, 391
Antarctic Treaty (1959), 443–44
Antitrust legislation, 137
ANZUS Pact (1951), 15, 89, 383
Appropriations Committee (US Congress),
    167
Arbenz Guzman, Jacobo, 86, 310
Argentina, 444, 498
    and Falkland Islands, 316
    and food power, 499–500
    and Non-Proliferation Treaty, 456
    nuclear technology, 449
Armed forces (US)
    issue of authority over, 225–34
    readiness, 416–18
Armed Services Committee (US Con-
        gress), 167, 191, 233, 350, 364
Arms control, 431–76
    after World War II, 443
    agreements for, 441–45
    before World War II, 438
    biological weapons, 459–61
    chemical weapons, 459–61
    comprehensive test ban, 447–48
    controlling arms proliferation, 457–59
    definition of, 432
    in Europe, 461–66
    explanation of, 432–33
    formulation of policy, 434–37
    and "hot line," 441
    impact statements, 437
    and Mutual and Balanced Force
        Reductions, 462–64
    negotiations, 440–42
    and Non-Proliferation Treaty, 456–57
    nuclear testing, 445–49
    objectives of, 433
    and preventive treaties, 443–45
    and SALT, 432, 436, 467–75
    and Soviet Union, 433–34, 439–76
    stability of, 432–33
    as threat to Pentagon, 435

and Vladivostok accord, 469–70
    worldwide progress of, 434
Arms Control and Disarmament Act, 434,
    437
Arms Control and Disarmament Agency
    (ACDA), 191, 235, 238, 267, 352,
    434–37, 451
    function of, 289–90
    and Limited Test Ban Treaty, 436
    and nonproliferation treaty proposal,
        436
Arms Export Control Act (1976), 421, 437
Arms transfers, 418–26
    benefits to US, 421–22
    criticisms of, 422–25
    curbing of, 425–26
    mechanisms of, 421
    recipients of, 418
Army (US), 310–11, 331, 417
    Army Intelligence, 335
    in West Germany, 416
Asia, 83
    and population growth, 484
Asian Development Bank, 297, 491
Aspin, Les, 350, 372
Associated Press, 188, 203
Association for the US Army, 167
Athens, 342
Atlantic Alliance, 57, 67, 78
Atlantic Monthly, 182
Atomic Energy Commission, 328
Atoms for Peace Plan (1953), 440, 452
Australia, 135
    and ANZUS Pact, 15
    as grain supplier, 485, 498
    nuclear technology, 449
    and SEATO, 15
Azores, 222

Baghdad, 503
Bahrein, 223, 349
Bailey, Thomas A., 113
Baltic Sea, 402
Baltimore Sun, 182
Bangladesh, 495
    hunger in, 480, 485
    US food aid to, 495
Barbary Pirates, 121, 226

Barnet, Richard J., 268–69
Baruch Plan, 438–40
Batista, Fulgencio, 86
Battle of the Atlantic, 309
Battle of Midway, 208
Bay of Pigs invasion (1961), 15, 86, 206,
    227
    and Castro, 207, 325
    failure of, 100, 150, 320
    and Kennedy, 188
Belgium, 57, 123
    as member of NATO, 56
Bentham, Jeremy, 134
Berlin, 17, 309
    Soviet blockade of, 13, 15
    West Berlin, 387
Big-stick diplomacy, 88, 232
Biological weapons, 459–61
Biological Weapons Convention (1972),
    460
Bissell, Richard, 317
Black Panthers, 335
B'nai B'rith, 157
Bolivia, 318
Bolling Commission, 366
Bombers and other aircraft
    AWACs surveillance aircraft, 413, 424
    B-1 bomber, 395, 398, 434
    B-52 bomber, 395, 402, 417
    F-15 fighter planes, 417, 424
    F-16 fighter planes, 413
    Nimrod, 413
    Tornado, 413
    TU-22M bomber, 473
Bonaparte, Napoleon, 29
Bonn, 412
Bosch, Juan, 86
Boxer Rebellion, 28, 29
Brandeis, Louis, 233
Brazil, 489
    as grain consumer, 488
    hunger in, 481
    and Non-Proliferation Treaty, 456
    nuclear technology, 449, 454
Brezhnev, Leonid, 21, 26
    and SALT, 467, 468
    and Vladivostok accords, 469
British Petroleum Co., 501
Brookings Institution, 303

Brown, Harold, 398, 433, 472
Browne, Malcolm, 188
Brussels, 505
Brzezinski, Zbigniew, 68, 77, 235, 303
    as special assistant to Carter, 243, 245,
        247, 257
Budget Committee (US Congress), 365
Budget and Impoundment Control Act
    (1974), 364–65
Bundy, McGeorge, 245
Bureau of Alcohol, Tobacco, and Fire-
    arms, 298
Bureau of Congressional Relations, 238
Bureau of East-West Trade, 299
Bureau of Economic Affairs, 238
Bureau of International Commerce, 299
Bureau of Narcotics and Dangerous
    Drugs, 239
Bureaucracy, 176
    and Bureaucratic Politics Model, 266–
        68
    influences on policymaker, 268–74
    and Unitary Actor Model, 265–66
    versus the president, 274–78
Bureaucratic politics, 302–05
Burke-Hartke Foreign Trade and Invest-
    ment Act, 159
Burma, 11
Bush, George, 330

California, 162, 526
Cambodia see Kampuchea
Cambon, Jules, 209
Camp David meeting (1978), 100
Canada, 57, 135, 410, 498, 505, 523
    as member of NATO, 56, 401
    nuclear technology, 449
Canal Zone, 353, 444
Cape of Good Hope, 94
Capitalism, 136–37
Caribbean, 411
Carter, Hodding, III, 286
Carter, Jimmy, 140, 174, 302, 398
    and ACDA, 434, 436
    and Afghanistan, 499
    and arms transfers, 422, 426
    and B-52 bombers, 395

Carter, Jimmy (*cont.*)
 boycott of Moscow Olympics, 20, 25
 campaign for reelection, 184–85
 "countervailing strategy," 390
 diplomatic recognition of China, 41
 dismissal of Young, 276
 energy conservation, 521, 522
 grain embargo, 495
 and hostages in Iran, 266
 human-rights policy, 20, 110, 274
 and India, 353, 355, 454–55
 member of Trilateral Commission, 78
 military policy, 145, 390–92
 and Mutual and Balanced Force
   Reductions (MBFR), 464
 and Neutrality Treaty, 354
 and neutron bomb, 62
 and nuclear proliferation, 353, 451, 455
 and Nuclear Regulatory Commission,
   454–55
 and Panama Canal Treaty, 295, 353
 and Persian Gulf, 391, 526
 presidential appointments, 224
 press conferences, 187–88
 and Rapid Deployment Force, 390–92
 role as policymaker, 273–74
 and SALT II treaty, 218, 354, 470–72
 and special assistant for national security, 68, 243, 245–46, 257
 and State Department, 281
 State of the Union address, 391
 and Third World, 90–91
 and US-Soviet relations, 185, 326
 and use of CIA, 318, 325–26, 330, 336
 and use of National Security Council,
   257
Casey, William, 326, 330, 332, 342
Case-Zablocki Act (1972), 349–50, 352
Castro, Fidel, 86–87, 100, 127, 194
 and Bay of Pigs, 207, 325
 CIA assassination attempts on, 333,
   337
Cater, Douglass, 206
Catledge, Turner, 207
Central America, 26, 62, 207
 and Reagan, 88
 use of intelligence in, 315
Central Intelligence Agency (CIA), 5, 12,
   217, 238, 239, 320–26, 335, 350

 as adviser to NSC, 251, 253
 assassination attempts on Castro, 333,
   337
 assassination attempts on Lumumba,
   333, 337
 and Bay of Pigs invasion, 188, 310, 333
 British liaison with, 319
 coordination of intelligence community,
   328–32
 covert operations, 324–25, 332–34
 creation of, 323
 directorate of administration, 324
 directorate of intelligence, 323–25
 directorate of operations, 324–25
 directorate of science and technology,
   324
 employment of the Mafia, 333
 estimates of Soviet military, 316, 399
 functions, 323
 in Chile, 86–87
 in Guatemala, 310
 in Indonesia, 311
 in Iran, 88, 310–11
 in Moscow, 314
 investigated by Rockefeller Commission, 335
 and Kennedy, 268
 National Intelligence Daily report, 315
 and National Security Act, 250, 290
 and North Vietnam, 316
 and the Pentagon, 327
 reporting facilities of, 190
 roles, 322
 training of Cuban brigade, 205
 training of military forces in Angola,
   333
 training of military forces in Laos, 333
 use of illegal methods, 320, 325, 332
 use of LSD, 335
Central Intelligence Agency Act (1949),
   323
Central Treaty Organization (CENTO)
   (1955), 15
Chamoun, Camille, 89, 228
Chemical warfare, 408–11
Chemical weapons (CW), 408–11, 459–61
Chernenko, Konstantin U., 26
Chiang Kai-shek *see* Jiang Jieshi
Childs, Marquis, 191

Chile, 86–88, 135, 317
    election campaigns in, 317, 333
    and election of Salvador Allende, 86–
        88
    US paramilitary operations in, 318, 352
China, 12, 28–44, 148, 163, 407
    attack on India (1962), 36
    Communist party, 29, 31
    Communist revolution (1949), 30, 32,
        89
    containment policy, 31
    Cultural Revolution, 38–39
    Great Wall, 40
    humiliation, 28
    invasion of Korea (1950), 31
    and Limited Test Ban Treaty, 446
    military spending, 399
    as most favored nation, 42
    Nationalist party, 30, 31
    Nixon visit to, 40–41, 76, 188–89
    and Non-Proliferation Treaty, 456
    and North Korea, 134
    nuclear explosions in, 449
    and Open Door Notes, 31
    propaganda against US, 31
    and recall of US diplomatic staff from
        (1950), 31
    recognition of, 372
    relations with Japan, 76–77
    relations with US and Soviet Union,
        44–48
    Sino-American détente, 38–44
    Sino-Soviet bloc, 32, 89
    Sino-Soviet split, 32–38, 316, 356
    and strategic war, 397
    support for Albania, 356
    and treaty of friendship with Japan,
        76–77
    and treaty of friendship with Soviet
        Union, 33
    and Treaty of Tlatelolco, 444
    US arms to, 418
    and US food policy, 494
    and US technology, 42
    US trade embargo against, 32
    US troops in, 227
    use of intelligence in, 315
    and war with Japan (1937–45), 30
Chinese Exclusion Law, 159

Christian Science Monitor, 182
Christopher, Warren, 369–70
Church, Frank, 372
Church Committee, 325, 329, 332–33,
    337–38
Churchill, Winston, 143, 250, 389
Civil War, 128, 139
Clark, William P., 235
Clark Amendment, 352, 357
Clarke, Duncan L., 436
Clausewitz, Carl Maria von, 130
Clifford, Clark, 164
Coal industry, 523–25
Cohen, Bernard C., 175, 192
Cohen, Eliot, 412
Colby, William, 325, 330
Cold War, 84, 85, 295, 356, 424, 439, 440
    origins of, 13–18
Colombia, 227
Colorado, 522
Commerce Department (Department of
    Commerce), 238–39, 267
    and Food for Peace, 496
    functions of, 298–99
    US Travel Service, 240, 299
Common Market see European Common
    Market
Communist Manifesto, 201
Communists and communism, 132, 148
    and "assured destruction," 387
    and brinkmanship, 382–85
    expansion and aggression, 15, 85, 134,
        227, 385, 387
    grand alliance between Soviet Union
        and China, 33
    in Eastern Europe, 56, 311, 462
    in France, 55
    in Guatemala, 310
    in Italy, 55, 310
    in Latin America, 86–88
    in State Department, 282
    victory in Indochina, 334
    "wars of national liberation," 387
Comprehensive test ban, 447–49
Conference of the Commission on Disar-
    mament, 459
Congress, 130, 167, 169, 190, 215, 220,
    375–78
    accepting bribes, 186–87

Congress (*cont.*)
    after World War II, 351–52
    appropriations, 217, 350
    and Arms Control and Disarmament
        Act, 435–37
    and Arms Export Control Act, 421
    authority over armed forces, 346–47
    ban on chemical weapons testing, 408–
        09
    budgetary process, 363–66
    committee system, 360–61, *see also com-
        mittees by name*
    confirming appointments, 347–48
    Constitutional powers of, 216–17
    diffusion of power, 360–63
    domestic bias, 359–60
    familiarity with public opinion views,
        173
    and Food Aid Convention, 490
    and food diplomacy, 480
    and Food for Peace, 496
    and foreign policy powers, 345–51
    improving foreign policy capabilities,
        373–75
    influence, 351–58
    information leaks, 370–71
    lack of information, 366–69
    lack of speed, 369–70
    legislation, 350
    legislative staff, 368–69
    and Nuclear Non-Proliferation Act, 454
    passing of Hawley-Smoot tariff, 115
    presidential evasion of, 221–34
    and Soviet Union, 356
    strengths, 371–73
    suitability for making foreign policy,
        358–73
    and War Powers Act, 347
Congressional Budget Office (CBO), 365–
    66, 369, 373
Congressional Research Service, 369
Connally, John, 65
Constitution, 213–21, 335
    and foreign policy, 215–21
    powers of Congress, 216–17
    powers of the president, 216–17
Constitutional Convention (1787), 215, 223
Consultative Group on International Agri-
    cultural Research, 491–92
Containment policy, 14, 17, 84, 85, 356,

382–85, 440
    and China's intervention in Korea, 31
    in the Far East, 89
    in the Middle East, 228
Conventional weapons, 405–07, 412
Coolidge, Calvin, 138, 347
Cooper, John Sherman, 229
Cooper-Church Amendment, 352
Corry, Edward, 87
Corwin, E. S., 217
Council on Foreign Relations, 154, 317
"Countervailing strategy," 390
Crabb, Cecil, 126, 377
C. Turner Joy (American destroyer), 228
Cuba, 218, 226, 397, 444, 473, 495
    and Castro, 86–87, 100, 127, 194
    and Kennedy, 266, *see also* Bay of Pigs
        invasion
    and Reagan, 88, 177
    Soviet missiles in, 310, 314, 332, *see also*
        Cuban missile crisis
    Spanish-American war, 122–23
    troops in Angola, 96
    US military operations in, 184, 227,
        294, 318, 346
Cuban missile crisis (1962), 15, 121, 155,
    221, 390, 441, 473
    and Congress, 218
    effect on Soviet Union, 398–99
    and Kennedy, 18–19, 121, 232, 370
    and the media, 194–95
Customs Bureau, 239
Customs Service, 298
Cutler, Robert, 244
Czechoslovakia, 356
    takeover by Germany, 8, 16

Daily Worker, 335
Daniels, Jonathan, 276
Darwin, Charles, *Origin of Species*, 136, 201
Daughters of the American Revolution
    (DAR), 335
Dawes, Charles G., 276
Declaration of Independence, 135
Defense Department (Department of
    Defense), 239
    and ACDA, 434, 436
    Air Force intelligence, 326–27

Army intelligence, 327
Bureau of Politico-Military Affairs, 280
on chemical warfare, 409
and congressional staffers, 372
creation of, 290
Defense Intelligence Agency, 326–27
and importance of Persian Gulf, 411
information resources, 162, 190
International Security Affairs (ISA),
    292–93
Joint Chiefs of Staff, 293–94
liaison with CIA, 323
and national security, 267
and National Security Act, 249
National Security Agency, 326–27
Naval intelligence, 326
Office of the Secretary of Defense
    (OSD), 292
on nuclear attack, 396
policy making, 238
and readiness problems, 416–18
reporting system, 367
Review Group, 253
SALT Task Force, 292
on Sino-Soviet dispute, 37
strength, 286
support of arms transfers, 421
view of Soviet military spending, 399–
    400
Defense Intelligence Agency (DIA), 315,
    326–27
Defense Reorganization Act, 290
Democratic party, 175
Deng Xiaoping, 39
Denmark, 56
DePorte, A. W., 64
Destler, I. M., 281–82, 287
Developmental Assistance Committee
    (DAC), 103
Dewey, George, 123
Diego Garcia, 223, 349, 391
Diem, Ngo Dinh, 333
Disarmament, 432, 438
Doig, Carol, 207
Doig, Ivan, 207
Dominican Republic, US military forces
    in, 86, 127, 218, 227, 232, 294, 346
Dresden 1 nuclear power plant (Illinois),
    525
Drug Enforcement Administration, 328

Dulles, Allen, 318–19, 325, 329
Dulles, John Foster, 89, 176, 244, 281, 286,
    385
    and brinkmanship, 383–84
Dye, Thomas, 165

Eastern Europe, 17, 130, 384
    and chemical weapons, 409
    and military spending, 399
    oil consumption, 515
    Soviet control over (1948), 13
    and strategic war, 397
East German Communist Party Congress,
    467
East Germany, 356, 384, 387
East-West Foreign Trade Board, 298
East-West relations, 58–59
    military, 401, 407–08
Economic agencies, 296–301
Economic development, 495
Economics and private enterprise, 136–38
Economic Support Fund, 288
Edward I, king of England, 523
Eglin Air Force Base, 310
Egypt, 100, 228, 371, 391
    and arms transfers, 418, 422, 423
    Aswan High Dam, 228
    and Food for Peace, 496
    invaded by Great Britain, France,
        Israel (1956), 57, 88
    and Israeli conflict, 495, 504–05
    nuclear technology, 449
    and "shuttle diplomacy," 505
    Soviet aid to, 228, 423
    US food aid to, 495
Einstein, Albert, 201
Eisenhower, Dwight D., 150, 228, 244,
    281, 305, 387
    Atoms for Peace program, 452
    and brinkmanship, 382–85
    farewell address, 166
    and massive retaliation, 61, 382–85
    military aid to Jordon (1957), 89
    Open Skies concept, 440
    and Outer Space Treaty, 443
    use of CIA, 318
    use of National Security Council, 251–
        58
    vs. bureaucracy, 277

Eisenhower Doctrine, 89, 228
Ellsberg, Daniel, 336
El Salvador, 26, 88, 177, 422
Energy, 500–27
    alternatives, 521–26
    coal, 523–25
    conservation, 521–22
    future outlook, 519–21
    natural gas, 522
    nuclear power, 525
    renewable sources, 525–26
    synthetic fuels, 522–23
Energy crisis, 65–66, 500
Energy Department (Department of
    Energy), 238, 239, 274, 328, 448
    and ACDA, 434
Energy Security Act (1980), 522
England see Great Britain
Environmental Modification Convention,
    437
Environmental Science Services Adminis-
    tration, 239
Erlichman, John, 224
Estonia, 13
Etheredge, Lloyd, 269–70
Ethiopia, 474
    hunger in, 480, 485
    US commitment to, 222, 349
Europe, 439, see also Eastern Europe;
        Western Europe
    arms control in, 461–66
    and arms transfers, 416, 425, 426
    and food power, 498
    as grain consumer, 486
    MBFR reductions in Central Europe,
        462–64
    military balance in, 401–05
    and nuclear arms control, 464–67
    oil imports, 391
    and population growth, 484
    Soviet forces in, 399
    and US food policy, 494
European Coal and Steel Community
    (1951), 56
European Common Market, 56, 64, 79,
    160, 492, 505
European Economic Community (EEC),
    56–57, 66, 78
Export-Import Bank, 159, 239, 297, 300
Exxon Co., 501

"Face the Nation" program, 189
Fairness Doctrine, 194
Falkland Islands, 198, 204, 316
Federal Aviation Administration, 239
Federal Bureau of Investigation (FBI),
    239, 328
    investigated by Rockefeller Commis-
        sion, 335
    use of illegal methods, 320, 335
Federal Communications Commission, 194
Federal Reserve System, 137
Federal Trade Commission, 137
Finan, James F., 410
Finland, 13
"Flexible response" doctrine, 385–88
Food Aid Convention, 490
Food and Agriculture Organization
    (FAO), 484, 488, 491
Food diplomacy, 480–500
    economic development, 481, 488–89
    and Food for Peace, 496
    food-population balance, 481–85
    food power, 498–500
    food reserve, 489–90
    poverty, 480–81, 488
    US food aid, 495–96
    US policy, 493–96
    and World Bank, 480
    and world food trade, 485–88
    and world hunger, 480–81, 485, 488–93
Food for Peace Program, 288, 297, 300,
    353, 496
Ford, Gerald, 293, 327, 469
    and SALT, 467
    use of CIA, 318
Foreign Affairs, 14
Foreign Affairs Committee (US Congress),
    355
Foreign Agriculture Service, 239, 496
Foreign Assistance Act (1974), 340, 352
Foreign Intelligence Advisory Board, 339
Foreign Military Sales (FMS), 421
Foreign policy (US), 3, 18, see also by
        country
    ambassador appointments, 219
    analytic model, 3–7, 26–27
    approaches to, 7–9
    appropriations and legislation, 219
    coordination problem, 237–39
    difficulties of, with Western Europe, 57

discussion, 96–99
effect of ethnic groups on, 162
effect of materialism on, 138
hardening, 30–32
and intelligence, 310–11
and limited arms control, 18
and the media, 181–210
military force of, 128–30
opinion-conversion process, 171–75
optimism and, 139–40
and policymakers, 237–41, 269–74
and power elite, 163–65
and pragmatism, 132–34
and presidential advisers, 234–35
and presidential predominance, 231–34
and pressure groups, 156–63
and private enterprise, 137–38
response to Third World nationalism,
    84–96
and role of public opinion, 145–56
since World War II, 218–19
and special assistant for National Secu-
    rity, 241–48
and technological exchange, 18
and trade, 18
treaty making, 218–19
and US Constitution, 213–21
war making, 218
Foreign Policy Association, 154
Foreign Relations Committee (US Con-
    gress), 233, 349, 361, 472
Foreign Service, 240, 280–84, 328, 331
Fort Meade (Maryland), 327
France, 5, 16, 17, 123, 281, 309, 371, 413
    control of Indochina, 15, 30
    as grain supplier, 485, 498
    invasion of Egypt (1956), 57, 88
    and Limited Test Ban Treaty, 446
    as member of NATO, 56, 57
    and Non-Proliferation Treaty, 456
    nuclear weapons and forces, 55, 57, 60,
        397, 402, 449, 453
    and Nuclear Suppliers Group, 454
    and SEATO, 15
    as sellers of arms, 425
    and Treaty of Tlatelolco, 444
    and Washington Naval Conference, 438
    withdrawal from Military Committee,
        414
Franck, Thomas M., 368, 376

Free University at Amsterdam, 489
Frei, Eduardo, 317
Freud, Sigmund, 201
Friendly, Fred W., 199
Fulbright, J. William, 229, 349, 372

Galbraith, John Kenneth, 189–90, 192
Gardner, Andrew, 194–95
Gasoline, US consumption, 521–22
Gelb, Leslie, 464
General Accounting Office (GAO), 369
General Agreement on Tariffs and Trade
    (GATT), 300, 492
General Dynamics Co., 166
General Services Administration, 239
Geneva Protocol, 408, 438, 459
Geneva Three-Power Naval Conference
    (1927), 438
George, Alexander, 269
George, Juliette, 269
Germany, 13, 227, 231, see also East Ger-
    many; West Germany
    after World War II, 439
    as example in foreign policy model, 5
    takeover of Czechoslovakia (1939), 8,
        16
Getty Co., 503
Gold standard, 115
Goldwater, Barry, 172
Grain, in world food trade, 485–88
Great Britain (United Kingdom), 5, 17,
    123, 142, 231, 309, 413
    and CENTO (1955), 15
    and comprehensive test ban, 448–49
    Destroyers-for-Bases deal (1940), 221
    gold standard, 115
    invasion of Eygpt (1956), 57, 88, 371
    and Limited Test Ban Treaty, 446
    as member of NATO, 56
    nuclear weapons and forces, 55, 397,
        402, 449, 453, 454
    oil prices, 510
    Parliament, 363, 374–75
    as sellers of arms, 425
    and Soviet overtures, 16
    Soviet spies in, 313
    and Treaty of Tlatelolco, 444
    and Washington Naval Conference, 438

Greece, 13, 14, 100, 355, 371, 422, 423
  as member of NATO, 56
Green Berets, 385–87
Greenland, 227
Greer (American destroyer), 227
Grenada, 88, 127, 218, 231, 294
Griswold, A. Whitney, 255
Gross national product (GNP), 68, 71
  Soviet, 311
Guam, 123, 388
Guam Doctrine, 389
Guantanamo Naval Base (Cuba), 444
Guatemala, 86, 127, 134
  US operations in, 222, 310, 318
Guevara, Che, 318
Gulf Co., 501
Gulf of Tonkin Resolution, 228–29

Hague Conferences (1899, 1907), 438
Haig, Alexander M., Jr., 246, 285–86, 348
Haiti, 227, 351
Halberstam, David, 188
Haldeman, Robert, 224
Hamilton, Alexander, 226, 297
Hanford nuclear power plant (Washington), 525
Hanoi, 402
Harper's, 182
Harrington, Michael, 155
Harris polls, 150
Harvard Business School, Energy Project, 521
Hawaii, 123
Hawley-Smoot tariff, 115
Hay, John, 349
Health and Human Services Department, 239
Hearst, Patricia, 202
Helms, Richard, 325, 329–30
Helsinki Conference on Security and Cooperation (1975), 20–21
Henry, Patrick, 214
Herbers, John, 193
Hersch, Seymour, 332
Hilsman, Roger, 240, 267
Himalaya Mountains, 480
Hiroshima, 402, 459
History, orthodox and revisionist views of, 13, 16, 17

Hitler, Adolf, 55, 116, 130, 309
  attack on Russia, 16
  invasion of Poland, 5
  and Non-Aggression Pact, 13, 16
  takeover of Czechoslovakia, 8
Ho Chi Minh, 15, 30, 85, 90, 336
Holt, Pat M., 377
"Holy Alliance," 114
Honduras, 88
Hoover Dam, 526
Hopkins, Harry, 224, 492, 495
House, Edward M., 224
House Appropriations Committee, 365
House Armed Services Committee, 154
House Committee on Intelligence, 319
House Foreign Affairs Committee, 349, 359, 361, 366, 369, 371
House International Relations Committee, 355
House of Representatives, 357, 372
  and Panama Canal, 355
House Select Committee on Intelligence (Pike Committee), 332
Housing and Urban Development Department, 239
Hudson Institute, 166, 449
Hughes, Barry, 165
Hughes-Ryan Amendment, 340–41, 352
Human rights observance reports, 353
Humboldt Bay nuclear power plant (California), 525
Humphrey, Hubert H., 173, 373, 437
Hungary, 273, 356, 384
Hunt, Howard, 336
Hussein, king of Jordan, 89, 355
Hu Yaobang, 39

ICBMs (intercontinental ballistic missiles), 331, 388, 392, 396, 467–72, 475
  Minuteman, 388, 396, 470, 472
  Titan, 388, 396
Iceland, 227, 414
  as member of NATO, 56
Immigration and Naturalization Service, 239
Imperialistic expansion, 123
India, 189, 192, 384, 459
  and arms transfers, 423
  attacked by China (1962), 36

and Carter, 454–55
and Food for Peace, 496
friendship treaty with Russia, 37
hunger in, 480
and Non-Proliferation Treaty, 456
nuclear weapons, 449, 453
Indian Ocean, 391, 445
Indochina, 8, 85, 90, 334, 352
Indonesia, 127, 271, 423
and Food for Peace, 496
hunger in, 480
US operations in, 311, 318
Inflation, 66–67
Institute for Scientific and Technological
Cooperation, 288
Intelligence (British), 316, 319
Intelligence (US), 309–42
analysts of, 315–16
communications intelligence (COM-
INT), 314
and Communist regimes, 313
community, 320–32, 340–41
counterintelligence, 312, 319–20
covert operations, 317–18
defined, 311–12
distribution of information, 316
electronic intelligence (ELINT), 314
failures, 310–11
functions, 312–20
human intelligence (HUMINT), 312
National Intelligence Estimates, 316
photographic intelligence (PHOTINT),
314, 324
policymaking role, 318
signal intelligence (SIGINT), 314, 324
spying, 313–14
successes, 310–11
techniques used to collect data, 313–14
Intelligence Identities Protection Act
(1982), 342
Intelligence Oversight Act (1980), 341, 348
Intelligence Oversight Board, 339
Intelligence Resources Advisory Committee (IRAC), 330
Inter-American Development Bank, 297,
491
Inter-American Treaty of Reciprocal
Assistance (Rio Pact) (1947), 15,
383
Interior Department, 239

Internal Revenue Service, 239, 336
International Atomic Energy Agency
(IAEA), 440, 444–45, 453–56
International Bank for Reconstruction and
Development see World Bank
International Communications Agency,
238, see also US Information Agency
International Development Cooperation
Agency (IDCA), 288–89
International Energy Agency (IEA), 66,
518–19
International Fund for Agricultural Devel-
opment, 491
International Military Education and
Training Program, 421
International Monetary Fund, 297
International monetary system, 517–18
International Press Institute, 184, 196
International Research Council of the
Center for Strategic and Interna-
tional Studies, 202
International Security Assistance, 437
International Trade Administration, 299
Interstate Commerce Commission, 137
Interstate and Foreign Commerce Committee, 364
Iowa, 485
Iran, 13, 134, 316, 391, 473
and CENTO, 15
and CIA, 310–11, 333
holding of American hostages (1979),
62, 66, 174, 208, 280, 518
nationalization of oil company, 504
nuclear technology, 449
overthrow of shah, 232, 331
political instability, 139
and US arms transfers, 418, 423–24
and US isolationism, 112
and US military and defense arrangements, 15, 127, 222, 294, 349
US paramilitary operations in, 318
US security pledges to (1959), 223
Iraq, 418, 504, 515
and CENTO, 15
nuclear technology, 449, 457
"Iron Curtain," 31
Isolationism, 112–18
Israel, 135, 161, 220, 238, 369, 495, 504–
05
and arms transfers, 418, 422, 425

Israel (*cont.*)
    attacked by Arabs (1973), 20
    defense arrangements with US, 15
    foreign aid, 100, 140
    invasion of Egypt (1956), 57, 88, 371
    and Lebanon conflict, 518
    and Nixon, 504–05
    and Non-Proliferation Treaty, 456
    nuclear weapons, 449, 457
    "shuttle diplomacy," 505
    and United Nations, 457
    West Bank settlements, 423
"Issues and Answers" program, 189
Italy, 134, 227, 310, 413, 425
    as member of NATO, 56
    non-leftist candidates in, 317, 333
    nuclear technology, 449
    and Washington Naval Conference, 438

Jackson, Henry M., 22–24, 372, 469, 473
Jackson-Vanik Amendment (1974), 22–24, 352
Jamaica, 342, 495
Japan, 12, 309
    after World War II, 439
    as ally of US, 53, 68
    and arms transfers, 418, 422, 425
    atom bomb dropped on, 17
    at war with China (1937–45), 30
    auto exports and industry, 72–73, 356
    Battle of Midway, 208
    and Carter's limit on Japanese exports, 73
    constitution, 69–70
    Diet legislature, 70
    demilitarization, 69
    democratization, 70
    economics, 68–69, 72–74
    and food power, 498
    foreign trade, 68–69
    government parties, 70
    as grain consumer, 486
    importance to America of, 68–69
    industry, 68
    inflation, 66–67
    and Israel, 505
    military, 55, 69, 74–75, 399
    and Nixon "shocks," 71
    and Nuclear Suppliers Group, 454
    nuclear technology, 75, 449, 453
    and OECD, 57
    oil consumption and imports, 391, 507, 515
    relations with China, 76–77
    relations with Soviet Union, 76
    relations with US, 68–79
    relations with Western Europe, 78–79
    and Roosevelt, 225
    and security treaties with US, 15, 70–71
    Self-Defense Force, 69–70, 74
    Socialist party, 70, 74
    tariffs, 72
    trade with US, 69, 71–74
    and treaty of friendship with China, 76–77
    US food aid to, 494
    and Washington Naval Conference, 438
    zaibatsus, 70
Jefferson, Thomas, 121–22, 135, 186, 226, 278
Jessup, Philip, 224
Jews
    organizations supporting Israel, 161–62
    restrictions on leaving Russia, 20–24
Jiang Jieshi, 13, 15, 30
    and treaty of friendship with Stalin (1945), 33–35
    and treaty of mutual defense with US, 40
John Birch Society, 335
Johnson, Loch, 222–23, 349
Johnson, Lyndon B., 245, 281, 285, 293
    election of 1964, 172–73
    "flexible response" doctrine, 385–88
    and Gulf of Tonkin Resolution, 228
    and National Security Council, 251, 256–58
    press conferences, 187
    use of CIA, 318
    and Vietnam, 150, 192, 231
    war on poverty, 155
Joint Chiefs of Staff, 192, 251, 253, 293–94, 338, 390
    and ACDA, 434
    and Defense Intelligence Agency, 327
Jordan, Hamilton, 224
Jordan, 89, 335, 437

Judiciary Committee (US Congress), 355
Justice Department, 193, 239
   Drug Enforcement Administration, 328

Kahan, Jerome, 384, 389, 394
Kampuchea, 8, 100, 150, 294, 480
Kansas, 485
Keliher, John G., 464
Kellogg-Briand Pact, 438
Keniston, Kenneth, 131
Kennan, George F., 13, 14, 25, 117, 118
Kennedy, Edward, 175
Kennedy, John F., 141, 240, 245, 267, 285,
   293, 304
   Alliance for Progress, 100–02
   and Bay of Pigs invasion, 188, 328
   and Congress, 231
   and Cuban missile crisis, 18–19, 174,
      232, 266, 370
   and "flexible response," 60, 385–88
   interested in Special Forces and Green
      Berets, 385–87
   and Khrushchev, 441
   and the media, 193, 205, 207
   military policy, 385–88
   need for arms control, 431
   and poverty, 155
   and public opinion, 150
   and secretary of state, 281
   sense of mission, 119–20
   and special assistant, 176, 244–45
   and State Department, 246
   use of CIA, 268, 318, 329
   use of National Security Council, 251,
      255, 257–58
   vs. bureaucracy, 277
Kennedy, Robert, 121, 193
Kennedy Round (1964–67), 64
Kennedy School of Government (Harvard
   University), 331
Khomeini, Ayatollah, 88, 208
Khrushchev, Nikita, 387, 441, 467
   and Cuban missile crisis, 19, 194
Kissinger, Henry A., 23, 24, 141, 154, 164,
   491
   and ACDA, 289, 436
   Necessity for Choice, 385
   as secretary of state, 224, 246, 286

and "shuttle diplomacy," 505
as special assistant, 188, 235, 242–43,
   245–47, 251, 347, 436
view of Allende's election, 87
Korea, 127, 226, 369, see also North Korea;
   South Korea
   invaded by China (1950), 31
   and National Security Act, 294
   and presidential powers, 220–21
   38th Parallel, 14, 134
   US intervention in, 15, 89, 382
   US military forces in, 70, 218, 346
   and War Powers Act, 230, 232
Korean War, 30–32, 40, 178, 382
Ku Klux Klan, 335

Labor Department, 239
Labor groups, 159–60
Lacquer, Walter, 202
Laird, Melvin, 293
Laissez-faire, 136–37
Langley Air Force Base (Virginia), 417
Laos, 8, 100, 134, 271, 318
   US commitment to, 333, 349, 387
Latin America, 83, 86–88, 114–15, 159,
   201, 318
   Alliance for Progress, 100–02
   hunger in, 480
   importance to American security, 86
   population growth, 484
   and Rio Pact (1947), 15
   and Treaty of Tlatelolco, 444–45
Latvia, 13
Lavelle, John D., 272
Le, Kong, 271
League of Nations, 115, 125, 129, 269, 438
League of Women Voters (LWV), 154,
   161
Lebanon, 89, 139, 150, 226, 294, 518
   US military forces in, 218, 228, 231,
      346, 357
Legalism-moralism, Kennan concept of,
   118
Legislative vetos, 353
LeMay, Curtis E., 384
Lenin, V. I., 183
Leningrad, 439
Levy, Walter J., 518

Lewis, William H., 423
Liberalism, 134–35
Liberia, 15
Libya, 342, 503
    oil production, 503, 504, 505, 515
Limited Test Ban Treaty (LTBT), 436,
    446–47
Lippmann, Walter, 155, 191, 194
Lithuania, 13
Locke, John, 134
Lockheed Aircraft Co., 166, 168
London Naval Conferences (1930, 1935),
    438
Los Angeles Times, 182
Lovett, Robert M., 155, 281
Lowell, James Russell, 119
Lumumba, Patrice, 127, 333, 337
Luxembourg, 56

MacArthur, Douglas, 31, 69, 134
Macartney, Lord, 29
McCarthy, Eugene J., 61, 167
McCarthy, Joseph, 282
McCone, John, 318, 329
McCormick, James M., 222–23, 349
MacDill Air Force Base (Florida), 391
MacFarlane, Robert C., 235
McNamara, Robert, 293, 327, 329, 385–88
Madariaga, Salvador de, 433
Madison, James, 206, 214, 226
Mafia, 333
Magsaysay, Ramon, 317
Maine (battleship), 122
Malraux, André, 30
Manchuria, 33
Manning, Bayless, 297, 373
Mao Tse-tung see Mao Zedong
Mao Zedong, 29, 38, 89
Marbury v. Madison, 214
Marchetti, Victor, 314, 320, 329, 331, 338–
    39
Maritime Administration, 239
Marks, John D., 314, 320, 329, 331, 338–
    39
Marshall Plan (1947), 15, 56, 382
Marxism-Leninism, 20–21, 39, 83, 132
Massive retaliation, 60, 382–85
Matthews, Herbert, 195
Meany, George, 73–74

Media
    and bureaucratic politics, 191–93
    channel of communication to other
        governments, 195
    commercialism, 197–99
    communication link within the govern-
        ment, 190–91
    critique of, 196–205
    expressing public opinion, 185–86
    and Fairness Doctrine, 194
    and foreign policy, 181–210
    influences on policy-making process,
        181
    informing the public, 184–85
    need for openness, 206–08
    need for secrecy, 208–10
    news definition, 199–202, 204
    newspapers, 181
    paucity of international news, 196–197
    as policymaker, 194–95
    policy promotion, 193–94
    and presidential press conferences,
        187–88, 192–93
    "prestige press," 181, 189, 194
    radio time, 197–98
    reporting after the fact, 203
    role in authoritarian and democratic
        political systems, 182–84
    suggestions for improvement, 204–05
    television, 182
    as watchdog over government, 186–89
    wire service copy, 203–04
Mediterranean Sea, 397, 402, 462, 466
"Meet the Press" program, 41, 189
Merchant Marine and Fisheries Commit-
    tee (US Congress), 355
Mexican War (1846), 226
Mexico, 126, 159, 227, 351
    oil production, 510, 519
    US food aid to, 494
Mexico City, 444
Meyer, Jean, 480
Middle East, 26, 89, 117, 237–38, 357, 437
    and arms transfers, 418, 422, 425
    as grain consumer, 488
    hunger in, 480
    Israel-Egypt conflict, 504–05
    oil production and supply, 58, 376,
        406, 498, 500–01, 510
    Palestinian refugees, 505

Soviet communism in, 228
US food aid to, 495
Middle East war (1973), 63, 66, 408–09,
  423, 474
Military
  appropriations bills since World War
    II, 350
  civilian control over, 294–95
  communications systems, 398
  military-industrial complex, 166–70
Military Assistance Program, 99, 421
Military policy, 381–426
  attitude toward military force, 128–30
  brinkmanship, 382–85
  and Carter, 390–92
  and Eisenhower, 382–85
  "flexible response" doctrine, 385–89
  and Kennedy, 385–88
  massive retaliation, 382–85
  military balance, 381
  "minimum deterrence," 389–90
  mutual assured destruction (MAD),
    388–89, 392–95
  and NATO, 381, 383–84, 401–15
  and Nixon, 388–90
  Rapid Deployment Force, 390–92
  "second-strike capability," 387–88
  since World War II, 381–95
  and Soviet Union, 381–426
  "sufficiency," 389
  and Warsaw Pact, 381, 401–15
Mill, John Stuart, 134, 206
Miller, Warren E., 173
Mills, C. Wright, 163
Minerals, 479, 528
Missile systems, 403, 434, see also ABMs;
    ICBMs; MIRV technology; SLBMs
  Honest John, 403
  Lance, 403
  Maverick, 424
  MX, 219, 245, 361, 369, 434, 448
  Pershing, 403
  Pershing II, 407, 467
  Roland II, 413
  Sidewinder, 424
  Soviet, 399–400, 417, 466, 473
  Titan II, 417
MIRV technology, 394, 396–97, 469–72
Mobil Co., 501
Mombasa, 391

Monroe, James, 115, 129
Monroe Doctrine, 115
Montevideo, 273
Moorer, Thomas, 390
Moralism
  and Bay of Pigs invasion, 121
  consequences of, 125–27
  and foreign policy, 120–27
  and Jefferson, 121–22
  and Spanish-American War, 122–23
Moscow, 96, 411, 433, 439
Mossadegh, Mohammed, 88, 310
Most-favored-nation (MFN) status, 6, 22
Munich Pact (1938), 8
Muskie, Edmund, 97, 280
Mutual and Balanced Force Reductions
  (MBFR), 462–64, 466

NAACP, 333
Nader, Ralph, 155
Namibia, 96
Nasser, Gamal Abdel, 57
National Aeronautics and Space Adminis-
  tration, 240
National Association of Manufacturers,
  159
National Cotton Council, 159
National Council of Churches of Christ in
  America, 161
National Enquirer, 182
National Farmers Union, 160
National Foreign Intelligence Board, 339
National Grange, 160
National Intelligence Daily (CIA), 315
Nationalism and nationalists, 501
  and Third World, 83–96
National Machine Tool Builders' Associa-
  tion, 159
National Press Club, 466
National Reconnaissance Office, 326
National Review, 185
National Rifle Association, 157
National Science Foundation, 240
National security, special assistant for,
  235, 241–48
National Security Act (1947), 249–50, 290,
  294, 329, 338
  creation of CIA, 323
National Security Agency, 327, 335

National Security Council (NSC), 237,
    245, 249–58, 290, 338–39
  Defense Program Review Committee,
    254
  54-12 Committee, 339
  40 Committee, 338–39
  Interdepartmental Groups, 252, 256
  members, 250–51
  Policy Review Committee, 257
  Review Group, 253, 256
  role, 249–50
  SALT Verification Panel, 254
  Senior Interagency Group, Intelligence,
    338
  Special Coordinating Committee, 257,
    338
  Undersecretaries Committee, 253–54,
    256
  Vietnam Special Studies Group, 254
  Washington Special Actions Group,
    254
National Security Industrial Association,
    167
National Student Association, 335
Navy (US), 331, 417
  Sixth Fleet, 462
Navy League, 166
Netherlands, 56, 505
Neustadt, Richard, 215, 275, 277
Neutrality Acts, 116, 129
Neutron bomb, 62, 407
New Deal, 110, 235
New International Economic Order, 84
New Republic, 185
Newspapers, 181, 189, 194
Newsweek, 154, 182, 185
New York, 162
New York City, 501
New York Times, 154, 190, 188, 192, 332,
    409
  "prestige press," 182, 189, 194
  Szulc on CIA, 205, 207–08
New Zealand, 15, 135
Nicaragua, 90, 177, 205, 227, 391
  covert assistance to, 88, 188, 207
Nigeria, 488
Nitze, Paul, 164, 473
Nixon, Richard M., 150, 173, 285, 293,
    336, 372

and ACDA, 289, 436
and biological weapons, 459–60
and chemical weapons, 408, 459–60
and Congress, 215, 231
foreign policy advice, 281
Guam press conference, 388
halt in bombing of North Vietnam, 272
and Kissinger, 243, 247, 253
military aid to Israel, 504–05
military executive agreements, 223
military policy, 388–90
"minimum deterrence," 389–90
"Nixon shocks," 65, 71
presidential appointments, 224
resignation, 178
signing of SALT I, 19, 468, 474
and special assistant, 188, 243, 245,
    251, 305
and State Department, 246, 268, 276
Trade Reform Act, 22
use of CIA, 318, 330, 339
use of National Security Council, 251–
    58
veto of War Powers Act, 347
Nixon Summit, 39–40
Noblesse oblige, 165
Non-Aggression Pact (1939), 13, 16
Non-Proliferation Treaty (NPT), 453, 454,
    456–57
Normandy invasion (1944), 16, 250
North Atlantic Council, 414
North Atlantic Treaty Organization
    (NATO), 15, 59, 63, 67, 148, 232,
    292, 319, 401, 413
  air power, 405–06
  alliance problems, 411–15
  antitank forces, 406–07
  and arms transfers, 418, 422
  burden-sharing, 411–12
  chemical warfare, 410–11
  conventional weapons, 405–07
  defense expenditures, 59, 411
  Defense Planning Committee (DPC),
    414
  formation, 56, 382
  High-Level Group, 61
  interoperability, 412–15
  member, 56
  Military Committee, 414

as "military museum," 412
military policy, 381, 383–84, 401–15
and Mutual and Balanced Force
    Reductions (MBFR), 462
naval forces, 406
and North Atlantic Council, 414
Nuclear Planning Group, 414
nuclear sharing, 414–15
and Persian Gulf, 392, 526
Special Group on Arms Control, 61
standardization of weapons, 412–15,
    426
Northern Ireland, 200
North Korea, 14, 134, 150, 221, 370
North Sea oil discoveries, 510
North Vietnam, 310, 387
Norway, 56, 510
Nuclear arms control in Europe, 464–67
Nuclear fuel cycle, 450–51
Nuclear Non-Proliferation Act, 353, 437,
    454
Nuclear reactors, 451–52
Nuclear Regulatory Commission, 454–56
Nuclear Suppliers Group, 454
Nuclear testing, 445–49
Nuclear war, threat of, 19
Nuclear weapons, 134, 382–85, 388–90,
    392, 395–401, 412
    proliferation, 449–61
    Theater Nuclear Forces (TNF), 402–
        05, 412, 466
Nunn, Sam, 372

Occidental Petroleum Co., 503
Office of Management and Budget
    (OMB), 248–49, 364–66
Office of Politico-Military Affairs, 238
Office of Strategic Services, 324
Office of Technology Assessment, 369
Office of the United States Trade Repre-
    sentative, 299–300
Ohira, Masayoshi, 77
Oil and oil industry, 517
    concessionary system, 501
    coordination of production and prices,
        509–10
    decline in prices, 517–18
    development of dependence on, 500–01

dominated by "Seven Sisters," 501–03
    Libyan embargo, 505
    Middle East supply, 500–01
    nationalization, 504
    and OPEC, 501–05, 508–15, 519
    Persian Gulf, 526–28
    Saudi Arabia, 504–05
    US dependence on, 501
    worldwide dependence on, 505–15
Olympics (Moscow, 1980), 20, 25, 63
Olympics (Munich, 1972), 202
Oman, 391, 422
Open Door policy, 31, 129
Open Skies concept (1955), 440–41
Opium War (1839–42), 28
Organization for European Cooperation
    and Development (OECD), 57, 65–
    66, 79, 103, 300–01, 488
    and International Energy Agency
        (IEA), 518–19
    oil consumption, 510–15
Organization of Petroleum Exporting
    Countries (OPEC), 66, 84, 238,
    297, 474, 491
    and food power, 498–500
    formation, 501–04
    goals, 503–04
    oil embargo, 508–09, 515
    oil price increase (1973), 504–05
    Teheran meeting, 505
Osirik nuclear reactor (Iraq), 457
Outer Mongolia, 33
Outer Space Treaty (1967), 443–45
Overseas Private Investment Corporation
    (OPIC), 159, 288, 300
Owen, Wilfred, 408

Pacific War, 208
Packard, Vance, 165
Pakistan, 15, 139, 455
    and Food for Peace, 496
    hunger in, 480
    and Non-Proliferation Treaty, 456
    nuclear technology, 449, 453
    US support to, 222, 349, 422, 423
Palestine Liberation Organization, 276,
    518
Panama Canal, 86, 91, 355

Panama Canal Commission, 353
Panama Canal Treaty (1977), 295, 353
Peace Corps, 240, 352
Pearl Harbor, 141, 227, 322
Peenemunde, 309
Pell, Claiborne, 437
Pentagon, 164, 237, 286, 435
    and bureaucratic politics, 191–92
    and comprehensive test ban, 447–48
    employees, 167
    and intelligence community, 327
    and wartime mobilization, 416
    and Washington Post, 188
Pentagon Papers, 336
People's Liberation Army, 37
People's Republic of China see China
Perkins, Dexter, 155
Persian Gulf, 12, 60, 75, 78, 315, 416
    and Carter, 391, 526
    oil supply, 411, 526–28
Philby, Kim, 313, 319–20
Philippines, 15, 127, 135
    election campaigns in, 317, 333
    hunger in, 480
    US acquisition of, 123
    US military bases in, 222, 349
Phoumi Nosavan, General, 271
Pillsbury, Michael, 78
Pinckney, Thomas, 135
Pine Bluff nerve gas plant (Arkansas), 409
Pluralism, 359
Poland, 26, 130
    Communists installed in Warsaw
        (1944), 13
    as grain consumer, 488
    invaded by Hitler (1939), 5
    Solidarity Union, 495
    and Soviet Union, 13, 474
Policymaking, 237–41
Political culture
    elements, 109–12
    influence of foreign policy, 111–12
    and US liberalism, 134–35
    and US optimism, 139–40
    and US pragmatism, 131–34
    and US private enterprise, 135–38
Population growth, 484
Portugal, 57, 349, 505
    as member of NATO, 56

Post Office and Civil Service Committee
    (US Congress), 355
Power elite, 163–65
Pragmatism, 131–34
Presidential power
    after World War II, 227, 346–47
    Constitutional, 216–17
    and foreign policy, 218–20, 363
    historical explanation, 220–21
Pressure groups, interest in foreign policy,
    156–63
"Prestige press," 181, 189, 194
Princeton University, 450
Pringle, Robert, 283
Private enterprise, 135–38
Protestant groups, 161, 164
Proxmire, William, 167–68
Public Health Service, 240
Public Law 480, 495, 496
Public opinion, government manipulation
    of, 176–78
Puchala, Donald J., 492, 495
Puerto Rico, 123, 444
Pulitzer Prize, 188
Pye, Lucien W., 37

Qadaffi, Muammar al-, 503

Rand Corporation, 166
Ransom, Harry Howe, 316–17, 337
Rapid Deployment Force (RDF), 390–92,
    418
Reagan, Ronald, 21, 25–26, 77, 110, 137,
    177, 246, 289, 304, 338, 357, 394,
    526
    and ACDA, 434, 437
    and bomber development, 395, 398
    and CIA, 326, 332, 336, 342
    and comprehensive test ban, 449
    lifting of grain embargo on Soviet
        Union, 301
    military spending, 294
    and MX missiles, 219, 398
    and neutron bomb, 62, 407
    and NSC, 255
    and nuclear proliferation, 455

objections to European pipeline, 58–59
reversal of Carter's policies, 91
and SALT II, 467, 472–73, 475
stand on Central America, 88
and START, 467, 472, 475
and State Department, 280–81
strategic arms proposal, 433–34
strategic balance, 398
and Trilateral Commission, 78
and US-Soviet relations, 326
and War Powers Act, 231
"zero option" proposal, 466
Republican party, 174–75, 348
Resource diplomacy, 479–530
energy, 479, 500–28
food, 479, 480–500
minerals, 479, 528
Reston, James, 191, 204–05
Rhodesia *see* Zimbabwe
Rio Pact *see* Inter-American Treaty of
Reciprocal Assistance
Robinson, Julian Perry, 409
Rockefeller Commission, 332, 335
Rogers, William P., 247
Roosevelt, Franklin D., 231, 235, 274, 276,
359
and Churchill, 142
entrance into World War II, 224–25,
227
Roosevelt, Theodore, 123–25
Rosenau, James N., 154
Rostow, Walt, 245
Rousseau, Jean Jacques, 134
Royal Dutch Shell Co., 501
Rumania, 13, 356
Rusk, Dean, 195
as secretary of state, 19, 155, 188, 227
and Kennedy, 244, 246
on State Department procedures, 285
Russia *see* Soviet Union
Russo-Japanese War (1904–05), 75

Saint Louis Post-Dispatch, 182
Sakharov, Andrei, 20
Sandinista National Liberation Front, 91
Satellites, 310, 326
Russian Cosmos, 311

Saudi Arabia, 237, 517
oil production and prices, 504–05, 515,
518, 521
and US arms transfers, 418, 422, 424
Scali, John, 195
Schlesinger, Arthur, 207, 208
Schlesinger, James, 293, 330, 402
Scoville, Herbert, Jr., 460
Seabed Arms Control Treaty (1971), 437,
445
Sea Power (Navy League journal), 166
Secret Service, 298, 328
Senate
and ACDA, 435–37
and Panama Canal Treaty, 354
and presidential appointees, 347
and SALT, 218–19, 467, 469, 472
and treaties, 218–19, 348–50
Senate Finance Committee, 23
Senate Foreign Relations Committee, 191,
223–24, 229, 285, 349, 366, 368, 371
Senate Internal Security Subcommittee,
194
Senate Preparedness Subcommittee, 227
Senate Select Committee on Intelligence
see Church Committee
Sequoia (yacht), 273
Shackley, Theodore, 330
Shanghai, 30
Shanghai Communiqué (1972), 40–41
Sheehan, Neil, 188
Siberia, 76
Sinkiang, 38
SLBMs (submarine-launched ballistic mis-
siles), 392, 396, 467–72
Smith, Adam, 135–37
Smith, Gerard C., 290, 436
Smithsonian Institution, 240
Socialist bloc, 25
Solidarity Union, 495
Solzhenitsyn, Alexander, 20
Somalia, 391, 422
Somoza Garcia, Anastasio, 90
Sorenson, Theodore, 176
South Africa, 91–95, 315, 505
and Non-Proliferation Treaty, 456
nuclear technology, 449, 457
South Asia, hunger in, 480, 485
Southeast Asia, 85, 225, 351, 388, 409

Southeast Asia Treaty Organization
    (SEATO), 15, 89, 383
South Korea, 14, 15, 74, 100, 127, 186,
    187, 458
    and Food for Peace, 496
    as grain consumer, 488
    nuclear technology, 449, 453
    and Truman, 266
    and US arms transfers, 418, 422
    US commitment to, 349
    US food aid to, 494
South Vietnam, 333, 350, 387
    and Food for Peace, 496
South-West Africa People's Organization
    (SWAPO), 96
Southwest Asia, 411
South Yemen, 418
Souvanna Phouma, Prince, 271
Soviet Union (Russia, USSR), 12, 55, 132,
    134, 168, 232, 407, 439
    aid to SWAPO, 96
    arms control and reductions, 348, 433–
        34, 439–76
    and arms transfers, 417–18, 423–26
    and Astronauts Rescue Treaty, 19
    and Baruch Plan, 439
    blockade of Berlin (1948), 13, 15
    bombers, 397, 400, 402, 473
    and Carter, 185, 326
    chemical warfare and weapons, 409–11,
        461
    and CIA estimate of GNP, 311
    combat troops in Cuba, 184
    Communist government recognized by
        US (1933), 16
    and comprehensive test ban, 448–49
    and Conference on Security and Coop-
        eration, 19
    construction of pipeline with Western
        Europe, 58
    control of Eastern Europe, 13, 130
    and détente, 18–20, 58–59
    deterioration of US-Soviet relations,
        340, 426
    emigration policy, 21, 22
    expansion, 411
    Far Eastern Fleet, 78
    and food power, 499–500
    as grain consumer, 486–88

and human rights, 20–21
installation of Hot Line (1963), 19
intervention in Africa, 59, 474
intervention in Angola and Ethiopia,
    474
intervention in Southwest Asia, 59
invasion of Afghanistan, 20, 25, 242,
    245, 315, 455, 472, 474, 495, 496,
    518
KGB, 26
Kremlin, 14, 354, 384, 401
and "limited adversary relationships,"
    25
and Limited Test Ban Treaty, 19, 446
military policy, 381–426
missile systems, 220, 331, 392, 398–
    400, 403–04, 417, 434
and Moscow-New York air link, 19
most-favored-nation status, 22, 352
and Mutual and Balanced Force
    Reductions (MBFR), 462
and NATO, 148
navy, 400
and Nonproliferation Treaty, 19
nuclear explosions, 449
nuclear weapons, 60
oil consumption, 515
and Outer Space Treaty, 19
and Persian Gulf, 526–27
and placement of missiles in Cuba,
    310, 314, 332
and Poland, 474
Politburo, 26
Red Army, 56, 250
rejection of Reagan's strategic arms
    proposal, 434
rejection of Reagan's "zero option"
    proposal, 466
relations with Japan, 76
relations with US and China, 44–48
and repayment of Lend-Lease loans,
    17, 21–22
and Rumania, 356
and SALT I (1972), 19, 21, 25, 467–69
and SALT II, 470–75
and Seabed Arms Control Treaty, 445
sharing scientific technological data, 19
Sino-Soviet bloc, 32, 89
Sino-Soviet split, 32–38, 316

spies, 313–14
Sputnik rocket, 60, 150
and START, 475
surrounded by hostile Communist
 nations, 36
and Threshold Test Ban Treaty, 446
and treaty of friendship with India, 37
and treaty of friendship with People's
 Republic of China, 33
and treaty of friendship with Vietnam,
 36
and Treaty of Tlatelolco, 444
and Treaty on Underground Nuclear
 Explosions for Peaceful Purposes,
 447
and US Congress, 356
and US grain and wheat agreements,
 160, 495
US-Soviet strategic balance, 395–401
and US strategic superiority over, 382
and US trade embargo against, 25
and Vietnam, 474
view of Chinese-Japanese relations, 77
and Vladivostok accord, 19, 469–70
weapons systems, 402–03
Spain, 15, 56
Spanish-American War (1898), 123, 226
Spanish Bases Agreement (1953), 349
Special Forces, "Green Berets," 385–87
Sputnik rocket, 60, 385, 443
Stagflation, 66
Stalin, Joseph, 56, 141–42, 439
 and Non-Aggression Pact (1939), 13,
  16
 and treaty of friendship with Jiang Jieshi (1945), 33–35
Standard Oil of California, 501
Stans, Maurice, 299
State Department (Department of State),
 6, 17, 157, 162, 175, 192, 238, 281,
 372
 and ACDA, 434, 436
 Bureau of Human Rights and Humani-
  tarian Affairs, 20, 350
 Bureau of Intelligence and Research,
  327–28
 Bureau of Politico-Military Affairs, 280
 Communists in, 282
 conditions of employment, 282–84

current issues, 281–88
described, 219–20
difficulties, 281–88
and Food for Peace, 496
foreign policy, 240
functions, 278–81
history, 278
internal procedures, 284–85
and the media, 189–90, 195
and Mutual and Balanced Force
 Reductions (MBFR), 464
organization, 278–81
policy making, 251
Policy Planning Staff, 132
recommendations for improvement, 287
reporting system, 367
and Review Group, 253
sharing of jurisdiction, 361
Stennis, John, 340
Stokes, Donald E., 173
Strategic Air Command (SAC), 383–84
Strategic Arms Limitation Talks (SALT),
 254, 289, 292, 310, 432, 436, 464,
 467–75
 SALT I (1972), 19, 21, 168, 219, 221,
  394, 467–70
 SALT II, 19, 24–25, 218, 467, 470–75
Strategic Arms Reduction Talks (START),
 26, 289–90, 467, 472, 475
Submarines
 Polaris, 388, 396
 Trident, 396–97, 434, 448, 472
Suez Canal, 57, 88, 371, 391
Sukarno, President, 271–72, 311
Supreme Court, 214, 353
Sweden, 425, 449
Switzerland, 449
Symbionese Liberation Army, 202
Symington, Stuart, 349
Synthetic Fuels Corporation, 522
Syria, 228, 418, 505
 nuclear technology, 449
Szulc, Tad, 205, 207–08

Tactical weapons, 402, 412
Taiwan, 30, 31, 32, 148, 188
 nuclear technology, 449
 and Shanghai Communiqué, 40–41

Taiwan (*cont.*)
    US diplomatic recognition of, 32
Taiwan Relations Act, 43
Tanks, coproduction of, 413
Tarapur nuclear reactor (India), 454
Tariffs, 115, 158–59
    European, 64
    Japanese, 72
Tatu, Michel, 45–46
Teheran, 266, 372, 505
Television, 182, 184, 194–95, 198–99
    coverage of terrorism, 201–02
Television News Reporting (CBS), 200
Tennessee Valley Authority, 240
Texaco Co., 501
Thailand, 15, 189, 387
    US commitment to, 349
Third World, 426
    anti-Western feelings, 83, 527
    attitudes toward US, 90, 95
    energy considerations in, 65–66, 376
    importance to US, 79, 83
    modernization, 84, 134
    nationalism, 83–96, 317
    Soviet interests in, 25, 356, 527
    US relations, policy, and aid, 12, 79–
        106, 133, 298
Three Mile Island (Pennsylvania), 525
Time, 182, 185
Tito, Marshal, 356
Torrijos Herrera, Omar, 353
Trade Expansion Act (1962), 64
Trade Policy Committee, 300
Trade Reform Act (1973), 22–24
Transportation Department, 240
Treasury Department, 6, 238, 267, 328
    and Food for Peace, 496
    functions, 297–98
    policy making, 251
Treaties, and the Senate, 348–50
Treaty of Tlatelolco (1967), 444–45
Treaty on Underground Nuclear Explo-
    sions for Peaceful Purposes (1976),
    447
Trilateral Commission, 77–79
Truman, Harry S., 141, 150, 275, 281, 383
    aid to France (1952), 85
    aid to Greece and Turkey, 382
    presidential appointments, 224

sent forces to Korea (1950), 89, 176,
    221, 266
    and special assistant, 243–44, 247
    vs. bureaucracy, 277–78
    and War Powers Act, 230
Truman Doctrine, 14–15
Turkey, 13, 14, 15, 100, 355, 382, 422, 423
    as member of NATO, 56
    US support to, 222, 349, 352, 423
Turner, Stansfield, 325, 330

Ultra code, 309
Unemployment, 66–67
United Auto Workers, 157
United Fruit Company, 310
United Kingdom *see* Great Britain
United Nations, 5, 31, 130, 161, 220, 224,
    269, 276, 439, 440, 445, 490
    Committee on Disarmament, 461
    Eighteen Nation Disarmament Com-
        mission, 459
    Food and Agriculture Organization,
        484, 488, 491
    human rights observance reports, 353
    and IAEA, 453
    and Israel, 457
    and Outer Space Treaty, 443
    and population growth, 482
    and South Africa, 93, 95, 457
    and World Food Conference, 490
United Nations Conference on Trade and
    Development (UNCTAD), 300, 492
United Nations Development Program
    (UNDP), 491
United Nations Educational, Scientific and
    Cultural Organization (UNESCO),
    196
United Press International, 188, 203
United States (America) *see also* Foreign
    policy *and by topic*
    agricultural groups in, 160–61
    attitude toward military force, 128–30
    business groups in, 158–59
    and consequences of self-image, 120
    contribution to France's war effort in
        Indochina, 15
    as counterforce in Greece and Turkey,
        14

defense arrangements with Iran, 15
defense arrangements with Israel, 15
defense arrangements with Liberia, 15
defense arrangements with Spain, 15
defense arrangements with Thailand,
    15
defense industries in, 422
devaluation of the dollar, 65
diplomatic recognition of Taiwan, 32
economic and military aid to Western
    Europe, 56
Europe's doubts of US commitment to,
    60–61
and food aid, 488
food policy, 493–96
food reserve, 490
as global power, 62–63
as grain supplier, 485–86, 498
as member of NATO, 56
national interests of, 12
and nuclear arms control in Europe,
    464–67
and nuclear explosions, 449
and Nuclear Suppliers Group, 454
nuclear weapons proliferation, 451–55
oil consumption, 66, 501, 505, 506–07,
    515
and Persian Gulf, 526
public opinion towards foreign policy,
    145–56
and "red alert," 474
relations with China and Soviet Union,
    44–48
relations with Japan, 68–79
relations with Third World, 79–106
relations with Western Europe, 53–67
security issues, 55–62
and security treaties with Philippines,
    South Korea, and Japan, 15
and security treaty with Taiwan
    (1954), 15, 32
and sense of mission, 119–20
and Soviet Union grain agreement, 495
support of CENTO (1955), 15
support of OECD, 57
as third-largest trading partner of
    China, 42
and Threshold Test Ban Treaty, 446
trade embargo against China, 32

and Treaty of Tlatelolco, 444
and Treaty on Underground Nuclear
    Explosions for Peaceful Purposes,
    447
and vision of self, 119
and Washington Naval Conference
    (1921–22), 438
and world hunger, 490–92
US Chamber of Commerce, 159
US-China Joint Economic Committee, 298
US Information Agency (USIA), 240,
    295–96, 304
US Intelligence Board (USIB), 330
US-Israeli Joint Committee for Investment
    and Trade, 298
US-Japan Trade Council, 355
U.S. News and World Report, 182, 185
US-Saudi Arabia Joint Commission on
    Economic Cooperation, 298
US-USSR Commercial Commission, 298
United Technologies Co., 166
Uruguay, 127, 281, 333
Utah, 408, 522

Vance, Cyrus, 41, 164, 208, 280, 286, 472
    and Brzezinski, 245, 303
Vanik, Charles A., 22–24
Venezuela, 501
Versailles Treaty, 218, 226
Veterans Administration, 240
Veterans of Foreign Wars, 166
Vietnam and Vietnam War, 8, 15, 20, 70,
    127, 168, 170, 188, 226, 370, 371,
    378, *see also* North Vietnam; South
    Vietnam
    American intervention in, 89–90, 391
    American policy in, 358
    American withdrawal from, 39
    chemical weapons, 459
    and CIA, 336
    Congress's view of, 355
    early years of war, 228–31
    infiltration routes in, 402
    and Joint Chiefs of Staff, 192
    and 1964 US presidential election, 172
    Paris peace agreement, 221
    and presidential power, 218
    public opinion of, 145, 372–73, 388

Vietnam and Vietnam War (*cont.*)
   and Soviet Union, 36, 474
   US expenditures in, 399, 411
   US involvement in, 15, 20, 57, 62, 85,
      133, 178, 294
   US isolationism after war, 112
   US military forces in, 347
Virgin Islands, 444
Vladivostok Accords (1974), 394, 467,
      469–70

Wall Street Journal, 182
War of 1812, 226
Warnke, Paul, 164, 434, 436
War Powers Act (1973), 230–31, 340, 347–
      48, 352, 370, 376
Warsaw Pact, 62, 401, 464
   air power, 405–06
   antitank forces, 406
   chemical warfare, 410–11
   conventional weapons, 405–07
   formation, 401
   military policy, 381, 401–15
   naval forces, 406
Washington, George, 113–14
Washington Naval Conference (1921–22),
      438
Washington Post, 154, 182, 188, 189, 190,
      192
Watergate, 187, 245, 378
   and CIA involvement, 312, 332, 340
   Congress's view of, 355, 365
Weinberger, Caspar W., 348, 401
Weisband, Edward, 368, 376
Welles, Sumner, 189
Western Europe, 12, 13, 15, 84, 411
   and arms transfers, 425, 426
   and chemical weapons, 461
   construction of pipeline with Russia, 58
   economic conditions, 55
   importance to US, 54–55
   inflation, 66–67
   and liberalism, 135
   military spending, 399
   oil consumption, 507, 515
   relations with Japan, 78–79
   relations with Soviet Union, 58–59
   relations with US, 53–67

   use of intelligence in, 315
   US troops in, 412
   and Warsaw Pact, 405–07
West Germany, 55, 85, 406, 412, 413, 425
   as member of NATO, 56
   nuclear technology, 449, 453–54
   US intelligence in, 309
   US troops in, 412, 416
   and Warsaw Pact, 401
Weyler, Valeriano, 122
White, T. H., 383
White House, 330, 367
   and ACDA, 435
   Oval Office, 356, 363
White House Staff, 235, 241, 245, 347
Wildavsky, Aaron, 168
Wilde, Oscar, 196
Willrich, Mason, 526
Wilson, Woodrow, 111, 115, 124, 129, 141,
      224, 269
Wolfers, Arnold, 62
Women's International League for Peace
      and Freedom (WILPF), 161
World Bank, 217, 288, 297, 298, 491
   and food diplomacy, 480
World Food Conference, 489–91
World Food Council, 491
World War I, 116, 127, 130, 438
   chemical weapons, 408, 411
   US delayed entry in, 162
   and US isolationism, 115
World War II, 5, 13, 67, 99, 117, 127, 128,
      129, 159, 221–22, 223, 310, 346–47,
      370, 418, 423, 438, 506, 523
   chemical weapons, 409
   code breakers, 208, 309
   end of, 130
   non-standardized armies, 414
   temporary end of US isolationism, 116,
      139
   US delayed entry in, 162
Worldwide Military Command and Con-
      trol system, 416
Wyoming, 522

Yalta conference (1945), 13, 16, 222
Yamani, Ahmed Zaki al-, 517
Young, Andrew, 276

Yugoslavia, 356, 496

Zablocki, Clement J., 359

Zaire, 481
Zhao Ziyang, 39
Ziegler, L. Harmon, 165
Zimbabwe, 112, 391, 505